W9-BOM-118

21st-Century Learning in School Libraries

21st-Century Learning in School Libraries

Kristin Fontichiaro, Editor

Libraries Unlimited

An Imprint of ABC-CLIO, LLC

A B C ● C L I O

Santa Barbara, California • Denver, Colorado • Oxford, England

Copyright 2009 by Libraries Unlimited

Library of Congress Cataloging-in-Publication Data

21st-century learning in school libraries / edited by Kristin Fontichiaro.
    p. cm.
    All articles were originally published in School library media activities monthly.
    Includes bibliographical references and index.
    ISBN 978-1-59158-895-5 (pbk : acid-free paper) ISBN 978-1-59158-896-2 (ebook) 1. School libraries—United States. 2. School librarian participation in curriculum planning—United States. 3. School libraries—Standards—United States. 4. Media programs (Education)—Standards—United States. I. Title. II. Title: Twenty-first century learning in school libraries.
Z675.S3F63   2009
027.80973—dc22   2009035571

13 12 11 10 9   1 2 3 4 5

This book is also available on the World Wide Web as an eBook.
Visit www.abc-clio.com for details.

ABC-CLIO, LLC
130 Cremona Drive, P.O. Box 1911
Santa Barbara, California 93116-1911

This book is printed on acid-free paper ∞
Manufactured in the United States of America

Contents

Acknowledgments xiii
Introduction xv

Chapter 1: 21st-Century Learning Standards 1
  Partnership for 21st-Century Learning Framework 1
  ASCD's Whole Child New Compact 2
  The ISTE NETS*S 2
  The AASL *Standards* 3
    The Importance of Language: The Partnership for 21st Century Skills and AASL
      Standards by Gail Formanack (September 2008) 6
    SLMAM Skills Correlations—New (2007) to Old (1998) by Deborah Levitov
      (February 2008) 9
    Standards for the 21st-Century Learner by Sharon Coatney (February 2008) 10
    Collaborative Planning for Information Literacy by *School Library Media Activities*
      Monthly (February 2008) 12
    Thirty Helens Agree: 2007 Research Supports AASL's *Standards for the 21st-Century*
      Learner by Marcia A. Mardis (June 2008) 13
    Dispositions: Getting Beyond "Whatever" by Barbara Stripling (October 2008) 16
    New Standards—Refreshing Our Work, AGAIN! by Betty Marcoux (March 2008) 20
Chapter 2: Meet the 21st-Century Learners 23
  Millennials and Kids 2.0 23
  Learner's Bill of Rights 24
    Millennials: Deal with Them! Part I by Stephen Abram (September 2007) 25
    Millennials: Deal with Them! Part II by Stephen Abram (October 2007) 27
    Kids 2.0 by Janice Gilmore-See (November 2007) 31
    Millennial Learners Build Knowledge Communities by Gail Bush (January 2008) 35
    Doesn't Everyone Have Rights to a Learner's Permit? by the Colorado School
      Library Leaders Learner's Bill of Rights Committee (May 2009) 38
    Learner's Bill of Rights by the Colorado School Library Leaders Learner's Bill of
      Rights Committee (May 2009) 40
Chapter 3: Envisioning a Vibrant Library Media Program 41
  Mission Statements: Shared Visions for Learning 41
  Visions 42
  What Should Great Student Learning Look Like in the School
    Library Media Center? 42

The Big Picture 42
  Hitch Your Wagon to a Mission Statement by Allison Zmuda (September 2007) 44
  About Mission by Susan Eblen (September 2007) 47
  Creativity Literacy: The Library Media Center as a Learning Laboratory by Gail Bush
    (February 2008) 54
  Principal Perspective, Part 2: The Library Media Program by Carl A. Harvey II
    (December 2008) 57
  What Does It Really Look Like when Students Are Learning in the Library Media
    Center? by Allison Zmuda (September 2008) 60
  There Is Knowledge to Be Gained by Ross J. Todd (June 2009) 63

Chapter 4: The 21st-Century School Library Media Specialist 67
  The Big Picture: What Does the Principal Want? 67
  School Librarians as Learning Specialists 67
  Who Are Our Role Models? 68
  How Do We Get Authority? 68
  What Do We Need to Do to Thrive Amid Change? 68
  Principal Perspective, Part 1: The Role of the Library Media Specialist by
    Carl A. Harvey II (October 2008) 69
  Reframing the Library Media Specialist as a Learning Specialist by Allison Zmuda
    and Violet H. Harada (April 2008) 72
  Impact as a 21st-Century Library Media Specialist by Peggy Milam Creighton
    (March 2008) 77
  Where Does Your Authority Come From? by Allison Zmuda (September 2006) 82
  Dancing Down the Rabbit Hole: Habits of Mind for Embracing Change
    by Kristin Fontichiaro (November 2008) 86

Chapter 5: Reading 89
  Millennial Readers 89
  Leisure Reading 89
  Supporting Reading Instruction 90
  Reading Instruction in the School Library Media Center 90
  Motivation and Reading 90
  Social Reading: Promoting Reading in the Millennial Learner by Leslie Preddy
    (January 2009) 92
  Urban Teenagers, Leisure Reading, and the Library Media Program
    by Sandra Hughes-Hassell and Ernie J. Cox (September 2008) 96
  Differentiated Instruction in Reading: Easier Than It Looks! by Liz Knowles
    (January 2009) 99
  Reading for Meaning: Questioning by Catherine Trinkle (January 2009) 102
  Reading for Meaning: Synthesizing by Catherine Trinkle (March 2009) 105
  Research-based Evidence: *The Role of the Library Media Specialist in Reading
    Comprehension Instruction* by Nancy Zimmerman (May 2005) 108
  Reading Incentives that Work: No-Cost Strategies to Motivate Kids to Read and Love It!
    by Ruth V. Small et al. (May 2009) 112

Chapter 6: Inquiry 117
  How Can Media Specialists Promote Inquiry-Focused Teaching? 118
  Inquiry: Not Just In the Library, Not Just for Research 118
  Information Inquiry by Daniel Callison (June 2002) 121
  Models, Part IV: Inquiry Models by Daniel Callison (December 2002) 126
  Student Inquiry in the Research Process, Part 1: Inquiry Research Basics
    by Leslie B. Preddy (November 2002) 130
  Student Inquiry in the Research Process, Part 2: Inquiry Research Orientation
    by Leslie B. Preddy (December 2002) 133

Student Inquiry in the Research Process, Part 3: Inquiry Research and Strategy
by Leslie B. Preddy (January 2003). 136
Student Inquiry in the Research Process, Part 4: Inquiry Research Investigation
by Leslie B. Preddy (February 2003). 139
Student Inquiry in the Research Process, Part 5: Inquiry Research Conclusion &
Reflection by Leslie B. Preddy (March 2003) 142
Inquiry: Inquiring Minds Want to Know by Barbara Stripling (September 2008). 147
Inquiry-based Teaching and Learning—The Role of the School Library Media
Specialist by Barbara Stripling (September 2008). 150
Critical Inquiry: Library Media Specialists as Change Agents by Kafi Kumasi-Johnson
(May 2007). 151
Engaging Students in Inquiry by Joan M. Yoshina and Violet H. Harada (April 2006) 155
Connecting Science Notebooking to the Elementary Library Media Center
by Kristin Fontichiaro and Sandy Buczynski (March 2009). 159
Chapter 7: Assessment. 163
Assessing *Information Fluency*: Gathering Evidence of Student Learning
by Barbara Stripling (April 2007) 166
Tools for the Assessment of Learning by Marjorie L. Pappas (May 2007) 171
Research Reflections, Journaling, and Exit Slips by Leslie Preddy (October 2008) 176
Sample Exit Slips for Elementary, Middle, and High School by Deborah Levitov
(October 2008) 178
Designing Learning for Evidence-Based Practice by Marjorie L. Pappas (January 2008). 180
Assessing Learning: *The Missing Piece in Instruction?* by Violet H. Harada and
Joan M. Yoshina (March 2006). 185
Building Evidence Folders for Learning through Library Media Centers
by Violet H. Harada (November 2006) 189
From Eyeballing to Evidence: Assessing for Learning in Hawaii Library Media
Centers by Violet H. Harada (November 2007) 194
Ohio's Foray into Evidence-Based Practice by Christine Findlay (October 2006) 200
Chapter 8: Collaboration 203
Collaboration Connections by Carl A. Harvey II (March 2008) 206
The Power and Spirit of Collaboration by Susan Vanneman (November 2006) 209
When Does Collaboration Start? by Gail Dickinson (October 2006). 211
Levels of Collaboration: *Where Does Your Work Fit In?* by Betty (Elizabeth L.)
Marcoux (December 2007). 214
Show Them What We Do: Strategies for Collaborative Teaching by Judi Moreillon
(September 2007) 218
Using Personality Traits and Effective Communication to Improve Collaboration
by Juanita Warren Buddy (May 2007). 221
Lesson Planning: The Ticket to Successful Teaching by Pat Franklin and
Claire Gatrell Stephens (September 2008). 225
Coteaching Published Lesson Plans: A Recipe for Success? by Judi Moreillon
(January 2009) 227
Collaboration: The Motown Method by Leslie Preddy (November 2008). 229
Collaboration: From Myth to Reality: Let's Get Down to Business! by Ross Todd
(March 2008) 232
Collaborative Planning by Deborah Levitov (November 2006) 237
Assessment Tool: Levels of Communication, Cooperation, and Collaboration with
Teachers by Deborah Levitov and Allison Zmuda (October 2006) 238

Chapter 9: Building a Toolkit of Instructional Strategies 239
    The Big Picture: The Value of Strong Lesson Design and Teaching/Learning Strategies. 239
    Strenghtening the Students' Research Process. 239
    Technology Strategies 241
    Beyond Academics: Developing Flexible Mindsets 242
        We Don't Have to Learn Anything; We Just Have to Find the Answer by Clara Hoover
            (October 2005) 244
        Authentic Learning by Daniel Callison and Annette Lamb (December 2004). 247
        Differentiated Instruction by Gail Bush (November 2006) 253
        Sift and Sort: *The Answers Are in the Questions!* by Kym Kramer and Connie Largent
            (April 2005) 256
        Questioning Revisited by Daniel Callison (February 2006) 261
        Red Light, Green Light: Guiding Questions by Deborah Levitov (October 2005). 265
        Assessing Questions by Deborah Levitov (January 2009). 266
        Primary Sources and Inquiry Learning by Marjorie L. Pappas (September 2006) 267
        Graphic Inquiry: Standards and Resources, Part I by Daniel Callison and Annette Lamb
            (September 2007) 271
        Graphic Inquiry: Skills and Strategies, Part II by Daniel Callison and Annette Lamb
            (October 2007) 275
        Cavemen Took Notes? by Leslie Preddy (December 2008) 280
        Brain Friendly Techniques: Mind Mapping by Cristine Goldberg (November 2004) 282
        The Power of Reflection in the Research Process by Peggy Milam (February 2005). 285
        Plagiarism by Daniel Callison (December 2005) 289
        Podcasting 101 by Kristin Fontichiaro (March 2007) 294
        Wikis and Collaborative Inquiry by Annette Lamb and Larry Johnson (April 2009). 296
        An Open Book: Life Online by Kathy Fredrick (December 2008). 300
        Mindsets: How Praise Is Harming Youth and What Can Be Done about It
            by Carol S. Dweck (January 2008) 302
Chapter 10: Elementary Lesson Plans 307
    Reading. 307
    Inquiry and Writing 307
    Social Studies 307
    Science 308
        Words Are Like Faces: An Exploration into Language and Communication
            by Judi Moreillon (April 2008) 309
        Tricking the Trickster: Recording and Comparing Story Elements by Judi Moreillon
            (September 2007) 311
        Promoting Inquiry with Emerging Readers Using Elephogs and Octobunnies
            by Kristin Fontichiaro and Debbie West (February 2009) 313
        Abigail and John Adams Online by Maureen Tannetta (October 2008). 316
        Science Notebooking in Action: Where Does Condensation Come From?
            by Sandy Buczynski and Kristin Fontichiaro (March 2009) 318
        Science Notebooking in the Library Media Center: Alternative Energy
            by Kristin Fontichiaro, Victoria A. Pascaretti, and Sandy Buczynski (March 2009) 320
Chapter 11: Secondary Lesson Plans 323
    Language Arts 323
    Government or Language Arts. 323
    Social Studies 324
    Science 324
        The Librarian Who Loves *LibraryThing* by Roberta Sibley (April 2009) 325
        Yo Socrates! Amend This! by Paula S. Eisen (October 2007) 327
        A Small World—Technology Connecting Kids to Kids by Ronda Hassig (June 2008). 331
        A Small World by Ronda Hassig (June 2008) 333

Fighting the Civil War with Primary Sources by Alan McCarthy and Sandra Sterne
(December 2006) 336
Interviewing Older Americans by Sandra L. Ricker (January 2009) 340
Designing Inquiry-Based Science Units as Collaborative Partners by Audrey Okemura
(November 2008) 341
Text-to-Self Connection: *The Lemonade Club* and Research into Diseases
by Catherine Trinkle (November 2008) 346

References 349
Recommended Reading 351
    Recommended Blogs for School Library Media Specialists 359
    Recommended Professional Journals 360
Index 363

Acknowledgments

First, thanks go to Marilyn Kiefer of the University of Michigan, whose question about moving forward with the AASL *Standards for the 21st-Century Learner* led to the idea of compiling *School Library Media Activities Monthly* (now *School Library Monthly*) articles into book format.

Thanks, too, to Sharon Coatney and Deb Levitov, who heard about the idea within 15 minutes of that conversation and agreed to it soon after. Sharon is a thoughtful editor who is highly skilled in helping bridge the gap between theory and practice. Whether offering me a weekly blog, adding me to a far-more-experienced-than-I advisory board, or giving me (and so many others) a chance to think through practice and write about it, Deb continues to challenge me to grow. This book developed concurrently with my co-guest editorship of the professional practice issue of *Knowledge Quest*. *KQ*'s editor, Debbie Abilock, co-guest editor Judi Moreillon, and I have burned up our e-mail accounts discussing school library media centers and the role of school library media specialists. The conversations have been tremendous. Cyndi Phillip appointed me to the AASL Learning Standards and Guidelines Implementation Task Force, chaired by Susan Ballard, which kept me on my toes as we developed strategies for implementing the AASL *Standards*. Sandy Buczynski, my coauthor on the book *Story Starters and Science Notebooking: Developing Student Thinking Through Literacy and Inquiry*, introduced me to science inquiry, which gave me an invaluable new lens through which to see inquiry in libraries. Marcia Mardis continues to stretch my thinking and was a once-in-a-lifetime teaching partner at the University of Michigan. I feel enormously fortunate to have these deep thinkers to learn from and with.

Thank you to the many school library media specialists, professors, AASL committee members, classroom teachers, blog and print readers, and others who have allowed me to stretch my wings, given me new ideas to consider, and allowed me to test my theories out loud. Special thanks to those involved with the 2008 conference of the International Association of School Librarianship, for which I served as program chair; the Wayne RESA media group in Southeastern Michigan; those who participated in the AASL Webinars on the *Standards for the 21st-Century Learner*, for which I presented the session on skills; ROM 17; and the Michigan Association for Media in Education, for giving me opportunities to clarify and articulate my thinking.

Thank you to my many colleagues in the Birmingham Public Schools, where the board of education has strongly supported school reforms to move us closer into 21st-century learning despite many years of state funding concerns. Special thanks to Stephen Palmer, Jennifer Martella, and Barbara Jones Clark, and to all of those who clucked sympathetically to see my bleary eyes after a late-night reading/writing session.

The American Association for School Librarians graciously gave permission for the *Standards for the 21st-Century Learner* to be quoted in selected articles in this book.

As always, thanks go to my family for their support.

Final thanks go to Blanche Woolls and the now-infamous bus ride in Lithuania where we met, and from which all of these opportunities have cascaded.

Introduction

This book began with a simple conversation. "Now that we've got the *Standards,* what are we supposed to *do* with them? What should I be communicating to my preservice school librarians?" asked a colleague. It was a great question, and one not just for preservice librarians but for practicing librarians as well. What would it look like to change our practice to be even more student-centered and inquiry-oriented than we had been in the past? As we talked, an answer emerged: collect the articles from *School Library Media Activities Monthly* and synthesize them into a book about 21st-century learning in school libraries.

The project has been nearly two years in the making. When the American Association of School Librarians (AASL) launched its *Standards for the 21st-Century Learner* (2007) at the National AASL Conference in October 2007, Deb Levitov, editor of *School Library Media Activities Monthly (SLMAM),* was preparing the February 2008 issue of the magazine. She asked Sharon Coatney, acquisitions editor for Libraries Unlimited, to write an article giving an overview for the new standards, while Deb went to work on a correlations chart that would help integrate the new standards into what was familiar. Once the chart was complete, it worked perfectly with Sharon's article, so both were published in tandem.

It was the beginning of an effort to search out authors who could bring more understanding and insight to the new standards for practicing library media specialists as well as professors in university programs and others in the field trying to understand the new standards and their implications. The voices of acknowledged leaders such as Ross J. Todd, Violet H. Harada, Barbara Stripling, and Marjorie Pappas blended with those of newcomers to share deeper knowledge of the new *Standards.* Some of the authors served on the committee that created the standards, others are library media specialists in schools that are trying to apply the standards, some are university professors, while others are library media specialist working in the publishing field. Others, like Allison Zmuda and Carol Dweck, added a unique and welcome perspective from outside the library media profession.

This is a book about meeting the learning imperative of our students. As such, we have concentrated on the part of school librarianship that focuses on teaching and learning. We've sifted through *SLMAM*'s recent publications to find the best articles and accompanying reproducible materials. Most of these articles were published within the past two years, although at times we have reached further back into the *SLMAM* archives and found articles that were remarkably prescient in anticipating this new journey into deep and meaningful school library learning.

This book may be used in preservice classes, in practitioner study groups, or as a stand-alone book for individuals. To facilitate use in adult learning groups, each chapter of this book features introductory comments, suggestions for advocacy, and discussion questions. An annotated bibliography of recommended readings is included at the end of the book.

We are grateful to all who have contributed to *SLMAM* (renamed *School Library Monthly* in September 2009) over the years as contributors, advisory board members, and readers (blog.schoollibrarymonthly.com). Thank you for what you have given to the magazine and to this book.

Deborah Levitov

Kristin Fontichiaro

Chapter 1

21st-Century Learning Standards

The [AASL] Standards represent a fresh look at what students should know as well as what they should be able to do with their library media specialists and library media programs. These standards are flexible enough to adapt to local situations yet forward-thinking enough to support students for years to come.

—Marcia A. Mardis, "Thirty Helens Agree" (see page 13)

This book focuses on building strong, vibrant student learning experiences in school libraries. It builds on the beliefs developed in *Standards for the 21st-Century Learner* (AASL *Standards*), a document released in October 2007 by the American Association of School Librarians (AASL), a division of the American Library Association (ALA).

To meet the AASL *Standards*, today's school libraries are no longer the quiet, books-only worlds of the past. Nor are today's school library media specialists (SLMSs; also known as school librarians or teacher librarians) meek, passive book lovers. School leaders should expect a SLMS to be a meaningful instructional partner in creating challenging instructional activities that make students active learners.

Before traveling to a foreign country, tourists often spend months getting to know their destination. They may acquire some common expressions in the native tongue, get to know some of the cultural behaviors specific to that nation, study a map to learn the relative location of the country's major cities and attractions, or learn the rate of currency exchange. Similarly, when school librarians begin to know the AASL *Standards*, it is important to become familiar with current visioning and standards documents for mainstream education. To look at the AASL *Standards* in isolation would be to deny their rich connections with other content areas and with the current postgraduation climate for students. Therefore, the SLMS begins by examining other contemporary visioning documents that work in parallel with the AASL *Standards*.

Partnership for 21st-Century Learning Framework

Over the past few years, businesses and educators have increased the frequency and intensity of their conversations about the skills and behaviors that businesses look for when hiring employees and how those skills and behaviors should be developed in students, particularly K–12 students. These meetings often focus on the mammoth shifts in the business world. Unlike graduates of the past, today's graduates do not anticipate taking a job after graduation from high school or college and staying with the same company for their entire careers. Former generations could anticipate a relative amount of stability; their world was mostly a local one. Now that industries are globalized, technology has made worldwide communication inexpensive and ubiquitous, and travel is still less expensive than it was in the past, the world has the capacity to change rapidly, as has been observed in the present. For example, many readers of this book clearly remember a world before cellular (or even touch-tone) telephones, computers, Internet, digital clocks, mp3 players (or even Walkmen!), GPS, e-books, or ATM machines.

1

Rapid technological advances have facilitated global-level employment and communication, shifting the employment landscape for white-collar or knowledge workers. These employees are now working more often in teams, perhaps even in teams that cross time zones, rather than working for individual advancement. For blue-collar workers such as those who work on assembly lines, the world has changed as their companies now compete against Third World economies and can no longer support a union payroll or resist making use of more accurate, less expensive automation.

As old jobs are phased out, new ones are invented, and it is this continual reinvention that promises to be a hallmark of the future for today's students. Educators and employers are realizing that the traditional curriculum may not be sufficient to meet that need. The Partnership for 21st Century Skills (P21; 21stcenturyskills.org) is one organization comprising both learning and commercial institutions that has examined a framework for the types of skills that graduates will need. The framework, released in fall 2007 and updated in January 2009 (21stcenturyskills.org/documents/framework_flyer_updated_ jan_09_final-1.pdf), discusses not only the skills and content areas crucial to success but also the support systems that need to be in place for that type of learning to exist.

For example, P21 holds that core subjects remain important but argues that students must also acquire an understanding of 21st-century themes such as a global economy and culture. In addition, students must acquire a set of behaviors to support a healthy life and career, such as critical thinking, creativity, innovation, and problem solving. Further, students need skills to navigate a never-ending flow of information via media outlets and the Internet, including information literacy, media literacy (the ability to interpret, evaluate, and synthesize messages delivered by media outlets), and technology skills.

Underlying these student skills is the recognition that the structures that support student learning must also change. Standards must reflect the core understandings students should gain; assessments should fairly examine students' level of mastery of those standards; curriculum and instructional outcomes should work to achieve those understandings; teachers need ongoing professional development to refine and update their pedagogy to meet diverse learner needs; and learning environments should be designed to be safe, stimulating, and user centered.

Many of P21's goals are reflected in *Standards for the 21st-Century Learner,* and it is no coincidence, given that AASL was included as a founding partner of P21. In "The Importance of Language: The Partnership for 21st Century Skills and AASL Standards" (beginning on page 6), Gail Formanack outlines the key partners and ideas of P21 and compares it with the AASL *Standards.*

ASCD's Whole Child New Compact

Similarly, the Association for Supervision and Curriculum Development (ASCD), a professional organization composed primarily of district administrators and curriculum leaders, rethought the role of school in a child's life. Perhaps as a reaction to the federal No Child Left Behind Act, which prioritized the acquisition of basic academic skills that could be assessed using standardized testing over holistic learning experiences, the arts, or inquiry learning, ASCD's New Compact reminded educators that children are more than academics. Success comes when students are not only acquiring content, but are healthy, safe, engaged, challenged, cared for, and prepared for a post-K–12 career or further study (ASCD n.d.)

The ISTE NETS*S

In 2007, the International Society for Technology in Education (ISTE), the largest educational technology professional organization in the United States, was refreshing its *National Educational Technology Standards for Students* (NETS*S). The refreshed NETS*S shifted focus away from the mastery of technology concepts and operations (e.g., ability to create a slideshow or send an e-mail) and instead looked at technology as a tool to further learning (e.g., how a wiki could foster collective knowledge or how a podcast could further the development of a child's written "voice"). Although knowing the nuts and bolts of technology and how to use it continues to be important, it is balanced by additional focus areas: use of technology to think creatively and innovatively; to communicate and to work collaboratively; to find, make sense of, and use information; and to behave ethically and as a digital citizen (ISTE 2007).

In these three documents (AASL *Standards*, New Compact, and NETS*S), there are recurring themes. Among these are a movement beyond basic skills and a movement to challenge students to think in new ways to meet new challenges. Many of these themes are further echoed in the AASL *Standards.*

The AASL Standards

The AASL *Standards* replace the *Information Power* (1998) documents, developed in partnership with the Association for Educational Communications and Technology (AECT). However, many of the values of the *Information Power* standards are echoed in the AASL *Standards* in greater depth and with an update to reflect the digital world of this century, as shown in Deborah Levitov's correlation chart on page 9. Sharon Coatney's article (beginning on page 10), "Standards for the 21st-Century Learner," shows how those values have transferred into the current document. Following the article, she suggests a template for collaborative lesson planning, "Collaborative Planning for Information Literacy," which can help scaffold the integration of the AASL *Standards* until doing so becomes second nature.

A remarkable characteristic of the AASL *Standards* is that they bring together so many disparate threads from research and best practice about maximizing the academic, social, collaborative, personal, and individual learning processes of the learner. Marcia A. Mardis, who coauthored the AASL *Standards*, reflects on the research in "Thirty Helens Agree: 2007 Research Supports AASL's *Standards for the 21st-Century Learner*" (beginning on page 13). Mardis's article succinctly demonstrates how richly the AASL *Standards* are embedded in best practice throughout the school setting.

The AASL *Standards*, available for free download at www.ala.org/aasl/standards, begin by outlining nine Common Beliefs. These Common Beliefs create a common foundational ground upon which school librarians and other educators can begin the conversation about 21st-century learning (Fontichiaro 2008a). The Common Beliefs can be summarized into these key areas: reading, inquiry, ethical behavior, technology, and equitable access to information and resources. They recognize that information literacy has become a more complex experience in light of changing formats and content, that students will need powerful toolkits to face a world of change, that learning is social, and that school libraries are essential to student learning (AASL 2007).

In his poem "A Valediction: Forbidding Mourning," John Donne (n.d.) describes a compass that has two feet: one stands firm and unmoving, which permits the other to stretch outward into new territory. The Common Beliefs can serve as the grounded "foot" that gives librarians the strength and conviction to extend into new areas of student learning as described in the four standards (discussed below). They can also serve as a litmus test for future hires or to assess a department's common understanding before leaping into a more in-depth study of the AASL *Standards* (Fontichiaro 2008b).

The AASL *Standards* document then is divided into four standards, which focus on the following: inquiry; critical thinking, synthesis, and making decisions; democratic and ethical behavior; and personal growth and creativity (AASL 2007). Although these four standards echo the values school librarians have set forth in the past, the real innovation of the standards comes when they are further broken down into substandards. Each of the four standards contains four subcategories: skills, dispositions, responsibilities, and self- assessment strategies.

Skills are those academic skills in which students engage and develop, such as gathering information, synthesizing, or using technology to communicate findings.

Dispositions are akin to character education traits or the Habits of Mind (Costa and Kallick 2009) and might be defined as the behavioral or mental toolkit that students develop and bring with them to a new situation. They might include perseverance, creative thinking, or persistence. When the AASL *Standards* were released, the dispositions were the most controversial. In an educational climate so focused on assessment, how does an educator assess these skills? Barbara Stripling addresses the importance of dispositions in "Dispositions: Getting Beyond 'Whatever'" (starting on page 16).

The third area is *responsibilities*. Similar to self-assessment, responsibilities work to shift the focus from the teacher as project leader to the student as manager of his or her own project.

Finally, *self-assessments* represent the student's ability to judge his or her own process and product and recognize areas for improvement. This metacognition helps students develop the ability to evaluate their own work independently, not merely judge their work's value according to adult (teacher or parent) feedback. The ability to self-evaluate is critical for workplace success, whether the student will become a plumber who needs to evaluate his work flow relative to his hourly fee or a politician who must constantly check her voting record against her beliefs and those of her constituency. Refer to chapter 7 for more discussion of developing students' abilities to know the quality of their own processes and products.

In "New Standards—Refreshing Our Work, AGAIN!" (starting on page 20), Betty Marcoux looks beyond the content of the AASL *Standards* and helps readers launch their journey to know, integrate, and support the goals of the new AASL *Standards*, including examples from other school districts.

Whereas the ASCD New Compact, P21, and NETS*S outline student learning in broad strokes, the AASL *Standards* paint with a finer brush. This finer level of granularity serves the school librarian well, as it names goals specifically, using educator-friendly language that can be understood both inside and outside the school library.

The AASL *Standards'* strong vision for student learning is a beacon toward which all school librarians can aspire.

GETTING TO ADVOCACY

Sharing the AASL *Standards for the 21st-Century Learner* can help administrators, stakeholders, and school board members see the school library through a new lens and begin to dismantle outdated visions of school libraries as quiet, sedate centers for teacher-prescribed lessons. Until they know the potential of school libraries, stakeholders are unable to speak on your behalf. Here are some public relations strategies for getting the word out and building a foundation upon which advocacy can develop:

1. Post a link to these documents on the school library's Web site or blog:

   a. AASL *Standards* (www.ala.org/aasl/standards)

   b. Scholastic's document *School Libraries Work!*, which summarizes over a dozen research studies showing the positive benefits of school libraries on student achievement (librarypublishing.scholastic.com/content/stores/LibraryStore/pages/ images/SLW3_2008.pdf)

   c. The Colorado Learner's Bill of Rights, endorsed by the Colorado School Library Leaders, which outlines ten aspects of learner-centered study to which school libraries can aspire (casl.wordpress.com/2008/ 11/08/colorado-learners-bill-of-rights/). The Bill of Rights, and an accompanying article, are also included in chapter 2 (beginning on page 38).

2. Share links to these documents in your school or district newsletter and show how these documents connect to local standards or curriculum in a way that will resonate with the readers/stakeholders.

3. Print out copies for the building administrator. Highlight the areas where the district is already strong and request a time to share a vision for further implementing the AASL *Standards*.

4. Request to speak to the board of education or board of trustees and encourage them to adopt the AASL *Standards* as a working document in the school or district. Even if it is not possible to be added to the formal agenda, most board meetings have a brief public comments period during which the information can be shared. Bring spare copies for the audience! Better yet, have teachers, administrators, or parents present—the ultimate goal of advocacy is to get others to speak for and about school library programs.

5. When a new district or school initiative is proposed, look for correlations between the AASL *Standards* and the new initiative. Advocacy, or creating an environment in which others speak about your value, is much more powerful than self-promotion. As a result, advocacy involves linking agendas and using language familiar to the stakeholders—speak to them and address their priorities. Find common ground (e.g., school improvement plans, the P21 initiative, local standards).

6. When attending district or regional meetings of school librarians, suggest convening a study group to discuss the AASL *Standards* and similar documents. "Getting Started with the Standards," authored by the AASL Learning Standards and Guidelines Implementation Task Force (Johns 2008), offers additional strategies for becoming familiar with the *Standards*. In addition, AASL's January 2009 publication, *Standards for the 21st-Century Learner in Action*, is a strong resource to show what the AASL *Standards* might look like when implemented. This provides a useful backdrop against which to begin your own work.

THOUGHTS FOR THE JOURNEY

1. Any school reform effort requires the collective thinking and dedication of many. Who can be identified in the building, district, or region as a study partner for moving forward?

2. What is the state of the school, district, or state school library curriculum? How do these documents support those existing curricula? What can be identified as areas that need to be updated or new areas for inclusion?

3. Has the school board seen or acted upon any of these documents? How?

4. Change can often provoke feelings of fear or anxiety. What concerns are raised about the new standards, especially the AASL *Standards for the 21st-Century Learner?*

5. Change is also exhilarating. What about these new standards, especially the AASL *Standards,* is exciting?

6. The AASL *Standards* signal a shift from teacher-centered instruction to student- centered learning. What evidence is there that student-centered learning is already happening in the school environment?

7. Preservice school librarians may be preparing to enter an environment in which the local culture is less familiar with 21st-century learning standards. As a newcomer to a school, how may existing gaps be bridged?

8. For administrators, what in these standards is already happening in the school setting? What is not? What can be done to support the implementation of these standards?

THE IMPORTANCE OF LANGUAGE

The Partnership for 21st Century Skills and AASL Standards

by Gail Formanack

Members of the school library media profession are fortunate to have new direction from two organizations that seek to define the type of educational experiences that will best benefit students as they prepare to continue to learn, live, and work in the 21st century. Both organizations, American Association of School Librarians (AASL) and the Partnership for 21st Century Skills, frame an educational experience that goes beyond traditional academic learning while putting a greater emphasis on critical thinking and problem solving. As the debate and commentary continue regarding the new *AASL Standards for the 21st-Century Learner*, it is important to compare the language used in both organizations' documents.

Members and Key Elements

The Partnership's member organizations include major corporations such as Apple, Microsoft, Dell, and Verizon along with education organizations such as the National Education Association (NEA), the Association for Supervision and Curriculum Development (ASCD), and AASL. The Partnership came into existence in 2002 and was initially supported by a two-year grant from the U. S. Department of Education. The Partnership for 21st Century Skills conducted extensive research and held outreach sessions with educators, employers, parents, community members, and students before creating a framework that they hope will result in a shared vision for education reform.

The Partnership believes that education needs to change if the United States is going to remain competitive in the global marketplace.

They have identified key elements of 21st century learning (Partnership for 21st Century Skills 2008):

▶ *Core subjects and 21st century themes:* The No Child Left Behind Act of 2001 identifies the core subjects as English, reading or language arts, mathematics, science, foreign languages, civics, government, economics, arts, history, and geography. The Partnership believe schools must go beyond basic competency in those areas by weaving in 21st century interdisciplinary themes that are critical to success but not typically emphasized in schools today: global awareness, financial, economic, business and entrepreneurial literacy, civic literacy, and health literacy.

▶ *Learning and innovation skills:* The following have been identified as essential to success in our increasingly complex life and work environments: critical-thinking and problem-solving skills; communication and collaboration skills; and creativity and innovation skills.

▶ *Information, media, and technology skills:* To be successful in an environment marked by access to an abundance of information and rapid changes in technology, individuals must be able to exhibit skill in information literacy, media literacy, and ICT (Information, Communications and Technology) literacy.

▶ *Life and career skills:* The following skills have been identified as important to incorporate into school experiences: flexibility and adaptability, initiative and self-direction, social and cross-cultural skills, productivity and accountability, leadership, and responsibility.

Support Systems

The Partnership also identified critical support systems that ensure mastery of the 21st century skills:

▶ *21st century standards and assessments:* Authentic assessments are the foundation of a 21st century education and must measure all of the skill areas listed above. Assessment of the 21st century skills must be integrated with the assessments of the core subjects. A balanced approach to assessment using effective classroom assessments along with high quality standardized testing can be a powerful tool to help both teachers and students gain success.

▶ *21st century curriculum and instruction:* Instructional materials and practice should produce mastery of 21st century skills.

▶ *21st century professional development:* Teachers should be provided with effective 21st century skills training and support for integrating these skills into classroom instruction.

▶ *21st century learning environments:* Students must have access to the tools that support the learning of the 21st century skills.

The Partnership has not written its own standards. Instead it advocates that states use existing frameworks and resources as they review and rewrite their own state standards. Its vision is that these 21st century skills be fully integrated into the teaching and learning of the entire curriculum as educators update how the core subjects are taught. They do not advocate that schools add a new class that teaches these skills separately. This vision is based on the belief that a rigorous curriculum in the core subjects is not enough to prepare students for a world that is characterized by rapid change and globalization. The 21st century skills they identify in the framework are designed to give young people the edge they need to compete successfully in an international economy.

Action Guide

The Partnership has published an action guide for state leaders to explain the framework and encourage states to create their own initiatives. The majority of their resources are available on their Web site (http://www.21stcenturyskills.

org). They have also launched *Route 21* which is an online, one-stop shop for 21st century skills-related information, resources, and community tools (http://www.21stcenturyskills.org/route21). For educators who need a more concrete idea of how these skills can be taught within the context of the core subjects, the Partnership has developed ICT Literacy maps for English, geography, math, science, and social studies. The maps identify tools and sample student outcomes for 4th, 8th, and 12th grade and should be helpful for not only content area teachers but also library media specialists.

▶ Learning has a social context.
▶ School libraries are essential to the development of learning skills (AASL 2007).

Four broad standards replace the nine standards found previously in *Information Power*. They are as follows:

▶ Inquire, think critically, and gain knowledge.
▶ Draw conclusions, make informed decisions, apply knowledge to new situations, and create new knowledge.
▶ Share knowledge and participate ethically and productively as members of our democratic society.

Library media specialists must step up and become instructional leaders by collaborating with classroom teachers in the design of learning experiences that require inquiry into essential questions tied to real-world, complex issues.

Linking to AASL Standards

In an examination of the language of the new *AASL Standards for the 21st-Century Learner*, it is important to note that there is also a focus on a foundation of critical thinking. This document begins by listing the following nine common beliefs:

▶ Reading is a window to the world.
▶ Inquiry provides a framework for learning.
▶ Ethical behavior in the use of information must be taught.
▶ Technology skills are crucial for future employment needs.
▶ Equitable access is a key component for education.
▶ The definition of information literacy has become more complex as resources and technologies have changed.
▶ The continuing expansion of information demands that all individuals acquire the thinking skills that will enable them to learn on their own.

▶ Pursue personal and aesthetic growth (AASL 2007).

The standards have statements under each that are divided into four categories: Skills, Dispositions in Action, Responsibilities, and Self-Assessment Strategies. Skill statements include some familiar concepts, such as 1.1.5 which reads, "Evaluate information found in selected sources on the basis of accuracy, validity, appropriateness for needs, importance, and social and cultural context." Some statements, however, reflect the impact of newer technologies, such as 4.1.7 which reads, "Use social networks and information tools to gather and share information" (AASL 2007).

Certainly the skills statements in the AASL standards further define and support the information literacy statements that are part of the Partnership's framework recognizing the important role these skills play in critical thinking. Information literacy skills provide the basis for students to be able to function optimally as life long learners.

Dispositions and Responsibilities

Dispositions in action are defined in the AASL standards document as "ongoing beliefs and attitudes that guide thinking and intellectual behavior that can be measured through actions taken." An example is 1.2.6 which states, "Display emotional resilience by persisting in information searching despite challenges" (AASL 2007).

In examining the language in the disposition statements, one sees terms such as adaptability, persistence, creativity, confidence, self-direction, flexibility, teamwork, social responsibility, and leadership.

Responsibility statements broaden the scope of the ethics standard found in *Information Power*. An example of a responsibility statement is 2.3.2 which states, "Consider diverse and global perspectives in drawing conclusions." Other terms found in the responsibility statements include ethical, legal, respect, contribute, and participate. The self-assessment strategy statements are a worthwhile addition to the document and should help focus instruction that leads to increased metacognition on the part of students. A sample statement is 3.4.3 which reads, "Assess own ability to work with others in a group setting by evaluating varied roles, leadership, and demonstrations of respect for other viewpoints" (AASL 2007). Other terms found in the self-assessment statements include monitor, adapt, reflect, assess, and evaluate.

Importance of Terminology

These are all terms that illustrate the overlap with the life and career skills part of the Partnership's framework. Some individuals who have commented on the new AASL standards have faulted what they consider are values-based statements and don't believe that they should be taught in school. However, the Partnership says there is ample evidence to indicate these skills are essential in the workplace and should be infused into the school curriculum. The new standards reflect many of the Partnership for 21st Century Skills of critical thinking and problem solving, creativity and innovation, and communication and collaboration.

In January 17, 2008, posted on his blog *Infomancy*, Christopher Harris defends the language of the new AASL standards against critics who have complained that the language is non-specific and vague. He also states that he believes the concerns about assessing the affective behaviors addressed in the standards have been overblown. Utilizing multiple forms of assessment, including observation, journals, and project logs, should allow teachers and library media specialists to gauge student success (Harris 2008).

This increased focus on a metacognitive approach to instruction is supported by the work of the National Center on Education and the Economy. They believe that students learn to take control of their own learning by defining goals and monitoring their own progress. Research has shown that students can be taught metacognitive strategies such as the ability to predict outcomes, note failures to comprehend, plan ahead, and activate background knowledge. The organization states that while the metacognitive approach is understood to be effective, it is under utilized in today's curricular materials and instructional practices. They believe these strategies must be taught in the context of subjects or within problem-based learning experiences because attempts to teach generic strategies in a class such as "study skills" frequently leads to a failure to transfer (Pelligrino 2006, 5).

The Role of the Library Media Specialist

"A language both reflects and affects a culture's way of thinking, and changes in a culture influence the development of its language" (Encyclopedia Britannica, s.v. "language"). The language in the new AASL standards and the vision for 21st century learning laid out by the Partnership for 21st Century Skills should allow library media professionals to think about how their current practices align with those outlined by these organizations.

Library media specialists must take a leadership role in shifting the educational culture away from one that values the collection and memorization of factual knowledge. Library media specialists must step up and become instructional leaders by collaborating with classroom teachers in the design of learning experiences that require inquiry into essential questions tied to real-world, complex issues. Efforts must be made to design assignments that incorporate reflection and self-assessment as integral parts of the process. Library media specialists must practice the same dispositions cited in the standards: openness to new ideas, teamwork, leadership, confidence, and flexibility. If teachers seem unwilling to make the shift, then the dispositions of persistence and emotional resilience will be necessary.

Substantive discussion about the language in both of these documents is needed to change the culture of library media centers.

References

American Association of School Librarians. *Standards for the 21st-Century Learner.* American Library Association, 2007.

Harris, Christopher. *Infomancy.* http://schoolof.infomancy/?p=465 (accessed February 18, 2008).

Partnership for 21st Century Skills. *Partnership for 21st Century Skills.* 2008. http://www.21stcenturyskills.org (accessed February 19, 2008).

Pellegrino, James W. *Rethinking and Redesigning Curriculum Instruction and Assessment: What Contemporary Research and Theory Suggests.* National Center on Education and the Economy, 2006.◄

Gail Formanack is the Supervisor of Library Services, Omaha Public Schools, Omaha, NE. Email: gail.formanack@ops.org

SLMAM Skills Correlations—New (2007) to Old (1998)

AASL Information Literacy Standards

AASL *Standards for the 21st-Century Learner* (2007). http://www.ala.org/aasl/standards

CORRELATED TO: **AASL/AECT** *Information Literacy Standards* (1998). AASL & AECT. *Information Power: Building Partnerships for Learning.* ALA, 1998.

The following correlations are made to help library media specialists match their previous knowledge of nine AASL Standards to the four new standards through a correlation process between "Indicators" from the 1998 Standards and "Skills" from the 2007 Standards. Although this only addresses skills, attention should also be given to the "Dispositions," "Responsibilities," and "Self-Assessments" outlined in the new standards.

Learners use skills, resources, and tools to:

1. Inquire, think critically, and gain knowledge.

1.1.1 Follow an inquiry-based process in seeking knowledge in curricular subjects, and make the real-world connection for using this process in own life. (1998: 1.5)

1.1.2 Use prior and background knowledge as context for new learning. (1998: 3.2)

1.1.3 Develop and refine a range of questions to frame the search for new understanding. (1998: 1.3)

1.1.4 Find, evaluate, and select appropriate sources to answer questions. (1998: 1.1, 1.4, 1.5, 2.4,)

1.1.5 Evaluate information found in selected sources on the basis of accuracy, validity, appropriateness for needs, importance, and social and cultural context. (1998: 1.2, 2.4)

1.1.6 Read, view, and listen for information presented in any format (e.g., textual, visual, media, digital) in order to make inferences and gather meaning. (1998: 1.4)

1.1.7 Make sense of information gathered from diverse sources by identifying misconceptions, main and supporting ideas, conflicting information, and point of view or bias. (1998: 1.2, 2.2, 2.3, 2.4, 7.1)

1.1.8 Demonstrate mastery of technology tools for accessing information and pursuing inquiry. (1998: 1.5)

1.1.9 Collaborate with others to broaden and deepen understanding. (1998: 9.3)

2. Draw conclusions, make informed decisions, apply knowledge to new situations, and create new knowledge.

2.1.1 Continue an inquiry based research process by applying critical-thinking skills [ ] to information and knowledge in order to construct new understandings, draw conclusions, and create new knowledge. (1998: none)

2.1.2 Organize knowledge so that it is useful. (1998: none)

2.1.3 Use strategies to draw conclusions from information and apply knowledge to curricular areas, real-word situations, and further investigations. (1998: 5.2)

2.1.4 Use technology and other information tools to analyze and organize information. (1998: 9.1)

2.1.5 Collaborate with others to exchange ideas, develop new understanding, make decisions, and solve problems. (1998: 9.1, 9.3)

2.1.6 Use the writing process, media and visual literacy, and technology skills to create products that express new understandings. (1998: 5.3, 6)

3. Share knowledge and participate ethically and productively as members of our democratic society.

3.1.1 Conclude an inquiry-based research process by sharing new understandings and reflecting on the learning. (1998: none)

3.1.2 Participate and collaborate as members of a social and intellectual network of learners. (1998: 9.4)

3.1.3 Use writing and speaking skills to communicate new understanding effectively. (1998: 3.4, 5.3,6, 9.1)

3.1.4 Use technology and other information tools to organize and display knowledge and understanding in ways that others can view, use, and assess. (1998: 9.1)

3.1.5 Connect learning to community issues. (1998: none)

3.1.6 Use information and technology ethically and responsibly. (1998: 7.2, 8.1, 8.2, 8.3)

4. Pursue personal and aesthetic growth.

4.1.1 Read, view, and listen for pleasure and personal growth. (1998: 3.4, 4.1, 5.1)

4.1.2 Read widely and fluently to make connections with self, the world, and previous reading. (1998: 4.1, 5.1)

4.1.3 Respond to literature and creative expressions of ides in various formats and genres. (1998: 7.1)

4.1.4 Seek information for personal learning in a variety of formats and genres. (1998: 4.1, 7.1)

4.1.5 Connect ides to own interests and previous knowledge and experience. (1998: 4.2)

4.1.6 Organize personal knowledge in a way that can be called upon easily. (1998: 3.4, 6)

4.1.7 Use social networks and information tools to gather and share information. (1998: 9.4)

4.1.8 Use creative and artistic formats to express personal learning. (1998: 4.2)

Permission to publish granted by the American Library Association to *School Library Media Activities Monthly* 24, no. 6, February 2008.

Standards
for the 21st-Century Learner

by Sharon Coatney

Standards for the 21st-Century Learner, the long anticipated and updated standards from the American Association of School Librarians, was unveiled by AASL President Sara Kelly Johns at the AASL National Conference in Reno, Nevada, in October 2007. Amidst the usual controversy associated with all things new and different, the new standards are, in reality, closely related to the 1998 AASL Information Standards for Student Learning (*Information Power: Building Partnerships for Learning*, ALA, 1998). The "*SLMAM* Skills Correlations" for AASL Standards can be found on page 58.

The following four new standards track pretty closely with the nine previous standards:

1. Inquire, think critically, and gain knowledge;

2. Draw conclusions, make informed decisions, apply knowledge to new situations, and create new knowledge;

3. Share knowledge and participate ethically and productively as members of our democratic society;

4. Pursue personal and aesthetic growth (*Standards for the 21st-Century Learner* 2007).

The updated standards are far more specific and the explanation of each standard is divided into Skills, Dispositions in Action, Responsibilities, and Self-Assessment Strategies.

The new, more specific divisions will help library media specialists effectively implement the new standards into their teaching. These new standards will prompt asking not only what skills are to be taught, but also how students can be assisted in developing self-assessment strategies and the necessary responsibilities and dispositions to successfully meet each

Sharon Coatney is a former library media specialist from Kansas. She is a past president of the AASL and Councilor at Large of the American Library Association. She is now the Senior Acquisitions Editor for Education and School Library Products at Libraries Unlimited/Teacher Ideas Press.

standard. The new format facilitates the acknowledgement that there are habits of mind that must be developed and put in place before skills can be attained by students. It is an important step in establishing the AASL standards at the forefront of current educational practices. For instance, in the first standard, "inquire, think critically, and gain knowledge," students are asked to develop skills to "find, evaluate and select appropriate sources to answer questions" (Skills 1.1.4). They must also demonstrate the disposition to "display emotional resilience by persisting in information searching despite challenges" (Dispositions in Action 1.2.6) as well as demonstrate the responsibility to "seek divergent perspectives during information gathering and assessment" (Responsibilities 1.3.2). Self-assessment strategies must be demonstrated to "monitor [their] own information-seeking processes for effectiveness and progress, and adapt as necessary" (Self-Assessment Strategies 1.4.1) (*Standards for the 21st-Century Learner* 2007).

The use of the terms "dispositions" and "responsibilities," as well as the inclusion of assessment strategies, more closely aligns these new standards to language and standards in the other content area curriculums. As library media specialists become more involved in instructional partnerships with other teachers, it becomes imperative that information literacy standards are positioned to align with these aspects of student learning. It is also extremely important that the language of the standards be understandable to the other educators. Successful collaboration with teachers begins with good communication; standards that are easily accessible and understandable to all teachers will enhance and enable the process. Accolades are due to the AASL Standards Writing Committee for their attention to these very important details and to the American Association of School Librarians for offering free downloads of the standards on their website.

The new standards, like the 1998 standards, are placed in context for the professional user through a statement of common beliefs and a description of the 21st-century learner. It is important to read and ponder these before analyzing the standards themselves. Standards are not developed in a vacuum; the education and cultural milieu does affect the current standards and these statements do a fine job of explicating the current situation.

In addition to providing definitions for key words used in the standards, helpful questions are provided for the library media specialist to ask about students. The following examples are taken from each of the four standards:

Skills

Key question: Does the student have the right proficiencies to explore a topic or subject further?

Dispositions in Action

Key question: Is the student disposed to higher level thinking and actively engaged in critical thinking to gain and share knowledge?

Responsibilities

Key question: Is the student aware that the foundational traits for 21st-century learning require self-accountability that extends beyond skills and dispositions?

Self-Assessment Strategies

Key question: Can the student recognize personal strengths and weaknesses over time and become a stronger, more independent learner? (*Standards for the 21st-Century Learner* 2007)

These questions along with the statement of common beliefs held by school library professionals draw a picture of the opportunities, responsibilities, and challenges facing today's library media specialists in preparing students to be 21st-century learners.

This information provides the necessary background knowledge for library media specialists to understand and implement the new standards—and that is where the fun really begins!

A lesson plan template design now includes skills, dispositions, responsibilities, and self-assessments in a myriad of possible combinations and integrated with the content area standards. For example, a study of DNA, or Democracy, or Dinosaurs can emphasize the skill of following a process model, the responsibility of connecting understanding to real-world situations, the disposition of maintaining a critical stance along with helping students monitor their own processes. The opportunity for creativity in implementing these new

standards is wide open. Library media specialists, who are among the most creative teachers in any building, should welcome these new standards.

See "Use This Page," page 2, for a lesson plan template that includes skills, dispositions, responsibilities, and self-assessments.

Standards for the 21st-Century Learner. ALA, 2007. http://www.ala.org/aasl/standards (accessed November 28, 2007).

Common Beliefs—Key Words:

"Reading is a window to the world.

Inquiry provides a framework for learning.

Ethical behavior in the use of information must be taught.

Technology skills are crucial for future employment needs.

Equitable access is a key component for education.

The definition of information literacy has become more complex as resources and technologies have changed.

The continuing expansion of information demands that all individuals acquire the thinking skills that will enable them to learn on their own.

Learning has a social context.

School libraries are essential to the development of learning skills."

(Standards for the 21st-Century Learner 2007)

Collaborative Planning for Information Literacy

Integrating the new AASL *Standards for the 21st-Century Learner* (2007). http://www.ala.org/aasl/standards

Curricular Area:_____ **Grade Level:** _____ **Timeline:** _____

LEARNING OBJECTIVES

Curriculum or Content Area Objectives: _____
_____

Information Literacy: (AASL Standards 1, 2, 3, 4): _____
_____

Skills (AASL Standards 1.1, 2.1, 3.1, 4.1): _____
_____

Dispositions (AASL Standards 1.2, 2.2, 3.2, 4.2): _____
_____

LEARNING GOAL FOR THE LESSON

Assessment for Students' Learning: What must students do to demonstrate their learning goal? (Harada 27) including Self-Assessment (AASL Standards 1.4, 2.4, 3.4, 4.4):_____
_____

Resources Needed: _____
_____
_____

RESPONSIBILITIES

Classroom Teacher:_____   Library Media Specialist: _____
_____   _____
_____   _____
_____   _____
_____   _____

Student (AASL Standards 1.3, 2.3, 3.3, 4.3): _____   Others: _____
_____   _____
_____   _____
_____   _____
_____   _____

Follow-Up: What evidence do you have that students achieved the learning targets? (Harada 25). What went well? What needs work? How did the collaboration go?_____
_____
_____

This page is based on "Use This Page" (*SLMAM*, November 2006: 2) and Violet H. Harada's "Building Evidence Folders for Learning through Library Media Centers" (*SLMAM*, November 2006: 25-30), and is related to the article written by Sharon Coatney in this issue (*SLMAM*, February 2008: 56-57).

Thirty Helens Agree:
2007 Research Supports AASL's
Standards for the 21st-Century Learner

by Marcia A. Mardis

Affirmation

A Canadian comedy troupe, Kids in the Hall, featured a recurring sketch on their long-running television show in which thirty women of various ages, sizes, and ethnicities, all called Helen, loudly proclaimed their agreement on issues ranging from "Punctuality is important," to "Good ideas should be written down." Just as the thirty diverse Helens agreed on a variety of topics, members of the American Association of School Librarians (AASL) used research from a variety of perspectives to affirm their important, new student standards, *Standards for the 21st-Century Learner* (2007).

New Student Standards and Research

These standards for students are the first step toward the national school library program standards revitalization. They include specific guidelines for implementation, professional roles, and program design and are to be released very soon. The *Standards* document resulted from a year of discussion, reading, community input, and forecasting. The *Standards* represent a fresh look at what students should know as well as what they should be able to do with their library media specialists and library media programs. These standards are flexible enough to adapt to local situations yet forward-thinking enough to support students for years to come.

The *Standards* embody core principles such as reading as a window to the world, inquiry as a learning framework, ethical information use, technology skills for future success, equitable access to information, broadening information literacy to encompass new media and technology, thinking skills for independent learning, learning as a social context, and school libraries as essential to learning (AASL 2007). These key understandings are also expressed in forward-thinking initiatives from the Association for Supervision and Curriculum Development's (ASCD) *The Whole Child: The Learning Compact Redefined* (2007) education initiative, the Partnership for 21st Century Skills' *Framework for 21st Century Learning*, and the International Society for Technology in Education's (ISTE) *National Educational Technology Standards for Students* (2007). Together, these documents represent a concerted effort of all educational stakeholders to coordinate visions and efforts for student development.

Research Links

Unlike prior annual research reviews, this review organizes research by each of the four standards and includes key U. S. and international education and library science studies. This broad approach reflects the widespread research support for the *Standards'* potential to prepare students to be global citizens.

Standard 1. Learners will use skills, resources, and tools to inquire, think critically, and gain knowledge (AASL 2007).

This standard ensures that students use the library to link what they are learning to what they already know. The link is made through questioning, using information reflective of various opinions, and applying information in ways that are ethical and easily communicated to others for feedback.

The premise underlying the first standard is that core curriculum is not sufficient for children to become successful, productive students and

Marcia A. Mardis, Ed.D., is an Assistant Professor at the Library and Information Science Program at Wayne State University in Detroit, MI. She was one of the authors of the AASL *Standards for the 21st-Century Learner*. Email: mmardis@wayne.edu

citizens. Indeed, a study of the change in teacher tasks in the United States conducted by Valli and Buese showed that the pressures of meeting the annual yearly progress goals mandated by the No Child Left Behind Act has narrowed the classroom curriculum and decreased creative, technology-infused, resource-based learning activities (2007). Activities and instruction in the library media center can provide students with opportunities to connect learning in different areas and build their abilities to express themselves and pursue their interests.

A study in England by Parker and Hurry suggested that elementary students' comprehension was improved when their teachers modeled, rather than led, questioning for reading assignments (2007). By seeing how to ask questions about a text and learning what types of questions to ask, students were able to work effectively in small groups with positive gains in their reading comprehension. This research was confirmed by a study of students with learning disabilities (LD) in a Washington high school (Lenz, et al. 2007). Due to large class sizes, teachers lacked the ability to work with LD students in a one-on-one format, but when teachers modeled strategies such as guiding questions and concept mapping, LD students applied these approaches for increased comprehension of informational texts as demonstrated on the state-mandated reading test.

Standard 2. Learners will use skills, resources, and tools to draw conclusions, make informed decisions, apply knowledge to new situations, and create new knowledge (AASL 2007).

When working toward this standard, students will organize and apply information to allow them to collaborate with others and draw meaningful conclusions. Students will use a range of resources to be productive, link their

conclusions to the world, and develop directions for future understanding.

In two recent studies in the United States, researchers examined the information management skills of new students at two universities through observations and interviews (Lohnes 2007; Wilber 2007). Both studies concluded that students did not apply traditional information seeking and organization skills, but rather, applied self-generated approaches to organization. The students discussed the incompatibility of the approaches to finding information they had been taught in school with the highly technology-mediated, Web-based interaction. Even with elementary level students, a quasi-experimental study conducted in Michigan showed that LD students benefited far more from the scaffolding provided by self-selected Web-based tools with their writing and organization skills than the traditional methods they had been taught in the classroom. These students requested access to computers outside the classroom to pursue their learning (Englebert, et al. 2007).

In Slovenia, a team of researchers led by Zuljian looked at the relationship between educators' philosophy of teaching and students' ability to work independently and draw wide-ranging conclusions (2007). The study results suggested that when teachers did not just practice student-centered learning, but also believed in student-centered learning, their pupils were more able to work independently, draw links between their class work and the world, and exhibit these traits in other classes.

Standard 3. Learners will use skills, resources, and tools to share knowledge and participate ethically and productively as members of our democratic society (AASL 2007).

This standard promotes the idea that student writing, technology use, collaboration, and communication should be oriented toward helping

students participate in the community and be globally knowledgeable. Students who meet this standard show leadership with informed decision-making and work with others in ways that respect diverse perspectives.

The growing number of English Language Learner (ELL) students is a tremendous opportunity for the library media center. While previous research has shown that ELL students at all grade levels excel in activities when they can express their knowledge through imagery or demonstration (Lee 2005), a pair of new studies suggested that elementary-level ELL students were best able to make gains in their reading and writing skills when they work collaboratively in small groups. Results of these studies also suggested that the native English speakers in the groups benefited from playing a teaching role and from learning language and culture from ELL students (Calhoon, et al. 2007; Kamps, et al. 2007).

Authentic problem-based approaches to learning ensure success in a range of curriculum areas. For example, a content analysis of AP calculus student work at a Nevada high school showed that students demonstrated more persistence in constructing and solving equations when the work related to a real world problem (Perrin 2007). Despite pushes for service-based curricula, student involvement in community-based issues most effectively comes from informal, self-initiated activities that reflect personal interests and values. A metasynthesis of literature relating to citizenship education throughout the world revealed that students were empowered in their communities and with social issues when they were encouraged to pursue self-directed, cross-curricular themes in informal learning environments like library media centers (Pike 2007). Students were more likely to demonstrate their "invisible citizenship" through creative expression and peer-to-peer communication.

Standard 4. Learners use skills, resources, and tools to pursue personal and aesthetic growth (AASL 2007).

This standard embraces leisure pursuits as worthwhile complements to school work and a support for student learning. It is recognized in this standard that the resources of library media centers are not just curriculum support entities, but also inspire students to read for pleasure and pursue their interests. Students can cultivate and pursue interests in the library media center and share their enthusiasm with others through a variety of media.

Surveys of 10th grade students and teachers conducted by Konings' research team in the Netherlands found that students desire to shape their learning environments and, when they feel as though they have had input, they are more successful and invested in their learning (2007). On the other hand, educators' perceptions of what learning environments should look like and contain was vastly different than students' preferences. The researchers concluded that student participation in the design of learning environments stimulated their commitment to and interest in school activities. Similarly, in an autoethnography of a first year high school teacher in Greece, the teacher asked students to describe factors that would make them more successful in learning ancient Greek. While the teacher expected students to ask for more learning support, students felt that their success would be best aided by learning in an environment they designed and in which they could pursue their personal interests in addition to their school work (Mitsoni 2006).

Common Goals

Library media specialists, technology specialists, teachers, school administrators, and community members have articulated guidelines that assure the same progressive and exciting future for our children. For library media specialists, the *Standards* not only represent a change, but also an unprecedented opportunity to support all education stakeholders with common goals for students and schools. It is exciting to see that while AASL, ASCD, the Partnership for 21st Century Learning, and ISTE converge on similar visions, researchers around the world have also been validating ways to enhance the relevance of library media centers for years to come.

References:

American Association of School Librarians. *Standards for the 21st-Century Learner.* http://www.ala.org/ala/aasl/aaslproftools/learningstandards/standards.cfm (accessed January 1, 2008).

Calhoon, Mary Beth, Stephanie Al Otaiba, David Cihak, Amber King, and Analise Avalos. "Effects of a Peer-Mediated Program on Reading Skill Acquisition for Two-Way Bilingual First Grade Classrooms." *Learning Disability Quarterly* 30, no. 3 (2007): 169-184.

Englebert, Carol Sue, Yong Zhao, Kailonnie Dunsmore, Natalia Yevgenyevena Collings, and Kimberly Wolbers. "Scaffolding the Writing on Students with Disabilties through Procedural Facilitation: Using an Internet-Based Technology to Improve Performance." *Learning Disability Quarterly* 30, no. 1 (2007): 9-30.

Kamps, Deborah, Mary Abbott, Charles Greenwood, Carmen Arrega-Mayer, Howard Wills, Jennifer Longstaff, Michelle Culpepper, and Cheryl Walton. "Use of Evidence-Based, Small-Group Reading Instruction for English Language Learners in Elementary Grades: Secondary-Tier Intervention." *Learning Disability Quarterly* 30, no. 3 (2007): 153-168.

Konings, Karen D., Mario J. van Zundert, Saskia Brand-Gruwel, and Jeroen J.G. van Merrienboer. "Participatory Design in Secondary Education: Is It a Good Idea? Students' and Teachers' Opinions on Its Desirability and Feasibility." *Educational Studies* 33, no. 4 (2007): 445-67.

The Learning Compact Redefined: A Call to Action. A Report of the Commission of the Whole Child. http://www.ascd.org/learningcompact (accessed January 1, 2008).

Lee, Okhee. "Science Education with English Language Learners: Synthesis and Research Agenda." *Review of Educational Research* 75, no. 4 (2005): 491-521.

Lenz, B. Keith, Gary L. Adams, Janis A. Bulgren, Norman Pouliot, and Michelle Laraux. "Effects of Curriculum Maps and Guiding Questions on the Test Performance of Adolescents with Learning Disabilities." *Learning Disability Quarterly* 30, no. 4 (2007): 235-243.

Lohnes, Sarah. "Situating the Net Gen: Exploring the Role of Technology in the Social Identity of College Students." Paper presented at American Educational Research Association, Chicago, April 2007.

Mitsoni, Fotini. "'I Get Bored When We Don't Have the Opportunity to Say Our Opinion:' Learning about Teaching from Students." *Educational Review* 58, no. 2 (2006): 159-170.

National Educational Technology Standards for Students: The Next Generation. http://www.iste.org/Content/NavigationMenu/NETS/For_Students/NETS_S.htm (accessed January 1, 2008).

Parker, Mary, and Jane Hurry. "Teachers' Use of Questioning and Modelling Comprehension Skills in Primary Classrooms." *Educational Review* 59, no. 3 (2007): 299-314.

Perrin, John Robert. "Problem Posing at All Levels in the Calculus Classroom." *School Science & Mathematics* 107, no. 5 (2007): 182-191.

Pike, Mark A. "Values and Visibility: The Implementation and Assessment of Citizenship Education in Schools." *Educational Review* 59, no. 2 (2007): 215-230.

Valli, L., and D. Bueses. "The Changing Role of Teachers in an Era of High-Stakes Accountability." *American Educational Research Journal* 44, no. 3 (2007): 519-558.

Wilber, Dana. "Mynetwork: Understanding the Links and Texts of College Students' New Literacies." Paper presented at American Educational Research Association, Chicago, April 2007.

Zuljian, Milena Valencic. "Students' Conceptions of Knowledge, the Role of the Teacher and Learner as Important Factors in a Didactic School Reform." *Educational Studies* 33, no. 1 (2007): 29-40. ✍

Dispositions:
Getting Beyond "Whatever"

by Barbara Stripling

"Whatever." This one word characterizes the public attitude of far too many students today. Many young people have developed an armor of nonchalance or "whatever" to counter the increasing pressures of testing-based accountability and classroom cultures of teacher-in-charge and students-in-step. This public attitude, however, does not accurately portray the private hopes and dreams of our young people. Most want to be successful, make choices, and be empowered to learn on their own. Our young people do not really think that "whatever" is an acceptable response, but they feel powerless to change the situation so that they can successfully pursue their own way.

One approach to countering this "whatever" attitude among youth today has been taken by the American Association of School Librarians (AASL). This association has taken a bold stance on the importance of attitudes and learning behaviors (also called dispositions) in its new national standards, *Standards for the 21st-Century Learner* (AASL, 2007). These standards go beyond a delineation of skills to include dispositions, responsibilities, and self-assessment strategies. All of these strands work together to enable learners to gain knowledge, solve problems, make decisions, create new knowledge, connect to others, pursue personal growth, and behave ethically and productively as members of our society.

What are dispositions?

The word, "disposition" is easily defined: "prevailing tendency, mood, or inclination; the tendency of something to act in a certain manner under given circumstances" (*Webster's Ninth Edition* s.v. "disposition"). Dispositions, then, are the emotions and attitudes that make us behave in a certain way. AASL recognized that even students with a high level of 21st-century skills are not successful in their learning unless they also have the dispositions to use those skills appropriately. As a concept beyond the denotation, "disposition" represents a complex interweaving of students' background and educational his-

tory, the environment of the classroom and school, the students' content knowledge and skill levels, and the teacher's ability to make the learning meaningful and engaging. Educators must, therefore, ensure that the context of school is conducive to the formation of positive learning dispositions.

The dispositions included in *Standards for the 21st-Century Learner* are assigned to the four learning standards according to the attitudes and behaviors most important for different phases of learning (AASL 2007). While learners are investigating and gaining knowledge (Standard 1), they must have the attitudes that propel them toward exploration (confidence, initiative), attitudes that enable them to be successful along the way despite the challenges of any inquiry process (adaptability, emotional resilience, persistence), and the behaviors that will enable them to respond both creatively and critically (creativity, critical stance). As learners move from gaining knowledge to drawing conclusions and applying knowledge (Standard 2), different learning behaviors become important—learners must be willing to figure out how to approach their knowledge from different directions (flexibility, divergent and convergent thinking, critical stance) in order to use it in new situations (personal productivity).

The expectation that learners will share their knowledge and participate ethically in groups is established in Standard 3. The dispositions required are related to the learners' willingness to demonstrate leadership, social responsibility, and teamwork. Learners who are pursuing personal and aesthetic growth (Standard 4) are more successful if they demonstrate the dispositions of active and engaged learners: curiosity, motivation, openness to new ideas, and the choice to read for pleasure and interest.

Why are dispositions important?

The dispositions outlined in the AASL Standards provide the catalyst needed for successful learning because just the acquisition of skills is not enough. Students may learn the skill of evaluating Web sites, for example, but they must also develop a critical stance and be disposed to use the evaluation skill each time they look at a Web site in order to consistently find good information. Students who are pursuing research and suffer predictable times of uncertainty and emotional lows will be able to push through to reach the next phase of their research successfully if they have developed emotional resilience (Kuhlthau 2005).

A number of educational researchers and writers have written about the importance of dispositions for learning. Art Costa and Bena Kallick have looked at successful learning behaviors and identified what they call "habits of mind" that lead to successful learning. Costa has defined habits of mind as "having a disposition towards solving a problem to which the solution is not readily apparent" (Project Q.E. 2001, 2). John Barell has listed the characteristics of thoughtful persons in his book *Teaching for Thoughtfulness*. These characteristics include many of the dispositions outlined in the AASL *Standards*, including confidence, persistence, and openness to others' ideas, curiosity, and cooperation with others in solving a problem (1995, 47).

A research study designed by David Conley to identify the knowledge and skills essential for success in the first year of college found that habits of mind are extremely important for students to bring to their university work; in fact, many of the university faculty participating in the study deemed habits of mind even more important than content knowledge. The habits of mind identified in the study coincide with many of the thinking skills and dispositions in the AASL *Standards*, including critical thinking, analytic thinking, problem solving, inquisitive nature, ability to deal with frustrating and ill-formed problems, drawing inferences and conclusions, and using technology to assist in learning (2005, 173). Deborah Meier summarized the power of dispositions by stating, "Educating kids for the 21st century means teaching them the habits of mind that will help them benefit from—and be benefits to—the world" (2003, 16).

Can dispositions be taught?

Dispositions are not taught explicitly. Instead, teachers structure learning experiences so that students practice the behavior that is an expression of the disposition. Over time, through a series of experiences that reinforce the targeted attitudes and behaviors, students can adopt the dispositions as their own personal habits of mind. For example, confidence and self-direction cannot be taught directly, but if students have a number of opportunities to determine their next steps and the teacher scaffolds these situations so that the next steps lead to success, then the students can develop attitudes of self-confidence and self-direction.

Dispositions are not grade-level specific, although some will be more appropriate at younger ages than others because of the natural development of emotional maturity. Teachers of primary-age children can focus on curiosity, while developing a critical stance may be introduced in late elementary/middle school. Unlike thinking skills (note Bloom's Taxonomy), dispositions are not taxonomically organized. Students do not have to become confident before they can be curious. There is, however, coherence to the development of dispositions because dispositions cannot be addressed in a one-time-only fashion. They must be introduced when appropriate and reinforced throughout the years of schooling so that they truly become embedded habits of mind for all students.

Dispositions are not observable until learners display behavior that expresses the underlying attitude. The dispositions in the AASL *Standards* are described as "Dispositions in Action" because for each disposition, a student behavior is defined that illustrates what that disposition might look like. For example, one way students can demonstrate initiative is by "posing questions and investigating the answers beyond the collection of superficial facts" (2007). Although students can display initiative in many other ways, the example given in the standards provides a clear model for teachers and library media specialists to understand how the disposition can be applied to a learning situation.

By expecting dispositions to be translated into action, teachers and library media specialists can assess students' development of these attitudes and learning behaviors. For example, students' self-direction, as well as their developing skills of investigation, can be assessed through a research log where students indicate the choices they have made with their reasons for making those choices and their plans for next steps.

What is the library media specialist's role in dispositions?

Library media specialists have a strong role in the development of dispositions through collaborative planning and teaching, building a supportive environment in the library media center, and facilitating a schoolwide culture of empowering learners.

Integrating Dispositions into Collaborative Planning and Teaching

The essential first step in integrating dispositions into instructional planning and teaching begins with the library media specialist and classroom teacher discussing dispositions, why they are necessary for successful learning, and which dispositions are most important for a particular group of students. Just as the number of skills taught within each unit of study is limited, so too must dispositions be focused within each unit.

In fact, based on the needs of a particular group of students, the library media specialist and teacher may decide to address one disposition for the whole year. For example, if they see that the students have a hard time adjusting when something goes wrong in their investigations, they may decide to focus the year on developing the disposition of adaptability. Early in the year, the library media specialist can model and students can

practice adaptability through a process of revising research questions to take advantage of available resources. Later in the year, the library media specialist or classroom teacher can teach a decision-making model for drawing conclusions where students can adapt their tentative conclusions as new information is acquired. Throughout the year, every time students are faced with challenges to their success in learning, they are reminded of adaptation strategies that can help them overcome or go around the barriers. By the end of the year, students will be mindful of the disposition of adaptability and some will have adopted it as a habit of mind.

The key to successful teaching for dispositions is that the library media specialist and teacher assess the needs of the students, focus on the appropriate disposition, decide the learning behaviors that would result from the disposition, and structure the unit and lessons so that students are taught strategies and given supports to succeed.

Strengthening Dispositions through the Library Environment

The library media specialist can carefully arrange the intellectual and physical environment of the library media center to reinforce the acquisition of dispositions. By offering opportunities for students to share book reviews with their peers, library media specialists help students demonstrate leadership and an appreciation for literature. By making a book display of biographies and photographs of famous people with a challenging question like "What makes a hero?," library media specialists can provoke curiosity and motivation to seek information. Library media specialists may also sponsor a public debate or open discussion in the library media center for students after they have completed their science projects on contemporary scientific issues. All students are, thus, encouraged to maintain openness to new ideas and diverse perspectives.

The library collection can also be developed with dispositions in mind. Books, media, and databases can be purchased to provoke curiosity, a critical stance, divergent thinking, creativity, social responsibility, reading motivation, and choice. One principal, for example, who wanted all her students to develop intellectual curiosity, said she would prefer that the library media center had one book entirely about hair styles than five books with generic overviews of fashion or grooming. The principal knew that students would be much more likely to catch the excitement of learning from an in-depth treatment of one topic than from short, non-specific paragraphs on various topics.

The arrangement of the physical facility can also foster the development of dispositions through spaces for conversation with classmates and other spaces designated for thinking and quiet study. Even signage and display spaces can lead students

to be open to new ideas, confident that they can locate resources on their own, motivated to read further about the display topics, and empowered to choose books that interest them.

Facilitating a Schoolwide Culture

Students will be more successful in developing dispositions for learning if the culture throughout the school emphasizes these dispositions. Library media specialists are in a position to impact the schoolwide culture because they can reach every teacher and every student. The first step for the library media specialist is to have a conversation with the principal, with examples ready to illustrate that teaching for dispositions can be integrated seamlessly into current instructional units—it's not "one more thing" for teachers to handle. Showing research about the impact of habits of mind and dispositions on learning and the necessity for students to acquire

these learning behaviors before college will help the administrator buy in to a schoolwide effort.

The next step is to provide professional development and facilitate conversations with teachers. Teachers may be convinced of the importance of teaching for disposition development if they recall their own stories—what triggered their own development and how that impacted their choices in school, college, career, and personal life. As a group, the teachers can then determine a coherent, schoolwide plan for the development of dispositions.

Moving from "Whatever" to "Yes, I can"

Students who have acquired the dispositions for learning outlined in *Standards for the 21st-Century Learner* can move from "Whatever" to "Yes, I can" and can be motivated to continue learning for academic and personal success. Through dispositions, all of our

students can become self-aware, motivated, and self-confident learners in the 21st century.

References::

American Association of School Librarians. *Standards for the 21st-Century Learner*. ALA, 2007.

Barell, John. *Teaching for Thoughtfulness*. Longman, 1995.

Conley, David T. *College Knowledge*. Jossey-Bass, 2005.

Kuhlthau, Carol Collier. *Seeking Meaning: A Process Approach to Library and Information Services*. Libraries Unlimited, 2004.

Meier, Deborah W. "Becoming Educated: The Power of Ideas." *Principal Leadership* 3, no. 7 (March 2003): 16-19.

"Project Q. E.: Encouraging Habits of Mind – Phase I." June 2001. http://www.mcdowellfoundation.ca/main_mcdowell/projects/research_rep/64_project_qe.pdf (accessed July 17, 2008).◄

Barbara Stripling is the Director of Library Services for the New York City Department of Education. Email: bstripling@schools.nyc.gov

New Standards—

Refreshing Our Work, *AGAIN!*

by Betty Marcoux

The standards for a school library media program have once again been revisited. The American Association of School Librarians (AASL) has released a new set of standards, and although the content is not totally new, the standards are streamlined. School library practitioners need to stay abreast of current thought represented in these new standards that are related to understanding the learning needs and behaviors of students.

This new set of standards places more responsibility on the student for their information behaviors and moves from nine standards to a crisp four (http://www.ala.org/aaal/standards). Yet, the National Council for Accreditation of Teacher Education (NCATE; http://www.ncate.org/) and the National Board of Professional Teaching Standards (NBPTS; http://www.nbpts.org/) continue to ask for even more in terms of student outcomes for the school library media program and professional library media specialist. These new standards move between the interests of the No Child Left Behind (NCLB; http://www.ed.gov/policy/elsec/leg/esea02/index.html) which emphasizes left brain function to the 21st-Century learning standards (http://www.21stcenturyskills.org), which center on the right brain approach to learning.

The constancy of all standards is, in itself, a message that these skills are important to student learning. HOW they are done and HOW they are demonstrated is why we have so many different sets of standards. The good news concerning the importance of standards to the educational process is that they are somewhat constant and don't seem to be going away, thus demonstrating that more than the school library profession sees these competencies as important for student learning. The bad news is that more and more influential people perceive that the school library program and profession aren't necessarily succeeding with these expectations and, rather than advocating collaboration and partnerships with the school library program, they are incorporating them without the inclusion of the school library program and professional. This attitude assumes that the professional and program can be either marginalized or eliminated without detriment to student learning needs.

This new set of AASL standards emphasizes the reading component as an uncompromising facet of all four standards. These standards also are prefaced by statements about inquiry, ethical behavior, technological prowess, and equality of access—all of which will be assumed behaviors in most educational settings. These standards are designed to be timeless by embracing the nature of expanding and morphing information needs and uses.

I think these four standards are great! They are a summation of what has been said by those in the field over many years. For example, Dresang's Radical Change Theory, Kuhlthau's Information Search Process Model, the Eisenberg/Berkowitz Big6/Super Three models, the Stripling/Pitts Brainstorms and Blueprints, and the Pappas/Tepe/Follett Pathways to Knowledge all address student information behaviors and information literacy strategies. Four major information literacy themes, however, emerge

Betty (Elizabeth) Marcoux, Ph.D., currently is on the faculty of the University of Washington Information School, and teaches in the area of school & youth librarianship. Formerly a K-12 teacher and library media specialist, she now works with current and future practitioners who dedicate themselves to children and young adult information services.

examining these models: defining the nature and scope of information literacy, establishing the value of information and its literacy, examining and planning for effective methods that instruct how to be information literate and, finally, defining how being information literate will positively impact information access and use. This new set of standards aligns well with these information literacy themes: Standards 1 and 2 address the nature as well as the scope of information literacy. They include how to work on effective methodology for making these two standards happen and how they can be achieved. Standard 3 addresses the value of information literacy in society today and tomorrow, especially as it reflects a democratic society. And Standard 4 addresses the use of information for growth, defining its impact on learning today.

Many library media specialists are just now beginning to understand and implement the work of the 1998 set of standards only to have new ones arrive on their desk. How can one possibly keep up with the renewal schedule while trying to implement what has al-ready been approved in the school district? It helps to realize that the new standards aren't completely new. In the world of ever updated and morphed information, these standards can be used to continue establishing the foundational nature of information access and use. While this new set will supplant former ones, there is merit in examining how these new standards interface with former standards and continue to mold the "bottom line" of student achievement. (See the "*SLMAM* Skills Correlations—New (2007) to Old (1998)" at: http://www.school librarymedia.com/articles/correlations2008v24n6.html). And, certainly, there are ways to blend the new standards with other standards.

One way to do this is to measure! Measure what is significant to the student—how can their growth in learning be demonstrated and impacted? Analyze the standards in terms of how to best measure them as well as how to link them to measurements currently being used. Consider it as a strategic combining of standards and measurements that are meaningful to all, including the purse string holders. Vi Harada, a faculty member of the University of Hawaii Graduate School of Library and Information Studies, captures the essence of measurement in her recent publication on assessment of student learn-ing (2005). In this publication, she ties real learning to inquiry more than to response. Measurement allows for this inquiry to occur. It is knowing which questions to ask and which questions will be used to find answers in terms of student achievement. Harada's work demonstrates how measurement reflects a desired outcome and is very beneficial to the school library program.

Another example of how to use measurement is to use these findings to drive the program and its place in the school unit. Sandra Nelson wrote about how to plan and get results for the public library (2001). These can easily be customized to reflect the interests and vision of the library media center and allow it to be even more integrated into the school unit.

A second way is to align these new standards with current standards in use and then share that information with all stakeholders, developing action plans based on what is already on the books and accepted. In Arizona this has been done with the Scottsdale School District (http://azla.wikispaces.com/). Interfacing the standards with what is already in practice allows the school library professional to determine how the new AASL *Standards* weave into the current curriculum/content standards of the state. In addition to allowing for multiple examples of content-driven process strategies to emerge within the valued standards of the school, this type of alignment allows many to see just how the information literacy standards interface. Thus, even though each school may have a different toolkit of standards to increase student learning, it is important to realize that the new

AASL standards fit well with them all. Library media specialists can also zero in on the significant content area standards used in a particular educational environment and demonstrate how they inherently interweave with the new AASL standards. They can identify which resources can be used to advance the issues of student achievement, and how they can be effectively used. Various lessons can be tied to standards and expectations in the school and state. Tools can also be identified to support student learning. THEN, after all of this identifying, learning outcomes can be identified to be paired with lessons taught that reflect the most valued standards for students. Just as we pair certain liquids with certain cheese and chocolate, so we pair standards and their expectations.

Library media specialists can continue to review and learn about the new standards. Look at them critically and see how they best interface with what is already happening in the school library program. See how they fit into the schema of 21st-century learning standards (http://www.21stcenturyskills.org), into the ISTE/NETS (National Educational Technology standards; http://www.iste.org/AM/Template.cfm?Section=NETS) and into the new theories about developmental information behavior of students. See how the affective characteristics of some standards lend themselves to reviving affective models of information while still embracing the cognitive model of student learning. See how these embrace the theory of Dan Pink's book, *A Whole New Mind*, that moves learning and doing from the rote world of the left brain to the creative, inquisitive risk world of the right brain (2005). These new standards seem to embrace more than the rote world of the information literate skilled and move one to the world of the information literate explorer.

The new standards also encourage student responsibility for their own learning by asking students to self-assess. Consider how the school library program and the library media specialist can support this self-assessment. Self-monitoring, a value-added commodity of the new standards, can be facilitated and embraced by the school library program. Self monitoring can also drive learning behaviors of the students and the faculty to determine the value of their learning.

Several issues haven't changed— the school library media program is still essential to student learning, the school library professional still drives the essence of quality programming, and the school still supports learning centered programs. On the other hand, several issues have changed—quantitative measurement of student progress is the coin of the realm for schools today whether we like it or not, and these four standards can provide everyone with a more comprehensible set of outcomes, and they offer a chance to align new technologies with new insights into student learning behaviors. This is the students' future—their world. We just facilitate their learning, exploration, and use of it.

As always, the time to act is now. While we work to cement our positions with federal and state legislation and examine what it is that today's student needs to know to succeed, let us use these standards to help us determine our roles in helping students be more success-ful learners. And along the way, we just may find that we are better learners when we understand and interface more productively with our students, our faculties, our stakeholders.

References:

American Association of School Librarians/Association for Educational Communication and Technology. *Information Power: Building Partnerships for Learning.* ALA, 1998.

American Association of School Librarians/American Library Association. *Standards for the 21st-Century Learner.* 2006. http://www.ala.org/ala/aasl-proftools/learningstandards/standards.cfm

Dresang, Eliza. *Radical Change: Books for Youth in a Digital World.* Wilson, 1999.

Eisenberg, Michael, and Bob Berkowitz. *Information Problem Solving: The Big Six Skills Approach to Library and Information Skills Instruction.* Praeger/Greenwood, 1990.

Framework for 21st Century Learning. http://www.21stcenturyskills.org

Harada, V. H., and J. M. Yoshina. *Assessing Learning: Librarians and Teachers as Partners.* Libraries Unlimited/Greenwood Press, 2005.

International Society for Technology in Education. *National Educational Technology Standards.* 1998. http://www.iste.org/AM/Template.cfm?Section=NETS

Kuhlthau, Carol. *Accommodating the User's Information Search Process: Challenges for Information Retrieval System Designers.* ASIS, 1999. http://www.asis.org/Bulletin/Feb-99/kuhlthau.html

Nelson, Sandra S. *The New Planning for Results: A Streamlined Approach.* American Library Association, 2001.

Pappas, Marjorie L., and Ann E. Tepe. *Pathways to Knowledge.* Follett Software, 1997. http://www.pathwaysmodel.com

Pink, Daniel. *A Whole New Mind: Why Right-Brainers Will Rule the Future.* Penguin, 2005.

Stripling, Barbara, and Judy Pitts. *Brainstorms & Blueprints: Teaching Library Research as a Thinking Process.* Libraries Unlimited, 1988. ✋

Chapter 2

Meet the 21st-Century Learners

We are dealing with a confident and talented generation. That's wonderful. They are, after all, our children—sons, daughters, nieces, nephews, and friends. They'll continue the chain that has been forged since time immemorial. We have a sacred trust in all sectors of libraries to make sure they can be the best they can be, that our communities can be great, and that we respect the traditions of our past while evolving to our vision of a better future.

—Stephen Abram, "Millennials: Deal with Them! Part II" (see page 27)

Ask any K–12 educator about today's students, and one answer comes up repeatedly: "They're not like the kids we used to teach." Indeed, today's learners are shaped by a digitally rich world full of video games, digital technologies, and constant connectivity via smartphones and cell phones. Many television commercials today have been reduced from 30 to 15 seconds in length. It's a jarring experience for older viewers, but not for many children and teens. They are used to high stimulus; a constant flow of information; multiple, simultaneous sensory inputs; and the ability to highly customize their environment, from personal playlists on their mp3 player to a custom ringtone, from their individual Webkins Web site to the custom background on their Gmail page (though texting is far more popular). They have a high degree of autonomy in their free time and may spend hours each evening in virtual worlds that are light years away from the face-to-face world of their parents. The linear approach to learning that is embraced by many of their teachers cannot keep pace with their mad-dash, hyperlinked world. They may display boredom or frustration in classrooms where they are not given choices as to how to direct their time or where they must shut down the devices such as mp3 players, IM, texting, or cell phones that link them to information and friends after hours.

At the same time, many of today's students hold onto a sense of idealism, community service, and leadership. Many yearn to make a contribution to the world around them, and community, environmental, and political activism are on the rise. In June 2009, for example, thousands of protesters both within Iran's borders and throughout the world expressed their concern via the microblogging site Twitter (twitter.com). Through their Tweets, by tinting their avatars green to signal support for democratic elections, or by changing their home location to Teheran in solidarity with the protesters (and making the protesters more difficult for Iranian censors to isolate), Twitter members used the site to engage with world events. In other words, their hyperlinked, virtual world does not equate to a lack of connection or concern about the human condition. Many students articulate that technology enhances their connectedness by making their interactions 24/7, not limited to face-to-face interactions.

Millennials and Kids 2.0

Many of these 21st-century learners were literally born in the 21st century and have been nicknamed "millennials." In a two-part series, "Millennials: Deal with Them!" (beginning on page 25), Stephen Abram defines millennials and their behaviors and outlines the imperative of school library media centers to meet millennial kids' needs. Janice Gilmore-See, in "Kids 2.0" (starting on page 31), provides an additional perspective on our current students and their need for both connectivity and creativity. She positions today's learners against the backdrop of a new technology-driven culture. Gail Bush considers how library media specialists can meet millennial needs and learning preferences. In "Millennial Learners Build Knowledge Communities" (beginning on page 35), she encourages school library media specialists to consider how their collections and practices can best meet millennials where they are.

Learner's Bill of Rights

Teachers from all types of classrooms know that the old strategies are no longer effective to reach today's students. With Google, instant messaging, and texting, students constantly have information at their fingertips, minimizing the need for rote memorization of dates and places. Simultaneously, with unlimited information so easily accessed, students have a new need: knowing how to make sense of boundless resources. Motivating diverse learners has risen in importance as well, as educators realize the power of students' desire to create, contribute, and engage in meaningful work.

How do educators articulate these new needs and advocate on behalf of their students? That was a question tackled by the Colorado School Library Leaders Learner's Bill of Rights Committee. In "Doesn't Everyone Have Rights to a Learner's Permit?" (beginning on page 38), the committee discusses the need factors that led them to create a list of ten rights for students. Their work resulted in "The Learner's Bill of Rights" (page 40). This is a powerful document, and permission is given to duplicate the Bill of Rights and share it with others. As the committee states, "the ideas in this document are a pathway to transform . . . daily teaching practices" (see page 39). An online version is available at the Colorado School Library Leaders' blog at casl.wordpress.com/2008/11/08/colorado-learners-bill-of-rights/. This would be a good link to make on any school library media center Web page or blog.

Understanding today's students—their new abilities, their increased diversity, their challenges and needs, and the world in which they live—is a key first step in designing learning that is meaningful, engaging, and deep for today's students.

GETTING TO ADVOCACY

Pose one of these questions for response on an interactive bulletin board: "What helps you learn best?" or "How does this library help you learn?" The results can help adult stakeholders hear from students—in their own words—about how they are benefiting from library media centers.

1. Photograph the results and share them with administrators and board of education members. Achieve the ultimate in advocacy and have students present the answers to board members. Advocacy is having others speak for and about school libraries.

2. Transcribe some of the quotes into a PowerPoint presentation. Play the presentation during Open House or parent–teacher conferences. If possible, have students present to parents, showing how they use library media center resources and apply information literacy skills and strategies.

3. Many computer operating systems have a built-in screen saver that allows you to customize scrolling text. Put some of the students' quotes onto the media center's computers.

THOUGHTS FOR THE JOURNEY

1. How has your school discussed "digital learners" or "millennials"?

2. What changes has your school community made to acknowledge "millennials"?

3. What changes has your school community opted *not* to make?

4. Does your school perceive digital learners as different from learners of the previous generation? Why or why not? How is this reflected in instructional methods?

Millennials: Deal with Them!
Part I

by Stephen Abram

I have been watching the next generation closely for many years. I even have and adore two members—a son, 21, and a daughter, 18. This next generation that includes my son and daughter is the biggest in history and already outnumbers the Boomers. As library media specialists and educators, therefore, we must care about them. In the past, we have sadly seen some of the consequences of the mutual disengagement of libraries and Generation X. It isn't pretty. Simply put, this "next" generation will comprise all of our student users (although there is emerging evidence that post-Millennials will be even more distinctive) and most of our college and university users—in short, our future. Furthermore, this is the one segment of the population that is actually growing through immigration. They will vote, run business and charities, fill government roles, and more. Because of these considerations, they are critical to the future of libraries and, indeed, the future itself.

I have commissioned, collected, and read dozens of reports on the demographics of this "next" group of library users. I have led dozens of focus groups and panels composed of these Millennials and have, therefore, probed and tested their preferences and behaviors. Believe me, they're different, and libraries must adapt. I know it's difficult because we, as library media specialists, must continue to offer services and collections for diverse demographic markets. We have to keep a foot in all camps to serve all of our users. But just as we now adapt to our aging users, we must also adapt to these new users as they emerge and engage in information discovery and research.

First, we must discard the idea that this is somehow a damaged

---

When dealing with millennials, we library media specialists need to consider the following statements very closely:
Thinking they are the same as other users is folly. Waiting for them to "get it" or self-correct is foolish. Ignoring the issue like an ostrich is professional suicide.

---

generation. It is largely a myth that they are performing more poorly in their education. As a matter of fact, their performance is likely ahead of previous generations. Secondly, there is a growing body of research that their IQs, their raw ability to access and use their intelligence, has grown markedly and at a level of statistical significance. In addition, MRI studies of their brains show that they use a greater degree and balance of their brains

Stephen Abram, MLS, is Vice President of Innovation for SirsiDynix. He is an SLA Fellow, president-elect of SLA, and the past president of the Ontario Library Association and the Canadian Library Association. He blogs at Stephen's Lighthouse: http://stephenslighthouse.sirsidynix.com. Stephen would love to hear from you at stephen.abram@sirsidynix.com

and have greater physical capacity through increased ganglia and folds of their brains. The majority of their education has been reinvented and shows great promise. They have better team skills, speaking and articulation skills, and problem-solving and process management skills. Conversely, they have weak general knowledge and fact skills which is not necessarily bad because actual raw facts decay rapidly in today's world. For example, the Periodic Table is not the same as it was when we went to school. Indeed, the number of planets has changed, the maps of nations have mutated on a seemingly daily basis, most knowledge is quite malleable in context today.

This "next" generation with so many new and different skills presents a huge opportunity for libraries! It's also a huge threat to society if we fail to meet their needs. If a whole generation shifts their information loyalties to Google™ and makes all of their future important decisions based on the most popular answer, or the one that advertisers want to promote, or the one that special interest groups or partisan politicians want, society is lost. This could be the result of a totally "Googled" generation.

So, the long and the short of it is that we have a window of opportunity to influence a generation. This opportunity only comes along, well, once in a generation. And this "next" generation is a big one. Do we believe in quality information? Do we believe in authoritative information? Do we select the best information? Can we improve the quality of the questions we ask? Can we create an information and entertainment environment that engages everyone and improves the

learning and community experience? The answer, of course, is Yes! The question is, How?

I don't pretend to know all of the answers. I do have some ideas, however, and I'll share a few in this article. And, frankly, I don't think any single approach is best and not just one thing will fix everything. It's all about attitude, approachability, engagement, and understanding.

The Eyes Have It

A study done by SirsiDynix and Kent State University in the spring of 2006 looked at students from grades one through twelve (See "Look in Their Eyes—Eye Tracking, Usability, and Children" by Greg Byerly, *SLMAM*, April 2007: 30-32). Through this study, we learned a great deal about this group. One of the more interesting studies was to take a subset of the students and use eye-tracking software to study how they interacted with websites. This type of study has been done for years, and we know Boomers have a typical page scanning pattern that differs from GenX and post-secondary students today. We discovered new patterns relating to comfort emerging in current K-12 populations. Scanning and reading comfort on the websites was of prime importance to members of this generation; otherwise, they were likely to just click by that site. Creators of advertising and news websites are rapidly learning that eyeballs are important in the virtual world. And stickiness and return visits are improved by paying attention to this basic premise. What works for members of other generations may not work for the "next" generation of users. What current generations find busy, distracting, and dense may delight them. We

have to learn to build for the real user beyond ourselves.

Format Agnosticism

Information in our libraries is organized according to a deep and traditional set of rules. We often organize by format with videos here, books here, and periodicals here. We then divide the online discovery engines by format—search for books in the OPAC, articles in the databases, videos by browsing the shelves. This method has worked for years, and we rarely needed to challenge it. The arrival of the Web and its simple, agnostic way of searching, however, has changed the expectations of a generation. Why do I even care about what format the information is in? If I'm going to mature in a world where nearly everything is digital (streaming media, books, magazines, newspapers, etc.) and on demand, I want my discovery and navigation tools to offer me everything at once—unlimited choices. Do discovery services in current libraries meet these expectations? It's time to focus on format agnostic discovery using new technologies like federated search, OpenURL resolvers, and social network influenced results.

Conclusion

Libraries must be the best they can be in dealing with this confident and talented "next" generation. Specific characteristics of this new generation will be addressed in Part II of "Millennials: Deal with Them!" (*SLMAM*, October 2007). These are characteristics that librarians from all areas will need to acknowledge in order to create libraries that can respond to and meet the needs of the Millennials and post-Millennials.✋

Millennials: Deal with Them! Part II

by Stephen Abram

"Millennials: Deal with Them! Part I" by Stephen Abrams was published in *SLMAM*, September 2007. For a continuation of this topic, visit the *SLMAM* blog with Kristin Fontichiaro (http://www.schoollibrarymedia.com).

More Choices and Delaying Choice

One consequence of the new world of abundant and almost limitless information is too many choices. In addition to the behaviors listed in Part I (*SLMAM*, September 2007: 57-58), another specific behavior of the Millennials is to delay choice until the last second. I have noticed with my own son and daughter that they don't commit to a Friday night social activity until almost past the point of no return. Technologies like mobile phones and instant messaging have found great favor with them because it is easy to delay commitment to a plan. I suppose my teen years were slightly slower versions of this trend with ubiquitous landlines and fast food. What can a library media specialist learn from this? Simple, don't expect them to commit in advance for library programs. Also, don't disappoint and disillusion them when they just show up.

Pathfinders and research skills training provided by library staff may be too directive for this generation. For example, Millennials like to explore two or three topics through several steps of a project like an essay or science fair topic before they choose just one topic. Choosing one topic and sticking to it through a process is as frustrating to them as them remaining noncommittal is to us. Viewed another way, they learn much more about the research process by exploring several paths. An alternative is to be aware of this preference and support the discovery process. Forcing choice too early meets neither their learning needs nor our agenda to have them discover advanced information fluency skills through experience.

Stephen Abram, MLS, is Vice President of Innovation for SirsiDynix. He is an SLA Fellow, president-elect of SLA, and the past president of the Ontario Library Association and the Canadian Library Association. He blogs at Stephen's Lighthouse (http://stephenslighthouse sirsidynix.com). Email: stephenabram@sirsi dynix. com

large scale. It actually might work better on a smaller, more social level. Oh yeah, look for Millennials where they are (schools, clubs, parks, malls), instead of just trying this in the library media center.

Internet Natives, Internet Immigrants

Mark Prensky wrote a seminal article on the key differences between those folks who learned the Internet and all its facets as adults (Digital Immigrants) and those who grew up immersed in it and who have never known another experience (Digital Natives) (http://www.marcprensky.com/writing/). Millennials are those folks, the Digital Natives, who have never really known a world without the Web. Therefore, our standard approach of asking patrons what they want doesn't work as well now. Ethnographic methods work the best. Just observe these students in a nonjudgmental manner and collect those observations and share them. Try to find insights. That's where the magic is. Become immersed in their world. Gaming nights or tournaments, rock the shelves concerts in the library media center, webpage design clubs, discussion groups, story hours, and the like all provide opportunities to observe and learn. It doesn't have to be formal and

Nomadic and Multi-taskers

This Millennial generation is nomadic and will only become more so. They have the tools and the advances through mobile Smart-Phones, GPS or location-aware services, wireless-based software that unfetters them from the ties that bound us—landlines, televisions, movie theaters, and desktop PCs. An untethered generation will present significant challenges as well as opportunities for libraries. Our primary image, as confirmed by the OCLC Perceptions report, is all about physical tethers—buildings, books, and reference desks. We know that is becoming more and more unrealistic every day, but perception is reality. So, what are the tools we need to invest in to adapt to this generation, to stay on their radar as valid and relevant information and learning partners? For starters, look at the following:
- Text messaging services
- Virtual Reference
- Instant Messaging

- Cross system collaboration, e.g., Public Library/School Board partnerships
- XML-based websites that display well on any device
- Presences on social network sites like MySpace, Facebook, and Bebo
- User-generated content such as YouTube and blogs
- Gaming programs and collections
- Round tables and collaboration spaces
- Engaging websites that meet daily needs for homework support and entertainment

So, here we are with a generation that can do and does many things at the same time. Some worry that they are in a state of continuous partial attention and lack the focus and concentration skills necessary for life. Some recent reports from Lee Rainie at the Pew Internet and American Life Project, however, indicate otherwise (http://www.pewinternet.org/).

They are conscious and capable of the need for quiet time and sanctuary. This might be part of the trend for this generation to be more religious and spiritual as well as highly concerned about their values, principles, and ethics. Anyway, this generation is growing up in a very noisy and media-driven world clamoring for their attention. Learning how to filter and choose what to pay attention to at a young age is a critical skill.

More Friends

Millennials today tend to have a wide circle of friends and acquaintances. This is easier to maintain with IM Buddies, email nicknames, and social networking websites. Because options like these are moving so quickly, libraries need to get on the train or be left at the station. I am talking about the social networking sites like MySpace, Bebo and Facebook. When something captures the attention and engagement of an entire generation, it is ignored at our peril. Facebook, by some estimates, engages over 90% of college and university students, at some institutions. MySpace is growing at over 200,000 new users daily. The average user visits twice a day for twenty minutes while contributing content of all types, posting to their blogs, organizing and attending events, and sharing their opinions throughout the social network. We are witnessing the birth of a transformational technology. By the way, nothing is new about the technology; it's just the Web 2.0 trends converging in a useful space aimed at a key target audience. Not putting libraries and library services in the path and spaces frequented by Millennials is foolhardy. Students are maintaining a supra-network of their friends and contacts that can exist beyond the context of their school or community and follow them for life. Need help? Ask the MySpace community. The library lesson here is simple. Talk to those librarians that have set up library MySpace pages this year and hear the stellar early results. Some even have the OPAC on their MySpace presences. Some have done parental awareness sessions and built anew their

connections across the generations. I've loved those library programs that taught kids how to pimp their MySpace pages while subtly teaching Internet safety skills. Marketers have a rule—be where the customers are.

Gamers

OK, let's get this part out of the way. Gaming, for the most part, is good. There are some bad games, but that's overplayed in the media. Only 15% of games sold were rated with a violence designation; 85% of games are rated E (Everyone E+10 for ages 10 and up) or T (teen for ages 13-17). The media hype may have us believing otherwise. Gaming, however, is not a passing fad—it's a twenty-plus billion dollar industry. According to the Entertainment Software Association in 2006, the average age of the gamer is 33 with 25% of adults over age 50 playing games and over 45% of gamers are women. The Pew Internet & American Life Project's recent report on *Teens and Technology* discovered that 81% of teens surveyed in

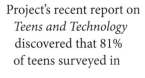

2005 said they played games online, and this doesn't even include other types of electronic gaming (http://www.pewinternet.org/). We must remain open to new formats such as games and how their role will play out in the content space. We already know that gaming skills improve the performance of surgeons, that gaming environments are showing up in R&D laboratories, and that gaming is proving to have positive military, safety, educational, and learning benefits. Yes, we must evaluate all new technologies thoughtfully and in an informed way. Let's make sure we hold this trend close to us and see how it evolves. The emergence of the gaming world based Second Life Library 2.0 is a great experiment to keep our eyes on.

And More

I could cover so much more about the opportunities presented by this "next" generation of Millennials. This generation also shows the following signs:

• They have greater respect and celebration of diversity (not just racial and religious but in other broader and more intangible ways).

• This group has a greater desire for a balanced life (perhaps because of their reaction to the Boomer role model). They actively seek a healthy lifestyle and exercise more than previous generations. They also have a strong family orientation combined with renewed traditional values.

• Politically, this group tends to be non-aligned, often describe themselves as independents, and make choices based on evidence and argument rather than party affiliation. While they are a reasonably conservative generation on many points for their own lives, they often tend to be socially liberal on issues like abortion and same sex relationships, and take a live-and-let-live attitude.

• This generation has a clear and sustainable optimism for their future combined with high expectations for themselves. They are very achievement-oriented, perhaps worrisomely too much so with very high parental expectations (the so-called helicopter parents), but as a possible consequence we are seeing a very high level of entrepreneurial attitudes and tendencies.

• They have a greater commitment to civic involvement with very high levels of participation in volunteer, church, and charitable activities.

• They have a love of reading, although perhaps not the traditional forms we measure. As graphic novels win Pulitzers and gaming magazines fly off the shelves and e-books, websites, and text games compete for the reader's attention, we might need to provide more diverse collections faster.

• They appear to be a generation that is evolving a new ethic around respect for intelligence, talent, inclusivity, and the individual. They are, notably a very direct generation. Their parents chose to raise strong and opinionated children. They tend to be very direct which can look impolite to older eyes but when reviewed later they appear to be just interacting in a way that is more direct than Boomers and GenX-ers. This creates challenges and friction if the behavioral generation gap between service staff and users is not ameliorated.

• Their learning styles are more diverse, and while the traditional strengths in mathematical/logical and text-based learning are still in evidence, there is growing confidence among experiential, physical, and graphical learners.

• As for social values, they appear to be developing a model of interaction that is both adaptive and flexible while preferring team and collaboration modes in their work. Working alone or silently is not an overall strength. Round tables in library media centers as well as small seminar spaces act like magnets.

Conclusion

We are dealing with a confident and talented generation. That's wonderful. They are, after all, our children—sons, daughters, nieces, nephews, and friends. They'll continue the chain that has been forged since time immemorial. We have a sacred trust in all sectors of libraries to make sure they can be the best they can be, that our communities can be great, and that we respect the traditions of our past while evolving to our vision of a better future.

Great Readings

If you've only got time for a few readings on the topic of this article, try these:

Books:

Beck, John C., and Mitchell Wade. *Got Game, How the Gamer Generation Is Reshaping Business Forever*. Harvard Business School Press, 2004 (hardcover). [In paperback as *The Kids Are Alright: How the Gamer Generation is Changing the Workplace*. Harvard Business School Press, 2006.]

Gee, James Paul. *What Video Games Have to Teach Us about Learning and Literacy*. Palgrave Macmillan, 2003.

Johnson, Steven. *Everything Bad Is Good For You, Popular Culture Is Actually Making Us Smarter*. Penguin Books, 2005.

References and Free PDFs:

Do They Really Think Differently: Digital Natives, Digital Immigrants Part 2. 2001. http://www.marcprensky.com/writing/Prensky%20-%20Digital%20Natives,%20Digital%20Immigrants%20-%20Part2.pdf

Sweeney, Richard. *Millennial Behaviors & Demographics*. 2006. http://www.library.njit.edu/staff-folders/sweeney/Millennials/Millennial-Behaviors-August-14-2006.doc

Abram, Stephen, and Judy Luther. "Born with a Chip." *Library Journal* (May 2004). http://www.libraryjournal.com/article/CA411572.html

Prensky, Marc. *Digital Natives, Digital Immigrants*. 2001. http://www.marcprensky.com/writing/Prensky%20-%20Digital%20Natives,%20Digital%20Immigrants%20-%20Part1.pdf#search=%22Prensky%2C%20Digital%20Natives%2C%20Digital%20Immigrants%22

Oblinger, Diana. "Boomers, Gen-Xers, and Millennials: Understanding the 'New Students.'" *Educause Review* (July/August 2003). http://www.educause.edu/ir/library/pdf/ERM0342.pdf#search=%22oblinger%22

Oblinger, Diana. *Educating the Net Generation*. Educause, 2005. http://www.educause.edu/educatingthenetgen/

Federman, Mark. *Why Johnny and Janey Can't Read, and Why Mr. and Ms. Smith Can't Teach: The Challenge of Multiple Media Literacies in a Tumultuous Time*. http://individual.utoronto.ca/markfederman/WhyJohnnyandJaneyCantRead.pdf#search=%22Mark%20Federman%2C%20Why%20Johnny%20and%20Janey%20Can%E2%80%99t%20Read%20and%20%22

Pew Internet and American Life Project. Many reports. http://www.pewinternet.org/

Blogs and Web Stuff:

Computers, Cell Phones and Multitasking: A Look Inside the Entertainment Life of 12-24 Year Olds. LA Times/Bloomberg, 2006. http://www.latimes.com/media/acrobat/2006-08/24767411.pdf

Ypulse Blog. http://www.ypulse.com/ ✋

Kids 2.0

by Janice Gilmore-See

Before you can create School Library 2.0, you must understand why it is necessary for your patrons living in the Web 2.0 world.

School Library 2.0 is a model for contemporary library media centers to change the way services are delivered to patrons. Does your library media program look the same as it did five or ten years ago? Are you developing programs for the millennial generation or are you reconstructing programs from your generation?

What are the factors that limit your ability to quickly change your library program to keep pace with the shifting student population? Even the best library media centers have barriers to service such as lack of physical space, time, budget, or staff. Before you learn how to use specific Web 2.0 applications, examine the philosophies behind

Web 2.0 tools to understand why they can be so successful with your library patrons.

How many of the following Web 2.0 phrases do you recognize when relating to the "digital native:"

The *digital native* values *ubiquitous connectedness*, desires *device independence*, insists on *personalization*, trusts the *wisdom of crowds*, and lives in *the long tail* of *the creative class*.

The World Wide Web has become the information choice for millions of computer users. The print reference collection, once the staple of information-seekers, often sits idle while the line for the computer grows. Search engines allow users uncomplicated and immediate access to an immense amount of online information through key-word and semantic searches.

The Internet, prior to 2003, primarily allowed people to type in Web addresses they knew, locate websites using search engines, and surf links from one page to another. The content, however, was controlled by the website owner. Regardless of the purpose of the webpage, users were basically pointers and clickers. A notable counterexample, however, was the eBay site which allowed sellers to post information and pictures of products for sale as early as 1995.

The term "Web 2.0" was credited to O'Reilly Media in 2004 and is used now to describe a second generation of Web-based services. It is often applied to an ongoing transition of the World Wide Web from a collection of static websites feeding information to users to a full-fledged computing platform serving continually-updated Web applications that get better as more people use it (O'Reilly 2005). Web 2.0 is a platform for personalized computing, networked social ex-

Janice Gilmore-See is the Acting District Librarian for La Mesa-Spring Valley School District, and currently attends the School of Library and Information Science at San Jose State University. Email: janicegilmoresee@lmsvsd.k12.ca.us

periences, participation in virtual communities, and creation of Web content itself, "characterized by open communication, decentralization of authority, [and] freedom to share and reuse" (Abram 2006).

Underlying Philosophies of Web 2.0

Digital Natives

Prensky, in "Digital Natives, Digital Immigrants," referred to cultural differences of digital natives, referring to the generation growing up with ubiquitous access to electronic media since birth (2001). Similar to the way native speakers have facility with the languages they learn growing up, digital natives naturally pick up technology skills. Digital natives are comfortable gathering information from many sources and intuitively navigate the Web using progressively sophisticated devices. Most digital natives spend more time staring at a screen of some sort than reading printed materials before adulthood.

On the other hand, digital immigrants are learning technology as adults. Most library media specialists are digital immigrants and must, therefore, cope with the very different approach to information gathering taken by their patrons. Just as immigrants are suspicious and wary of the customs and practices they find when they move to a new country, digital immigrants often question the beliefs and values they observe in the online world. For example, one way to

appeal to digital natives is to make content editable whenever possible. This, however, requires the library media specialist to trust students to make good choices about what they post for the rest of the school community to see. The poor choices evident on such sites as MySpace (among other social sites) cause many digital immigrants to worry that the virtual world is dangerous and unsuitable for student use.

Tech-savvy library media specialists willing to be early adopters of 2.0 technologies are often stymied by school policy. Generally, policy decision-makers are digital immigrant administrators and conservative school boards that fear the worst-case scenarios of technology misuse. Schools that block access to the newest technologies and applications, however, are creating roadblocks that keep students from rich technology experiences that are more readily available to students in affluent and middle-income homes. Library media centers are a natural place to introduce Web 2.0 tools as a bridge to span the digital divide.

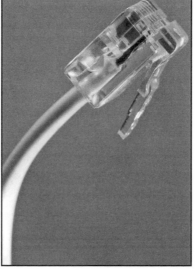

WEB 1.0—A one-way street; the information superhighway.

Online news • Online information • Online commerce

Ubiquitous Connectedness and Device Independence

Broadband and wireless technologies allow users to stay connected continuously with a wide variety of devices. Pervasive computing is the goal of the digital native, meaning that information is accessible from any device at any time in any place. This includes computing devices of all types: cell phones, e-Book Readers, PDAs, game consoles, TVs, cameras, iPods, and all sorts of hot new gadgets that are now capable of connecting to the Web. Organizations like Amazon.com, which claims to have "the Earth's biggest selection" and Google™, whose mission is "to organize the world's information and make it universally accessible and useful," leave library media centers with their limited hours and programs at a loss when competing for the digital native's attention.

Personalization

Digital natives also want to have their services personalized. One good example of personalization is the Amazon.com recommendation engine. Amazon uses the purchasing patterns of their large customer base to suggest other items that may be of interest based on an individual's searches. They also allow customers to submit product reviews. Library media centers can use these same sorts of tools to help students find additional materials based on their previous check-outs as well as allow them to post their good finds for others to see.

Wisdom of Crowds

Surowiecki explains in *The Wisdom of Crowds* that many complex cognitive projects are best solved by large groups of "reasonably informed, unbiased, and engaged people. The group's answer is almost invariably much better than any individual expert's answer, even better than the best answer of the experts in the group. The reason for this superiority is that each individual brings to the problem some valuable unique knowledge or perspective. Any errors in that knowledge or perspective are balanced against those of others in the group, so the collective wisdom of the group is likely to be extremely accurate, reliable, knowledgeable, and predictive" (Surowiecki 2004).

This theory accounts for the success of *Wikipedia*, which boasts over seven million articles in 251 languages. It is updatable by anyone at any time thus allowing the "wisdom of crowds" to accumulate the biggest storehouse of knowledge ever. Breadth of content flourishes because the process is electronically collaborative, distributed across the world, and participation is voluntary. The professional library community has been highly critical of *Wikipedia*, pointing out potential problems with reliability, accuracy, quality, bias, and inconsistency, as well as vulnerability to vandalism. Even though scholarly studies (Viegas, Wattenberg, and Dave 2004) conclude that vandalism is relatively short-lived, and that *Wikipedia* is generally as accurate as other encyclopedias, libraries and academia continue to snub it. Could it be that digital immigrant librarians are simply uncomfortable with the wisdom of crowds? Digital natives use and rely on these tools, and their acceptance is based on its comprehensive nature. Furthermore, depending on the currency of the topic, the term they are seeking may not even exist in print.

WEB 2.0—A complex transportation system with expressways and toll roads, including driver-created entrances and exits connecting boulevards, streets, and avenues.

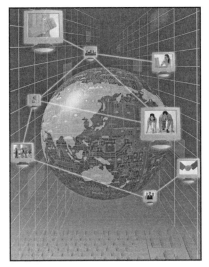

Social Networks

Instant Messaging

Podcasts • Mashups

Telecommunication

Blogs • RSS Feeds • Wikis

Audio, Picture, and Video Sharing

Gaming and Virtual Environments

Collaboration and Productivity Tools

The Long Tail

The term "The Long Tail" (the statistical distribution illustrated in the diagram below) was introduced by Chris Anderson in his October 2004 *Wired* magazine article of the same name as an explanation for the success of the Internet and Internet commerce in popular and niche markets. In this distribution, a high-frequency population is followed by a low-frequency population, which gradually "tails off." In many cases the infrequent events—the long tail, represented by the light gray portion of the graph—can cumulatively outnumber the initial portion of the graph, such

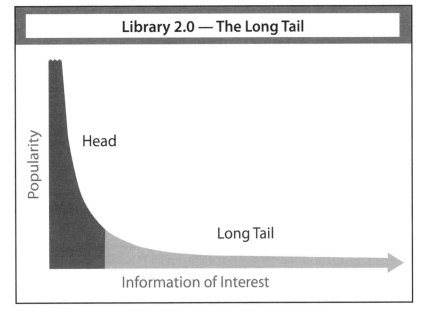

that in aggregate they comprise the majority (Anderson 2004).

Using the library media center as an example, the dark gray portion of the graph would represent the most popular circulating items in the library. The light gray portion represents all the other books that were only checked out by one or two students. Even though the popular items represent a good portion, the diverse needs and interests of students allow those infrequently checked out items to account for the majority of the total circulation.

Students turned away in the past when they were looking for eclectic or unpopular information now have access to it via the Web. Young adults can find books on unconventional subjects, independent music and video productions, obscure genre movies, and the like. Moreover, they can find others with the same interests and create micro-communities. Digital natives use

Library media specialists can begin to understand the unique perspective of the digital native information seeker by sampling and experimenting with the tools they use. Sign up for a social bookmarking account (http://www.del.icio.us) to get a taste of the 2.0 world. Consider taking the free online learning experience called School Library Learning 2.0, a program for CSLA members and friends (http://schoollibrarylearning2.blogspot.com/).

Web 2.0 tools to support personalized searches, express themselves, and share recommendations with others they trust.

The Creative Class

Dr. Richard Florida, Professor of Public Policy at George Mason University, believes that there is an emergent class of people (knowledge workers, intellectuals, artists, and scientists, among others), which he calls the creative class (2002). These people have a different perspective about technology, and especially about borrowing the work of others and using it to create new works. These people are creative by nature and tend to cluster in big cities where they can find communities and jobs that embrace this culture. Digital natives are a natural part of the creative class and ensure the further growth of Web 2.0 products. Library media centers located in these cities and suburbs will be especially impacted as parents look for schools that support their child's academic and recreational goals. Students who often know more about technology than their teachers or library media specialists want to do more than just view information; they want to personalize it, organize it, change it, create it, and share it with others. The challenge then is to find ways to use these student strengths to help increase engagement in school.

Ready for School Library 2.0?

Does your library media center exist like a one-way street with the library media specialist initiating all the programming? How long will this keep the attention of your digital native learners? School Library 2.0 begins when library media specialists use Web 2.0 tools

to invite participation from the students, teachers, and parents in design and delivery of library programming. The active and empowered library patron is a significant component of School Library 2.0 with information and ideas flowing back and forth between the library media specialist and the patrons. Library services now can evolve and improve through this technology and overcome the traditional barriers to service.

Note: Special thanks to Chris Walsh from the Infinite Thinking Machine (http://www.infinitethinking.org/) for bringing this message forth at the CUE conference and inspiring library media educators to use technology to create innovative instructional programs.

Resources

Abram, Stephen. "Web 2.0, Library 2.0, and Librarian 2.0: Preparing for the 2.0 World." *SirsiDynix One Source E-newsletter* (January 2006). http://www.imakenews.com/sirsi/e_article000505688.cfm?x=b6ySQnR,b3B5r7pL

Anderson, Chris. "The Long Tail." *Wired* 12, no. 10 (October 2004).

Florida, Richard. *The Rise of the Creative Class: and How It's Transforming Work Leisure, Community and Everyday Life.* Perseus Books, 2002.

O'Reilly, Tim. "What Is Web 2.0?" O'Reilly Media (September 2005). http://www.oreilly.com/go/web2.

Prensky, Marc. "Digital Natives, Digital Immigrants." *On the Horizon* 9, no. 5 (2001).

Surowiecki, James. *The Wisdom of Crowds: Why the Many Are Smarter than the Few and How Collective Wisdom Shapes Business, Economies, Societies and Nations.* Little, Brown, 2004.

Viegas, Fernanda, Martin Wattenberg, and Kushal Dave. *Studying Cooperation and Conflict between Authors with History Flow Visualizations.* MIT Media Lab and IBM Research, 2004.

Millennial Learners Build Knowledge Communities

by Gail Bush

We hear the whispers from our academic library buddies. News of millennial learners infiltrating our colleges and universities with wireless weapons designed to derail linear learning abound. The lack of focus on depth of content and reflection is stunning and continuous; partial attention does not write a research paper. And yet, with all this opportunity for connectivity, we must rejoice in the seemingly natural appetite for access of all kinds. After all is said and done, this access may be our best link to the future leaders of society.

A full quarter of the American population, who were not even alive before the advent of Pacman, is now firmly attuned to a completely computerized existence. Our current high school students do not remember a time

before cell phones, and our current elementary students cannot imagine what we did before we had the Internet available 24/7. It seems that if we look closely at this new breed, we see that there is an engagement with others, seeking information that we will do well to address. How millennial learners choose to spend their cognitive

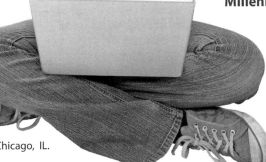

capital has few limits short of bandwidth and wi-fi. Let us as library media specialists then concentrate on the "learner's choice" and appreciate that the learning laboratories we develop in our library media centers serve these needs with relevance and authenticity. Let our library media programs reflect the demands of the outside world for thinkers who make connections with information to build knowledge communities.

How exactly do we justify an independent learning environment when our teachers still feel the age-old pressure to cover the curriculum from Plato to NATO to prepare for standardized testing? Look to the millennial learners; look to those connected students who are learning and building and growing in new ways to prepare for the global challenges of rapid societal change and uncertainty.

Millennial Learners Defined

Reports vary, debates continue, but a consensus of the studies of millennial learners produces an emerging definition. These learners, born between 1979 and 1994 (some say between 1982 and 2000), com-

Gail Bush is a faculty member and director of the Center for Teaching through Children's Books at National-Louis University in Chicago, IL. Email: Gail.Bush@nl.edu

prise 27% of the population and are impelled to be connected with each other through any means. Their attention is partial, their reflective skills are challenged, and they tend to appreciate shallow breadth as opposed to narrow depth of content. Divergent perspectives see millennial learners as both socially isolated and networked and as both technologically facile and operating in only the two dimensions of sight and hearing (based on computer usage). While it is risky to make generalizations about learning styles, there are trends for us to explore as we seek to best serve them. Perhaps thinking about traits and attributes helps us to understand that students who have an unbridled hunger for information-seeking display certain behaviors that we welcome in our independent learning environments.

Instructional Strategies for Information Literacy

Each of the broad categories of the national information literacy standards—information literacy, independent learning, and social

responsibility—suits this discussion of millennial learners in distinct ways. The concept of students as knowledge builders moves to the center of learning so that we recognize what we offer is of value, and we can discard old habits that are no longer relevant. We must still keep in mind that we strive to serve all students.

Information Literacy

The universe of inquiry within the library media center is the perfect home for millennial learners. What is the problem that needs to be solved? What is my task at hand? This area is one that perplexes the best of us. While we understand that we teachers need to focus on curriculum content at some point during each semester or school year, there should be a time when lessons are designed for students to create information-seeking strategies. The motivation to seek the most accurate and appropriate information is a natural part of intellectual curiosity to some but certainly not all students. This is especially true for many millennial learners who are accustomed to pre-packaged sound bites. Finding problems, solving them, and perhaps redefining them are the activities of researchers everywhere. Industrious students take ownership when this responsibility is their own—when task definition means more than being given a list of topics and told to choose one. With the teacher-prescribed list of topics, the cart of books pulled, and the inevitable pathfinder, the student is denied any opportunity to define the information need and any relevance the lesson might have is diluted by spoon-feeding information. Too many students

feel that they "power down" in school. No call for that sentiment in the information power center of the school.

Independent Learning

We library media specialists should plan for the widest, deepest, highest learning environment possible. We should have a range of materials and resources that previously would have been impossible. We can create a playground for the mind and a laboratory for learning by availing ourselves of a learning environment from the richness of the community. We can invite "human" resources whenever possible. We can collaborate with the public library so that members of their book club and members of the school library book club are reading together. We can join with the film club to match books with movies. We can make connections in an authentic way to stimulate the connections that the millennial learner makes naturally. We can review the collection development policy checking for the acquisition of a variety of formats. We can include resources like Jackdaws (http://www.jackdaw.com) that provide facsimiles of primary source documents organized by themes. We should budget for high quality photography paper to print out photos and realia from the American Memory Project of the Library of Congress (http://www.loc.gov). We can also provide a variety of areas for students to be in solitude amongst the stacks and also to work in groups, to read magazines, and to work in privacy. We can commend students as they confer within the group structure as a corporate problem-solving team would operate, but at the same time, welcome the lone student who seeks quiet and peace. The variety of environments we provide both physically and virtually will aid in serving our young information architects as they design their personal learning spaces.

Social Responsibility

Perhaps the most important lesson coming out of libraries today is the value of relevant, accurate, authoritative information as a building-block to knowledge. Whether they are available in print or online, resources used in research do not spontaneously generate. Someone wrote the original document, the article, the column, the caption, the title, the review, the annotation. Someone created the graphic, the icon, the image. If it is used, it should be cited. If the student is not sure, he/she should be told to cite it. We are in good company with our friend David Loertscher in suggesting that plagiarism is a moot issue once the bird units are effectively banned (2004). Gathering information from sources and citing them is just the beginning for a unit that is inquiry-based, problem-based, authentic, and engages

learning. If an entire end-product for a project can be plagiarized by a student, we need to look at that assignment to see where it could be revised to require higher order research skills. Even at the youngest ages, students can read and summarize informational text that is then compared and contrasted. For students of all ages, let the library media center be a place where they learn how to behave appropriately around information. This lesson hits home to many students as they author information that is readily available online and that might itself be susceptible to plagiarists. Treat students as published authors. Millennial learners as contributors to knowledge communities have a healthy respect for intellectual property when they experience ownership over their ideas and information.

Traits of millennial learners that endear them to information specialists include hopefulness about the future, goal-orientation for seeking information, civic-mindedness that makes the information relevant to a more socially just world, and inclusive thinking beyond traditional lines of ethnicity and class. The more we learn about emerging technologies as tools for building knowledge communities the more our students will come to understand the value of the library in their lives. Aim for being facile with a variety of formats of information while keeping a professional perspective of matching the content to the best available medium. Library media specialists can stay open, provide access, and realize that the news they hear will not feel like an ending but rather like an exciting new beginning.

References

Abram, S. "Millennials: Deal with Them!" *Texas Library Journal* 82, no. 3 (2006): 96, 98, 100-103.

American Association of School Librarians and Association for Educational Communications and Technology. *Information Power: Building Partnerships for Learning.* American Library Association, 1998.

Bush, G. "Just Sing: Creativity and Technology in the School Library Media Center." *Knowledge Quest* 30, no. 2 (2001): 18-21.

Bush, G. "Envisioning Information Literacy Standard 10." *Knowledge Quest* 34, no. 5 (2006): 19-21.

Heyboer, K. "To Teach Tech-savvy Millennials, Forget 'Boring' Books and Lectures." *The Star Ledger* (October 2006): A1.

Howe, N., and W. Strauss. *Millennials Rising: The Next Great Generation.* Vintage Press, 2006.

Lippincott, J. K. "Net Generation Students and Libraries." *EDUCAUSE Review* 40, no. 4 (2005): 56-66.

Loertscher, David, et al. *Ban Those Bird Units.* LMC Source, 2004.

McHale, T. "Portrait of a Digital Native." *Technology & Learning* 26, no. 2 (2005): 33-34.

Oppenheimer, T. "The Computer Delusion." *The Atlantic Monthly* 280, no. 1 (July 1997): 45-62. http://www.tnellen.com/ted/tc/computer.htm (accessed May 16, 2007).

Raines, C. "Managing Millennials." *Generations at Work.* 2002. http://www.generationsatwork.com/articles/millenials.html (accessed May 16, 2007).

Williams, L., E. Kolek, and M. Kluge. "Is Being 'Plugged In' Changing Campus Life? A Conversation." *Student Affairs On-Line* 3, no. 1 (Winter 2002). http://www.studentaffairs.com/ejournal/Winter_2002/ (accessed May 16, 2007).

NOTE: Many thanks to Ms. Susan Dobinsky, Niles North High School faculty member, Niles, IL, for generously sharing her 2007 millennial learner research.

Doesn't Everyone Have Rights to a Learner's Permit?

by the Colorado School Library Leaders Learner's Bill of Rights Committee

The word "rights" often conjures up emotions and images and a sense of entitlement. The word "rights" might be preceded with other words such as "civil," "constitutional," or "human." *Merriam-Webster* defines a right as "something to which one has a just claim: as the power or privilege to which one is justly entitled." What about applying these ideas of rights to learners? Doesn't everyone have rights to a "learner's permit?"

A Changing World

The world is currently undergoing dramatic change—politically, technologically, and economically. Thomas Friedman opened our eyes, in his book *The World Is Flat*, to the dramatic change taking place as we shift to a global economy and marketplace (2007). Competition from countries that can produce more items faster and cheaper than the United States is just beginning to make us re-evaluate the skills we are currently teaching students to be competitive and thrive in this marketplace.

Our students are changing as well—having been born into a highly connected, technological world, they have learned how to network, communicate, and navigate in this high-tech environment that seems foreign to many of their library media specialists and teachers. So, while governments and departments of education rally around the battle cry to test – test – test and focus on school accountability, what is happening with the students? They are becoming disillusioned.

According to "The Silent Epidemic: Perspectives of High School Dropouts," a report by Civic Enterprises in association with Peter D. Hart Research Associates for the Bill & Melinda Gates Foundation, each year, almost one third of all public high school students fail to graduate from public high school (2006). This report is available at http://www.civicenterprises.net/pdfs/thesilentepidemic3-06.pdf /.

Furthermore, students are not gaining the 21st-century skills that they need to be competitive in this high-tech, globally connected society. In the study conducted by The Partnership for 21st Century Skills, "Are They Really Ready to Work," 69.6% of employers reported high school graduates are deficient in critical thinking and problem solving skills (http://www.21stcenturyskills.org/documents/FINAL_REPORT_PDF09-29-06.pdf).

An Idea is Born

A group of innovative thinkers in Colorado recognized the opportunity and the need to address both of these issues: lack of student motivation and declining skills. While pondering a vision statement to accompany the new *Standards for the 21st-Century Learner*, it became clear that something was missing in the standards, the educational

> By using the *Standards for the 21st-Century Learner* in conjunction with the Learner's Bill of Rights, teachers can develop and maintain a collection of open-ended assignments in which students have a vested interest in their learning.

plans, and the accountability processes in our education system (AASL 2007). Fundamentally, that missing item was—learner's rights.

As the American Association of School Librarians (AASL) unveiled the *NEW Standards for the 21st-Century Learner* in Reno at the Bi-Annual Conference, October 2007, the Colorado library media specialists and other educators immediately stepped forward to embrace the new standards.

A committee made up of thirty

library media specialists, school district library and technology directors, state library consultants, department of education managers, and other concerned educators from across the state met to decide if they wanted to adopt the AASL standards as the Colorado learner's standards. After studying the standards and engaging in a lively discussion, the committee members unanimously voted to adopt the standards. Without delay, the committee began to work on developing sub-committees that would disseminate information and educate Coloradans about these new standards.

A Vision sub-committee was created and they developed several important documents, one of which was the Vision Statement:

> "We [all learners] exist to inquire, create new knowledge, share knowledge and participate productively, and pursue personal and organizational growth."

As the vision committee began brainstorming this statement for the *Colorado 21st Century Learner Standards* document, one of the members, Jody Gehrig, Director of Libraries, Denver Public Schools, suggested that what was really needed was a learner's bill of rights! The committee agreed that it was an idea worth pursuing.

Creating the Learner's Bill of Rights

Representatives from across the state of Colorado gathered and a tiny brainstorm developed into the *Learner's Bill of Rights*. It was critical to the group for the document to be written in a simple and straight-forward language. The document is intended to be a road map and a learner's permit giving students' permission to become 21st-century learners. The committee worked to ensure that it was representative of the standards addressed in *AASL's Standards for the 21st-Century Learner*, International Society for Technology in Education's (ISTE) *National Educational Technology Standards for Students*

(NETS), and *Partnership for 21st Century Skills' Standards*.

After the Learner's Bill of Rights was developed, feedback was gathered from a larger audience. The document was posted in the AASL forum, shared with the Colorado Association of School Libraries (CASL) through their Web site, and discussed at a meeting of the Colorado School Library Leaders (CoSLL) meeting. The feedback was overwhelmingly positive and only minor edits were made. The Learner's Bill of Rights was endorsed by CoSLL and shared with library leaders at the Colorado Department of Education (see "Use This Page," page 2).

Next Steps

In taking the next steps to promote this document, the committee members considered how these rights impact all learner audiences. In order to truly bring this document to life, it is important to specify how the document works for library media specialists, teachers, other learning specialists, and students. A future expansion of the Learner's Bill of Rights will provide links and ideas to help library media specialists, teachers, and other educational specialists enhance their collaboration, improve their instruction, and essentially ensure that the rights of the learner are being met.

By using the *Standards for the 21st-Century Learner* in conjunction with the Learner's Bill of Rights, teachers can develop and maintain a collection of open-ended assignments in which students have a vested interest in their learning. Library media specialists can begin to communicate with teachers so they understand that the Learner's Bill of Rights is not just one more thing they need to do, but instead understand that the ideas in this document are a pathway to transform their daily teaching practices.

Students can refer to their learner rights via posters, Web sites, bookmarks, etc., and both identify skills that they in-

nately possess and those that they need to acquire or expand in order to improve their ability to think and learn.

By writing descriptions and examples of learner's behaviors for each right in simple terms, all users should be able to obtain a deeper understanding of the intentions of the document and slowly begin to revolutionize how learning takes place.

If anyone would like to participate in describing these learner rights in action or share a story of this "right" from a teaching practice, the wiki *Colorado Learner's Bill of Rights* is available for both visitors and contributions (http://colearnersbor.pbwiki.com/). The journey forward of this Learner's Bill of Rights ensures that every student in Colorado and elsewhere has the right to a "learner's permit."◄

The Learner's Bill of Rights Committee:

Chair: Jody Gehrig, Director of Libraries, Denver Public Schools, Denver, Colorado

Mary Beth Bazzanella, ET/IL Specialist, Jefferson County Public Schools, Golden, Colorado

Cheri Hilton, Teacher Librarian, South High School, Denver Public Schools, Denver, Colorado

Nance Nassar, School Library Senior Consultant, CO Department of Education, State Library, Denver, Colorado

Carol Peterson, Educational Technologist-ITC, Poudre School District, Fort Collins, Colorado

Nancy White, ET-IL Information Literacy Specialist, Academy 20 School District, Colorado Springs, Colorado

Learner's Bill of Rights

The learner has the right to:

1. question and be curious.

2. have personal ideas.

3. choose how to learn and share understanding.

4. plan and participate in learning at an appropriate level.

5. grapple with challenging ideas or concepts.

6. access the information and resources needed.

7. participate in and contribute to a learning network.

8. think critically, solve problems and make decisions.

9. make mistakes and learn from them.

10. reflect on learning.

The "Learner's Bill of Rights" was published with permission of CoSLL.

Chapter 3

Envisioning a Vibrant Library Media Program

Such directions challenge us to reconceptualize the school library, not so much as a space where information is organized, provided and accessed, (which of course is important), but rather as the school's physical and virtual learning commons where inquiry, thinking, imagination, discovery, and creativity are central to students' information-to-knowledge journey, and to their personal, social and cultural growth.

—Ross J. Todd, "There Is Knowledge to Be Gained" (see page 63)

What does a successful school library program look like? The answer is far more complicated than it appears. Like jewels, strong programs have many facets, and no two are exactly alike. A program's strength and vibrancy result from the convergence of many factors: a building's unique learning culture, the personality and passions of the building staff and school librarian, the learning needs of the students, local or state curriculum, the AASL *Standards for the 21st-Century Learner,* and available funding, among others. This chapter examines a variety of perspectives on the elements that create a vibrant library media center as well as strategies for articulating and sharing those elements.

Mission Statements: Shared Visions for Learning

Mission statements, a practice adopted from corporations, are short, one- to two-sentence goal statements, often created by schools as part of a school reform or school accreditation effort. Some mission statements focus on educating the whole child, whereas others prioritize educational excellence, college preparedness, an appreciation for diversity, or character education. These mission statements delineate the most important values of a school and point to a school or district's most sacred values.

In "Hitch Your Wagon to a Mission Statement" (beginning on page 44), Allison Zmuda discusses how important it is for school libraries to align their practices with the school's mission statement. Zmuda also discusses the frequent scenario in which the school librarian may be interested in reform that has not yet come. Being that many mission statements are a result of the collective ideas of building staff, connecting the library program to the staff-endorsed mission is a useful strategy to help staff see the benefits of a quality library program.

In "About Mission" (page 47) Susan Eblen, in collaboration with her colleagues in the Simsbury (Connecticut) Public Schools' Library Media Department, discusses how her department worked with Zmuda to design a philosophical framework for their K–12 learning. Eblen's colleagues worked collaboratively to create a departmental mission statement that, through e-mail conversations and face-to-face meetings, developed into a list of goals, essential questions, and exit outcomes. None of these would have been possible without the mission statement as a guiding light.

Visions

Another approach to defining a library is through a vision. Gail Bush, in "Creativity Literacy: The Library Media Center as a Learning Laboratory" (beginning on page 54), envisions school libraries as a place for constructivist learning: learning that is student centered and in which students create knowledge rather than "receive" it. School libraries are ideal laboratories that can give students literal and mental "space" for exploration and creativity.

Key to the success of any school library media program is an administrator who sees how that program can benefit student learning. When Carl A. Harvey II's principal came to North Elementary in Indiana, he had never before worked with a certified school library media specialist. In "Principal Perspective, Part 2: The Library Media Program" (beginning on page 57), Principal Vince Barnes tells us that he quickly learned how valuable his library media specialist was. In their questions and answers, Harvey and Barnes discuss how the administration builds support for school libraries and for the school library media specialist's teaching—and the resulting payoff. Barnes should know: North Elementary was voted the 2007 School Library Media Program of the Year by the American Association of School Librarians.

What Should Great Student Learning Look Like in the School Library Media Center?

When visitors come to a school, the principal or tour guide inevitably makes a stop in the school library media center. The visitors see "busy" students in the library media center, but what are they busy doing, and what *should* they be busy doing? That key question is explored in Zmuda's article, "What Does It Really Look Like When Students Are Learning in the Library Media Center?" (beginning on page 60). She argues that we must continue to move students beyond passive learning and into active engagement with knowledge construction. Zmuda shows, with piercing clarity, what low-learning and vibrant-learning environments look like. Her keen observations give practicing library media specialists a document to share with colleagues and administrators to spark a conversation about *real* library-based learning.

The Big Picture

Concluding this chapter is an article by Dr. Ross J. Todd of Rutgers University, "There Is Knowledge to Be Gained" (beginning on page 63). Todd starts with a specific example of a revitalized library (renamed a learning commons) in the Boston area; he then paints a vivid portrait of a reconceptualized school library media center. Building on the Productive Pedagogy framework of Gore, Griffiths, and Ladwig (2002), which has intellectual quality, relevance, supportive environment, and recognition of difference as its core tenets. Todd maps each to vibrant school library media centers. It is a powerful vision indeed, one that begs discussion and sharing with colleagues.

GETTING TO ADVOCACY

Before reaching out to stakeholders and asking them to support and speak out for school libraries, school library media specialists must first look inward and inventory their programs' current status. Having a solid vision and mission for the library media program is an essential step to creating an advocacy plan that involves stakeholders. Library media specialists must know where they are going and why before they can link the library agenda with the priorities of potential advocates.

1. Read the school's mission statement. Identify key values that are also represented in the library media statement. If connections are absent, ask administrators, teachers, students, or parents to help rewrite the library's mission statement to better demonstrate the link between the library and the school. Involving those outside the library media center can help you identify and grow future advocates.

2. Find the library media department's mission statement. If none exists, consider requesting that this be added to an upcoming departmental meeting agenda. If it exists, consider revisiting it so that it reflects the AASL *Standards* while also linking to the district mission. Build future advocates for the department by inviting others to contribute to the mission statement.

3. Consider how the library media center can be described in a single sentence to a visitor to the school. Would it be described as, "A rigorous research environment?" "A place where children revel in stories?" or something else? Invite colleagues to help create this definition. One way to visualize this statement is to think about a message that could be placed on T-shirts ordered for the library. What would they say? As a jumpstart, play around with the T-shirt templates, complete with color graphics, available at VistaPrint (www.vistaprint.com). This could be an exercise in creating the mission statement with others.

4. Post the library media center's mission statement prominently in the library and online: on the door, at the circulation desk, on the blog or Web site, or on a bulletin board.

5. Most professionals have business cards. Consider ordering inexpensive business cards featuring the library mission statement. VistaPrint (www.vistaprint.com) can help with adding a custom logo. Moo Cards (www.moo.com), slightly more expensive, features favorite Flickr photos on the backs of cards. Imagine conversations that can arise upon presentation of a business card featuring the storytime area, computer lab, reading tent, or writing castle!

THOUGHTS FOR THE JOURNEY

1. What are the benefits of vision or mission statements?

2. Who should be involved in creating the library media program mission statement?

3. How can mission statements be used to connect your work to that of the entire school?

4. Sometimes, schools create mission statements as a response to a district/trustees directive, but once the directive has passed, they are no longer referenced. How could you help your staff reconnect with or revamp the vision?

5. What do you hope your administrator will see when he or she visits the school library?

Hitch Your Wagon to a Mission Statement

by Allison Zmuda

The Power of Mission
A mission statement drives the work of the school when it creates strong internal accountability among staff members for student learning. This means that staff believe they are responsible for student performance while maintaining a sustained focus on a handful of improvement efforts. This is a commitment to collaborating with one another to analyze student work as well as each other's instructional practices, and to acquiring new knowledge and skills (even if it means unlearning old ones).

The call for schools to redefine, recommit, or reclaim their mission is being trumpeted by researchers, business leaders, and educators across the nation. One of these calls to reconsider the purpose of schools comes from David Conley, Director for the Center of Education Policy Research at the University of Oregon and Executive Director of the Educational Policy Improvement Center. He warns of the significant gap between high school work and college readiness by stating, "Research suggests that one of the major reasons that students falter in college is the gap between their high school experiences and college expectations. Many first year students find that their college courses are fundamentally different from their high school courses. College instructors expect students to draw inferences, interpret results, analyze conflicting source documents, support arguments with evidence, solve complex problems that have no obvious answer, draw conclusions, offer explanations, conduct research, and generally think deeply about what they are being taught" (National Research Council 2002). In the later 2006 report *Are They Really Ready to Work?*, the top areas identified by employers as crucial to workplace success are as follows:

1. Critical thinking/problem solving
2. Information technology application
3. Teamwork/collaboration
4. Creativity/innovation
5. Diversity (Conley 2007).

Vivien Stewart, Vice President of Education of the Asia Society, calls on schools to prepare students for the world community. She says, "Our challenge is to hone students' critical thinking skills and to familiarize students with key concepts that they can apply to new situations. In this way, they can make sense of the explosion of information from different sources around the world and put factual information into context" (2007).

Despite all this clamor for a more rigorous, performance-based, global-minded mission to drive the work of schools, many structures and staff have remained unchanged. According to Professor Richard Elmore, none of this should come as a surprise. He states, "The core of schooling remains relatively stable in the face of massive changes in the structure around it. Schools legitimize themselves with their various conflicting publics by constantly changing external structures and processes, but shield their workers from any fundamental impact of these changes by leaving their core intact. This accounts for the resilience of practice within the context of constant

Allison Zmuda is an Educational Consultant with Education Connection in Litchefield, CT. She was the keynote speaker at the Treasure Mountain Research Retreat #12, Pittsburgh, PA (October 2005) and the AASL Fall Forum "Assessing Student Learning in the SLMC" in Warwick, RI (2006). Email: azmuda@hughes.net

institutional change" (2004).

A mission statement can be an important response to these concerns about the purpose of the school organization; its purpose is to cause student learning as defined by a set of goals. In their new book *Schooling by Design*, authors Grant Wiggins and Jay McTighe delineate the range of goals for learning by stating, "Students are meant to leave school as not merely learned, but inquisitive; not merely knowledgeable, but capable of using their education for good ends; not merely with technical skills but with the appropriate habits of mind that determine whether the skill is used wisely, unwisely, or not used at all when needed. Again, content mastery is not the primary point of teaching even when mission refers to academic goals" (2007).

The Impact of Mission on Library Media Centers

The push for schools to become more accountable for the learning results they produce has created significant pressure on staff to analyze the relationship between the teaching design and the students' performance. The push for schools to be more mindful of preparing students for the challenges of college and the workplace has highlighted the need for information literacy and technology to be a meaningful component of curriculum designs and instructional practice. Likewise, the push for schools to engage all learners in authentic, complex tasks that mirror the real world has elevated the research process from a procedure

that is carried out only in a library to an inquiry-based framework that supports learning in all subjects. Library media specialists should see their work as "the school's work," not just because their classroom space and resources are shared by all, but because the significance of the learning conducted in the library media center is at the heart of the school's purpose. That assumes, however, that the work being conducted in the library media center lives up to the promise of the mission—does it require students to be critical and creative thinkers? Adept problem solvers? Fluent and respectful communicators? Or does the work, instead, simply highlight the autonomous practices that live in the building?

Library media specialists typically are expected to collaborate with everyone. Because the teacher holds the proverbial key to the classroom door, he or she also has the access to the students. If there is no access to students, there is no opportunity to cause student learning. Real collaboration is, however, based on a mutual understanding from all parties. Each party brings to the table a unique and important contribution that makes the collective work richer than any individual effort. Without this mutual

respect, collaboration does not occur. Thus, results are minimized (if not obliterated), and the opportunity of the library media specialist to engage students in work relevant to established information literacy goals is lost. Library media specialists must, therefore, bend over backwards to accommodate classroom teacher requests in hopes that these "good will gestures" will open the door to more meaningful forms of collaboration.

On the larger scale of school reform, library media specialists openly wish that "things were different" but are largely resigned to the fact that they aren't. Therefore, the cost of pushing for "something more" can feel not only uncomfortable but unbearable and ultimately

unproductive. Today's "systemic constraints," however, do not mitigate the desire or the responsibility to achieve the mission of the school. In his monograph to the international best seller *Good to Great*, Jim Collins advises, "It might take decades to change the entire systemic context, and you might be retired or dead by the time those changes come. In the meantime, what are you going to do now?...You must retain faith that you can prevail to greatness in the end, while retaining the disci-

> *The good news is that library media centers are increasingly being looked to as an untapped source of potential learning, a place where students can engage in work that is purposeful, powerful, and personalized. The challenge is how to make sure that the increased attention brings results in real change in instructional practice instead of superficial "parallel play."*

pline to confront the brutal facts of your current reality. What can you do today to create a pocket of greatness, despite the brutal facts of your environment?" (2005). Such reform efforts require much more than additional initiatives, policies, and structures; they require fundamental changes in how we work together to cause student learning. The solution requires more than time, money, and additional staffing; it requires clarifying how staff dedicate instructional minutes to focus students on significant tasks that will prepare them for an ever-increasingly complex, connected, and global world where communication, collaboration, critical thinking, and creativity are prerequisites for success.

The Importance of Candor

Candor requires staff to speak openly about gaps between the status quo and the mission of the school. Renowned businessman Jack Welch asserts that lack of candor damages the relationships between people because of the inability to honestly communicate about difficult issues. He further states, "Instead they withhold comments or criticisms. They keep their mouths shut in order to make people feel better or to avoid conflict, and they sugarcoat bad news in order to maintain appearances. They keep things to themselves, hoarding information. That's all lack of candor and it's absolutely damaging" (Welch 2005). Welch's assertion may appear counterintuitive. Many library media specialists would contend that it is more damaging to speak their minds to their colleagues about the need for more authentic collaboration, more

cognitively demanding work for students, more focused tasks (in design, in directions, and in grading criteria), and more feedback about how students performed as measured by an established set of indicators. Holding on for the right moment, the safe moment, the teachable moment flies in the face of professional responsibilities to the short-term obligation to the students in the school right now and also to the long-term obligation to grow the system.

Clearly there are ways of engaging teachers in conversations that are tactful but still direct. But this desire to grow people must be accompanied by the necessary courage and compassion when discussing difficult issues. This is the role of a coach—someone who articulates (and models) a vision of what quality looks like and then provides the support needed to grow each person to that point. Coaches must not only care about the people they work with but also must be able to separate out the performance from the performer. In other words, library media specialists in this coaching role must navigate precarious conversations through nurturing relationships with individual staff without compromising the clarity of the message or hedging on the difficulty and depth of the change. Higgins states, "Coaches know that significant change demands energy from them and the learners over a long time. They know that any deeply ingrained faulty skill will get worse before it gets better. Performers must be willing to take a step back to be able to take greater steps forward later. It is never easy and coaches prepare learners for this challenge in the beginning" (2003).

Leading the Way

The authority and leadership for this type of collegial coaching does not come from the job title or hierarchy of employees but rather from the system's internal accountability to accomplish the mission of the organization. The good news is that library media centers are increasingly being looked to as an untapped source of potential learning, a place where students can engage in work that is purposeful, powerful, and personalized. The challenge is how to make sure that the increased attention brings results in real change in instructional practice instead of superficial "parallel play." This requires nothing less than a fundamental change in "beliefs, norms and values about what it is possible to achieve, as well as in the actual practices that are designed to bring achievement"(Elmore 2007). But the payoff for the hard work can inspire the school community because the mission statement finally has become much more than words on a wall; this statement has become the mantra for how we do business.

Resources

Collins, J. *Good to Great and the Social Sectors: A Monograph to Accompany Good to Great.* HarperCollins, 2005.

Conley, D.T. "The Challenge of College Readiness." *Education Leadership* 64, no. 7 (April 2007).

Elmore, R. F. *School Reform from the Inside Out: Policy, Practice, and Performance.* Harvard Educational Press, 2004.

Higgins, A. *Best Coaches, Best Practices: Your Path to Personal Excellence.* Higgins House, 2003.

Stewart, V. "Becoming Citizens of the World." *Education Leadership* 64, no. 7 (April 2007).

Welch, Jack. *Winning.* Harper Business, 2005.

Wiggins, G., and J. McTighe. *Schooling by Design.* Association for the Supervision of Curriculum and Development, 2007.

About
MISSION

by Susan Eblen

"Would Susan Eblen and Lois Garrison please come up to the podium to read their LM philosophy statement?" This request came from Allison Zmuda at the beginning of her keynote presentation, "Who Gives You the Authority to Do What You Are Doing?" on Sunday morning at the very end of the AASL Fall Forum "Assessing Student Learning in the SLMC" (2006) in Warwick, Rhode Island. A year earlier, Zmuda had announced the battle cry, "Who gives you the authority?" during David Loertscher's Treasure Mountain Workshop preceding the AASL Conference in Pittsburgh, Pennsylvania.

Our hearts beating quickly, Lois and I made our way to the podium to address the crowd of about five hundred library media specialists from forty-nine states. Zmuda had been the catalyst and support behind our district's curriculum rewriting. It was easy to make a connection to Allison's succinct observations about the work of library media specialists and it was very affirming to read our philosophy statement out loud to our peers.

The purpose of this article is to retrace the steps that led to the development of this philosophy statement as well as to focus on our library media department's satisfaction with the process.

First, subject area "vertical teams" were formed by the Simsbury School District in 2003 to rewrite a standards-based curriculum for all students. Department supervisors and curriculum leaders participated in professional development sessions using *Understanding by Design*, a model by Grant Wiggins and Jay McTighe (1998).

During the spring of 2004, secondary-level department supervisors and selected teachers were invited to an all-day workshop to design "enduring understandings and essential questions" for their content areas based on Connecticut State Standards. The entire library media department, composed of five elementary and two secondary library media specialists, collaborated in developing "enduring understandings and essential questions" based on the current Connecticut State Information Technology Literacy Frameworks. By the end of September 2005, we made final edits to this document (see Figure 1: UbD Framework w/Standards, page 18).

Library media specialists then drafted a philosophy statement during department meeting times, professional development times, and via e-mail throughout the fall of 2005. Secondary library media specialists continued to draft a list of skills, ("By Twelfth Grade, students will know and be able to") based on the philosophy statement (see Figure 2: First Philosophy/Goals Statement, page 19). These skills connected to the recently drafted State of Connecticut Information and Technology Literacy Standards (http://www.sde.ct.gov/sde/lib/sde/Word_Docs/Curriculum/itf.doc).

This article was a collaborative effort by all members of the Simsbury Library Media Department: Lois Garrison, Diane Philippe, Jamie Sepa, Susan Zenick, Lea Macaro, Janet Roche, Maureen Snyder and Susan Eblen. Susan Eblen is the Library Media Department Supervisor for Simsbury Public Schools, Central School. Email: seblen@simsbury.k12.ct.us

Figure 1: UbD Framework w/Standards

Library Media Curriculum Framework – September 2005		
CT K-12 Information Technology Content Standards	**Enduring Understandings: Students understand that:**	**Essential Questions**
Responsible Use: Students will demonstrate the responsible, legal and ethical use of information resources, computers and other technologies.	• The way information is presented and represented is a reflection of academic integrity.	• Why do I need to cite sources to give credit?
Definition and Identification of information needs: Students will define their information needs and identify effective courses of action to conduct research and solve problems.	• There are numerous ways to solve information problems. • The quality of the question determines the quality of the results. • Asking questions leads to identifying important problems to be solved.	• Why question? • What is your job when you are looking for information? • What makes a good research question? • How do I know what questions to ask? • Where do I read first? • What are the benefits of being a skeptic?
Information processing: Students will apply evaluative criteria to the selection, interpretation, analysis, reorganization and synthesis of information from a variety of sources and formats.	• Information is available in many formats; spoken, visual and written. • Information is the currency of meaning. • Information is evaluated depending on information need.	• How do I conduct research? • What plan do I use? • How is solving an information problem like the job of a detective? • What is the big idea? • How do I know if information is reliable?
Application: Students will communicate ideas, information or conclusions by using technologies to create written, visual, oral and multimedia products.	• Information can be interpreted and manipulated. • Information skills require independent learning.	• How can I manipulate information to shape others' thoughts? • How do I figure out what is real? • What skills are necessary to make me a critical thinker? • What skills are necessary to make me an independent user of information? • How is my work in the library different from my work in the classroom? • How can I use what I learn in the library to be more successful in the classroom? • How can I use what I learn in the library to be more successful in life?
Technology Use: Students will use technologies for productivity, problem-solving and learning across the content areas.	• Literacies are multiple in nature and change rapidly.	• What technology do I use? • How does technology enhance my learning?
Assessment: Students will assess the effectiveness and efficiency of their own choices and uses of information and technology for problem-solving and communications.	• Students understand that all learning involves active participation and ownership.	•How do I know when I'm done? • What would I fix or change next time? • What is my job when I'm looking for information?
Literature Appreciation: * This standard was added by the Simsbury Library Media Department.	• Information is the currency of meaning. • "Free voluntary reading" makes a better reader. • There are different types of reading materials available. • Reading can be for many purposes and reasons, i.e. information needs, reading for pleasure, etc.	• Why do I read? • How does literature depict life? • Why do people view the same information differently? • How does reading affect my thinking, feeling and acting?

In May 2006, Zmuda shared another version of the original Understanding by Design document (Figure 1, page 18), in which she had added a column with embedded tasks developed from her curriculum writing sessions with teams of high school teachers. We library media specialists focused for several hours on "what we do," further analyzing our day-to-day teaching in detail. We emerged from this meeting with a clearer understanding of where we needed to go and how to create more consistent and meaningful collaboration with classroom teachers. Specifically, these were the steps we designed:

- Defined State Standards in our own terms, e.g.,
  Responsible Use: Students will demonstrate the responsible, legal, and ethical use of information resources, computers, and other technologies = ethical problem-solvers.
- Brainstormed a list of key ideas about our work.
- Divided into small groups and prioritized the ideas.
- Formed small groups and created a graphic organizer to explain the relationship of key ideas and shared this with the whole group (see Figure 3: All Learners in the 21st Century, page 20.)
- Synthesized the models, coming to consensus on a model that represented our program.
- Created a philosophy statement with Zmuda.
- Drafted goals based on the philosophy statement and State Information Technology Standards.

By immersing ourselves in the documents we created, we made the entire process more successful, intense, and rewarding. We had a working draft to guide our collaborative work by the end of the day. This document was yet another confirmation of the need to weave information literacy skills across the curriculum and through the grades. We walked away with a better understanding and clarity about what we do, helping us articulate our curriculum with key constituents (see Figure 4: Final Philosophy/Goals Statement, page 21.)

During the fall and winter of the 2006-2007 school year, our process continued. Library media specialists spent professional development

Figure 2: First Philosophy/Goals Statement

Students need to have information communication and technology (ICT) skills to understand and live in the 21st century. Simsbury Public Schools' library media specialists (LMS) believe all students can think critically and creatively using information and communication technologies to solve problems effectively and efficiently.
ICT transcends any discipline. Developing these skills allow students to ethically access, manage, integrate, evaluate, create, and communicate information.

LMS promote ICT to enhance productivity and personal development within their learning communities.

By developing information literacy skills, students by graduation will be able to:

- become effective and efficient users of ideas and information.
- compete globally.
- become independent learners.
- think critically and creatively, in order to solve problems, conduct research and make choices effectively and efficiently.
- access, manage, integrate, evaluate, create, and communicate information.
- enhance productivity and personal development.
- prepare for the information-and technology-rich world.
- identify relevant and reliable sources.
- perform successful search strategies to find information in print or electronic media.
- evaluate information.
- use information found on the Internet by skimming and taking notes.
- publish their ideas.
- use information ethically: citing sources to avoid plagiarism, respect for intellectual property, obey copyright laws, and comply with the Acceptable Use of Technology Policy.
- stay safe while online.
- locate, access and use print and complex electronic sources on the Internet and in databases.
- improve test scores, particularly attaining higher reading scores.
- appreciate and enjoy a wide range of literature, media, and technology.

Figure 3: All Learners in the 21st Century (Inspiration Diagram)

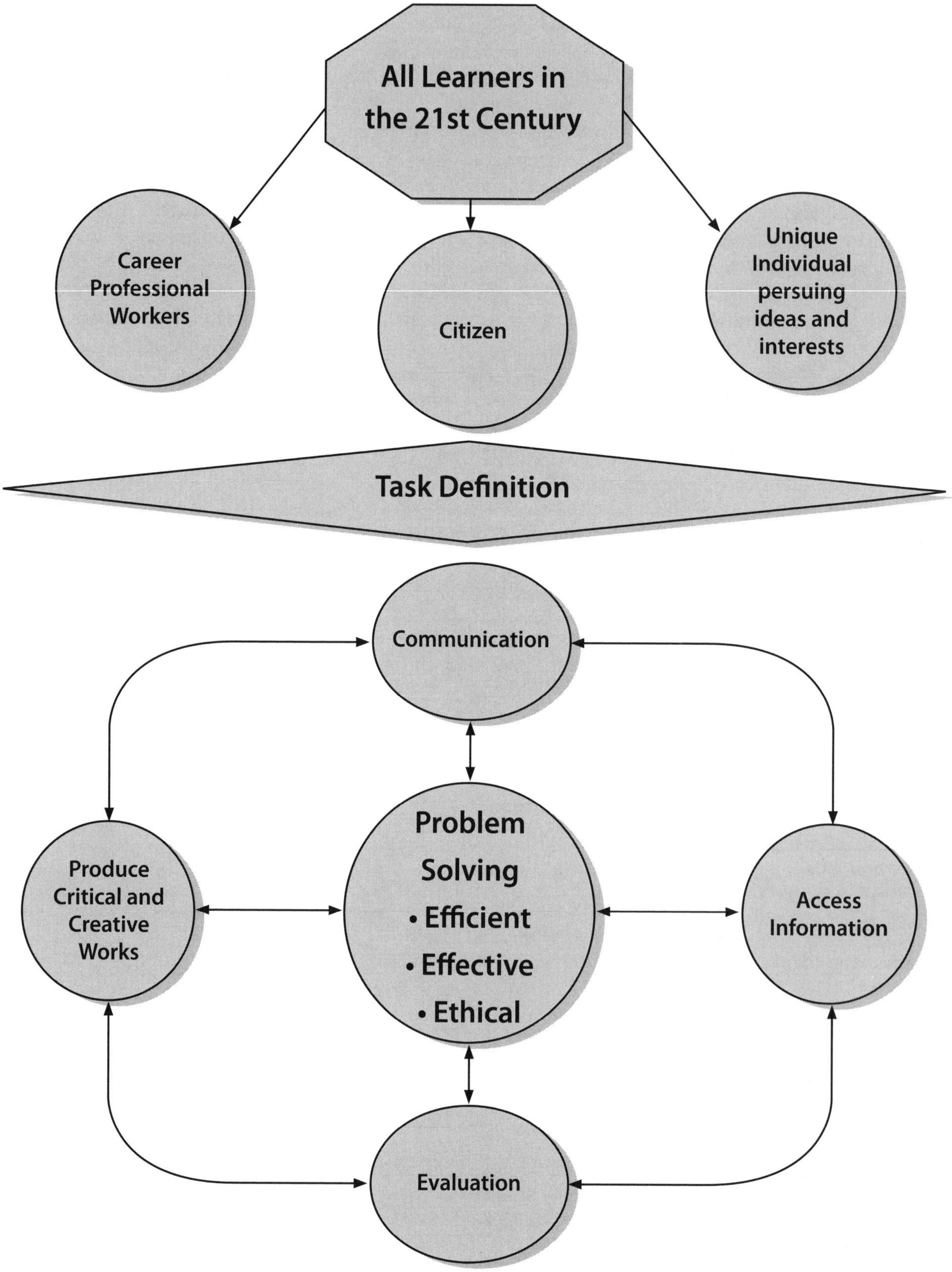

time working with our synthe-sized version of the Connecticut Information Literacy Standards to create aligned knowledge and skills. We decided we needed more focus and direction so arranged to meet with Zmuda again in February 2007. At this meeting, library media goals became "deliverables," and knowledge and skills became "competencies." We created a chart mapping deliverables to competencies and matched them to grades and subjects (see Figure 5: Goals & Competencies Chart, pages 22-23). This chart enables the library media department to track when, how, and where the competencies are embedded and taught.

As with any changes to philosophy and curriculum frameworks, the next step is to get the administration and department supervisors on board. We are currently planning a presentation for the fall of 2007. Through this collaborative effort with administrators, curriculum leaders, and library media specialists, the students of Simsbury Public Schools will be well on their way to becoming 21st century learners.

References:

"Information and Technology Literacy Framework." Connecticut State Department of Education, January 2006. http://www.sde.ct.gov/sde/lib/sde/Word_Docs/Curriculum/itf.doc (Accessed May 10, 2007).

Wiggins, Grant, and Jay McTighe. *Understanding by Design*. 2nd ed. Association for Supervision and Curriculum, 2005.✍

Figure 4: Final Philosophy/Goals Statement

Simsbury Public Schools Library Media Framework

Education provides learners the opportunity to acquire knowledge and skills to enrich their lives. A more rigorous and relevant form of accountability emerges when information is applied in search for a solution to a problem, to better understand a problem, or to create new knowledge. The foundation of our library media program is to facilitate the competence of learners as unique individuals with interests and ideas, citizens, and future members of the workforce. The development of that competence comes from the learner's clarity of task, ability to access information and literature, evaluate and synthesize information, produce critical and creative works, and communicate to an intended audience. Underlying this work is the learner's ability to critically think and problem solve in an efficient, effective, and ethical manner.

Library media specialists design both stand alone and collaborative learning experiences to provide all students with the opportunity to achieve the goals articulated in the Connecticut State Department of Education's Information and Technology Literacy Framework. The success of all students is dependent upon the quality and consistency of the collaboration between the library media specialist and classroom teachers. Library media specialists dedicate their professional efforts not only to ensure vital media and tools are available to students and staff, but also to ensure that students and staff make the use of these media and tools an integrated and meaningful part of teaching and learning.

By the end of grade 12, all students will be able to:

Generate and identify questions to focus task. (Standard 1)

Develop plans for accessing information/literature and monitor effectiveness of plans making necessary adjustments. (Standard 2)

Make efficient information choices based on the range of prior experiences and the nature of the task. (Standard 2)

Use search engines, indexes, directories and databases to access information/literature. (Standard 2)

Critically evaluate a source to determine the degree that it is readable, reliable, relevant or recent (Standard 3)

Organize and synthesize information both w/in a source and/or across a variety of sources. (Standard 3, 4, 6)

Identify and use the appropriate technological tools to communicate information, ideas and findings. (Standard 4, 5, 6)

Communicate information, ideas and findings that are both appropriate and effective for the intended audience. (Standard 4, 5, 6)

Use tools, language, and media in accordance with established laws, policies and citation guidelines. (Standard 6)

Evaluate work using established criteria to determine whether it meets quality expectations. (Standard 4, 7)

Reflect on the process and product to determine overall effectiveness and develop actions for the next time. (Standard 4, 7)

Figure 5. Goals & Competencies Chart

Students by Grade 12 will know or be able to:

Goals or Deliverables	Competencies	Grades K-2	Grades 3-6	Grades 7-8	Grades 9-12
ELA Standard I	Read and respond to written, oral, and visual text				
I. Generate and identify questions to focus task.	Pose questions to define and refine a task				
II. Develop a plan for accessing information/literature and monitor the effectiveness of plans making necessary adjustments.	Efficiently navigate LMC for a given purpose *based on knowing the organizational structure*				
	Use strategies to locate and access information from a variety of sources				
	Identify and use key vocabulary of print sources to efficiently locate and access information				
	Identify and use key vocabulary of electronic catalog, search engines, and databases to efficiently locate and access information				
	Use Boolean logic, keywords, and phrases to search				
	Identify and use key vocabulary of free internet sources to efficiently locate & access information and verify authorship				
III. Make efficient information choices based on the range of prior experiences and the nature of the task.	Use strategies to select appropriate reading materials based on: personal preferences, reading level, nature of task and prior knowledge				
IV. Use indexes, directories, search engines and databases to access information/literature.	Use the electronic card catalog to survey and locate materials				
	Identify and use key vocabulary of print sources to efficiently locate and access information				
	Identify and use key vocabulary of electronic catalog, search engines, and databases to efficiently locate and access information				
	Use Boolean logic, keywords, and phrases to search				
	Identify and use key vocabulary of free Internet sources to efficiently locate and access information and verify authorship.				

Figure 5. Goals & Competencies Chart (continued)

		Grades K-2	Grades 3-6	Grades 7-8	Grades 9-12
	Navigate an electronic resource to efficiently locate and access information				
V. Critically evaluate a source to determine the degree whether it is readable, reliable, relevant, or recent.	Evaluate relevancy of information for a given task				
	Evaluate reliability of text given the nature of the task, point of view, author and evidence contained in it.				
VI. Organize and synthesize information both within a source and/or across a variety of sources.	Identify and prioritize relevant information				
	Record and organize accurate, "trackable" information				
	Use information to produce new knowledge				
	Use information to solve/better understand the nature of a problem, phenomena, or period				
	Use information to develop the logic of an argument in order to create, recreate or refute a point of view				
VII. Identify and use the appropriate technological tools to communicate information, ideas, and findings.	Use Boolean logic, keywords, and phrases to search				
	Identify and use key vocabulary of free internet sources to efficiently locate and access information and verify authorship				
	Navigate an electronic resource to efficiently locate and access information				
IX. Use tools, language, and media in accordance with established laws, policies, and citation guidelines.	Use all materials responsibly				
	Select, check out, and return LMC materials				
	Use appropriate citation format to document sources				
X. Evaluate work using established criteria to determine whether it meets quality expectations.	*Complete self-evaluation using rubrics, exit tickets, etc.*				
XI. Reflect on the process and product to determine overall effectiveness and develop actions for the next time.	*Complete self-evaluation using rubrics, exit tickets, etc.*				

Creativity Literacy:
The Library Media Center as a Learning Laboratory

by Gail Bush

School library scholars wrap their curricula around principles of constructivism for good reason. That educational philosophy dictates that learners create their own meaning, bringing past experiences to bear. Since each student embodies unique experiences, it follows that in the constructivist pattern of thought, knowledge built will in turn be unique to that person. Following this thought, might we not think every student to be creative? After all, each one is creating knowledge. A creative thinker does create, in fact, he/she is prolific. The most creative are considered to go beyond the ordinary, take all knowledge within a domain, and persist to a place that is particularly expressive in a manner viewed by others as exceptional in some fashion. As educators, we know creativity when we see it in student work. The criteria we inherently use include appropriateness of expression within the knowledge base. If we want students to aspire toward creativity, they, therefore, need the background knowledge to succeed.

Gail Bush is a faculty member and director of the Center for Teaching through Children's Books at National-Louis University in Chicago, IL. Email: Gail.Bush@nl.edu

Aspects of constructivism that guide effective library media programs provide the basis for our role as the school's learning laboratory especially in using online sources. This environment of inquiry has a heightened relevance now that online information sources are in need of constant evaluation. Because of the constant connectivity to online sources, students need to develop the capacity to question authority and authenticity. As independent learners, students require an adaptable environment where they may seek strategies to define their information needs; indeed, each learner constructs knowledge, but based on what information and from which source?

The library media center provides a flexible environment for learning in solitude or in social engagement. The library media center also comes equipped with a professional educated in providing guidance and facilitation to the information seeker. Print resources are current, visually engaging, and offer a variety of divergent perspectives on topics of study. Media services are available to produce end products that best communicate student learning. Opportunities to demonstrate understanding through performance or product are supported along with the physical space for various educators engaged in assessment to come together around content, process, and product. The hard lines between and among disciplines and subjects within disciplines soften as all knowledge has a place in this physical, virtual, and intellectual space—the library media center as a learning laboratory.

The creativity literacy that we seek to impart is not just relegated to those creative types who are considered geniuses within their areas of expertise and talent. Each child has an innate creative appetite. On the other hand, education is often unfortunately blamed for squeezing the creativity out of our children. Some classroom teachers might not be eager to highlight creative aspects of demonstrating understanding. Appealing to the characteristics commonly identified with creativity can guide us in our quest to reclaim the value of creativity literacy. We can come to understand how the library-media-center-as-learning-laboratory may also serve our teachers as the best place to think creatively.

Autonomy and Independence

There is a sense of confidence, perhaps sometimes misguided, that creative spirits exude. They might not have the content knowledge that help to support their claims, but they have a strength in their autonomy of thought that is worthy of encouragement. The independent thinker might also be considered disruptive in a classroom setting, but in the library media center, the independent thinker should feel right at home amongst multiple perspectives, a variety of formats, and many literacies and intelligences included in every endeavor. The library media specialist thinks broadly about interdisciplinary opportunities that might engage the independent thinker. Autonomy of thought might manifest itself in selecting a different process or end-product for an assignment. Collaborating with teachers to support differentiated instruction in the library media center can foster autonomy and independence in our students.

Wonderment and Playfulness

Somehow linear learners seem more methodical while creative thinkers have a stronger sense of

playfulness about intellectual matters. If the library media center is not a learning laboratory, then how about having a learning playground in the library media center? This would be a place to play with ideas and new concepts and interpretations of history as well as application of the past to the present and future. All these ideas are welcome in the library media center learning playground. There is a passion that may be fed through poetry about war or the beautiful stories found in young adult novels of families caught in refugee camps. The peace that can be found in misery, as well as the loneliness of fame, attract

thinkers who turn assumptions on their heads, dissect the known, and enjoy predicting the unknown. Again, collaborating with teachers to add elements of scenario-building or role-playing adds interest to these learners. Traits of wonderment and playfulness may also be supported through the collection in seeking resources that allow students to play with ideas through technology or read from vastly different viewpoints. A wide range of end products supports invention and exploration.

Humor and Wit

Laugh and learn and grow together with creative thinkers. Knock-knock jokes never get old, and the elegant simplicity of a political cartoon that combines content knowledge and wit engages creativity in some of our students. Playing with words, creating anagrams and acronyms, rewriting fables and fairytales with a modern twist are all intriguing to those creativity literate learners. Delicious ambiguity and incongruity are downright frightening to some learners but they provide opportunities for relating to content in new and interesting ways to other learners. Invite irony, write puns, reward wit, use satire and other novel combinations of ideas. Humor is not only healthy, it allows us to see the world in a different light. Sharing humor has become a popular aspect of the online community with funny videos and parodies that spread like wildfire. Before collaborating with other educators, it is advisable to prepare a few specific ideas for infusing humor into a particular lesson plan or unit of study.

Persistent and Prolific

Creativity literate learners are creative. They have a desire to continue to work toward a goal with which they are engaged. They might not want to move on even when the time has come to do so. They have many ideas and may need time to try them out and produce many creative products as they continue to strive toward greater challenges. Transitions might not come easily to creative students who do not see the value in stopping their creative endeavor. It is possible, therefore, within the library media center to provide flexible time. Before and after school and lunch hours might be used on occasion where they are not usually available. As educators, we might think creatively about fostering this prolific propensity while seeking a balance that best serves the student.

The Creativity Literate Library Media Specialist

This era of accountability in education feels oppressive to many who work diligently to make our libraries havens of independent learning. Now more than ever, we need the support of our fellow educators. Use the ideas in this article to collaborate with colleagues who share a commitment to broaden the learning experiences for students. There are so many opportunities for differentiation—both for those thinkers who want to collect facts and for those who want to play with ideas. Strong instructional design will find a place for those with varying attributes to work together to build a meaningful social learning experience. Opportunities are also ripe for older and younger student partners especially when humor and wonderment are ingredients in the mix. Think broadly, share the possibilities with colleagues, expect the unexpected, and keep moving forward. British journalist Graham Greene wrote that "there is always one moment in childhood when the door opens and lets the future in." In our schools, we know exactly which door to open.

References

American Association of School Librarians and Association for Educational Communications and Technology. *Information Power: Building Partnerships for Learning*. American Library Association, 1998.

Bush, G. "Just Sing: Creativity and Technology in the School Library Media Center." *Knowledge Quest* 30, no. 2 (2001): 18-21.

Bush, G. "Creativity Literacy in the School Library: Tapping our Inner Resources." In *Educational Media and Technology Yearbook*, edited by M. Orey, V. J. McClendon, and R. M. Branch, 225-233. Libraries Unlimited, 2006.

Callison, D. "Creative Thinking." *School Library Media Activities Monthly* 15, no. 4 (December 1998): 41-44.

Dewey, J. *Experience and Education*. Macmillan, 1938.

Greene, G. *The Power and the Glory*. Heinemann, 1940.

Meador, K. S. *Creative Thinking and Problem Solving for Young Learners*. Libraries Unlimited, 1997.

Puccio, G. J., and M. C. Murdock. "Creative Thinking: An Essential Life Skill." In *Developing Minds: A Resource Book for Teaching Thinking*, edited by A. Costa, 67-71. 3rd ed. Association for Supervision and Curriculum Development, 2001.

Sternberg, R. *Defying the Crowd: Cultivating Creativity in a Culture of Conformity*. Free Press, 1995.

Torrance, E. P., and H. T. Safter. *Making the Creative Leap Beyond*. Creative Education Foundation, 1999.

For Further Reading: Creativity Literacy References Compiled by Gail Bush

Amabile, T. M. *Creativity in Context*. Westview Press, 1996.

Andreasen, N. C. *The Creative Brain: The Science of Genius*. Penguin, 2005.

Callison, D. *The School Buddy System: The Practice of Collaboration*. American Library Association, 2002.

Callison, D. "Creativity Literacy in the School Library: Tapping our Inner Resources." In *Educational Media and Technology Yearbook*, edited by M. Orey, V. J. McClendon, and R. M. Branch, 225-233. Libraries Unlimited, 2006.

Callison, D. *Key Words, Concepts and Methods for Information Age Instruction: A Guide to Teaching Information Inquiry*. LMS Associates, 2002.

Costa, A., ed. *Developing Minds: A Resource Book for Teaching Thinking*. 3rd ed. Association for Supervision and Curriculum Development, 2001.

Csikszentmihalyi, M. *Creativity: Flow and the Psychology of Discovery and Invention*. HarperCollins, 1996.

de Bono, E. *Lateral Thinking: Creativity Step by Step*. Harper & Row, 1970.

Eisner, E. *Think with Me about Creativity*. Owen, 1964.

Feldman, D. H. "The Development of Creativity." In *Handbook of Creativity*, edited by R. Sternberg, 169-188. Cambridge University Press, 1998.

Gardner, H. *The Unschooled Mind: How Children Think and How Schools Should Teach*. Basic Books, 1993.

Gardner, H. *Creating Minds: An Anatomy of Creativity Seen through the Lives of Freud, Picasso, Stravinsky, Eliot, Graham, and Gandhi*. Basic Books, 1993.

Jackson, P. W., and J. W. Getzels. *Creativity and Intelligence*. John Wiley & Sons, 1962.

John-Steiner, V. *Notebooks of the Mind: Explorations of Thinking*. 2d ed. Oxford University Press, 1997.

Langer, E. J. *The Power of Mindful Learning*. Perseus, 1997.

Kraft, U. "Unleashing Creativity." *Scientific American Mind* 16, no. 1 (2005): 16-23.

McGilly, K., ed. *Classroom Lessons: Integrating Cognitive Theory*. MIT Press, 1994.

Meador, K. S. *Creative Thinking and Problem Solving for Young Learners*. Libraries Unlimited, 1997.

Nickerson, R. S. "Enhancing Creativity." In *Handbook of Creativity*, edited by R. Sternberg, 392-430. Cambridge University Press, 1998.

Perkins, D., and S. Tishman. *The Thinking Classroom: Learning and Teaching in a Culture of Thinking*. Allyn and Bacon, 1995.

Ritchhart, R., and T. Blythe. *Creativity in the Classroom: An Educator's Guide for Exploring Creative Teaching and Learning*. Disney Learning Partnership, 1999.

Ritchhart, R., and T. Blythe. *The Power of the Creative Classroom*. Disney Learning Partnership, 2001.

Sternberg, R. *The Nature of Creativity*. Cambridge University Press, 1988.

Sternberg, R., and L. O'Hara. "Creativity and Intelligence." In *Handbook of Creativity*, edited by R. Sternberg, 251-272. Cambridge University Press, 1998.

Torrance, E. P. *Guiding Creative Talent*. Prentice-Hall, 1962.

Wilks, S. *Critical & Creative Thinking: Strategies for Classroom Inquiry*. Heinemann, 1995.

Principal Perspective, Part 2:
The Library Media Program

by Carl A. Harvey II

Every summer, a group of friends and I head to a nearby outdoor music venue to enjoy a Jimmy Buffett concert. It is always one of our favorite summertime events. We sit on the lawn listening to Jimmy sing his signature songs. But, when I stop to think about it, I realize that the show is much more than just Jimmy. Sure, it's his lead voice, but there is also the Coral Reefer Band, the technicians, the stage hands, the managers, the ticket-takers, the security personnel, the songwriters, and the fans that all combine to make it a wonderful experience. I think that the library media program is very much like this Jimmy Buffett concert experience. The library media specialist is the lead voice, but there are teachers, parents, students, administrators, and community members that all work together to make it an amazing program. If any one of these groups isn't working, the program can falter.

Being a Catalyst

Just as my friends and I attend the concert to see the performer Jimmy Buffett, we library media specialists are the catalysts to attract people to the library media program. We in the library media profession are constantly grappling with how we separate the quality of the program from the quality of the library media specialist. How do we help administrators value library media programs? How do we advocate for the library media program without it seeming that we only hope to save our jobs as library media specialists? Stating these questions is far easier than providing answers, but the questions do spark conversations that we need to have.

This, the second of a series of interviews with my principal, Vince Barnes at North Elementary School, gives library media specialists a chance to hear a

Principal Vince Barnes (left) visits Carl Harvey's library media center at North Elementary daily.

principal's perspective of the library media specialist and the library media program and help us begin to address the previous questions.

I admit I had a bit of uneasiness when Vince was first hired because I learned that his experience with library media programs was virtually non-existent. How would that impact the program we had developed at North? I think you'll see that he quickly became the strongest ally of the library media program and me. The following questions were answered by Vince, the high school principal, and my remarks follow.

The Library Media Program

Q: How do you help teachers see the potential of the library media program?

A: Well, I think the first thing is that I make sure the right person is in the library media program. If a school has an effective library media specialist, then the library media program will be effective. Also, it helps to have part of the school improvement plan dedicated to how you can infuse media and technology into the improvement goals.

The school improvement plan is a key document that drives what is happening in today's schools. We were fortunate when the template was designed for programs in our district, [that] one of the columns listed was Media/Technology strategies. As our plan is revised, I work with teachers to revise these strategies. I make sure, too, that as I suggest ideas for projects, share resources, etc., I make connections back to our school improvement plan.

Q: What do you value most in the library media program and why?

A: I value most that it promotes the love of reading and learning for our students. The library media center is an exciting place for our students to learn by reading, researching, listening, engaging in technology, etc. The library media center is truly the hub of activity at our school. There are so many activities taking place in the library media center that excite children about reading and learning.

I never have to invite Vince to visit the library media center. Most days he makes two trips through every classroom and learning space in our building. Our students are very familiar with him and know that he is aware of what they are learning and that he values what they are doing. So, he easily can see what is happening in the library media program. If I'm not working with a class when he stops in, I ask him questions, share a tidbit of information, or have a short discussion. For me, it is easy because he is so visible. For a library media specialist who doesn't have a principal that stops by often, it is important to communicate in other ways but to make sure that the principal knows the great things that are happening.

Q: How does the library media program fit into your school?

A: As I said earlier, the library media program seems to be the center of our school learning! As an elementary school, we are very focused on literacy and the library media center supports [that] in many ways. Because of the quality of the library media program provided by the teachers, library media specialists, and the aides in the library media center, it allows our library media program to be that integral part of our school learning.

This team approach is key. Each of our grade levels sits down and plans out the next week together. Most often this is before or after school. I can't always make it to each planning session each week, but I strive to be there as often as possible. Besides me, the resource teachers also attend, so it is a powerful group of educators who share ideas, strategies, and resources. Our best collaborative projects have come from those planning sessions.

Q: How does the library media program connect to school improvement?

A: The library media program enhances our school improvement by infusing media and technology into each of our goals. Our staff is well aware of the power of technology and media with today's children, thus we use it often to enhance the lessons being learned.

This year we continue our focus on literacy and literacy stations. As our teachers continue to refine and set up stations, training sessions on all needed technology tools and resources will be offered through the library media program. Connections will be intentionally made between the school goals and the library media program. Showing how the library media program can help with those strategies and goals is critical.

Q: **Besides your current building, what other experiences have you had with library media programs?**

A: I have not had much experience with an effective library media program. My previous schools only had a library that was very traditional and run by parent volunteers and open limited hours during the school day. The library was an afterthought. The library did not enhance teaching and learning at all.

Q: **Where did you learn about library media programs?**

A: I learned most about the importance of library media programs from our library media specialist. His constant communication with the teachers and me showed me the importance of the library media program in the overall vision of our school. He makes it his mission to engage me in learning about the importance of the library media program to the overall continuous school improvement. His ongoing collaboration with the teachers also shows me the importance

of this level of collaboration.

I'm sure Vince would tell you he knows more than he ever wanted to know about library media programs, but I try to make sure that in all our conversations he sees the connections we make to learning in our building. He gets emails, voicemails, visits to his office, visits to my office, newsletters, reports, etc. I use all communication vehicles possible so that he knows what we're doing and why it is important. I bring back what I learn from conferences and tell him how these ideas are helping us. One of the professional development presenters we work with says, "As good as we are; we can get better!" and that is what I keep in mind when I communicate with Vince. How can we keep moving our program forward?

Q: **How did you come to value school library media programs?**

A: Due to our library media specialist's vision and implementation of an effective program at North Elementary, I was able to see the value of the library media center as it supports our teachers and students in the area of literacy. It also supports our parents with a parent library section in our library media center. The daily use by the students and teachers sold me on the value of school libraries. Before working at North, I would have said, "Sure I think library media programs could be important to schools." But now that I have seen a national award-winning one in place, I would fight for the program because of its importance to student learning.

I honestly know that if I go to Vince with an idea, the rationale, and the connection to what we're doing, he will do anything he can to make it happen. Sometimes that includes helping find funding sources; sometimes it is being the voice to the teachers so they get behind it; sometimes it involves him stepping back and letting us run with it.

Conclusion

Now, think back to the Jimmy Buffett concert analogy. Tickets for Jimmy's concerts sell out in minutes. He doesn't need to do very much advertising or try to convince people his concerts are good, and they should attend. Library media specialists can take a lesson from Jimmy. By creating dynamic programs where instructional calendars fill up each week, we create a legion of "fans" (administrators, students, parents, teachers, etc.) that will become the advocates for the library media program.

Related Resources:

Hartzell, Gary. *Building Influence for the School Librarian: Tenets, Targets, and Tactics.* Linworth, 2003.

Hartzell, Gary. "Why Should Principals Support School Libraries?" *ERIC Digest* (Nov. 2002). ERIC ED470034.

Harvey, Carl A., II. *No School Library Left Behind: Leadership, School Improvement, and the Media Specialist.* Linworth, 2008.

Harvey, Carl A., II. "What Should a Teacher Expect a School Library Media Specialist to Be?" *Library Media Connection* (February 2005).

Hughes-Hassell, Sandra, and Violet H. Harada. *School Reform and the School Library Media Specialist.* Linworth, 2008.

McGhee, Marla W., and Barbara A. Jansen. *The Principal's Guide to a Powerful Library Media Program.* Linworth, 2005.

Zmuda, Allison, and Violet H. Harada. *Librarians as Learning Specialists: Meeting the Learning Imperative for the 21st Century.* Libraries Unlimited, 2008. ◄

Carl A. Harvey II is the library media specialist at North Elementary School in Noblesville, IN. Email: carl@carl-harvey.com

What Does It Really Look Like

When Students Are Learning in the Library Media Center?

by Allison Zmuda

Walk into any library media center and you will, no doubt, see lots of students busily working on classroom assignments. While these students may be focused and industrious, the real question is what drives their work, and are they learning? Student learning comes from active efforts to construct knowledge that requires them to pursue inquiries, locate and evaluate evidence, make connections, analyze patterns, reconcile apparent discrepancies, deliberate about language, communicate thinking, and, finally, revise their work. The focus of this article is on the need to transform passive learning found in student efforts to just locate information to active engagement in constructing knowledge. This transformation begins with the library media specialist's collaboration with colleagues.

Owning the Problem

Many students regard the assignments they are given in the library media center comparable to completing "forms"—little more than bureaucratic exercises that are part of the daily drudgery of school. They may be committed to recording an answer to the question or a response to the prompt but remain uncommitted to the unavoidable struggle required in knowledge construction. They may become impatient with library media specialists for not telling them where they can find what they are looking for, or how to document their research the right way, or when they have enough information and can move on to the next part.

Such disengagement inhibits true learning; it prevents students from the responsibility as well as the opportunity to build their intelligence. Mel Levine worries about the impact this disengagement has on the child's future success. He states, "Many students emerge from high school as passive processors who simply sop up intellectual input without active response. Some passive learners, although able to scrape by academically, endure chronic boredom in school and later suffer career ennui. Their habit of cognitive inactivity can lead to mediocre performance in college and later on the job" (Levine 2007, 19). The solution to the problem then is more than collaborating with classroom teachers to produce authentic research tasks; it also requires constant analysis of how students are working to ensure that they can learn something from the experience.

When I recently conducted a workshop in Western New York, library media specialists and their partner classroom teachers lamented that when students are given robust research-based assignments, they still behaved as if these assignments were low-level search and retrieval tasks. My challenge to them was to describe what these learners look like so that the library media specialist and classroom teacher can more effectively design and facilitate research-based instructional experiences that will cause learning.

Not only do students misunderstand their job as learners, but they seldom get to experience a true sense of accomplishment that comes from constructing their own understanding and becoming steeped in knowledge. Eleanor Duckworth states:

Of all the virtues related to intellectual functioning, the most passive is the virtue of knowing the right answer. Knowing the right answer requires no decisions, carries no risks, and makes no demands. It is automatic. It is thoughtless… Knowing the right answer is overrated. It is a virtue—there is no debate about that—but in conventional views of intelligence it tends to be given far too much weight (1996, 64-65).

Recently, when I was conducting an observation in the library media center, I saw a group of students diligently recording information on a particular research topic of their choice. I asked each of them what was most interesting in what they had found so far and got blank stares. When I probed further, one student finally remarked, "I think you misunderstand the assignment. We don't have to find things interesting. We just have to find things."

The Inevitable Joy and Pain of Knowledge Construction

When students are working to locate information to answer a question, they may be temporarily engaged in the "hunt" but find little intellectual satisfaction from their efforts. When students are really researching, however, the "hunt" is altogether different. Instead of being driven to find what they believe to be a predetermined answer, they are in the pursuit of truth. They work to find out what "really happened," how something "really works," or what "really matters." They work to persuade an audience, to communicate information and ideas, to describe an event, object, or life. And this hunt is inevitably frustrating. They find sources that disagree with each other, point them in different directions, and challenge the validity of their original research question or thesis.

So what do students look and sound like when they are truly engaged in a research task that is likely to cause learning? Collaborating with classroom teachers to describe these learners is a significant step in answering that question and elevating the quality of student work in the library. Indicators, developed by both classroom teachers and the library media specialist, can be used to monitor student learning and appropriately scaffold instructional interventions so that students can successfully complete the task. Development of indicators can be based on the following reflective prompts:

What does it looks like when students are working on a robust research task where little learning is likely to result?

►They look for direct answers to indirect/complex inquiries.
►They follow an orderly, linear process or execute a plan from start to finish without reflecting on whether it's working.
►They copy what they find without thinking about it.
►They work to complete the task as quickly as possible.
►They confuse quantity of information with quality of research.
►They view every published source as valid (both to the inquiry and as an authority on the subject).
►They focus more on the "bells and whistles" of the task than the substance.
►They operate with an overly narrow or broad inquiry that they are unable to refine.
►They collect details without thinking about connections and areas of incongruence or information gaps.
►They assume that if they find the "answer" in one source that they have "finished" looking.

If students are really researching then...

- How would they move around the library?
- What kinds of questions would they ask teachers and the library media specialist?
- What kinds of conversations would they have with their peers?
- What would they find interesting?
- How long would it take them to complete a task?
- What would they find frustrating?
- How would they work to overcome obstacles?
- Who would they want to collaborate with?
- How would they document what they found?
- How would they work to organize and develop their ideas and information?

It is important to note that research is only one type of learning that takes place in the library. A similar process could be applied to other types of learning in the library such as communicating information and ideas to an audience and pursuing personal and aesthetic growth through reading (see *AASL Standards for the 21st-Century Learner*).

In addition to observing students as they work on a task, it also is of vital importance that the learning environment is conducive to knowledge construction. Vi Harada and I have delineated features of such learning environments in our book *Librarians as Learning Specialists* (Libraries Unlimited, 2008). These features include the following examples:

- Opportunities to pursue areas of interest and curiosity as part of the curriculum.
- Conferences between staff member and individuals or small groups of learners based on their current level of work or understanding of ideas.
- Student development of plans to achieve goals and a feedback cycle of planning, evaluation, and reflection to determine whether the plan is having the intended effect and make necessary adjustments.
- Physical spaces conducive to the nature of the work—collaborative space to think and develop ideas together; quiet places to read, process, analyze, reflect, and create work; white board/SMART board space to visually illustrate concepts; and visual cues that provide vital information about procedures, protocols, and strategies.
- Assignments completed in a range of ways based on a combination of what the student needs, his or her preferred way of working, and the focus of the learning goal.
- Students measure current work (both their own and their peers) based on a set of established criteria and articulate adjustments that would improve the quality of the work.
- Students routinely explain both to one another and to staff how they arrived at a conclusion and are as curious about the process as the result (Zmuda and Harada 2008).

Key Actions to Make This Start to Happen Now

It is possible to create learners who are actively searching to make meaning, who are internally motivated to pursue an answer, who are evaluating information to determine its relevance and its credibility, and who are taking care to correctly document their findings. There are four key actions that library media specialists can begin to take today to make this more likely to happen:

1. Describe what it looks like when students are really doing the assignment and when they only appear to be doing it.
2. Develop instructional interventions that refocus passive efforts to active struggles.
3. Examine assignment directions, scoring tools, and revision opportunities to ensure that they communicate the value of making connections, analyzing evidence, developing ideas using information, drawing conclusions and refining work.
4. Examine library practices and policies to ensure that they facilitate the unavoidable risk-taking, messiness, impulsiveness, analysis, frustration, and joy that come from the pursuit of a curiosity.

While this may seem like a solitary endeavor at times, library media specialists can consistently work to enlist others in envisioning what "success" looks like and strive to create the conditions (feedback and then space) necessary for others to reflect on the implementation of successful practices. Both students and teachers alike will begin to see that a true sense of accomplishment in the library media center comes from the genuine struggle to make meaning.

Works Cited

American Association of School Librarians. *Standards for the 21st-Century Learner.* 2007. http://www.ala.org/ala/aasl/aaslproftools/learningstandards/standards.cfm (accessed June 2008).

Duckworth, Eleanor. *The Having of Wonderful Ideas and Other Essays on Teaching and Learning.* 2d ed. Teachers College Press, 1996.

Levine, Mel. "The Essential Cognitive Backpack." *Educational Leadership* 64, no. 7 (2007): 16-22.

Zmuda, Allison, and Vi Harada. *Librarians as Learning Specialists: Meeting the Learning Imperative for the 21st Century.* Libraries Unlimited, 2008.

Zmuda, Allison, and Vi Harada. "Reframing the Library Media Specialist as a Learning Specialist." *School Library Media Activities Monthly* 24, no. 8 (April 2008): 42-47. ◄

Allison G. Zmuda is an education consultant who has worked with schools throughout the United States and Canada. Email: zmuda@competentclassroom.com

"There Is Knowledge to Be Gained"

by Ross J. Todd

A Library Media Center Transformed

The Chelmsford High School Learning Commons had an official opening ceremony in December 2008. It was an event attended by community and state dignitaries, including Susan Fargo (Massachusetts State Senator), Paul Cohen (Town Manager), Donald Yoeman (Superintendent of Schools), and school library colleagues Dr. Carol Gordon (Rutgers University) and Dr. David Loertscher (San José State University). (See the *Boston Globe* story and readers' comments: http://www.boston.com/news/education/k_12/articles/2008/12/08/new_learning_commons_defies_commonplace/). I was privileged to speak at this ceremony and was part of the group witnessing the exciting transformation of a library media center into a vibrant and challenging center of instruction where the primary goal is to help students in the information-to-knowledge journey.

The development of the Learning Commons and the transformation of the existing library media center were through the leadership of library media specialist Valerie Diggs. The school faculty and students are excited about the transformation and see it as a place for a rich variety of initiatives that engage students in learning through diverse resources, information technology, and collaborative instruction. This statement by John F. Kennedy, "We set sail on this sea because there is knowledge to be gained," is in a prominent place and clearly signals the intent of the Learning Commons.

The entrance to the Learning Commons is a vibrant and colorful wall with framed covers of books and other information products created by former students. In other parts of the commons, the most prominent signage is "Ask," "Think," and "Create." It is an inspiring place in its conceptualization, design, and potential for collaborative, cooperative, and constructive learning. It symbolizes an inspiration to all who come by—an invitation to set sail on a knowledge journey, encouraged by the success of those who have come before.

Learning Commons

Loertshcer, Koechlin, and Zwann, in their book *The New Learning Commons: Where Learners Win!*, posit that in a learning commons, "the focus is on inquiry based learning journeys" and supporting "a schoolwide culture of inquiry fostering 'habits of mind' and 'learning dispositions' conducive to success" (2008, 16). Kuhlthau, Maniotes, and Caspari state that at the heart of preparing students for a global information environment, the focus is on inquiry,

where students can "draw on the knowledge and wisdom of the past while using the technology of the present to advance new discoveries for the future" (2007, 1). Prensky, in his provocative article "Turning on the Lights" says that a 21st-century learning process occurs when children do not just power up their devices, they power up their minds (2008, 42), creating a school where children are led "out of the intellectual darkness and into intellectual light" (2008, 41) and where learning is deep, meaningful, and relevant to their present and future lives.

Knowledge-Centric Paradigm

The conceptualizing of and structuring of a learning commons shifts both the thinking of what a library media center is as well as its learning imperative in the school. Rather than being defined in terms of collections and instructional activities that focus primarily on an information-centric paradigm—the finding, accessing, and evaluating of information—the primary focus of a learning commons is on engaging learners in an active process of discovery, inquiry, and creativity, developing deep knowledge and understanding, and actively engaging in critical thinking and problem solving. This is a knowledge-centric paradigm for library media centers.

This type of paradigm is outcome focused, where the growth of student knowledge, achievement, and success are central to the role of the library media center. I welcome the new AASL *Standards for the 21st-Century Learner* because the focus is on inquiry, engagement, thinking, reflection, and the development of deep knowledge and understanding. This gets to the core of constructivist learning and defines the central focus of the library media center. The new standards place particular emphasis on the growth of knowledge where learners are actively searching for meaning and understanding, directly involved and engaged in the discovery of ideas for themselves, constructing knowledge for themselves, encountering alternative perspectives and conflicting ideas, and taking ownership and responsibility for mastery of curriculum content and skills.

As I reflect on these outcomes, I think they are consistent and timely with a growing educational trend worldwide. Educational systems are currently grappling with the direction education is going, and focusing on questions such as how to respond innovatively to needs of learners, increase intellectual engagement and relevance, strengthen learning and teaching, equip students with the skills and knowledge—cognitive and cultural, social and linguistic—that have power and salience in the world. These systems are building a culture of high expectations for optimal student learning outcomes supported by teachers' continuous professional development, and working collaboratively in teams across learning areas and developing strong links with their communities. Serious questions are beginning to emerge on why education is failing our students, and how it can be reformed in ways that pave a brighter future for our students.

For example, on February 6, 2009, the New Jersey Department of Education made available for public review and comment a draft of the revised "Core Curriculum Content Standards for New Jersey" in nine content areas. The revised content standards emulate some of the key educational trends identified above. They focus on Big Ideas, Enduring Understandings, and Essential Questions, and seek to integrate 21st-Century Knowledge and Skills by incorporating a strong emphasis on technology integra-

tion, interdisciplinary connections, and infusion of global perspectives. Even more importantly, they seek to explicitly promote the use of innovative learning strategies by integrating supportive technologies, inquiry- and problem-based approaches, and higher order thinking skills. Against the backdrop of the new AASL *Standards for the 21st-Century Learner,* there is a synchronicity that is timely and opportunistic for all library media specialists. There is a significant challenge being put forward, a challenge that clearly resonates in the *Standards for the 21st-Century Learner* and echoed in Kennedy's statement, "We set sail on this sea because there is knowledge to be gained."

Reconceptualizing the Library Media Center

Such directions challenge us to reconceptualize the library media center, not so much as a space where information is organized, provided, and accessed (which, of course, is important), but rather as the school's physical and virtual learning commons where inquiry, thinking, imagination, discovery, and creativity are central to students' information-to-knowledge journey and to their personal, social and cultural growth. It is inquiry, thinking, discovery, and creativity that characterize the work of library media specialists. In the context of the rich development of the technological and information environments for our students, we must not lose sight of the core work of library media centers, which I believe centers on transforming information to deep knowledge and deep understanding. This is a knowledge-centric outcome, not an information-centric outcome. And this is constructivist learning.

The *Standards for the 21st-Century Learner* challenge us to reflect on the nature and focus of the pedagogy that takes place in the library media center as well as the way that we construct the learning environment to engage students in meaningful learning. Does it focus

on information or knowledge? Does our instruction focus on the "finding" and the "found," or does it focus on the "understood?" Does it focus on the getting of information, or does it focus on engaging with information to create deep knowledge and understanding as well? The new learning standards challenge us to think about what we teach in library media centers as well as the outcome of our teaching.

I have been reading about the Productive Pedagogy framework developed by Gore, Griffiths, and Ladwig (2002). Based on a series of research studies in Australia, productive pedagogy is concerned with what is being taught and the quality of learning produced. Gore, Griffiths, and Ladwig sought to develop a model of productive pedagogy that results in high-quality student learning and improved learning outcomes. As a framework for quality teaching and learning, it is built around four fundamental principles: Intellectual Quality, Relevance, Supportive Environment, and Recognition of Difference. Unquestionably, these principles underpin AASL's *Standards for the 21st-Century Learner.*

▶ **Intellectual quality** centers on the development of higher order thinking, depth of knowledge, depth of understanding, ability to engage in substantive conversation, ability to recognize knowledge as problematic, and reading literacy grounded in language, grammar, and technical vocabulary. These are essential dimensions of pedagogy that are essential to enabling students to move from accessing, finding, and collecting information, to engaging with it in critical, reflective, analytical, and constructive ways to create deep understanding for themselves.

▶ **Relevance** is about learning that is linked to students' background knowledge and connected to real-life contexts where students solve intellectual and real-world problems and integrate knowledge from diverse fields to develop new understandings. Relevance is a highly important dimension in inquiry-based learning and in engaging students in research-based tasks. Ownership of the research task, engagement, interest, and motivation are directly related to how relevant students see their learning tasks.

▶ **A supportive classroom environment** is about providing a socially supportive and positive learning environment where students have a say in the pace, direction, and outcome of their learning tasks, where they are engaged and on-task, where performance criteria are made explicit, where diverse cultural backgrounds are brought into play, and where a sense of community, identity, and active citizenship are fostered.

▶ **Recognition of difference** refers to the dynamics of learning as an inclusive social and cultural process of community and identity building, where diversity and difference are recognized and integrated as part of the teaching and learning process (Gore, Griffiths, and Ladwig 2002, 375-387).

A Framework for Library Media Centers

The dimensions of productive pedagogy, as developed by Gore, Griffiths, and Ladwig (2002) are shown in the table (below and on page 58). It is a useful framework for library media specialists and their school community so they can reflect on their library media center and how it functions, particularly in the context of the new standards.

The Productive Pedagogy framework presented here provides a useful set of questions for engaging the whole school in conversation about the direction the library media center is headed as well as the active contribution that it can make to the learning agenda of the school. I am inspired by a quote from Oliver Wendell Holmes, distinguished poet, professor, and physician: "I find the great thing in this world is not so much where we stand, as in what direction we are moving" (http://www.quotationspage.com/quote/29470.html). He also said, "The main part of intellectual education is not the acquisition of facts but learning how to make facts live" (http://quotationsbook.com/quote/11936/). This is

the future of library media centers—the Learning Commons—the connection to the curriculum, the lives of our students, and their present and future world.

References:

American Association of School Librarians. *Standards for the 21st-Century Learner.* American Library Association, 2007.

Gore, J. M., T. Griffiths, and J. G. Ladwig. "Towards Better Teaching: Productive Pedagogy as a Framework for Teacher Education." *Teacher and Teaching Education* 20 (2002): 375-387.

Kuhlthau, C. C., L. K. Maniotes, and A. K. Caspari. *Guided Inquiry: Learning in the 21st Century.* Libraries Unlimited, 2007.

Loertscher, David V., Carol Koechlin, and Sandi Zwann. *The New Learning Commons: Where Learners Win! Reinventing School Libraries and Computer Labs.* Prepublication Draft. Hi Willow Research & Publishing, 2008.

Prensky, Marc. "Turning on the Lights." *Educational Leadership* 65, no. 6 (March 2008): 40-45.◄

Ross J. Todd, Ph.D., is Associate Professor, Director of the MLIS Program, and Director of Research for the Center for International Scholarship in School Libraries (CISSL) and School of Communication, Information & Library Studies (SCILS) at Rutgers, The State University of New Jersey. Email: rtodd@rci.rutgers.edu

Productive Pedagogy Dimensions (Gore, Griffiths, and Ladwig 2002), Items, and Key Questions for Library Media Specialists and Classroom Teachers

INTELLECTUAL QUALITY	
Higher order thinking	Are higher order thinking and critical analysis a strong part in the instructional initiatives in the library media center? Do information literacy initiatives focus on "the found" or/and "the understood"?
Depth of knowledge	Do lessons, whether individual or in collaboration with classroom teachers, cover central concepts and their complex relations in any depth, detail, or level of specificity? Do they facilitate the collection of descriptive facts about a topic, or do they enable deep understanding of the complex relationships of a topic to be developed?
Depth of students' understanding	Do the work and response of the students provide evidence for understanding of concepts or ideas? Is there evidence of the knowledge outcomes as a result of instructional interventions? How are the knowledge outcomes of the library media center charted? What evidence-based strategies form professional work?
Substantive conversation	Is the library media center a place of sustained dialogue among students, teachers, and the library media specialist? Is it a place where help is readily available for students at all stages of their information-to-knowledge journey? Is constructive critique and feedback part of the learning experience in the library media center? Is the whole school community engaged in substantive conversation about the library media center and its strategic role in learning?

Continued ▶

Productive Pedagogy Dimensions, Items, and Key Questions for Library Media Specialists and Classroom Teachers (continued)

Knowledge as problematic	Are students engaged in examining diverse viewpoints and perspectives, and critically evaluating ideas, and not just examining information sources? Do they know how to deal with problematic knowledge and to construct their own positions, viewpoints, perspectives, and conclusions?
Meta-language	Do students show mastery of complex concepts in their creative output and use the language of the discipline with understanding and ease?
RELEVANCE	
Knowledge integration	Does the instructional work of the library media specialist build on prior/ existing knowledge of students, and not just focus on isolated library media center concepts? Is library media center learning centered on curriculum or library itself?
Link to background knowledge	Is there an attempt to connect with students' background knowledge? How is learning made relevant to the knowledge and experience of the students? How is this background knowledge connected to current learning requirements?
Connection to the world beyond the classroom	Do lessons and the assigned work have any resemblance or connection to real-life contexts? Does it really matter if students never know?
Problem-based curriculum	Is there a focus on identifying and solving intellectual and/or real-world problems? Do students see the relevance of their information literacy instruction to the real world?
SUPPORTIVE CLASSROOM ENVIRONMENT	
Students' direction of activities	Do students have any say in the pace, direction, or outcome of the research tasks they undertake? Are they given an opportunity to choose broad topics within a curriculum theme? Do they have an opportunity to negotiate the focus questions? Do they choose how they will represent their deep knowledge in the product that they create?
Social support for student achievement	Is the library media center a socially supportive, positive environment? Is it rule focused and driven? Is it a welcoming help center? Does it support just-in-time learning? Does it provide opportunities, systems, and spaces for collaborative learning?
Academic engagement	Are students engaged and on task? How does the library media center environment and actions sustain in students "the will to know"?
Explicit quality performance criteria	Are criteria for student performance made explicit? In negotiating research tasks with classroom teachers, is there an emphasis on demonstrating engagement with information, critical thinking, and problem solving, as well as the nature and scope of the knowledge product?
Student self-regulation	How is time management, project management, and knowledge production management facilitated with and for the students as they undertake their research and creative production?
RECOGNITION OF DIFFERENCE	
Cultural knowledge values cultures	Are diverse cultural knowledge brought into play? Does the library media center collection respect and value diverse knowledge? Is a safe environment provided for students to explore complex, conflicting ideas in safety and anonymity?
Public representation of inclusive participation	Are deliberate attempts made to increase the participation of all students of different backgrounds? Is the library media center a welcoming place for all? Does the library media center celebrate difference and diversity, or homogeneity?
Narrative	Is information literacy instruction empowering students to construct new knowledge for themselves, actively engaging them in presenting, analyzing, and interpreting information to build personal knowledge, or does it focus on the collection of facts?
Group identities in learning community	Does teaching build a sense of community and identity?
Active citizenship	Are attempts made to foster active citizenship? Is the library media center a vital connection between the world of students, the curriculum, and life and living for the future?

Chapter 4

The 21st-Century School Library Media Specialist

Library media specialists must refocus their job descriptions and their daily practice so that they target direct contributions to improve the achievement of all learners on defined curricular goals.

—Allison Zmuda and Violet H. Harada, "Reframing the Library Media Specialist as a Learning Specialist" (see page 72)

When many parents, teachers, and administrators were in school, their librarian was too often a bystander in their education, a behind-the-scenes member of the faculty who managed a quiet, studious environment. As the vision for the learning that takes place in school libraries continues to grow, school library media specialists (SLMSs) continue to push past that old paradigm.

With the advent of the AASL *Standards for the 21st-Century Learner,* SLMSs once again embarked on a journey of self-evaluation to refine and refocus the many roles they play throughout the school community. At the heart of this self-reflection is the question, "What kind of professional is needed to implement the visionary program (described in chapter 3), with robust student learning experiences (as defined in chapter 1)?" This chapter explores the many roles played by successful SLMSs as they strive to meet the new AASL *Standards.*

The Big Picture: What Does the Principal Want?

This chapter begins with "Principal Perspective, Part 1: The Role of the Library Media Specialist," an interview between school library media specialist Carl A. Harvey II and Vince Barnes, his building administrator. In this interview (page 69), Barnes outlines the qualities he looks for in an excellent SLMS. A quality he sees as most important is a commitment to ongoing school improvement. He identifies the unique leadership perspective of the media specialist as someone who interacts with all classes in the school and multiple curriculum committees.

School Librarians as Learning Specialists

Many SLMSs transitioned into the role after years of experience as classroom teachers, and many states require that they be highly qualified not only as librarians but as teachers as well. It is no surprise, then, that they feel a special affinity with the teaching part of their job. Ironically, this double certification is often overlooked by stakeholders, whose outdated perceptions of school librarianship cloud their ability to see the full potential of these professionals.

In "Reframing the Library Media Specialist as a Learning Specialist" (beginning on page 72), Allison Zmuda and Violet H. Harada throw down the gauntlet, challenging SLMSs and their administrators to look past the role of librarian-as-resource-provider or passive observer of teacher-centered learning. Instead, they provoke a conversation about SLMSs as agents of learning and specialists in instructional design. Their essay is both a tantalizing view of potential and a demand for rejecting the status quo.

The rigors of the AASL *Standards* require that librarians not only teach, but teach to promote student-centered, complex learning. Engaging students in inquiry, questioning, problem solving, resource evaluation, reflection, and synthesis means a new instructional paradigm is needed. Preparing for this new role may require a paradigm shift for the SLMS and for the staff.

Who Are Our Role Models?

Who can we look to as models? Peggy Milam Creighton suggests several in "Impact as a 21st-Century Library Media Specialist" (beginning on page 77). Building on Malcolm Gladwell's identification of mavens, connectors, and salespeople in *The Tipping Point* (2000), she points to specific leaders in the field and identifies the activities, programs, and technology tools those leaders use in their leadership work.

How Do We Get Authority?

How can a SLMS get a foothold? This can be a challenge for library media specialists entering schools where collaboration or inquiry are not easily identifiable in the school culture. Allison Zmuda suggests that the journey begin with data. In "Where Does Your Authority Come From?," Zmuda (beginning on page 82) outlines possible data to collect and strategies for taking action based on that information.

What Do We Need to Do to Thrive Amid Change?

To face transitions positively, Kristin Fontichiaro suggests looking inward. Just as the AASL *Standards* promote the development of a dispositions toolkit for students, SLMSs need an inner toolkit to adapt to a change-filled professional future. In "Dancing Down the Rabbit Hole: Habits of Mind for Embracing Change" (beginning on page 86), Fontichiaro maps the Habits of Mind of Arthur Costa and Bena Kallick (2009) to the practice of SLMSs. Having a framework like this can help to anchor a SLMS during transformational times.

GETTING TO ADVOCACY

1. In "Where Does Your Authority Come From?" (page 82), Zmuda suggests that SLMS view every interaction with teachers as a collaborative one. Doing so can work toward establishing rapport and trust. Who could you call on now to write a supportive paragraph for the school newsletter, media center blog, or board of education packet?

2. In discussing the Habit of Mind of humor, Fontichiaro (page 86) recommends rest and self-care. School library media specialists have a tendency to martyr themselves for the good of the cause. Try to self-advocate for your own need for balance. A vital school library media program cannot thrive when the SLMS is exhausted! This is also why it is so important to grow advocates—so the library media specialist does not have to be the only voice.

THOUGHTS FOR THE JOURNEY

1. Creighton (page 77), identifies national school library leaders who demonstrate leadership as mavens, connectors, and salespeople (Gladwell 2000). Who can be identified locally as fitting these categories? What can be learned from observing them in practice?

2. Fontichiaro (page 86) includes Costa and Kallick's (2009) trait of metacognition. How can metacognition be incorporated into professional practice?

3. Zmuda and Harada state, "There is no upside to library media specialists collaborating with classroom teachers on tasks that are bad business. If library media specialists participate in the design and orchestration of these types of tasks . . . they become accomplices in the assignment of yet another task that dilutes inquiry" (Zmuda and Harada 2008). This is a revolutionary statement. How does one balance between the pressure to collaborate and the pressure for improved instruction?

4. Do you perceive yourself as a learning specialist? Why or why not?

Principal Perspective, Part 1:
The Role of the Library Media Specialist

by Carl A. Harvey II

A friend of mine often remarks, "We are all one bad administrator away from being out of a job." That's not the most positive statement, but any of us who have had the opportunity to work under different administrators know that the pendulum of support can swing—sometimes quickly and abruptly. I've been very fortunate. Of the four administrators I've had the pleasure to work for, all of them were supportive of the library media program and the role of the library media specialist. A great deal of the success of our library media programs can be attributed to the administrators who have had the vision and foresight to help these programs excel.

When other library media professionals meet or hear about my current administrator, Vince Barnes, they often say, "Can we clone him?" While science probably hasn't quite hit that mark yet, I find through every conversation I have with Vince that I learn a little bit more about education and how I can take what I'm doing and move it up another notch.

Library Media Specialist Carl Harvey and Principal Vince Barnes

This article is Part One of a series of three articles based on a conversation with Vince about library media centers. Parts Two and Three will be in the December and February issues of *SLMAM*, respectively. I think his perspectives will help other administrators learn more about library media programs and provide insight to library media specialists

from the administrator's vantage point. The articles will be divided into three themes: Part One will focus on the role of the library media specialist, Part Two will look at the library media program, and Part Three will look at the administrator. Each question and answer is followed by my analysis.

Vince Barnes began his current position as the principal at North Elementary in 2004. Previously he was with the Indiana Department of Education and prior to that he was a principal in a private Catholic school. His early experiences as a principal and teacher were in private schools where parent volunteers ran libraries, so his first experience working with a certified library media specialist has been at North Elementary.

Questions for an Administrator

Q • What do you feel are the • qualities you want and need in a library media specialist?

A • I want the library • media specialist to fully understand the importance of continuous school improvement. As part of this understanding, he/she needs to realize that the more you align the curriculum, instruction, and assessment with each other, the more a school will continue to improve. In order for the library media specialist to have a full understanding of this concept, he/she needs to be involved in curriculum development, collaboration with teachers, and the school improvement process.

Vince's comments focused on teaching and learning. Nothing was mentioned about the ability to catalog materials, order books, or any of the countless other tasks that have to be done to run a library media center. If you asked him the question again, focusing on teachers instead of library media specialists, the answer would be much of the same. Each teacher—no matter what subject or role in the school—assumes the administrator has no idea about all the other "stuff" they have to do. While that may be true, administrators know that the main focus of every staff member is on teaching and learning. Why would we assume that it would be any different for the library media specialist?

Q • What unique skills • can the library media specialist contribute to a school?

A • They can see the overall • picture because they work with all grade levels and all areas of curriculum. They are not pigeonholed into one subject area or grade level. Also, library media specialists needs to have a strong commitment and understanding of curriculum, instruction, and assessment. Above all, this person needs to be able to work with all types of people throughout the school setting— teachers in all areas and grades, district administrators, building administrators, and support staff. The library media specialist should be an educational leader of the building.

Library media specialists often talk about being the only person in the building with their particular job—which is true. However, if one takes time to think about it, the person whom they have the most in common with is actually not the classroom teachers, but the administrator. Working with all the teachers, support staff, students, parents, etc. gives the library media specialist that same global look of the building that the principal has. When you talk with administrators, what kind of conversations do you have? Are they more focused on little details, or are the conversations about instruction, teaching, professional development, resources, and technology? While I'm sure sometimes I bug Vince with what he must think are stupid little details, I also know that we talk about how we can keep moving our school forward. Our similar perspectives make it easy to see the big picture when often times the classroom teacher can only see the impact from his/her classroom or grade level point of view.

Q • The educational system • in the United States is quite focused on standards and achievement tests right now. How can the library media specialist contribute to these goals?

A • By being a part of the • school improvement process. If he/she understands this process like I described above, he/she can infuse media and technology into these school improvement goals, thus making the learning for students more accessible and meaningful.

As library media specialists look for ways to collaborate with teachers, school improvement plans are the most critical starting place. Recently, I had an email conversation with another library media specialist who was worried about the literacy block their school was implementing as part of the school improvement plan. He wondered if the teachers would still come to the library media center for check-outs and how he would get the opportunity to collaborate with them with such a fixed block for literacy instruction. He began by taking the right steps to be a part of the literacy block. He attended the literacy block training, he examined the instructional materials the teachers were using, and he used that as a springboard to begin the conversation of how the library media program could be an integral part of this new program. Since school improvement plans are driving what teachers are doing in schools today, library media programs need to be aligned to the plans and show the connections needed to help reach the established goals. School improvement plans are another opportunity to open the door to collaboration.

Q • Many school districts • use the standard teacher evaluation form for evaluation of the library media specialist? If you were to design an evaluation customized for the library media specialist, what would you put on the evaluation form?

A • I would use the same type • of evaluation for the fact that a library media specialist is a teacher. I would probably add to it information that is also pertinent to the job, i.e., budget of the library media center, etc.

When our district went to a new evaluation form a few years ago, the library media specialist was given the opportunity to look at the new form and modify it to fit the position. After a few discussions, it became clear we didn't need another form. Our new form was divided into four areas: planning and preparation, classroom environment, instruction, and professional responsibilities. Every role and task performed by a library media specialist fell into one of these areas. Using the form, Vince can comment on the "library jobs," but the focus of the evaluation is on teaching and learning which supports his view that library media specialists must have skills that focus on teaching and learning.

Q: What role do you envision the library media specialist serving on the school leadership team?

A: Leader of the process—but, of course, this can only happen for any one faculty member if he/she has the respect from other staff members and he/she is seen from other staff members as competent and they are confident in their work.

Okay, I know I'm a glutton for punishment some days. My hand automatically (sometimes without knowing it) rises when there is a call for volunteers. I love working with teachers on curriculum. I love working with our school improvement process. I love getting a chance to always add my two cents about how the library media program can help. Although it isn't possible to be on every committee in the building, it is important to be represented as much as possible. Without having a part in the educational decision-making process, how can the library media program be seen as an integral part of instruction?

Q: What is your preferred communication method with members of your staff about sharing ideas for programs, school concerns, etc.?

A: I use a variety of methods for communication including weekly memos, newsletters, one-on-one conversations for concerns, Professional Learning Communities meetings, staff meetings, etc.

Finding the right opportunity to talk with your administrator can sometimes be difficult. Depending on the size of your school, the administrator may not be available on a moment's notice. Vince has the "open door" policy, so quite often, as I wander through the front office I pop in with a comment or question. In addition, Vince makes two trips through every instructional space every day. He is out where teachers and students can readily talk and interact with him. So, I also know that if I haven't made it to the office and need to talk with him, he will make it in the library media center at some point during the day. Emails also work well as I know he hates it when his in box is full. I've learned what methods work best for communicating with Vince. Other colleagues of mine find that if they schedule a regular meeting with the administrator, that works best. The key is to figure out what method your administrator prefers.

Q: What do you value most in your library media specialist and why?

A: He is always looking for ways to make learning more meaningful for students and teaching more meaningful for teachers. He is always forward thinking and proactive—not waiting for teachers to ask for help—he tells them what they need, even when they have no idea they need it. This is done in a collaborative manner with co-teaching and plenty of support. He also helps teachers with new skills in technology and media by gradually releasing them, i.e., teach a skill for them with the students, then helping the teacher teach it, then having the teacher teach it independently.

As library media specialists, we know our plates are full with all kinds of jobs and responsibilities. It takes effort and perseverance every day to keep our library media centers running efficiently and effectively. As we consciously make decisions each day to prioritize the tasks at hand, the most important things that should float to the top of the list are those things that relate directly to teaching and learning. How can we make the most impact for students? That is what administrators need and want to see.

Additional Resources:

Hartzell, Gary. *Building Influence for the School Librarian: Tenets, Targets, and Tactics.* Linworth Publishing, 2003.

Hartzell, Gary. "Why Should Principals Support School Libraries?" *ERIC Digest* ED470034 (November 2005). ERIC Clearinghouse on Information and Technology, Syracuse, NY.

Harvey, Carl A., II. "Aligning School Library Media and Principal Agendas." *School Library Media Activities Monthly* 23, no. 9 (May 2007): 48-49.

Harvey, Carl A., II. *No School Library Left Behind: Leadership, School Improvement, and the Media Specialist.* Linworth Publishing, 2008.

Harvey, Carl A., II. "Under the Radar." *School Library Media Activities Monthly* 24, no. 10 (June 2008): 47-48.

Harvey, Carl A., II. "What Should a Teacher Expect a School Library Media Specialist to Be?" *Library Media Connection* (February 2005): 23.

Hughes-Hassell, Sandra, and Violet H. Harada. *School Reform and the School Library Media Specialist.* Linworth Publishing, 2008.

McGhee, Marla W., and Barbara A. Jansen. *The Principal's Guide to a Powerful Library Media Program.* Linworth Publishing, 2005.◄

Carl A. Harvey II is the library media specialist at North Elementary School in Noblesville, IN. Email: carl@carl-harvey.com

Reframing the Library Media Specialist as a Learning Specialist

by Allison Zmuda and Violet H. Harada

Preparing students to meet the challenges of the 21st century has solidified the need for information literacy and technology as meaningful components of curriculum designs and instructional practices. The survey report *Partnership for 21st Century Skills* states that, when polled, voters rank the following areas as high priorities for schools (2007):

- computer and technology skills
- critical thinking and problem solving skills
- ethics and social responsibility
- written and oral communications
- teamwork and collaboration
- lifelong learning and self-direction
- leadership
- creativity and innovation
- media literacy
- global awareness

In today's schools, a host of learning specialists joins classroom teachers in working with students. These specialists have no formal classroom assignments, but they provide instruction for students, and, frequently, training for teachers. They range from library media specialists and reading resource teachers to technology coordinators and math coaches. As learning specialists, library media specialists, because of their deep content expertise about the nature of inquiry and the construction of knowledge, are uniquely suited to develop 21st-century student learning skills. What would it look like if learners could determine their information needs, solve problems, read for pleasure, effectively and ethically use in-

formation and ideas, debate merits of a point of view, and create quality written and oral communications?

Such clarification of what the learners must do to achieve mission goals defines for all staff what good business looks like in the library media center. Good business is work (instructional activities and assessments) that develops student learning around the goals that are most important (again as defined by the mission). The recently published *Standards for the 21st-Century Learner* requires students to construct knowledge through the exploration and analysis of ideas, information, and point of view, and to communicate their learning through authentic, transfer-oriented tasks (AASL 2007). In his research of student learning in Ohio, Ross Todd found strong evidence that:

> Students unequivocally recognize that when school librarians have a clearly defined role as an information literacy specialist, their opportunities for learning are enhanced. This role is a very active, learning-centered role where school librarians actively contribute their expertise to that of the classroom teachers to enable students to transform infor-

Allison G. Zmuda is an education consultant who has worked with schools throughout the United States and Canada. Email: zmuda@competentclassroom.com

Violet H. Harada is a professor in the University of Hawaii's Library and Information Science Program. Email: vharada@hawaii.edu

mation into personal knowledge (Todd, 2006).

Bad business is work that is irrelevant, tangential, or counter-productive. These activities or assessments require students to collect information or resources in the library media center and then leave. The superficiality of this acquisition is doomed to fail. Students will not become wiser, more skillful, or more strategic; they will not become more prolific or powerful as communicators; they will not become more mindful of the validity of alternate points of view or the persuasive use of data. Bad business takes up precious resources of the library media specialist because of the time it takes to prepare and organize the resources as well as the orchestration and oversight of the experience. Major features of bad and good business practices are delineated in Table 1.

There is no upside to library media specialists collaborating with classroom teachers on tasks that are bad business. If library media specialists participate in the design and orchestration of these types of tasks, even though they know that it is "bad business," they become accomplices in the assignment of yet another task that dilutes inquiry to the level of answering the questions on a worksheet, reduces deep reading to counting the number of pages read, and prostitutes construction of knowledge to a cut-and-paste exercise. The library media specialist must insist that every learning experience in the library-classroom aligns with the learning goals of both the classroom teacher's curriculum and the library media curriculum. The key to depersonalizing this transformation of "bad business" to "good business" comes from the continued insistence that this isn't about what the teacher or library media specialist prefers, but what the learner requires. The mission statement and AASL *Standards for the 21st-Century Learner* should be prominently featured in all aspects of the learning environment—physically hung on the walls, judiciously placed in curriculum binders and planning materials, and prominently displayed on the school and library media websites. The library media specialist also should use the learning goals as a touchstone in every conversation with staff. Such relentless consistency both models and reinforces to staff that the focus on the goals of learning is a "disciplined mindset" that ensures that what students are asked to do on a daily basis is challenging and worthy of the attempt.

How the 21st-Century Mission Affects the Job Description of the Library Media Specialist

In their upcoming book, *Librarians as Learning Specialists: Meeting the Learning Imperative for the 21st Century*, Zmuda and Harada contend that library media specialists must refocus their job descriptions and their daily practice so that they target direct contributions to improve 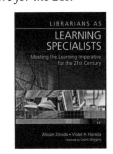 the achievement of all learners on defined curricular goals. The job description of a library media specialist predictably includes key components that appear in those of many other learning specialists employed in schools. A comparative analysis of reading, technology, mathematics and librarian job descriptions is shown in Table 2 (see page 44).

While the parallels are evident in theory, will this "reframing" resonate with library media specialists? The authors tested out the viability

Table 1. Bad and Good Business Practices for Library Media Specialists	
Moving away from bad business where…	**Moving toward good business where…**
Success is defined by the number of staff who collaborate with the library media specialist.	Success is defined by the quality of the work completed in the library media center.
Success is defined by doing whatever is asked in order to be recognized as valuable or important.	Success is defined by investing resources only in those tasks that are central to the library mission.
Success is defined by helping students find what they are looking for.	Success is defined by engaging students in the construction of deep knowledge through the exploration of ideas and information, conducting of investigations, and communication and evaluation of findings.
Success is defined by the number of instructional sessions held in the library media center.	Success is defined by the student learning that resulted from completion of work centered on subject area and information literacy goals.

of the concept through countless conversations with library media specialists and their supervisors throughout the United States. In one such exploratory conversation at a state-level conference, Zmuda asked over 100 library media specialists to participate in a KWL activity on their ideas, concerns, and insights about being viewed as a learning specialist. This discussion is summarized in Table 3 (see page 45).

How This Affects the Design, Implementation, and Analysis of Student Learning

Instructional designs are always in a state of flux. While there are core practices, strategies, and re-

Table 2. What Learning Specialists Do		
Assessment and Instruction (with students)	**Curriculum, Assessment, and Instruction (with staff)**	**Program Development, Leadership, and Management**
• Provide instruction for individuals or small groups of students. Such instruction tends to be supplemental to that provided by the classroom teachers. • Work on short-term basis with targeted students, then provide strategies/processes for classroom teachers to follow. • Provide instruction, using research-supported programs.	**Curriculum** • Serve on curriculum committees. **Assessment** • Assist in the development of assessment instruments (retelling protocols and running records) and selection of assessment instruments. • Assist in interpretation of test results with teachers and parents. • Share results of assessments with public. **Instruction** • Discuss and share ideas with teachers about help for struggling students, and materials and ideas that enhance performance. • Hold collaborative planning sessions to develop lessons and strategies for working with students. These are held either on a systematic, regular basis, as needed, or "on the fly." • Demonstrate strategies for teachers, observe, and provide feedback. • Participate in observations (teachers observing each other) for professional growth. • Provide a "friendly ear" for teachers who want to talk about issues, problems, or ideas that they have about instruction and assessment for their students.	**Development and Leadership** • Provide professional development for teachers as part of the school staff development program; also teach classes that teachers can take for credit. Work with teachers in planning and conducting professional development in the schools. • Work closely with the principal in setting a schedule and making decisions about professional development. • Serve as mentor to new teachers by modeling, providing feedback, and coaching. • Work with special educators and serve on instructional support or pupil personnel teams. • Lead study groups (read a professional book or article and then discuss). • Serve as a resource to allied professionals, parents, other community members, volunteers, and tutors. • Serve as a resource for parents (communicate with parents, providing and accessing information); conduct workshops on how they can work with their children; provide workshops for parents of preschool students. • Work with other school specialists. • Work with volunteers (provide training sessions, coordinate schedules, recruit). **Management** • Maintain center or location for various materials. • Look for and assist in the selection of new materials (including development of criteria for determining quality of those materials); assist in the piloting of new materials. • Coordinate program schedules.

sources that constitute the basis of the learning experiences, teachers and library media specialists must constantly monitor and adjust their work in light of their increased knowledge of the nature of their learners and the learning. This design cycle of construction, analysis, and adjustment is grounded in the essential question: How do I know if what I did today worked? For an instructional design to "work," a teacher or library media specialist must investigate:

- Did the instructional experience(s) cause the desired learning for every learner?
- What evidence do I have to that effect?
- Will the learning likely transfer to future learning experiences?

Ross Todd stated in an interview in 2006:

In the current educational climate there is a very clear mandate for a shift from putting our

K What do we know a learning specialist to be?	W What are we curious or concerned about if the library media specialist is reframed as a learning specialist?	L What have we learned so far about what reframing the library media specialist as a learning specialist will require?
• Someone who believes that all students can be successful learners. • Someone who is up on the latest trends in teaching and learning. • Someone who has work experience in both the classroom and the library media center. • Someone who uses assessment data to determine student strength and weaknesses to inform future instruction. • Someone who can diagnose learning problems and design ways to address them. • Someone with deep content expertise about how people learn. • Someone who works with staff and students. • Someone who constantly reflects on his/her own practice and how to improve. • Someone who is able to break things down into small, manageable pieces. • Someone who is fluent with the curriculum goals across grade levels and subject areas. • Someone who can coach performance (from staff and students) through the design of challenging and motivating tasks. • Someone who seeks out new learning experiences, tools, and resources because of what the learners need.	• How do we articulate our role in an effective way so the message is heard? • How do we use professional learning communities to facilitate work? • How much do we really know about how different types of learners learn in the library media center? • How can we earn respect of staff and the larger system as a learning specialist? • How does the learning specialist fit into the hierarchy of the school or district organization? • Who has the authority to make decisions about what instruction will look like in the library media center? • How do we increase the number of teachers who want to collaborate with us in the design, implementation, and evaluation of learning? • How do we hone our leadership skills so that we can improve the effectiveness of our collaborative work with staff? • How do we elevate the quality of instructional and assessment practices in the school/district? • Who are the other learning specialists in the school? What relationship do we have with one another? What relationship should we have? • How do we facilitate learning while running the library media center?	• Just because it isn't happening in front of us doesn't mean it isn't happening—the teacher's classroom is an extension of the work in the library media center. • We will never be considered learning specialists without collecting evidence of student achievement in our classroom. • Because disengaged learners learn nothing, we have a responsibility to "fix" instructional designs that are low-level, information retrieval tasks. • A learning specialist, like any teacher-leadership position, is an inherently precarious, messy job because it lives somewhere between the administrative ranks and the teaching ranks. • Without a clear job description (on paper and in practice), it is impossible to know whether we are doing the right things. • Staff think that we are what they see us do—if they only watch us organize, sort, manage, and support, they will not see us as learning specialists.

Table 3. Insights and Issues of Library Media Specialists as Learning Specialists

Note: Specific contributions to the KWL chart were made by audience participants at a breakout session facilitated by Allison Zmuda on November 15, 2007, including but not limited to the reflections of: Debra Kay Logan, Hilda Weisburg, Dee Giordan, Linda Piscione, Pat Slemmer, Diane Drayer Beler, Pat VanEs, Christine Lopey, and Dawn Henderson.

emphasis on finding and accessing to knowledge building. It's where education is going. We are talking about standards-based education. We are talking about accountability. We are talking about evidence of achievements. There is incredible emphasis on meeting curriculum standards, knowledge-based outcomes. Our instructional interventions need to put a richer emphasis on those knowledge-based outcomes. How do we pedagogically intervene in the information experience of a child, to enable them to go beyond the amassing of facts to the interrogation of those facts and to develop deep knowledge? That's a very complex task (Kenney 2006).

What makes this inquiry even more complex is the inevitable reality that what "works" for one student does not work for all students. Staff must work to troubleshoot inevitable learning problems so that students have additional opportunities to improve performance through highly focused remediation, extension, and enrichment. Again, library media specialists as learning specialists are uniquely situated to collaborate in this effort through their development and dissemination of resources, curriculum leadership, and participation in professional learning communities. They also possess valuable skills in designing and analyzing instructional activities and assessments tasks, modeling of processes and "best practices," and coaching of improved staff and student performance.

How This Affects Our Short-Term and Long-Term Efforts

A mission-centered mindset

requires a constant analysis of whether the daily practices of the library media specialist are having the desired effects on student achievement. Such analysis will inevitably uncover areas of "misalignment" where significant resources are expended to support the development of work and acquisition of materials that are tangential to established curricular goals. This "misalignment" plagues not only the work of the library media specialist but of all educators. In their seminal work on schooling and leadership, Grant Wiggins and Jay McTighe state:

One failure of conventional schooling and of school reform in general relates to the deeply held belief that if we just get good people trying hard to do good things, it will all work out. The truth is otherwise: excellence in leadership as well as in teaching is a function of constant and deliberate self-correction, mindful of clear and agreed-upon goals while unflinchingly seeking out feedback and thus dealing with the brutal facts of reality. The school reforms of the past twenty-five years continue—and continue to be needed—because many schools are far from facing the information that cannot be ignored. That information is of two kinds: feedback about how deeply and effectively students are learning and are engaged, and feedback suggesting that many time-honored actions and policies in school are dysfunctional—counter to mission (2007, 179).

Library media specialists who reframe themselves as learning specialists will find the recognition,

respect, and collaboration they seek when they put an end to "bad business" practices that divert focus from the mission. This charge will not be easy. It will be fraught with difficult conversations, political strategizing, repeated modeling, relentless data collection and analysis, and candid feedback. But the rewards of good business will be spectacular: the sound of students engaged in the construction of knowledge and the communication of thinking, the opportunity to see that the investment of resources positively affects student performance on higher-order tasks and staff teaching practices, and the sense of satisfaction that the library media center is the most information-rich, inquiry-rich, resource-rich, pedagogically-rich classroom in the building.

References

American Association of School Librarians. *Standards for the 21st-Century Learner.* http://www.ala.org/aasl/standards (accessed November 18, 2007).

Kenney, Brian. "Rutgers' Ross Todd's Quest to Renew School Libraries." http://www.schoollibraryjournal.com/article/CA6320013.html (accessed November 15, 2007).

Partnership for 21st Century Skills. "Beyond the Three Rs: Voter Attitudes toward 21st Century Skills." http://www.21stcenturyskills.org/documents/p21_pollreport_2pg.pdf (accessed November 15, 2007).

Todd, Ross. "It's All about Getting A's." http://www.cilip.org.uk/publications/updatemagazine/archive/archive2006/january/toddjan06.htm (accessed November 15, 2007).

Wiggins, Grant, and Jay McTighe. *Schooling by Design.* Association for Supervision and Curriculum Development, 2007.

Zmuda, Allison, and Violet H. Harada. *Librarians as Learning Specialists: Meeting the Learning Imperative for the 21st Century.* Libraries Unlimited, 2008. 🖑

Impact as a 21st-Century Library Media Specialist

by Peggy Milam Creighton

Note: The text in italic bold represents the hotlinks to each resource. This article is available on the *SLMAM* website with the hotlinks in place (http://www.schoollibrarymedia.com).

Library media specialists have ***big roles*** to fulfill as program administrators, information specialists, teachers, and instructional partners. But what about the more mundane tasks accomplished every day? These small things do make a big difference. In his book *The Tipping Point: How Little Things Can Make a Big Difference*, author ***Malcolm Gladwell*** details these routine behaviors that reap big rewards (2000). Gladwell identifies three types of people who can make a difference: mavens, connectors, and salesmen. He explains, "Mavens are data banks. They provide the message… Connectors are social glue: they spread it…" "Salesmen," he continues, they are the ones "with the skills to persuade us when we are unconvinced of what we are hearing…" (2000). When I read this, I immediately thought of individuals who fit into these three categories. But I wondered, "How do these analogies apply to library media specialists?" Eventually, I realized these categories identify the habits of exemplary library media specialists and make a big difference in the success of their practice.

Peggy Milam Creighton, Ed.S., NBCT, is the library media specialist at Compton Elementary School in Powder Springs, GA. Email: peggymilam@hotmail.com.

Characteristics of Media Mavens
wise
insightful
understanding
technology models
lifelong learners
data collectors
professional achievers
program developers
consultants
advisors
information gatherers
authorities
gurus
experts

Media Mavens

Surely, everyone knows some library media specialists who are mavens. An article entitled "Mavens" in *Wikipedia* identifies Gladwell's mavens as "intense gatherers of information." I think school library mavens are the wise ones who reap the information harvest for the benefit of others. Library media specialist mavens recognize that they have insight into what students enjoy reading and use that information to support reading instruction. They understand that they play a key role in modeling technology tools, so they adopt ***My Space, You Tube, Flickr***, and ***Peanut Butter wiki*** and teach others. Library media specialist mavens become ***Google Earth*** gurus, ***Frappr*** mapping fanatics, and ***Library Thing*** catalogers. Media mavens are experts at using the ***Library of Congress, Search Systems, The Institute for Library and Information Literacy Education***, and the ***National***

Center for Education Statistics to locate information. They use their knowledge of the curriculum to make information more accessible to their students. They create pathfinders such as those created by the multitalented Master Maven *Joyce Valenza* to better serve their staff and students.

Library media mavens seek to increase their knowledge to better serve their patrons. They gather data to assess their programs, as master mavens *Joan Yoshina* and *Violet Harada* have done. Media mavens continue to grow professionally by *Ninging* with others, *Hitchhiking* professional development, *Feedburning* informative blogs and podcasts, and learning in a *MUVE*.

Library media mavens put their wisdom to work developing unique programs that attract patrons with special needs, community partners, parents, and others in their community. Library media mavens podcast story times, such as Master Maven *Sarah Chauncey* has done. Library media mavens stream video of their *school news shows* so working parents can tune in, offer *Homework Help Hotlines* by phone, *blogs*, or with Instant Messaging. For all the patrons they serve, mavens play a role as consultants, advisors, information gatherers, authorities, and niche-fillers. As such, they are valuable members of their staff, valuable members of their communities, valuable collaborators, and valuable program administrators.

Library Media Connectors

Perhaps most readers can identify some connectors. Gladwell says, "Sprinkled among every walk of life… are a handful of people with a truly extraordinary knack of making friends and acquaintances. They are Connectors" (2000). The article "The Tipping Point" in *Wikipedia* says that Gladwell's connectors are "those with wide social circles. They are the hubs of the human social network…."

Connectors blog their thoughts and ideas, bringing countless minds together to comment on the same issue virtually, such as Connoisseur Connector and self-proclaimed curmudgeon Alice Yucht has done with her *Alice in Infoland* blog. Connectors have a way of drawing others in and making them joiners, such as Connoisseur Connector Lisa Perez has done with her *virtual meetings in Second Life*.

School library media connectors make themselves available to serve on technology committees, attend team meetings, and write School Improvement Plans. As connectors, they willingly offer to assist the principal, to mentor new staff members, or to tutor after school.

Connectors are champions of causes that are important in the school library world: they lobby for bills such as the *SKILLS Act*; they become *National Board Certified Teachers*, conference speakers such as Connoisseur Connector *Gail Dickinson* or published writers such as the prolific Connoisseur Connector *Doug Johnson*. They serve in professional organizations as *Sara Kelly Johns* does, mentor new media specialists as *Carl Harvey II* does, or teach online as *Annette Lamb and Larry Johnson* do. Connectors, like Connoisseur connector *Barbara Stripling*, are role models who pave the way for others to follow.

Connectors are innovators, such as Connoisseur Connector *Peter Milbury*. They see connections others have missed and share ideas, like *Shonda Brisco* and *Diane Chen* do. They promote programs that enrich instruction during the day and in *After School Programs*. They volunteer for things others avoid, assist with difficult behavior problems, or provide timeout space. Library media specialist connectors are not afraid to try new combinations and blaze new trails to forge a relationship.

Connectors build communities both in person and virtually. Connectors use collaborative technology tools to draw folks together: they post literary and school-related events on *Google calendars* and share them, create blogs to keep patrons informed, open *Facebook* accounts, share *Nings*,

Characteristics of Connectors

bloggers
assistants
tutors
lobbyists
writers
role models
volunteers
teachers
joiners
mentors
champions of causes
speakers
innovators
trail blazers
community builders

and use *Twitter* as a virtual reference tool with Instant Messaging help.

Library media specialist connectors share their knowledge with others. They create videos and post them to *Teacher Tube*, such as Connoisseur Connector "Dr. Loopy" a.k.a. *Doug Valentine* has done. They post their favorite websites to *Del.icio.us* for others to access, communicate their experiences on *LM_net* or *Teacher-Librarian wiki* or *School Library Media Activities Monthly* blog and share what they have learned so others can learn it, too.

Library Media Specialist Salesmen

It is most likely that readers know some library media specialists who are salesmen. According to Gladwell, salesmen are the ones "with the skills to persuade us when we are unconvinced of what we are hearing…" (2000). The article entitled "The Tipping Point" in *Wikipedia* says salesmen are "charismatic people with powerful negotiation skills. They exert 'soft' influence rather than forceful power."

As salesmen, library media specialists are writers and advocates of all things related to school libraries, such as Super Sales people

Ken Haycock, *David Loertscher*, and *Blanche Woolls*. School library salesmen are the promoters of new trends in technology resources, such as *Joan Frye Williams*, and, like Super Salesmen *David Warlick* or *Michael Stephens*, they are compelling and magnetic. Library media specialist salesmen possess superior marketing skills, such as Super Saleswoman *Jill Stover*, who has led the way in "thinking outside the book" with her unique marketing strategies. School library media specialist salesmen create slogans, write mission statements, create contests, and schedule events that attract new patrons and keep veteran patrons coming back.

Library media specialist salesmen use research to convince others of their authority, such as Super Salesmen *Keith Lance* and *Ross Todd*. They use their diverse skills to differentiate their programs from the rest. If they are writers, they publish promotional material—newsletters, brochures, *flyers*, blogs, wikis, websites, PowerPoints, and *bookmarks*. Storytellers, such as *Toni Buzzeo*, take every opportunity to demonstrate their skills—at Parent Night, on the school news, on the Web, at the Talent Show, at

the fall fair. The artsy ones create banners, t-shirts, signs, and even *sculptures*. Those who think they lack the talent to do it themselves use prepared kits from the *American Library Association* or the *American Association of School Librarians*.

School library media specialist salesmen are visionary, such as Super Saleswoman *Debbie Abilock*—they introduce new technology trends and model their use. They convince reluctant adopters to try new things, maximize use of their *space* and their resources, and make their programs sound inviting. School library media specialist salesmen are hawkers, clowns, attention-getters, magnets, speakers, promoters, and advertising executives. School library media salesmen are the dynamos who convince others not to lose out by not joining in.

Implications for Library Media Specialists

So what can be learned from these three types of people? Some of the most successful library media specialists are the ones who find their niche, and whether they are mavens, connectors, or salesmen, these library media specialists have made a difference by meeting a need. They model technology tools such as *My Space*, *Teacher Tube*, *Flickr*, *Google Earth*, *Library Thing*, and *Peanut Butter wiki*. They podcast, stream video, IM, and Twitter. They search the Library of Congress, stay abreast of legislation such as the SKILLS Act, become National Board Certified and mentor others to do the same. They speak, write, research, and promote all they can, and convince patrons to take advantage of it. What if all

Characteristics of Salesmen

persuaders
negotiators
advocates
compelling
marketers
publishers
convincing
clowns
unique
charismatic
writers
promoters
magnetic
researchers
visionaries
hawkers
attention-getters
dynamos

of us could join with the collective chorus of library media specialist voices who are currently making a difference in their daily practice? What if we could all lead "octopus programs" such as *Kelly Kuntz,* past President of the Oregon Educational Media Association envisioned when she said, "A strong library program would be like an octopus. It would work its way into every classroom, and if you tried to cut off the tentacles you couldn't because it was so interwoven into the fabric of the school…."

Resources:

Print

Gladwell, M. *The Tipping Point: How Little Things Can Make a Big Difference.* Little, Brown, 2000.

Internet (in order of mention in article)

Roles of the SLMS. http://www.ala.org/aaslTemplate.cfm?Section=informationpower&Template=/ContentManagement/ContentDisplay.cfm&ContentID=19930

Malcolm Gladwell. http://www.gladwell.com

Wikipedia "mavens." http://en.wikipedia.org/wiki/Maven

My Space. http://www.myspace.com

You Tube. http://www.youtube.com

Flickr. http://www.flickr.com

Peanut Butter wiki. http://pbwiki.com

Google Earth. http://earth.google.com

Frappr. http://www.frappr.com

Library Thing. http://www.librarything.com

Library of Congress. http://www.loc.gov

Search Systems database. http://www.searchsystems.net

The Institute for Library and Information Literacy Education. http://.ilile.org

National Center for Education Statistics. http://nces.ed.gov/

Joyce Valenza's pathfinders. http://www.sdst.org/shs/library/pathmenu.html

Violet Harada article. http://www.schoollibrarymedia.com/features/articles/Nov06.html

Teacher Librarian ning. http://teacherlibrarian.ning.com/

Professional Conference summaries. http://www.hitchhikr.com

Feedburner Aggregator. http://www.feedburner.com

Second Life multi-user virtual reality environment. http://secondlife.com/

Sarah Chauncey's podcasts. http://www.grandviewlibrary.org/StoryTelling.aspx

School news shows. http://mes.wcs.k12.va.us/morning_news.htm

Homework help hotline. http://www.putnamcityschools.org/hefner/homework.html or http://mhms-media.blogspot.com/2006_10_01_archive.html

Wikipedia "connectors." http://en.wikipedia.org/wiki/The_Tipping_Point_(book)

Alice in Infoland. http://www.aliceinfo.org/

Virtual meetings in Second Life. http://slurl.com/secondlife/Info%20International/127/233/34/

SKILLS Act. http://www.ala.org/ala/aasl/aaslissues/SKILLS_Act.cfm

NBCT. http://www.nbpts.org

Gail Dickinson. http://education.odu.edu/eci/dir/vitae/g_dickinson.shtml

Doug Johnson. http://www.doug-johnson.com/

Sara Kelly Johns. http://fromtheinsideout.squarespace.com/

Carl Harvey II. http://www.nobl.k12.in.us/media/NorthMedia/LMS/NORTHLMC/HARVEY.HTM

Annette Lamb/Larry Johnson. http://eduscapes.com/lamb/

Barbara Stripling. http://www.schoollibraryjournal.com/article/CA499368.html

Peter Milbury. http://www.school-libraries.org/milbury/

Shonda Brisco. http://txschoollibrarians.ning.com/profile/ShondaB

Diane Chen. http://deepthinking.blogsome.com/

After School Programs. http://teacher.scholastic.com/products/bookflixfreetrial

Google calendars. http://www.google.com/calendar

Facebook. http://www.facebook.com

Ning. http://www.ning.com

Twitter. http://twitter.com

Teacher Tube example. http://www.teachertube.com/view_video.php?viewkey=3c2807e1dd9963eda16d

Doug Valentine. http://teacherlibrarian.ning.com/photo/photo/listForContributor?screenName=drloopy

Del.icio.us example. http://del.icio.us/peggymilamcreighton

LM_Net wikispaces. http://lmnet.wikispaces.com/

SLMAM Blog on Web 2.0. http://blog.schoollibrarymedia.com

Teacher Librarian Wiki. http://teacherlibrarianwiki.pbwiki.com/

Wikipedia "salesmen." http://en.wikipedia.org/wiki/The_Tipping_Point_(book)

Ken Haycock. http://slisweb.sjsu.edu/people/faculty/haycockk/haycockk.php

David Loertscher/Blanche Woolls. http://www.gale.com/reference/about-reviewers/blanche-woolls-david-loertscher/index.htm

Joan Frye Williams. http://www.infopeople.org/workshop/instructor/56

David Warlick. http://davidwarlick.com/wordpress/?page_id=2

Michael Stephens. http://tametheweb.com/

Jill Stover. http://librarymarketing.blogspt.com/

Keith Lance. http://www.lrs.org/documents/resumes/kl_res.pdf

Ross Todd. http://www.scils.rutgers.edu/~rtodd/

Library flyers. http://www.ed.gov/pubs/parents/LearnPtnrs/library.html

Library bookmarks. http://www.gale.com/free_resources/marketing/find_yourself/

Toni Buzzeo. http://www.tonibuzzeo.com

Library sculpture. http://www.olc.org/marketing/6wcpl.htm

ALA/AASL Marketing kits. http://www.ala.org/ala/pio/campaign/prtools/campaignforamericaslibrariesprogramwashingtondc/marketing_workbook.pdf Or http://www.ala.org/ala/pio/campaign/schoollibrary/schoollibrary.htm

Debbie Abilock. http://www.noodletools.com/debbie/bio/

Space. http://www.edfacilities.org/rl/libraries.cfm

Kelly Kuntz. http://www.nwrel.org/nwedu/09-01/link.asp ✋

Student Learning in the Library Media Center
What am I here for? What are my students here for?

Basic Task Description	Individual/Teacher Expectations	Areas of Information Literacy (check those that apply)
		☐ Define and clarify ☐ Locate and retrieve ☐ Select, process, and record data ☐ Analyze ☐ Synthesize ☐ Share and use ☐ Reflection

What areas of Information Literacy are new for you/your students?

What areas do you/your students have experience in but still may have questions about?

What areas do you/your students have a lot of experience and success in?

For more information about this page, see the article "Where Does Your Authority Come From?: Empowering the Library Media Specialist as a True Partner in Student Achievement" by Allison Zmuda (*SLMAM*, September 2006, pages 19-22).

Where Does Your Authority Come From?

Empowering the Library Media Specialist as a True Partner in Student Achievement

by Allison Zmuda

The library media center has long been a beloved and specialized learning environment for students, a place rich with opportunities to pursue specialized inquiries, interests, and ideas. It is the most natural venue in schools for differentiation, integration of technology, and collaboration. In recent years, state and national standards for information literacy and technology have delineated a framework for what students are expected to know and be able to do as a result of their work in the library media center. Noted education researchers, system leaders, and authors as well as foundations have further bolstered the importance of the library media center as an integral part of 21st century learning so that students are prepared for the demands of the workplace. There has never been a more exciting or potentially powerful time to be a library media specialist.

There is, however, one fundamental problem that has existed for years and has frustrated specialists for years: How do we get the authority to teach students? If they don't come to the library media center at all or come for a meaningful purpose (i.e., a task where students are expected to work in critical and creative ways to collect, analyze, and synthesize information), then how can students be expected to achieve the standards?

True authority does not come from the superintendent, principal, or even the teachers worked with every day; it comes from a very large achievement gap. This achievement gap is the chasm between the academic expectations for learners and the current achievement levels of students within the school. Most specialists have been aware of this gap for years and many have vocalized those concerns and, consequently, lobbied for broader access to students and more resources. The major stumbling block, however, is that without data to illustrate this gap, it looks like a rhetorical contention based on the unabashedly biased viewpoint of those professionals that seem to have the most to gain. So, to claim the authority needed to close this achievement gap, it is important to get the data to show the current student achievement levels, compare that to state/national standards for learning, and then propose short-term

Allison Zmuda is an Educational Consultant with Education Connection in Litchfield, CT. She was the keynote speaker at the Treasure Mountain Research Retreat #12, Pittsburgh, PA, October 2005. Email: azmuda@hughes.net

and long-term ways to close those gaps.

What kind of data are we talking about?

A reliable measure of student achievement requires getting a collection of different types of evidence. For example, the amount of time a student has spent in the library media center is a necessary, but not sufficient, piece of information because seat time alone is not a predictor of learning success.

> **Questions to guide the data collection process:**
> 1. What do we have to find out?
> 2. What data are currently available?
> 3. What new data do we need?
> 4. How do we obtain data?
> 5. How can we collect data in a valid and reliable form?
>
> **Guidelines to support the effort:**
> • Measure what is necessary, not what is convenient
> • Keep focused on what is being evaluated: student learning, not individual educators
> • Involve key stakeholders in dialogue about the intent of the data collection process (before, during, and after)
> • Involve staff in the collection and analysis
> • Use data to produce a collective mandate for change

Examples of powerful data sources include:
- Existing information literacy requirements (how much time students at each grade level are required to be in the library media center and the focus of that requirement—orientation vs. development),
- Analysis of state content standards in all subject areas to determine how many require information and technology literacy,
- Required core assessments completed by all students in a grade level/course to evaluate incorporation of information and technology literacy,
- Daily attendance figures in the library media center (also accounting for how many times the center was full which limited the use for others)
- Percentage of teachers who bring students to the library 0-2, 3-5, and 6+ times per year,
- Nature of the tasks students are working on (i.e., classify by level on Bloom's taxonomy).

Now that I have the attention of the staff, what do I do next?

Once the preliminary data is collected and communicated, the next challenge is how to act on that information in a way that enlists the support of classroom teachers and leaders to raise student achievement. It is critical to keep the focus on the results so that staff see subsequent actions (both on a daily basis and in long-term planning) as a necessary means to achieve the desired end. Whatever the status quo currently looks like (nature of relationships with teachers, existing resources, level of support from school, system, and state leaders), two conditions must be met to positively impact student achievement:
- Library media specialists view every point of contact with a teacher and his/her respective students as a true collaboration of content areas.
- Library media specialists view the collection, analysis, and reflection on student achievement data as a primary part of their work.

Condition #1: Library media specialists view every point of contact with a teacher and his/her respective students as a true collaboration of content areas.

Collaboration rooted in trust and respect among committed adults is the most essential condition for meaningful change in any organization. "Without trust and respect, there is no real learning and dialogue about the need for change" (Wagner 1997, 29). The library media specialist must never sacrifice the opportunity to develop information literacy skills just to pacify or cajole a teacher to come to the library media center. Not only does this deference diminish student clarity about what research and synthesis involves, but also relegates the specialist to a supporting role instead of a meaningful partner in the professional learning community. Specialists must communicate the vision and expectations for student learning in the library media center so that teacher and student alike are clear on what is expected when they work in this environment. (See Figure 1).
- When staff come together to

Figure 1
(See reproducible on page 2).

Student Learning in the Library Media Center What am I here for? What are my students here for?		
Basic Task Description	Individual/Teacher Expectations	Areas of Information Literacy (check those that apply)
		☐ Define and clarify
		☐ Locate and retrieve
		☐ Select, process, and record data
		☐ Analyze
		☐ Synthesize
		☐ Share and use
		☐ Reflection
What areas of Information Literacy are new for you/your students?		
What areas do you/your students have experience in but still may have questions about?		
What areas do you/your students have a lot of experience and success in?		

work on any task, they must first be clear about what they are doing and why they are doing it. This provides the opportunity for classroom teacher and library media specialist to envision what the student learning outcomes will be, thus creating potent internal accountability. (See Figure 2.)

- Teamwork is not something that should be talked to death upfront—it can happen quickly if teachers are required to do the work together and the suc-

cess of the work is measured by the established outcomes.

- Staff should be expected to "surface problems to which they have no immediate solutions" so that the organization can learn (Elmore 2005). This requires more than complaining about a concern; it requires that each issue be collectively scrutinized to identify root causes and possible action steps. Once action steps are identified, both teacher and specialist understand what

they are supposed to do and how those actions will impact the work of the team.

The legacy of these opportunities is that members of the staff come to trust that the increased capacity they have together eclipses their best individual efforts. They not only see the powerful connections that already bind them together, but work much more proactively to maximize the power of these connections.

Condition #2: Library media specialists view the collection,

Figure 2: Nature of Teacher/Library Media Specialist Collaboration

	Isolated Event	Coordinated Effort	Partnership
Design	Teacher approaches library media specialist to reserve space in the library for students to complete a task using resources.	Teacher solicits information/ideas about what resources are available to support student work for the assigned task.	Teacher comes to specialist with an idea for a research task or with a topic and works with the specialist to further develop the idea.
Execution of Instruction	Teacher supervises student work in the library media center. Specialist provides class with a basic orientation of available resources (if appropriate) and may have made a list of relevant resources if given enough lead time. Teacher and students ask for assistance from the specialist as questions/problems arise.	Teacher and specialist provide support to students during the completion of the task: teacher primarily on the task parameters and grading expectations, specialist primarily on how to access/use resources.	Teacher and specialist each provide support to students during the completion of all aspects of the task: orienting them to the resources at hand; supporting their use of the resources and their efforts to collect, analyze, and synthesize information; and the clarification of task parameters/grading expectations.
Evaluation of Student Work	Teacher evaluates student work. Task parameters and grading expectations may or may not have been shared with the specialist in advance.	Teacher evaluates student work (the grading expectations were shared with the specialist prior to the students work in the library media center).	Teacher and specialist score student work together using a common rubric that includes criteria both within the teacher's content area and information literacy.
Reflection and Next Steps	Specialist waits to find out how it went—receives anecdotal information from teacher and/or student(s) but does not see student work or analysis of student achievement.	Teacher shares information with specialist on how it went. May submit a sample of student work or a copy of the task for the specialist's binder. Next steps are reserved until the teacher has another task in mind that requires the specialist's support.	Based on student achievement of the task, teacher and specialist draw conclusions about what the next task(s) should focus on to meet academic expectations both within teacher's content area and information literacy.

analysis, and reflection on student achievement data as a primary part of their work.

Devoting more time to assessment of student achievement requires spending less time on other tasks. The question is how much priority is given to the analysis of student work by both the library media specialist and the school in general? There is a growing body of research that a powerful library program positively impacts student achievement scores as much as 10-20% (Loertscher and Lance 2003). To realize such gains, however, the focus of the specialist must be broader than merely daily operations. That focus requires more personnel assistance, both in the form of volunteers and paid assistants, however, it is much more cost effective to have the most expensive employee(s) in the library media center focused on the most important priorities of the learning environment.

When teachers bring their students in as an "isolated event" (Figure 2), library media specialists can still evaluate student performance on information and technology literacy standards with or without involvement of the classroom teacher. The challenge is to have a way of evaluating students that is highly efficient (because of a minimal amount of time to supervise many different students with whom there are differing degrees of familiarity). One of the most promising practices for this is to track student work into a basic database using a handheld device (i.e., Palm). Imagine a basic database that has the names of all of the students in the school (this can interface with existing school software) and the information literacy standards for each grade level(s). A basic rating system such as Novice

Learner, Apprentice Learner, or InfoStar (2004) by Koelichn and Zwaan could be adopted so that library media specialists could evaluate student performance with or without collaboration from the supervising teacher. This would provide critical data about the overall proficiency of students to use as leverage for more time and broader access to students for improvement of student achievement. It also would reveal which students have greater opportunities to learn because of the frequency and quality of their access to the library media center.

When teachers and library media specialists work as part of a "coordinated effort" (Figure 2), specialists can advocate including a strong information literacy component to classroom assessments and rubrics either designed on behalf of or in conjunction with the individual teacher. This should be a natural pairing because information literacy is embedded in virtually all subject area content standards and requires limited additional effort/planning time on the part of the classroom teacher. Not only can specialists coordinate with teachers on this one-on-one basis, but also at the department/content level by applying the same approach to the development or refinement of core assessments (i.e., research requirement, I-search project, family tree visual, Web-Quest). By analyzing existing tasks and student work samples, specialists can propose revisions to the task and scoring criteria so that the focus is sharpened on targeted information and technology literacy skills in addition to department/grade level expectations.

When teachers and library media specialists work in "partnership"

(Figure 2), there is a powerful opportunity to ensure that the tasks require students to demonstrate their competency in the subject. "The goal of competency makes clear that the aim of education is not the ability to acquire and retain information—the traditional formulation... [it is the] ability to do something with what you know—to apply information in the search for a solution to a problem or to create new knowledge—creates an expectation of more rigorous forms of accountability and assessment"(Wagner 1997, 45). This partnership involves teacher and specialist working together in the design, delivery, and evaluation of student learning. While this is the most time consuming of all three forms of collaboration, it does maximize the effectiveness of the instruction and can have the most significant impact on student achievement.

To some, this article may be an untenable proposal; to others, it is a call to action; and to still others, it is a confirmation of what they have been saying all along. Regardless of individual perspectives on this issue, the fact is that without the authority to work with students in a rigorous, relevant, and consistent manner, no curriculum document on the national, state, or local levels will ever impact student learning.

Resources

Koechlin, Carol, and Sandi Zwann. *Build Your Own Information Literate School.* Hi Willow Research and Publishing, 2003.

Loertscher, David V., and Keith Lance. *Powering Achievement: School Library Media Programs Make a Difference: The Evidence.* 2nd ed. Hi Willow, 2002.

Wagner, Tony. *Making the Grade: Reinvesting in America's Schools.* Routledgefalmer, 1997. ✋

Dancing Down the Rabbit Hole: Habits of Mind for Embracing Change

by Kristin Fontichiaro

In Lewis Carroll's *Alice in Wonderland*, Alice acts on her curiosity and follows the White Rabbit down the Rabbit Hole and into a new world of magic, fear, and adventure. In some ways, we library media specialists are all like Alice this year. As we work to integrate a host of new standards and examine our work, a new and wonderful world beckons, yet it is scary to consider whether we really want to follow the bottle's "Drink Me" command.

This past school year, 2007–2008, has brought a banner harvest of new research and guidelines not only regarding the work of our students, but also for our role as facilitators of high-quality student learning experiences.

Our role as technologists morphed as the International Society for Technology in Education (ISTE) "refreshed" its National Educational Technology Standards for Students (NETS*S) in 2007, followed by the National Educational Technology Standards for Teachers (NETS*T) in July 2008. The 1998 ISTE standards focused primarily on technology operations and tools and the student's ability to make those tools work. Student interaction with technology was often tightly structured by teachers, with students "following the steps." The refreshed NETS*S, on the other hand, look forward to the 21st-century career paths of our students—careers that will require collaborative work around the corner or around the world, creative and innovative solutions, problem solving, and ethics (ISTE 2007). Students envision and design their work. The NETS*T encourage teachers to facilitate and model this new kind of working, a far cry from the days of tips sheets and predetermined computer procedures (ISTE 2008).

Similarly, we were given a vision for today's learners when AASL released the new *Standards for the 21st-Century Learner* in October 2007. The AASL Standards encapsulate the NETS*S and also paint a far richer and more complex picture of meaningful student learning. More attention is focused on cognitive processes such as problem-solving, evaluation, and critical thinking. A fourth standard builds on students' intrinsic interests and motivations by focusing on learning for personal growth. Each standard is fleshed out in four categories: cognitive skills (the "thinking" skills), dispositions (the mental behaviors the students call upon when faced with an unfamiliar situation), self-assessments (the ability to self-monitor), and responsibilities (developing students' abilities to hold themselves accountable for quality work and work practice) (AASL 2007). It is a rich vision of a well-rounded, highly-skilled student.

The AASL Standards' focus on personal and aesthetic growth was echoed by the Association for Supervision and Curriculum Development (ASCD), which continued its Whole Child campaign to refocus the national debate on all aspects of student learning, not just those content areas and skills of standardized tests. Healthy lifestyle, creative thinking, inquiry, engagement, and opportunities for growth are all key components (ASCD 2008).

The momentum continued to build beyond the institutional level. Individuals such as Wiggins and McTighe continued to redefine the way we think about schools and their purpose. They wrote, "The mission of high school is not to cover content, but rather to help learners become thoughtful about, and productive with, content. It's not to help students get good at school, but rather to prepare them for the world beyond school—to enable them to apply what they have learned to issues and problems they will face in the future" (Wiggins and McTighe 2008). They proposed that curricular planning focus on acquiring knowledge, making meaning of that knowledge, and then transferring that knowledge into new situations. In other words, the focus shifts from a checklist of content to cover to the cognitive skills students develop in order to use content meaningfully.

This thought is echoed by Treffinger, who argues that creative and critical thinking—two different mindsets with different purposes—should be at the heart of 21st-century teaching (2008). Students need practice grappling with content and making meaning of it but also thinking in new and creative ways—an intriguing dichotomy that echoes the "left brain/right brain" thinking debate of decades past.

All of these examples point to the fact that our educational climate is about to change—and fast.

How Do We Get There?

How do library media specialists adapt to these changes and develop the skill sets to model creativity (NETS*T)? Guide inquiry (AASL)? Promote transfer (Wiggins and McTighe)? Develop critical thought (Treffinger)? All while continuing to administer a facility, nurture a collection, and develop collaborative relationships with staff and students?

First, it takes committing to the fact that ongoing learning is a responsibility of the profession. Professional learner is one of five roles Levitov outlines for library media specialists (the others are visionary, leader, connector, and teacher) (2007).

Next, a series of behaviors must be identified that scaffolds and focuses our energies. For this, the Habits of Mind of Costa and Kallick poses a useful model (2008). In their research, Costa and Kallick identified sixteen key traits that are found in successful people, regardless of their age or career path. These sixteen traits (clustered into twelve in this article) serve as dispositions for library professionals, much as the AASL Standards outlines dispositions for students. They help library media specialists develop strong mental behaviors to use in a changing educational world and thrive in it.

The Habits of Mind

The following examples from Costa and Kallick's book illustrate how their twelve "habits of mind" relate to the library media specialist.

Persisting

Success can come slowly as library media specialists work to develop a 21st-century culture in schools. Staying the course and not giving up at the first road block are essential. But persistence does not mean that there is a single "right" path to travel. Persistence can mean identifying alternate routes or detours and validating them as legitimate pathways to the same outcome. Professional reading—in print, online, or on blogs—can nourish us on that journey.

Thinking and Communicating with Clarity and Precision

Messages are customized for the audience. Statistics are quoted to administrators and library media specialists gush over the latest adventure novel

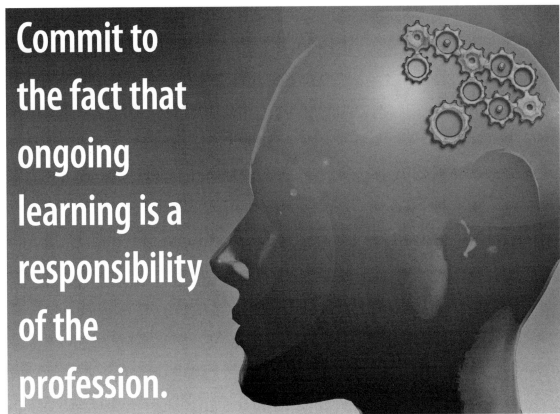

Commit to the fact that ongoing learning is a responsibility of the profession.

with kids. The library media center has a virtual counterpart where the vision can be shared with others.

Taking Responsible Risks and Managing Impulsivity

The line must be walked between innovation and thoughtfulness. An "educated guess" can be acted upon, but the guess is built on knowledge and experiences. The library media specialist takes a step back and reflects before adopting the latest trend outright. Decision-making is modeled for students to gather facts before taking action. Perhaps, the decision to buy a new tool or technology for everyone is based on piloting it.

Gathering Data through All Senses

Students are observed interacting with the collection and with technology, teachers' needs are attended to, personal instincts are honored as a result of reading about educational trends, or "feeling the vibe" of a situation. Technology tools like online surveys, comments on blogs, and podcasts with stakeholders help get a clear status report.

Listening with Understanding and Empathy, Thinking Flexibly, and Thinking Interdependently

The needs of users are put first. If hockey biographies don't circulate in the 920s, we move them to the sports section, where kids scour the shelves. Students' personal growth can be developed by building print and digital resources that resonate with them, and teachers can be supported by listening to what they need to enhance teaching and learning. Multiple perspectives and the willingness to change when needed should also be considered. Recognition that the library media program is part of a school's interdependent web and that the actions of the library media specialist can resonate either positively or negatively throughout the school community is important.

Creating, Imagining, Innovating

As the NETS*T propose, library media specialists must model the process approach of the researcher. Processing of ideas can result in adding programs, rethinking library media center layout, buying graphic novels, or investing in digital audio books. Students know the library media specialist is curious and eager to learn and grow. Teachers know they can come to the library media specialist for new twists on familiar lessons or to get a jumpstart with a new resource or technology tool.

Responding with Wonderment and Awe and Finding Humor

Library media specialists can commit to being "in the moment" by recognizing outstanding work and embracing "Aha!" moments in students and staff. These moments can be documented on blogs or in email. When exploring new technologies and resources with teachers and students, the library media specialist must save time for play and wonder. They must also take care of emotional, spiritual, and physical health to feel comfortable, confident, and well-rested enough to enjoy work.

Thinking about Thinking (Metacognition)

Professionalism and programs improve when library media specialists take time to reflect on thought processes, efficiency, and decision making.

Striving for Accuracy and Precision

No matter how much creativity and innovation go on in the library media center, it is important to recognize that an organized digital and print collection accelerates the speed at which learn-

ers are connected with the resources they need. Dewey doesn't need to be abandoned for drama games—there is room for both. Library media specialists recognize that accuracy builds trust, and that accurate online calendars, Web pages, and OPACs are important symbols of trust.

Questioning and Posing Problems

Recognition that at the heart of all authentic research is questioning is in line with the AASL Standards. Library media specialists model questioning in personal work by identifying gaps, choosing areas for instructional improvement, and developing testable hypotheses such as the following: "Would that circulate more if ___?" "How could I better support ___? "How can I motivate students to ___?" "What if ___?" As technology specialists, it is important to be healthy skeptics: "That's a cool tool, but does it help kids learn or want to learn?" "Does it make learning more efficient or meaningful?" "Reduce stress on teaching?"

Applying Past Knowledge to New Situations

Library media specialists should honor what has been learned and use it to scaffold new initiatives and behaviors.

Remaining Open to Continuous Learning

Library media specialists recognize that professional organizations, digital or face-to-face conferences, networking, and ongoing professional reading keep minds fertile and flexible—ready for what comes next (http://www.habits ofmind.net).

Conclusion

Just as Alice discovered, change and the unknown can be scary and magical at the same time. But these changes can be less scary when library media specialists realize that by committing to the certainty of change, the necessity of ongoing professional growth, and the development of Habits of Mind, the flexible toolkit needed to thrive is gained.

References

American Association of School Librarians. *Standards for the 21st-Century Learner.* American Library Association, 2007.

Association for Supervision and Curriculum Development (ASCD). *ASCD Whole Child.* http://www.wholechildeducation.org/ (accessed July 11, 2008).

Costa, Arthur L., and Kallick, Bena. *Habits of Mind.* http://www.habitsofmind.net (accessed July 11, 2008).

International Society for Technology in Education (ISTE). *NETS for Students 2007.* http://www.iste.org/Content/NavigationMenu/NETS/ForStudents/2007Standards/NETS_for_Students_2007.htm (accessed July 11, 2008).

International Society for Technology in Education. *NETS for Teachers 2008.* http://www.iste.org/Content/NavigationMenu/NETS/ForTeachers/2008Standards/NETS_for_Teachers_2008.htm (accessed July 11, 2008).

Levitov, Deborah. "One Library Media Specialist's Journey to Understanding Advocacy: A Tale of Transformation." *Knowledge Quest* 36, no. 1 (2007): 26-31. (accessed July 11, 2008, from Wilson SelectPlus).

Treffinger, Donald J. . "Preparing Creative and Critical Thinkers." *Educational Leadership* (online only). http://www.ascd.org/portal/site/ascd/template.MAXIMIZE/menuitem.c00a836e7622024fb85516f762108a0c/?javax.portlet.tpst=818d37ec925d82800173fc106210 8a0c_ws_MX&javax.portlet.prp_818d37ec9 25d82800173fc1062108a0c_viewID=article_ view&javax.portlet.prp_818d37ec925d828 00173fc1062108a0c_journalmoid=f9ef56a 18b6ba110VgnVCM1000003d01a8c0RCR D&javax.portlet.prp_818d37ec925d82800 173fc1062108a0c_articlemoid=844056a18 b6ba110VgnVCM1000003d01a8c0RCRD &javax.portlet.begCacheTok=token&javax. portlet.endCacheTok=token (accessed July 11, 2008).

Wiggins, Grant, and Jay McTighe. "Put Understanding First." *Educational Leadership* (May 2008): 36-41.◄

Kristin Fontichiaro is a library media specialist with the Birmingham (Michigan) Public Schools. She is the author of *Podcasting at School* (Libraries Unlimited, 2008) and *Active Learning Through Drama, Podcasting, and Puppetry* (Libraries Unlimited, 2007. She can be reached at font@umich.edu or on the *SLMAM* blog (http://blog.schoollibrarymedia.com).

Chapter 5

Reading

Don't just say that reading matters; show students that reading matters in everyone's life.

—Leslie Preddy, "Social Reading: Promoting Reading in the
Millennial Learner" (see page 92)

Throughout their history, library media specialists have been champions of reading. From readers' advisory to reading incentive programs to book-based competitions, no one doubts librarians' commitment to books and their readers. This value continues in the AASL *Standards for the 21st-Century Learner*. The first Common Belief articulates how reading can connect readers to the greater world, and Standard 4 reinforces the value of reading widely for both learning and personal pleasure.

However, the new millennium has brought new challenges. The ubiquity of the Internet in many students' lives is redefining what is meant by "reading." Digitized databases and texts, audio books, and informational Web sites stretch the traditional print definition. Does perusing a Web site about video game strategies count as reading? How can library media specialists support the social generation of learners? How can readers be developed in communities where reading is not actively modeled in homes? How can individualized instruction be supported so it meets students where they are? And what opportunities do library media specialists have in the instructional role to reinforce reading skills as part of the daily practice? These questions are at the core of this chapter.

Millennial Readers

Some pundits claim that millennials read less than those in previous generations. But further exploration may indicate that millennials are reading, but that the formats of what they are reading are quite different. Students are reading texted messages instead of letters, for example. Millennial learners have high standards for what they choose to read and are passionate about their choices. Successful school-based reading can facilitate millennial-friendly reading. Leslie Preddy's article, "Social Reading: Promoting Reading in the Millennial Learner" (beginning on page 92), discusses the impact of sustained silent reading in Preddy's middle school and the lessons learned from her students. She advocates for anytime, anywhere reading discussions; modeling enthusiasm for reading; entertaining "hooks" like video booktalks; opportunities for peers to share reading experiences with one another; reading aloud; choice in reading; a tantalizing-to-teens collection; and the types of incentives that can further develop a love for reading.

Leisure Reading

Sandra Hughes-Hassell and Ernie J. Cox advocate for choice in reading in "Urban Teenagers, Leisure Reading, and the Library Media Program" (beginning on page 96). They show how librarians can stimulate the interests of urban readers and help them want to read. Troubled by less-than-optimal standardized test scores among urban teens, the authors step back from the data and identify practical suggestions to engage these students in reading. They encourage school librarians to refocus collection development, to redefine "reading" to encompass online reading and nontraditional texts, and to strengthen the home-school library connection. Although their article focuses specifically on urban environments, their suggestions can be adapted to many others.

Supporting Reading Instruction

Liz Knowles, in "Differentiated Instruction in Reading: Easier Than It Looks!" (beginning on page 99), provides an overview of how reading *differentiation*—the practice of customizing educational content or delivery according to the needs of each individual student—might look at various school levels and points out how the school library media specialist can support those efforts through readers' advisory, loaning books to classrooms for use, organizing reading incentive programs, and assisting students as they test their reading comprehension skills during research projects.

Reading Instruction in the School Library Media Center

Judi Moreillon (2007) has called upon the profession to engage in a meatier, more deliberate instructional role in developing reading comprehension skills and strategies, one in which library media specialists are active co-instructors on reading comprehension and the development of reading skills.

In "Reading for Meaning: Questioning" (beginning on page 102), Catherine Trinkle examines the leading strategies for reading comprehension, maps them to the AASL *Standards,* and shows how student-generated questions and the researched answers can support classroom instruction on reading comprehension. Trinkle's "Reading for Meaning: Synthesizing" (beginning on page 105) discusses how this high-level thinking skill can help students transfer guided synthesis in the language arts curriculum to new texts and situations discovered during research in the library media center. Thoughtfully designed library experiences move students beyond a language arts anthology or controlled-vocabulary-leveled readers and help students develop skills with authentic texts that ignite their curiosity and motivation.

In "Research-based Evidence: The Role of the Library Media Specialist in Reading Comprehension Instruction" (beginning on page 108), Nancy Zimmerman looks at recent literature on reading comprehension and suggests how the school library media specialist can help by creating a culture of readers and modeling strategies.

Motivation and Reading

At the core of many conversations about how to develop a culture of readers is the issue of motivation and incentives. Ruth V. Small, along with her graduate students at Syracuse University, reflects on the frequent practice of assigning extrinsic rewards for reading in schools that use such programs as Accelerated Reader. In "Reading Incentives that Work: No-Cost Strategies to Motivate Students to Read and Love It!" (beginning on page 112), Small identifies concerns with such programs, which include cost of implementation, the low level of intellectual engagement needed to pass a quiz, the use of prizes based on reading accuracy, and selection from a reading list that is often set by corporate employees, not educators. The article outlines research about the negative impact of extrinsic motivation on performance and identifies free alternatives to motivate students to read. Her bibliography can guide readers to research that may be helpful in their own school environment.

Twenty-first-century school library media specialists must support the development of reading skills and dispositions in students. Simply supporting "pleasure reading" is not enough. Simply giving out reading points is not enough. We must actively develop collections to meet all readers, support classroom instruction, and model and support the development of reading strategies.

GETTING TO ADVOCACY

1. Reading is one of the most powerful ways to bring the community into your school library media center to see what is happening. At the elementary level, consider scheduling evening events to which children and their parents can come and share reading time together. Help working parents see the library in action. At the secondary level, open up the library media center to faculty book clubs, parent book clubs, or parent-student book clubs.

2. Have students advocate for your resources by creating hallway posters, podcasts, or booktalks on the school broadcast.

THOUGHTS FOR THE JOURNEY

1. What are you currently doing in your school library to promote reading for pleasure? To support reading comprehension? To promote reading for information?

2. What role do you play in supporting readers who are below grade level? Above grade level?

3. What resources do you have that support differentiated instruction or multiple intelligences in students?

4. What do you identify as the top reading needs of your school? Your school's top strengths?

5. Many schools feature an annual author or illustrator visit. Beyond exciting children about reading, how do these visits support reading instruction? How could they support reading instruction?

6. Some library media specialists state that they are "reading teachers" or "the reading experts" of the school. How do library media specialists differ from reading specialists? From classroom teachers who teach reading skills or comprehension strategies? How are they the same?

7. Preddy (page 92) discusses the role of incentives to motivate student reading yet warns that such incentives should relate to reading. What are some examples of meaningful incentives? Inappropriate incentives? Compare and contrast her ideas with those of Small (page 112).

8. If you are a preservice library media specialist, what resources can you identify (reviews, professional journals, experts, etc.) that will help you strengthen your ability to support reading as a lifelong habit and reading for comprehension?

Social Reading:
Promoting Reading in the Millennial Learner

by Leslie Preddy

Reading is not traditionally thought of as a group activity. But, why not? People love to talk. People love to share experiences. People love to find things they have in common with other people. Reading promotions can take advantage of this human trait! Inspiring the next generation to be readers requires the socialization of reading. Embracing children and young people's present day need

for community and socialization engages lifelong reading habits. Because this generation needs, and even thrives on, social interaction, reading must become social, too.

Students' minds today are attracted to entertainment and all things social. Just observe them in their natural habitat (outside of school hours) and witness them hanging out. It becomes obvious that socializing has become a multi-tasking phenomenon. Young people watch a movie while simultaneously talking and texting. They hang out with friends while keeping a texting finger at the ready so they can twitter. They talk on the phone while blogging and surfing social networking Web sites. To engage the reading attitudes of this generation, educators (aka reading motivators) need to adapt some old tricks and add new tricks to their bag to meet these Digital Natives where they live—the world of social interaction and social technology.

According to the Office of Education Research and Improvement, evidence-based education requires the "integration of professional wisdom with the best available empirical evidence in making decisions about how to deliver instruction" (2008). Educational instinct, that gut feeling that says spending time promoting and advocating the importance of reading, sets the right direction, but more proof than professional intuition is needed. In order to initiate change or validate current practices, it is also required to examine best practices and research. Research about reading and literacy emphasizes the importance of reading and its impact on the quality of life for all children, all young people, and all adults, as indicated by the following information:

- ▶A person without a high school diploma or equivalent earns 98% less than a person with a bachelor's degree and "educational attainment is positively related to… literacy." (Planty 2008; US Department of Education 2007).
- ▶A developed literacy in reading is an essential, determining factor for entry-level workplace and college readiness and success, according to the ACT Assessment. College includes trade, technical, 2-year, or 4-year colleges (ACT 2006).
- ▶Fifty-seven percent of prison inmates began their current incarceration without a high school diploma or equivalent and "incarcerated adults had lower average… literacy than adults in the same age group living in households" (Greenberg 2007).
- ▶According to "Reading at Risk: A Survey of Literary Reading in America," literary reading is dropping, with young adults marking the sharpest decline. The report further concludes that there is a correlation between reading literature for pleasure and education and income levels (2004).

What does all this mean? Being literate and finding enjoyment in leisure reading is correlated to educational success, work fulfillment, and lifetime income. Developing a literate generation of lifelong readers is an important part of this generation's growing into self-sufficient adults.

In 2004, Perry Meridian Middle School in Indianapolis, Indiana, engaged in an action research project to pilot a local reading intervention program, SSR with Intervention. The program proved to successfully improve student's reading attitudes, comprehension, and state standardized test scores. What the educators learned was vital to successfully developing a lifelong reader. This process requires meeting the reader's emotional needs through reading, developing relationships, and creating reading role models (Preddy 2007). The three R's necessary to impact the next generation—reading, relationships, role models—are explained below.

▶**Reading.** Kids today are busy. They have time commitments placed on them socially and by home and school. Time is an important factor. Finding time to read together with friends and family throughout the school day is difficult. Finding that time to read, however, is imperative. Carving fifteen to twenty-five minutes out of a school or class day makes a difference. Most things in life require practice in order to gain skills, do it well, and establish the habit. Establishing time to read for pleasure during the school day ensures students get to practice and develop the reading habit. Promoting a home reading log also encourages families to continue the practice and experience at home while also giving the student reading experiences outside of the traditional school day.

▶**Relationships.** Developing reading relationships gets to the heart of what children and young people cherish—socialization. They need to have discussions about what people are currently reading with teachers, peers, family, mentors, role models, and virtual friends. They need to get into the habit of sharing reading experiences and viewing it as common place as talking about last night's game, movie, blog, or TV show. Reading discussions do not have to be formal or lengthy; short and sweet can be just as effective, but the conversations must occur in order to breed reading into this generation's hearts and minds.

Talk about reading in the hall, cafeteria, gymnasium, bus, classroom, bathroom, and any other place people are talking. What are you reading and how can you share it with him? What is he reading? What has he heard others are reading?

▶**Role Models.** Be a reading role model. Don't just say that reading matters; show students that reading matters in everyone's life. Warm up class by revealing something interesting you

read the night before. Read aloud snippets of something you found appealing, entertaining, valuable, refreshing, educational, or down-right fun. Put a sign up at your desk or door announcing to students what you are currently reading. Frequently take advantage of the time in class when everyone is completing a silent reading assignment to model reading by positioning yourself toward the front of the class and reading something in their presence. Carry reading material with you wherever you go so students are reminded that an effective reader keeps reading material nearby. Reward students and classes with free reading time and read alongside them throughout the reading reward time (Preddy 2007).

Millennial learners are a lot of fun to be around and are energizing to educate. Embracing student's reading habits and motivating them is absolutely enjoyable and adds life to a day as an educator. These millennial learners are digital natives who have never experienced life without the Internet or instant gratification. Children born into generational poverty (i.e., those living in two or more generations of poverty) through necessity, live for the moment and value people (Payne 2007). Digital natives and those in generational poverty combined create our school's millennial population. As millennial learners, they share the same values, interests, and abilities which, when met, can successfully develop uninterested students into lifelong readers.

Meeting their needs requires entertainment, participation, control, auditory skills, and incentives. The millennial educators get the joyful job of finding ways to relate reading to millennial learners' values, interests, and abilities.

Based on what is known about millennial learners (digital natives) and Ruby Payne's (2003) research on generational poverty and the traits of an effective reader (Gardiner 2005), student traits can be used to an educator's advantage. Students thrive on entertainment, participation in learning, feelings of control and choices, auditory skills, and appropriate rewards and incentives. Developing lifelong readers requires educators to adapt, change, or continue tactics that include interactive technology and active engagement through games, conversation, and social networking. The following are examples of how educators can promote social reading:

▶**Entertainment.** Today's youth need and demand to be entertained. As a colleague says, they want a rollercoaster in the classroom every day. Find ways to make a reading rollercoaster for your school or classroom. Develop or buy reading board games that require students to talk about what they are currently reading as they play the game. Set up a schedule for a readers' café where kids can eat, hang out, and read before school, during lunch, or after school. Provide live booktalks and reading recommendations. Create booktalk and

recommendation posters and displays. Host family reading events where the student and a significant adult read the book prior to the event, then attend a party full of games and activities to celebrate the book. Host brown bag book clubs for students to attend during school. Create video and audio book promotions to publish on the Internet.

▶**Participation.** Involve students in reading conversations throughout the building: classroom, hallway, cafeteria, and library media center. Allow students to share book experiences with others students in a relaxed atmosphere by giving them the opportunity to read aloud a passage or booktalk a book that mattered to them. Set up virtual places on the Internet for students to discuss reading. Host a wiki for book review and summary postings. Find out whether your library media center's online library catalog has the capabilities to post student book reviews, then campaign and train staff and students to utilize the service. Get students involved in schoolwide reading promotion events like author visits, one book-one school, the state's student choice award, and reading madness month. Find ways for students to be involved in group sharing and student-led sharing opportunities. Host a book exchange party where students bring a book they loved, booktalk it, then trade with the other attendees so everyone goes home with a different book.

▶**Control.** Feeling control over their lives also means they need freedom of choice with what they read. Get kids together with similar tastes in reading by hosting a genre book club. They can share a book they've read in a particular genre and feel as if they're not being told to read one particular title or type of book. Set up a "Give One, Take One" display so students can donate books they no longer want and swap for another book. Allow options in the classroom and instead of telling them what they have to read, give them three to five books to pick from either as a class or as an individual student. Keep the library media center well-stocked with a wide range of interesting reading materials, have multiple copies of popular titles, and stay current and up-to-date with reading and literary trends.

▶**Auditory Skills.** Students have excellent auditory skills. Because their listening comprehension is higher than their reading comprehension, read aloud to them as a group or do paired reading. No matter what age, read aloud to the students while they either just listen to you or have copies to follow along with you as you read. By reading aloud you model tone, inflection, punctuation, pronunciation, and pacing. In addition, you can interact with the simple and complex thinking of an effective reader, pulling on prior knowledge, asking questions, and answering questions throughout the reading. Make audio books and bookcasts available. Post audio booktalks online or find ways to have them out and available in the library media center.

▶**Incentives.** Reward students, but reward appropriately. Some argue that students shouldn't be rewarded for reading, because that is what they are supposed to do anyway, and that's not how the real world works. It can be argued, however, that incentives are appropriate because the real world does offer rewards. The incentive could be a smile, praise, or physical reward. For this generation, remember to reward them for meeting a reading or literacy goal, or for participating in a reading event, but be sure the incentive equals the task. To appropriately reward a student or a reader, the reward should be related to what the students need to value. If students are to value reading, then the reward should relate to reading. Incentives could be a pass to the library, extra reading time, a free book to add to their home bookshelf, a gift certificate to a local bookstore, a fieldtrip to a local bookstore, bookmarks, paperback book covers, etc. The external motivation derived from a school creating a culture and climate of reading helps students develop their intrinsic desires to read (Preddy 2007)

In order to reach a new generation of readers, find ways to make reading social. Find pleasure in training staff in the ways of reading engagement. Delight in finding ways to make reading socially acceptable, common-place, entertaining, and interactive in your school for yourself, your staff, and your current and future students. Read, talk, play, and have fun!

References:

Greenberg, E., E. Dunleavy, and M. Kutner. *Literacy Behind Bars: Results from the 2003 National Assessment of Adult Literacy Prison Survey (NCES 2007-473)*. U. S. Department of Education. Washington, National Center for Education Statistics, 2007. http://nces.ed.gov/pubs2007/2007473_1.pdf (accessed October 21, 2008).

Payne, Ruby. *A Framework for Understanding Poverty*. 3rd rev. ed. Aha Process, 2003.

Planty, M., W. Hussar, T. Snyder, S. Provasnik, G. Kena, R. Dinkes, A. KewalRamani, and J. Kemp. *The Condition of Education 2008 (NCES 2008-031)*. National Center for Education Statistics, Institute of Education Sciences, U. S. Department of Education, 2008. http://nces.ed.gov/programs/coe/2008/pdf/20_2008.pdf (accessed October 21, 2008).

Preddy, Leslie. *SSR with Intervention: A School Library Action Research Project*. Libraries Unlimited, 2007.

Przeclawski, Gail, and Christina Woods. "Literacy and Generational Poverty." AASL National Conference Session 1275, October 26, 2007.

"Reading at Risk: A Survey of Literary Reading in America." Research Division Report #46. National Endowment for the Arts, 2004. http://www.nea.gov/pub/ReadingAtRisk.pdf (accessed October 21, 2008).

"Reading between the Lines: What the ACT Reveals about College Readiness in Reading." ACT, 2006. http://www.act.org/path/policy/reports/reading.html (accessed October 21, 2008).

SLJ Leadership Summit 2006. "Learning in the 21st Century: The Role of the School Library Media Program." Chicago, November 2-3, 2006.

U. S. Department of Education, National Center for Education Statistics. *The Condition of Education 2007 (NCES 2007-064)*. U.S. Government Printing Office, 2007. http://nces.ed.gov/programs/coe/2007/pdf/18_2007.pdf (accessed October 21, 2008).

Whitehurst, Grover P., Assistant Secretary. "Archived Information: Evidence-Based Education (EBE)." Office of Education Research and Improvement. http://www.ed.gov/offices/OERI/presentations/evidencebase.html (accessed October 21, 2008). ◄

Leslie Preddy is the library media specialist at Perry Meridian Middle School in Indianapolis, IN. She is the author of *SSR with Intervention* (Libraries Unlimited, 2007) and co-author of *The Blue Book on Literacy and Instruction for the Information Age* (Libraries Unlimited, 2006). Web site: http://www.lesliepreddy.com; Email: lpreddy@msdpt.k12.in.us

Urban Teenagers, Leisure Reading, and the Library Media Program

by Sandra Hughes-Hassell, and Ernie J. Cox

Schools serving urban youth face a growing literacy crisis. A study by Balfanz, Spiridakis, and Neild found that as many as 70% of eighth graders attending urban middle schools had a reading comprehension below grade level (2002). These reading difficulties can affect the entire school experience. As Biancarosa and Snow point out, in the era of the No Child Left Behind (NCLB) Act performing below grade level in reading carries increasingly higher stakes for retention and ultimately the withholding of high school diplomas (2006). Leisure reading is one tool that can support the literacy development of these youth (Krashen 2004; McGrath 2005).

Developing a leisure reading program that is relevant and responsive to the lives of urban teenagers requires an understanding of the unique motivations, interests, attitudes, influences, and preferred reading materials of urban teens. The focus of this article are the findings of two surveys on the leisure reading habits involving 798 low income, minority urban middle school students. (Hughes-Hassell and Pradnya 2006; Hughes-Hassell and Lutz 2006). The surveys investigated five aspects of urban teen leisure reading: (1) Do urban teenagers read in their leisure time?; (2) If they read, what do they read, when do they read, and why do they read?; (3) What topics and types of characters or people do they like to read about?; (4) How do they obtain their reading material?; and (5) Who encourages them to read? Table 1 (page 57) provides demographic data for the survey participants.

In general, these urban teenagers appear to engage in leisure reading, though for some readers it might be only an occasional pursuit. They also appear to recognize the value of reading. In their comments to the open-ended survey questions, many of them acknowledged the importance of reading to their success in school, college, and the workforce.

Not surprisingly, the teens prefer reading materials that are relevant to their lives. Magazines that deal with topics of interest to them, books about teenagers like themselves, and the Internet, which they view as not only providing more relevant, up-to-date information, but doing so in a "social" manner, were among their favorite items.

Most of the teens view reading as a solitary activity and do not see themselves as part of a community of readers. When asked if they ever talked to their friends about the things they were reading, most responded no. The only discussions they reported having with teachers revolved around the books they were reading for class.

The teenagers also appear to read very little during the summer. This is particularly troubling since research shows that summer reading is critical to learning, especially for low performing and/or disadvantaged students.

Implications
Collection Development

When urban adolescents are invited to read, library media specialists must remain open to their reading interests by providing and promoting the reading materials about topics that are of interest to them. According to information from the survey, magazines are the most preferred form of leisure reading. While many media centers have magazine sections available, they tend to contain the usual suspects—*National Geographic*, *Time*, and perhaps *Sports Illustrated*. The surveys show, however, that many urban teens read magazines that have not been part of this traditional periodicals collection such as *Black Beat*, *Latina*, *Low Rider*, *Sister to Sister*, *Slam*, *Urban Latino*, and *Word Up*. Not all of these titles have an obvious or immediate connection to curriculum, but they are a vital part of the literacy support system. Encouraging teachers to make curriculum connections using magazines such as these would help urban teens connect their own interests to the inquiry process.

Reading about celebrities, sports figures, and musicians is also popular, so nonfiction books can provide avenues for exploring pop culture. Today's nonfiction books contain quality pictures, lots of captions, and sidebars—features that make them especially appealing to teens who have short attention spans, prefer visual mediums, or are reluctant readers. While many professional journals contain reviews of nonfiction, the real "pop" stuff often does not get reviewed. The best way to locate it is to visit a bookstore, or better yet, have students select titles from an online bookstore (Jones et al. 2004).

Finally, it is critical to respect urban students' culture and heritage by providing culturally relevant resources. The kinds of materials that have been found to be most effective with adolescent students of minority groups are those containing authentic portrayals that students can identify with, including characters, settings, and situations, or themes that students are keenly interested in and that are relevant to their lives (Henry 1998). Many of the student's favorite titles are part of a growing genre of books known as Street Lit. These titles are not often found in most library media centers because of their controversial content, however, library media specialists can use teens' interest in books like *Flyy Girl* (Tyree 1993) and *True to the Game* (Woods 1994) to introduce them to urban young adult titles that are less sexually graphic, violent, or morally derisive (Morris et al. 2006).

Student Engagement

Literacy grows out of relationships—whether these are teen to teen, parent to child, sibling to sibling, teacher to student, or mentor to mentee (Zirinsky and Rau 2001). In order to sustain and encourage the reading habits of adolescent readers—even the most avid readers—educators must extend the reading community (Aronson 2001).

The Internet is one tool that can be used to create a community of readers. The Internet has made it possible for teens to interact with readers from around the world, communicate with authors, and explore the "text-worlds" of their favorite books (Mackey 2001). Many African American and Latino authors and illustrators have developed webpages for teens (e.g., Nikki Grimes, Gary Soto, Jacqueline Woodson, Jess Mowry, and Sandra Cisneros). Additionally, many school and public libraries have also established book discussion blogs and MySpace pages aimed at adolescents.

It is important to give teenagers time during the school day to read. This is particularly important for economically disadvantaged students who often have to work to improve financial conditions at home, and may not have a place or the resources to read texts of their choice outside of school (Fisher 2004).

Books and other reading materials should also be aggressively marketed to urban teens. Many of the students indicated that they enjoy reading but are unable to locate materials they like. Booktalks, podcasts, and book trailers are all excellent ways to introduce teens to appealing reading material. Tatum suggests that educators develop lists of "must-read" texts for black adolescent males (2005). Library media specialists can also develop similar "must-read" lists for other cultural groups.

Finally, provide access to books during the summer. Access to books has been found to be positively associated with the amount of independent reading students do in the summer (Kim 2004), yet there is large disparity between access based on socioeconomic status and ethnicity (Neuman and Celano 2004). To address this disparity, school districts might consider keeping library media centers open in the summer, asking private foundations for funding to purchase literacy materials for low income youth, and developing packets of materials that students can borrow for the summer.

Student Home Life

Parents play a significant role in developing and sustaining the leisure reading habits of children and adolescents. Chandler found that this was particularly true for youth from working class backgrounds who often experience confusion because of a disconnect between literary experiences at home and school (1999). Parents can be involved as book club organizers and library volunteers. Most importantly, they can encourage the continuation of literacy development in the home environment. Library media specialists can offer family literacy training workshops to help create a continuum of support for adolescent reading.

Table 1. Demographic Data for Study Participants					
	Total Number of Participants	Male	Female	Ethnic/Racial Background	
School 1	214	95	119	Caucasian	21%
				African American	73%
				Hispanic/Latino	3%
				Asian American	3%
School 2	584	275	309	Caucasian	7%
				African American	27%
				Hispanic/Latino	66%

Conclusion

Input, stimulation, and encouragement from teachers and library media specialists are key factors in helping urban teens develop into successful readers. Neuman and Celano found that well-trained, caring librarians can help close the "literacy divide" (2004). In a study of Philadelphia public libraries, they identified five qualities of excellent librarians:

►They make an effort to know students, call them by their first names, and develop a personal relationship that extends beyond the child to the family.

►They push students to reach beyond their current abilities and to read beyond their current level.

►They often do "over-the-shoulder" teaching, helping children as they learn to use computers and as they work on their homework.

►They do not just point to materials; they teach children how to use the materials.

►In the most difficult circumstances, they form writing clubs, chess clubs, and reading groups. They plan field trips and other activities to attract and retain their young patrons (2004, 85).

Library media specialists who adopt these qualities as part of their professional practice can better understand and respond to the unique needs of urban teens in library media centers.

References

Allington, Richard L., and Anne McGill-Franzen. "The Impact of Summer Setback on the Reading Achievement Gap." *Phi Delta Kappan* 85, no. 1 (September 2003): 68-75.

Aronson, Marc. *Exploding the Myths: The Truth about Teenagers and Reading.* Scarecrow Press, 2001.

Balfanz, Robert, Kurt Spiridakis, and Ruth Curran Neild. *Will Converting High-Poverty Middle Schools to K-8 Schools Facilitate Achievement Gains?* A research brief for the School District of Philadelphia. Philadelphia Education Fund, 2002.

Biancarosa, Gina, and Catherine E. Snow. *Reading Next—A Vision for Action and Research in Middle and High School Literacy: A Report to Carnegie Corporation of New York.* 2nd ed. Alliance for Excellent Education, 2006.

Chandler, Kelly. "Reading Relationships: Parents, Adolescents, and Popular Fiction by Stephen King." *Journal of Adolescent and Adult Literacy* 43, no. 3 (November 1999): 228-239.

Fisher, Douglas. "Setting the 'Opportunity to Read' Standard: Resuscitating the SSR Program in an Urban High School." *Journal of Adolescent and Adult Literacy* 48, no. 2 (October 2004): 138-150.

Henry, Annette. "'Speaking Up' and 'Speaking Out': Examining 'Voice' in a Reading/Writing Program with Adolescent African Caribbean Girls." *Journal of Literacy Research* 30, no. 2 (June 1998): 233-252.

Hughes-Hassell, Sandra, and Pradnya Rodge. The Leisure Reading Habits of Urban Adolescents. *Journal of Adolescent and Adult Literacy* 51, no. 2 (2007): 22-34.

Hughes-Hassell, Sandra, and Christina Lutz. What Do You Want to Tell Us About Reading? A Survey of the Habits and Attitudes of Urban Middle School Students Toward Leisure Reading. *Young Adult Library Services* 4, no. 2(2006): 39-45.

Jones, Patrick, Michelle Gorman, and Tricia Suellentrop. *Connecting Young Adults and Libraries.* Neal-Schuman, 2004.

Kim, Jimmy. "Summer Reading and the Ethnic Achievement Gap." *Journal of Education for Students Placed at Risk* 9, no. 2 (April 2004):169-188.

Krashen, Stephen. *The Power of Reading: Insights from the Research.* Libraries Unlimited, 2004.

Mackey, Margaret. "The Survival of Engaged Reading in the Internet Age: New Media, Old Media, and the Book." *Children's Literature in Education* 32, no. 3 (September 2001):167-189.

McGrath, Anne. "A New Read on Teen Literacy." *U.S. News and World Report.* 20 February 2005. http://www.usnews.com/usnews/culture/articles/050228/28literacy.htm (accessed May 5, 2008).

Morris, Vanessa J., Sandra Hughes-Hassell, Denise E. Agosto, and Darren T. Cottman. "Street Lit: Flying off Teen Fiction Bookshelves in Philadelphia Public Libraries." *Young Adult Library Services* 5, no. 1 (Fall 2006): 16-23.

Neuman, Susan B., and Donna Celano. "Save the Libraries!" *Educational Leadership* 61, no. 6 (March 2004): 82-85.

Tatum, Alfred W. *Teaching Reading to Black Adolescent Males: Closing the Achievement Gap.* Stenhouse, 2005.

Zirinsky, Driek, and Shirley A. Rau. *A Classroom of Teenaged Readers: Nurturing Reading Processes in Senior High School.* Longman, 2001.◄

Sandra Hughes-Hassell, Ph.D., is an associate professor at the School of Information and Library Science at the University of North Carolina at Chapel Hill (email: smhughes@email.unc.edu) and Ernie J. Cox is a library media specialist and doctoral student at the University of North Carolina (email: ejcox@email.unc.edu).

Table 2. Survey Findings

72% indicated that they engaged in reading as a leisure activity.
Females were more likely to read for pleasure than males.
The majority of the students indicated that they read in their spare time for three main reasons: fun and relaxation, to learn new things, and because they were bored.
Those who did not enjoy reading seemed to prefer other activities rather than simply rejecting the act of reading.
Magazines were clearly the preferred leisure reading material for both males and females. Other preferred materials included comic books, graphic novels, and the Internet.
Celebrities, "people or characters like me," sports figures, and musicians are among the most popular topics for the respondents' leisure reading.
Students indicated that they get their reading material from three primary sources: the library media center (71%), the public library (53%), and the classroom (53%).
When asked who encourages them to read, 70% of the teens chose parents, 63% selected teachers, 27% chose library media specialist, and 13% chose public librarian.

Differentiated Instruction in Reading: Easier Than It Looks!

by Liz Knowles

Differentiated instruction has been around for over fifteen years and, like many educational practices, the attention to it is cyclical. Most recently, Carol Tomlinson has been the master providing many books, articles, and workshops for educators about how to embrace differentiation. Others advocating differentiation include Carolyn Chapman, Laura Robb, and Gayle Gregory. There is even an annual National Conference on Differentiated Instruction sponsored by Staff Development for Educators, a business founded in Peterborough, New Hampshire, in 1986, by Jim and Lillian Grant.

What Is Differentiated Instruction?

The most important premise of differentiated instruction is recognition that even in a group of students with the same chronological age, each child is different. Today's students have many differences: background knowledge, learning styles, interests, and skills, to name a few. One-size-fits-all learning is no longer seen as the way to teach students. Tomlinson stated that differentiation can be accomplished in three areas: content (what the students need to learn), process (how they are going to learn), and product (how they are going to demonstrate that they have learned) (1999). This approach to teaching requires the teacher to assess where the students are and start from that point by providing information and lessons in ways that solidly connect with the child's learning style and interests.

Differentiated instruction relies on frequent informal assessments and teachers talking to their students to discover their interests, learning styles, and what they find easy and difficult. Curriculum quality is essential. Learners must be respected and teachers should be "teaching up" by giving their students challenging, stimulating, and thought-provoking material while supporting those who need assistance.

What Are Some Best Practices for Teaching Reading?

Experts who have shared lists of best practices in teaching reading include Harvey Daniels, Steven Zemelman, Regie Routman, and Marie Carbo. One of the most important factors is access to reading material. Most experts agree that students cannot be successful at reading without actually having blocks of time to read and lots of great choices! Library media centers providing books for rotating classroom collections are a must as well as parental support and access to books at home from a very early age.

Students also need to have ample opportunities to discuss the books they read—with a reading partner, in small groups, and in the form of booktalks to their peers. All teachers and library media specialists need to understand that reading aloud to students should not stop at 3rd grade—it should continue into the high school years. Taking time out of precious class time to share a good book demonstrates the value and importance of reading. To validate the importance of the reading-writing connection, a reading log is essential not only for keeping a record of titles read but also for reflections about each reading experience.

What About How Reading Is Taught? Is It Only Taught by Primary Grade Teachers?

Learning to read is a strange phenomenon. Everyone knows of young children who seemingly taught themselves to read through constant exposure to lots of books and lots of people reading aloud to them. Some parents can teach their children to read by labeling things around the house and creating language experiences based on family events, trips, and life in general. Some children learn quickly at school. Others struggle.

One thing is clear: early and continual exposure to lots of books and oral language makes it easier for children to learn to read. Phonemic awareness does not need to be taught to the vast majority of beginning readers; phonics instruction should be completed early in first grade and replaced by word analysis (contextual clues, syllable patterns, affixes). Class time should be spent reading not doing worksheets and drills.

There are many ways to teach reading and many programs and tools are available. The most important point is that there is no one right way to teach children to read. It is important that the teacher has a full "bag of tricks" in order to provide the appropriate tools for success for each student. Once the basic decoding skills are taught and the child has a good solid sight word vocabulary, the

remaining years are spent fine-tuning.

Teachers in middle and high school must provide their students with strategies for dealing with challenging texts, unfamiliar material, and important information using a variety of sources. When content area texts are evaluated using the readability level test, it is understandable why many students have difficulty comprehending the content and vocabulary. Even middle and high

school students who are proficient in math can have difficulty with math tests based on inaccurate reading of word problems and directions!

How Is Differentiated Instruction Used to Teach Reading?

It seems that reading has always

been taught by using reading groups based on the students' proficiency in oral reading and comprehension. Each class had three groups and depending on the grade level, phonics was sometimes used as well as sight words. Then reading programs became more the norm, some of which wanted the whole class to read the entire story together, stopping frequently to question, summarize, and then predict what would happen next before continuing the reading. At other times students were taught to read using only phonics and decodable texts. It has since been discovered that phonics is not a reading program but just one tool in a large toolbox of techniques for teaching reading.

With differentiated instruction in reading, one of the most important factors is student choice in selecting literature. The classroom teacher and the library media specialist are keys to providing good books and the tools for students to select the "just right" book. Skills can be pretested and then taught using literature rather than worksheets as the lesson format.

There is currently a great deal of information about guided reading instruction where the teacher works with small flexible groups teaching reading strategies. Leveled books are the key component in this type of reading program. These books are not selected from a collection of chapter books/novels and then leveled. Instead, they have been carefully written in accordance with standardized criteria for each level including difficulty level and words selected from an appropriate list (like controlled readers).

It has been confirmed by such reading experts as Krashen, Allington, and Routman that the only way to learn to read is by using real literature and by helping children to select "just right" books. In order to provide the best possible climate for reinforcing beginning readers' improvement, it is necessary to focus on children's literature, having books in classrooms, and teaching kids to know if a book is "just right" for them. Students can and should select and read challenging books successfully if the topic is of great interest to them.

Where Do Library Media Specialists Fit in the Quest for Differentiated Instruction in Reading?

What about the role of library media specialists in differentiated instruction in reading? Library media specialists work closely with teachers to provide exciting choices for students. They explore all the most recent titles and share them. They know the reading habits of students and help to guide them to the kind of books they are interested in or to books by an author they like. They provide access to national programs for the entire student population. These programs include National Library Week, Teen Read Week, Read across America, Banned Books Week, Teen Tech Week, Reading across Continents, One Book - One School, and Read for the Record.

Since library media specialists have huge collections of learning resources, in many formats and learning levels, it stands to reason that they can assist students in understanding these resources and effectively using them. Library media specialists can assist students in reading to find information for reports and projects. They can help students read to learn by showing them how to use a cataloging system, other databases, reliable search engines, and Web sites. Once the students have found these materials, library media specialists can help them search inside the books for tables of contents, indices, glossaries, and lists of references. They teach using Bloom's Taxonomy by helping students to understand, analyze, synthesize, and evaluate the material they find in their research. They help the students find meaning in the information.

So What Needs to Be Done to Create Successful, Lifelong Readers?

Teaching children to read and then fostering the enjoyment of reading throughout the middle and high school years is definitely a challenge in today's high-tech culture. Utilizing differentiated instruction for reading allows teachers to work with the students at their level and through their particular interests and styles in order to provide stimulating and appropriate titles and learning experiences. This makes reading exciting and worthwhile instead of boring or frustrating. It is our responsibility to make the best connections to books for our students at school in order to foster a love of reading.

The entire school community must get involved and that includes all faculty and administrators. The school setting should have comfortable areas to read inside and outside. Time should be made for all school reading, guest readers, and book clubs of all sorts. If there is a school Web site, a TV Studio, and a Parents' Association—all should reflect and support a commitment to reading enjoyment. Preparing our children to be lifelong readers is everyone's responsibility.

Parents must be involved in this effort too. They should read aloud daily to and with their children and then engage them in discussing the story. Frequent trips to the public library and/or bookstore are recommended. At both locations, children can participate in story times.

The data about reading for pleasure is disturbing. It states that not enough teens, young adults, and adults read for pleasure. Reading for pleasure is significant in the development of good readers and good readers are good test-takers and good writers, they have well-developed vocabularies, and they do well in the workplace. For this reason, it is imperative that we work diligently to make reading a pleasure for a lifetime!

References:

Allington, Richard. *What Really Matters for Struggling Readers: Designing Research-Based Programs.* Longman, 2001.

Atwell, Nancie. *The Reading Zone: How to Help Kids Become Skilled, Passionate, Habitual, Critical Readers.* Scholastic, 2007.

Carbo, Marie. *Becoming a Great Teacher of Reading: Achieving High Rapid Reading Gains With Powerful, Differentiated Strategies.* Corwin Press, 2007.

Daniels, Harvey, and Marilyn Bizar. *Teaching the Best Practice Way, Methods that Matter, K-12.* Stenhouse, 2005.

Hudak, Tina. "Are Librarians Reading Teachers, Too?" *Library Media Connection* (February 2008): 10-14.

Knowles, Elizabeth, and Martha Smith. *Reading Rules! Motivating Teens to Read.* Libraries Unlimited, 2001.

Krashen, Stephen. *The Power of Reading: Insights from the Research.* Libraries Unlimited, 2004.

Robb, Laura. *Differentiating Reading Instruction: How to Teach Reading to Meet the Needs of Each Student.* Scholastic, 2008.

Routman, Regie. *Reading Essentials: The Specifics You Need to Teach Reading Well.* Heinemann, 2003.

Tomlinson, Carol. *The Differentiated Classroom: Responding to the Needs of All Learners.* ASCD, 1999.

Tovani, Cris. *Do I Really Have To Teach Reading? Content Comprehension, Grades 6-12.* Stenhouse, 2004.

Walpole, Sharon, and Michael McKenna. *Differentiated Reading Instruction: Strategies for the Primary Grades.* Guilford Press, 2007.

Zemelman, Steven, Harvey Daniels, and Arthur Hyde. *Best Practice: New Standards for Teaching and Learning in America's Schools.* Heinemann, 1998.◄

Liz Knowles, Ed.D., is the director of professional development for Pine Crest School in Boca Raton, FL. She is the author of *Differentiating Reading Instruction Using Children's Literature* (forthcoming, Libraries Unlimited). Email: eddrknow@aol.com; Web site: http://www.talkaboutkidsbooks.com

Reading for Meaning: Questioning

by Catherine Trinkle

Library media specialists are great questioners. The professional journals are full of fellow practitioners grappling with both philosophical and practical issues as they seek to answer their questions and spark meaningful discussion. These questions include…

How do we make the connection between reading to learn and learning to read?

How do we help student researchers in the media center who may not be able to read successfully the documents we help them find?

How do we get teachers, whose plates are already full with curricular demands, into the library media center to do research projects that use technological resources they may not be comfortable using themselves?

What does the *AASL Standards for the 21st-Century Learner* mean for students?

And finally, how do research and reading comprehension work together?

The answer is in the questioning!

Creating Thinkers

In these days of ever-changing curriculum, as administrators strive to find programs that will help students become better readers and better test-takers, an essential question remains: How do we help students become deep thinkers while helping them master grade-level reading skills?

The *AASL Standards for the 21st-Century Learner* is on the table for discussion and library media specialists have many questions about the included standards' efficacy and implementation. These standards will prove very helpful to the library media specialist willing to become familiar with them, connect them to best practices in reading, and align them to their local curriculum. The standards lead library media specialists to ask themselves questions such as those in the first paragraph of this article. And questioning is a good thing.

Teachers who think they have too much on their plates might steer clear of the library media center if they think the new AASL standards are just something else to add to their list of curricular goals. But, if they can be shown that work in the library media center helps them teach the very skills they are covering and that they will have a partner in that teaching and assessment, they might come to understand that their burden has been lightened. This is profound at the elementary level where pressure has never been greater for students to master skills at each grade level. At the secondary level, every teacher is now seen as a reading teacher, and language arts skills are expected to be reinforced in every curricular area. Even P.E. teachers are having students write in journals.

In the library media center, reading strategies and writing skills are embedded in the research process and reading comprehension strategies taught by language arts teachers. These strategies can also be applied in other areas of the curriculum thus providing a way for students to use them in a different setting.

What Are the Reading Comprehension Strategies?

The following strategies are taken from Ellin Keene's "Mosaic of Thought, The Report of the National Reading Panel: Teaching Children to Read"(2000) and Robert Marzano's *Classroom Instruction that Works* (2001). They are also each deeply embedded in the new *AASL 21st-Century Standards* (2007).

1. Good readers use metacognitive strategies, such as stating their purpose for reading, previewing the text, checking for understanding, and using fix-up strategies to think about and have control over their reading. Fix-up strategies include: skipping ahead, rereading, asking questions, using a dictionary, reading the section aloud, making personal connections or connections to the subject, using text features (keywords, words in bold or italicized words, pictures and captions, diagrams and charts), predicting, thinking about what you've read, making a mental picture, deciding if this section is necessary or can be skipped.

2. Good readers use graphic and

semantic organizers to make meaning from informational text as well as fiction.

3. Good readers ask questions.
4. Good readers answer questions.
5. Good readers summarize what they have read. To summarize, students determine what is important and put it into their own words.
6. Good readers connect what they are learning to what they already know and to their prior experiences.
7. Good readers visualize, or make pictures in their brains as they are reading. When they realize they are no longer making these visual images, they understand that they are no longer really reading.

The chart below, "Reading Strategies Correlated," provides examples of how reading strategies and concepts in the *AASL Standards for the 21st-Century Learner* can be correlated.

Clearly, teaching reading comprehension strategies and teaching the research process are not mutually exclusive academic disciplines. Rather, they are one and the same.

AASL Standards for the 21st-Century Learner offers an exciting articulation of what library media specialists do best by describing what is being taught, or what should be taught, in the library media center. When teaching the research process, whether using Big6™, I-Search, or another carefully developed process, the new standards are being implemented and strategic reading comprehension skills are being taught in the context in which they were originally introduced. Thus, students are being given the opportunity to practice the skills as they are acquired.

Questioning Skills

An essential literacy skill is asking questions. Just as the library media specialist asks questions, so must students. Because reading comprehension strategies should be taught directly and explicitly, students need to be told that they should ask questions throughout their research and that all questions are valid (National Reading Panel 2000). Asking questions is no easy task for many students. Many would rather simply copy from a text than to ask their own questions and seek the answers through reading. When research projects are carefully designed and each step taught explicitly with teacher modeling, students can go beyond copying and cut-and-paste to create original research.

The I-Search approach, for example, begins with students posing questions about their research topics. Students are encouraged to think of everything they know about their topics (connect to prior knowledge) and then generate questions. Students might skim and scan text to get new ideas for questions. All this is done at the initial stage of research. This approach is similar to the Big6™ approach whereby students begin by defining the task and asking themselves questions such as "What do I need to know?" and "What do I need to accomplish?" Questioning continues during the research process as students create new questions based upon new knowledge, add questions based upon discussions with peers and instructors, or make new connections to information. The following information from *AASL Standards for the 21st-Century Learner* supports the importance of questioning during any research process:

1.1.3 Develop and refine a range of questions to frame the search for new understanding.

1.2.1 Display initiative and engagement by posing questions and investigating the answers beyond the collection of superficial facts.

1.2.4 Maintain a critical stance by

Reading Strategies Correlated

The following information is taken from the *AASL Standards for the 21st-Century Learner* (2007).

Reading Strategy:	AASL Learning Standard:
Metacognition	1.2.5 Demonstrate adaptability by changing the inquiry focus, questions, resources, or strategies when necessary to achieve success. 1.4.1 Monitor own information-seeking processes for effectiveness and progress, and adapt as necessary.
Graphic & Semantic Organizers	4.1.6 Organize personal knowledge in a way that can be called upon easily.
Ask Questions	1.2.1 Display initiative and engagement by posing questions and investigating the answers beyond the collection of superficial facts.
Answer Questions	4.2.2 Demonstrate motivation by seeking information to answer personal questions and interests, trying a variety of formats and genres, and displaying a willingness to go beyond academic requirements.
Summarize	1.1.7 Make sense of information gathered from diverse sources by identifying misconceptions, main and supporting ideas, conflicting information, and point of view or bias.
Connect to Prior Knowledge	4.1.5 Connect ideas to own interests and previous knowledge and experience.
Visualize	4.1.8 Use creative and artistic formats to express personal learning.

Excerpted from *Standards for the 21st-Century Learner* by the American Association of School Librarians, a division of the American Library Association, copyright © 2007 American Library Association. Available for download at http://www.ala.org/aasl/standards. Reprinted with permission.

questioning the validity and accuracy of all information.

2.2.2 Use both divergent and convergent thinking to formulate alternative conclusions and test them against the evidence (2007).

Convergent questions can be answered simply by reading the text. They are low on Bloom's Taxonomy as the answers are fact based, and there is a concrete answer. The questions students ask will begin with "who," "what," "where," and "when," and the answers may be brief until students learn to

example of a divergent question is "How does global warming on Earth affect the solar system?"

An exciting Web-based teaching resource to help students learn to ask questions is Into the Book, a project produced by the Wisconsin Educational Communications Board (http://reading.ecb.org/teacher/questioning/index.html). Under the Questioning section, there are five questioning strategies and videos for each strategy. Four single-session lesson plans are offered. The lesson on Thick and Thin Questions

McKenzie's Web site offers explanations and graphic organizers for seventeen types of questions to help the library media specialist and teacher guide students to higher level thinking.

Summary

While library media specialists are not reading teachers, the work they do with students in the library media center helps students become better readers. Library media specialists can help students create good questions and read for meaning, thus making the reading and research connection clear and strong to the school community. In this way, library media specialists can become both a vital teaching partner and a valuable resource for students and teachers.

The February 2009 SLMAM article entitled "Reading: Searching for Meaning" will detail how students can apply reading comprehension strategies to make connections in their search for answers.

> When research projects are carefully designed and each step taught explicitly with teacher modeling, students can go beyond copying and cut-and-paste to create original research.

provide supporting detail for more interesting answers. Students in every grade ask convergent questions about their research topics. An example of a convergent question is "What is global warming?"

As students progress through school, they are able to ask more divergent questions, which can have many different answers. Students apply the same skills they learn to be good readers when they ask these higher level questions. They infer; draw on prior knowledge; make connections to self, other texts, and the world; and most importantly, they think about their thinking as they struggle to come up with big questions. Just as it takes practice to become a strong reader, it takes practice to come up with these big research questions. By-products of the instruction given by library media specialists are those grand conversations between the media specialist and student and between students as they discuss their research topics. Divergent questions might begin with "suppose," "what if," "imagine that," and "how would." An

would be excellent to help students learn the difference between convergent and divergent questions.

Jamie McKenzie developed his Questioning Toolkit back in 1997, and it is as useful today as ever to help students learn to ask relevant questions (http://fno.org/nov97/toolkit.html). McKenzie states in the introduction that instruction in questioning should begin in kindergarten. This strengthens the role of the library media specialist in helping students apply the same skills they learn as good readers to being good researchers in the library media center. It is also true that library media specialists can help students become better readers by teaching them to become better researchers. Again, students apply their reading skills in a new exciting context—one outside of Basal readers and worksheets. It puts them in control of their learning as they choose topics of interest and ask questions they wonder about. Library media specialists can help them ask questions they never knew they had!

References:

American Association of School Librarians. *Standards for the 21st-Century Learner*. ALA, 2007. http://www.ala.org/aasl/standards (accessed October 10, 2008).

Keene, Ellin. *Mosaic of Thought: The Power of Comprehension Strategy Instruction*. 2nd ed. Heinemann, 2007.

McKenzie, Jamie. "Questioning Toolkit." *The Educational Technology Journal* 7, no.3 (November/December 1997). http://fno.org/nov97/toolkit.html (accessed October 10, 2008).

Marzano, Robert. *Classroom Instruction that Works: Research-Based Strategies for Increasing Student Achievement*. ASCD, 2001.

"Teaching Children to Read: An Evidence-Based Assessment of the Scientific Research Literature on Reading and Its Implications for Reading Instruction." National Reading Panel, 2000.

Wisconsin Educational Communications Board. *Into the Book*. http://reading.ecb.org/teacher/questioning/index.html. (accessed October 10, 2008).◄

Catherine Trinkle is the library media specialist at Avon Community School Corporation in Avon, IN. Email: CATrinkle@avon-schools.org

Reading for Meaning: Synthesizing

by Catherine Trinkle

Library media specialists have used and applied reading skills terminology now popularly found in No Child Left Behind documentation and *A Nation at Risk* long before that terminology became an integral part of these documents. The current focus on reading skills includes using such strategies as graphic organizers, note taking, skimming, questioning, and summarizing. When readers use multiple reading skills, they are synthesizing; and they are bringing together new ideas and information along with their prior knowledge to form deeper knowledge and understanding of content and the author's purpose. These strategies have long been effectively used by library media specialists.

When researchers apply these same reading skills to the research process, they synthesize information to create new meanings and original thinking. These essential skills are very familiar to library media specialists who teach them through the research process and project-based learning in the library media center. It is also important to ensure that these skills are taught through collaboration so that carts of books are not just delivered to the classroom without any input from the library media specialist. This process emphasizes the importance of having a certified library media specialist in the library media center.

Reading/Information Literacy Skills

Shared Responsibility

When the library media specialist is teaching a student how to "seek information for personal learning in a variety of formats and genres" (*Standards for the 21st-Century Learner* 4.1.4), she is also teaching students to assess prior knowledge, making connections to what they already know. While using strategies to help students "draw conclusions from information and apply knowledge to curricular areas" (*Standards for the 21st-Century Learner* 2.1.3), the library media specialist can simultaneously teach students to make connections between the text and their own knowledge, between the text and what is going on in the world, or between the text and other material the students have read. What may have seemed to be a traditional library skill, to "maintain a critical stance by questioning the validity and accuracy of all information" (*Standards for the 21st-Century Learner* 1.2.4), can be seen as an opportunity for the library media specialist and classroom teacher to teach students how to ask questions about what they read and to determine the author's intent. In this way, the classroom teacher can share the responsibility for teaching essential reading skill with a fellow professional trained to teach those same skills in a different context, beyond the reading Basal or worksheet, thus transferring and applying skills in new settings.

Skill Transfer

Teaching skills out of context is necessary so that those skills become embedded in the student's schema. Rhoder, in the article "Mindful Reading: Strategy Training that Facilitates Transfer," explains that mindful learners are highly active and engaged and are in control of their learning (2002). They use reading strategies to connect

their personal experiences with the texts they encounter in school. To get students to this level of independence, Rhoder believes the classroom teacher or reading teacher cannot be expected to work alone. Instead, "promoting active, mindful reading and teaching students to use strategies is every teacher's responsibility" because those strategies

the differentiated needs of students are met through a carefully designed lesson; each student can find a variety of information and resources at his or her level, apply reading skills necessary for understanding the texts they have chosen, and synthesize their readings to make new meaning at whatever reading level they happen to be.

late these skills, teachers understand the steps students need to take to read for information, recognize the terminology used to teach those steps, and are more comfortable teaching students directly and explicitly about doing research from start to finish. Students, in turn, know what is expected of them and exactly how to do what is asked of them.

An approach to research that allows students to build on prior knowledge, make connections from the known to the new, and requires students to ask specific, thought-provoking, and meaningful questions about their subject is the best way to ensure that students will not simply be copying from a text or turning in a paper they wrote for another class. This approach allows students to create original work that is interesting to them and their readers. It helps students apply reading skills as they read for meaning—a skill that can be used throughout their lives.

synthesis : the dialectic combination of thesis and antithesis into a higher stage of truth
(Merriam-Webster Dictionary)

can't be taught one-time in one teacher's classroom (Rhoder 2002, 498). Instead, all teachers must teach these strategies continuously, over time, in multiple classrooms and across grade levels. This is easily made possible for library media specialists who are often the only teacher students see from one grade level to the next.

Rhoder emphasizes that texts used to teach reading strategies should be at the student's instructional level, that teachers should model the strategies and provide practice using real-world tasks, that students should work through one or two strategies at a time in order to become skilled at transferring the strategies to different situations, and that students must have "lots of opportunities to experience success by working hard so they understand that effort can lead to accomplishment" (2002, 499). Rhoder further emphasizes that reading strategies should be taught and then practiced by students out of context of the content area so that students learn how to use each strategy for the many reading purposes they encounter in and out of school (2002). In the media center, students have the opportunity to synthesize, or merge new knowledge with their prior knowledge, not from single-volume texts and Basal readers, but from a plethora of resources offered at a multitude of reading levels. Thus

The Research Process

Teaching reading strategies in the library media center equates to teaching reading strategies out of context. It makes perfect sense that classroom teachers and library media specialists collaborate often to help students become better readers and deeper thinkers but also learn content knowledge at the same time. In this way, library media specialists can help teachers do their jobs more effectively. They can show the teaching staff that the research process and reading comprehension strategies are mutually supportive and that when combined with student learning in the library media center, students benefit. Just as content area teachers would be remiss in telling students simply to read a section of text and answer questions on a worksheet, library media specialists cannot stop at telling students to take notes as part of a research project. It cannot be assumed that students know how to take notes or how to do so without copying directly from the source. Research instruction that does not articulate each step of the process, in detail, fails to help students complete research tasks reliably. Library media specialists must use best practices in reading instruction to articulate the necessary skills that are only implied by most research approaches. When library media specialists articu-

Note Taking and Summarizing

Students should be taught effective note taking and summarizing strategies to effectively answer their questions. Both require students to determine what is important from a text, decide what is not important in a text, and restate in their own words a condensed interpretation of the text. The benefits are huge. Summarizing and note taking require students to analyze what they have read and to think deeply about what is important and what is not, what they understand versus what remains unclear, what makes sense to them and what doesn't connect with prior understanding. This is what it means to synthesize: to determine what is important, rearrange information to retell it in a new way, and to create a new body of work. As a result, when students synthesize information, summarize, and take notes, they gain knowledge and understanding that are retained in long-term memory.

Marzano recommends that students be given a variety of choices for taking notes (2001). Some students might prefer to take notes in an outline format while others prefer webbing. He emphasizes research that shows student achievement on tests increases with the amount of information students take in their notes (2001).

As any library media specialist who has written book reviews knows, summarizing is difficult work. It takes practice and because it cannot be mastered within a few lessons, library media specialists can co-teach this skill both before and during research projects. It must be recognized that classroom teachers are not solely responsible for teaching this reading skill. It is also a research skill and by modeling summarizing and requiring students to summarize throughout the process of note taking and writing, library media specialists share the responsibility for teaching this essential skill.

Synthesizing

Whereas summarizing and note taking require students to deconstruct an author's messages and meanings, synthesis has them do the opposite. When readers and researchers synthesize, they bring various parts together to form a new whole, a new meaning, a new message. When they synthesize, students create original work. They can articulate their original thinking through writing or speech, or they can make a model depicting their original thinking. The key here, of course, is that students create original work. Marzano stresses that when it comes to synthesizing, unlike note taking, having less information becomes important. For synthesis, a student must:

- ▶delete trivial and redundant material
- ▶substitute superordinate terms for lists (tree is the superordinate for birch, oak, and maple)
- ▶write a topic sentence (Marzano 2001, 32).

This is an appealing aspect of research for library media specialists and avoids assignments that require little

more of students than finding information in a written work and copying that information into their notes. In order to bring students to a higher level of thinking, research projects and assignments that are carefully designed and instructed include reading comprehension strategies within the research process.

Assignments must be scaffolded and include teacher modeling. Employing these strategies will not result in longer research projects, however. When teaching these reading/research strategies, there is less time off-task, as students will know at each step exactly what is required of them. They will spend less time claiming they don't know what to do because the library media specialist and classroom teachers will have modeled how to do each step. Students won't waste precious time looking for more books and Internet sites, claiming that they "don't have enough information" because they will have carefully chosen needed resources to help them answer their questions, and they will know how to find the answers to their questions within those resources.

Summary

The same reading strategies taught by classroom teachers to develop strong readers are the strategies also used by library media specialists to teach the research process. Both reading and research involve asking and answering meaningful questions, summarizing and note taking, connecting prior knowledge to new information, visualizing, predicting, rereading, skimming and scanning, using keywords and text features, and

determining importance. Each is like a puzzle piece; when the student puts the pieces together, the information has been synthesized to create new meaning and unique insights. Library media specialists who are well versed in these reading strategies offer teachers partners in teaching the strategies, library media centers full of differentiated resources to match the needs of readers, and the experience to help students use those resources to make new meanings and create wholly original work.

References:

American Association of School Librarians. *Standards for the 21st-Century Learner.* ALA, 2007. http://http://www.ala.org/ala/aasl/aaslproftools/learningstandards/AASL_Learning_Standards_2007.pdf (accessed July 7, 2008).

Marzano, Robert. *Classroom Instruction that Works: Research-Based Strategies for Increasing Student Achievement.* Association for Supervision and Curriculum Development, 2001.

Rhoder, Carol. "Mindful Reading: Strategy Training that Facilitates Transfer." *Journal of Adolescent & Adult Literacy* 45 (2002): 498–512.◄

Catherine Trinkle is the library media specialist at Avon Community School Corporation in Avon, IN. Email: CATrinkle@avon-schools.org

Research-based Evidence:

The Role of the Library Media Specialist in Reading Comprehension Instruction

by Nancy Zimmerman

In 1999, the Office of Educational Research and Improvement (OERI) of the United States Department of Education charged the RAND Reading Study Group (RRSG) with developing a research agenda to address pressing literacy issues. Published in 2002 after much investigation, the RRSG concluded that evidence-based practices in the teaching of reading comprehension are sorely needed as part of the larger context of reading instruction in the United States. The RRSG, summarizing the state of research and research-based practice in reading comprehension, defined "reading comprehension as the process of simultaneously extracting and constructing meaning through interaction and involvement with written language," and argued that preparation of teachers often does not adequately address children's needs for reading comprehension instruction. The RRSG stated that "many children who read at the third grade level in grade three will not automatically remain proficient comprehenders in latter grades. Therefore, teachers must teach comprehension explicitly, beginning in the primary grades and continuing through high school" (RRSG 2002, xii).

Of late, more research appears in publication concerning the explicit reading comprehension instruction called for by the RRSG. Yet despite the growing knowledge base regarding the value of instruction designed to enhance comprehension, teachers spend inadequate time and attention on comprehension instruction in both the elementary and upper grades (Block 2002). Although the majority of this research and writing is directed at classroom teachers and reading specialists, school library media specialists, as required by their teaching role, also must accept responsibility for teaching comprehension strategies. As noted educator Sterl Artley implores, "Every teacher a teacher of reading" (Sweet 2003, xii). This does not mean that every teacher should be teaching students to read words, but rather every teacher, including library media specialists, should be teaching students to read with purpose and in context. Learning science, math, history,

and/or literature, whether written in text or hypertext, requires specific ways of reading. Library media specialists must take it upon themselves to develop their own knowledge base in the teaching of comprehension strategies so that they may participate fully in explicit reading comprehension instruction to increase student learning.

In the scope of this article it is not possible to instruct library media specialists in all the individual reading comprehension strategies currently discussed in the professional literature. Rather, each library media specialist must study, learn, and practice using and teaching these many strategies, those "planful approaches readers bring to organizing and monitoring their activities as readers" (Sweet 2003, 100). For example, Keene (1997) names connecting the known to the unknown, determining importance, using sensory images, delving deeper with questions, and inferring meaning as strategies and Sweet (2003) details strategies of self-questioning, monitoring for understanding, predicting, using context clues to define unknown words, and using sensory images. At the end of this article are multiple sources replete with information for learning these strategies and for effective ways to utilize them in direct instruction of students. Instead, what this article attempts to do is highlight the unique ways library media specialists are poised to contribute to comprehension instruction in their schools beyond teaching these specific strategies and to equip library media specialists with research-based evidence supporting that role.

Creating a Reading Culture: Access, Interest, and Motivation

The simple truth is that students want to be where there is a welcoming, supportive instructional environment and the school library media center, with its critical resources, should be such a place. Students are more motivated to read when interesting and appropriate texts are readily available. Employing an abundance of diverse, inter-

Nancy Zimmerman, Ph.D., is an Associate Professor with the School of Library and Information Science at the University of South Carolina in Columbia, SC.

esting texts for reading instruction and surrounding students with print materials of all kinds in a warm instructional climate promotes reading and learning. Diverse texts translate to different types of materials in a variety of formats and genres at levels of appropriate complexity. Providing materials that children are interested in reading in the format they like, including comic books, paperbacks, video or audiotapes, and magazines, stimulates reading and provides just as much or more reading value as traditional textbooks (Krashen 1993, McQillan 1998, Sweet 2003). Research has shown that enriching the library media center with a large collection of interesting reading materials and providing ready access to those materials results in more reading (Krashen 1993, Sweet 2003). Fitzgibbons (1996), conducting evaluative research of a reading motivational campaign, found that access, and hence motivation to read, was enhanced if books were kept in a well-designed and organized library media center, and even more if books from the center were used in rotating (not static) classroom collections. These findings should come as no surprise to library media specialists. Evaluation, selection, acquisition, and organization of reading material that is of interest to students, age and content appropriate, and integral to the curriculum is the particular purview of the library media specialist and one of the primary ways that library media specialists contribute to the reading program.

Library media specialists create a friendly, productive, user-oriented learning environment that is conducive to reading and learning. A peek in the door of the library media center shows evidence of student ownership and is "a buzz of activity" as learners seek out quality books and materials and interact with each other (Donham 1998). Library media specialists actively promote the library media center and its reading services and are visible in the center and the greater learning community collaborating with students, parents, teachers, and administrators, so that all know they are welcome.

Library media specialists must be cognizant of barriers or perceived barriers to library media center access and work to eliminate them, such as restrictive checkout policies and rigidly scheduled classes. Even in mandated restrictive settings, library media specialists can create a warm and welcoming environment for students, break out of standard old modes of operation, and seek innovative ways to provide more open access. For example, if students are regularly scheduled for "library time" regardless of instructional need, library media specialists could take that opportunity to provide reader's advisory services and help students learn to thoughtfully select books and other materials of interest to them that they will read more eagerly. Library media specialists

also might allow that time to be used for reading discussion circles or other activities that promote social interaction among students with each other and with the literature. Research findings demonstrate that those teachers, and by extension library media specialists, who provide opportunities for student access, student choices, and collaborative, interactive learning in a welcoming environment increase motivation for reading and comprehension of text (Bond 2002).

Keene found that most well-written books are usable for just about all reading comprehension strategies and "all children need strategy instruction if they are reading sufficiently challenging materials" (1997, 249). Most teachers, when teaching or modeling reading strategies, select a group of books or materials from which students can choose. Limiting text selection occurs only at times for a specific purpose, such as for an author or genre study or because a discussion group wants to read the same title. Again, expertise in book evaluation and selection is the strength of the library media specialist and this knowledge makes library media specialists valuable collaborative partners to teachers seeking those "just right" materials.

Library media specialists are skilled reader's advisors. They know quality materials, the literature, the collection, the curriculum, and the teachers and students. A prime and never-ending responsibility of the library media specialist as reader's advisor and reading teacher is to teach students to make wise, challenging book selections that will facilitate growth as a reader. Keene (1997) cautions library media specialists to consider three critical factors when helping learners select those "just right" for them books: the child's schema and background knowledge which affects readability; the child's interests which affects motivation and attitude toward reading; and a variety of reading materials, specifically different genres, authors, increasing difficulty, etc., which are necessary for students to acquire strategic reading skills. Keene also recommends permitting students to "field test" books and materials for inclusion of those factors and allowing students to stop reading materials that do not meet their needs. Library media specialists also can develop recommended lists of quality books and materials on a given topic for those times when preselection for a specific purpose is necessary.

Building Background Knowledge

The research literature supports a compelling fact: what students already know is one of the strongest indicators of how well they will learn new information. Researchers commonly refer to what a person already knows as "background knowledge" (Marzano 2004). According to Keene

(1997), linking the known to the unknown is one of the most effective comprehension strategies. In order to boost student learning then, the background knowledge of students must be increased. Utilizing quality resources and the library media specialist's knowledge of those resources, the literature, and the curriculum, the library media specialist is poised to provide varied academically enriching literary experiences that will help build a student's background knowledge. For example, reading aloud to students, even in high school, from different genres including informational and poetry books, and activities such as one-on-one reading with a mentor-reader partner and literature discussion groups, can be carried out in the library media center and contribute to the development of background knowledge. These literary occasions serve to increase the depth of student experiences and allow them opportunities to process information several times and in different ways. Repeated cognitive exposure significantly impacts content retention and even the briefest instructional encounter might be enough to provide students with the kernel of understanding that will deepen as they encounter the subject further (Marzano 2004).

Research on the multidimensional nature of background knowledge provides some insight for library media specialists' efforts to enhance that knowledge. To develop background knowledge that will impact student achievement in specific academic subjects, the information critical to those specific academic areas must be the target of instruction. Given that the 1999 National Assessment of Educational Progress found that students do less well with informational texts than with narratives and that informational reading is the most representative of the mature reading required of adults, increasing student proficiency with expository text is vital. Yet, studies show us that teachers lack strategies for helping students comprehend informational text (Block 2002). With their knowledge of the curriculum and informational resources that support that curriculum, library media specialists play an important role in facilitating and conducting purposeful content specific instruction. In addition, as experts in the text structure of information sources, library media specialists can share strategies for ensuring student attention to both the external physical organization of text and the internal structure of the content and ideas. Students that learn to use the external organization of informational text, such as paragraph and section headings, tables of content, indices, and captions, and basic expository structures, such as compare and contrast, sequence of events, and description, are more able to comprehend and retain key ideas (Block 2002). Additionally, library media specialists are technologically savvy and can teach students how to adapt comprehension strategies used for making meaning from informational text to use with Internet sites and hypertext information. Learning that involves the reader and requires active participation, such as having students generate their inquiries and information seeking around what they want to know, can shift the task from memorizing content to the construction of meaning. The library media specialist is particularly equipped to offer models and provide practice for understanding informational text.

Modeling Strategies and Behaviors

Modeling is critical. The most important thing for students to see library media specialists (and others) do is read. Equally critical is to share the joy of reading with students through reading aloud, talking about books, and modeling strategies for successful reading. Students are often oblivious to the processes that proficient readers use to make sense of text. Many relatively fluent readers with fairly good recall of what they read do not engage with texts at deeper levels or actively relate what they read to their life experiences, their background knowledge, or other authors and texts they have read (Dudley-Marling 2004, Keene 1997). Keene recommends explicitly teaching and modeling for students how to make connections between the texts they are reading and their background knowledge and experiences: how to make text-to-self (relating texts to your own experiences), text-to-world (relating texts to your knowledge about the larger world), and text-to-text (relating texts to other texts you have read) connections. Modeling reading behaviors, like use of comprehension strategies, is a powerful way to show students how to think about reading. Modeling joyful reading encourages students to discover their own delight so they may gradually assume responsibility for their own book selection, reading, and comprehension behaviors.

Conclusion

This is a critical period of accountability for schools and teachers. Library media specialists can contribute much to the teaching of reading comprehension strategies that enable students to be proficient, challenged readers and learners. Library media specialists contribute most significantly by providing access to a quality organized collection, creating a nurturing reading culture, providing opportunities for readers to build background knowledge, and modeling and explicitly teaching reading behaviors and comprehension strategies.

References

Block, Cathy Collins, and Michael Pressley. *Comprehension*

Instruction: Research-based Best Practice. New York: Guilford Press, 2002.

Donham, Jean. *Enhancing Teaching and Learning: A Leadership Guide for the School Library Media Specialist*. New York: Neal-Schuman, 1998.

Dudley-Marling, Curt, and Patricia Pugh. *A Classroom Teacher's Guide to Struggling Readers*. Portsmouth, NH: Heinemann, 2004.

Fitzgibbons, S. A. *Reading Excitement and Paperbacks Project (REAP): REAP Revisited Evaluation Project*. Bloomington, IN: Indiana University, 1996.

Keene, Ellin Oliver, and Susan Zimmermann. *Mosaic of Thought: Teaching Comprehension in a Reader's Workshop*. Portsmouth, NH: Heinemann, 1997.

Krashen, Stephen. *The Power of Reading: Insights from the Research*. Englewood, CO: Libraries Unlimited, 1993.

Marzano, Robert J. *Building Background Knowledge for Academic Achievement: Research on What Works in Schools*. Alexandria, VA: Association for Supervision and Curriculum Development, 2004.

McQuillan, Jeff. *The Literacy Crisis: False Claims, Real Solutions*. Portsmouth, NH: Heinemann, 1998.

Rand Reading Study Group (RRSG). *Reading for Understanding: Toward a R&D Program in Reading Comprehension*. Santa Monica, CA: 2002. Available: http://www.rand.org/multi/achievementforall/reading/readreport.html

Sweet, Anne Polselli, and Catherine E. Snow, eds. *Rethinking Reading Comprehension*. New York: Guilford Press, 2003. ✍

Reading Incentives that Work:
No-Cost Strategies to Motivate Kids to Read and Love It!

by Ruth V. Small with Elizabeth Angelastro, Susanne Bang, Sharon Bainbridge, Colleen Brindamour, Joanne Clarke, Christine Cordova, Brooke Dittmar, Elizabeth Hubbard, Deborah McHugh, Teena Lauth, Kimberly Lee, Kathleen Mauldin, Brianna Pannell, Natalie Panshin, Marie Sarro, Megan Stasak, Jennifer Sullivan, April Yannarelli

A World of Rewards

In education, it is possible to find dozens of examples of "forced" reading incentive programs, such as "Accelerated Reader" (AR) and "Earning by Learning." These types of programs categorize student reading levels, provide limited reading lists coordinated with those reading levels, assess student reading through computer-based tests, and award tangible prizes when they pass the test. Those who perform best get the most rewards while those who perform less well get fewer (or no) rewards.

The problems with such reading incentive programs is that they require students to select books from a pre-established list only, test them on facts presented in the books, and award points to those who pass the test, allowing students to cash in the points for tangible prizes. If students were industrial workers trying to increase the number of widgets being produced, this might be appropriate behavior modification. But, students are learners who, it is hoped, will develop a sustained love of reading. Reading is not a simple mechanical skill to be repeated. Instead, it is a personal act that should result in aesthetic pleasure, a gain of knowledge, or both.

Typically, these "silver bullet" programs add even more stressful testing to an already test-heavy educational system, reward achievement but not effort, award unrelated prizes that have little or no long-term meaning or impact on lifelong reading behaviors, and are costly to implement.

Yet, many schools flock to programs that focus on quick results and promise higher test scores, despite the lack of evidence of long-term learning impact or potential negative effects. In this article, some of the research on the use of extrinsic rewards in schools will be reviewed, some real-life examples will be included, and the five characteristics of reading incentive programs described above will be addressed. Finally, some effective, tried-and-true, no-cost alternative strategies will be shared that can be used to motivate long-term student reading behaviors.

What the Research Says

While much of the early research on the use of extrinsic rewards was conducted in the workplace, most of the current research focuses on using extrinsic rewards to motivate learning. These rewards are typically used (like punishments) to control and manipulate behavior. Here's an example of one such program, as described by a school media graduate student intern. The program was schoolwide and is described as follows:

> In the library, the teacher-librarian offers stickers to K-1 classes… Each time a student raises his/her hand and offers an idea, she gives that student "wings," which is a sticker. For one class, I forgot at first and we started our discussion. Only a few kids were offering comments or answers, then the teacher-librarian came over and observed and grabbed the stickers to give out for me. Suddenly, 3/4 of the class had their hands in the air and I couldn't seem to end the discussion to get to the next task…

The consensus of research results on extrinsic rewards indicates that they seldom have any positive long-term effects on learning and that they can actually have a negative impact (Johnson 1999; McCullers, Fabes, and Moran 1987). For example, Pavonetti, Brimmer, and Cipielewsi found that children who did not have an AR program during their elementary years read significantly more in middle school than those who did have an AR program (2002/2003).

McQuillan points to several studies that found once the extrinsic incentives are taken away, participants have a lower intrinsic interest in the task than their non-rewarded counterparts (1997). Whereas extrinsic rewards have been shown to increase productivity in tasks that are repetitive and uncomplicated (like writing spelling words), these rewards actually had negative effects on tasks of concept attainment, insight learning, and creativity (McGraw 1978). The following example from a school media graduate student shows her reflections on her own experiences as an elementary student:

> My elementary school had a reading incentive program where, after reading a certain number of books, we could win a free personal pizza from a pizza store… I remember how some of my classmates would read (or skim!) as many books as they could get their hands on, just so that they could win the Book It certificate. After that program ended (I think around 4th or 5th grade), reading became "boring" and "dorky" and so on.

Furthermore, giving extrinsic rewards sends the message that the task or behavior is not, in and of itself, interesting and valuable, rather it says that the task must be unpleasant, since a reward is required to do it and that reading is perceived as a means to an end rather than its own reward (Carter 1996). The following example is from a parent:

> Last year my daughter's school sent home a form that we were supposed to mark for every fifteen minutes we read together and we were supposed to read one of each kind of book on the list… I felt our reading time was devalued by the expectation of accountability it created over valuable reading time that was ours, not theirs.

Research meta-analyses (e.g., Rummel and Feinberg 1988; Wiersma 1992; Tang and Hall 1995) found substantial support for the general hypothesis that expected tangible rewards made contingent upon doing, completing, or excelling at an interesting activity undermine intrinsic motivation for that activity (Deci, Koestner, Ryan 1999). When extrinsic rewards were given contingent

on performance of a task that would otherwise have been undertaken purely out of interest, individuals lost interest in the task (Beswick 2002).

The use of rewards with contingencies (e.g., limits, imposed goals, competitions) seems to be most detrimental to the motivation, performance, and well-being of the individuals subjected to it. Edward Deci, arguably the most recognized and productive researcher on intrinsic motivation, conducted experiments in which groups of subjects were asked to complete a puzzle. One group was paid for completing the task while those in the other group were not. The results found that the presence of an extrinsic reward such as money increased motivation temporarily for the task, but once the reward was removed, motivation dropped to a level even lower than before the reward was introduced. Not only did the subjects in the control group spend increasingly more time working on the puzzle (signifying a growing level of intrinsic motivation), but they also voluntarily returned to work on the puzzle during their free time, while the subjects in the experimental group did not (1971).

Since that initial research, Deci and his associates have published more than 100 additional research studies in which they found additional support for their initial findings that tangible extrinsic rewards undermine intrinsic motivation, with one exception (2006). When there is little intrinsic motivation to begin with (i.e., for students who are not intrinsically motivated), using extrinsic rewards can be effective for helping students internalize and identify with the value of tasks that were once considered boring or unpleasant (Deci and Ryan 1985). As Small states, "Extrinsic rewards are short lived and should be used judiciously, and only until students move to a more intrinsic orientation… the ultimate goal is for students to be motivated by their own sense of pride in their learning accomplishments and achievements rather than by some external reward" (2005, 19-20).

Limited Choice of Reading Materials

Choice is the key to a person feeling self-determined (Deci 1995). Some reading incentive programs take away what should be a leisure time, free-choice activity by dictating what books a child can/cannot read, making reading "for pleasure" just one more stressful school "subject." For teacher-librarians, this puts external limits on their library collections and detracts from library programs (like booktalks) that motivate students to try new and unfamiliar authors and genres. In addition, many teacher-librarians and teachers have found that social interaction featuring books (for example, book club discussions and booktalks) increases students' intrinsic motivation to read (Manning, 2005; Williams, Hedrick, and Tuschinski, 2008). So, why not let kids read what's important to them? Practicing reading by reading more titles more often is what helps build skills, while loving what is being read is what builds a lifelong motivation to read.

Testing

Testing kids on what is supposed to be a free-choice activity extends the current testing environment in education. Most of the tests also measure right-wrong, factual information exclusively for an activity that often requires the use of imagination, critical thinking, and interpretation skills (Brown 2003). Few of these tests ask students what they like to read, how much they enjoyed a particular book, and if they would like to read similar books. The test results do little to inform teachers and teacher-librarians about students' reading interests.

Unrelated Prizes

Many reading incentive programs offer extrinsic rewards for what should be an intrinsically pleasurable activity, thereby implying that the act of reading is only valuable if one gets "paid" for it. Often the rewards have little or

no relationship to the task itself (stickers, candy, video games, pizza parties, bicycles).

Some Little- to No-Cost Reading Incentive Strategies that Work

Many of the elaborate, formal reading incentive programs can be costly. In harsh economic times, it makes sense to offer other reading incentives that excite children about reading but cost little or no money. The library is a place where students can select reading materials that are personally interesting and relevant to them. There are many effective, low-cost motivational strategies that can be used that only require commitment and consistency. Following are some easy-to-implement examples.

▶Model good reading habits as a powerful way to motivate kids to read. Sustained Silent Reading (SSR) and Drop Everything and Read (DEAR) are examples of programs that, if implemented correctly, can have a positive impact on student reading motivation, and development. The best part is that it's free! Following is an example of a "mini-DEAR" time implemented in one library media center:

One middle school librarian I observed treated every other library period as a DEAR time. She might start with a booktalk, then would expect every student to select some reading material (magazines, newspapers, and books were all acceptable—some of the more reluctant readers were apt to pick up *SI for Kids* while more enthusiastic readers would work on novels). As soon as all the kids [checked out materials], she would join the group and also read (thus providing a good model).

▶ Use a "Parents As Reading Partners (PARP)" program in the school as a way to allow students to read with other adults. Substituting the word "People" for "Parents" is more inclusive.

▶ Demonstrate genuine excitement and enthusiasm for reading. Such activities as storytelling, booktalks, and book trailers (promoting a book through video) introduce students to a range of reading materials and motivates them to read. Share personal, intrinsic

motivation by talking about a favorite book. Following is an example shared by a school media graduate student from her fieldwork:

I recently watched the librarian where I am doing my fieldwork read *One Grain of Rice* by Demi to a group of second graders. He first prefaced the book by saying it was about math and listened to them say "ugh." Then he went on to build the book up as one of his favorites… He built it up so much that they couldn't help being interested, and sure enough, they loved the book. It is a great book, but his modeling excitement about the book was a huge motivator. Really, there's no substitute for that.

▶ Find creative ways for students to share favorite books and other reading materials with peers (e.g., present their own booktalks, create book trailers to be housed on the library media center's Web site, or write book reviews for the school newspaper).

▶ Keep track of each student's interests and then introduce a range of related reading materials (e.g., fiction and nonfiction books, Web sites, videos). Create a chart listing students and their interests as a reference. Give students access to the chart so they can add to it at any time.

▶ Think of "reading" in the broadest sense. It doesn't matter if students want to read books, magazines, e-books, Web sites, or comic books as long as they're reading and loving it. Stefl-Mabry states,

…school library media special-

ists know that to survive in the twenty-first century students need to be familiar with a wide variety of reading and informational material in an extensive array of formats: books, magazines, newspapers, radio, television, movies, electronic sources, databases, Web pages, blogs, and so on. Innovations in traditional printing techniques along with advances in electronic technologies have transformed the ways in which we live, learn, play, and are governed (July 2006).

▶ Select rewards for students unlikely to have intrinsic motivation (e.g., they have experienced repeated learning failure, they are unsure of their skills), that are related to the activity (e.g., books, bookmarks, public library cards) or that ultimately become part of the learning experience. Here are a couple of diverse examples:

Children pick out books of interest and start to read. When they need to put their books away and leave the library, the teacher-librarian gives them a bookmark of their choice. If the student has not started reading the book in the library, they will receive bookmarks from their classroom teacher. This creates extrinsic motivation to start their book, but they need to sustain their motivation intrinsically.

A group of second graders come into the library to do research projects on dinosaurs. They will be working in small groups to find information. For one of the research steps, student groups turn in a topic sheet that includes the type of dinosaur they would like to research and what they hope to learn. Once that sheet is turned in, a small toy representation of their chosen dinosaur is given to each member of the group, not only as a reward for completing that part of the assignment but also an incentive to find out more.

▶ **P**rovide verbal praise or encouragement for good reading behaviors. These types of verbal rewards can increase intrinsic motivation by affirming students' ability, thereby building their self-efficacy.

Conclusions

Intrinsic motivation is the enthusiasm to engage in a task for its own sake out of interest and/or enjoyment; it is the basis of authentic human motivation. It energizes and sustains behavior through the spontaneous satisfaction one feels as a result of accomplishing a task and attaining one's internal goals or expectations (Keller 1979). Extrinsic rewards often undermine students' intrinsic motivation. Teacher-librarians can provide a learning environment that nurtures students' intrinsic motivation for reading by modeling reading behavior, demonstrating an enthusiasm for reading activities, understanding what motivates students to read, offering the full range of literacy formats, and providing praise and reinforcement for students engaged in reading activities.

References:

Beswick, David. "Management Implications of the Interactions between Intrinsic Motivation and Extrinsic Rewards." February 2007. http://www.beswick.info/psychres/management.htm. (accessed February 25, 2009).

Brown, Carol. "Guiding Elementary Students to Generate Reading Comprehension Tests." *TechTrends* 47, no. 3 (2003): 10-15.

Carter, Betty. "Hold the Applause." *School Library Journal* 42, no. 10 (1996): 22-25.

Deci, Edward L. "Effects of Externally Mediated Rewards on Intrinsic Motivation." *Journal of Personality and Social Psychology* 18 (1971): 105-115.

Deci, Edward L. *Why We Do What We Do: Understanding Self-Motivation*. A Penguin Book, 1995.

Deci, Edward L. "The Rewards Controversy. Self-Determination Theory." University of Rochester. Psychology Department. November 27, 2006. http://www.psych.rochester.edu/SDT/cont_reward.html. (accessed February 25, 2009).

Deci, Edward L., Richard Koestner, and Richard M. Ryan. "A Meta-Analytic Review of Experiments Examining the Effects of Extrinsic Rewards on Intrinsic Motivation." *Psychological Bulletin* 125 (1999): 627-668.

Deci, Edward L., and Richard M. Ryan. *Intrinsic Motivation and Self-Determination in Human Behavior*. Plenum, 1985.

Johnson, Doug. "Creating Fat Kids Who Don't Like to Read." *Book Report* 18, no. 2 (1999): 96.

Keller, John M. "Strategies for Stimulating the Motivation to Learn." *Performance & Instruction* (October 1987): 189-195.

Kohn, Alfie. *Punished by Rewards: The Trouble with Gold Stars, Incentive Plans, A's, Praise, and Other Bribes*. Houghton Mifflin, 2001.

Krashen, Stephen. "The (Lack of) Experimental Evidence Supporting the Use of Accelerated Reader." *Journal of Children's Literature* 29, no. 2 (2003): 9, 16-30.

Lepper, Mark R., David Greene, and Richard E. Nisbett. "Undermining Children's Intrinsic Interest with Extrinsic Rewards: A Test of the 'Overjustification' Hyposthesis." *Journal of Personality and Social Psychology* 28, no. 1 (1973): 129-137.

Manning, Maryann. "Coaxing Kids to Read." *Teaching PreK-8* 35, no. 6 (2005): 80-81.

McCullers, John C., Richard A. Fabes, and James D. Moran III. "Does Intrinsic Motivation Theory Explain the Adverse Effects of Rewards on Immediate Task Performance?" *Journal of Personality and Social Psychology* 52, no.5 (1987): 1027-1033.

McGraw, Kenneth O. "The Detrimental Effects of Reward on Performance." In *The Hidden Costs of Reward: New Perspectives on Psychology and Human Motivation*, edited by M. Lepper and D. Greene. Lawrence Erlbaum, 1978.

McQuillan, Jeff. "The Effects of Incentives on Reading." *Reading Research and Instruction* 36 (1997): 111-125.

Pavonetti, Linda M., Kathryn M. Brimmer, and James F. Cipielewski. "Accelerated Reader: What are the Lasting Effects on the Reading Habits of Middle School Students Exposed to Accelerated Reader in Elementary Grades?" *Journal of Adolescent and Adult Literacy* 46 no. 4 (2002/2003): 300–311.

Rummel, Amy and Richard A. Feinberg. "Cognitive Evaluation Theory: A Meta-Analytic Review of the Literature." *Social Behavior and Personality* 16 (1988): 147-164.

Small, Ruth V. *Designing Digital Literacy Programs with IM-PACT: Information Motiva-

tion, Purpose, Audience, Content, Technique. Neal-Schuman, 2005.

Stefl-Mabry, Joette. "Computer-Aided Reading Promotion: Accelerated Reading - Silent Sustained Reading Camouflaged in a Computer Program?" *The Best of ERIC*. School Library Media Research, July 20, 2006. http://www.ala.org/ala/mgrps/divs/aasl/aaslpubsandjournals/slmrb/editorschoiceb/bestoferic/besteric.cfm (accessed February 24, 2009).

Tang, Shu-Hua and Vernon. C. Hall. "The Overjustification Effect: A Meta-Analysis." *Applied Cognitive Psychology* 9 (1995): 365-404.

Wiersma, Uco J. "The Effects of Extrinsic Rewards in Intrinsic Motivation: A Meta-Analysis." *Journal of Occupational and Organizational Psychology* 65 (1992): 101-114.

Williams, Lunetta. M., Wanda.B. Hedrick, and Linda. Tuschinski, L. "Motivation: Going Beyond Testing to a Lifetime of Reading." *Childhood Education* 84, no.3 (2008): 135-141.

The authors would like to acknowledge the input of these additional graduate students who shared their ideas and opinions about extrinsic rewards for reading in IST 663: Integrating Motivation & Information Literacy at Syracuse University, fall 2008: Jennifer Abrams, Lesley Ann Belge, Rebecca Buerkett, Kathryn Buturla, Mira Dougherty-Johnson, Sara Edwards, Elizabeth Jurkiewicz, Sylvia Kendrick, Allison Livermore, Beth Miles, and Christine Santimaw.◄

Ruth V. Small, Ph. D., is Laura J. & L. Douglas Meredith Professor at Syracuse University's School of Information Studies. This article was created as a result of a class discussion on extrinsic rewards with school media graduate students sharing their research findings and personal and professional experiences.

Chapter 6

Inquiry

Educators in all subject areas are recognizing the power of inquiry to provoke deeper learning.

—Barbara Stripling, "Inquiry: Inquiring Minds Want to Know" (see page 147)

On notable change in the AASL *Standards for the 21st-Century Learner* is that the phrase "information literacy," which was used in the *Information Power* documents, does not appear in the content of the AASL *Standards* beyond a reference in the Common Beliefs (AASL 2007). Instead, the more expansive process of inquiry is present. Using the term "inquiry" rather than "information literacy" for school library learning is beneficial to the school library media specialist (SLMS). First, it renames the research process using terminology that is more familiar to classroom teachers. Inquiry is not unique to classroom learning; indeed, it is present in many subject areas, particularly science, and so using a familiar term gives classroom colleagues a new sense of common ground with the SLMS. Second, a commitment to inquiry also indicates a library media specialist's interest in being a collaborative teaching partner throughout the student's learning experience, from initial question development through reflection. Unfortunately, a pitfall of "information literacy" was that it could be misconstrued to mean simply the finding and reading of information or a series of mini-lessons. Inquiry, on the other hand, encompasses the entire experience of questioning, discovering information, synthesizing it, and reporting it.

Using the term "inquiry" does not mean tossing out current information literacy skills, but it gives a new, more comprehensive context in which those skills can be embedded. Using "inquiry" rather than "information literacy" in conversations with stakeholders may be one way to help them understand that SLMSs are integral to the learning process, not merely demonstrators of isolated skills such as constructing a database search. Inquiry, quite simply, goes deeper.

Inquiry is one of the most prized student-centered learning experiences. It begins with students' questions, not teacher-driven ones. Inquiry is not a series of responses to teacher-provided questions; instead, the student's curiosity is nurtured and supported. When a student engages in inquiry about a topic of personal curiosity, his or her self-driven need motivates deeper exploration, a move beyond the collection of superficial facts, which sustains student interest even when the learning journey encounters the inevitable snags. The research process gives students a structure in which to explore ideas and perspectives of interest, process those ideas, and create a work product that represents original thought and synthesis. Inquiry is constructivist. During inquiry, students work alone or in collaborative groups to discover, explore, understand, synthesize, and create new deep and thoughtful learning.

This chapter begins with two articles by Daniel Callison that build a firm foundation of inquiry. The first, "Information Inquiry" (beginning on page 121), provides an overview of the stages of inquiry, and the second, "Models, Part IV: Inquiry Models" (beginning on page 126), shows various processes and models for building inquiry learning units. Next, in a five-part series (beginning on page 130), Leslie Preddy dives deeply into inquiry, detailing each phase.

As Stripling notes in "Inquiry: Inquiring Minds Want to Know" (beginning on page 147), inquiry lies at the heart of the AASL *Standards*. Having a strong conceptual understanding of the inquiry process and its learning objectives is essential before teachers and school library media specialists can engage students in a meaningful inquiry experience.

How Can Media Specialists Promote Inquiry-Focused Teaching?

Stripling's "Inquiry-based Teaching and Learning—The Role of the School Library Media Specialist" (beginning on page 150) gives an overview of how library media specialists can impact inquiry-focused teaching and learning both within and outside the school library media center. She provides specific strategies that include collaboration, pedagogy, collection development, and taking a leadership role via professional development, reflection, and modeling.

Kafi Kumasi-Johnson's "Critical Inquiry: Library Media Specialists as Change Agents," (beginning on page 151) suggests an active approach to promoting inquiry. Critical inquiry goes beyond academic change to social change. She points out that SLMSs need to transform their practices to "make it real" for their students. This can mean busting no-talking myths, offering up authentic collaborative environments like book clubs, or creating forums for authentic student expression.

In "Engaging Students in Inquiry" (beginning on page 155), Joan M. Yoshina and Violet H. Harada outline their inquiry process and provide an example of how fourth-grade students pursued their interest in learning more about hurricanes and natural disasters following the recent Asian tsunami and Hurricane Katrina. By exploring their own questions, students remain motivated throughout the search process, pursue knowledge beyond the collection of superficial facts, and gain greater levels of understanding.

Inquiry: Not Just In the Library, Not Just for Research

It is easy for the school library media specialist to assume that he or she is the sole promoter of inquiry in the school setting. Such an assumption is incorrect. Many curriculum areas promote an aspect of inquiry, though each area's procedures may appear different. The library media specialist can make a connection to this deep thinking process by partnering with those in other curriculum areas both inside and outside the library.

For example, the scientific method is a structured experimental approach grounded in inquiry. In fact, the Stripling Inquiry Model (discussed in chapter 7) closely maps to the scientific method. One method of documenting the planning, execution, and reflective processes of the scientific method is known as science notebooking. In "Connecting Science Notebooking to the Elementary Library Media Center" (beginning on page 159), Kristin Fontichiaro and Sandy Buczynski demonstrate how closely aligned science notebooking is to the inquiry process outlined in the AASL *Standards*. This correlation opens up new avenues for approaching science colleagues for collaborative work. When the cognitive processes of inquiry are prioritized over the requirement that library collaborations must involve library resources, we can create new and valuable ways to support student learning, wherever it happens in the school. Additional articles on inquiry in the content areas are found in later chapters of this book.

GETTING TO ADVOCACY

Making stakeholders aware that the SLMS is invested in rich student learning is a key step to building support. Moving past the stereotypical concept that library media specialists are more than book people or resource managers is key, especially given that many decision makers came of age at a time when school libraries were quiet places for students to complete teacher-prescribed work or where paraprofessionals circulated materials but did not teach. Systematically reinforcing this new image over time is essential to build support for the library media program before budget cuts jeopardize the program's future. Ongoing communication is central to building advocacy.

1. Use the values of inquiry to reach out to colleagues with whom you have not previously connected. Using "inquiry" instead of, or in addition to, "information literacy" to define what you can offer in a collaborative partnership can help classroom teachers envision a richer partnering experience with you.

2. Create a newsletter article, bulletin board, or bookmarks that discuss how school librarians support inquiry. This is a vehicle that can be used to gain initial interest and can lead to working collaboratively with others. This in turn will lead to building advocates who understand the important role the library media specialist plays in teaching and learning related to inquiry. Show how current information literacy skills play a crucial role in the inquiry process and be sure that classroom colleagues know that the school library can be part of the bigger inquiry picture. Become a member of the school improvement/instructional planning team so that the library media program becomes an ongoing part of the discussion related to academic goals. Help others see the library media program through their agenda—what is important to them.

3. Recognize that many students engage in below-the-radar, unstructured inquiry by checking out a series of books on a similar topic to pursue personal curiosity. If your circulation policy sets a limit on the number of items that may be circulated at one time, consider how you will meet these students' informal inquiry needs and whether the policy can be flexibly adjusted to meet those needs. Make this part of a discussion with the administrators and teachers in your building. Involve them in the decisions so they have a better understanding of how this influences the learning goals for students. In this way you begin to build advocates.

4. Partner with the public library to provide additional resources for students. Saving a busy parent a trip to the public library—or, if media center resources are limited, having them be greeted by a public librarian aware of their research needs—helps build a future advocate for the school library media center. Be sure to move from the one-way messages and actions that are at the level of "do unto" others (PR) to involving parents in the process of planning what happens in the library media program. Once involved, they may communicate information to other parents about the partnership with the public library and why it is important and helpful to their children's learning. This can be as simple as a note in the parent newsletter or a posting on the school Web site.

5. Consider how library resources can support parent needs as well. In the current economic climate, access to high-speed Internet connections or to up-to-date circulated materials may be more limited than in the past. How could the school library media center help? Could some materials be circulated directly to parents? Could parents bring their laptops to school to access the school's wireless Internet connection? This does not necessarily mean additional work for the school library media specialist. Savvy high school students might be able to lead parents in a resume-formatting workshop, for example.

6. Could your library accommodate senior patrons? Many high schoolers must complete a service project, and technology training for senior citizens in the school computer labs could be a way to earn needed service credits. Consider courses for senior citizens about eBay, checking e-mail, using Skype's free voice-over Internet service to connect with grandchildren, or podcasting to capture oral histories. Senior citizens have higher-than-average voter turnout, so connecting them with the activities of the school could have a significant impact the next time the district seeks a millage renewal.

THOUGHTS FOR THE JOURNEY

1. How can display space in and around the school library media center showcase the process and the products of inquiry?

2. Inquiry is practiced on a regular basis by many professions, such as medical researchers, attorneys, and corporate investors. How could you harness the leaders in your community to help demonstrate the real-world need for increased inquiry in your school?

3. Beginning SLMSs sometimes feel overwhelmed at the number of classroom colleagues who will not engage in inquiry because they need that time to master discreet skills that will be assessed on a standardized test. How could mini-inquiry lessons replace longer inquiry units to better adjust to this reality and show how the discreet skills are part of the process? Throughout the 2009–2010 school year, *School Library Monthly* will run a series called "Nudging Toward Inquiry," which recommends small changes that can be made to existing non-inquiry units that gradually help the teacher move toward deeper instruction.

4. How can the inquiry process be used to reach out to novice teachers? What stereotypes might need to be overcome?

5. Stripling's six-step inquiry process—Connect, Wonder, Investigate, Construct, Express, and Reflect—has similarities to and differences from other research models such as those listed in the sidebar. How is Stripling's approach similar to or different from the research model you are currently using?

**LEADING INQUIRY AND
INFORMATION PROCESSING MODELS
OF THE PAST 25 YEARS**

- Kuhlthau's Information Search Process (1985, 1989)

- Eisenberg and Berkowitz' The Big6™ (1988)

- Stripling and Pitts' Research Process Model(1988)

- Pappas and Tepe's Pathways to Knowledge Model (1995)

- Yucht's Flip It! Model (1997)

- McKenzie's Research Cycle (2000)

Information Inquiry

by Daniel Callison

The components of information inquiry tie together the essential methods that must be practiced by both teacher and learner in order to meet basic information and media literacy skills.

When integrated with academic content areas across the curriculum and supported by the knowledgeable use of modern information technologies, information inquiry can result in learners who are fluent in selection and application of methods to address their information needs. These learners are fluent in that they have mastered the concepts and components of information literacy to the degree that they can adjust to and address future changes as the Information Age continues to evolve.

The Five Components of Information Inquiry

A component represents a part of a compound or complex whole. The components described here are based on the essential concepts for information inquiry—those ideas for actions to be taken by the learner to acquire and apply knowledge. Elements of inquiry, especially in the learning process associated with the scientific method, are further defined in the key word "Inquiry."

Questioning. This component rests on natural curiosity held by most humans from birth. Who? What? Where? When? How? But most of all, Why? This component, as it interacts with the other four, becomes a more refined skill set. The result is the ability to ask more refined, focused, relevant, and insightful questions.

Questions trigger the interactions that can eventually lead to greater understanding of an environment, a situation, a problem, an issue, or actions of a person or group. Today, these questions are raised in an environment dominated by a flood of information, often unorganized, misleading, and overpowering. Understanding meaning and solution, however, are the indicators of the end of the inquiry process. Conclusions are the basis for a beginning to another set of questions. Information inquiry is based on a continuous questioning cycle, the essence of lifelong learning.

Exploration. Closely tied to questioning, exploration is the action taken to seek answers to the questions. In many cases, no specific questions are on the agenda, but the drive to satisfy curiosity moves the learner to reading, viewing, listening to, and searching through information. As the information inquiry elements interact and the abilities of the human mature, exploration becomes the action to gain information related to specific questions. Exploration becomes a systematic search for and examination of resources and information.

Sources of information, in whatever format the learner can gain access, are examined, accepted, and discarded based on gaining satisfaction. Over time and through many cycles of these elements, information needs and tasks become more focused. As a result, exploration involves a more discriminating process to seek and select information. Mature abilities gained through practice and experience result in more efficient use of time to search, examine, and reflect.

Assimilation. This component involves the actions to absorb and fit information to that which is already known, believed, or assumed by the learner. In some cases, assimilation means reinforcing or confirming what is known. In many cases that apply information inquiry methods, assimilation involves an altering of what has been accepted as knowledge by the individual learner or group of learners.

Inquiry makes learning more than a gathering of facts. Assimilation through inquiry leads to consideration of a wider range of perceptions and options. As the learner matures, assimilation involves linking a host of diverse information to that previously known and applying that information to meet different future situations. Assimilation involves accumulation of knowledge, alteration of accepted knowledge, and constant consideration of alternatives.

New information assimilated with previ-

—Continued

Daniel Callison, Ed.D., is Professor and Executive Associate Dean at Indiana University School of Library and Information Science, 755 W. Michigan UL 1110A, Indianapolis, IN 46202; (317) 278-2376; Toll Free (866) 758-7254; Bloomington (812) 855-1490; http://www.slis.indiana.edu/Faculty/callison.html

ously held information is accepted as knowledge—new knowledge on the part of the individual learner even if not new to many others. Such is also accepted as knowledge whether the information is right or wrong. The learner assimilates or comprehends a meaning and thus the information is retained as knowledge, not just a fact without relevance.

Inference. This component involves the actions or processes for deriving a conclusion from facts and premises. Inference may involve personal choice and actions taken based on conclusions that seem most relevant and meaningful for the situation. On a personal basis, inference is usually an internal message to the self, and not one that is conveyed in a formal manner to others.

In other cases, inference may involve a wider communication of conclusions. The inference either is shared among members of a group working on the same tasks in a cooperative effort, or the inference is presented to those who might need a recommendation for action or need to evaluate the learner's ability to address a problem and communicate a solution.

A sharing of the conclusions may lead to further assimilation of more information for both the presenter and the audience. Presentation of inferences often refines the meaning of the conclusions and may be delivered to an audience to both inform them and often to persuade them. In nearly all cases, inference will raise new questions for exploration.

Information within the inference component is most useful when it becomes evidence. The information may come from observation, literature review, expert or witness interview, data from survey, or experimental study, and range in levels from slight association to clear cause and effect. Evidence is necessary to support a claim, notion, plan for change, or hypothesis. Without evidence, inference that leads to conclusions and recommendations can not be made. Evidence may be necessary to justify the status quo or accepted norm. Evidence always is necessary to justify change.

Reflection. This component raises the question that brings the interactions of the elements to a complete cycle, "Have I been successful in answering my question?"

Further, other questions that involve assessment of the information inquiry process extend from reflection. Were the resources used the best possible? What new questions have resulted and how should they be explored? Is what has been accepted as new knowledge meaningful to me or to others? Has this knowledge been understood to the extent that the communication process is complete? What evaluation of the application of this cycle in

information inquiry do others have to offer?

As the learner matures in his or her ability, reflection will be used more and more within each element as well as an overall action. Reflections to assess exploration, assimilation, and inference are formative in that the the learner is aware of the consequences of actions in one component on the limitations or opportunities in other components. Reflection on a summative nature allows the learner and teacher to consider decisions connected across the entire project.

The learner who masters self-reflection becomes more likely to be not only a true independent learner, but also one who can help others master the information inquiry interactions. The teacher who masters both formative and summative assessment processes will provide more clarity to his or her guidance and feedback in judgment of learner actions. The teacher as a model of reflective behavior will serve as a mentor who learns from mistakes as well as success.

Inquiry

Inquiry is a learning method that has survived the ages and has served as an instructional tool that enables humans to survive and prosper. Inquiry is based on techniques similar to the scientific method involving systematic observation and documentation to draw a conclusion. It is the practice of these techniques that constitutes teaching methods for the Information Age.

Teaching is the opportunity to provide meaningful situations for learners to experiment and deal with information problems. Teachers—whether classroom instructors, library media specialists, student peers, or parents—will best instill inquiry skills when they are seen as models of the process. It is essential, therefore, that current and future teachers master the information inquiry process and information literacy skills.

Not every information problem requires the use of the inquiry method in order to derive a solution. Certainly we learn from observation, example, and directions. Often by trial and error, we sift through solutions that seem to best fit the problem and often transfer that solution to similar problems. Many important skills and facts are mastered through routine practice. Memorization and meaningful application of these skills and facts makes for efficient learning in many situations.

Raising questions that challenge the norm or that involve some new area not included in the prescribed knowledge base requires methods which will take the teacher and the student on an systematic path. The elements of information inquiry help to define this path.

Methods associated with inquiry serve to both provide practice in question formulation, information exploration, assimilation of new information with previously understood information, inference of solutions or conclusions, and reflection on what was learned and how.

Depending on the ability and maturity of the learner, the complexity and importance of the problem and other factors, such as time and resources meeting the information need, may need to be very quick and direct or may take a lifetime. Information inquiry is the companion to lifelong learning, while experience and common sense combine to address many short-term problems. Application of information inquiry methods are likely to add value to experiences and add wisdom to common sense.

Information Environments

Everyone faces problems related to information, and nearly every problem faced is related to information. Often associated with the need to answer a question, information problems are as varied as the tasks we attempt to complete and the needs we face every day. These problems are common in three settings that most of us find ourselves at some stage in life: academic, personal, and workplace.

The academic setting, involving tasks in typical school environments, is the main one used in this column to illustrate information problems and the techniques to address those problems. In some cases these techniques are steps the student can take on his or her own, while many others require interventions and guidance on the part of the teacher.

In the academic setting, problems can be real or contrived. Real information problems may be personal needs concerning how to enroll in a course or how to prepare for an exam. Other information problems may be simulations or exercises assigned as learning experiences. Typical of these are term papers and reports that involve the use of multiple resources beyond the textbook.

Although best practices would suggest that these resource-based information problems are stronger learning situations when they are as authentic as possible, the report assignments at any grade and across disciplines leave a lot to be desired in terms of challenging students and teachers to use multiple resources effectively and efficiently. Awareness of new resources, their location, and some practice in an exercise to extract and organize facts are often the only results.

As the student leaves the academic environment and enters the workplace, authentic takes on new meaning. While simulations and perhaps even field experiences in school took

the student closer and closer to the "real world," on-the-job information problems soon convince most people that not everything necessary for job survival was taught in school.

At its best, however, information inquiry can establish a foundation for trouble-shooting strategies that transfer from the academic to professional job and even personal settings. While the details of the problems may differ, methods to address the information problems in real life are similar enough to support initial success in the real world. The former student soon finds that information decisions that may need to be made come faster, may actually effect the personal lives of many others, and that repeated wrong decisions lead to termination of the job, not just a corrected paper.

Personal information needs are present throughout our lives, from birth to death. Thus, many elements of information inquiry are reflected in the constant questions raised by preschoolers. Information preferences often are displayed as well, as the child may seek out information sources that they find to be safe, reliable, and reinforce what they want to hear. These are habits that learners carry with them as they learn to explore the information world in more detail through academic situations. Learning to be critical and open-minded is a combination of skills that is often difficult for even the best students to master.

Information Problems

Information problems range from simple with quick answers to complex questions without any hope of answers. Building on experiences with locating and extracting information to address questions leads to a fundamental ability to match resources to information need.

Starting in elementary grades, students can formulate questions that can be addressed through basic reference materials, simple Internet searches, further examination of the content of their textbooks, and even phone calls to local experts on the topic if necessary. Question posed. Resource located. Acceptable response found. Such exercises can instill awareness of the value of different resources as well as confidence in information location if the student is successful.

Most students gain even more confidence by taking command of raising their own questions. Thus, beyond the worksheets and set reference questions for practice, students at an early age should be encouraged to branch out from the standard questions posed and begin to personalize what they seek to learn. These are the first steps in inquiry—stating one's own questions and determining resources of preference.

—Continued

While much of what will help introduce the novice to information resources includes practice single resource questions, inquiry does not really blossom until multiple resources are used to check and verify facts or perspectives.

As the novice enters the more complex information inquiry tasks, he or she is likely to raise the following types of questions:

- What must I do? How much and how soon?
- What must I use? How many and where are they?
- How will my answer be evaluated?

Other questions, such as those following, illustrate information problems expressed at higher levels of consideration. Although most students may not phrase their information need in the exact terms that follow, those who mature in the information inquiry process will explore ways to address not only these questions but many more.

- What is my need? What questions must be addressed? What do I know now and what do I want to find out?
- How do I locate the information I need? Where is the information most likely to be found and who might help me locate it?
- What methods will help me search effectively so I can locate the most useful information? What methods help me work efficiently so I can save time in searching and have more time to read, interpret the information, and fit it with what I already know?
- How much information do I need? How complete should my answer be? Who must I satisfy with the information—me, my teacher, my classmates, my parents, my boss?
- How much time do I have to determine an answer? To what extent might I seek additional resources if time is available? Does the information I have located give me any leads or links to additional information? When do I have enough information?
- What is the acceptable level of evidence? Is one document, website, or article enough? Should the information be current and from an accepted expert? Do I need a second source to confirm the first?
- How do I apply this information to solve my problem? Should I gain opinions from others as to the usefulness and validity of the information?
- Is the information for me personally and to meet my own interests or needs, or must I also communicate the information to others? Who are these others? Teachers? Classmates? Employers? Do I present my interpretation of the information in different ways to different audiences? Do I know their understanding of the problem and their likely understanding, acceptance, or rejection of my conclusions?
- If an abundance of information is found, how do I decide what to select and what to exclude? If very little or no relevant information is found, and the questions are ones I must or want to address, how to I go about gathering original data?
- After finding information that seemingly supports my belief and information or that seemingly counters what I believe, how do I determine which to accept and use? How do my own perceptions and biases fit against the perceptions and biases found in the information I have located?
- Based on all possible information, primary and secondary, it is not possible to come to a conclusion. What can be learned from this and what might be done differently next time I try to answer these or similar questions?

These questions illustrate a wide range of information problems. They suggest challenging tasks. All the more reason that students should be introduced to efficient ways to search for information as early in their academic lives as possible.

Literacy and Fluency

Information literacy is a set of skills through which the student demonstrates the ability to recognize when information is needed and to take steps that lead to location and selection of information that can be used effectively to address the need. The resourcefulness to move through this process with confidence and the abilities to adjust to different databases and deal with a variety of technology-based information systems are signs of information fluency.

While information literacy represents command over those skills that are needed at a given age level to function in academic settings of the Information Age, information fluency represents the ability to move beyond to levels of independent skill acquisition. Well-versed in the use of information technologies, those who are information fluent are able to express themselves creatively, to reformulate knowledge, and to synthesize new information.

Jamie McKenzie describes the student who has moved to the fluent stage as the ability to "move across a menu of strategies until one works. [These students] do not allow themselves to get stuck in one place trying the same wrong tool or strategy over and over again, harder and harder. They are toolmakers and tool-shapers [they can formulate their own strategies when necessary] as well as tool-users" (51).

The interactions that take place through information inquiry are the methods and techniques that help the student become information literate and eventually strive for fluency.

For Further Reading

Association of College and Research Libraries. *Information Literacy Competency Standards for Higher Education.* http://www.ala.org/acrl/ilintro.html (Viewed June 1, 2001).

Breivik, Patricia, and J. A. Senn. *Information Literacy: Educating Children for the 21st Century.* New York: Scholastic, 1994.

Kuhlthau, Carol Collier. *Seeking Meaning: A Process Approach to Library and Information Services.* Norwood, NJ: Ablex, 1993.

McKenzie, Jamie. *Beyond Technology: Questioning, Research and the Information Literate School.* Bellingham, WA: FNO Press, 2000. http://fno.org or http://questioning.org

Neuman, Delia. "Beyond the Chip: A Model for Fostering Equity." *School Library Media Quarterly* 18, no. 3 (1990).

http://www.ala.org/aasl/SLMR/slmr_resources/select_neuman.html (Viewed June 4, 2001).

Schement, Jorge Reina, and Terry Curtis. *Tendencies and Tensions of the Information Age.* New Brunswick, NJ: Transaction Publications, 1995.

Spitzer, Kathleen L., Michael B. Eisenberg, and Carrie A. Lowe, eds. *Information Literacy: Essential Skills for the Information Age.* Syracuse, NY: ERIC Clearinghouse on Information & Technology, 1998.

Toffler, Alvin. *The Third Wave.* New York: Morrow, 1980.

Tyner, Kathleen. *Literacy in a Digital World: Teaching and Learning in the Age of Information.* Mahwah, NJ: Lawrence Erlbaum Associates, 1998.

Wurman, Richard Saul. *Information Anxiety.* New York: Bantam Books, 1989.

Models, Part IV:
Inquiry Models

by Daniel Callison

WebQuest

Bernie Dodge has defined WebQuest as an inquiry-oriented activity in which some or all of the information with which learners interact comes from resources on the Internet, optionally supplemented with videoconferencing. He states there are two levels of WebQuests, based on Marzano's dimensions of learning.

For Short Term WebQuests, the goal is knowledge acquisition and integration. At the end of the WebQuest, a learner will have grappled with a significant amount of new information and made sense of it. A Short Term WebQuest is designed to be completed in one to three class periods.

For a Longer Term WebQuest, the goals include extending and refining knowledge. As a result of this learning experience, the student has analyzed a body of knowledge deeply, transformed it in some way, and demonstrated an understanding of the material by creating something to which others can respond. This experience will require a week to a month in a classroom setting.

The templates for developing a WebQuest have grown to be more complex over years of experimentation by thousands of students and teachers. The basic idea remains, however. Each WebQuest site provides:

- A clear task description,
- Links to resources needed to address the problem,
- Examples of the process to accomplish the task,
- Guidance on how to sort and display information gathered,
- Conclusion and summary of what the learner accomplished, and
- Encouragement to move to higher learning domains.

Dodge favors WebQuests that draw on the following thinking skills defined by Robert Marzano in order to extend and refine knowledge:

Comparing—Identifying and articulating similarities and differences between or among things.

Classifying—Grouping things into definable categories on the basis of their attributes.

Inducing—Inferring unknown generalizations or principles from observations or analysis.

Deducing—Inferring unstated consequences and conditions from given principles and generalizations.

Analyzing Errors—Identifying and articulating errors in one's own or others' thinking.

Constructing support—Constructing a system of support or proof for an assertion.

Abstraction—Identifying and articulating the underlying theme or general pattern of information.

Analyzing Perspectives—Identifying and articulating personal perspectives about issues.

Marzano identifies two more dimensions of learning:

Using Knowledge Meaningfully—The application of knowledge in order to complete a meaningful and constructive task during which skills of decision-making, problem-solving, invention, investigation, and experimental inquiry are applied.

Productive Habits of Mind—This is the highest dimension of learning according to Marzano as the learner has matured in development of habits that regulate his or her behavior and approach to new tasks.

Critical thinking:

be accurate and seek accuracy

be clear and seek clarity

maintain an open mind

restrain impulsivity

take a position when the situation warrants it

—Continued

Daniel Callison, Ed.D., is Professor and Executive Associate Dean at Indiana University School of Library and Information Science, 755 W. Michigan UL 1110A, Indianapolis, IN 46202; (317) 278-2376; Toll Free (866) 758-7254; Bloomington (812) 855-1490; http://www.slis.indiana.edu/Faculty/callison.html

VOLUME XIX, NUMBER 4/DECEMBER 2002

respond appropriately to others' feelings and
level of knowledge

Creative thinking:

persevere

push the limits of your knowledge and abilities

generate trust and maintain your own standards of evaluation

generate new ways of viewing a situation

Self-regulated thinking:

monitor your own thinking

plan appropriately

identify and use necessary resources

respond appropriately to feedback

evaluate the effectiveness of your actions

Key Resources

Dodge, Bernie. *The WebQuest Page at San Diego State University.* http://edweb.sdsu.edu/webquest/webquest.html (Viewed June 28, 2001).

Marzano, Robert J. *A Different Kind of Classroom: Teaching with Dimensions of Learning.* Alexandria, VA: Association for Supervision and Curriculum Development, 1992.

Marzano, Robert J., and others. *Dimensions of Thinking: A Framework for Curriculum and Instruction.* Alexandria, VA: Association for Supervision and Curriculum Development, 1988.

Minnesota's Inquiry Process

Mary Dalbotten and her staff at the Minnesota Department of Children, Families, and Learning applied the model for information problem-solving developed by Eisenberg and Berkowitz to the Learning Profile for Inquiry portion of the state's curriculum. Across all areas of the curriculum, the inquiry process was applied as one of ten strands for student learning. The other strands involved reading, writing, the arts, mathematics, science, cultures, decision-making, managing resources, and languages. In all areas of the curriculum, Dalbotten found there were standards and learning activities for students to raise questions and apply data analysis that would imply possible answers. Data is broadly defined to include narrative or testimonial evidence as well as quantitative evidence.

Minnesota's Inquiry Process

1. Generate Questions: Pose significant questions.
2. Determine Feasibility: Identify strategy and method to address questions.
3. Collect Data: Apply method to locate or generate new data.
4. Reduce and Organize Data: Select data which is more relevant, and organize to meet questions.
5. Display Data: Present data in visual form to summarize and communicate findings.
6. Compile Conclusions and More Questions: What new questions come from this process?

Key Resource

Dalbotten, Mary S. "Inquiry in the National Content Standards." In *Instructional Interventions for Information Use,* edited by Callison, McGregor, and Small, 30-82. San Jose, CA: Hi Willow Research, 1998.

Indiana's Student Inquiry Model

Based on Callison's elements of Information Inquiry, Leslie Preddy has developed and tested a model for basic student inquiry through Indiana schools. Supported by the Indiana Department of Public Instruction, Preddy links activities back to the elements of Information Inquiry through these processes:

Exploration

Orientation

Strategy

Investigation

Conclusion

Key Resource

Preddy, Leslie B. *Student Inquiry in the Research Process.* http://www.msdpt.k12.in.us/etspages/pm/imc/Inquiry/index.htm

Constructivist Learning Models for Inquiry

David Jonassen, professor of instructional systems at Pennsylvania State University, is one of a growing number of instructional design theorists who believes that learning environments for effective advanced knowledge acquisition are best developed on the principles of constructivist learning theory. Although usually placed within higher education, his viewpoint has implications for secondary and elementary school settings as well. Writing in 1992, Jonassen stated:

"Constructivism holds that the mind is instrumental and essential in interpreting events, objects, and perspectives on the real world, and that those interpretations comprise a knowledge base that is personal and individualistic. The mind filters input from the world in making those interpretations. An important conclusion from constructivistic beliefs is that we all conceive of the external world somewhat differently, based on our unique set of experiences with that world and our beliefs about those experiences" (139).

A model that represents the attributes of meaningful learning under constructivist theory includes:

Active—manipulative, observant, interactive experiences and engagement in the activities to experience and learn by doing.

Constructive—articulative and reflective so that learners try to deal with new experiences that present new ideas, information, or methods than they have experienced previously.

Intentional—reflective and regulatory to

meet a goal, and the learner articulates what goals are to be or have been reached.

Authentic—complex and contextual so that the learning tasks are challenging and not overly simplified.

Cooperative—the learning tested, refined, and shaped through collaboration and conversation as the learner shares ideas with others in order to receive and give constructive feedback.

James Carey, professor of library and information science at South Florida University, has applied the constructivist approach to instructional design for facilitating the education of students in information literacy.

Teaching Problem-Solving Skills in the School Media Center Context

Skills	Teacher Role	Student Outcomes
Library	(Explain) sets of tools for accessing, manipulating, creating, and reporting information in a variety of formats.	Find information from multiple resources and use it in preparing reports or presentations.
Information	Teach library skills and a process by which students can be guided in their solution of information problems.	Apply a generic solution strategy to a variety of information problems, and construct new meaning through the interaction between what they know and the new information that they encounter.
Information Literacy	Create learning environments and cooperative group structures in which the natural outgrowth of curiosity is the collaborative construction among students of effective information problem-solving strategies.	Construct personal solution strategies for information problems, and generalize, test, and adapt those strategies in new problem situations.

Carey also applies principles of the constructivist learning approach to the more traditional instructional model.

Comparing Traditional Instructional Design with Constructivist Learning

1. Traditional: Teacher provides a motivational introduction.
   Constructivist:
   - Foster motivation through ownership by giving students choices in the content they explore and methods they use for exploration.
   - Situate the problem in a meaningful (authentic) context that is rich in content and interest.

2. Traditional: Teacher states what is expected, reminds students of what they should know.
   Constructivist:
   - Problem scenarios emphasize constructing process over finding answers.
   - Scenarios require reflective thought, looking back to incorporate foundational knowledge into new knowledge.

3. Traditional: Teacher presents the new content with examples that will help the students recall for application.
   Constructivist:
   - Use cooperative learning so that students can negotiate the meaning of what they are learning.
   - Design problem scenarios of high complexity requiring use of multiple process strategies and knowledge skills.
   - Encourage multiple perspectives and interpretations of the same knowledge.
   - Situate the problem in authentic contexts.

4. Traditional: Provide students with opportunity to practice new skills.
   Constructivist:
   - Problem scenarios are generative rather than prescriptive; that is, students construct their own investigation and knowledge acquisition rather than following steps of a prescribed process.
   - Encourage group participation for trying out and negotiating new knowledge and process.

5. Traditional: Provide student with information about how well they are doing in their practice.
   Constructivist:
   - Balance the potential frustration of aimless exploration with just enough facilitation to ensure progress; facilitation techniques include modeling, scaffolding, coaching, and collaborating, but fade as students become more skillful.
   - Facilitate group interaction as needed to ensure peer review of knowledge and process.

6. Traditional: Teacher provides a review and relates new skills to real-world applications and upcoming lessons.
   Constructivist:
   - Students have opportunities to explore multiple, parallel problem scenarios which they will apply to a new scenario of information (need) processes they have previously constructed.

7. Traditional: Teacher provides tests, performance checklists, rating scales, attitude scales, or some other means of measuring mastery of new skills. —Continued

Constructivist:

- Suggest tools that students can use to monitor their own construction of knowledge and processes; students should be reflective and critically review previous learning and newly constructed positions.
- Standards for evaluation are not absolute, but must be referenced to the student's unique goals, knowledge, and past achievement.
- The ultimate measure of success is transfer of learning to new, authentic environments.

Carey's Model for Problem Solving and Life Skills

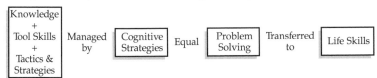

Key Resources

Carey, James O. "Library Skills, Information Skills, and Information Literacy: Implications for Teaching and Learning. *School Library Media Quarterly Online.* Vol. 1. 1998. http://www.ala.org/aasl/SLMQ/skills.html

Jonassen, David H. *Computers as Mindtools for Schools: Engaging Critical Thinking.* New York: Prentice Hall, 1999.

Jonassen, David H. "Evaluating Constructivist Learning." In *Constructivism and the Technology of Instruction,* edited by T. M. Duffy and D. H. Jonassen. Hilsdale, NJ: Lawrence Erlbaum Associates, 1992.

Jonassen, David H., Kyle L. Peck, and Brent G. Wilson. *Learning with Technology: A Constructivist Perspective.* Upper Saddle River, NJ: Merrill, 1999.

The Research Cycle

Jamie McKenzie opens his book *Beyond Technology* with this statement:

"Questions and questioning may be the most powerful technologies of all. How might this be so? Questions allow us to make sense of the world. They are the most powerful tools we have for making decisions and solving problems, for inventing, changing, and improving our lives as well as the lives of others. Questioning is central to learning and growing. An unquestioning mind is one condemned to 'feeding' on the ideas and solutions of others. An unquestioning mind may have little defense against the data smog so typical of life in this Information Age" (1).

McKenzie's message is central to the inquiry process. Too often students are asked to use resources to "find out" or "cut and paste" without the challenge to raise and answer their own questions. Learning to formulate questions both as an individual and with groups is the most essential skill in the research cycle. He sees students in a more productive mode when they move through the Research Cycle several times before they begin to determine what they will report.

The Research Cycle

Determine the essential questions

Determine subsidiary questions

Develop a research plan—what sources are needed?

Gather information—skim and select

Synthesize and evaluate findings

Revise questions

Revise plan and revisit or locate more sources

Gather information again

Sort and sift information again

Synthesize to invision, propose, or invent and evaluate again

Revise questions and focus

Revise plan for access to most relevant sources

Gather more precise information

Sort and sift to show meaning

Synthesize to infer and evaluate

Report findings

Key Resource

McKenzie, Jamie. *Beyond Technology: Questioning, Research and The Information Literate School.* Bellingham, WA: FNO Press, 2000. See also http://fno.org and http://questioning.org (Viewed June 28, 2001).

Student Inquiry in the Research Process

Part 1: Inquiry Research Basics
by Leslie B. Preddy

"Inquiry" seems like such a small, unassuming word that it can be overlooked as inconsequential. It's not a word that is used often in casual conversation with friends or co-workers. It's not even fun to say—it is actually a little awkward when you think about it. But the meaning behind that one little word in relation to student research has far-reaching potential. When trying to make sense of the world around us, and helping students make sense of that world as well, inquiry is a powerful word with even more powerful tools. Inquiry is a method to employ that allows students, teachers, and library media specialists to work together toward becoming independent thinkers.

A Planning Guide for Information Power: Building Partnerships for Learning (ALA/AASL 1999) defines inquiry as "the process for formulating appropriate research questions, organizing the search for data, analyzing and evaluating the data found, and communicating the results in a coherent presentation." It gets to the heart of that which we, as library media specialists and educators, are concerned: valuing the process a researcher goes through as much, if not more, than the final product. Inquiry is a method for recognizing the need to teach ourselves and others to think things through as we question, read, analyze, investigate, reflect, internalize, hypothesize, and present our findings and theories in a way that is audience appropriate. It is a way to get away from just reporting the facts and more toward developing the skills necessary for students to become independent thinkers with a self-awareness and ability to problem solve throughout life.

> *"One seeks to equip the child with deeper, more gripping, and subtler ways of knowing the world and himself."*
>
> —Jerome Bruner, Psychologist, 1961

Planning for Inquiry

Planning for an inquiry research project is a collabo-

Leslie B. Preddy is library media specialist at Perry Meridian Middle School in Indianapolis, IN. E-mail lpreddy@msdpt.k12.in.us
"Student Inquiry in the Research Process" (http://www.msdpt.k12.in.us/etspages/pm/imc/Inquiry/index.htm?1025700207264) was developed with a grant from the Indiana Department of Education-Office of Learning Resources based on the elements of information inquiry designed by Dr. Daniel Callison, Indiana University, and LMS Associates.

rative effort between the library media specialist and classroom teacher. A teacher's passion for a particular subject, the curriculum, and standards initiate the inquiry topic and should be used as a basis for inquiry research. For optimum success, the inquiry topic should be an integral part of the standards and curriculum.

Collaboration between the classroom teacher and library media specialist should include sharing roles and responsibilities, with a clear understanding of the division of and sharing of tasks. Expect to spend time planning, designing, implementing, and assessing. Just as students will be expected to do during the inquiry project, keep a collaboration log, journal, notebook, or folder and put all inquiry research collaboration expectations, guidelines, and requirements in it. It doesn't need to be fancy, typed, or formally structured; it just needs to be kept together so that it is easily accessible at the point of need. Be willing to make modifications as necessary to suit the needs of the collaborative teacher's teaching styles or student's learning styles. Recognize that collaborative planning for inquiry is a fulfilling, challenging, and creative process, not traditional and mechanical. Share a willingness to evaluate jointly and revise the inquiry research unit. Enjoy being collaborative partners and benefit from the opportunity to learn from one another and grow as educators.

To be effective, the library media specialist must be willing to set aside or postpone other administrative responsibilities and routine activities to devote attention toward the inquiry unit, students, and classroom teacher. This requires focusing on the role of teacher-library media specialist instead of administrator-library media specialist. To be approachable, useful, and needed, appear available, interested, and focused on the inquiry unit and people.

National Goals, Standards, Best Practices

Inquiry is a component of curriculum, national goals and standards, and many state standards. It is not something to teach in addition to everything else, but rather a method to gain perspective and focus energy. Students will become better researchers and be able to adapt the process learned to real-life strategies. Inquiry is imbedded in the national standards of all of the major disciplines. With modifications for the student's cognitive ability level, it is an effective and natural technique for the inquisitive from childhood through adulthood.

Curriculum Standards for Social Studies. http://www.socialstudies.org/standards/toc.html

Information Literacy Standards for Student Learning. http://www.ala.org/aasl/ip_nine.html

National Education Technology Standards for Students. http://cnets.iste.org/index2.html

National Health Education Standards. http://www.aahperd.org/aahe/pdf_files/standards.pdf

National Science Education Standards. http://stills.nap.edu/html/nses/

Principals and Standards for School Mathematics. http://standards.nctm.org/

Standards for the English Language Arts. http://www.ncte.org/standards/standards.shtml

Educator Roles for Inquiry

Using the inquiry method requires educators to break out of the tradition teaching role and to wear a number of professional hats: Appraiser, Coach, Guide, Instructor, Motivational Speaker, and Role Model.

Appraiser—As appraiser, the classroom teacher and library media specialist continually observe and evaluate student efforts, abilities, and learning throughout the process. Assessments can be made through a variety of means: rubrics, observations, checklists, interviews, surveys, self-evaluations, and peer evaluations.

Coach—As a coach, the classroom teacher and library media specialist use coaching methods, similar to those employed by an athletic coach, to help students practice and progress toward research autonomy. A coach demonstrates for the student how to succeed with techniques and strategies, and then gives plenty of time to "warm up" and "practice." Act as a student's coach as he or she moves through the research inquiry process. Continue verbal encouragement and inspiration along the way. Be observant and go to the aid of students in need.

Guide—As guide, the classroom teacher and library media specialist observe student inquiry activity and help lead students through difficult spots. Ideally, educators should guide in a way that requires the student to solve his or her own problems by using techniques like the Socratic Method. A guide does not have or give all of the answers, but may help with which route the student should travel to get to a destination.

Instructor—As instructor, the classroom teacher and library media specialist conduct lectures and discussion to establish a basic knowledge about the subject from which to build. Work collaboratively to develop students' reading and study skills, to develop students' capacity to distinguish differences between report writing and research, and to develop students' abilities to generate age-appropriate, researchable questions. The instructor gives students opportunities to practice using supporting evidence, analytical thinking, and drawing conclusions. The instructor develops mini-lessons to be taught as the need arises in relation to research methods, instead of teaching in an artificial environment.

Motivational Speaker—As a motivational speaker, the classroom teacher and library media specialist take on the role of empowering and inspiring students as individuals, small groups, or whole classes to succeed and to continue when things get rough. Give students the encouragement that elicits the desire and will to excel. Instill in students the self-esteem that is sometimes crucial for having the drive necessary to proceed on the quest for answers. Encourage the students to believe in themselves enough to make it through the more difficult situations that arise when researching.

Role Model—As a role model, the classroom teacher and library media specialist demonstrate throughout the inquiry process information literacy and inquiry skills and methods. Lead by example through modeling methods, techniques, and expected behavior. Go through the inquiry research process alongside the students.

Moving Toward Inquiry Research

Topic Selection & Questioning—Inquiry research should be generated from the student's base knowledge by building on what they know instead of what they don't know. Take the classroom time necessary so that the students have the opportunity to learn enough about the curricular topic, or general theme, to have a foundation of interest from which to generate their inquiry research questions. Allow students the intellectual opportunity to select and specify a topic, or category, to investigate that is not only related to what they have been learning in class, but also of interest to them. With ownership of what is being researched comes the unexpected responsibility for what and how he or she is learn-

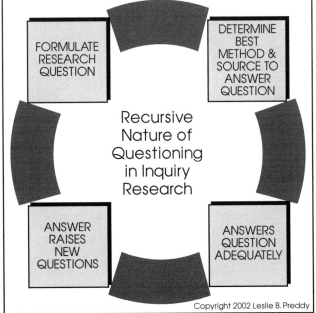

Recursive Nature of Questioning in Inquiry Research

FORMULATE RESEARCH QUESTION

DETERMINE BEST METHOD & SOURCE TO ANSWER QUESTION

ANSWER RAISES NEW QUESTIONS

ANSWERS QUESTION ADEQUATELY

Copyright 2002 Leslie B. Preddy

—Continued

ing. Many state and national standards are written in the context of student's generating their own questions to investigate. For example, Indiana's English/Language Arts academic standard 7.4.5 states, "Research and Technology...Identify topics; ask and evaluate questions; and develop ideas leading to inquiry, investigation, and research."

Interpret, Analyze, Evaluate—Help students understand how to interpret what information is important and should be kept and what should be disregarded through the inquiry research process. Give students the training and tools necessary to acquire the skills that allow for age-appropriate interpretation, analysis, and evaluation of information. Give students the skills required to develop, implement, analyze, and interpret interviews, surveys, and questionnaires. Help students learn how to use a variety of traditional and nontraditional resources that allow them the opportunity to learn about the resources available in their community: home, school, local, state, national, international, and virtual.

Students as Learners and Teachers—Be observant and encourage peer mentoring and tutoring. A person learns and retains more from teaching, so give those students with the experience and ability the freedom to take those teachable moments and show a peer how to do something they've all ready learned. In my experience, the students surprise me every year with what they can teach each other. I often see what I had taken just a moment to show one student, applied by that student to help his or her peers. I see students that would not normally be considered by the classroom teacher as a positive role model or classroom leader actively helping other students, even if it's something as small as sharing a book they've come across that they think will help a peer. Students should be given an opportunity to demonstrate expertise with their peers. If a student has a gift for navigating the Web, editing video, locating key information in a book, or other talents, allow him or her to relate that information to peers in need. Learn not to underestimate the value of peer information sharing. Include a formal situation for peer counseling, where students can be paired up and share research findings and how they anticipate presenting or reporting their thoughts and findings. As a component to the project conclusion, allow for peer evaluation and self-evaluation. Students will take peers' comments as sincerely and often as more legitimate than an adult's. Obligating students to evaluate themselves requires the student to internalize and self-analyze, which is vital for self-awareness and future research success.

Evaluating Inquiry Research

The inquiry research process should be evaluated separately from the students' final research product. For inquiry to be most effective and fulfilling, the classroom teacher and library media specialist should devote the time and effort necessary to jointly evaluate students.

Inquiry Process—Evaluate the research process as much as the final product. The inquiry process can be formally evaluated through the student's ability to meet deadlines throughout the project, on-task behavior, select and locate traditional and nontraditional sources, daily reflections, ask for help when appropriate, keep a research notebook or journal, peer assessments, and self assessment.

Inquiry Product—Offer a variety of product options for reporting and presenting inquiry research findings that meet the needs of the auditory, visual, and kinesthetic learner. The product should be evaluated for its written and oral aspect, aesthetics, accuracy, and coherency. Evaluation can be done by the students, educators, administrators, community leaders, field experts, and peers.

Suggested Readings on Inquiry in the Research Process:

Callison, Daniel. "Key Words in Instruction: Inquiry." *School Library Media Activities Monthly* 15, no. 6 (February 1999): 38-42.

Callison, Daniel. "School Library Media Programs and Free Inquiry Learning." *School Library Journal* (February 1986): 20-24.

Owens, Roxanne Farwick, Jennifer L. Hester, and William H. Teale. "Where Do You Want to Go Today? Inquiry-based Learning and Technology Integration." *The Reading Teacher* 55, no. 7 (April 2002): 616-625.

Joyce, Marilyn, and Julie Tallman. *Making the Writing and Research Connection with the I-Search Process: A How-To-Do-It Manual.* (How-To-Do-It Manuals for Librarians, No 62.) New York: Neal Schuman, 1997.

References:

Brazee, Ed. "Collaborating on Curriculum: Why It Matters, How It Works." *Middle Ground* (August 2000): 33-37.

Callison, Daniel. Interview. July 17, 2001.

Callison, Daniel. "School Library Media Programs and Free Inquiry Learning." *School Library Journal* (February 1986): 20-24.

Carey, James O. "Library Skills, Information Skills, and Information Literacy: Implications for Teaching and Learning." *School Library Media Quarterly.* http://www.ala.org/SLMQ/skills.html

Gordon, Carol. "Students as Authentic Researchers: A New Prescription for the High School Research Assignment." *School Library Media Researcher.* Vol. 2, 1999. http://ala.org/aasl/SLMR/vol2/authentic.html

Holland, Holly. "Reaching All Learners: You've Got to Know Them to Show Them." *Middle Ground* (April 2000): 10-13.

Indiana Academic Standards. http://www.doe.state.in.us/standards/welcome2.html

Kuhlthau. Carol C. "Implementing a Process Approach to Information Literacy: A Study Identifying Indicators of Success in Library Media Programs." *School Library Media Quarterly* 22, no. 1 (Fall 1993). http://www.ala.org/aasl/SLMR/slmr_resources/select_kuhlthau1.html

Loertscher, David V. *Taxonomies of the School Library Media Program.* 2nd ed. San Jose, California: Hi Willow Research and Publishing, 2000.

A Planning Guide for Information Power: Building Partnerships for Learning. Chicago: American Association of School Librarians, 1999.

Wisconsin Education Media Association, with additional scenarios by Paula Montgomery. "Information Literacy: A Position Paper on Information Problem Solving." American Association of School Librarians, 1993, 1999. http://www.ala.org/aasl/postitions/ps_infolit.html

Wolcott, Linda Lachance. "Understanding How Teachers Plan: Strategies for Successful Instructional Partnerships." *School Library Media Quarterly* 22, no. 3 (Spring 1994). http://www.ala.org/aasl/SLMR/slmr_resources/select_wolcott.html

Student Inquiry in the Research Process

Part 2: Inquiry Research Orientation

by Leslie B. Preddy

This and future installments of the "Student Inquiry in the Research Process" series are devoted to a concrete, hands-on, classroom teacher/library media specialist collaborative model for implementing the inquiry approach to the research process into the classroom and school library media center.

Inquiry Research Orientation

Inquiry research begins with the orientation phase. Orientation is building the foundation of knowledge, which gives the teachers and students a point of reference for the topic. The topic that will be used for the inquiry is found in the curriculum, standards, and textbooks. The curriculum, classroom lessons, discussions, and lectures lead to the student inquiry. Educators give students the background information necessary to successfully begin and complete investigative activities. It is essential to student success to give students enough background knowledge of the topic so that they can develop questions for the inquiry.

One key to building a successful foundation is for the classroom teacher and library media specialist to agree upon a common language as they plan collaboratively. Students will become distracted and confused easily if different educators refer to the same issues in instruction in different ways and with different key words, especially if it is a new concept for students. For example, what terms will you use to refer to the process of locating information in a book? What terms will you use in relation to analyzing a source for facts, opinions, bias, and understanding?

Be willing to alter the sequence and scope of activities and lessons based on the cognitive abilities of the students. Some classes may be more successful during the orientation phase if the process is adapted to their

Leslie B. Preddy is library media specialist at Perry Meridian Middle School in Indianapolis, IN. E-mail: lpreddy@msdpt.k12.in.us "Student Inquiry in the Research Process" (http://ntserver1.msdpt.k12.in.us/etspages/pm/imc/Inquiry/index.htm) was developed with a grant from the Indiana Department of Education-Office of Learning Resources based on the elements of information inquiry designed by Dr. Daniel Callison, Indiana University, and LMS Associates.

needs by the educator facilitating class discussions instead of using individual worksheets. Allow the students to make decisions and develop ownership of their learning as a group.

Research Journal

An organizational journal is indispensable when teaching students of any age how to research. A research journal is a tool used to help students develop enough structure to organize their thoughts and activities while still allowing for creativity and independent thinking. It can be made out of many things: folder, notebook, large envelope, or three-ring binder.

The research journal contains the expressly written guidelines, expectations, activities, and deadlines. The classroom teacher and library media specialist should brainstorm and plan together to develop a research journal that is appropriate for the age/grade level, resource, and project, and suits the educators' teaching styles.

Together, the class reviews the entire contents of the research journal before the inquiry research begins. The journal will be submitted at the end of the inquiry for a grade. It will be used to evaluate the student's organization skills and completion of all steps of inquiry, as well as a reference for educators when grading the process and evaluating the final product.

Timeline

The classroom teacher and library media specialist jointly develop a timeline for the project. The timeline clearly states for students a daily schedule of events: where they will be working, when things are due, on what work to focus, etc. If possible, during the intensive investigative phase of the inquiry, research on alternate days or only use part of the week for the research. This will give the classroom teacher and the library media specialist time to review the research journals and provide feedback, follow-up, and remediation as necessary. Spacing out the research time also will provide students with the opportunity to remove themselves from the process, which is often how clarity and brainstorms occur for emergent inquirers.

Journal Checklist

Students will keep everything they do related to the inquiry in their research journals, which allows the educator and students to be more organized and therefore allows for more time on task. The journal checklist will give the student a detailed list of what needs to be kept in the journal, so that there is a concrete understanding from the beginning of what the educator expectations are: timeline, classroom lecture and discussion notes, all inquiry worksheets, rubrics, notes for every source used, daily reflections, primary sources, peer evaluation, storyboard, annotated bibliography, self-evaluation, etc.

Process Rubric

Develop the mindset that the process is important and should be evaluated just like the final product. Incorporate those expectations into a rubric for the purpose of evaluation.

Product Rubric

Educators are strongly encouraged not to share what the final product options are until the research time has almost concluded. In this way, students will be focused on finding the answers to their research questions, instead of what they will produce. Throughout inquiry, student ownership of what is being learned is vital, so one adaptation that can be made is that each class, with the educator's facilitation, develops their own rubric for evaluating the final product.

Pre-Searching Activities

Students will select a topic of inquiry following a method of pre-searching, as developed by Virginia Rankin. Pre-searching is preparing students for research with basic training and techniques that require an instruction time commitment from the classroom teacher and library media specialist, but will improve students' abilities to accept ownership for the process and to research independently.

Brainstorming

Brainstorming occurs after the class has been oriented to the curricular topic through classroom instruction. It requires focusing on what is all ready known about the topic. As a class, think about the broad curricular topic and write down every word that comes to mind related to that topic. Some words will be very broad in scope, others quite specific, and a few that may seem insignificant. All the words that students generate should be written down. The educator should not add or suggest any words. Next, students are given a large, general encyclopedia article related to the topic and a pre-search worksheet that will provide practice in finding citation information as well as skimming and note-taking. Walk students through finding and completing bibliographic information, and then provide a mini-lesson on how to skim a resource for information. Provide a limited amount of time for students to skim the article for more words to add to their brainstorm list. Once the allotted time is up, come together as a class to add words to the list previously created by the class.

Categories

Creating categories allows students to take a large topic and look at it in smaller components. Categorizing takes the brainstormed list of words and organizes them into logical groupings. The class, as a group, generates broad categories from the brainstorming list into which most or all of the words will fall. Group words by a common characteristic and give each category a name. Individuals, small groups, or an entire class may place the brainstorm words into the categories. Some words may be applicable to more than one category.

Questioning

Ownership of learning begins with students developing their own researchable questions. This can be done as individual students, small groups, or an educator-led classroom discussion. Developing a researchable question that is age-appropriate, is answerable, and can be answered with the resources available is an acquired skill that requires time and patience on behalf of the educator. The first time in a school year that the classroom teacher and library media specialist work with a particular group of students to develop those researchable questions will require a lot of attention and focus devoted to the orientation phase of inquiry research.

Give students an opportunity to review the category names and contents. Each student should think about which category/categories are interesting and what he or she already knows about that category. Using basic question starters of who, what, when, where, why, and how, the students begin developing questions related to the category in which they're interested. These should be questions to which they don't already have the answer, but would like to find the answer. Even though this is the developmental stage of formulating questions, students should think in terms of questions that are interesting enough to them that their interest will be held long enough to complete the research. (See sample questioning worksheets, page 26.)

The classroom teacher and library media specialist should jointly review students' questioning worksheets in order to gain a better understanding of students' independent questioning levels.

Skimming for Information

Skimming and scanning for information is a method to be introduced in the orientation phase and reviewed and reinforced throughout the inquiry process. When introducing skimming skills, develop an overhead or poster with key skimming and scanning for information terms listed. Allow time for a mini-lesson to instruct students on what each applicable term is and where or how to find it in a traditional resource. Allow each student to have a resource, and walk them through, as a class, the who, what, when, where, why, and how

—Continued

for each skimming and scanning term. Allocate time in the mini-lesson for students to locate each skimming tool within the resource.

```
┌─────────────────────────────────────────────────────┐
│ Skim & Scan for Information                           │
│ Things to look for:                                   │
│ Contents page              Charts                     │
│ Index                      Graphs                     │
│ Your Inquiry Research Keywords  Statistics            │
│ Guidewords                 Summary Boxes              │
│ Words in Bold or Italics   Timeline/Chronology        │
│ Pictures and Captions      Glossary                   │
└─────────────────────────────────────────────────────┘
```

Conclusion

This has been an overview of the first of a five-phase inquiry research process that includes Orientation, Exploration, Strategy, Investigation, and Conclusion and Reflection. In the next installment of "Student Inquiry in the Research Process," hands-on strategies for the Exploration and Strategy phases will be introduced.

Suggested Readings on Inquiry in the Research Process:

Callison, Daniel. "Questioning." *School Library Media Activities Monthly* 12, no. 6 (February 1997): 30-32.

Callison, Daniel. "Schema and Problem-Solving." *School Library Media Activities Monthly* 14, no. 9 (May 1998): 43-45.

References:

Duncan, Donna, and Laura Lockhart. *I-Search, You Search, We All Learn to Research.* New York: Neal-Schuman, 2000.

"First Steps in Library Research: The Pre-Search Presented by Pre-Search Creator Virginia Rankin." *Library Instruction Round Table.* American Library Association, 1992. Video program: 20 min.

Kramer, Kym, library media specialist. Fishback Creek Public Academy/Elementary, Indianapolis. Interview. January 11, 2001.

Langhorne, Mary Jo, ed. *Developing an Information Literacy Program K-12.* New York: Neal-Schuman, 1998.

Rankin, Virginia. *The Thoughtful Researcher: Teaching the Research Process to Middle School Students.* Englewood, CO: Libraries Unlimited, 1999.

Stanley, Deborah B. *Practical Steps to the Research Process for High School.* Englewood, CO: Libraries Unlimited, 1999.

Questioning Worksheet Samples

Secondary

```
┌──────────────────────────────────────────────────────┐
│ NAME: _____ DATE: _____             │
│                                                       │
│                   Questioning                         │
│                                                       │
│ General Topic we have been studying:                  │
│ _____          │
│                                                       │
│ One category that really interests me:                │
│ _____          │
│                                                       │
│ This category interests me because:                   │
│ _____          │
│ _____          │
│                                                       │
│ List all the questions for this category to which I   │
│ don't already have the answer:                        │
│                                                       │
│                                                       │
│                                                       │
│ One category that really interests me:                │
│ _____          │
│                                                       │
│ This category interests me because:                   │
│ _____          │
│ _____          │
│                                                       │
│ List all the questions for this category to which I   │
│ don't already have the answer:                        │
│                                                       │
│                                                       │
│                                                       │
│ At home tonight, discuss with your family your two    │
│ category choices. Listen to your family's suggestions │
│ and ideas. Think about it.                            │
└──────────────────────────────────────────────────────┘
```

Elementary

```
┌──────────────────────────────────────────────────────┐
│ NAME: _____                │
│                                                       │
│                   Questioning                         │
│                                                       │
│ In class, I learned about                             │
│ _____          │
│ _____          │
│ _____          │
│                                                       │
│ I am still curious. I want to learn more about        │
│ _____          │
│ _____          │
│ _____          │
│                                                       │
│ One question I have is                                │
│ _____          │
│ _____          │
│ _____          │
│                                                       │
│ One question I have is                                │
│ _____          │
│ _____          │
│ _____          │
│                                                       │
│ Tonight, I'm going to show this to my family. We will │
│ talk about my ideas and what I am learning.           │
│                                                       │
│ My family thinks                                      │
│ _____          │
│ _____          │
│ _____          │
│ _____          │
│ _____          │
└──────────────────────────────────────────────────────┘
```

Student Inquiry in the Research Process

Part 3:
Inquiry Research and Strategy

by Leslie B. Preddy

This and future installments of the "Student Inquiry in the Research Process" series are devoted to a concrete, hands-on, classroom teacher/library media specialist collaborative model for implementing the inquiry approach to the research process into the classroom and school library media center.

Inquiry Research Exploration & Strategy

Student inquiry in the research process begins with an orientation phase where students are learning about a theme in the curriculum and how to narrow that theme into a specific interest of inquiry. From there, students move toward the exploration and strategy phases where, based on an interest that has developed through curriculum and instruction, inquiry develops into research questions that are refined based on available resources and the ability level of each individual student.

Exploration

A key role in information inquiry is allowing each student to take a leadership role and ownership of what will be learned and researched by developing his or her own, personalized interest in the topic through question development. National education and state subject areas have standards written with the expectation, either clearly stated or implied, that students develop the ability to create age-appropriate, researchable questions. This is a learned task that may be difficult to teach students whose research skills have been cultivated in a traditional environment of having an assignment handed to them with a specific topic to research as well as exactly what details must be found and how findings

Leslie B. Preddy is a library media specialist at Perry Meridian Middle School in Indianapolis, IN. E-mail lpreddy@msdpt.k12.in.us "Student Inquiry in the Research Process" (http://www.msdpt.k12.in.us/etspages/pm/imc/Inquiry/index.htm?1025700207264) was developed with a grant from the Indiana Department of Education-Office of Learning Resources based on the elements of information inquiry designed by Dr. Daniel Callison, Indiana University, and LMS Associates.

should be reported. This scenario causes learning to occur in an artificial environment that does not allow for students to develop the ability to analyze, internalize, and interpret information critically, efficiently, creatively, or effectively.

Exploration is when a curricular topic is explored as students cultivate a topic for inquiry. Fostering interest begins with learning how to develop a topic into questions for inquiry. This will require a lot of attention and class time initially, but as the school year progresses, each subsequent inquiry will require less time devoted to exploring and developing questions. The classroom teacher and library media specialist will need to work as a team to help students come to terms with their topics and what questions are not only of interest, but also researchable with the resources and information available.

In the final step of the exploration phase, students combine and narrow preliminary questions down to the ones that interest them the most. The classroom teacher and library media specialist review these refined questions before the next inquiry session. The educators spend that evening reviewing all questions and recommending changes and/or revisions. Students take these helpful hints for success from the classroom teacher or library media specialist and write a final draft of the selected questions on a strategy sheet as the students move toward the next phase of inquiry research, Strategy.

Contract

The classroom teacher and library media specialist jointly develop a contract to share with students during the exploration phase of inquiry research. The contract is a vital tool for communicating to parents the role that research will be taking in their child's life.

The contract includes a simplified rubric with clearly stated, minimal expectations for the parent and child to review together. The rubric outlines in general terms basic, satisfactory, and proficient guidelines for student work in effort, information inquiry, written product, oral presentation, final product or project, bibliography, and research journal. Knowing these expectations in advance provides another opportunity for the student to take ownership of his or her learning. Requiring the contract be taken home, reviewed, and signed by a parent provides the guardian with an advance glimpse of where his or her child's efforts will be focused for the immediate future.

Strategy

The strategy gives students the opportunity to become more aware of the information world as they learn about a variety of resources, traditional and nontraditional, and select those that are most appropriate for answering each specific question of inquiry.

To develop a strategy, students take the questions created and revised in the exploration phase, remove the least appealing question, and refine what is left into a strategy. This encourages a student to have some personal thought and internalize his or her research actions.

Strategy intentionally allows students the opportunity to finalize research questions. This is when the educator helps students formulate key words related to each question that will be used to locate information in a resource as well as when skimming and scanning for information in that resource. This is an excellent opportunity for educators to introduce or review the variety of formats of information and resources. Take time to show students how to look at each individual question and make an educated guess as to which resource types might be best to use initially as an answer to the question being attempted. Require the student to internalize his or her decision by explaining why he or she thinks those specific resource types might be best for answering that specific question.

INFORMATION TOOLS	
Almanac	Map
Atlas	Museum*
Audio	Museum Curator*
Autobiography*	Newspaper Article
Biography	Nonfiction
CD-ROM	Online Database
Chart	Organizations
Diary* or Journal*	People
Dictionary	Photograph*
Distance Learning*	Political Cartoon
Encyclopedia	Public Library
Illustration	Questionnaire*
Internet	Survey*
Interview*	Television
Letter*	Timeline
Magazine	Video
*example of a Primary Source	

Daily Reflection

Provide students an occasion every day for self-analysis. Giving students this chance to reflect personally on

what he or she is doing, thinking, and still needs to do is an invaluable use of instructional time. Toward the end of each research session, provide the students ample time for detailed response to age-appropriate and intellectually suitable questions similar to the following:

- What did I do today?
- What question was I trying to answer?
- What problem, if any, did I have today?
- Explain something new I learned (for example, successfully learning a new research technique, how to use a specific resource or a resource never used before, something I didn't know about my topic).
- New questions that I now have about my topic.
- People that helped me today and what they did to help (teacher, student, parent, sibling, library media specialist, etc.).
- How do I feel about today?
- What do I need to do next?

The library media specialist and/or classroom teacher should collect the Daily Reflections every day during information inquiry in order to read through them each evening. At least one comment should be placed on each Daily Reflection before it is returned to the student the next school day. By not being hypercritical, educators will allow students the comfort and personal growth experience of knowing that they may place any personal feelings on the Daily Reflection, even if those feelings are critical of an educator, the instruction, or the assignment. This is an opportunity for educators to quickly understand what a student's current research ability level is, as well as where weaknesses in instruction exist. Employing this step will help the educators know whether a student is doing okay, requires remediation of particular research techniques, is growing frustrated and needs help, deserves a pat on the back for being excited about something new that he or she has learned about the topic or learned to do, or needs some emotional encouragement and is feeling discouraged. A Daily Reflection aids the educator with understanding the classroom research climate and quickly establishes a need to either remediate the class with a review of a particular skill or advance to more complicated research and inquiry skills.

Conclusion

During the Inquiry Exploration Phase and Strategy Phase is when the educators and students instinctively feel the need to discuss the outcome, or what final product will be required at the conclusion of the research. Save this excitement by discussing what the final product will be, the expectations related to the final product, and the product rubric until the final phase of the research, which is when the students actually will begin working on the product. Be prepared to respond to students who may be frustrated the first time an educator withholds the details of the concluding product.

Gathering the information is separate from analyzing it. During exploration and strategy, educators need to reinforce with students that finding the answers to

—Continued

their research questions should be the focus. Each student needs the opportunity to learn that research requires hard work, focus, and dedication. Allowing students to concentrate on and worry about the end product before the research has even begun is detrimental to developing information literacy and instilling a lifelong desire and pleasure of learning for the sake of learning.

Suggested Readings on Inquiry in the Research Process:

Callison, Daniel. "Questioning." *School Library Media Activities Monthly* 8, no. 6 (February 1997): 30-32.

Pappas, Marjorie. "Learning Communities." *School Library Media Activities Monthly* 15, no. 7 (March 1999): 30-32.

Rankin, Virginia. "The Thought that Counts: Six Skills that Help Kids Turn Notes into Knowledge." *School Library Journal* 45, no. 8 (August 1999): 26-29.

References:

"First Steps in Library Research: The Pre-Search Presented by Pre-Search Creator Virginia Rankin." *Library Instruction Round Table.* American Library Association, 1992. Video program: 20 min.

Kramer, Kym, library media specialist. Fishback Creek Public Academy/Elementary, Indianapolis. Interview. January 11, 2001.

Lincoln Public Schools Guide to Integrated Information Literacy Skills. Lincoln, Nebraska: Lincoln Public Schools.

Rankin, Virginia. *The Thoughtful Researcher: Teaching the Research Process to Middle School Students.* Englewood, CO: Libraries Unlimited, 1999.

Student Inquiry in the Research Process

Part 4:
Inquiry Research Investigation

by Leslie B. Preddy

This, past, and future installments of the "Student Inquiry in the Research Process" series are devoted to a concrete, hands-on, classroom teacher/library media specialist collaborative model for implementing the inquiry approach to the research process into the classroom and school library media center.

The Investigation Phase

The Investigation Phase is when a student is engaged authentically in using investigative research methods as the student attempts to find answers to inquiry questions. Think of the information inquiry task as an investigation, or systematic examination, not a traditional school research assignment. During the investigation a student should be expected to think about what he or she is doing and learning as a variety of sources are used to try to find answers to inquiry questions.

Educators and students need to look beyond the confines of a traditional source to find answers to inquiry questions. Students will be expected to understand what primary sources and secondary sources are, and when it is best to use each. Students will need to receive guidance on how to interpret primary sources and how a primary source can be significant for the further understanding of a topic. Train students how to conduct an interview, survey, or questionnaire. Research sessions should conclude with a daily reflection (daily reflection is further explained in last month's issue of *School Library Media Activities Monthly*).

The library media specialist and classroom teacher should observe and note students with certain abilities

Leslie B. Preddy is a library media specialist at Perry Meridian Middle School in Indianapolis, IN. E-mail lpreddy@msdpt.k12.in.us
"Student Inquiry in the Research Process" (http://www.msdpt. k12.in.us/etspages/pm/imc/Inquiry/index.htm?1025700207264) was developed with a grant from the Indiana Department of Education-Office of Learning Resources based on the elements of information inquiry designed by Dr. Daniel Callison, Indiana University, and LMS Associates.

and have the students share their expertise with students that need help in that particular area.

Source Notes

Information inquiry means dynamically thinking about and being engaged actively in the quest for knowledge. This requires students to not only relate citation information and take notes, but also to think about the usefulness of the source. As educators, we can no longer assume that students are thinking past gathering information; we must require the student to think beyond. Students will use source notes to store citation information, notes, data, interpretation, analysis, hypothesis, thoughts, ideas, and concerns. The process of using a source should conclude with the student summarizing the source, what was most useful about the source, and what was most difficult about using the source. Educators will instruct students on how to read for understanding, take notes, and evaluate whether a source is useful. These are key skills that need to become imbedded in students so that they can become independent learners.

Based on findings and personal insights, students will meet with either the library media specialist or classroom teacher and discuss the need to adjust questions, or develop new ones for further inquiry or re-analysis. As Virginia Rankin, in *The Thoughtful Researcher*, says, "Sometimes an answer itself becomes the topic for consideration."

Primary Sources

A primary source is a firsthand or direct source. It may be a significant or historical document without interpretation or explanation. It may be a person who was actually a participant or observer. It may be a person's journal diary, letter, or memoir. It may be a historic home, site, or artifact. It may be mass media: a film, video, audio, or photograph taken at the time or place documenting what happened. It may be a book, magazine, or newspaper article published/written at a particular time in history about an event occurring at that time. It may be a correspondence or interview of someone who was there for an event. Primary sources can be accessed through an agency, archive, book, distance learning, e-mail, exhibit, government entity, historic site, library, monument, museum, organization, primary source website, questionnaire, report, speech, or survey.

When looking at a primary document, the student needs to think about the beliefs, opinions, political climate, and scientific and medical knowledge of that time and place. There are key issues to keep in mind when reviewing and evaluating a primary source, although not every question is appropriate for every primary source:

- What type/kind of primary source is it? (Photograph, Letter, Speech, etc.)
- Who wrote, designed, built, created, or published it? What was his or her name(s), if you know? How was the person(s) significant?
- Who were the key participants?
- Who was the intended audience?
- Who lived in, visited, read, or heard it?
- For what was it used?
- Why did they? What was their motive?
- When did they?
- Where was it written/designed/created?
- What was occurring locally at the time?
- What was occurring around the world at the time?
- What sort of impact did it have locally? Globally?
- How does it impact us today?
- What are the facts about it that are important to your inquiry research?

Interview

Instruction for interviewing etiquette and procedures should be reviewed before a student conducts an interview. Either a parent or educator should assist a student in locating an appropriate interviewee and scheduling the interview. All interviewees and interview questions should be approved by the school library media specialist or classroom teacher before the interview takes place. The interview can be handled through distance learning/videoconference, letter, e-mail, fax, or telephone.

Who should a student interview? Choose somebody that is well-respected, educated, and informed about the topic. When contacting the person to see if they are willing to participate in an interview, identify the project, the school, and the grade level. Explain what the assignment is, why his or her input is needed, and what will be done with the information.

What does a student ask? The questions asked should be questions that the student has not been able to find the answer to through other research means. The questions should not be answerable with a simple yes or no and should never be personal or embarrassing for the interviewee. An educator should review questions for appropriateness and authenticity before the interview.

How should the interview be conducted? All ques-

tions should be prepared in advance. The student should listen carefully to the answers given, without interrupting, and take notes that are legible and include the key ideas. Whenever necessary, the student should repeat what was said for clarification to confirm that he or she understood correctly. Students should write down the words exactly if it will be used as a quote, and should ask for names or words not known to be spelled or explained.

Immediately following the interview, the student should review all notes from the interview and transcribe them. Any interview should conclude with a thank you letter from the student detailing his or her appreciation and explaining how much the interview helped with a better understanding of the topic.

Community Resources

The library media specialist and classroom teacher should develop and annually update a packet of primary resources in the community specifically created to aid parents and students. The packet should include community resources, sites and museums, and Internet resources. The handout of "Resources in the Community" should be an annotated list of specific and general primary resources in the community appropriate to the topic to suggest to students. Include as many specifics as appropriate: address, phone, available hours, requirements and cost for admission/use, contact name, Internet address, e-mail address, etc. Before distributing the packet to parents and students, educators should regularly update and confirm the information for each resource. Be sure to include any necessary updates to the hours of operation, fees, and other operational details. Also include an annotation of the organization's procedures, policies, and resources available to the public that relate to the general curricular topic upon which the student's inquiry is based.

Storyboard

Toward the conclusion of the investigation, students will begin to organize their thoughts and information. As the research is drawing to a close, share with students for the first time what their final product options are for presenting their newfound expertise.

Collaboratively, educators should guide students through the process of selecting the appropriate product for their inquiry. Be creative about final product options to provide for a variety of learning styles and for student choice. The library media specialist and classroom teacher should want the student to share in a way that provides the opportunity for each individual to be successful. While working on how to disseminate the information, students answer:

- Who is my audience? With whom will I be sharing my product?
- What is the best way to share my knowledge? What should my written, verbal, and/or visual product be?
- Why do I think this will be the best way for me to share my expertise?

As students select a final product format, each stu-

—Continued

dent will complete a storyboard for an activity/graphic, static display, or writing as appropriate to help with organization. A storyboard is something that students can easily relate to when put into the perspective of how filmmakers use a storyboard to lay out the sequence of events for a film or cartoon. The storyboard provides the necessary structure a student requires as he or she begins to get the research in order. A storyboard will work as a blueprint and allow students to draft a general idea for how to present inquiry findings before actually beginning the final product. The storyboard should be completed in preparation for the peer conference, while there is still research time available, since completing the storyboard may help a student realize gaps in the information that need further investigation.

Peer Conference

Students will think about what others are learning and assist fellow students through an informal conference where students can share what has been learned and give advice for what needs to be done. A peer conference gives students an opportunity to verbalize the research and product in a nonthreatening setting. This process is done while there is still research time available and before the final product is created. Through sharing the source notes and storyboard with a peer, a student will synthesize the inquiry through an informal presentation and discussion with a peer, relating both what he or she has learned and concluded through the investigation. The peer will interact to help the student understand what needs more clarification and what may be confusing to an outsider about his or her newfound expertise.

The library media specialist or classroom teacher will give the necessary guidance on how to evaluate a peer productively and positively during the conference. Students will need to understand how to be respectful of a peer's feelings, ideas, and research. Teach students how to accept constructive criticism and listen to advice in a positive and accepting manner. While the peer being evaluated is summarizing his or her research and storyboard, the reviewer should be thinking about:

- Does your peer seem to care about and be interested in the topic? How did your peer make you feel about the topic?
- Did your peer support the information with research? Were there supporting facts and/or examples?
- What could your peer do to help others understand the topic? Give suggestions for improving facts and information.
- What was organized well? What was confusing?
- On the storyboard, what was most effective? What was least effective?

Just like a student would take notes during an interview or on a source note, the student should take notes about what his or her peer suggests is good and bad with the research and storyboard. Upon completion of the peer conference, the student should decide what advice is worth taking, i.e., what changes the stu-

dent will make and what needs further research based on his or her peer's advice.

Conclusion

The Investigation Phase is when a student is most likely to become lost or lose focus. The classroom teacher and library media specialist should work together to reduce that risk. Incorporate before- or after-school help sessions in the library media center. Conference and consult with students needing guidance. Remain vigilant and facilitate impromptu help sessions and tutoring for those in need. Regularly check student's notes, research journals, and daily reflections. Take action as necessary for off-track individuals, groups, or classes.

Educators will need to be observant of research challenges. Educators should notice students with inquiry questions that are difficult to answer with the resources available to them. Information challenges will need to be taken into account when evaluating the final product and research process. Students that fight to find the answers that are eluding them should not be penalized, but instead rewarded and encouraged for their tenacity.

Suggested Readings on Inquiry in the Research Process:

Callison, Daniel. "Key Words in Instruction: Analysis," *School Library Media Activities Monthly* 15, no. 8 (April 1999): 37-39.

Callison, Daniel. "Key Words in Instruction: Interview," *School Library Media Activities Monthly* 15, no. 7 (March 1999): 40-41, 44.

McDowell, Dan. "Process Guide #4: Primary Source Documents." http://projects.edtech.sandi.net/staffdev/tpss99/processguides/HowToPrimaryS.html. (Last accessed July 27, 2001).

Small, Ruth V., and Marilyn P. Arnone. "Website Quality: Do Students Know It When They See It?" *School Library Media Activities Monthly* 15, no. 6 (February 1999): 25-26, 30.

References:

Brooks, John I. "John I. Brooks III—Primary Source." http://register.uncfsu.edu/f_broos/Frms/WkbkP.htm (Last accessed July 27, 2001).

Duncan, Donna, and Laura Lockhart. *I-Search, You Search, We All Learn to Research.* New York: Neal-Schuman, 2000.

Joyce, Marilyn Z., and Julie I. Tallman. *Making the Writing and Research Connection with the I-Search Process.* New York: Neal-Schuman, 1997.

Langhorne, Mary Jo, ed. *Developing an Information Literacy Program K-12.* New York: Neal-Schuman, 1998.

Lincoln Public Schools Guide to Integrated Information Literacy Skills. Lincoln, NE: Lincoln Public Schools.

Rankin, Virginia. *The Thoughtful Researcher: Teaching the Research Process to Middle School Students.* Englewood, CO: Libraries Unlimited, 1999.

Stanley, Deborah B. *Practical Steps to the Research Process for Middle School.* Englewood, CO: Libraries Unlimited, 2000.

Stripling, Barbara K., and Judy M. Pitts. *Brainstorms and Blueprints: Teaching Library Research as a Thinking Process.* Englewood, CO: Libraries Unlimited, 1988.

Whitson, Bill. Revised by M. Phillips. "Library Research Using Primary Sources." http://www.lib.berkeley.edu/TeachingLib/Guides/PrimarySources.html (Last accessed July 27, 2001).

Student Inquiry in the Research Process

Part 5: Inquiry Research Conclusion & Reflection

by Leslie B. Preddy

This is the final installment of the "Student Inquiry in the Research Process" series. The series has been devoted to a concrete, hands-on, classroom teacher/library media specialist collaborative model for implementing the Information Inquiry approach to the research process into the classroom and school library media center.

Conclusion & Reflection

Students, classroom teachers, and library media specialists work hard throughout the inquiry process. The time has come to conclude the research journey. Research wraps up with the logical organization of information and development of a final product and presentation to fellow students, parents, and possibly even community members. The conclusion of the research, product development, and presentation is followed by reflection: reflection of peers, reflection of self, reflection of educators, and reflection upon the process. Using the inquiry research process means not only doing, but always thinking, analyzing, and internalizing the who, what, when, where, why, and how of what we did, and concluding with a sense of accomplishment.

Organization and Dissemination

As students move toward finalizing inquiry research, they will begin to organize their source notes in order to develop their storyboard (see "Student Inquiry in the Research Process, Part 4") into a final product. Organizing notes is an acquired talent that most have difficulty achieving.

No matter what their age, students need ongoing and repeated assistance getting and staying organized. With a research journal in hand, which should include all of their source notes, a large part of the organizational aspect of this monumental task has been accomplished. However, students must learn to prioritize and

Leslie B. Preddy is a library media specialist at Perry Meridian Middle School in Indianapolis, IN. E-mail lpreddy@msdpt.k12.in.us "Student Inquiry in the Research Process" (http://www.msdpt. k12.in.us/etspages/pm/imc/Inquiry/index.htm?1025700207264) was developed with a grant from the Indiana Department of Education-Office of Learning Resources based on the elements of information inquiry designed by Dr. Daniel Callison, Indiana University, and LMS Associates.

manage the material and notes they have collected. This is critical in getting the final product off to a successful start.

In order to develop a meaningful final product that is clearly based on the research questions a student developed, the classroom teacher and library media specialist will outline a few simple steps for a student to follow.

1. Each student should choose a large space that is conducive to his or her ability to focus in which to spread out work. The space may be a table, the floor, the public library, student's bed, or kitchen table. Whatever type and wherever the space is that makes the student most comfortable is as important as the need for it to be free of distraction. Workspace needs to be large enough to be able to spread out the contents of the research journal.

2. A student's strategy (see "Student Inquiry in the Research Process, Part 2") clearly states the initial, critical research questions. The completed strategy should be referred to in order to organize the source notes into stacks by inquiry research question. This also will give the student a clear indication of whether each question was answered, answered adequately, and whether a question generated another question for consideration that now should be included in the final product.

3. Once the source notes are organized into piles by strategic question, notes should be read. One pile at a time, the question and each and every source note the student wrote related to that question should be read.

4. Once all source notes for a question are read, the student needs to put himself or herself in reflective mode and think about each note that was written. The student should give him or herself an opportunity to digest each word, concept, thought, and fact that at some point the student thought was important in the information gathering process, but may or may not be important now as he or she thinks of organizing the gathered data into a final product.

5. After reflecting on all the information gathered for a particular question, the student should retain only the information that still seems important and answered the intended question thoroughly, thoughtfully, and with some personal insight. The question a student should

be asking himself or herself is whether the information that seemed important enough to write down when taking notes is still vital now that the final product is being developed.

6. Once the student has thoroughly weighed the information gathered related to a question, he or she should disregard, or get rid of, any information that no longer seems useful or important. This can be done mentally or by using a pencil to draw a line gently through words on a source note that no longer seem important.

7. Steps three through six should be repeated until all organized source note piles have been reviewed.

Once the notes have been thoroughly reviewed, the final product can be constructed based on the drafted storyboard (see "Student Inquiry in the Research Process, Part 4"), the information remaining in the source notes, and a student's learning style and creativity. Within the final product, the student should be answering his or her initial, strategic inquiry questions. Each student also should be expected to detail the research adventure. Could all questions be answered, or could they be answered to the student's or educator's satisfaction? Finally, as part of the reporting process, the student should be able to explain intelligently, as age-appropriate, what efforts were made and research challenges faced.

Peer Evaluation

A key component to information inquiry is the opportunity to present the research quest and final product to a peer or peers who will evaluate the final product and research openly, honestly, and critically. Ideally, the peer, or peers, also should have been through the inquiry research process. Dissemination of knowledge occurs with the presentation of the final product, which may, and should, include an oral reporting aspect. People often learn best by teaching, so giving students an opportunity to reverse teacher-student roles and become the instructor expands the opportunity for growth and learning to occur exponentially. A student always needs feedback from the library media specialist and classroom teacher, but inquiry research demands a third party, a peer reviewer, to also critique the product, presentation, and process.

There are vital questions that a student needs answered in order to learn successfully from the adventure and digest suggestions for ways to improve future ventures. Without this piece, a means to improving future research will be lost. A student needs to know not only what needed to be improved, but also what was done well. It is important for a student to understand where his or her talents are, which may be different than what he or she always has assumed. It also is important to know what he or she needs to put effort toward in order to become more successful in future endeavors. Peer evaluators should respond to the following questions:

- What appear to be your peer's researching strengths?
- What was done well in the presentation?
- What was done well in the final project's product?
- What did your peer seem to know best about his or

her research topic?
- At the conclusion of the presentation, was the peer able to summarize the topic?
- What were your opinions of your peer's inquiry topic before the presentation?
- What were your opinions of your peer's inquiry topic after the presentation?

Peer Evaluation			
OVERALL			
Adequate coverage of topic	needs improvement	satisfactory	excellent
The student theory/thesis is clear	needs improvement	satisfactory	excellent
Includes supporting facts & examples	needs improvement	satisfactory	excellent
Supported information with research	needs improvement	satisfactory	excellent
Does he/she seem to care about topic	needs improvement	satisfactory	excellent
Organization	needs improvement	satisfactory	excellent
Spelling, Grammar, Punctuation	needs improvement	satisfactory	excellent
Understandable annotated bibliography	needs improvement	satisfactory	excellent
ORAL PRESENTATION			
The oral presentation begins well	needs improvement	satisfactory	excellent
The oral presentation ends well	needs improvement	satisfactory	excellent
Able to hold audience interest	needs improvement	satisfactory	excellent
Spoke loudly, clearly, & with expression	needs improvement	satisfactory	excellent
Eye contact with audience	needs improvement	satisfactory	excellent
FINAL PROJECT/PRESENTATION			
The final project/product is organized	needs improvement	satisfactory	excellent
Final project/product is neat	needs improvement	satisfactory	excellent
Final project/product is creative, colorful	needs improvement	satisfactory	excellent
Original work (not plagiarized)	needs improvement	satisfactory	excellent
Able to hold interest	needs improvement	satisfactory	excellent

Annotated Bibliography

One aspect of the concluding and reflecting phase of the inquiry process is for the student to complete an age-appropriate annotated bibliography. A student develops a bibliography in order to give credit to sources appropriately. A student annotates the bibliography in order to give in-depth thought to the source's content and ease of use, as well as personal thoughts and opinions of the source.

Educators should expect and plan for students that are uncomfortable with bibliographies. Developing an annotation may be a completely foreign experience for them, so the library media specialist and classroom teacher will need to devote time to introducing and reviewing with students how to develop a personalized and valuable annotation appropriate for each citation formulated.

Allow students a chance to draft out their citation and annotation on a worksheet similar to the example on page 26. It is important for students to be given the time to practice with the format, layout, and language necessary for a successful annotation and citation. It will take both the library media specialist and classroom teacher thoroughly explaining the how-to and circulating throughout the room during the rough drafting of the annotated bibliography in order to give students the one-on-one attention necessary for success.

The annotation is not intended to be complex, but instead thoughtful and personalized to each individual's experience with the source. Students can create an appropriate and useful annotation of two to three sentences by answering the following questions:

- What was the specific format of the source? (book, encyclopedia, interview, online database, questionnaire, survey, video, etc.) —Continued

- How did I find this source?
- Where did I find this source? (community, public library, school library media center, home, etc.)
- Generally, what kind of information could be found in the source?
- What information did I find in or with it that was important to me?
- What did I really like about this source?
- What did I find difficult about using this source?
- What are my personal feelings about this source?
- How might I use this source in the future?

```
┌─────────────────────────────────────────────┐
│             Annotated Bibliography            │
│ General topic we have been studying _____│
│ Specific topic I chose for my research _____│
│                                               │
│ • Citation #1                                 │
│ _____│
│ _____│
│        ANNOTATION: _____│
│ _____│
│ _____│
│                                               │
│ • Citation #2                                 │
│ _____│
│ _____│
│        ANNOTATION: _____│
│ _____│
│ _____│
│                                               │
│ • Citation #3                                 │
│ _____│
│ _____│
│        ANNOTATION: _____│
│ _____│
│ _____│
│ _____│
│                                               │
│          "Student Inquiry in the Research Process"  │
│ © 2002  Permission to Duplicate for Education Use Only  Leslie B. Preddy │
└─────────────────────────────────────────────┘
```

Rubrics

Assessment tools in the form of rubrics are the instrument used by both the educators and the students to gauge successes and failures in the process and product. *Information Literacy Standards for Student Learning* (1998) defines rubrics as "a scaled set of criteria that clearly defines for the student and the teacher what a range of acceptable and unacceptable performance looks like." Rubrics take the guesswork out of evaluating student work and progress by describing expected behavior and action. Expectations for excellence and quality are established and shared with students beforehand. Educators should share samples of prior students' excellent, average, and poor work. Students know what grade or points each level of effort will procure for them because the rubric includes criteria for what the educator thinks is exemplary, satisfactory, and unacceptable. An educator's goal for using a rubric as an assessment tool should be to give a student the opportunity to understand the teacher's guidelines and expectations clearly.

Inquiry lends itself admirably to assessing the research process as well as the final product and presentation. The research process is more important, and should be given more weight in grading, than the final prod-

uct. The final product is a byproduct, and the actual true measure of learning should be the research process of finding, analyzing, internalizing, and interpreting information in a logical and coherent fashion. It is challenging to put concrete measures, necessary and expected by parents, students, and fellow educators, on a process. A tangible tool, like the research journal (see "Student Inquiry in the Research Process, Part 2"), is an invaluable measure of the process. Giving concrete significance of the process can be created with a rubric or checklist that empowers and values the research process by requiring the use of a research journal and using the contents of the journal (which contains all worksheets, handouts, daily reflections, peer and self-evaluations, etc.) and educator observations throughout the process of on-task, age-appropriate behavior. These are standards by which to measure progress and process.

The final product and presentation should be evaluated for accuracy, consistency, quality, analysis, supporting evidence, organization, referencing, and the ability to answer the strategy questions. A four-point rubric, with zero equaling no effort and four excellent could be used when evaluating the final product for:
- written—technical and content;
- oral—technical and presentation; and
- product—artistic/aesthetic and technical content.

Self Evaluation

Every student should complete a self-evaluation in order to gain a better understanding of the process and the quality of the final product, as well as who he or she was before the inquiry and what he or she has become. Self-evaluation is not a simple task. The classroom teacher and the library media specialist need to provide students thorough training on evaluating themselves critically, analytically, and compassionately. Students must be taught how to be detailed and use supporting evidence for the evaluation to have merit and offer the potential for self-growth.

Students should respond to the following questions in a thoughtful, reflective, and professional manner.
- What did I learn about my topic that I didn't know before? If I had more time, what would I still like to learn about my topic?
- What was my best and worst research question? Why do I think it was the best/worst?
- Which question helped me find really interesting information? What was it about this question that led to such interesting information? Why do I think the information was so interesting?
- How did I know for what information to look? What did I learn about how to find information that I can use again?
- What source or type of source did I find most and least useful? What was good/bad about it?
- What source or type of source did I use that I had never used before? How did I find it? How did I learn how to use it? What was good/bad about it?
- What community resources did I use? How did they help?

- When searching for information in the future, what would I do differently and what would I do the same?
- What part of the research journal was most useful and helped me stay on task?
- What did I do very well this time? What aspect of the instruction helped me the most?
- What could I do better next time? What would help me do better next time?
- Which people (students and/or adults) were most helpful? How did they help?
- What made my work better this time? When was I most creative?
- Do I like my final project? Do I like my final presentation? Why or why not? What would I do differently and what would I do the same?

Conclude the self-evaluation segment with each student writing an essay detailing the inquiry experience. Included in the essay should be the step-by-step of what the student did, the technical how-to of what was learned, and the personalized experiences of the student.

Self Evaluation			
The books I used were	helpful	a little helpful	no help
The Internet was	helpful	a little helpful	no help
My teacher was	helpful	a little helpful	no help
My library media specialist was	helpful	a little helpful	no help
My partner was	helpful	a little helpful	no help
Nontraditional resources were	helpful	a little helpful	no help
Resources in my community were	helpful	a little helpful	no help
My research on my project was	okay	better than usual	my best
My effort was	okay	better than usual	my best
My writing was	okay	better than usual	my best
My oral presentation was	okay	better than usual	my best
My final project/product was	okay	better than usual	my best
My bibliography was	okay	better than usual	my best
My organization skills were	okay	better than usual	my best
I liked doing my project.	yes	somewhat	no

Educator Evaluation

At the conclusion of the inquiry process, students have an opportunity to evaluate honestly the inquiry research as a unit, the classroom teacher, and the library media specialist. An educator evaluation plays a pivotal role for students and teachers. This is the opportunity for students to make judgments and give biased opinions about the topic, the inquiry process, the product, and the educators. This is the students' chance to tell the educators what they really think without threat of recrimination. It is an opportunity for the educators to take an honest look at the assignment and instruction through the eyes of students. It gives the educators an opportunity to re-evaluate and re-examine instruction based on flaws and misconceptions outlined by students.

- Should this unit be taught again? Why do you feel that way?
- What was the best thing that your classroom teacher did? What was the least helpful? Was your teacher helpful, a little helpful, or no help?
- What was the best thing that your library media specialist did? What was the least helpful? Was your library media specialist helpful, a little helpful, or no help?
- Which research lesson was most helpful? What made it so helpful? When thinking about doing research in the future, was what you've learned and done for this research helpful, a little helpful, or no help?
- Which research lesson was least helpful? What do we need to do to make it better?
- What about the research journal was most helpful? What was least helpful? Overall, was your research journal helpful, a little help, or no help?
- Being honest with yourself and us, do you think there was enough time? Where was there too much? Where was there too little?
- What did we do well? What do we need to do better? What other suggestions and comments do you have for us?

Just as the classroom teacher and school library media specialist require students to evaluate each other, themselves, and the unit, the collaborating educators also must complete a self-evaluation in order to gain a better understanding of the process, the quality of instruction, and the collaborative roles. In order for the inquiry unit to have future merit, the educators must model expected behavior through an evaluation and offer further opportunity for self, collaborative, and professional growth.

- Will we teach this unit again? What did I/we do very well this time? What made it work well? What do we need to do better?
- Did we allow ourselves enough unit planning and collaborative planning time?
- What did students have difficulty doing properly that I/we may need to spend more time teaching in the future?
- What aspect of instruction did I/we do successfully? Which aspect of instruction do I/we need to improve?
- Was the instructional time appropriate? When was there too much? When was there too little?
- What part of the research journal was most useful to me/us when helping students through the process? To students? To evaluation?
- What was my favorite experience? What was my collaborative partner's favorite experience?
- What did I learn about myself when planning collaboratively? What were my strengths and weaknesses? How will my collaborative partner's strengths make up for my weaknesses in the future? How well did I work with my collaborator?
- What did I learn about my collaborative partner? What were my partner's strengths and weaknesses? How will my strengths make up for my collaborative partner's weaknesses in the future? How well did my collaborator work with me?
- Which community resources were most helpful and accommodating?
- Which sources did I/we find most helpful when working with students? Which sources could I/we not have lived without?

—Continued on page 51

Student Inquiry...

• What source, or type of source, was successful that I/we had never had a student use before?

Conclusion

Classroom teacher and library media specialist collaboration to teach information inquiry and student learning leave all involved with a sense of accomplishment and of overcoming a worthwhile challenge. Inquiry allows for reflection from everyone and provides an opportunity to analyze what happened in order to make decisions on what to do next time. Educators need to take the time to select examples, both good and bad, from all phases of the inquiry process for future reference. It allows an opportunity for students to show off by placing final products on display or hosting an open house function at which students can present their research process and findings to family, peers, and the community.

Using the Information Inquiry approach to research is a powerfully fulfilling experience for students and educators. As Julie Sumrall, Freshman Intensive English Teacher at Jefferson High School in Lafayette, Indiana, says, "Grading the final paper was not such an overwhelming task this year because I already knew the students had been successful. I knew they had learned something. They were familiar and comfortable with the library and the inquiry process. This was what was important to me and what I had struggled with in the past. The final written paper, then, became less a measure of learning." Information Inquiry lends itself admirably to assessing the research process as well as the final product and presentation. It develops skills in students that are taken to future projects, future grade levels, and continued into adulthood. It is the process, not the final product that is most important. As the conclusion and reflection phase of inquiry concludes, so too does the journey, a research adventure.

Suggested Readings on Inquiry in the Research Process:

Callison, Daniel. "Key Words in Instruction: Authentic Assessment." *School Library Media Activities Monthly* 14, no. 5 (January 1998): 42-43, 50.

Callison, Daniel. "Key Words in Instruction: Cooperative Learning." *School Library Media Activities Monthly* 14, no. 3 (November 1997): 39-42.

Callison, Daniel. "Key Words in Instruction: Rubrics." *School Library Media Activities Monthly* 17, no. 2 (October 2000): 34-36, 42.

Callison, Daniel. "Key Words in Instruction: Synthesis." *School Library Media Activities Monthly* 15, no. 10 (June 1999): 39-46.

References:

Callison, Daniel. Interview. July 17, 2001.

Feder-Feitel, Lisa. "Rubrics Are Red Hot!: What Rubrics Can Do for You and Your Students." *Creative Classroom* (November/December 2000): 54-56.

Information Literacy Standards for Student Learning. Chicago: American Library Association, 1998.

Joyce, Marilyn Z., and Julie I. Tallman. *Making the Writing and Research Connection with the I-Search Process.* New York: Neal-Schuman, 1997.

Langhorne, Mary Jo, ed. *Developing an Information Literacy Program K-12.* New York: Neal-Schuman, 1998.

Lincoln Public Schools Guide to Integrated Information Literacy Skills. Lincoln, NE: Lincoln Public Schools.

Rankin, Virginia. *The Thoughtful Researcher: Teaching the Research Process to Middle School Students.* Englewood, CO: Libraries Unlimited, 1999.

Stanley, Deborah B. *Practical Steps to the Research Process for High School.* Englewood, CO: Libraries Unlimited, 1999.

Stripling, Barbara K., and Judy M. Pitts. *Brainstorms and Blueprints: Teaching Library Research as a Thinking Process.* Englewood, CO: Libraries Unlimited, 1988

Sumrall, Julie. Interview. January 14, 2002.

Inquiry:
Inquiring Minds Want to Know

by Barbara Stripling

The old yellow journalism adage, "Inquiring minds want to know," actually has more than a kernel of truth to it. Both experience and research tell us that students engaged in inquiry are more motivated to pursue learning on their own than students who are fed pre-organized information that they are expected to remember. Inquiry lies at the heart of the new standards issued in 2007 by the American Association of School Librarians, entitled *Standards for the 21st-Century Learner*. To understand and implement the new standards, library media specialists need to have a clear conception of "inquiry" and its implications for teaching and learning through the library media center.

Inquiry is a process of learning that is driven by questioning, thoughtful investigating, making sense of information, and developing new understandings. It is cyclical in nature because the result of inquiry is not simple answers but deep understandings that often lead to new questions and further pursuit of knowledge. The goal of inquiry is not the accumulation of information; it is the exploration of significant questions and deep learning.

What is the difference between inquiry and information literacy?

The American Association of School Librarians (AASL) and the Association for Educational Communications and Technology (AECT) issued standards for information skills called *Information Literacy Standards for Student Learning* in 1998. These standards clearly outlined the skills necessary for students to access, evaluate, and use information; become information literate and independent learners; and display social responsibility in the use of information. The new 2007 standards broaden the concept of information literacy by incorporating the skills necessary for a more constructivist view of learning, in which students are empowered to ask meaningful questions and follow a path of discovery to construct their own understandings, draw conclusions, create new knowledge, and share their knowledge with others. These new standards emphasize that the questioning, critical thinking, and creative generation of new knowledge are as important to students' learning as their information finding.

Inquiry, as defined by the new standards, is a way of learning that involves more than the application of skills. Also necessary for inquiry are dispositions (attitudes toward learning), responsibilities, and self-assessment or reflection.

Together, all of these domains encompass a full picture of the requirements for the 21st-century learner.

Why focus on inquiry?

The emphasis on inquiry is a natural extension of John Dewey's ideas of learning through experience—that learners draw meaning by connecting one experience to another and to the future and by reflecting on and organizing the ideas that emerge from the experiences (Dewey 1938, 20, 27, 43, 45-7, 49, 87). Dewey's ideas are the basis of what is now called constructivism, in which learners are expected to construct their own meaning and teachers are expected to frame an environment that stimulates learners to question and discover rather than passively to receive information delivered to them (Brooks and Brooks 1993, 30).

Increasingly, educators in all subject areas are recognizing the power of inquiry to provoke deeper learning. Selected books on the subject of using inquiry as the core concept are listed in the references. Library media specialists, whose primary focus is helping students learn the process skills to read and discover the world, have often struggled in the past to gain recognition from their education colleagues about the importance of process skills for learning content. With the rising emphasis on inquiry-based teaching and learning in all content areas, classroom teachers are accepting more readily the integrated teaching of process and content. In fact, as information explodes and teachers recognize that they can never deliver all the important information in their subject area, a new consensus is forming about the necessity of teaching students how, rather than what, to learn. Linda K. Jordan probably expressed the views of many teachers when she said this about science inquiry: "Although inquiry may not be the only way to teach science, many science educators believe that it may be the best way for students to learn science" (Audet and Jordan 2005, 43).

What is the underlying process of inquiry and what skills are most important?

Most models of inquiry follow the same general cycle (Audet and Jordan 2005, 14; Stripling 2003, 7; Kuhlthau, Maniotes, and Caspari 2007, 17-20; Short et al. 1996, 18, 157):

- ▶ Tap into prior experience, background knowledge
- ▶ Generate intriguing questions or problems that can be investigated
- ▶ Develop a plan for investigation
- ▶ Select resources—select, analyze, and evaluate information that addresses the questions or problems
- ▶ Organize information, find patterns, draw conclusions and new understandings
- ▶ Create demonstration of learning and share with others
- ▶ Reflect on the process and product of learning; generate new questions

All research is messy and recursive; inquiry is more so because no one knows the end. Even if students are inquiring about a topic that has been studied before, the new understandings that are gained are unique to those students and to the connections that they make. Throughout the process, students reflect on what they are observing and finding out. They may change direction, ask new questions, challenge the inconsistencies they discover, seek new perspectives, and fill gaps in their information.

The skills included in the AASL *Standards for the 21st-Century Learner*

outline an active discovery process for all learners as revealed by the verbs used in the indicators—inquire, use, think critically, apply, create, share, read, pursue, develop, evaluate, make sense of, demonstrate, organize, listen, collaborate, conclude, connect, respond, and seek (2007). The attitudes toward learning, called dispositions in action, are also stated in active terms (e.g., display, demonstrate, maintain a critical stance, employ, use, and show) so that educators can gauge the degree to which students are displaying the habits of mind that lead to successful inquiry and learning. Because the aim of inquiry is active discovery, library media specialists and classroom teachers can employ formative assessment to track the actions of students and assess their progress in attaining and using skills and dispositions throughout the inquiry cycle.

How does inquiry differ across content areas?

Although the process of inquiry is much the same as it is applied in various content areas, the emphasis may be on different types of thinking. In mathematics, for example, inquiry in the curriculum focuses on problem-solving and reasoning. Students are expected to look for patterns and relationships that explain the physical world. The patterns/relationships exist as truths that are not dependent on the time (when), the place (where), or the reason (why) of the problem; therefore, students must be concerned with accuracy and logical reasoning, not with point of view or context (Stripling 2003, 23-24).

Science students are expected to

question, hypothesize, and investigate the natural world. Their inquiry is guided by a search for accurate and replicable evidence in order to confirm or refute a hypothesis and draw conclusions about the truth. Similarly to mathematics, the evidence is evaluated for its credibility and accuracy, not its point of view or social context. Identifying misconceptions is particularly important for science inquiry because most people tend to form theories about the way the world works through simple observation rather than investigation. Fallacious theories are not easily replaced unless they are brought to the surface and countered with more accurate information (Stripling 2003, 21-23).

Inquiry in history and the social sciences focuses on people and their interactions with the world. As a result, students must assess the evidence for

Increasingly, educators in all subject areas are recognizing the power of inquiry to provoke deeper learning.

point of view, social and historical context, authoritativeness, credibility, and other qualitative factors. In the social sciences, students inquire to find multiple truths as representative of different perspectives and different time periods. Inquiry in the social sciences is concerned with the interplay of "Why?," "Who?," "Where?," "When?," "What caused?," "What resulted?," and "How good or bad?" rather than the "How?" or "What?" of science and math. Interpretation of evidence and drawing conclusions in social-science inquiry are very complex processes that must be based on students carefully evaluating the evidence without succumbing to their own personal biases. It may be important for students to identify their own point of view before social-science inquiry, just as students in science must identify their own misconceptions (Stripling 2003, 24-27).

Inquiry in language arts and literature is based on interpretation of evidence that includes weighing the social context, determining point of view and author's purpose, questioning, identifying main ideas and supporting details, making inferences, and synthesizing. Inquiry about literature (both fiction and nonfiction) must be very text-based with background material used as a context for interpretation of the text. Inquiry in the language arts classroom that is not tied to literature often provides a rich opportunity for students to choose any researchable subject of personal interest. The skills most important for individualized inquiry will vary according to the subject chosen (Stripling 2003, 27-29).

See "Use This Page" (page 2) for a more specific outline of the role of the library media specialist implementing inquiry-based teaching and learning.

What is the role of the library media specialist in inquiry-based teaching and learning?

The goal of inquiry-based teaching is that all students develop an "inquiry stance" with more emphasis on asking good questions than finding the answers (Cochran-Smith and Lytle 1999). The payoff in terms of in-depth learning is profound: "Students can and do learn about subjects in teacher-centered classrooms, but they learn best in a learner-centered environment that emphasizes inquiry" (Audet and Jordan 2005, xiii).

Every inquiry learning experience should start with a challenging problem or question (often generated by the students) that is meaningful and worthy of deep exploration. Questions that are connected to students' own lives and their prior knowledge are the most intriguing and authentic, and, therefore,

motivating to students. Once students have constructed new understandings based on their investigations, they should be given opportunities to apply them to new situations.

To achieve this level of inquiry-based learning, the library media specialist's role involves collaboration, teaching, and collection development, as well as leadership and professional development. There are many ways the library media specialist can approach these roles. In terms of collaboration, the library media specialist must work with teachers to help restructure the curriculum, foster cross-curricular connections, and incorporate AASL *Standards for the 21st-Century Learner*. Library media specialists as teachers must be able to establish learner-centered environments, foster active and reflective learning, and enhance and support student learning while focusing on AASL *Standards for the 21st-Century Learner*. Through collection development, library media specialists must provide the resources (physical and virtual) required to meet the demands of an inquiry approach to learning and teaching. They must also be leaders by fostering and encouraging inquiry throughout the school and by providing and participating in professional development opportunities related to inquiry-based teaching and learning.

Why focus on inquiry?

Inquiry is certainly not a panacea for all of the issues that students, teachers, and library media specialists face in our schools today. Library media specialists who understand the inquiry process and how it contributes to learning across the curriculum, however, will be prepared to integrate inquiry experiences whenever they are appropriate. Each time students participate in a successful inquiry activity and acquire new skills of questioning, investigation, and discovery, the library media center has fostered a culture of inquiry in the school and enhanced the understanding of content and the acquisition of lifelong learning skills—the

true intent of AASL's new *Standards for the 21st-Century Learner*.

References

American Association of School Librarians. *Standards for the 21st-Century Learner*. American Library Association, 2007.

American Association of School Librarians and Association for Educational Communications and Technology. *Information Literacy Standards for Student Learning*. American Library Association, 1998.

Audet, Richard H., and Linda K. Jordan (eds.). *Integrating Inquiry across the Curriculum*. Corwin Press, 2005.

Bransford, J. D., A. L. Brown, and R. Cocking, eds. *How People Learn: Brain, Mind, Experience, and School*. National Academy Press, 1999.

Brooks, Jacqueline Grennon, and Martin G. Brooks. *In Search of Understanding: The Case for Constructivist Classrooms*. ASCD, 1993.

Cochran-Smith, M., and S. Lytle. "Relationships of Knowledge and Practice: Teacher Learning in Communities." *Review of Research in Education* 24, no. 8 (1999): 249-305.

Dewey, John. *Experience and Education*. Simon and Schuster, 1938.

Donham, Jean, Kay Bishop, Carol Collier Kuhlthau, and Dianne Oberg. *Inquiry-Based Learning: Lessons from Library Power*. Linworth Publishing, 2001.

Kuhlthau, Carol C., Leslie K. Maniotes, and Ann K. Caspari. *Guided Inquiry: Learning in the 21st Century*. Libraries Unlimited, 2007.

Mills, Heidi, and Amy Donnelly. *From the Ground Up: Creating a Culture of Inquiry*. Heinemann, 2001.

National Research Council. *Inquiry and the National Science Education Standards: A Guide for Teaching and Learning*. National Academy Press, 2000.

Short, Kathy G., et al. *Learning Together through Inquiry: From Columbus to Integrated Curriculum*. Stenhouse Publishers, 1996.

Stripling, Barbara K. "Inquiry-Based Learning." In *Curriculum Connections through the Library*, edited by Barbara K. Stripling and Sandra Hughes-Hassell. Libraries Unlimited, 2003.

Weinbaum, Alexandra, et al. *Teaching as Inquiry: Asking Hard Questions to Improve Practice and Student Achievement*. Teachers College Press and National Staff Development Council, 2004.◄

Barbara Stripling is the Director of Library Services for the New York City Department of Education. Email: bstripling@schools.nyc.gov

Inquiry-based Teaching and Learning— The Role of the Library Media Specialist

by Barbara Stripling

An extension of "Inquiry: Inquiring Minds Want to Know"

Collaboration

Collaboration underpins the success of any library media program. The library media specialist and classroom teachers must support each other because inquiry takes more time, the path may be unpredictable, the teacher is not always in control, students need a lot of support throughout the process, students need resources beyond the classroom on an unpredictable variety of subjects, and amid all the complexities, students must be surrounded by a safe and well-organized learning environment.

Through collaboration, the library media specialist can:

- ▶ Help restructure the curriculum so that inquiry and problem solving are integrated into all subject areas.
- ▶ Foster connections across curriculum areas, a focus on broad concepts instead of isolated facts, and the true blending of content and process.
- ▶ Incorporate the American Association for School Librarians (AASL) *Standards for the 21st-Century Learner*.

Teaching

The goal of inquiry-based teaching is that all students develop an "inquiry stance" with more emphasis on asking good questions than finding the answers (Cochran-Smith and Lytle 1999).

Library media specialists can:

- ▶ Establish a learner-centered environment by gradually releasing responsibility to the students.
- ▶ Integrate the teaching of habits of mind (Audet and Jordan 2005, 89-90) with inquiry and communication skills to foster both active and reflective learning.
- ▶ Enhance students' effectiveness in learning when they pay attention to the learning environment of the library and attend to four main areas that comprise a climate that fosters inquiry (Bransford, Brown, and Cocking 1999, 121):
  1. Learners' skills, attitudes, prior knowledge, interests.
  2. Knowledge formation through connections among ideas, focus on big concepts and intriguing questions, integration of skills and dispositions.
  3. Assessment by both teacher and student of process and content of learning.
  4. Community of learners that surround the learning experiences with sharing, interchange of ideas, listening to and challenging the ideas of others.
- ▶ Scaffold and support students through the difficult process of inquiry, but also challenge superficial ideas and uncritical acceptance of evidence if students are to reach as high as they can in their learning (Donham 2001, 3).
- ▶ Integrate and implement AASL's *Standards for the 21st-Century Learner*.

Collection Development

Inquiry is obviously dependent on availability of instructional materials and equipment. Inquiry is, in fact, a major incentive for a school to invest in a library media center.

Library media specialists can:

- ▶ Provide both physical and virtual resources that are tied closely to curriculum areas of emphasis by involving teachers in the selection process. For example, Web sites that are particularly good for specific units can be made available for easy access through the library home page, wikis, portals, and special bookmarking sites like *del.icio.us*.
- ▶ Place special emphasis on providing access to multiple perspectives and on offering materials for in-depth study, not superficial grazing.
- ▶ Advocate for technology that is essential for access to a wide variety of resources.
- ▶ Assist in providing guidance and instruction in the use of technology for learning.
- ▶ Assist in providing guidance in the use of books and periodicals.
- ▶ Assist in incorporating students' use of technology for inquiry learning involving social tools to share and build on the ideas of others, and to demonstrate their learning to a broader community.

Leadership and Professional Development

In effective professional development, teachers are guided to (National Research Council 2000, 91-98):

- ▶ Do inquiry themselves multiple times;
- ▶ Reflect on their own inquiry experiences;
- ▶ Develop conceptual understanding of their content area and of inquiry;
- ▶ Be a part of a collaborative community of inquiry;
- ▶ Assess their own teaching practices and content priorities in terms of effectiveness of student learning; and
- ▶ Rethink instructional time to build in inquiry experiences.

Library media specialists can:

- ▶ Provide professional development (in the form of workshops, study groups, mentoring, or collaborative planning) that offers teachers opportunities to participate in inquiry-based experiences and hone their own skills and confidence in inquiry-based teaching.
- ▶ Take a leadership role in fostering inquiry throughout their school community by communicating with administrators about the attributes and requirements of inquiry-based teaching and learning, so that the administrators support teachers and foster a schoolwide culture of inquiry.
- ▶ Seize every opportunity to reach out to parents and interpret inquiry-based teaching and learning for them through newsletters, parent/teacher conference nights, special workshops and programs, and presentations of student projects (Inquiry Nights).

See reference list in previous article.

Join Kristin Fontichiaro at the *SLMAM* blog for ongoing discussion and information related to AASL's *Standards for 21st-Century Learner* (http://blog.schoollibrarymedia.com/).

Critical Inquiry: Library Media Specialists as Change Agents

by Kafi Kumasi-Johnson

Isn't inquiry inherently critical? What distinguishes a critical approach to inquiry from other types of inquiry? When you ponder these questions, you engage in one of the basic activities of a critical mind—questioning. However, critical inquiry is much more than simply asking questions. Rather, it deals with an understanding of the meaning and significance of the questions asked in relation to larger social issues. Yet, as Shulman (1981) points out, in the field of education there is no clear definition or methodology of inquiry. As such, there is no clear (or agreed upon) understanding of what constitutes inquiry. Consequently, critical inquiry is often articulated in complex ways. To address this challenge, this column describes some of the key concepts and strategies of critical inquiry that are relevant to the work of school library media specialists in secondary settings. This approach to inquiry is rooted in critical theory and calls upon library media specialists to become change agents who provide spaces for students to openly question, challenge, and investigate social and cultural issues.

Kafi Kumasi-Johnson is a doctoral student in curriculum studies at Indiana University, Bloomington, with a minor concentration in School Library Media. She has served as a secondary library media specialist in the Detroit public schools. E-mail: kkumasij@indiana.edu

Inquiry as a Contextual Practice

Even if educators agreed upon a definition of inquiry, the classroom instructional strategies used to implement inquiry-based learning would vary across the curriculum. Each discipline has its own set of concepts, methods, and procedures. For instance, in science classrooms, disciplined inquiry generally involves using some aspect of the scientific method (McPherson 2001). In disciplines such as history, teachers often rely upon logical reasoning and role-playing to help students understand the actions and decisions made by historical figures (Foster and Padgett 1999). Since library media specialists are not bound to teach a particular content area, they have a unique opportunity to forge a new kind of inquiry within the library media center that can both complement and extend the efforts of classroom teachers. Critical inquiry is well suited to the work of the library media specialist because it strikes a balance between substantive information problem-solving and the reflective, process-oriented approaches to inquiry that are familiar to librarians. A critical perspective on inquiry (and literacy) presumes that knowledge is value-laden and that no information problem is neutral, but is embedded within issues of power and privilege (Giroux 1998). The goal of critical inquiry in the library media center is to help students understand relationships between power and domination underlying various information problems, and to help students develop creative ways to work toward social justice (Slater, Fain, and Rossatto 2002).

Exploring Critical Inquiry and the Role of the Library Media Specialist

Traditional approaches to inquiry in the library media center have been problem-based and process-oriented but have not necessarily been critical. For example, Mike Eisenberg and Bob Berkowitz's Big6™ inquiry model, which has become closely tied to school library media instruction, is described as an information problem-solving strategy or process model that can be used to "handle any problem, assignment, decision, or task" (Eisenberg and Berkowitz). Yet, within this model, the information problem itself does not always come under scrutiny, and the library media specialist often takes on a peripheral role as resource support staff rather than teacher. A student may identify a seemingly mundane, noncritical information problem such as "how to build a garden" and never be challenged to investigate important social issues related to that problem, such as who can build a garden and who cannot. In contrast, a critical approach to inquiry would challenge the library media specialist not only to help students identify resources to solve mundane informational problems, but also to help students identify inquiry topics that are rooted in macro-level societal concerns that deal with issues of race, class, and gender (among others).

The critical-inquiry approach benefits library media specialists by expanding their role to new and exciting possibilities for working with students. Students also stand to benefit greatly, especially those students whose culture and history have been marginalized in schools. Research suggests that when educators design curriculum and instructional activities that affirm the home and community literacy practices of students of color, these students are more likely to perform better academically and become more engaged with school (Ladson-Billings 1995).

If you are still unsure of what critical inquiry might look like in your library media center, the following is a brief set of activities, suggestions, and ideas for making it real.

Define Critical Inquiry for the Learning Community

Given that the terms "inquiry" and "critical" are used in so many different contexts, it is important for the library media specialist to help students, teachers, and parents understand how critical inquiry is used in the learning community and how it differs from other learning strategies. The library media specialist should convey that critical inquiry is about educating students as scholars who disseminate their ideas in various scholarly and community forums. Also, critical inquiry can be presented as a shift in the traditional roles and expectations of students. Instead of thinking of students strictly as receivers of information, students become teachers who are capable of raising important questions and investigating real life concerns and, in turn, educate their community.

Making it real. Prepare a handout or newsletter for staff and students that explains the library media specialist's role in preparing students to think critically and to utilize the library media center as a resource for investigating real-life issues. Invite the staff to visit the library media center and share examples of students engaged in critical inquiry.

Demystify the Concept of Inquiry and Make Critical Inquiry Relevant for Students

The idea of "doing" research may be off-putting for many students. Likewise, inquiry may be seen as an academic chore if it is not introduced skillfully. The library media specialist should take time to demystify the concept of inquiry and make it relevant for students. One approach is to draw from students' real-life experiences to help them see that they already engage in inquiry in their daily lives.

Making it real (a scenario): A group of African American youth, who attend a predominately white high school, are overheard complaining about their teachers' and administrators' perceived lack of support and cultural sensitivity. The library media specialist, in collaboration with several classroom teachers, recognizes this as an opportunity to explore the concept critical inquiry with students. After visiting the library media center, students learn that critical inquiry is about educating their communities and participating in social change. With this new understanding, students share examples of critical inquiry in their communities and surmise that social and political activism is key to critical inquiry. Classroom teachers and the library media specialist plan a set of curricular activities that culminate in a written proposal that outlines their plans to establish an African American student organization. In addition, the library media specialist organizes the schools' first annual African American Read-In (see http://www.ncte.org/prog/readin/107901.htm) as a way to allow students the opportunity to continue to explore additional information while celebrating the African American literary tradition.

Rethink the Library Space

Critical inquiry is not simple and often involves facilitating group discussions and other learning activities that require noisy behaviors. In order to support these kinds of learning experiences, the library media specialist should relax policies that may preclude these activities from occurring in the library media center.

Making it real: Prepare signs for your library media center that indicate "Critical Inquiry=Good Noise in the Library Media Center!"

Integrate Literature and Audio-Video Resources

Novels are a great way to engage in critical inquiry projects while utilizing the library media center's resources. The library media specialist can select one or two pieces of children's and young adult literature that address complex social issues and use them as the basis for helping students address real-world issues. Utilizing a variety of audio-visual materials (CD's, music videos) and online multimedia resources (e.g., http://www.Youtube.com) can be a great way to evoke conversations and help students see how larger social issues connect to real-life situations and those that play out in popular culture.

Making it real: Host an after-school book club and bring in music and videos that tie into the novels' theme. For example, in reading the novel *Born Blue* by Hans Nolan, the library media specialist can extrapolate on the theme of Blues music within the novel by bringing in music by artists like Etta James and Billy Holiday. Also, because the novel deals with issues of African American culture and identity, students may conduct extended research on identity and the issues many African American girls face, particulary those relating to hair and skin complexion. The video documentary *A Girl Like Me* (2006) is an example of an electronic resource that might be used for this topic.

Integrate Social and Cultural Questions into the "Information Environment"

Information inquiry has been described as the process of searching for information and applying information to answer questions. Callison (2002) suggests that these questions tend to be tied to one or more of three information environments: personal, academic, and workplace. While this description of information provides a useful overview, it does not include two very important areas from which students, particularly students of color, tend to generate questions—social and cultural environments. A critical approach to inquiry would bring to the foreground students' social and cultural informational concerns and has the potential to reach a large population of students whose literacy resources are often marginalized in schools (Mahiri and Sablo 1996; Osborne 1996).

Making it real: Talk to students about the questions and issues related to their cultural identity and ethnic background that they are struggling with. Create opportunities for critical inquiry and social action in the library media center around these issues.

Provide Scaffolding, Social Action, and a Community Forum

A critical inquiry approach to library instruction can help offset the perception among some administrators that library media specialists do not directly impact student learning (Hartzell 1997). The library media specialist, in collaboration with teachers, should allot time for students to come to the library media center for brainstorming sessions that encourage them to raise questions and engage in social action related to real-world issues. Critical inquiry in the library media center will help other educators, parents, and community members see that the library media specialist can impact student achievement and influence social change. Also, critical inquiry can provide a forum for students in which to share their ideas with their community. These culminating events should not be seen as school presentations, but rather as scholarly forums where students articulate their ideas, entertain questions, and engage in critical dialogue.

Making it real: Examples of culminating inquiry projects might include a political demonstration; a video documentary; a panel session; or a literary reading/performance.

These suggestions for implementing critical inquiry in the library media center require a shift in the way inquiry is perceived and discussed by the school library media profession. If library media specialists, as critical educators, provide spaces for students to critically engage, investigate, and act on pressing issues in the world around them, then they are effectively working toward becoming agents of social change.

References

A Girl Like Me. http://www.youtube.com/results?search_query=a+girl+like+me&search=Search (accessed December 18, 2006).

Callison, D. *L551 Information Inquiry for Teachers.* 2002 course syllabus. http://www.slis.indiana.edu/syllabi/fall_2002/l551_callison.html (accessed December 21, 2006).

Eisenberg, Mike, and Bob Berkowitz. *Big6™: Information Skills for Student Achievement, 2001-2005.* http://www.big6.com/ (accessed December 15, 2006).

Foster, S. J., and C. S. Padgett. "Authentic Historical Inquiry in the Social Studies Classroom." *Clearing House* 72, no. 6 (1999): 357-363.

Giroux, H. "Literacy and the Pedagogy of Voice and Political Empowerment." *Educational Theory* 38, no. 1 (1998): 61-75.

Hartzell, G. "The Invisible Librarian: Why Other Educators Are Blind to Your Value." *School Library Journal* 43, no. 11 (1997): 24-29.

Ladson-Billings, G. "Toward a Theory of Culturally Relevant Pedagogy." *American Educational Research Journal* 32, no. 3 (1995): 465-491.

Mahiri, J., and S. Sablo. "Writing for Their Lives: The Non-School Literacy of California's Urban African American Youth." *The Journal of Negro Education* 65, no. 2 (1996): 164-80.

McPherson, G. R. "Teaching the Scientific Method." *The American Biology Teacher* 63, no. 4 (2001): 242-45.

Osborne, A. B. "Practice into Theory into Practice: Culturally Relevant Pedagogy for Students We Have Marginalized and Normalized." *Anthropology and Education Quarterly* 27, no. 3 (1996): 285.

Shulman, L. S. "Disciplines of Inquiry in Education: An Overview." *Educational Researcher* 10, no. 6 (1981): 5-12, 23.

Slater, J. J., S. M. Fain, and C. A. Rossatto. *The Freirean Legacy: Educating for Social Justice.* P. Lang, 2002.

Engaging Students in INQUIRY

by Joan M. Yoshina and Violet H. Harada

The past year may be remembered as "the year of the natural disaster." Beginning with a tsunami of biblical proportions, news coverage has been dominated by scenes of devastation brought about by hurricanes, earthquakes, floods, and disease. Whether they are directly involved or merely bystanders to these catastrophic events, children have felt the effects. They want to know why these tragedies occur and how to protect themselves when they do happen. They express concern for the victims they have come to know through the news media, and they wonder what they can do to help.

In a technologically advanced, media-saturated culture such as ours, children are often confronted with realities that are as disturbing as they are real. As educators, we search for ways to deal with events that are so compelling that everything else drowns in the tide. The question becomes: How can we bring these events into the learning environment in a manner that is responsive to the needs of students and at the same time

addresses required standards and meets federal guidelines?

Some educators have found success through inquiry learning—a student-centered approach that provides opportunities for students to make choices that help determine the direction of their learning. Barbara Stripling describes inquiry as a framework for learning that is "active, shared, and based on the pursuit of student-generated questions" (2003, 5). Inquiry allows students to construct personal knowledge about issues and problems that is both personally meaningful and important to learn about.

Involving Students in Inquiry

In an inquiry environment, students help to negotiate the direction of the learning. Typically, students help to determine what they will learn, how they will learn, and how their performances will be measured. The challenge for educators is to create an environment that encourages students to pose thoughtful questions about problems and issues that they care about.

We work with teachers at one school who use the news

media to develop what they call "a culture of inquiry." Students routinely search newspapers, magazines, and selected Internet sites looking for issues that spark their interest and curiosity. Three questions guide the daily discussion of current events:

- Why is the event important?
- How does this event affect us?
- What questions do I have beyond what was covered in the piece?

Fourth graders at the school generated a list of potential topics that included events like Hurricane Katrina, the Asian Tsunami, and the earthquake that devastated Pakistan. After a discussion of the relative importance of these topics, the library media specialist suggested that the class form investigative teams to study different types of natural disasters. Teachers and students agreed to the more generative topic on the following grounds:

- Natural disasters are important to learn about.
- Students will have a choice of topics to investigate.
- The broader topic provides opportunities to compare and contrast different types of events.
- Students will be able to examine the connections

Joan M. Yoshina is a retired school library media specialist, who has worked in elementary and secondary library media centers in Hawaii. Email: byrony@hgea. net. Violet H. Harada is a professor in the University of Hawaii's Library and Information Science Program, 2680 East West Road, Honolulu, HI 96822. Email: vharada@hawaii.edu.

between human activities and the occurrence of catastrophic events.

Framing the Inquiry

Questioning is at the heart of inquiry. The best topics are those that generate meaningful questions that can be used to frame the investigation. Essential questions promote understanding by moving instruction away from "a succession of activities...to a focus on ideas and major issues" (Harada and Yoshina 2004, 12). Good essential questions share the following characteristics:

- They are open-ended. (There is no one right answer.)
- They focus on big ideas rather than facts.
- They point out what is important to learn about the topic.
- They lead to other questions.

In our example, the instructional team decided to involve students in the process of identifying essential questions for the natural disasters unit. Teachers facilitated the discussion by first having students brainstorm what they wanted to know about natural disasters. From a long list of questions, the children worked in groups to determine which met the criteria for essential questions. They decided that the following were central to their inquiry:

- How do natural disasters affect our lives?
- How should we prepare for natural disasters?

Each team created a web to organize the inquiry around questions related to these essential questions. As new information was uncovered, additional questions were added to the web. The final version of the web created by the team investigating hurricanes is represented in Figure 1.

Assessing Performance

Inquiry involves students in learning what is active, observable, and measurable. Many educators have promoted the performance task as a way of measuring student outcomes by examining their products and performances (Wiggins and McTighe 1998, Wiske 1994, Harada and Yoshina 2005). Clear performance tasks have several things in common:

- They provide a context for the presentation or performance.
- They identify a real audience.
- They define the requirements for the final product or performance.
- They describe the student's role in the process.

The fourth grade instructors asked students to consider ways in which they could share their knowledge of natural disasters as well as their compassion for the victims. Stories were shared about children around the world who had initiated projects on

FIGURE 1: EXAMPLE OF STUDENTS' QUESTION WEB

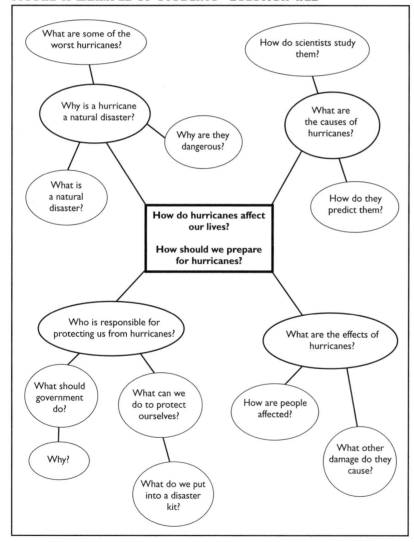

behalf of disaster victims. Students considered the pros and cons of different projects and offered their own ideas about how to make a difference. Instructors incorporated students' ideas into a performance task that stated the context for the presentation, described the audience, outlined expectations for the final product, and explained the student's role (Figure 2).

The performance task provides a context for students to demonstrate what they know, what they are able to do, and what they care about. In an inquiry environment, instructors also work with students to determine the criteria for a successful performance. Fourth graders examined models of presentations from previous projects and identified the characteristics that made some displays more effective than others. With guidance from their teachers, students agreed to the following criteria for their projects:

- The information must be accurate.
- The information has to come from different kinds of sources.
- The information has to answer the essential questions.
- The display has to be attractive and easy to read.
- The display should include pictures that show why the event is a natural disaster.
- The disaster kit should include enough food, water, and other essential items to last at least a week.

The instructors used these criteria to create tools for monitoring progress through different phases of the inquiry. The school library media specialist designed a checklist to guide students through the information search process. An example of how a student completed the checklist is shown in Figure 3.

Developing Inquiry

The goal of inquiry is the construction of new knowledge. Stripling provides a framework that clarifies how cognitive skills are involved in knowledge construction:

- *Connect:* Students connect the topic to their prior knowledge and personal experience.
- *Wonder:* Students ask meaningful questions to focus the inquiry. They make predictions and form hypotheses.
- *Investigate:* Students plan the search. They access sources. They evaluate information. They take notes. They cite sources.
- *Construct:* Students use

FIGURE 2: PERFORMANCE TASK FOR NATURAL DISASTERS UNIT

Context: We will sponsor a booth on natural disasters for "Make a Difference Day."

Audience: Parents, teachers, students, and people who visit the booth.

Final product and/or performance: We will make disaster kits containing items every family should have on hand in case of an unexpected emergency. We also will create visual displays about natural disasters that have affected people around the world. Throughout the day, we will be collecting donations for the Red Cross to help victims of disaster.

Student's role: To prepare for this event, each of us will be expected to:
- Work with a group to gather information related to a natural disaster.
- Help to create a display that provides important informaton about the natural disaster.
- Make a disaster kit to use in case of an emergency. Provide a list showing the contents of this kit.
- Answer questions about our display and help to collect donations.

FIGURE 3: STUDENT EXAMPLE

Criteria	What I did	How I did it	Problems I had
Chooses a natural disaster to research	I chose hurricanes because lots of people lost their houses to Hurricane Katrina.	I watched TV and looked at *Time for Kids* on the Internet.	I didn't have a problem. I wanted to help the hurricane victims.
Asks questions to guide search	I asked: What causes hurricanes? Why are the dangerous? How do they forecast them?	We made a web with the essential questions in the middle. I added my qustions to the web.	I had a hard time thinking of "How" and "Why" questions. But I got ideas from my team.
Finds information in different sources	I used books, TV, encyclopedias, *Yahooligans!news*, and *Time for Kids*.	I used the OPAC to find books. I looked at the bookmarks for Internet sites.	I didn't have enough time to look at all the books and Internet sites.
Takes notes from sources	I took notes on the causes of hurricanes and why they are dangerous.	I used the contents page and index to locate information. I took notes in my own words.	I am having a hard time understanding how scientists forecast hurricanes. The reading is hard.
Organizes information for the display	I worked with my group to decide how we will present the information. We each took one question to write about.	I used separate note pages for each question so I looked at my notes for "Why are they dangerous?"	We're still not sure how to lay out the information on the display board.

information to build personal knowledge. They create products and plan performances.

- *Express:* Students communicate their knowledge with real audiences.
- *Reflect:* Students reflect on what they are learning, how they are learning, and problems they are having (2003).

Periodic visits to our fourth grade class provide glimpses of students engaged in the serious business of constructing personal knowledge. This is what we might see at different phases of the inquiry:

Connect

Students pour over magazines and newspapers and access the news through selected websites, including *Yahooligans! News, Time for Kids, Kidsnewsroom.org,* and *Science News for Kids.* They examine a map of the United States that uses color-coded dots to indicate the occurrence of natural disasters. They discuss their interest in particular topics and share questions that they have.

Wonder

Students respond to readings and media presentations by posing questions that lead to additional information and deeper understanding. They help identify essential questions for the unit, and they create webs in which they record their personal questions. As new information is uncovered, they push the inquiry forward by asking additional questions.

Investigate

Students seek information for the purpose of constructing personal knowledge. In the inquiry environment, students ask their own questions, plan the search and presentation, and access information in both primary and secondary sources. They evaluate sources and information for accuracy, relevance, and accessibility. They read for information, and they take notes to answer questions.

Construct

Students use information to validate predictions, test hypotheses, express a point of view, and suggest solutions to problems. At this stage, students organize their information for an effective presentation, create drafts, and plan their displays. They collect items for their disaster relief kits and make a list telling why each item is needed. Importantly, they use feedback to improve their products.

Express

Students share their knowledge with authentic audiences. Participation in "Make a Difference Day" lends a sense of purpose to the project that makes learning meaningful. Students express empathy for the victims by collecting donations. They share information through their visual displays. They help their families by creating disaster kits. They expand their understanding and clarify their ideas through conversations with visitors to the display.

Reflect

Students keep reflection logs where they write about their topic choices and the questions they have. During the investigation phase, they use their logs to compare resources and pose questions about problems they encounter. At the completion of the project, they share their thoughts about the entire experience by responding to prompts: What went well? What should we do differently? What have we learned about natural disasters?

Conclusion

Library media specialists who are committed to collaboration may find an opportunity through inquiry, a student-centered approach that focuses on big ideas that spring from students' questions and observations about the real world. The ultimate goal of inquiry is for students to construct personal knowledge about topics that are meaningful to them. Constructing knowledge involves questioning, planning, investigating, and creating products and performances—all components of the information search process. Inquiry projects that are developed through school library media center/classroom partnerships are powerful initiatives that challenge students to form personal meaning and motivate them to take thoughtful action.

References

Harada, Violet H., and Joan M. Yoshina. *Assessing Learning: Librarians and Teachers as Partners.* Libraries Unlimited, 2005.

Harada, Violet H., and Joan M. Yoshina. *Inquiry Learning through Librarian-Teacher Partnerships.* Linworth, 2004.

Stripling, Barbara K. "Inquiry-based Learning." In *Curriculum Connections through the Library,* edited by Barbara K. Stripling and Sandra Hughes-Hassell, 3-39. Libraries Unlimited, 2003.

Wiggins, Grant, and Jay McTighe. *Understanding by Design.* Association for Supervision and Curriculum Development, 1998.

Wiske, Martha. "How Teaching for Understanding Changes the Rules in the Classroom." *Educational Leadership* 51, no. 5 (February 1994): 19-21. ✋

Connecting Science Notebooking to the Elementary Library Media Center

by Kristin Fontichiaro and Sandy Buczynski

The *Standards for the 21st-Century Learner* paints a vibrant image of motivated, student-driven work (AASL 2007). The Common Beliefs in this document state, "Inquiry provides a framework for learning," and Standard One articulates that students will "Inquire, think critically, and gain knowledge." As the standards unfold, they further define the inquiry process: activating students' prior knowledge, connecting the process to real-world applications, reviewing and evaluating information, and synthesizing new understandings into a final work product. Inquiry, rather than information literacy, is the term at the core of the new *Standards*. This nomenclature change connects library-based work more strongly to the teaching strategies of classroom teachers.

What Is Inquiry?

The term "inquiry" can be viewed from two perspectives. Inquiry refers to the abilities students develop when designing and conducting investigations and the understanding they gain through this process about the nature of science. Inquiry also refers to teaching and learning strategies that enable students to master content concepts (NRC 2000).

Young children are innate inquirers as they explore the world around them. Capturing this sense of wonder in a structured approach to problem solving is the essence of inquiry-based instruction. Rather than following a prescribed series of steps and arriving at "the correct answer," students develop, carry out, and reflect on their own processes to arrive at understanding. Through inquiry, students view the problem through multiple lenses, develop understanding from multiple perspectives, and deepen collective class understanding.

Knowledge is in the head of the learner who can only construct what he or she knows on the basis of his or her own experience. Inquiry-based instruction provides that experience.

Science Inquiry

Library media specialists are not the sole standard-bearers for inquiry; science teachers are deeply committed to inquiry as well. Guided by the National Science Education Standards, science teachers are charged with providing three kinds of scientific skills and understandings. Students need to:

- ►Learn the principles and concepts of science,
- ►Acquire reasoning and procedural kills of scientists, and
- ►Understand the nature of science as a particular form of human endeavor (NRC 2000).

Inquiry pedagogy helps science teachers achieve these goals. Teachers build science lessons on the principle that learners do not enter classrooms as blank slates; rather, they bring with them preconceived ideas about how the world works. To provide learners with constructivist experiences that place them in the center of their learning, encouraging them to explore and relate concepts to their own experiences, science teachers routinely design lesson plans using the 5E model (Ansberry and Morgan 2005). Developed by the Biological Sciences Curriculum Study (BSCS), 5E lesson design is in five phases:

- ►Engage (capture student interest)
- ►Explore (through common concrete experiences)
- ►Explain (students articulate ideas in their own words and listen to each other)
- ►Elaborate (address misconceptions and generalize concepts to a broader context)
- ►Evaluate (self-evaluation and summative assessment) (BSCS 2006).

In the 5E model, the student takes on much of the responsibility for asking questions, thinking creatively, explaining possible solutions, and applying new vocabulary. The teacher is a facilitator, providing time for students to observe and investigate, asking for evidence and clarification from students, and encouraging students to self-assess their own learning.

Bringing Science and the Library Media Center Together

To maximize students' learning, science teachers and library media specialists can work together to pursue quality cognitive experiences for elementary students via inquiry and science skills. The two share a deep responsibility for promoting reasoning skills, content acquisition, and curiosity in students. Realizing that students must have a deep foundation of factual knowledge and a means to organize that knowledge in ways that allow retrieval and application, science notebooking represents an ideal method for capturing mutual educational objectives.

What Is Science Notebooking?

Science notebooking is a process tool used to scaffold inquiry as well as provide an ongoing record of the students' procedural and cognitive processes. Using the steps of the long-established scientific method, the notebook is a place where students formulate explanations from evidence, analyze trends and patterns, and draw conclusions based on relevant

evidence. These science notebooks facilitate inductive thinking through a series of sense-making strategies. The use of multiple modalities—text, graphs, charts, scientific drawings, procedural lists, sketches, and observations—gives students the opportunity to think through ideas and data in many ways. This approach facilitates differentiation for English Language Learners and for students with special needs (Klentschy 2008). In addition, repeated use of science notebooking develops many types of writing: expository, procedural, and reflective. In a science notebook, students write for themselves, rather than for an instructor audience. By doing so, science notebooks empower students and give them ownership; they recognize their notebooks as a place to record their own processes and discoveries in their own voices. This is a significant shift away from extrinsically-motivated, teacher-assigned tasks.

Science notebooking is not a curriculum; its process can be used with existing science kits (Campbell and Fulton 2003) or to document the investigation of original measurable questions. While the content and design of each inquiry project may be different, the linear series of science notebooking steps remains the same: awakening prior knowledge, introducing initial scientific concepts and vocabulary, developing measurable questions, identifying variables, drafting procedural steps, creating a useful data organizer, conducting the experiment, recording data, processing the data to establish a claim with supporting evidence, and synthesizing a conclusion.

As in quality library inquiry, the instructor's role is not to give out worksheets or predetermined procedures; instead, they provide overarching scaffolding via the notebooking process and support students' efforts to organize and make sense of their work. Throughout the notebooking process, instructors are actively involved in formative assessment. Rather than assigning grades to the notebooking process, instructors give feedback via conferencing, constructive comments, and reflective opportunities for students. In this application of science notebooking, the summative assessment is in the form of an authentic, real-world product (such as a brochure, letter, podcast, or monologue) that brings the thinking process full-circle and demonstrates the students' level of applied conceptual understanding.

A simple, marble-covered composition notebook is ideal for science notebooking. Because the stitched binding keeps papers in a fixed order, the notebook is an enduring record of current understanding and past thinking, becoming a cognitive portfolio that can span many projects over multiple grade levels.

How Can the Library Media Specialist Be Involved?

When library media specialists become partners in science inquiry, they have new opportunities for reinforcing the values found in the AASL Standards. The correlation is remarkably strong, and Table 1: Using Science Notebooking to meet the AASL Standards (see page 27) shows how closely science notebooking supports the inquiry process outlined in the AASL Standards. Co-teaching halves the student-to-teacher ratio and facilitates greater levels of student support via feedback, conferencing, and

personalized, differentiated instruction. Library media specialists can share their expertise in designing meaningful questions and provide companion resources. Those students who have developed new questions or further interest in a topic can work intensively with the library media specialist to pursue these interests. For some inquiry projects, specifically those dealing with physical science (e.g., motion and design and physics), the larger tables of the library media center create a wonderful ad hoc laboratory.

Lesson Plans with Science Notebooking

Check out the two lesson plans related to science notebooking in this issue of *SLMAM*. One lesson plan was developed from a perspective of hands-on science, "Science Notebooking in Action: Where Does Condensation Come From?" (pages 12-14) and one was developed from the perspective of library media research, "Science Notebooking in the Library Media Center: Alternative Energy" (pages 14-16). These lesson plans show the strong correlation between science inquiry and the AASL Standards and demonstrate how working with hands-on science can develop the skills needed for research.

Conclusion: Joining Forces

In the transition from *Information Power* to AASL's *Standards for the 21st-Century Learner*, library media specialists are changing from instructors who focus on finding information to guides who help students make meaning from and enhance conceptual understanding. When library media specialists step outside the traditional confines of the library media center, they can find a dynamic partnership with science teachers and co-create active learning environments. Science notebooking encourages authentic engagement that reinforces the nature of science and results in more resonant student learning. Hands-on inquiry, like quality library inquiry, strengthens students' cognitive toolkit, brings new knowledge, and develops lifelong habits of mind.

References:

American Association of School Librarians. *Standards for the 21st-Century Learner.* ALA, 2007. http://www.ala.org/ala/mgrps/divs/aasl/aaslproftools/learningstandards/standards.cfm (accessed November 9, 2008).

Ansberry, K., and E. Morgan. *Picture-perfect Science Lessons: Using Children's Books to Guide Inquiry.* National Science Teachers Association Press, 2005.

Biological Sciences Curriculum Study (BSCS). *BSCS Science: An Inquiry Approach.* Kendall/Hunt, 2006.

Buczynski, S., and K. Fontichiaro. *Story Starters and Science Notebooking: Developing Children's Thinking through Literacy and Inquiry.* Teacher Ideas Press, in press.

Campbell, B., and L. Fulton. *Science Notebooks: Writing about Inquiry.* Heinemann, 2003.

Klentschy, M. *Using Science Notebooks in Elementary Classrooms.* National Science Teachers Association Press, 2008.

National Research Council (NRC). *Inquiry and the National Science Education Standards: A Guide for Teaching and Learning.* National Academy Press, 2000. ◄

Kristin Fontichiaro is an elementary library media specialist for the Birmingham (Michigan) Public Schools and author of *Podcasting at School* and *Active Learning through Drama, Podcasting, and Puppetry* (Libraries Unlimited) . She blogs about 21st-century learning in school libraries for *School Library Media Activities Monthly* (http://blog.schoollibrarymedia.com). Email: font@umich.edu

Sandy Buczynski is an associate professor of science education at the University of San Diego in San Diego, California. She coordinates the Math, Science and Technology Education graduate program and teaches courses in science pedagogy and curriculum design. Email: sandyb@sandiego.edu

Together, they are the authors of *Story Starters for Science Inquiry: Developing Student Thinking through Literacy and Inquiry,* to be released in Spring 2009 by Teacher Ideas Press. They thank Marcia Mardis for her assistance with this article.

Notebooking Stage	What Happens	Role of the Library Media Specialist	AASL Standards Correlation
Planning for Learning	The teacher selects a science concept focus and, optionally, finds a story that introduces students to a content-based problem needing solution. The teacher and library media specialist select an inquiry focus (e.g., questioning, predicting, making meaning of data, conclusion, etc.) that will be especially monitored.	Provides age-appropriate introductory content materials and/or stories related to the scientific problem. Plans co-teaching, formative assessments strategies, project, and rubric with teacher.	Common Belief 8: Learning has a social context. Common Belief 9: School libraries are essential to the development of learning skills.
Story Starter, Connecting to Science, Inventory Walk, Vocabulary	The teacher taps into and strengthens prior knowledge. In Story Starters and Science Notebooking, teachers present a story that introduces a science concept and problem to be solved. The teacher introduces basic science concepts, begins vocabulary development, and reveals materials available for students to use in designing an investigation.	Provides cameras so students can create labeled photo display of inventory items as a visual reference throughout inquiry. Recommends books for additional reading. Co-leads discussions.	1.1.2: Use prior and background knowledge as context for new learning. 4.1.5: Connect ideas to own interests and previous knowledge and experience.
Questioning	Students generate an open-ended measurable question. Counting, cause and effect, or comparison questions are effective. Avoid "yes/no" questions.	Guides students in designing open-ended questions that will lead to fruitful exploration.	1.1.3: Develop and refine a range of questions to frame the search for new understanding.
Formulating a Prediction	Based on the measurable question, students determine what they think a logical outcome will be and then make a prediction (via writing or drawing) about the direction of that outcome.	Assists students in creating an "if, then" statement that reflects the student's vision of a possible outcome of the experiment.	1.2.1: Display initiative and engagement by posing questions and investigating the answers beyond the collection of superficial facts.
Identifying Variables	Students identify the experimental elements (variables) that will change, be measured as a result of that change, and remain constant.	Guides students in their efforts to identify variables using word clues such as "if, then."	Belief 7: The continuing expansion of information demands that all individuals acquire the thinking skills that will enable them to learn on their own.
Designing the Procedure	Students further define their experimental process by visualizing the steps they will take to test their prediction. In a sequential manner, students write or sketch steps to be followed during the experiment.	Helps students visualize steps needed to gather data, reviews procedural thinking for thoroughness and materials needed, monitors for gaps.	4.4.3: Recognize how to focus efforts in personal learning.
Creating the Data Organizer	Students reflect on their variables and consider the types of data they will need to collect in order to test their prediction. They create an empty graphic organizer (table, chart, graph, etc.) for use during the experiment.	Provides examples of graphic organizers. Helps students envision data to collect. Monitors that the organizer relates to the procedure and prediction.	2.1.2: Organize knowledge so that it is useful.
Conducting the Experiment, Recording Data and Observations	In groups, students conduct the experiment and record data. In addition, they sketch images of the experiment in progress and record observations.	Circulates throughout groups to monitor progress, discusses progress with students, gives oral feedback, and assists students with accurate measuring.	3.2.2: Show social responsibility by participating actively with others in learning situations. 3.2.3: Demonstrate teamwork by working productively with others.
Claims and Evidence	Students review data, looking for patterns or trends that lead them to make an assertion (claim). Students justify their claim with data (evidence) collected during the experiment. The cognition in this step moves students away from reliance on prior knowledge and into consideration of collected data.	Helps students make meaning of data and distinguish between inference and evidence. Assists with using technology to sort data, calculate, or construct graphs to make patterns/ trends visible.	1.1.6: Read, view, and listen for information… to make inferences & gather meaning. 2.1.4: Use technology and other tools to analyze and organize information.
Conclusion	In their notebooks, students compare their claims and evidence to their original prediction. They determine whether their original prediction was supported and what new scientific knowledge they have gained. Students reflect on possible experimental errors. The notebook will be used in subsequent steps as a reference in creating a work product that demonstrates what has been learned.	Collaboratively guides students through this thinking process. Reminds students that unsupported predictions are not failures and provides examples of "failures" that yielded new discoveries.	2.4.2: Reflect on systematic process, and assess for completeness of investigation. 2.4.3: Recognize new knowledge and understanding. 3.4.1: Assess the process by which learning was achieved in order to revise strategies and learn more effectively in the future.
Project	Students use findings to create an authentic work product (brochure, podcast, monologue, etc.) that requires them to apply content knowledge, interpret results of investigation in context of original problem, take a different perspective (speak from another voice), or use technology to communicate findings. Students receive rubrics in advance to guide them in identifying quality work. Students have opportunities to re-submit final project after constructive feedback.	Provides support or co-teaches necessary writing or technology skills. Supports student work in creating the final product that demonstrates level of conceptual knowledge. Shares in evaluating student work and revising the project for resubmission.	2.1.6: Use the writing process, media and visual literacy, and technology skills to create products that express new understandings. 3.1.1: Conclude an inquiry-based research process by sharing new understandings and reflecting on the learning. 3.4.2: Assess the quality and effectiveness of the learning product.
Next Steps	Like real scientists, students consider what new hands-on or library inquiries they might like to explore next. Future investigations are recorded in the same science notebook, creating a long-term portfolio of student thinking.	Works with groups to pursue new hands-on or library inquiry. Shares evidence of learning with administrators. Plans next inquiry with teacher.	2.4.4: Develop directions for future investigations.

Excerpted from *Standards for the 21st-Century Learner* by the American Association of School Librarians, a division of the American Library Association, copyright © 2007 American Library Association. Available for download at http://www.ala.org/aasl/standards. Reprinted with permission.

Chapter 7

Assessment

School library media specialists must consider not just how many lessons they conduct but whether students have actually been learning the skills taught.

—Violet H. Harada and Joan M. Yoshina, "Assessing Learning:
The Missing Piece in Instruction?" (see page 185)

For many years, behind closed doors, school library media specialists would say, with a sigh of relief, "Thank goodness we don't have to do *grading*. It's part of why I became a librarian." Perhaps decades ago, this was true. But in today's era of high-stakes standardized testing, tight school budgets, and accountability for student learning, SLMSs can no longer secretly congratulate themselves for abdicating the assessment portion of their teaching role. Nor can they limit their data to circulation statistics or the number of visitors; those numbers no longer tell a compelling story about the role of the library media center in student learning.

To appeal to administrators and decision makers, school librarians must engage in work that assesses the impact of their work and the growth of their students. Assessment is not solely the purview of adults: the AASL *Standards* promote the development of self-assessment strategies among students. They must speak the language that other educators speak: the language of student learning. *Evidence-based practice* asks library media specialists to gather evidence—or data—about student learning and to adjust the approach to meet gaps in student understanding and conceptual mastery.

Assessment is one facet of evidence-based practice. Assessment is a process of determining what students have learned as a result of instruction. The face of assessment has changed in the past few decades. In the past, assessment came at the end of a unit, such as grading a project or scoring a test, a process known as *summative assessment*. If students had not mastered the content as evidenced on the test or project, it was too late. Today's assessment options are far more diverse. It is not necessary to wait until a project's conclusion to tell students about the quality of their work and work processes. *Formative assessment* defines a variety of opportunities for students to receive feedback about their work in progress. Formative assessment lets school librarians and teachers correct misconceptions, praise efforts, recommend alternative resources, and question student conclusions before a final project is completed. This results in higher student mastery and conceptual understanding. A third type of assessment, *diagnostic assessment*, takes the pulse of students' prior knowledge. When compared with the summative assessment, diagnostic assessment can reveal what has been learned as a result of instruction. Whereas many assessments are quantitative in nature, assigning letter grades or numerical scores, qualitative data can have equal or greater meaning.

How do students, librarians, and administrators know that students are learning in the school library media center, or whether students are simply going through the motions? How do educators know that they are measuring student cognition, not merely a student's ability to follow directions? What evidence is there that library media specialists' instructional practice is working? These are questions that Barbara Stripling addresses in "Assessing Information Fluency: Gathering Evidence of Student Learning" (beginning on page 166). Using her Inquiry Model as an example, Stripling opens a conversation about how student learning can be gauged using diagnostic, formative, and summative assessment.

Marjorie L. Pappas's "Tools for the Assessment of Learning" (beginning on page 171) echoes Stripling's ideas and offers a variety of tools, including logs, writing prompts, checklists, and organizers, that reveal student thinking and provide opportunities for instructors to assess for gaps in understanding and plan interventions.

Leslie Preddy, a middle school library media specialist, explores how students can become more self-aware while educators gain perspective on progress in "Research Reflections, Journaling, and Exit Slips" (beginning on page 176). Sample exit slips by Deborah Levitov (beginning on page 178) provide ready-to-duplicate examples for easy implementation.

Pappas continues the conversation with "Designing Learning for Evidence-Based Practice" (beginning on page 180), which brings the backward design approach of Wiggins and McTighe (2005) into the library media center. Though this article was published before the advent of the AASL *Standards,* the ideas remain sound. The process begins by identifying exit outcomes. Once the outcomes are envisioned, the teaching team decides how learning will be assessed, what formative and self-assessment strategies will be folded in, which instructional methods would be most effective to lead students to the desired outcome, and how to reflect on the student work. Finally, evidence is documented and shared with stakeholders.

One of the leading voices in assessment in school libraries is Violet H. Harada. In "Assessing Learning: The Missing Piece of Instruction?" (beginning on page 185), she and Joan M. Yoshina bring the assessment conversation to a practical level, demonstrating what assessment might look like with specific elementary and secondary examples.

Harada continues the conversation with "Building Evidence Folders for Learning through Library Media Centers" (beginning on page 189), reporting on a cohort of Hawaiian school library media specialists and their efforts to gather evidence and artifacts that demonstrate improvement in the student learning experience. Evidence folders, a collection of documents and artifacts, become a tool with which school library media specialists communicate what students are learning. Unlike a portfolio, which documents the educator's work, an evidence folder focuses on students.

Harada's third article, "From Eyeballing to Evidence: Assessing for Learning in Hawaii Library Media Centers" (beginning on page 194), takes its title from a library media specialist who traditionally used "eyeballing" to guess at student progress rather than taking a more systematic approach of developing measurable evidence of student learning. She reveals what school librarians in Hawaii discovered when they began to implement more rigorous assessment structures and how they led to more rigorous teaching. Backward design, or beginning with the end in mind, is crucial to this work, echoing Pappas's "Designing Learning" article. Harada also discusses the importance of helping students learn to self-evaluate more effectively.

Finally, Christine Findlay reports about the work of the Ohio Educational Library Media Association (OELMA) in systemically approaching evidence-based practice. Based on the landmark OELMA study led by Ross Todd and Carol Kuhlthau of Rutgers University, which surveyed students about their perceptions of their learning in school libraries, OELMA leadership began to systematically train school librarians to collect evidence of student learning, using the theme, "Can You Find the Evidence-Based Practice in Your School Library?" Findlay's article, "Ohio's Foray into Evidence-Based Practice" (starting on page 200), discusses the rollout and impact of OELMA's strategies.

As these articles outline, assessment is key to the long-term growth of students and the long-term viability of SLMSs and school library media centers.

GETTING TO ADVOCACY

1. Ask that your name be added to the teacher's name on assignment sheets and rubrics so that parents and administrators have an additional opportunity to see you as an instructional partner. In staff meetings and curriculum-related planning sessions, it is most powerful to have teachers discuss how they have worked with the library media specialist to meet learning objectives. In this way they become active advocates, and it isn't just the library media specialist delivering the messages. Classroom teachers listen best to other classroom teachers.

2. Offer to help design rubrics so that they reflect both the process and the product of library learning. This benefits students and shows classroom colleagues how the goals of the library link to and match the goals of the classroom.

3. Work with teachers to add a student self-assessment column to the rubric, thus empowering students' long-term self-evaluation skills. Then ask students to share their new understandings with stakeholders at an open house or other public event.

4. Recognize and acknowledge effort. Building rapport, trust, and collegiality are at the heart of recruiting advocates in students, teachers, administrators, and others.

THOUGHTS FOR THE JOURNEY

1. How can you ensure that you are assessing student growth and learning, not just assessing whether or not students followed a teacher-directed procedure?

2. How do you handle a situation in which the student has a grossly different perspective on his or her achievement than you do?

3. What strategies for formative assessment are you currently using? What strategies from this chapter might be useful to adopt?

4. What kinds of data are most useful for a fellow teacher to see? For a parent? For a building administrator? For a school board member? What is important to each of these groups of stakeholders? How can you better see their perspective?

Assessing

Information Fluency:

Gathering Evidence of Student Learning

by Barbara Stripling

Do you ever feel like the character portrayed by Patrick Swayze in the movie *Ghost* who has difficulty making himself heard by anyone who is not a fellow ghost? How many times have you tried to tell your teachers and administrators about the positive effect of information skills on student learning, only to be ignored because you do not have evidence to back up your claims? By assessing students' ability to apply information skills to class assignments, library media specialists can provide the evidence that will foster schoolwide attention to students' information fluency. At the same time, library media specialists will be solidifying their essential contribution to both teaching and learning.

Barbara Stripling is the Director of Library Services for the New York City Department of Education, NY. Email: bstripling@schools.nyc.gov.

What Is Information Fluency?

Information fluency is the ability to access, make sense of, and use information to build new understandings. The term "information fluency" is now accepted in the field as a replacement for "information literacy" because students must not only know the skills, but also apply the skills fluently in any personal or academic learning situation.

Information fluency skills make sense to students when they are engaged in a coherent process of inquiry and learning. Students want to be able to seek and find information to answer their questions. They want to be empowered as independent learners who can navigate the growing area of information and transform what they find into knowledge and understanding.

This process of inquiry and

learning is a recursive cycle of thought. One model to summarize this learning framework is provided in Table 1 (Stripling 2003, 8), below.

How Can Information Fluency Be Assessed?

Library media specialists can assess students' ability to apply information skills at each phase of an inquiry process by using three main types of assessment: diagnostic, formative, and summative. Since information skills should be taught when students have a reason to use them, the assessment of information skills should be integrated into real content-learning situations and should not be isolated from curriculum and instruction in the classrooms.

Why Use Diagnostic Assessment?

Diagnostic assessment is most often used during the Connect phase (See Table 1, below) of inquiry because it is important to identify pre-existing knowledge and skills as well as misconceptions in order to set goals for new learning. Techniques that teachers use to diagnose prior knowledge of content can also be used successfully to measure the following student information skills: pre-tests, pre-performance tasks, the "Know" part of a K-W-L (Know-Wonder-Learned) chart, or a concept map.

Pre-tests are especially valuable for bringing misconceptions to the surface. Research has shown that unless learners recognize their own misconceptions, they are not likely to replace them with more accurate or detailed knowledge. At an early elementary level, for example, the library media specialist starting to teach how a library is organized might give a set of cards with pictures of various objects in different colors and sizes to groups of students with the instructions to group the cards as they would be organized in a library. Once students have shared their work, the library media specialist can determine whether students think books are organized by color, size, or category. A follow-up class discussion can alert students to their own misconceptions about the way a library is arranged.

Another diagnostic assessment is a pre-performance task, a task assigned to students before any direct instruction. The most commonly used activity for orientation to the library, a scavenger hunt, can easily turn into a mindless game with limited impact on learning; however, if a scavenger hunt is used as a pre-performance task, the library media specialist will be able to assess students' existing knowledge. This assessment of students' existing knowledge on how to locate items in the library can be used to design future lessons that build on what students already know.

How Does Formative Assessment Lead to More Effective Instruction?

Formative assessment is the measurement of knowledge and skills during the process of learn-

TABLE 1

Stripling Inquiry Model	
Phases	**Inquiry Strategies**
Connect	Connect to self, previous knowledge Gain background and context Observe, experience
Wonder	Develop questions Make predictions, hypotheses
Investigate	Find and evaluate information to answer questions, test hypotheses Think about the information to illuminate new questions and hypotheses
Construct	Construct new understandings connected to previous knowledge Draw conclusions about questions and hypotheses
Express	Apply understandings to a new context, new situation Express new ideas to share learning with others
Reflect	Reflect on own learning Ask new questions

ing (the Wonder, Investigate, and Construct phases of inquiry) in order to inform the next steps. The magic of formative assessment is that it engages both library media specialists and students in thinking about the learning/inquiry process while it is happening so that adjustments can be made immediately as needed. Although some formative assessment tools are developed and administered by the library media specialist (ungraded exams, checklists, rubrics, exit cards, observation checklists, and consultations), others will be developed by the students as a normal part of their inquiry process. These are the very same tools that they use to question, challenge, evaluate, organize, and reflect on the information they are gathering (inquiry framework questions, evaluation templates, graphic organizers, and learning log notetaking sheets).

One example of formative assessment administered by the library media specialist is an exit card. The library media specialist hands each student a card in the last five to ten minutes of class time in the library media center. For example, upper elementary and secondary students are given a specific question to answer about their progress or new understandings (e.g., What was the most interesting idea you learned today?, What question(s) are you having trouble answering through your research?, What source did you find today and how did you decide it was valuable?, Where are you in your inquiry process, and what's your next step?). Lower elementary students can be asked to rate their own progress on simplified tasks (Did you find five facts about your animal today?) with their name and a smiley or frowny face. The students hand in the cards as they leave. The library media specialist responds on the back with specific suggestions, provocative questions, ideas for next steps, or general encouragement.

An observation checklist is another example of formative assessment delivered by the library media specialist. Because information fluency assessment is largely a measure of students' ability "to do," library media specialists can develop checklists of observable behaviors that signify students' use of information fluency skills. Checklists measure completion of work, but generally they are not a good instrument to measure quality of work. Observation checklists are most valuable when developed as a matrix with students' names on one side and the observable behaviors on the other. (See Checklist Example to the left.)

Students should be empowered to do formative assessment for themselves. Library media specialists, however, can facilitate student reflection on the process of inquiry by providing Inquiry Framework Questions (New York City Department of Education, Office of

Checklist Example	Geraldo	Chymeka	Steven	Stephanie	Jamal
Elementary:					
Predicted what a book would be about from its title					
Took notes on at least two facts to answer each question					
Used pictures to find answers to questions					
Secondary:					
Developed at least three focusing questions					
Set up notetaking log sheets with a question at the top of each					
Found and took notes from a magazine article					
Found and took notes from two books					
Evaluated a website using the criteria established by the class					

Library Services). Students can self-regulate their progress through the recursive process of inquiry by considering each question before they decide to move to the next phase. For example, before moving to the Wonder Phase, a student may ask:

- Do I know enough about the idea or topic to ask good questions?
- Am I interested enough in the idea or topic to investigate it?

Before moving to the Investigate Phase, a student may ask:

- Can my question(s) be answered through investigation?
- Will my question(s) lead me to answers that will fulfill my assignment or purpose for research?

Before moving to the Construct Phase, a student may ask:

- Have I located sources with diverse perspectives?
- Have I found enough accurate information to answer all my questions?
- Have I discovered information gaps and filled them with more research?
- Have I begun to identify relationships and patterns and thoughtfully reacted to the information I found?

How Can Summative Assessment Leverage Collaboration?

Summative assessment is the measurement of knowledge and skills at the end of a process of learning (during the Express and Reflect phases of inquiry as mentioned in Table 1) in order to determine the amount and quality of learning. Summative assessments of information fluency are most effective when integrated into summative assessments of content learning. When library media specialists can demonstrate the integral nature of information fluency skills to the success of the final product, then teachers can see the added value of the library media program and the applicability of information skills for their classroom instruction.

Teachers and library media specialists can use a variety of summative assessment choices such as authentic projects (connected to the real world), presentations, exhibitions, performance tasks, portfolios, and process folios that enable students to demonstrate their new understandings. In each case, the checklist or rubric used for evaluation should be designed by both teachers and library media specialists to include the information fluency skills essential to the creation of the product. Other summative assessment tools are completed by the students themselves, reflecting their new understandings about the content and the inquiry process. These tools include concept maps, final reflections, documentation of their content and process learning, and self-assessment with checklists and rubrics.

Summative assessment products can be designed for different levels of thinking, depending on the requirements of the assignment and the depth of learning expected. Library media specialists can collaborate with classroom teachers to design assessment products that challenge students to think, connect, construct, and demonstrate their learning in creative and enjoyable ways. By designing creative assessment products that incorporate information fluency skills, library media specialist/teacher teams solidify the connection between library and classroom instruction and strengthen student interest and success.

Table 2, Assessment Levels & Information Fluency Skills (page 29), illustrates two levels of research products and notes the information fluency skills that might have been taught with the unit.

What Guidelines Should Be Followed in Developing Assessments of Information Fluency?

Library media specialists who want to assume a leadership role in assessment in their schools and make the assessment of information fluency skills a vital part of teaching and learning throughout the school can follow six simple guidelines:

- *Establish clear information fluency learning goals*—State explicitly the information fluency skills that students are expected to learn within each research unit.
- *Define clear criteria for successful application of information fluency skills*—Provide teachers and students with models of successful employment of the skills.
- *Align goals and criteria with assignment*—Ensure that the skills being taught are essential and integral to the classroom teacher's assignment.
- *Move to student self-assessment*—Empower students to assess their own inquiry process.
- *Make assessments a natural part of teaching and learning throughout the process of learning*—Use diagnostic,

formative, and summative assessments to strengthen the teaching of information fluency skills and move students toward confidence and independence in their own learning.

Assessment is a critical element of effective teaching. Library media specialists who are able to provide evidence that students have learned information fluency skills will be more successful in their teaching and more integral to the instructional program of the school. Through assessment, library media specialists have the potential to transform their role from invisible and unheard ghost to the most sought-after partner in the school.

References

Harada, Violet H., and Joan M. Yoshina. *Assessing Learning: Librarians and Teachers as Partners*. Libraries Unlimited, 2005.

Hart, Diane. *Authentic Assessment: A Handbook for Educators*. Addison-Wesley, 1994.

Lewin, Larry, and Betty Jean Shoemaker. *Great Performances: Creating Classroom-Based Assessment Tasks*. ASCD, 1998.

New York City Department of Education, Office of Library Services. *Information Fluency Continuum*. http://schools.nyc.gov/NR/rdonlyresBD4FDF5F-F45F-43AE-90BB-410BDBC641AF/6513/INFOFLUENCYCONTK12Final102006.pdf

Newmann, Fred M., et al. *A Guide to Authentic Instruction and Assessment: Vision, Standards, and Scoring*. Wisconsin Center for Education Research, 1995.

Shepard, Lorrie A. "Linking Formative Assessment to Scaffolding." *Educational Leadership* 63, no. 3 (November 2005): 66-70.

Stiggins, Richard J. *Student-Centered Classroom Assessment*. 2nd ed. Merrill, 1997.

Stripling, Barbara. "Expectations for Achievement and Performance: Assessing Student Skills." *NASSP Bulletin* 83, no. 605 (March 1999): 44-52.

Stripling, Barbara K. "Inquiry-Based Learning." In *Curriculum Connections Through the Library*, edited by Barbara K. Stripling and Sandra Hughes-Hassell. Libraries Unlimited, 2003.

Stripling, Barbara K., and Judy M. Pitts. *Brainstorms and Blueprints: Teaching Library Research as a Thinking Process*. Libraries Unlimited, 1988.

TABLE 2

Assessment Levels & Information Fluency Skills
Adapted excerpt from Barbara K. Stripling and Judy M. Pitts (1998).

Level	Sample Assessment Products	Information Fluency Skills
Recalling *Recalling and reporting the main facts discovered;* *Making no attempt to analyze the information or reorganize it for comparison purposes*	• <u>Select</u> 5-10 accomplishments of the person you have researched. Produce a "Hall of Fame" (or "Hall of Shame") poster with your biographee's photocopied picture and list of accomplishments. • <u>List</u> five "Do's and Dont's" about a social issue that you have researched.	• Identifies main ideas and supporting details. • Develops own point of view and supports with evidence. • Uses common organizational patterns to organize information (compare/contrast).
Analyzing *Breaking a subject into its component parts (causes, effects, problems, solutions);* *Comparing one part with another*	• <u>Characterize</u> your researched historical person in an obituary which makes clear his/her role in the conflicts of the day. • Write a letter to the editor <u>scrutinizing</u> a local issue. Support your opinions with specific details from your research.	• Recognizes multiple causations for same issues or events. • Presents conclusions to answer the question or problem. • Verifies all facts through use of multiple sources. • Develops own point of view and supports with evidence. • Utilizes different organization structures as appropriate for point of view and conclusions.

Tools for the Assessment of Learning

by Marjorie L. Pappas

Accountability is huge today!! Teachers and administrators are fully engaged in providing evidence that Susie and Johnny can meet the achievement levels set by state standards. Where are library media specialists in this scenario? The curriculum of the school library media program is typically based on information literacy standards, but which standards? The *Information Literacy Standards for Student Learning* (AASL/AECT 1998) are the national standards, but do states or school districts have standards? Before library media specialists can assess students, they need to identify the curriculum and/or standards that students are expected to apply as they gather and use information for projects, research papers, and personal interest.

Many state standards include knowledge and skills relevant to information literacy. Some standards include library media as a separate content area, while others have integrated library media skills and knowledge throughout all content areas. For example, *Information Literacy: Florida's Library/Media Curriculum Connections* is a separate document with guidelines for information literacy skills across all grade levels. Ohio and North Carolina have similar documents. The *Illinois Learning Standards* include information literacy within the English Language Arts Performance Descriptors as one of the strands. When state standards do not include separate library media standards, library media specialists sometimes conclude that there are no standards for their program, but that is inaccurate. A close examination of content areas within state standards usually identifies relevant standards. Library media specialists in Indiana developed a *Correlation of the Information Literacy Standards* (AASL/AECT 1998) and Indiana's Academic Standards. This document correlates each of the *Information Literacy Standards* with the content standards. References to resources within INSPIRE, the Indiana virtual library, are noted in red text below each relevant standard. The value of this document is priceless because it enables collaboration between classroom teachers and teacher librarians to increase student achievement.

Teacher librarians can achieve the same type of correlation by working with classroom teachers to map the curriculum using the *Information Literacy Standards* as part of that process. Curriculum mapping shows the connections between the content area curriculum and the library media curriculum.

What Is Assessment?

Information Power positions the school library media program within the context of constructivist learning theory and authentic learning. This approach engages students in problem-solving and inquiry projects that require students to be critical thinkers and decision makers (AASL/AECT 1998). The traditional testing approach evaluates students' ability to regurgitate information, but it does not provide evidence of their applying a process or thinking skills.

Assessment is the process of gathering evidence to show student understanding of information lit-

Marjorie L. Pappas, Ph.D., is a writer, consultant, and virtual professor from Danville, KY. Email: mlpappas@adelphia.net

eracy. Assessment documents focus on thinking rather than on evaluating or measuring rote knowledge. The tools of assessment can range from an observation to a checklist or a portfolio. Library media specialists use assessment tools to assess a skills lesson or a project that is the culminating activity for a complex lesson or unit.

Formative assessment takes place throughout a learning activity. A library media specialist who is teaching a lesson on using an index might stop at various places in the lesson and ask questions to check for understanding. Students might be engaged in gathering information, using a specific database, or recording information on a log template. The library media specialist meets briefly with small groups to talk about their note-gathering process. Each of these is an example of formative assessment, such as checking for student understanding at various stages in the lesson.

Summative assessment assesses student learning at the end of a learning activity. For example, students are studying weather patterns and they gathered local weather data over multiple weeks. Working collaboratively with the classroom teacher, the library media specialist demonstrated several weather websites and helped design an organizer that would enable students to organize their data showing patterns and trends in weather systems. The weather organizer and a written report documenting the results were the summative assessments for this unit. The assessments demonstrated knowledge of both the science and information literacy standards.

What Are Assessment Tools?

Assessment tools enable both learning and assessing. Many tools facilitate the learning process and provide evidence of new skills and understandings. Tools can include logs, checklists, rating scales, organizers, matrices, concept maps, brainstorming webs, and rubrics (Harada and Yoshina 2005).

Logs and Reflection

Students write logs to show the steps or process they follow to complete a task or project. For example, students are studying deserts and need to gather information about the animals and their habitats. Working in small groups, they culminate the project by creating a diorama depicting the ecosystem within a specific desert. Students keep a daily log of their research process. Each day their teacher asks them to write a log entry in response to a prompt (see Figure 1, page 23).

Writing prompts are important because they provide a focus for the students' writing and evidence of students' ability to meet the lesson or unit objectives. One of the objectives for the unit on deserts is that "students will locate resources appropriate for their research topic." The writing prompt (see Figure 1) requires students to reflect on their resources and select those that are the most useful. The process of writing a log enables students to think about the steps involved in gathering and using information. This process involves metacognition, thinking about how we think and learn.

Checklists and Rating Scales

Checklists are a list of the requirements, characteristics, steps, and behaviors that result in a positive outcome from a task or project. Checklists are a tool for both students and teacher(s). Students can use the checklist to determine if they followed all the steps and requirements of the project prior to submission. The teacher uses the checklist to assess the project. Typically, checklists include a definite "yes" or "no" indicating the student met or did not meet the requirement. Checklists sometimes include a note column enabling the teacher to write a comment about some or all of the requirements or characteristics (Harada and Yoshina 2005).

A rating scale includes criteria for assessing the process and content that reflects a successful product or performance. The rating scale is similar to a rubric and is useful when it is possible to rate student performance along a continuum. However, the rating scale does not describe the variance of levels for each criterion. Rating scales are easier to write than rubrics, but they do not provide students with as much assessment information.

JoAnn Floyd (2007) created a biography lesson that engages students in creating a timeline of a person studied. The lesson, "Putting It on the Line!", includes an example of a rating scale that assesses the organizer and timeline required as products in the lesson (see Figure 2, page 23).

Organizers

Organizers are visual representations of content that show the interrelationships of specific relevant information. Organizers allow learners to deconstruct concepts and visually demonstrate relationships. Hyerle (1996) suggests that the higher orders of thinking, analysis, and synthesis of information require learners to "organize, break down, and reformulate, [which] are the steps upward toward evaluative thinking." Hyerle adds that "even the lowest level of Bloom's taxonomy—knowledge—is defined as the basic organization of content." Information is traditionally presented in a linear manner, which makes it difficult for learners to construct relationships between concepts. Organizers, as visual representations of content, provide learners with the tools to understand relationships.

Organizers, tools of learning and assessment, enable and provide evidence of thinking. Organizers are visual tools, thus there are an infinite number of possibilities for shapes and designs. When an important outcome of an organizer is assessment, library media specialists need to construct the organizer(s) to reflect the learning objectives of the lesson.

Constructivist learning theory places great importance on help-ing learners make a connection to prior knowledge. Brainstorming webs and KWL charts are organizers that enable a connection with prior knowledge. For example, students who are beginning a unit on immigration might start their learning experience by developing a brainstorming web. The classroom teacher and/or the library media specialist begins the brainstorming session by asking students who they know that has recently immigrated to the United States. The discussion progresses and the brainstorming web develops on the whiteboard as students make connections with their knowledge about people and issues related to immigration (see Figure 3, page 24).

Thinking Skill Organizers

Examples of thinking skill organizers include classification, sequence, comparison, conclusion, problem solving, and inference.

The "Animal to Animal—A Comparison" lesson engages students in gathering information and developing a chart that compares animals using the criteria of appearance, habitat, diet, and other facts (Aspelund 2007, 16). (See Figure 4, page 24.)

The sequence or timeline organizer can be applied to many learning activities. The historical timeline is one of the more obvious options, but the charting of a sequence of events covers a variety of activities, for example, plot of a fiction book or drama, steps of a process, or the important events in the life of a famous person (see Figure 5, page 24).

One of the more classic shapes for a comparison organizer is the Venn diagram. Two circles overlapping allows for similar characteristics in the overlapping sections with differences in the outer parts of the circles (see Figure 6, page 25).

Process Organizers

Organizers can be used to facilitate and assess a process. The brainstorming web is a useful tool in

FIGURE 1. LOG OF DESERT RESEARCH

Teacher's prompt: Which resources gave you the most useful information?

Student's log entry: We found a really great website about the Sahara Desert. There were pictures of the animals living there. Also pictures of the food they eat.

FIGURE 2. SAMPLE CHECKLIST (Taken from the lesson plan by JoAnn Floyd, *SLMAM*, February 2007: 11-13.)

Assessment of Graphic Organizer and Biographical Timeline				
Criteria	Exemplary	Proficient	Developing	Unacceptable
Graphic Organizer lists at least 5 or more significant events.				
Graphic Organizer includes a corresponding date for each event.				
Timeline accurately reflects the information detailed in the organizer.				
Appropriate graphics are included.				
Timeline is neat and information is well spaced.				
Proper spelling and punctuation are evident.				
The source is given credit.				

FIGURE 3: BRAINSTORMING WEB

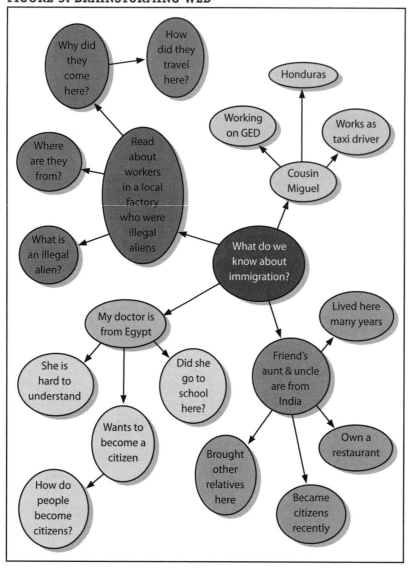

FIGURE 4: COMPARISON CHART (From a lesson plan by Carol Aspelund, *SLMAM*, January 2007: 15-17.)

Compare Two Animals		
	Animal Name	Animal Name
Appearance		
Habitat		
Diet		
Other Facts		

FIGURE 5: SEQUENCE OR TIMELINE ORGANIZER

the early stages of an information-seeking process. The KWL chart also enables a connection to prior knowledge while incorporating questioning as learners brainstorm what they know and want to know.

Note taking or the recording of information is typically a challenge for students. A note-taking form or organizer provides students with a visual structure for recording information. The T-chart is a two-column organizer that focuses students on concise notes in column one and reflection about those notes in column two (see Figure 7, page 25).

Other process organizers include a searching matrix, a planning organizer that lists specific steps for completing the research project with a column for specific strategies, and the date for completing each step.

Conclusion

Assessment tools give library media specialists snapshots of evidence that demonstrates student understanding of the Information Literacy Standards. Over time the evidence provide a more complete picture of learners' ability to gather, evaluate, and use information to solve problems, make decisions, and think critically. Used in conjunction with the evidence gathered by classroom teachers, library media specialists can show how the library media program supports the content standards and student achievement.

References

American Association of School Librarians/ Association for Educational Communication and Technology. *Information Power for Student Learning*. Chicago: ALA, 1998.

Aspelund, Carol. "Science: Animal to Animal—A Comparison." *School Library Media Activities Monthly* 23, no. 5 (January 2007): 15-17.

Bloom's Taxonomy: Sample Questions. http://www.officeport.com/edu/bloomq.htm (accessed January 29, 2007)

Harada, Violet H., and Joan M. Yoshina. *Assessing Learning: Librarians and Teachers as Partners.* Libraries Unlimited, 2005.

Hyerle, David. *Visual Tools for Constructing Knowledge.* ASCD, 1996.

Floyd, JoAnn. "Reading/Language Arts: Putting It on the Line!" *School Library Media Activities Monthly* 23, no. 6 (February 2007): 11-13.

Illinois Learning Standards. English Performance Descriptors and Classroom Assessments. Illinois State Board of Education. http://www.isbe.net/ils/html/descriptors.htm (accessed January 29, 2007)

Indiana's Academic Standards. Indiana Department of Education. http://www.doe.state.in.us/standards/welcome2.html (accessed January 29, 2007)

Information Literacy: Florida's Library Media / Curriculum Connections. Florida Department of Education. http://www.firn.edu/doe/instmat/ilflmcc.htm (accessed January 29, 2007)

Library Guidelines. Ohio Department of Education. http://www.ode.state.oh.us/GD/Templates/Pages/ODE/ODEDetail.aspx?page=3&TopicRelationID=340&ContentID=2489&Content=17495 (accessed January 29, 2007)

Additional Resources

Callison, Daniel. "Organizers." *School Library Media Activities Monthly* 16, no. 5 (May 2000): 36-39.

Graphic Organizers. [Smart Card]. Kagan Cooperative Learning, 1998. http://www.kaganonline.com/Catalog/SmartCards1.html

Harada, Violet H. "Building Evidence Folders for Learning through Library Media Centers." *School Library Media Activities Monthly* 23, no. 3 (November 2006): 15-29.

Harada, Violet H. "Working Smarter: Being Strategic about Assessment and Accountability." *Teacher Librarian* 33, no. 1 (October 2005): 8-15.

Harada, Violet H., and Joan M. Yoshina. "Assessing Learning: The Missing Piece in Instruction." *School Library Media Activities Monthly* 22, no. 7 (March 2006): 20-23.

Harada, Violet H., and Joan M. Yoshina. "Engaging Students in Inquiry." *School Library Media Activities Monthly* 22, no. 8 (April 2006): 22-25.

Harada, V. H., and Joan M. Yoshina. *Inquiry Learning through Librarian-Teacher Partnerships.* Linworth, 2004.

Hyerle, David. *A Field Guide to Using Visual Tools.* ASCD, 2000.

Koechlin, Carol, and Sandi Zwaan. *Build Your Own Information Literate School.* Hi Willow Research, 2003.

Organizing Thinking Books 1 & 2: Organizers on CD. The Critical Thinking Co. http://www.criticalthinking.com/getProductDetails.do?code=c&id=06808

Pappas, Marjorie L. "Organizing Research." *School Library Media Activities Monthly* 14, no. 4 (April 1997): 30-32.

Pappas, Marjorie L. "State Landmarks." *School Library Media Activities Monthly* 19, no. 9 (May 2003): 22-25.

Pappas, Marjorie L. "Writing Editorials." *School Library Media Activities Monthly* 19, no. 10 (June 2003): 20-24.

Parks, Sandra, and Howard Black. *Organizing Thinking: Books 1 & 2.* Critical Thinking Co, 1992.

Web Sites—Organizers

Concept Mapping and Inspiration. The Virtual Institute. http://www.ettc.net/techfellow/inspir.htm

Graphic Organizers. Houghton Mifflin, 2000. http://www.eduplace.com/kids/hme/k_5/graphorg/

Graphic Organizers. North Central Regional Laboratory, 1988. http://www.ncrel.org/sdrs/areas/issues/students/learning/lr1grorg.htm

Graphic Organizers: Activity Bank. S.C.O.R.E. http://www.sdcoe.k12.ca.us/score/actbank/torganiz.htm

Learning Resources: Graphic Organizers. Annette Lamb, ed. 2003. http://eduscapes.com/tap/topic73.htm

Region 15 Graphic Organizers. http://www.region15.org/curriculum/graphicorg.html

Write Design Online: Graphic Organizers. http://www.writedesignonline.com/organizers/ ✋

FIGURE 6: VENN DIAGRAM

United States

Declared independence from Great Britain
Spanish influence in SW
Growing Hispanic population
Health care system is private
Sections are a warmer climate

Early settlers—English
English language is prominent in both
Democratic government

Canada

Remains part of British Empire
French culture and language
Health care system is public
Colder climate, parts near the Arctic Circle

FIGURE 7: T-CHART FOR NOTE TAKING

Bibliographic Citation:	
Author	Publisher/date
Title	
Brief Summary Notes	Reflection/Evaluation Comments

Research Reflections, Journaling, and Exit Slips

by Leslie Preddy

Taking the time to think about the effectiveness and quality of what has been done, what is being done, and what still needs to be done is an essential and natural part of being a lifelong learner. It is, therefore, important to teach students how to successfully reflect upon experiences and evaluate their interactions with resources, events, and themselves throughout the research process. The speed of information access as well as students' automatic acceptance that all information is good information makes the opportunity to digest the moment and contemplate the future in research even more important.

Giving students an occasion every day for self-analysis through the strategies of reflection, journaling, or exit slips provides the chance to personally reflect on what they are doing, what they are thinking, and what still needs to be done. It is an invaluable use of instructional time. Using one of these strategies allows students the necessary practice to look back on their experiences until they are capable of doing this independently and intuitively as an effective and efficient researcher does. These practices provide opportunities for educators to quickly understand individual student researchers, as well as where weaknesses in instruction exist.

Reflections

In a reflection, the educator poses a group of simple questions that require students to write a brief response. Questions can be developed to give students a chance to personally reflect and self-analyze what has just been done, what needs to be done, roadblocks, successes, personal thoughts, and feelings. Examples of some questions to include are:
- What did I do today?
- Titles of the resources I used today were…
- What question was I trying to answer? or Research question/s I was working on today were…
- What problem, if any, did I have today? or The biggest problem I had today (with myself, other people, or the research itself) was…
- What was something new I learned? (For example, successfully learning a new research technique, how to use a specific resource, a new resource never used before, something I didn't know about my topic,…)
- What new questions do I now have about my research topic, final product, or a research skill?
- Who were helpful people I encountered today and what they did they do to help me (teacher, student, parent, sibling, library media specialist, etc.)?
- How do I feel about today? or Today I feel _____, because…
- What, specifically, do I need to do next? or What I need to do next… (be specific—for example, name the title of the source that I want to use and the research question I will start my research time using)

Journaling

The educator can use journaling to provide students with an opportunity to reflect on the research day through an age-appropriate paragraph or essay response to an experience-to-self or experience-to-world question, similar to text-to-self and text-to-world questions.

Journal prompts appropriate for any project are:
- Pretend you are writing a note to a friend and you include a paragraph about this research project. What would you say?
- Tell how you feel about your abilities throughout this research project. Describe your strengths. Describe your weaknesses. What steps do you need to take to build those weaknesses into strengths?
- Today you were interviewed by another student about your research. You shared what you have learned, facts, and interesting details about your famous person. Describe how you feel about your interview. Explain what you think you did well. What did you forget to talk about and wish you had? On the back of this paper draw a picture of your person doing what you think he/she did best.

- Brainstorm all the ideas you have for your final project. Include possible slogans, materials needed, and other ideas that will make your project unique and stand out.
- Write as if you were taking notes for research. List tips and strategies for effective note-taking. In addition, tell what you have found most interesting so far about your topic.
- Today you worked with key words. Why is it important to keep key words in mind when reading for the answers to research questions?
- How well do you like your questions? How do you think the questions will help you while you become an expert on this topic? Which question do you think is most interesting and why?

Journal prompts can also be written very specifically for a particular project. Examples of project-specific questions are:

- Hero or Biography: Explain one or more ways the person you are researching is similar to you and one or more ways he or she is different.
- Social Concerns: What organizations are you learning about that exist to fight against this problem? What do you propose is a good way to get involved? If you could start your own organization, what would it be about and why? How would it solve problems?
- Indians of North America: Why do you think researching about the ancient Native Americans is important to being an American citizen today?

Exit Slips

The educator can use exit slips if time is limited for reflection. An exit slip can take just the last few moments of research time as students prepare to transition to the next activity or class. An exit slip is a small slip of paper requiring fill-in-the-blank responses:

- The research skill I was taught today was…

- A research skill I already knew and used today was…
- Help! A question I have about my project, my research, the assignment, or today's events is…

Intersperse these fill-in-the-blank responses with questions that require students to circle an emoticon (happy, okay, sad, frustrated) to reflect the day's feelings:

- The skills taught today were helpful:
- My personal effort in class today:
- My classroom teacher and library media specialist were busy today helping students research and stay on task:

Through reflections, journaling, and exit slips, an educator can learn more about his/her students as researchers. These strategies provide structure and guided opportunities for students to record and communicate. Written reflections often help students identify and organize thoughts and build self-confidence for successfully managing today's information needs. An educator might learn that a particular student is doing okay, requires remediation with a particular research technique, is enthusiastic and excited about something learned, or frustrated and feeling discouraged. Written communication can also help an educator manage time for constructive feedback as well as provide a clear assessment tool for knowing where students are and what needs to be reinforced. These strategies can help an educator focus on critical problems and better management of communication with students.

References:
Callison, Daniel, and Leslie Preddy. *The Blue Book on Literacy and Instruction for the Information Age.* Libraries Unlimited, 2006.◄

Leslie Preddy is the library media specialist at Perry Meridian Middle School in Indianapolis, IN. She is the author of *SSR with Intervention* (Libraries Unlimited, 2007) and co-author of *The Blue Book on Literacy and Instruction for the Information Age* (Libraries Unlimited, 2006). Website: http://www.lesliepreddy.com; Email: lpreddy@msdpt.k12.in.us

Sample Exit Slips for Elementary, Middle, and High School

Shown here are examples of exit slips. These examples provide one method that might be used to address the dispositions, responsibilities, and self-assessments of the *AASL Standards for the 21st-Century Learner* (2007) and serve as an extension to four of the lesson plans in this issue as well as the article by Leslie Preddy, "Research Reflections, Journaling, and Exit Slips" (*SLMAM*, October 2008: 22-23), the article by Deb Logan, "Being Heard…Advocacy + Evidence + Students = Impact!" (*SLMAM*, September 2006: 46-48), and examples from Kristin Fontichiaro's book, *Podcasting at School* (Libraries Unlimited, 2008).

To guide the development of Exit Slips, the following questions should be answered:
- ▶What are the targeted learning goals for students?
- ▶What are the targeted information literacy standards and skills?
- ▶What behaviors are you looking for in the learner?
- ▶How do you expect the student to show responsibility?

The exit slips can be established with questions or statements, whatever seems most effective for the age group or the desired response.◄

High School

(Lesson Plan: "Banned Books" by Pat Franklin, see pp. 13-14)
Disposition 1.2.4; Responsibility 1.3.2; Self-assessment: 1.4.3

What did you learn about the use and power of language? _____
_____
_____

How will you use what you learned in the future?
_____
_____
_____

How do you know if information is reliable and accurate? _____
_____
_____

What remaining questions do you have? _____
_____
_____

Middle School

(Lesson Plan: "It's a Two-Minute Mystery" by Dianne Ritz-Salminen, see p. 11)
Dispositions: 1.2.5, 3.2.3; Responsibilities: 1.3.4; Self-assessment: 2.4.1

Helpful resources I used today were _____
_____

My strategy for choosing the best information was to _____
_____

Ways our group worked well together were_____
_____

I contributed to the group work by_____
_____

A way we could improve working as a group would be_____
_____
_____

Elementary School: Intermediate

(Lesson Plan: "Abigail and John Adams Online" by
   Maureen Tannetta, see pp. 17-18)
Dispositions: 1.2.1, 2.2.4, 4.2.2; Responsibilities: 1.3.1,
   1.4.2, 3.3.4; Self-assessment: 2.44, 3.4.3

I learned that a cause of the Revolutionary War
was _____
_____
_____

An important question that I answered was ____
_____
_____

I would like to know more about _____
_____
_____

I showed extra effort in my work by _____
_____
_____

I could have done better by_____
_____
_____

Elementary School: Primary

(Lesson Plan: "Book Knowledge 101" by Tamilah
   Richardson, see pp. 12-13)
Responsibility: 2.3.2; Self-assessment: 2.4.3

I can find the front cover of a book.

I can find the back cover of the book.

I can find the title page of a book.

Designing Learning for Evidence-Based Practice

by Marjorie L. Pappas

Assessment and evidence-based practice have become hot topics today, but the bottom line for busy library media specialists is how they effectively apply to what is happening or needs to happen in the library media center. How can information literacy lessons be designed to provide evidence that students have met the objectives of the lesson? What is backwards design? What are appropriate assessment tools, and how are these applied within a lesson? How do library media specialists select appropriate instructional methods? How do library media specialists use the evidence of student learning?

Connecting to State Standards

The No Child Left Behind Act (NCLB) has placed a significant focus on standards. "Standards establish what students need to know and be able to do to be proficient at various levels in their education" (Pappas 2007, 19). Understandably, classroom teachers are focused on effectively covering their content area standards and are often reluctant to add information literacy skills to their lessons because they see no direct connection to the state achievement tests. However, a close examination of many state standards documents shows a significant correlation between the *Information Literacy Standards* (AASL and AECT) and content area standards. Library media specialists who found those correlations in their state standards and developed information skills lessons focused on those correlations with appropriate assessment are accumulating evidence that demonstrates the effectiveness of the library media program. As an increasing number of states are replicating the Colorado Study, a growing body of evidence suggests that high quality school library media programs can increase academic achievement scores by as much as 20% (Lance 2001, 6).

Designing Learning with Backwards Design

The Designing Learning for Evidence-Based Practice matrix (Figure 1, page 21) provides a sequence of steps or a process for designing learning with documentation or evidence of the learning outcomes.

Backwards design is a concept developed by Grant Wiggins and Jay McTighe (2005), and it includes the following elements:

- What do we want students to learn? (standards and objectives)
- How will we know if learning has occurred? (assessment tools or strategies)
- How will we facilitate the learning process? (responsibilities of library media specialist, classroom teacher, and students)

Zmuda uses the concepts of backwards design to create a form that library media specialists can use to "communicate the vision and expectations for student learning in the library media center" (2006, 2).

Select Standards and Objectives

Ideally, the process would begin with identifying the appropriate state

Marjorie L. Pappas, Ph.D., is a part-time virtual professor in the Professional Development Studies program, School of Communication, Information and Library Studies at Rutgers University. She is also the author of articles on inquiry learning and assessment and the co-author of *Pathways to Knowledge and Inquiry Learning* (Libraries Unlimited, 2002). Email: Marjorie.pappas@gmail.com

standards. Library media specialists who are collaborating with a classroom teacher in the planning process would select content standards that correlate with the *Information Literacy Standards* and develop relevant objectives for the lesson.

What about the library media specialist, however, who is teaching information skills with limited or no collaboration with the classroom teacher? Should evidence-based practice apply only in those situations when collaboration is possible? Zmuda suggests that "when teachers bring their students in as an isolated event, library media specialists can still evaluate student performance on information and technology literacy standards with or without involvement of the classroom teacher" (2006, 22). Library media specialists in the elementary grades who now operate with fixed schedules might find this evidence useful when advocating for a change to a partially flexible schedule.

Assessment of Student Learning

Determining what students will do to demonstrate their new skills or knowledge is the next step of design process. The library media specialist and classroom teacher have a variety of assessment tools and strategies from which to choose (see Figure 1, below).

Todd's research findings suggest that checklists completed by both the library media specialist and the student are an important assessment strategy in evidence-based practice (2003). Checklists are both learning and assessment tools that enable students to engage in self-checking to determine if all of the requirements are completed. Todd's research also found that "some school librarians indicated that they used rubric strategies where students' performance in final products were scaled according to a set of criteria that clearly defined what range of acceptable to unacceptable performances and/or information products look like" (12).

Pappas states, "Organizers are visual representations of content that show the inter-relationships of specific relevant information" (2007, 22). Organizers, including webs, matrices, and KWL charts enable students to visually demonstrate thinking skills, e.g., comprehension, analysis, synthesis, and evaluation.

Harada suggests the log is a valuable tool for self-assessment and reflection that enables students to monitor their own learning (2006, 35). However, the construction of writing prompts is critical to using logs or journals as assessment strategies. The writing prompts should closely correlate with the objectives of the lesson. For example, a lesson that focuses on evaluating websites might include the following writing prompts for student logs:

- Which three Web resources were the most valuable for this research project?
- What are some examples of quality features that represent the evaluation criteria on those three websites?

The selection of assessment tools for a specific lesson must reflect the learner outcome(s) included in the objective(s). For example, the lesson

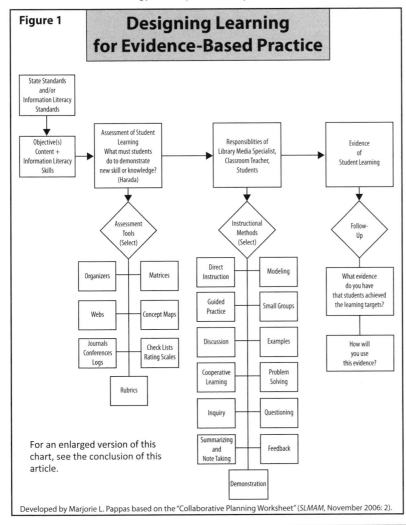

Figure 1

Designing Learning for Evidence-Based Practice

State Standards and/or Information Literacy Standards

Objective(s) Content + Information Literacy Skills

Assessment of Student Learning What must students do to demonstrate new skill or knowledge? (Harada)

Assessment Tools (Select)

Organizers | Matrices
Webs | Concept Maps
Journals Conferences Logs | Check Lists Rating Scales
Rubrics

Responsiblities of Library Media Specialist, Classroom Teacher, Students

Instructional Methods (Select)

Direct Instruction | Modeling
Guided Practice | Small Groups
Discussion | Examples
Cooperative Learning | Problem Solving
Inquiry | Questioning
Summarizing and Note Taking | Feedback
Demonstration

Evidence of Student Learning

Follow-Up

What evidence do you have that students achieved the learning targets?

How will you use this evidence?

For an enlarged version of this chart, see the conclusion of this article.

Developed by Marjorie L. Pappas based on the "Collaborative Planning Worksheet" (*SLMAM*, November 2006: 2).

objective requires students to use the catalog to find books in the library media center. The organizer might be a matrix that includes several topics with a space to write the author, title, and call number of several books about those topics. Or, if students are required to gather information about the life of a prominent colonial American, one assessment tool might be a timeline of significant events in that person's life.

Organizers and matrices are typically constructed of different shapes and, thus, are limited only by the creativity of the library media specialist or classroom teacher.

Performance tasks and products are often used as assessments. The product or task alone, however, does not provide sufficient evidence of learning. A rubric, checklist, or rating scale should be used to assess both the quality of the product or performance and the content.

Selection of Instructional Methods

The next step in the design process is determining the appropriate instructional method(s) or the responsibilities of the classroom teacher, library media specialist, and student (see Figure 1, page 21).

Direct instruction is typically some form of lecture ranging from an audio approach to a multimedia presentation. There are also situations when direct instruction is the most efficient method for delivering information to students. However, this is one-way communication and unless the speaker is incredibly dynamic, students frequently tune out after a short period of time.

Indirect or individualized instruction typically causes the learner to become more mentally engaged. A short lecture followed by a demonstration or modeling and then some form of guided practice are much

more likely to produce a longer rate of retention.

Inquiry, problem solving, or cooperative learning approaches cause students to take some responsibility for gathering information and applying that information to the construction of a product or performance task. The challenge with these methods is that students—often working in small groups—are usually engaged in slightly different learning experiences, each of which require facilitating or coaching by the library media specialist or classroom teacher. Scaffolding strategies, therefore, become very important with these instructional methods. Scaffolding can include pathfinders (to help students gather information), carefully written instructions that include information about incremental tasks and the requirements of the end product or performance. Checklists that detail steps in the process and requirements of the task are useful to guide students and to assess both the process and end product. Daily logs or journals that include writing prompts can engage students in thinking about new understandings while providing information about the process they followed throughout the learning activity.

Marzano's research on instructional strategies that work would be a useful resource for library media specialists (2001). The list of strategies includes the following:

- Summarizing and Note Taking
- Homework and Practice
- Nonlinguistic Representations
- Cooperative Learning
- Setting Objectives and Providing Feedback
- Cues, Questions, and Advance Organizers (Table of Contents, iii).

This is an intriguing list because these strategies are often applied in lessons developed by library media

specialists. For example, summarizing and note taking are both part of information literacy skills.

Marzano suggests that nonlinguistic representations include mental models, graphic organizers, descriptive patterns, physical models, drawn pictures and pictographs, and engagement in kinesthetic activity (74-83). These strategies relate to visual literacy that is important today as our world grows increasingly more visual.

The category, Cues and Questions, relates to engaging students in questioning and higher level thinking. Questioning and critical thinking are inherent in inquiry learning and information literacy skills.

Marzano's discussion about advance organizers reflects David Ausubel's theories related to strategies enabling students to make connections with their prior knowledge. Library media specialists typically use brainstorming webs and KWL charts for this purpose.

Evidence of Student Learning

When the lesson is completed, the next step is to gather the assessment tools to compile and analyze the data. Harada suggests that spreadsheets are useful for recording data. Reflections on each lesson and the compiled data by classroom teachers and library media specialists also provide useful anecdotal information. Quotations from students' reflections might also be included in evidence folders, which could include examples of lessons, student work, sample logs, and examples of assessment tools (Harada 2006).

The next step is to make a list of those students whose assessments suggest they were not successful in fulfilling the objectives of the lesson. A lesson can be planned to reteach those skills with a follow-up activity for that group of students.

Recording Your Evidence

Data collected using student assessments, reflections, notes from student conferences, and reflections from library media specialists and classroom teachers is not the same as quantitative test data. Information in evidence folders is qualitative, i.e., descriptive. However, over a period of time, this qualitative data can be very informative.

Library media specialists will need a framework for tracking this data for a longitudinal picture of patterns and trends. Many school districts have developed an information skills curriculum. When a district curriculum exists, a spreadsheet can be created that includes the list of skills by grade level as a list in the first column. Column labels might be Proficient (3 points), Satisfactory (2 points) and Novice (1 point). This spreadsheet can be replicated for the appropriate number of grades and classes. After each new skill lesson, the assessment results can be aggregated by those three rating scales and the scores recorded on the spreadsheet. Columns for percentages would provide additional information.

One interesting variable to track would be the level of collaboration associated with each lesson. Zmuda and Levitov have proposed the "Assessment Tool: Levels of Communication, Cooperation, and Collaboraton with Teachers" that can help library media specialists with this sort of tracking (2006).

Koechlin and Zwaan also have included a chapter in their recent book, *Build Your Own Information Literate School,* that provides examples of forms for recording the results of information skills evidence (2005). One section includes lists of documents from students, classroom teachers, and library media specialists that could be collected as evidence.

Using and Communicating Evidence

Lessons can be evaluated based on the results of the evidence. Assessment data and reflections from students will be very useful for revising each lesson. A form should be created that can be used by the library media specialist and the classroom teachers to evaluate each lesson. A section might be included for evaluating the library media center's resources used for the lesson. The form should be short and easy to complete to accommodate the busy schedules of classroom teachers.

Periodically, information from evidence folders and spreadsheet records can be included in newsletters to both parents and faculty. Individual class data can be shared with each classroom teacher. It is important to communicate this information with teachers and principals so that they will develop an understanding of the value of the library media curriculum as it intersects with the school content area curricula. Once evidence is acquired, library media specialists should communicate, communicate, communicate!

References

AASL and AECT. *Information Power: Building Partnerships for Learning.* ALA, 1998.

Harada, Violet H. "Building Evidence Folders for Learning through Library Media Centers." *School Library Media Activities Monthly* 23, no. 3 (November 2006): 25-30.

Harada, Violet H., and Joan M. Yoshina. *Assessing Learning.* Libraries Unlimited, 2005.

Harada, Violet H., and Joan M. Yoshina. *Inquiry Learning through Librarian-Teacher Partnerships.* Linworth, 2004.

Koechlin, Carol, and Sandi Zwaan. *Build Your Own Information Literate School.* Hi Willow Research, 2003.

Lance, Keith Curry, and David V. Loertscher. *Powering Achievement: School Library Media Programs Make a Difference.* Hi Willow Research, 2001.

Levitov, Deborah D., and Allison Zmuda. "Assessment Tool: Levels of Communication, Cooperation, and Collaboration with Teachers." *School Library Media Activities Monthly* 23, no. 2 (October 2006): 2.

Marzano, Robert J., Debra J. Pickering, and Jan E. Pollock. *Classroom Instruction that Works: Research-Based Strategies for Increasing Student Achievement.* ASCD, 2001.

Pappas, Marjorie. "The Impact of Standards-Based Education on School Library Media Programs." In *School Reform and the School Library Media Specialist,* edited by Sandra Hughes-Hassell and Violet H. Harada. Libraries Unlimited, 2007.

Pappas, Marjorie L. "Tools for the Assessment of Learning." *School Library Media Activities Monthly* 23, no. 9 (May 2007): 21-25.

Todd, Ross J. "Evidence-Based Practice: Overview, Rationale, and Challenges." In *We Boost Achievement! Evidence-Based Practice for School Library Media Specialists,* edited by David V. Loertscher. Hi Willow Research, 2003.

Wiggins, Grant, and Jay McTighe. *Understanding by Design.* 2nd ed. ASCD, 2005.

Zmuda, Allison. "Where Does Your Authority Come From? Empowering the Library Media Specialist as a True Partner in Student Achievement." *School Library Media Activities Monthly* 23, no.1 (September 2006): 19-22.

Organizer Resources

Graphic Organizers Activity Bank. SCORE. http://www.sdcoe.k12.ca.us/score/actbank/torganiz.htm

Graphic Organizers in the Classroom. Developed by Annette Lamb and Larry Johnson. Teacher Tap. http://eduscapes.com/tap/topic73.htm

The Virtual Institute: Concept Mapping and Inspiration. New Jersey Department of Education's Technology Fellowship Institute. http://www.ettc.net/techfellow/inspir.htm

Tools for Reading, Writing and Thinking. Greece Central School District. http://www.greece.k12.ny.us/instruction/ela/6-12/Tools/Index.htm ✤

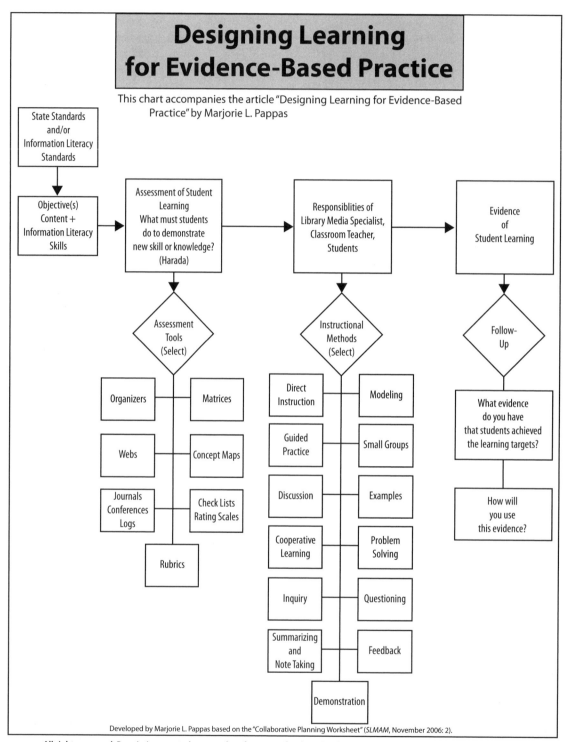

Designing Learning for Evidence-Based Practice

This chart accompanies the article "Designing Learning for Evidence-Based Practice" by Marjorie L. Pappas

State Standards and/or Information Literacy Standards

Objective(s) Content + Information Literacy Skills

Assessment of Student Learning
What must students do to demonstrate new skill or knowledge? (Harada)

Responsiblities of Library Media Specialist, Classroom Teacher, Students

Evidence of Student Learning

Assessment Tools (Select)

Organizers | Matrices

Webs | Concept Maps

Journals Conferences Logs | Check Lists Rating Scales

Rubrics

Instructional Methods (Select)

Direct Instruction | Modeling

Guided Practice | Small Groups

Discussion | Examples

Cooperative Learning | Problem Solving

Inquiry | Questioning

Summarizing and Note Taking | Feedback

Demonstration

Follow-Up

What evidence do you have that students achieved the learning targets?

How will you use this evidence?

Developed by Marjorie L. Pappas based on the "Collaborative Planning Worksheet" (*SLMAM*, November 2006: 2).

Assessing Learning: *The Missing Piece in Instruction?*

by Violet H. Harada and Joan M. Yoshina

School library media specialists from all levels often gather at district meetings to share their war stories. You'll hear the following concern from elementary folk, "We have to teach the same skills over and over again because the students just don't remember them." At the same time, the middle school professionals chime in, "Whatever you teach the students at the elementary level, they still can't use the library when they come up to us!" Then the school library media specialists in the high schools add their concerns by stating, "What are you folks teaching the students in the lower schools? The students are pretty clueless when we get them."

Does this mean that school library media specialists have not been actively teaching information skills? Obviously, not! If anything, school library media specialists at all levels have been investing long hours in preparing and implementing lessons. They try to coordinate these lessons with teachers, and, in the best-case scenario, they collaboratively plan and deliver the instruction.

The missing piece in this sce-nario is whether students have actually been learning. The questions central to whether this student learning is successful are as follows:

- What have they been learning?
- How well have they been learning?
- How can we verify they are learning?

This shift from a teaching focus to a learning focus is a crucial one. School library media specialists must consider not just how many lessons they conduct but whether students have actually been learning the skills taught (Harada 2005). The following are critical questions in assessing learning:

- What do we assess? The important first step is to identify our specific learning target.
- What are we looking for? We need to develop criteria that help us assess how well students achieve the target. The criteria should be stated clearly in terms of the desired behaviors and must be written in language that the students can understand.
- How do we conduct the assessment? We need to select a strategy or tool, which can range from simple checklists to detailed rubrics, to conduct the assessment.
- How will students demonstrate their understanding? We need to design a performance task for students. By participating in this hands-on activity, students can demonstrate their achievement of the learning target.
- How can we use the results to adjust or modify our teaching? By utilizing concrete evidence of what students can and cannot do allows us to use that evidence to improve our instruction.

Here are two examples that briefly describe how student performance in the library media center might be assessed.

Elementary School Example

A second grade class is curious about the endangered animals and plants in their state. They want to identify these species and determine how they came to be endangered. They also want to know if there are ways to save them from extinction. Working in pairs, the students want to create a portable exhibit of their find-ings for display and presentation during the school's annual Learning Fair held in the cafetorium. Maggie, the school library media specialist, works with Sally, the

Violet H. Harada is a professor in the University of Hawaii's Library and Information Science Program; 2680 East West Road; Honolulu, HI 96822. Email: vharada@hawaii.edu. Joan M. Yoshina is a retired school library media specialist who has worked in elementary and secondary library media centers in Hawaii. Email: byrony@hgea.net.

teacher, at several points in the unit. One of the skills Maggie volunteers to teach is generating relevant questions. Maggie's approach to assessment involves the following steps:

1. Identify the learning target. Maggie defines an observable target such as the following: A second grade student will be able to generate at least four relevant questions about a specific endangered animal or plant in the state.

2. Develop criteria for assessment. Maggie writes the criteria for the questions as "we can" statements that the students can readily understand. They include:
- We can write at least one question that asks for a description of our animal.
- We can write at least one question that asks for a comparison of our animal with another endangered animal.
- We can write at least one question that asks how it survives.
- We can write at least one question that asks why it is endangered and how it might be saved.

3. Select an assessment tool. Maggie determines that a checklist (Figure 1) using the above criteria is the easiest way to check for student understanding.

4. Design a performance task. The students work in pairs to generate question webs that show whether they can create at least four questions that meet the established criteria. They use the checklist to assess their own webs. Maggie and Sally also use the checklist to assess the students' webs. Figure 2 is an example of a student web.

5. Use the assessment results to improve instruction. As Maggie and Sally examine the students' webs, they collect the following evidence:
- All students can write questions that require a description of their animals.
- About 80% of them can write

Figure 1: Checkllist for Questions

We can write a question that relates to	For student: Yes or no? Comments?	For teacher/LMS: Yes or no? Comments?
1. Describing our animal		
2. Comparing our animal with another endangered animal		
3. Explaining how it survives		
4, Telling why it is endangered and how it might be saved		

Figure 2: Sample of Question Web

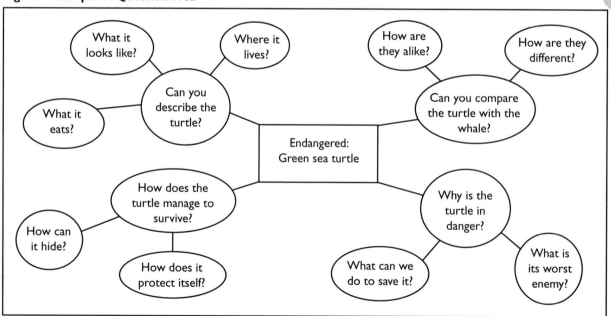

questions that compare their animal with another endangered animal.

- About 50% of them can write questions that ask about the animals' survival tactics.
- About 50% of them can write questions that ask why the animal is endangered and how it might be saved.

By examining the assessment data, Maggie and Sally decide to have a debriefing session that focuses on the questions that students need to revise. They first introduce examples of clearly worded questions and questions needing more work. They compare the two types of questions and discuss how the second type of question might be improved. Once students seem to grasp how they might revise their own questions, they begin working on them. Maggie and Sally circulate among the students to provide guidance and feedback.

Secondary School Example

Seventh graders in a 7-12 school are building time capsules that they will open as seniors. The language arts, social studies, and science teachers work together as a core team on this project. They present the following scenario to the students:

You are organized as four-member teams to create a time capsule that you think captures something important in today's world. Each member of the team must contribute an artifact to the team's time capsule. It can be a photograph, videotape, or actual item that identifies a person, event, or issue that you believe has significantly influenced our thinking or our lifestyles. Along with the artifact, each team member

will include a 500-word message that describes the person, event, or issue; and supports why you have made this particular selection for the time capsule. The time capsules will be stored on campus and reopened at a special ceremony when you are graduating seniors.

The teachers invite their school library media specialist, Brad, to join them. They realize that students must use a variety of resources for background information on their choices. Brad offers to help students hone their note-taking skills. His assessment plan follows:

1. Identify the learning target. Brad identifies his target as: A seventh grade student will be able to take accurate notes that are relevant to his or her information need.

2. Develop criteria for assessment. Brad invites the students to identify criteria for effective note taking. They brainstorm suggestions. Brad and the teachers also have input. Students and instructors ultimately decide on the following three criteria:

- Notes must be relevant. They must answer the questions that students have posed.
- Notes must come from reliable sources. Students must carefully cite all of their sources.
- Notes must be written in the students' own words. To do this, students must be able to identify key words and key phrases in the sources they use. They must be able to paraphrase and summarize the information.

3. Select an assessment tool. Brad takes the lead in drafting a rubric that is based on the above

note-taking criteria. He encourages feedback from both students and teachers before finalizing the rubric (Figure 3).

4. Design a performance task. Students spend four sessions in the school library media center using print and electronic resources. The teachers require students to write their notes on note-taking organizers (Figure 4). The students maintain separate organizer sheets for each question. They use the rubric to assess their own notes. Brad and the teachers divide their assessment work so that they each examine the notes from approximately twenty students.

5. Use the assessment results to improve instruction. When Brad and the teachers examine the students' notes after the first note-taking session, they realize that many students are copying phrases that they don't really understand. The language arts teacher volunteers to spend more time with the students on clues within texts that might help them make sense of their notes. At the midpoint, the instructional team members discover that students are not digging deeply enough for information that supports their selections for the time capsule. To provoke more thinking and discussion about this, the social studies and science teachers have the students critique each other's notes and share where more information might be crucial. Brad works with student teams that need to retrieve more information as a result of the critiquing sessions.

Concluding Tips

If the notion of assessment is daunting, start small. Work with one teacher. Work on one unit.

Focus on specific skills within the unit. The point is to start somewhere and build.

There is no need to start from scratch in devising assessment tools. In two of the books that we have co-authored, we offer numerous examples of assessment instruments that might be used with a range of information literacy skills (Harada and Yoshina 2004, Harada and Yoshina 2005).

There are also numerous websites that include useful assessment models. For example, a Prentice-Hall site provides samples of rubrics for both process and product assessment (http://www.phschool.com/professional_development/rubrics.html). Tools for examining use of primary sources and cooperative learning projects are especially helpful. Another example is the links to teacher created rubrics offered by the School of Education at the University of Wisconsin-Stout (http://www.uwstout.edu/soe/profdev/rubrics.shtml). This site includes exceptional rubrics that assess holistic thinking. It also covers rubrics for an impressive range of student products including dioramas, editorials, oral histories, and reflective journal entries.

In Summary

Providing tangible evidence about the power of learning through libraries is an enormous challenge facing our profession. It is a challenge we cannot afford to ignore if we are to be an integral part of the school's teaching and learning community.... Assessing for learning cannot be an afterthought but must be a central part of our mission. (Harada & Yoshina 2005, 144).

References:

Harada, Violet H. "Working Smarter: Being Strategic about Assessment and Accountability." *Teacher Librarian* 33, no. 1 (October 2005): 8-15.

Harada, Violet H., and Joan M. Yoshina. *Assessing Learning: Librarians and Teachers as Partners.* Libraries Unlimited, 2005.

Harada, Violet H., and Joan M. Yoshina. *Inquiry Learning Through Librarian-Teacher Partnerships.* Linworth, 2004.

Professional Development-Hot Topics-Assessment. http://www.phschool.com/professional_development/assessment/rubrics.html

Teacher Created Rubrics for Assessment. http://www.uwstout.edu/soe/profdev/rubrics.shtml

Figure 3: Note Taking Rubric

Criteria	Exemplary	Proficient	Needs Work
Notes must be relevant.	All information relates directly to my questions. I have enough details to support all major points.	All information relates directly to my questions. I need more details to support my major points.	My information does not always relate to my questions. I need more details to support my major points.
Notes must come from reliable sources.	I use resources that my instructors and I recognize as reliable.	I am not sure about the reliability of one resource.	I am not sure about the reliability of more than one resource.
Notes must be written in my own words.	I can identify key words and phrases that help me use my own words. I can explain the meaning of all words that I use.	I can identify key words and phrases that help me use my own words. I can explain the meaning of most words that I use.	I need help with identifying key words and phrases. I need help with the meanings of many words that I use.

Figure 4: Note Taking Organizer

Questions addressed:	
Citation(s) for source(s) used:	
Key words or phrases taken from source	Elaboration in my own words

Building Evidence Folders for Learning through Library Media Centers

by Violet H. Harada

The controversy over the 65% Solution underscores the public's perception that library media centers do not provide vital instructional programs. This legislation, enacted in states such as Texas, Kansas, and Louisiana, pumps 65% of a state's educational budget into direct classroom resources (Toppo 2006). Unfortunately, library media specialists are classified as non-instructional support personnel according to the National Center for Education Statistics (NCES). Because of this, the American Association of School Librarians has produced a position statement on the instructional classification of library media specialists in hopes of including certified library media specialists as part of the NCES "instruction" classification (http://www.ala.org/ala/aasl/aaslproftools/positionstatements/instclass.htm).

Even without the 65% Solution, however, library media programs are frequently on the chopping block when school budgets shrink. A principal in that predicament recently told me, "I would love to keep my library media specialist but I have to consider my priorities. I need to retain the positions and programs that show my students are actually learning." Indeed!

When building level administrators and school advisory councils meet to wrangle over budgets, they seek to support programs that demonstrate positive student growth in areas of high need. The big question is whether you, as a library media specialist, are able to produce this type of evidence. While many library media specialists spend a major portion of their week engaged in instructional activities, the impact of their teaching is often invisible (Harada and Yoshina 2006). The following are critical questions that library media specialists must wrestle with:

- How does your library media center support student learning?
- What compelling evidence do you have that students have achieved the learning targets?

For library media specialists who have been comfortable with traditional forms of reporting, responses to the above questions require a dramatic paradigm shift from an object-oriented approach to a student-oriented approach of assessment and evaluation. The object-oriented approach centers on evaluation reports that include statistical counting of "things" such

Violet H. Harada is a professor in the University of Hawaii's Library and Information Science Program; 2680 East West Road; Honolulu, HI 96822. Email: vharada@hawaii.edu

as new acquisitions, circulation figures, and numbers of instructional sessions and planning meetings. The student-oriented approach focuses on assessment of student performance. It involves not only what students learn but also the degree to which student learning is demonstrated (Harada and Yoshina 2005).

The Hawaii Experiment

Library media specialists in Hawaii, like many of their colleagues elsewhere in the nation, are exploring ways to design and implement this type of student-oriented assessment. As one elementary library media specialist stated:

I teach at least four classes a day but I haven't really addressed the issue of assessment. I informally eyeball what the kids are doing as I circulate among them but that's about it. I am now realizing this is not enough. At the last faculty meeting, my principal asked the entire faculty to focus on evidence of student learning. I sat there thinking, I know I have been doing a good job of teaching but I also know that I haven't been collecting or communicating evidence of what the kids are actually learning in my library media center. That is going to be my big challenge this year.

To tackle the issue of assessment in Hawaii's school library media centers, twenty-four K-12 library media specialists are currently participating in a pilot project to develop evidence folders. These folders are intended as communication tools with key stakeholder groups in the school community. The data and information included in the folder center on the library media

center's contribution to academic achievement.

This pilot project, entitled "School Librarians Help Students Achieve: Here's the Evidence!," is the collaborative brainchild of the Hawaii Association of School Librarians, the University of Hawaii's Library and Information Science Program, and the Hawaii Department of Education's School Library Services. This year-long professional development initiative incorporates face-to-face sessions and online communication via a listserv and a website.

The project employs a practice-based approach that centers on library media specialists using lessons and curricula from their own schools as the artifacts for improvement (Ball and Cohen 1999). They have opportunities to critique each other's work and offer suggestions for improvement in face-to-face sessions. Using the online tools, they continue the dialogue, exchange ideas, and provide critical support to one another as they strive to create evidence folders for their own school library media programs. The rest of this article describes the approach they are taking and the steps involved in constructing these evidence folders.

A Strategic Approach to Assessment

The core of the evidence folder is the synthesis and analysis of student learning that results from library instruction. The library media specialists in Hawaii realize that they cannot formally assess all of the lessons they teach; therefore, they are employing a strategic tactic to assessment (Harada 2005). They begin by asking themselves the fol-

lowing questions:

What are the most critical learning gaps that my students are facing at this time?

How does my teaching support the classroom teachers' efforts to close the gaps?

These questions are essential ones because they force library media specialists to consider the value of what they teach from the perspective of the classroom.

For all of the Hawaii schools, these gaps are rooted in the mandates of No Child Left Behind (U. S. Department of Education n.d.) and in the state's content and performance standards (Hawaii State Department of Education 2005). At the same time, the library media specialists are prudently taking baby steps forward through building their evidence folders. In getting started, they have each selected one or two lessons that are clearly aligned with the identified learning gaps in their respective schools.

Through participation in this project, they are aware that effective assessment is not simply a matter of adding a rubric to an existing lesson plan. To build stronger assessment components into the lessons, they have adopted a "backward mapping" strategy that requires an outcome-focused examination of existing instruction (Wiggins and McTighe 1998). The reflective process involves the following:

• Connecting the selected lesson to the state's content and performance standards.

This is an important first step because it clearly indicates that the library instruction reinforces the skills and dispositions that the classroom is also trying to achieve.

- Stating the learning goal of the selected lesson.

  The learning goal must precisely identify the learner(s) and the specific concept or skill being learned.
- Describing the performance task.

  The task answers the question: What must students do to demonstrate their understanding of the learning goal? It describes the task and the desired level of performance.
- Creating a tool or strategy to assess the quality of student performance.

  An effective tool allows the student and the instructor to clearly identify what is being learned and determine how well it is being learned. Checklists, rating scales, and rubrics are among the tools used. Graphic organizers including K-W-L charts, concept maps, and Venn diagrams are also valuable tools for assessment purposes. For more detailed information on these various instruments, refer to the list of assessment resources at the end of this article.
- Compiling and analyzing assessment data.

  The use of a spreadsheet program is one effective way to enter and tabulate assessment scores for a class. Spreadsheets also allow you to merge assessment data from several classes if you are developing a composite profile by grade level or by course. An added advantage of spreadsheets is that you can easily create graphs and charts with the information.
- Reflecting by instructors on ways to improve their teaching strategies based on assessment data. Importantly, the tabulated data helps the library media specialist

answer the following questions: What did most of the students learn well? What was problematic for them? Based on the assessment findings, how might I modify my instruction to improve student learning?
- Reflecting by students on ways to improve their own learning skills.

  A key aspect of assessment is students gaining the confidence and know-how to accurately reflect on their own progress and achievement. By engaging in self-assessment, the students ask themselves the following questions: What did I do well in this lesson? What was hard for me and why? How might I do things differently?

  Figures 1, 2, and 3 (pages 28-29) elaborate on various aspects of an outcome-focused approach to assessment.

Evidence Folders

As mentioned earlier, the selected lessons and resulting student performances form the guts of an evidence folder. It is important to remember that the audiences for the folder are stakeholder groups that influence decision making at the school level, i.e., administrators, school advisory boards, and teaching colleagues. The language used should be jargon-free and clear to non-educators.

Key components of an evidence folder include the following:
- A brief description of how the library's mission connects with the school's mission
- A brief description of the school's major learning targets for the school year
- A brief description of how instruction in the library media center connects with school's

learning targets
- Samples of lessons taught in the library media center that connect with the school's learning targets
- Samples of student work for each lesson included in the folder
- Displays of compiled assessment data that communicate what students learned from these lessons
- Samples of commentary from students about possible future improvements
- Samples of commentary from instructors about possible teaching improvements

Figures 4 and 5 (page 30) provide tips and suggestions for developing evidence folders.

Summary

Unlike a portfolio, which is primarily intended for self-assessment, an evidence folder is a way to communicate what students learn through the library media center to other members of the school community. It can be a paper document; it can also be rendered electronically. The critical message is that library media centers contribute directly to student achievement. Assessment, therefore, is not an incidental but a central part of the process.

Resources for Assessment

Andrade, H. G. "Using Rubrics to Promote Thinking and Learning." *Educational Leadership* 57, no. 5 (February 2000): 13-18.

Davies, Anne. *Making Classroom Assessment Work.* Connections, 2000.

Donham, J. *Assessment of Information Processes and Products.* Follett Software, 1998.

Gregory, K., C. Cameron, and A. Davies. *Self-Assessment and Goal-Setting for Use*

Figure 1: Using an Outcome Based Approach to Assessment

Note: The sample responses below are based on a grade 4 lesson using the OPAC.

Steps in outcome-based approach	Sample responses
1. Connect the selected lesson to the state's content and performance standards.	This lesson is linked directly to a language arts standard: locating sources–finding age-appropriate resources to complete a research project.
2. Develop a clear learning goal.	Fourth grade students will demonstrate their ability to access information by using the OPAC to find resources for their projects.
3. Describe the performance task.	Working individually, a student will use appropriate subject headings in his or her OPAC search to locate at least two resources that are useful for the assignment.
4. Create a tool to assess the quality of student performance.	Students use a graphic organizer that has been developed by the library media specialist to complete this particular assignment. (Refer to Figure 2.)
5. Compile and analyze assessment data.	The library media specialist uses a spreadsheet to compile data on the class' work. (Refer to Figure 3.)
6. Instructors reflect on findings.	Based on the compiled data, the library media specialist and the classroom teacher decide to differentiate the instruction. Students, who "met" or "exceeded" the requirements, move on with the teacher's assistance and begin gathering information. The library media specialist confers with students, who "approached" or "did not meet" expectations, to help them with keywords and locational skills.
7. Students reflect on findings.	Students also rate themselves on the assignment. They have an opportunity to write reflective comments about how well they performed.

in Middle and Secondary School Classrooms. Connections, 2000.

Herman, J. L., P. R. Aschbacker, and L. Winters. *A Practical Guide to Alternative Assessment.* Association for Supervision and Curriculum Development, 1992.

Luongo-Orlando, K. *Authentic Assessment: Designing Performance-Based Tasks.* Pembroke Publishers, 2003.

Northwest Regional Educational Laboratory. *Assessment Home – Toolkit 98.* http://www.nwrel.org/assessment/toolkit98.php (accessed August 9, 2006).

Pappas, M. "Organizing Research." *School Library Media Activities Monthly* 14, no. 4 (December 1997): 30-32.

Pearson Prentice Hall. *Professional Development-Hot Topics-Assessment.* http://www.phschool.com/professional_development/assessment/rubrics.html (accessed August 9, 2006).

Schrock, K. *Kathy Schrock's Guide for Educators: Assessment and Rubric Information.* http://school.discovery.com/schrockguide/assess.html (accessed August 9, 2006).

Stefl-Mabry, J. "Building Rubrics into Powerful Learning Assessment Tools." *Knowledge Quest* 32, no. 5 (May-June 2004): 19-23.

Stiggins, R. *Student-Centered Classroom Assessment.* Prentice Hall, 1997.

Strickland, K., and J. Strickland. *Making Assessment Elementary.* Heinemann, 2000.

U.S. Department of Education. *Rubistar: Rubistar Rubric Generator.* http://rubistar.4teachers.org/ (accessed August 9, 2006).

University of Wisconsin-Stout. *Teacher Created Rubrics for Assessment.* http://www.uwstout.edu/soe/profdev/rubrics.shtml (accessed August 9, 2006).

Cited References

American Association of School Librarians. "Position Statement on Instructional Classification." http://www.ala.or/ala/aasl/aaslproftools/positionstatements/instclass.htm (accessed August 8, 2006).

Ball, D. L., and D. K. Cohen. "Developing Practice, Developing Practitioners: Toward a Practice-based Theory of Professional Education." In *Teaching as the Learning Profession: Handbook of Policy and Practice,* edited by L. Darling-Hammond and G. Sykes, 3-32. Jossey-Bass 1999.

Harada, V. H. "Working Smarter: Being Strategic about Assessment and Accountability." *Teacher Librarian* 33, no. 1 (October 2005): 8-15.

Harada, V. H., and J. M. Yoshina. *Assessing Learning: Librarians and Teachers as*

Figure 2: Graphic Organizer for OPAC Lesson

Subject headings found in OPAC	Titles of resources found with subject headings	Call numbers for resources

I rate my work as follows:
  ☐ 4 (Exceeded) = I found more than 2 resources using appropriate subject headings.
  ☐ 3 (Met) = I found 2 resources using appropriate subject headings.
  ☐ 2 (Approaching) = I found 1 resource using an appropriate subject heading.
  ☐ 1 (Not met) = I was not able to find a resource using an appropriate subject heading.
Student's comments:

My library media specialist rates my work as follows:
  ☐ 4 (Exceeded) = Student found more than 2 resources using appropriate subject headings.
  ☐ 3 (Met) = Student found 2 resources using appropriate subject headings.
  ☐ 2 (Approaching) = Student found 1 resource using an appropriate subject heading.
  ☐ 1 (Not met) = Student was not able to find a resource using an appropriate subject heading.
Library media specialist's comments:

Partners. Libraries Unlimited, 2005.

Harada, V. H., and J. M. Yoshina. "Assessing Learning: The Missing Piece in Instruction?" *School Library Media Activities Monthly* 22, no. 7 (March 2006): 20-23.

Hawaii State Department of Education. *Hawaii Content & Performance Standards III Database*. http://standardstoolkit.k12.hi.us/index.html (accessed August 8, 2006).

U.S. Department of Education. *No Child Left Behind*. http://www.ed.gov/nclb/landing.jhtml (accessed August 8, 2006).

Toppo, G. "States Sign On to '65% Solution' for Funding Schools." *USA Today*. http://www.usatoday.com/news/education/2006-04-10-65-percent-solution_x.htm (accessed July 20, 2006).

Wiggins, G., and J. McTighe. *Understanding by Design*. Association for Supervision and Curriculum Development, 1998. ✋

Figure 3: Grade 4 Class Performance on OPAC Lesson

Student	Exceeded	Met	Approaching	Not Met
Anderson	x			
Bailey		x		
Carson	x			
Davies				x
Emerson		x		
Farantino		x		
Gee		x		
Hong	x			
Lopez		x		
Martinez			x	
O'Reilly			x	
Omura			x	
Thompson	x			
Viloria		x		
Zilonis				x
TOTALS	**4**	**6**	**3**	**2**

From Eyeballing to Evidence:
Assessing for Learning in Hawaii Library Media Centers

by Violet H. Harada

The development of "library evidence folders" for assessment purposes was featured in a previous *SLMAM* article, "Building Evidence Folders for Learning through Library Media Centers" (Harada, November 2006). The project developers challenged participants to change their mindsets from "eyeballing student performance" to designing and implementing measurable evidence of student learning. These developers were part of a collaborative yearlong project that brought three organizations together: Hawaii Association of School Librarians (HASL), the Hawaii Department of Education's School Library Services (SLS), and the University of Hawaii's Library and Information Science (LIS) Program.

Since the publication of that article and the 2006 AASL Fall Forum that focused on assessment, various state library leaders have contacted the Hawaii project developers expressing their desire to conduct similar assessment training in their own regions. This article will focus on this growing and heartening interest in assessment as central to student learning.

To briefly recap, the Hawaii initiative began with a weeklong summer institute in 2006 and continued into the fall and spring in the form of individual consultations and online communication with a pilot group of twenty-four K-12 library

media specialists. The goal was to create more effective instruction that targeted key learning goals in the schools. This follow-up article summarizes critical lessons learned, accomplishments achieved, and continuing work identified by the Hawaii group.

Lessons Learned

Building rigor. The library media specialists were advised to take a "strategic approach" to assessment. This meant identifying lessons that directly connected with learning gaps in their respective schools. For all of them, this involved standards that students were not achieving in the state tests. It was not surprising, therefore, that they selected information-related lessons that dealt with the language arts standards since youngsters were having problems in various aspects of reading and writing. However, a pivotal insight for the library media specialists was that the lessons they identified were not the "conventional library lessons." For example, these were not the lessons on parts of the book at the elementary level or the one-shot orientation sessions at the secondary level.

As a group, they began to under-

Violet H. Harada is a professor in the University of Hawaii's Library and Information Science Program; 2680 East West Road; Honolulu, HI 96822. Email: vharada@hawaii.edu

stand that instruction must challenge students to strengthen skills in higher order thinking and knowledge construction. In short, even before they wrestled with the issue of assessment, they had to tackle the issue of what was worth learning. As one library media specialist noted:

> It might have been obvious to my colleagues, but it was a huge aha discovery for me that so many of my existing lessons were really superficial. As an elementary librarian, I was spending a lot of my instructional time on scavenger hunts in the library and craft-making sessions based on books I read to the students. While the kids had fun and loved the time they spent with me in the library, I realized that I wasn't really addressing deeper learning issues such as how to help them generate meaningful questions as they read literature or how to make intelligent inferences from a text.

Table 1 (below) provides examples of the shifts in teaching emphases of the Hawaii group based on new understandings about the learning needs of students.

Planning with the end in mind. Project planners emphasized the importance of starting with clearly stated learning targets and designing performance tasks that facilitated students achieving these targets. They also stressed that the criteria to assess whether or not students reached these goals had to be aligned with the learning targets. Importantly, both targets and assessment criteria were written in language that the students understood. The library media specialists in the group admitted that they had not previously designed lessons in this way. One of them confided:

> I have always started by hunting for lesson ideas from other librarians and from the Internet. I hate to admit this but I never started with a clearly stated target. I sort of intuitively knew why I was doing a lesson but I didn't spend much time actually thinking about this. And I only did informal assessment... you know, observing the class as they worked. Working "backward" was a tremen-

dous design challenge for the group. After re-thinking a particular lesson, a library media specialist remarked:

> This is giving my brain a real workout!! After yesterday's session, I went home and kept thinking about my lesson. I began to realize that the reason why this particular lesson had never worked the way I wanted was because I had not done this kind of backward mapping. I had always tagged on my goal after I had my lesson idea in place. It's no wonder that the lesson itself did not match the goal! In addition, I did not assess what the students did except by eyeballing the group.

To facilitate planning in this backward fashion, a lesson template was devised that put standards, goals, and assessments before the lesson procedure itself (see Table 2, below).

Library media specialists paid special attention to numbers 5, 6, 7, and

TABLE 1. Moving Toward More Rigorous Teaching	
Prior Focus	**Current Focus**
Location and retrieval of information: identifying parts of a book.	➤ Assessment of appropriate information retrieval techniques: identification of text features in informational resources that are useful in efficient retrieval of needed information.
Organization of information: creating an outline or learning a specific method of note taking.	➤ Making sense of information: identifying a main idea and supporting details.
Appreciation of literature: conducting read-aloud and booktalk sessions.	➤ Interpretation of literature: making inferences, analyzing character motivation.
Creation of bibliographies: developing citations.	➤ Demonstration of ethical responsibility: developing citations within the context of the legal and ethical implications of intellectual property rights.

TABLE 2.
Contents of Lesson Template

Designing the learning plan
1. Title of lesson
2. Grade level
3. Content standards addressed—including benchmarks
4. Information literacy standards aligned with content standards
5. Specific learning target for the lesson
6. Criteria to assess achievement of the learning target
7. Performance task or object that will be assessed
8. Tool to use in assessing how well students achieve the learning target
9. Lesson procedure
10. Resources for the lesson

During and after implementation
11. Assessment results
12. Reflection on what worked and ways to improve this lesson

8 on the template: learning target, assessment criteria, performance task, and the tool used to assess student performance. Without clear alignments of these critical instructional elements, they encountered problems in actually implementing their lessons. For example, one library media specialist found that her pretest of the students' ability to analyze a literary character did not actually measure one of her critical learning targets of being able to infer personality traits. By reflecting on what was happening, she was able to modify the assessment tool before administering it to a second class.

Involving students in assessment. While the library media specialists recognized the importance of students participating in the assessment process, they frequently struggled with when and how to involve the students. They raised pragmatic questions such as: Can students as young as kindergarten and first grade be involved? When do I find the extra time to let the students do this? Can they accurately assess themselves? As the school year progressed, the library media specialists gradually uncovered the following answers to these types of questions:

- ***Age of students.*** An elementary library media specialist teamed with one of her kindergarten teachers to see what the youngsters understood about "finding information." They decided to have the students create a wall-sized concept map to assess student knowledge. At the beginning of their mini-research project, the students simply knew that a person had questions and looked in books to find the answers. By the end of the project, however, the concept map included the following critical components: thinking about what is already known, looking in more places

(not just books), not making up the information, and sharing the information with other people. By creating the concept map, the students could see their own progress. They were particularly excited about showing their parents what they had learned during the parent conference session.

- ***Time to assess.*** Library media specialists found that involving students in assessment did not have to take an inordinate amount of "extra" time. Some of them used simple checklists that students completed as they worked on a particular activity. This kept the students focused and on task. Several of them also experimented with exit passes. Depending on the learning target, students were given slips of paper (passes) with spaces for their names, dates, and one question connected to the learning target. For example, following a lesson on main ideas, the question on the exit pass was: Can you describe one way to identify a main idea in an article? Students could quickly write a response on their passes and share them as they exited the library media center.

- ***Accuracy of student assessment.*** Everyone discovered that learning how to accurately assess one's own progress was in itself a crucial learning process. It did not matter whether the library media specialists used surveys, rubrics, or other forms of assessment. At the beginning, students frequently over-rated themselves. Both the teachers and library media specialists began to realize that they had to follow up with class debriefing sessions and conferences to facilitate student growth in this area. One library media specialist noted that "we had to go over

how to use the rubric, criterion by criterion, and we had to have samples of student work for the kids to begin understanding how to look at their own work with a more discriminating eye."

Starting small. At the beginning of the Hawaii project, almost all of the library media specialists indicated they wanted to build assessment into major portions of their program, i.e., incorporate formal assessment measures across all grade levels or with entire departments. They were advised to start with a workable piece of their larger goals. For some, this meant targeting just one teacher. For others, it meant focusing on a single skill or concept that aligned with classroom teaching priorities. As one library media specialist reflected at the end of the year:

At first, I wanted to do something with all of the freshmen students in my high school. As I thought about this and learned more about what would be involved in assessing their work, I realized that I was being overly ambitious in this first year. You know what I mean—I had to get my toe in the water before diving in the pool! So I decided to work on one particular skill that the teachers wanted taught and started my assessment work with two of the teachers that I knew would follow through in their classrooms. By doing this, I made things doable for myself. This also made it possible for me to succeed without killing myself in the process!

Being resourceful collaborators. Lack of time to meet with teachers was a persistent challenge for all the library media specialists. At the same time, they empathized with the classroom teachers who felt the pressures of meeting the mandates of No Child Left Behind. While they squeezed joint meetings into wedges of time before and after school, some of the library media specialists were fortunate enough to meet with teachers during the teachers' prep time. In most cases, however, the library media specialists had to be resourceful and flexible. Many of them found email a valuable means of discussing lessons. One library media specialist devised an online lesson template that became a handy tool for asynchronous discussions with her teachers. In many of the schools, teachers were devising curriculum maps across grade levels and within departments. These maps were valuable documents for the library media specialists. They could use them as initial indicators of classroom learning targets and begin to plan ways to help busy and stressed-out teachers meet these targets.

Achievements Accomplished

Equal partners in teaching and learning. By working on assessment as an essential component of their work with students, the library media specialists discovered that teachers and administrators began viewing the library media specialist's efforts with different eyes. The author uses pseudonyms below but the examples are real ones:

- Jane devised a simple observation checklist for a lesson that she conducted on understanding the sequence of events in a biography. While Jane was teaching the class, she asked the teacher if she could help out by using the checklist to assess the students. The teacher agreed to do this. In the process, she realized that Jane's checklist was a valuable tool for measuring individual student progress and that working as a team had mutual benefits. The teacher took the assessment data back to class and used it to help students who had

encountered difficulties during the lesson.

- Lorna's teachers were very concerned about the students' inability to write adequate reader responses to literary pieces. Knowing this, Lorna volunteered to reinforce reader response skills through her instruction in the library media center. First, however, she conducted a pre-assessment of what students could already do by having them submit samples of previous responses. Based on her analysis of their work, she helped the teachers identify specific weaknesses in the students' samples. As a team, they devised criteria checklists that helped the youngsters focus on elements of a successful reader response. Together, they also introduced and reinforced thinking and writing skills students needed in a yearlong effort toward improvements.

- Velma devised a learning matrix that displayed how the lessons she taught in the library media center aligned with the standards being emphasized in the classrooms. She included examples of lesson plans and her fledgling efforts to assess for learning in a few of the lessons. She shared her products with both the administrator and the faculty. The teachers were impressed and asked Velma if they might include her lesson plans and assessments in their class portfolios as evidence of learning that extended beyond the classroom.

- Darlene was already working with a team of high school teachers on research projects when she joined the pilot group. She was motivated to do this because "assessment was the missing piece in our

high school projects." Throughout the school year, she shared her work in assessment with the other members of her high school team. She is currently serving on a special task force to devise a "skills progression matrix" for the senior projects at her high school.

- When Carol joined the Hawaii pilot group last year, she was nervous and apprehensive about her ability to devise and implement learning assessments. She started small by tackling a specific skill on character analysis in literature. Her teachers were pleased with the assessment results, and this emboldened Carol to work with more classes and teachers. When the principal invited her to join a school team focusing on student assessment for the upcoming school year, she said, "I was ready!"

Emerging leaders. The ability to assess for learning is more a mantra than a reality in many schools; teachers know they should be doing it but they are not sure how best to do it. When library media specialists have training in this area, they can emerge as potential teacher leaders. Here are examples from the pilot group:

- At one high school where every teacher and resource specialist is expected to produce an evidence folder, the library team members serve as mentors to faculty members who might need additional support.

- An elementary library media specialist was selected by the faculty and administration as a member of the school team that attended a national assessment conference in Oregon.

- Another elementary library media specialist was recommended by her principal to join a state cohort training program for promising teacher leaders.

- A high school library media specialist has taken the initiative to organize a study group on student assessment in her own complex.

Continuing Work

Pursuing professional inquiry. The library media specialists involved in this project realize that their work as instructional designers is just beginning. They continue to wrestle with the alignment of learning targets, assessment criteria, and tools for assessment. As one of them noted, "This is much harder than I imagined. I now realize how easy it is to use vague terms and have only the muddiest idea about what you actually mean!"

They still struggle to craft precise and measurable criteria in assessing how well students actually perform. As they work on more lessons, they find themselves asking increasingly complex questions such as: What am I actually trying to measure? Are there other ways to assess students' achievement of this target? How do I design this experience so that it facilitates the learning I want to see happen? What does the assessment data really tell me? Caught up in this type of inquiry, one of the

library media specialists reflected: I started off with assessment but now I realize that I need to know much more about ALL elements of teaching that results in real learning. I guess I didn't know how much I didn't know! There are all sorts of questions I am now asking myself. This is scary and exciting at the same time.

Collaboration at the state level. Through our work on this project, the developers have realized the importance of embracing a shared vision and collaborating to achieve that vision. Follow-up efforts on this initial work have included the following:

- Conducting a summer one-day clinic in 2007 for the pilot group. This was an opportunity to reunite members of the group and reflect on lessons learned as well as to share next steps.
- Mounting a second summer institute in 2007 for a new cohort of library media specialists. While the author coordinated the original institute, two HASL members took the lead this year. They also involved members of the pilot group to join the sessions and serve as informal mentors. The

results were hugely positive.

- Collaborating on a first-time effort to produce a multi-year plan for professional development that unites the three organizations in a comprehensive effort to strengthen library media specialists as important teaching partners in 21st century schools. The SLS unit is coordinating this initiative and involving HASL and LIS to leverage the resources and talents from these groups.

Conclusion

The Confucian adage, "The journey of a thousand miles begins with a single step," fittingly captures the initiative described in this article. The Hawaii project marks the beginning of a journey that has not been without its hurdles and stumbling blocks. Importantly, however, the rich lessons that are learned along the way hold immeasurable promise for students to succeed as critical learners. At the same time, these experiences are also raising expectations to excel as model teachers who are also lifelong learners.

Cited Reference

Harada, V. H. "Building Evidence Folders for Learning through Library Media Centers." *School Library Media Activities Monthly* 23, no. 3 (November 2006): 25-30.

Recommended Readings

Harada, V. H. "Working Smarter: Being Strategic about Assessment and Accountability." *Teacher Librarian* 33, no. 1 (October 2005): 8-15.

Harada, V. H., and J. M. Yoshina. *Assessing Learning: Librarians and Teachers as Partners.* Greenwood/Libraries Unlimited, 2005.

Harada, V. H., L. Kam, and L. Marks. "School Librarians Help Students Achieve: Here's the Evidence!" *MultiMedia & Internet@Schools* 14, no. 2 (March/April 2007): 25-28.

Stiggins, R. J. *Student-Involved Assessment for Learning.* 4th ed. Pearson/Merrill Prentice Hall, 2005.

Todd, R. J. "School Libraries and Evidence: Seize the Day, Begin the Future." *Library Media Connection* 22, no. 1 (August 2003): 12-18.

Wiggins, G., and J. McTighe. *Understanding by Design.* Association for Supervision and Curriculum Development, 1998.

Acknowledgments
The author expresses special gratitude to the other members of the Hawaii team for their vision and leadership in this project.
From the Hawaii Association of School Librarians:
Linda Marks, 2007 president, and Lynette Kam, 2007 vice president in charge of programming.
From the Hawaii Department of Education's School Library Services:
Donna Shiroma, unit director, and Hilary Apana-McKee, specialist.

Questions:
Getting to the Heart of Assessment

The following questions were formulated from the article "From Eyeballing to Evidence: Assessing for Learning in Hawaii Library Media Centers" by Violet H. Harada (*SLMAM*, November 2007: 21-25). The list can be used by library media specialists to help develop and examine their assessment practices.

What is worth learning?

- ⇥ What are the standards that students are not achieving?
- ⇥ Do identified lessons help students develop higher order thinking and knowledge construction?
- ⇥ Are the learning targets clearly stated?

What are the performance tasks?

- ⇥ Do the identified performance tasks facilitate students achieving the learning targets?
- ⇥ Is the learning experience designed to facilitate the desired learning?

Have the students achieved the identified learning targets?

- ⇥ What is being measured?
- ⇥ Are learning targets really being assessed?
- ⇥ Are the results measurable?
- ⇥ Is the selected assessment tool the best choice?
- ⇥ Are the learning targets, assessment criteria, performance tasks, and the tool used to assess student performance in clear alignment?
- ⇥ When will the assessment be conducted?
- ⇥ How much time will it take?
- ⇥ What do the assessment data really reveal?

What about the students?

- ⇥ How will the students be involved in the assessment?
- ⇥ Are the assessments and the learning targets written in language that the students can understand?
- ⇥ Do students understand the assessment process?

Ohio's Foray into Evidence-Based Practice

by Christine Findlay

As I begin this article about Ohio's work with Evidence-Based Practice (EBP), a popular quote keeps coming to my mind. The quote, "The more things change, the more they remain the same," is sometimes meant to be comforting, but unfortunately, when it comes to library media centers in Ohio, this familiar quote brings no comfort. We are still struggling to establish the value of library media centers and certified library media specialists.

Our school library association, Ohio Educational Library Media Association (OELMA), has been working for many years to gather evidence in hopes of convincing our state government of the need for a certified library media specialist in every school. Our latest efforts began in 2002 when the board of OELMA applied for a grant to do a state study. We wanted to know what a study would reflect about our library media centers after reading the results of the Colorado and Alaska studies. Board members of OELMA, however, decided to take a little different slant with our study so, therefore, began work with Dr. Ross Todd and Dr. Carol Kuhlthau of Rutgers University on the Student Learning through Ohio School Libraries Research Project.

Since then, many articles have been written about the study and the results. I have included a list of resources at the end of this article rather than discussing them now. I do, however, want to describe the progression of events that led OELMA to a practical implementation of the results.

The study was actually a student survey with an analysis of the students' responses. Students from grades three to twelve, in schools where the library media center was perceived to be effective, answered a series of questions about how the media center helped them. The survey wasn't about how many visits were made to a media center or if the resources were bountiful. Rather, it was about how students perceived the help they received in the center; it was about student learning outcomes.

For the most part, library media specialists were pleased with what they learned from the survey. Even though everything was not perfect, students did seem to recognize the type as well as the significance of the help they received in the library media center. There were, however, some surprises. One in particular was that library media specialists didn't connect quite as strongly with the promotion of reading as they anticipated. Some experienced a little aha moment: "Aha! I've worked so hard at helping with research that they forget I know books!" That was speculation, of course, but it seemed like a possibility.

Christine Findlay is a school library media specialist at the Central Resource Center of the Centerville City Schools in Centerville, Ohio, and a Past President of the Ohio Educational Library Media Association. Questions about OELMA's EBP modules can be addressed to her at christine.findlay@centerville.k12.oh.us

After the survey was analyzed and the results were dispersed throughout the state to administrators, boards of education, teachers, elected officials, etc., the dust settled and our next thought was "So....what now?" We had our study. We had spread the good news about effective library media centers in Ohio. Would it make a difference in such issues as attitudes, number of positions, and budgets, that are a daily reality?

OELMA's Board then invited Dr. Ross Todd to discuss the findings of this study with library media specialists in the state. Gradually, we came to realize that in this culture of testing and data-driven decision making, we needed to collect specific data about student learning outcomes. More importantly, we needed to do so at the local level if we wanted support for the library media program in our particular school districts.

As library media specialists, we have all kinds of statistics that describe the library media center (number of books, circulation data), but these statistics don't tell us how the media center is important to student learning. Dr. Todd pointed out that we needed data similar to the data gathered by classroom teachers. For example, if Mrs. Smith brought her class to the library media center and the library media specialist taught information skills, what exactly did students learn? How did it impact their projects? Was there any evidence that what was taught actually helped students achieve?

OELMA next contracted with the two Ohio Study Project Managers, Gayle Geitgey and Ann Tepe, who worked with Todd to create a staff development mod-

ule for library media specialists. The module, *Can You Find the Evidence-Based Practice in Your School Library?*, was designed to help library media specialists look critically at their own programs through Evidence-Based Practice (EBP). Todd, along with Geitgey and Tepe, presented the first EBP workshop at the OELMA State Conference in 2004. Working as a team, they explained why library media specialists need to gather evidence of learning results. Various methods of gathering the evidence were explored along with how this evidence can be used effectively.

This pilot presentation was evaluated and participant feedback was highly favorable so it was expanded to a full-day workshop. An OELMA Speaker's Bureau was formed to provide the workshop.

Beginning with the summer of 2005 in partnership with Wright State University (WSU) for a graduate credit option, OELMA held the first Advanced Summer Institute for Professional Development. Dr. Todd returned to Ohio and worked with Geitgey and Tepe to provide a day of special training for eight self-selected library media specialists. They were trained as presenters of the module and made available through the Speaker's Bureau.

A debriefing was held after these training sessions and again the module was tweaked. Plans

were put into place for how the speakers could deliver the EBP module. It was decided that a school district, an OELMA region, another state association, or just a group of library media specialists could contact the OELMA office to plan an EBP Workshop. They would be given the names of the trainers and could contact the trainer of their choice. The OELMA office would take the responsibility for registering the participants and photocopying the participant materials. The trainers would be paid a portion of each participant's fee.

It has now been a year since the creation of the Speaker's Bureau and it has worked well. We have been able to offer the EBP Workshop in many areas of the state and by May 2006, over 150 library media specialists had participated.

Feedback from participants continues to be very positive with many library media specialists stating that it was the most relevant professional development they had ever experienced. Others said it would immediately change how they approached instruction in their library media center. Everyone seemed to ask the same questions: "Now that I understand EBP and how to gather the evidence of student learning, how do I track it and communicate the results with my administration? How do I use the evidence to im-

Because the Ohio study was funded with Library Services and Technology Act (LSTA) funds, the survey, the results and an EBP CD are available on the OELMA website (http://www.oelma.org/StudentLearning/default.asp).

prove my program?" Many participants, in their evaluations, asked for a follow-up session on EBP.

Like most professional associations, OELMA functions on a very limited budget. It takes time and money to develop training modules. Luckily, Wayne State University was interested in a partnership leading to a WSU research grant. This grant provided funding for the development of the second EBP module, *Developing Strategies for Establishing Evidence-Based Practice in Your School Library*, and a summer workshop to pilot the new module.

We are constantly made aware of the fact that we must be proactive in the library media profession. There can be many state reports with very supportive findings about library media centers. There can be better graduate programs training new library media specialists to work with our students in the Information Age. But, it is still clear that in the final analysis the library media program is often the area viewed as nonessential for academic achievement. When we are told a position has been eliminated, it is too late to gather the evidence of student learning outcomes. It is, therefore, essential for library media specialists to understand and use the tools of EBP in this age of No Child Left Behind and data-driven decision making.

The next stage of the OELMA EBP plan calls for training so participants, using our state standards and *Excel*-based software, can work in a lab setting to use the data they have gathered to assess student learning in their library media centers. Building on their knowledge of EBP and the tools provided, participants will begin to map out a plan for how they can design and transform student learning through library media instruction and present the results of that transformation to administration.

It is time to retire that old adage that "the more things change, the more they remain the same." In Ohio, we want to empower our library media specialists to use the tools that show the difference they make in student achievement. This plan incorporated through the EBP modules is to work each year to build on our strengths and improve our weaknesses as we gather evidence and document how library media centers make a difference to our students. Stay tuned! Ohio is not ready to give up on school library media centers!

Following is a list of some excellent resources on the concept of Evidence-Based Practice to use when advocating for the value of library media centers. For more information on OELMA's Evidence-Based Practice modules, please contact info@oelma.org.

Barron, Daniel D. "Evidence-Based Practice and the Library Media Specialist." *School Library Media Activities Monthly* 20 (2003): 49-51.

Everhart, Nancy, and Debra K. Logan. "Building the Effective School Library Media Center Using the Student Learning through Ohio School Libraries Research Study." *Knowledge Quest* 34 (2005): 51-54.

Harada, Violet H., and Joan M. Yoshina. *Assessing Learning: Librarians and Teachers as Partners*. Libraries Unlimited, 2005.

Kenney, Brian. "Ross to the Rescue." *School Library Journal* 52 (2006): 44-47.

Kuhlthau, Carol C. "The Center for International Scholarship in School Libraries—CISSL at Rutgers." *School Library Media Activities Monthly* 21, no. 5 (2005): 49-51.

Langhorne, Mary Jo. "Show Me the Evidence!" *Knowledge Quest* 33 (2005): 35-37.

Oatman, Eric. "Overwhelming Evidence." *School Library Journal* 52 (2006): 56-59.

Ohio Educational Library Media Association. http://www.oelma.org/StudentLearning/default.asp (accessed May 27, 2006).

Pascopella, Angela. "Heart of the School." *District Administration* 41 (2005): 54-58.

Todd, Ross J. "Irrefutable Evidence." *School Library Journal* 49 (2003): 52-54.

Whelan, Debra Lau. "13,000 Kids Can't Be Wrong." *School Library Journal* 50 (2004): 46-50.

Young, Terrence, comp. *School Libraries Work!* Scholastic Library, 2006. ✋

Chapter 8

Collaboration

Collaboration is a dynamic, interactive process among equal partners who negotiate instructional goals to impact student achievement.

—Judi Moreillon, "Show Them What We Do: Strategies for Collaborative Teaching" (see page 218)

The AASL *Standards for the 21st-Century Learner* can be daunting when one approaches them as an individual educator. Luckily, of the many topics that have been discussed in the pages of *School Library Media Activities Monthly* (now *School Library Monthly*), perhaps none has been mentioned more frequently than collaboration, or the process of co-teaching that occurs between a school library media specialist and a teacher. As the articles in this chapter point out, collaborative teaching can, at a minimum, shrink the student-to-teacher ratio and, at its finest, result in far-improved instructional design that yields higher student achievement. Collaboration is a key strategy to achieving the deep student learning envisioned by the AASL *Standards*.

Collaboration takes many forms, and there are many approaches to accommodate various school configurations. Whether a school serves young learners or college-bound seniors, whether the school librarian works on a fixed schedule or has flexible scheduling to accommodate as-needed instruction, collaborative opportunities can be found everywhere.

Collaborations can stretch beyond classroom teachers. Physical education, music, art, and other educators who serve as "specialists," as well as the counselor or social worker, are all potential partners. Who better to help lead a lesson on cyber bullying, for example, than the counselor who is an expert on face-to-face bullying? Who better to partner on an art history lesson than the art teacher and the library media specialist, who brings an expertise of digital art resources available for free online?

With professional development initiatives such as professional learning communities or PLCs (DuFour 2004), lesson study (Lewis et al. 2004), humanities classes team-taught by language arts and social studies teachers, special education initiatives to partner classroom and special education teachers, and others, collaboration is by no means limited to work with the library media specialist. School librarians are facing perhaps the richest opportunity ever to align their collaborative desires with existing school reform efforts.

Despite these trends, collaboration is easier said than done. School or district culture may reinforce an egg-carton approach to education, one that prioritizes teachers working alone in their classrooms over partnering with colleagues. Teachers and administrators may harbor outdated assumptions about the roles of school library media specialists and may not see them as equal teaching partners. Evaluation of teachers may not reward those who work together to design meaningful learning experiences for students.

How do SLMSs lay the groundwork for collaborative opportunities? Carl A. Harvey II suggests that it begins with SLMS preparedness. In "Collaborative Connections" (beginning on page 206), he suggests that school librarians begin by gathering curriculum guides and maps, keeping track of past material requests or collaborations in order to offer them again next year, attending curriculum meetings, looking for partners, and maximizing information conversations. In "The Power and Spirit of Collaboration" (beginning on page 209), Susan Vanneman stresses that a prepared library media specialist can help relieve teachers' workload and pressure and lead to joyful partnering.

In "When Does Collaboration Start?" (beginning on page 211), Gail Dickinson identifies three tiers of working together in deepening levels of partnership: cooperation, coordination, and collaboration. New library media specialists, who often struggle most to reach a level of collaboration among more senior teachers, can recognize that early cooperation efforts, such as teaching information skills in isolation or providing books on a cart for a teacher to use, can later develop into coordinated efforts like booktalking upon request, and further into fully developed collaborative lessons and units, where responsibility for planning, instruction, and assessment is shared equally between the instructional partners.

Betty (Elizabeth) L. Marcoux offers a different tiered system for collaboration in "Levels of Collaboration: Where Does Your Work Fit In?" (beginning on page 214). Marcoux identifies a Pyramid of Collaboration. Beginning with the lowest level of interaction, the pyramid's levels are

- **consumption,** in which students use library resources to meet other objectives;

- **connection,** in which library media specialists are aware of the school schedule but have no role in carrying it out;

- **cooperation,** in which there is minimal coordination and minimal interaction with students);

- **coordination**, in which the teacher plans the lesson, but a portion of the lesson is taught by the library media specialist; and

- **collaboration,** which echo's Dickinson's definition of lessons that are jointly designed, facilitated, and evaluated.

What can collaboration look like? And how can different collaboration models be used to demonstrate the value library media specialists can add to student learning? Those are the questions asked by Judi Moreillon in "Show Them What We Do: Strategies for Collaborative Teaching" (beginning on page 218). Moreillon points out that collaboration isn't *what* we do, but *how we do it.* There are many potential "hows": dividing the class into two groups with two instructors, having one lead teacher and one supporting teacher, developing learning centers for independent student work, parallel teaching, alternate teaching, and team teaching. Recognizing that collaboration can look different in different situations may relax the anxiety of many SLMSs, who worry that they are not "collaborating right."

One of the unspoken fears of some educators is that library media specialists will "take over" their classroom, overshadow their own instructional style, or imply that the teacher was not effective enough to teach the lesson alone. Whether these fears have validity or not, perception is reality, as the saying goes. Personality and pedagogical styles can cause friction if they are not acknowledged. "Using Personality Traits and Effective Communication to Improve Collaboration," by Juanita Warren Buddy (beginning on page 221), describes strategies for identifying personality traits and work styles and for meeting those differences with improved communication techniques.

Pat Franklin and Claire Gatrell Stephens offer a template for conversations between teachers and librarians that help to align expectations in "Lesson Planning: The Ticket to Successful Teaching" (beginning on page 225).

Judi Moreillon's "Coteaching Published Lesson Plans: A Recipe for Success?" (beginning on page 227) suggests that using a published lesson plan can minimize friction over pedagogical styles and allow a collaborative team to focus on building a working relationship.

Leslie Preddy's "Collaboration: The Motown Method" (beginning on page 229), suggests a 1960s Motown group as a metaphor for back-and-forth co-teaching.

Ross Todd confronts the elephant in the room. In "Collaboration: From Myth to Reality: Let's Get Down to Business. Just Do It!" (beginning on page 232), Todd points out an unfortunate reality. Despite the number of publications and research studies that outline the benefits of collaborative teaching, there is far less team teaching going on in American school libraries than is desirable. He references numerous research studies on collaboration in school libraries that bear out this uncomfortable truth. He then discusses the outcome of a research project evaluating a collaboration development project at Kent State University's Institute for Library and Information Literacy Education and the seven key insights that emerged.

Finally, two tracking documents are presented (beginning on page 237). The first, "Collaborative Planning," by Deborah Levitov, can help structure the process of planning a collaborative lesson. "Assessment Tool: Levels of

Communication, Cooperation, and Collaboration with Teachers," by Deborah Levitov and Allison Zmuda, can help a SLMS track the levels of teamwork between the SLMS and classroom teachers.

GETTING TO ADVOCACY

Advocating for collaborative teaching requires a delicate hand, so that teachers do not misinterpret your efforts as self-aggrandizement. Consider these strategies to help develop a culture of collaboration in your school:

1. Follow the behind-the-scenes strategies described by Carl Harvey and Susan Vanneman. Do your homework so that you are prepared for collaborative conversations.

2. Seize the moment: if formal planning sessions are not part of building culture, take advantage of informal conversations in the hall or teacher's lounge.

3. Download Scholastic Library Publishing's *School Libraries Work!* (www2.scholastic.com/content/collateral_resources/pdf/s/slw3_2008.pdf). This document contains summaries of major reports and studies showing the impact of school libraries—and collaboration—on student achievement. Identify studies within the document that could be shared with administrators to support your desire for a more collaborative community.

4. Attend as many curriculum meetings at the school and district level as possible to become aware of curriculum issues and to offer the resources, instructional support, and involvement of the school library media center.

5. Recruit teachers to share student learning that results from collaborative efforts.

6. When discussing the benefits of collaboration, speak from the perspective of what students will gain. Nobody wants to collaborate to improve the perception of school libraries, but they will collaborate if it makes their teaching easier and improves their students' achievement.

THOUGHTS FOR THE JOURNEY

1. What existing structures support collaboration in your school or district?

2. What barriers to collaboration exist? How could these barriers be minimized?

3. Collaboration begins small. A few well-developed efforts at collaboration will lead to further collaboration later. Be selective about whom to approach for these early attempts at collaboration—who would be a good person for first efforts?

4. How will you showcase the results of a positive collaboration? How can you leverage those positive results?

5. What curriculum or school improvement committees are present in the school? How can you become involved?

6. What is your administrator's position on collaboration? If collaboration is not a visible value in your school, what is the best way to "sell" it to him or her? As Juanita Warren Buddy points out in her article, different personalities respond in different ways. What is the personality or work style of your administrator? What is the best way to "sell" collaboration to him or her? Who could help you?

Collaboration Connections

by Carl A. Harvey II

O f all the buzz words used in the school library media profession, "collaboration" evokes the strongest feelings—and not all of those feelings are positive. Some library media specialists are not convinced that collaboration is an essential part of their programs, yet collaboration seems to be essential in many other professions. In fact, there are very few professions where people can work in isolation, because most careers require workers to collaborate and work with colleagues. The practice of taking a class to the library media center with the library media specialist doing his or her own thing, in isolation, should be long gone. Excuses like problems with scheduling, lack of support staff, and an insufficient budget are not acceptable. What is most important is student learning and the most effective learning takes place when teachers and library media specialists collaborate.

Carl A. Harvey II is the library media specialist at North Elementary School in Noblesville, IN. Email: carl_harvey@mail.nobl.k12.in.us

During a workshop a few years back, a library media specialist shared an absolutely wonderful poetry unit. She had a fixed schedule and taught this unit during National Poetry Month in April. But, when she was asked if it correlated to the time when the classroom teachers taught poetry, she was perplexed. Why would that matter? Imagine the increased impact on students if while they were learning about poetry in the classroom, the library media specialist was reinforcing it in the library media center. The students would certainly have had a much richer experience if the two teachers had taken time to collaborate. Instead, poetry was taught at two different times of the year and it is possible the two teachers shared contradictory information.

The Look of Collaboration

In the ideal scenario, the library media specialist and teachers would have sat down together and planned their units. If they were working with a fixed schedule, they could have correlated their topics and skills so that students had multiple chances to practice and reinforce their learning. If they were working with a flexible schedule, they could have met and determined what types of lessons and projects to co-teach and co-assess.

Collaboration isn't always easy. Teachers and library media specialists understand this when they see students doing group work. In this form of collaboration, students often struggle with dividing out the tasks, and some students seem to be doing all the work, while others do none of the work. It is also difficult to deal with a variety of personalities and come to a common consensus. Adults have these same struggles when collaborating. But, just as students doing group work discover, a group of teachers and the library media specialist can work together to make a stronger project that results in better instruction for students.

Figuring out where to start is often the most difficult part. Experience says that most teachers are not going to come running to the library media specialist ready to collaborate. Most teachers did not witness this type of collaboration when they were in secondary school nor did they have any training for this sort of collaborative teaching during their college years. So, the burden of beginning collaboration falls on the library media specialist. The library media specialist has to be the one to

- start the conversation.
- articulate the possibilities.
- open the door and let people into the library media center.
- begin to break down hurdles and obstacles.
- be positive about the potential.

Following are some ways to potentially crack the wall between isolation and collaboration.

Plans

Most teachers have lesson plans, syllabuses, or a yearlong curriculum map to guide their teaching. Ask for a copy. Create a binder with plans organized by grade levels or departments. Take time to read them. Make notes of potential connections that could be made with the library media program. Each month, review the plans for what is coming up and

email teachers, put notes in mailboxes, or have face-to-face conversations about the curriculum topics. For example, a note might say, "I see in your curriculum map that in January you are going to be talking about penguins, and all of these fabulous arctic animal books were added to the collection last fall. Any chance there might be a research project we could do together?" or "I just got this fabulous picture book in that would be great to introduce as your next novel in class."

Document and Gather Data

Even those teachers who are not inclined to want to collaborate can provide the library media specialist with options (even if unintentionally). When a request comes in for a collection of books, keep a copy of the titles pulled. Just knowing a theme or topic being discussed can be the spark for a project. When the materials are sent to the teacher, include a note about potential projects or ideas that could correlate to those materials. Start a calendar and track titles pulled. This information can be a springboard for making contacts with teachers for the next school year. The library media specialist might say, "Oh, it is almost October. Do you need those ocean resources again for November? We'd be glad to get those, and how could I help with incorporating information literacy skills with this unit?"

Meetings

Whenever meetings are suggested as an option, often the first thought is who wants to attend another meeting. However, if the teachers in the building get together on a regular basis to plan instruction, the library media specialist should be there as much as possible. Many times, at the elementary level, entire grade levels plan together. Some do this during preparation periods, but others use time before or after school. Make a calendar and try to attend as many of these sessions as possible. Sometimes, there is little the library media specialist can add or the connection to the library media program may be remote; however, just knowing what the teachers are covering and how can provide a wealth of information. It is also important to consider that the more visible the library media specialist, the easier it is to collaborate. Attending planning meetings provides a forum where the library media specialist can suggest applicable ideas for instruction.

From resources to potential co-teaching, planning sessions can be invaluable opportunities for sharing. If the library media specialist is on a fixed schedule, connecting to teachers during their planning times is more problematic. One way to do this is to have one teacher serve as the "library" contact. The library media specialist could share ideas with that contact that could be taken to the planning meeting. The administrator could also provide for periodic times to cover the library media specialist's classes with a substitute so the library media specialist can attend these planning meetings. When faced with obstacles, the important thing is to think of possible solutions instead of wallowing in the problems.

Beyond Classroom Teachers

It is also important to remember there are other teachers in the building besides just classroom teachers. There are also special area and special needs teachers who can be potential connections for collaboration. An example is a resource teacher who sometimes works with small groups of students yet he or she wants to keep students engrossed in the same topic/content covered in the classroom. He or she can work with the library media specialist to find resources and develop activities and projects to do in the library media center. Art, music, and physical education teachers as well as other teachers beyond the core subject areas can be targets for collaboration. A conversation with a music teacher at my building a few years ago turned into a collaborative effort that has resulted in a project at each grade level during music class. Library media specialists should always look for different possibilities for collaboration.

Technology

Whether teachers like it or not, technology continues to have a major impact on the instruction in today's schools. Many teachers need help learning what technology is available and how to use it with students. Library media specialists can provide staff development on technology and, at the same time, model using technology effectively with students. Teachers can then begin to identify how they can use it in their own instruction. Once teachers decide to use technology with their students, they often need a strong support network. This provides another opportunity for the library media specialist to collaborate with teachers.

Informal Conversations

Conversations in the hallway, chats in the teachers' lounge, discussions during lunch, or even after-school social events can all lead to potential collaboration. Teachers like to get together; they like to talk. They talk about their day, students, lessons, family, hobbies, etc. Not every conversation leads back to the library media program, but every conversation provides additional information that may lead to something down the road. It is important that the library media specialist find time to eat in the lounge, attend social functions, and be visible in the halls before and after schools. They should strive to be part of the conversation. They can share what is happening in the library media center as well as hobbies and interests. This helps create an environment of trust and collegiality that will make it easier to collaborate.

Library media specialists have to be the initial instigators of collaboration. But, once the seeds are sown and the instruction is a success, teachers will want to come back for more and more. Collaboration is not a silver bullet that will make every library media program a critical component of the school; however, collaboration does build allies. These allies can be very useful if the program is threatened with budget or staffing cuts. These allies know that when teachers and library media specialist collaborate to co-plan, co-teach, and co-assess, it builds a stronger and richer learning experience for students. This should be the ultimate goal.

The Power and Spirit of Collaboration

by Susan Vanneman

Collaboration is the power and spirit of successful, thriving library media programs. It is the reason some library media centers pulse with activity and are alive with active learners. When in place, collaboration seems magical, but in reality it is the result of hard work, dedication, and planning. What can library media specialists do to make this "media magic" happen in their centers?

✳ KNOW WHAT IS HAPPENING in your building! Knowledge of curriculum objectives and of how the collection supports the curriculum is essential. Library media specialists need to know the curriculum and the timeline for the instruction. Have access to current, enticing support materials as a powerful lure for first time, as well as long-time collaborating partners. Keep the staff informed with newsletters, signs, listserv notices, and individual contacts when new materials are added to the collection and when new electronic resources or strategies become available. Curriculum needs must be a purchasing priority. Library media specialists need to serve on curriculum committees and play an active role in curriculum staff development.

✳ REACH OUT to teachers! Don't wait for them to come to you. Be creative—think of specific processes, strategies, and resources that can integrate with their instruction and share those ideas. Some teachers may not be familiar with a specific research path or process, so introduce it to them, and they and their students will soon understand the power of the process. You will then have an ongoing collaborating partner.

✳ HAVE A PROCESS for planning collaborative instruction (see "Collaborative Planning" in this issue, page 2). This lets teachers know up front that you are organized and understand good instructional practice and design. Be flexible and offer to plan before school, after school, whenever, to meet the needs of the teacher or team. This formal approach may not always continue as you establish long-term partners, but it is a step that will clarify objectives and initially lead to successful collaboration. A collaborative plan should include who, what, when, where, and how it will be done.

✳ KNOW STRATEGIES for enhancing the instructional objectives of your partner(s). You should have a repertoire of strategies that will help students have successful experiences in the library media center. Your contributions to collaboration with the teacher and resulting student success should include reading for information skills, note taking tips, ethical research practices, and skills for using technology as a research tool. The teacher can provide the more exact content expertise in the relationship. Successful collaborators recognize the talents and strengths of the individuals and plan instruction accordingly.

✳ REMEMBER that exemplary practices for teaching information literacy strategies are more meaningful when they are:
  ✳ embedded and relevant to student needs;
  ✳ described and modeled;
  ✳ teach students when, why, and where they can use strategies;
  ✳ repeatedly practiced; and
  ✳ reinforced through feedback (Pressley 1995, 2-3).

✳ UNDERSTAND that collaboration means viewing your work with the teacher as a partnership that requires trust and respect.

Susan Vanneman is a National Board Certified Teacher in Library Media and is the library media specialist at Robin Mickle Middle School in Lincoln, NE.

This partnership is an opportunity for the students to benefit from the attention, knowledge, perspectives, and skills of two teachers. Students enjoy seeing teachers work together in this relationship and appreciate the more immediate assistance and reinforcement it makes possible. Collaboration helps students gain the skills needed to be independent users of information.

✳ BE TOTALLY DEDICATED to being a teaching partner; stick with the students and teacher(s) through every piece of the instructional sequence. The library media specialist should be an active partner in the instructional design and the rubric devised should reflect both the content and process of the project. Both partners owe it to each other and the students to always be prepared, on time, and engaged in the process.

✳ REFLECT DAILY on your work so that your collaborative efforts and instruction can be adjusted to the student needs. Make note of changes for the next time you collaborate. At the conclusion of the collaboration, systematically evaluate each part of the process and make revisions for your next effort together (see "Assessment Tool: Levels of Communication, Cooperation, and Collaboration with Teachers" in *SLMAM*, October 2006, page 2).

If ever the power and spirit of collaboration were essential, it is now when the workload and pressure on teachers seems to be growing and justification of staffing and budget for library media centers are challenged. The emergence of state standards has increased the need for and importance of collaborative efforts by teachers and library media specialists. Quality instruction and increased academic excellence can be the outgrowth of successful collaborative efforts. Library media specialists who want dynamic programs need to be the change agents and proactively work to engage teachers in the process of collaboration. The "magic" of collaboration is careful planning and attention to the process. Successful collaboration requires enormous effort and repeated practice, especially in the beginning, but participants in the process find that it is a joyful way to interact with colleagues and students and gets easier with time.

Resource:

Presseley, Michael, and Christine McCormick. *Cognition, Teaching, and Assessment*. HarperCollins, 1995. ♦

When Does Collaboration Start?

by Gail Dickinson

The concept of the library media specialist as a teacher of information skills has been present since the very beginning of the profession. *Information Power* presents the teaching of information skills as a function of the collaborative relationship between library media specialist and classroom teacher (AASL/AECT 1998). Another book, *Library Power*, reaffirmed the power of this collaborative partnership (Zweizig & Hopkins 2000). The research literature is helpful to library media specialists in understanding the process by which students develop skills in information use (Kuhlthau 2004) and in identifying the instructional methodologies helpful in the teaching of information skills (Eisenberg and Berkowitz 1988; Macrorie 1988). The research literature, however, is less helpful for new library media specialists who have not yet developed the relationships with classroom teachers on which collaborative information skill instruction can be built.

Gail K. Dickinson, Ph.D., is Associate Professor in the Department of Educational Curriculum and Instruction at Old Dominion University, Norfolk, VA. Email: gdickins@odu.edu

To find more assistance, we have to go outside the school library profession. Marilyn Friend and Lynne Cooke's writings are helpful for creating a scaffold for the collaborative teaching of information skills integrated into classroom content (Friend and Cooke 1996). They define collaboration as a "style for direct interaction between at least two coequal parties voluntarily engaged in shared decision-making as they work toward a common goal" (1996, 6). This definition of collaboration delineates a series of goals for beginning library media specialists to develop a relationship with classroom teachers where there are opportunities for direct interaction through face-to-face planning meetings, email, chat, or by other forms. Blanket memos to the faculty or general announcements at faculty meetings are not examples of direct action. Direct interaction is based on direct contact with one or more specific teachers for the purpose of establishing a collaborative relationship.

Inexperienced library media specialists or those new to collaborative processes may be daunted by the need for the process to be co-equal, for the decision making to be shared, and for the result of the shared planning to be a common goal. True collaboration, as defined above, does have those elements and can be achieved after years of experience and with increased confidence gained by successful collaborations as well as lessons learned from unsuccessful attempts. There is a continuum for collaboration that sets the stage for the collaborative experience scaffold. This continuum begins with Cooperation, moves into a more interactive stage with Coordination, and reaches the final level with true Collaboration (Callison 1999; Dickinson 2006).

The Handshake of Collaboration

If true collaboration can be thought of as a handshake, then the continuum of collaboration that follows might be helpful as an analogy:

- Cooperation is two hands stretching towards each other, but with only the fingertips touching. The classroom teacher is reaching out to the library media specialist by acknowledging upcoming units or resources needs, and the library media specialist is responding by preparing lists of resources available or providing those resources at the proper time. The library media specialist may also develop isolated information skills lessons for the class in the hope that students may remember to apply the skills at the proper time. If the hands do not exactly meet, or if one hand retracts slightly, it does not affect the instruction on either side. The classroom teacher can teach without the

resources, and whether or not the students learn the skills a week or a month before application is not a problem. Even if the unit is cancelled or abbreviated, the information skills instruction can be taught as planned. The students will use the information someday.

Cooperation is important, but it is not Collaboration.

- Coordination is a deeper level of the collaborative process and can be visualized by hands crossing at the wrist or arm. The library media specialist steers the information skills little red wagon to meet the

Teaching Collaborative Processes

Skills are best learned when the application is direct and immediate. That holds true for student learning of information skills and it is also true for pre-service library media specialists learning the skills for collaboration. Preparation of information skills lessons and practice teaching to other prospective library media specialists are useless in the most important part of the collaborative process—the direct interaction with a classroom teacher to propose an integrated information skills unit. The continuum of collaboration applied to school library media preparation could be the following:

- **Cooperation.** In the Cooperation stage, school library candidates (students in school library media preparation programs) would learn ways to provide resources for teachers and to teach students (PK-12) in the school library program. Some sample activities might be creating newsletters and webpages to advocate for school library media programs, learning about children's and young adult literature, and learning about information skills processes including the development of isolated information skills lessons.

- **Coordination.** When the prepared candidates move to the Coordination stage, they can apply the content curriculum to the provision of resources or instruction, or to specific student or teacher needs. Sample activities might be development of mediagraphies based on state curricula, the performance of storytelling or booktalking to PK-12 students, or preparation of instructional lessons to coordinate with classroom content.

- **Collaboration.** In order to ensure that library media specialists are prepared for true collaboration, they must have had at least one true collaborative experience. Development of a co-planned, co-taught, and co-assessed integrated information skills unit in conjunction with a practicing classroom teacher and then taught to PK-12 students provides the only authentic experience to ensure that candidates are prepared for the job. Many school library media programs require that the instruction is videotaped so that the supervised experience can provide the highest level of value as a learning experience. Because teaching in a library media center is different from teaching in an enclosed self-contained classroom, some classroom teachers find the transition to library media specialist difficult.

classroom teacher steering the classroom content little green tractor. They plan to meet at the crossroads at the same day and same time. Coordination takes cursory planning and some level of interaction. It is a deeper level of collaborative planning than just Coordination, but each instructional package is still separate. If the classroom teacher or the library media specialist arrives at the crossroads a little early or a little late, it doesn't matter. Each has a contained instructional goal that is only indirectly dependent on the other. Coordination is important, but it is not Collaboration.

- True Collaboration can be thought of as a handshake. When two hands are clasping each other, it is difficult to tell where one hand stops and the other starts. The collaboration represented by the handshake is based on co-planning, co-teaching, and co-assessment of student learning progress in the mastery of classroom content and the process of information location and use. A handshake is a symbol of trust and of friendship as well as a reflection of common interest. So, too, is Collaboration.

Friend and Cook also provide some clarity in the definition of co-teaching (1996, 45). Team teaching, where the classroom teacher and the library media specialist are present in the same physical space and share the responsibility for joint instruction, is not the only definition of co-teaching. In any of the stages described, the approach to co-teaching may also be teacher/support in which either the classroom teacher or the library media specialist takes the lead in instruction. These roles may alternate based on whether the instruction is content-based or information skills-based. Another common practice is to approach collaboration by station teaching, i.e., by dividing the class so that some students remain in the classroom or another part of the library media center for content instruction while some are under the supervision of the library media specialist for information skills instruction or research.

When to Start Collaboration

The collaborative information skills instruction scaffold can be applied to classroom teachers as well as library media specialists. Library media specialists may want to map the teachers on the scaffold and identify who are at the cooperation stage, who have progressed to the coordination stage, and who are true collaborators. Some teachers, of course, are off the scaffold entirely because they have never acquired the trust in the first place or have lost the trust necessary to cooperate with any education professional outside of their own classrooms. Victories come in small stages—maybe seeing collaborative relationships move from one stage to another or being able to place a teacher who was previously uncooperative at the beginning level.

The job description of the library media specialist as teacher does not specify a waiting period before beginning collaboration. The collaborative continuum must start with day one on the job. To do otherwise would be equal to a fifth grade teacher deciding to put off math instruction until the second or third year of teaching, when he or she has a better understanding of the curriculum, the students, and the instructional processes of the school. It doesn't work that way for classroom teachers, and it shouldn't work that way for library media specialists. The job of the library media specialist is to become familiar with the curriculum, the collection, and the students and, at the same time, perform all functions in the job description at the highest possible level. We can't wait several years to become familiar and confident at program administration duties before fulfilling the rest of the job description. Students of all ages stream in and out of our library media center doors. We have one chance, just one year, to catch them at each grade level. An opportunity lost is a generation lost.

References

American Association of School Librarians/Association for Educational Communication and Technology. *Information Power: Building Partnerships for Learning.* ALA, 1998.

Callison, Danny. "Collaboration." *School Library Media Activities Monthly* 15, no. 5 (January 1999): 38-40.

Dickinson, G. K. *Achieving National Board Certification for School Library Media Specialists; a Study Guide.* ALA, 2006.

Eisenberg, M., and R. E. Berkowitz. *Curriculum Initiative: An Agenda and Strategy for Library Media Programs.* Linworth, 1988.

Friend, M., and L. Cooke. *Interactions: Collaboration Skills for School Professionals.* 2nd ed. Longmans, 1996.

Kuhlthau, C. C. *Seeking Meaning: A Process Approach to Library and Information Services.* 2nd ed. Libraries Unlimited, 2004.

Macrorie, K. *The I-Search Paper.* Boynton/Cook, 1988.

Zweizig, D., and D. M. Hopkins. *Lessons from Library Power: Enriching Teaching and Learning.* Libraries Unlimited, 2000. ✋

Levels of Collaboration:
Where Does Your Work Fit In?

by Betty (Elizabeth) L. Marcoux

Action in library media centers today often involves collaboration with the classroom and the administration, as well as links to learning standards. Smith spoke about the need to have a collaborative environment in a school to positively affect instruction (1990). There is also significant research that speaks to the benefits of collaboration. A study in Colorado suggests there is evidence that student achievement is 20% higher in schools where there is collaboration compared to schools where there isn't collaboration (Lance 2000).

Collaboration and Academic Concerns

Several academic areas of concern are enhanced by collaboration. They are the following:

Student achievement

An increase in student achievement in collaborative settings has been established in studies such as Judith Warren Little's in 1990 where she found that collaboration between teachers was directly linked to student achievement. More recently, a study of collaboration indicated that test scores were directly impacted in relationship to the degree to which library media specialists and classroom teachers worked together (Lance 2003). This study also indicated that collaboration between teachers and library media specialists is more likely when the library media specialist is a school leader.

Teacher professional development

An article by Vi Harada discussed the challenges of teacher collaboration (2001). She suggested that there are concepts on collaboration that can be implemented and documented in ways that allow them to impact teacher evaluation and create an environment of shared teaching values with a positive impact on student learning. In the state of Washington there is a push to place the library media center in the middle of teacher learning about the classroom-based assessments in social studies (http://www.wlma.org/cbas). Several summer institute programs that instruct about the collaboration between the social studies classroom teacher and the library media specialist are being held throughout the state and are being taught by library media specialists to classroom teachers. This is an example of the opportunities available to library media specialists to interact more concertedly with classroom teachers for the purpose of increasing student achievement through collaboration.

Collaborative schools

Collaborative schools are valued and sought after in teaching environments (Leonard and Leonard 2003). While there may be frequent evaluation and feedback, it is usually informal and thus the opportunity to be an impromptu mentor to other teachers is more likely and less threatening. Teachers practicing communication skills with other teachers tend to be more likely to collaborate, and this is one of the factors in the current No Child Left Behind professional teacher

Betty (Elizabeth) L. Marcoux, Ph.D., currently is on the faculty of the University of Washington Information School, and teaches in the area of school and youth librarianship. Formerly a K-12 teacher and library media specialist, she now works with current and future practitioners who dedicate themselves to children and young adult information.

standard requirements (http:www. ed.gov/nclb/overview/intro/exec-summ.html). Teachers are viewed as part of a community (the school) of learners who engage in a learning process more actively when there are elements of cooperative learning and development. Empowering students is valued by teachers as it allows them to have input into what impacts students and their work. Novice teachers also benefit from being empowered as it gives them a sense of supportive mentoring where mistakes and inadequacies are not judged but used to launch into alternative and perchance better teaching methodology. Novice teachers maximize their rewards through elements of peer collaboration that allow them to seek advice and guidance as well as assistance—resulting in better teacher and learning.

Educational improvement

Collaboration means a shared event or experience. In schools this can be translated to mean jointly contributing to the belief that school quality is largely based upon what happens at the site. A book written in 1998 by Sarasen and Lorentz spoke about the need to institutionalize a level of collaboration in the school for educational improvement. Instruction was seen as most effective in a school environment that had norms of collegiality and continuous improvement. A wide range of practices and structures enabled educators to work together and move toward educational improvement.

Collaboration Characteristics

There are a variety of characteristics that define collaboration behaviors between educators. Significant ones are the following:

Frequent, continuous conversation about teaching and its practice

The ability to have peer conversations about what will work, won't work, could work better, etc. pedagogically increases the awareness of involved parties about what is best for student learning in that situation. Sharing information about the learners helps with the planning, implementation, and evaluation of a learning experience. Collaborative methodology allows for this to happen.

> "Collaboration is the process of shared creation: two or more individuals with complementary skills interacting to create a shared understanding that none had previously possessed or could have come to on their own" (Fullen 1993).

Frequent use of peer observation and critique of teaching

Peer assessment is a threatening behavior, but one that can potentially be of great benefit to both the assessor and the assessee. A library media center can be a strong venue for such observation and critique and can lead to more concerted and stronger collaboration between the teacher and the library media specialist. Knowing the hazards as well as the opportunities of a learning situation helps to give insights not only to those with daily connections, but builds respect and understanding for what is occurring as well as what might occur. Sharing this information in a nonthreatening environment helps everyone develop and fine-tune their educational approaches.

Joint planning, design, research, evaluation, instruction preparation

There is evidence in the research that the use of communication between information agencies who share common audiences and goals is more effective in designing meaningful learning opportunities. In the state of Washington, the Connecting Learners to Libraries Initiative asked school and public libraries serving the same student populations to develop and implement coordinated projects between their agencies (Washington State Library 2007). The results suggest that awareness of each other's environment as well as the joint planning and design of their work benefited the students at both sites.

Peer coaching

A recent study by Meyers, Fisher, Marcoux with tweens (those between the ages of 9-13) found that while they benefited from a consistent message, they were often more successful sharing the message with their peers than were the adults (2007). This suggests that peer coaching may have more value to the peer than adult coaching in some circumstances, and that having student assistants work with each other as well as other students may have more learning value to them than previously understood. Specifically, increasing these interactions may have value.

Ingredients of Successful Collaboration

There are six elements of successful collaboration: the environment, the characteristics of mentoring, the process or structure of collaboration, communication, a shared purpose, and resources. Each element has an analysis that determines the level of collaboration. For instance, resources can be a reactive set of reading materials, office tools, writing tools—all minimal in terms of facilitation—to a maximum of a discussion about the resource types needed and how to best use them for that purpose. The environment may be minimally the four walls of the classroom or maximally the classroom expanded to include the entire learning environment appropriate to the lesson.

There are five different levels of collaboration. Each lesson can be analyzed to determine the level of collaboration it encompasses: consumption, connection, cooperation, coordination, ultimate collaboration. This, of course, is NOT taking into consideration the level of isolation, the antithesis of collaboration—something experienced in schools where there is no connection between the library media center and the classroom.

Definitions for these types of collaboration are as follows:

Consumption: Students consume library resources for typing, printing, photocopying, weekly reading quotas, etc.

Connection: The library staff is informed about the lesson in terms of what it is and/or when it will occur in the library media center but has no input into the design or timing of it.

Cooperation: The library staff is informed about the lesson goals, its expected outcome, its due date, and the criteria for assessment. There is minimal consultation about types of resources to be used and timing of the project. The library staff works with the students on how to use the resources and how to do their research.

Coordination: The library staff has informed the library media center about the lesson goals, its expected outcome, the timing of the project, and how it will be evaluated. The library staff has shown students not only how to use the resources but has participated in facilitating their use. The library staff has worked with the students on how to do their research and how to develop their projects.

Collaboration (Ultimate): The library staff and the classroom teacher have jointly planned and implemented the entire lesson. Teaching is shared on all aspects of the lesson, and student assessment/evaluation is done jointly. There is evaluation of both content mastery and also resource use. Students are also assessed on their information literacy process.

Fullen pointed out the successful connection of a learning organization with its ability to form and reform alliances that have similar agendas (1993, 97). He advocated for sharing information. He believed that being dependent on sharing created an outcome that contributed to higher [learning] standards. Malone looked at collaboration from a business lens, but also talked about the flow dependency of one activity leading to the production of another resource or activity which came about only because of this interaction (2004).

A Movable Feat

It is possible to move up the collaboration continuum to a higher level or degree of collaboration. It is also important to know that not all lessons need or should be at the "ultimate collaboration" level. Assess the level needed for the particular library media program. Determine which lessons have potential for moving to a higher level of collaboration. Determine how to get there.

When assessing the level of collaboration, consider how this lesson could move up the collaboration pyramid and become part of the post-project/lesson assessment. In designing the lesson for the "next" time, these are the issues that will be taken into consideration by both the library media specialist and the classroom teacher. A record of the event(s) with documentation of what has occurred will assist both to develop a closer style of collaboration and increase the visibility of the work both are doing.

Is This You?

There are two streams of thought in terms of collaboration: proactive and reactive. The differences are sug-

Diagram 1

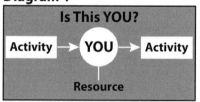

Diagram 2

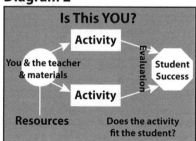

gested in Diagram 1. In this diagram, "you" are focused upon the activity and responding to it. This is a reactive stance and common in school library media programs. Few connections are made between students learning other than to suggest support for what someone else has put in place to create the learning opportunity.

Diagram 2 suggests a more active stance. It suggests that "you" are a part of the planning, implementing, and ultimately the evaluation of the learning event. It even suggests evaluation of the actual activity to see how well it matches/fits the student learning objective.

Pyramid of Collaboration

A Pyramid of Collaboration (see below) of the various levels of collaboration and a Collaboration Assessment Tool (see page 24) will allow you to determine what level best fits the work being done. Used in determining best practices between collaborating factors of the public and school libraries, and also used in various Washington state site schools to increase collaboration, this instrument is offered for your use. Please inform the creator of this instrument as to its use and value to your program.

The most important part of the collaboration equation is YOU! Work on identifying the issues that help

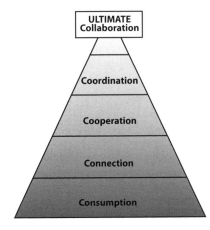

or hinder collaboration. Identify the major stakeholders needed to do collaboration. Do an assessment of what is happening now. Then, examine various options that match with the assessment findings. When you have this information, consider holding focus meetings to confirm findings and plans. Once that has happened, do it and evaluate what you do. Remember, in the end, the effort needed for collaboration must result in enough reward so that there is reason for all involved to continue to support the process.

Conclusion

To collaborate is to share—to collaborate at different levels is to share the responsibility for learning with more and more input. While there are other ways of approaching collaboration, this model allows for greater collaboration between the classroom and the library media center. It involves the school library staff interacting with the teaching staff. It is moving from information literacy expertise to information process expertise. The move means working with the classroom teacher as much as students. It means facilitating the Internet and database use as guided research tools full of resources. The focus of the school library staff is from that of the knowledge holder to the knowledge manager.

The newer model of collaboration involves working with others to determine the social costs and implications of information to the student learning environment. It means considering social perceptions of the audience, relationships between the instruction and the learning, developmental challenges, and greater understanding of how to best devise (and evaluate) learning opportunities that achieve the target more readily.

According to the study by Meyers, Fisher, and Marcoux, there is a richness in providing for information seeking practices that resonate clearly with students if these practices are socially and developmentally mediated and facilitated (2007). The library media speciallist can effectively work in these areas of differentiated learning. Collaboration makes this happen more frequently.

References:

Fullen, M. *The Learning Organization and its Environment: In Change Forces: Probing the Depths of Educational Reform*. Falmer Press, 1993.

Harada, Violet H. "Professional Development as Collaborative Inquiry." *Knowledge Quest* 29, no. 4 (March/April 2001): 13-19.

Leonard, L., and P. Leonard. "The Continuing Trouble with Collaboration: *Teachers Talk. Current Issues in Education* [On-line] 6, no. 15 (September 17, 2003). http://cie.ed.asu.edu/volume6/number15/

Lance, K. Curry. "How School Librarians Help Kids Achieve Standards." *Library Research Services* (April 2000). http://www.lrs.org/documents/lmcstudies/CO/execsumm.pdf

Little, J. W. "The Persistence of Privacy: Autonomy and Initiative in Teachers' Relations." *Teachers College Record* 91, no. 4 (April 1990): 509-536.

Malone, T. *The Future of Work: How the New Order of Business Will Shape Your Organization, Your Management style, and Your Life*. Harvard Business Press, 2004.

Meyers, E. et al. *Social in-Social out: The Information Worlds of Millenials*. In press, 2007.

No Child Left Behind. *Executive Summary*. 2001. http://www.ed.gov/nclb/overview/intro/execsumm.html

Sarasen, S. B., and E. M. Lorentz. *Crossing Boundaries: Collaboration, Coordination, and the Redefinition of Resources*. ERIC ED412660, 1998.

Smith, S. C., and J. J. Scott. *The Collaborative School: A Work Environment for Effective Instruction*. Eric SuDoc ED 1.310/2:316918, 1990.

Washington State Library. *Connecting Learners to Libraries Initiative*. 2007. http://www.secstate.wa.gov/library/libraries/projects/connecting/ 🖐

Show Them What We Do:
Strategies for Collaborative Teaching

by Judi Moreillon

Through LM_NET, the school library blogosphere, face-to-face and electronic meetings of the American Association of School Librarian's Affiliate Assembly, colleagues from across the country share best practices and concerns for the present and the future of our work. I have observed that one perennial online conversation centers on students, classroom teacher colleagues, or administrators who do not know what we library media specialists/teacher-librarians actually DO. Consequently, if we assume that everyone is "from Missouri" and must be SHOWN the benefits of classroom-library collaboration, the responsibility to clearly communicate what we DO falls fully and squarely on our shoulders.

This responsibility, however, presents several challenges to library media specialists/teacher-librarians who work within the constraints of fixed library schedules. In schools where library media specialists/teacher-librarians provide classroom teachers planning time and teachers do not stay in the library media center with students during their "library lessons," this lack of knowledge is understandable. Even if classroom teachers and administrators are provided copies of "our" lesson plans, they have not actually SEEN what happens when we work with students.

Ideally, open-access, flexibly scheduled library media programs are the best setting for demonstrating our impact on student achievement, but this impact can also be observed in a fixed schedule environment if classroom teachers are required to remain in the library media center with their students. This collaborative approach to teaching shows we are committed to developing and refining effective instructional practices within our schools.

Collaboration

Collaboration describes HOW educators work together rather than WHAT we do. Collaboration is a dynamic, interactive process among equal partners who negotiate instructional goals to impact student achievement. Classroom-library collaboration can occur in the planning, implementation, and assessment stages of teaching. Ideally, it happens during all three. It is, however, during the implementation stage that library media specialists/teacher-librarians have golden opportunities to SHOW students, classroom teacher colleagues, and administrators exactly what we DO.

During standards-based lessons, collaborators can work in isolation from one another or they can assume different co-teaching roles. When collaborators tackle the task of "assigning responsibilities" for components of the lesson, library media specialists/teacher-librarians can suggest co-teaching strategies that lower the student-to-teacher ratio. This approach increases support for individual students, provides models for cooperative learning, and makes effective small group and individual reading, writing, and researching conferences possible. If one of our goals is for students, classroom teachers, and

Judi Moreillon, Ph.D., is the author of *Collaborative Strategies for Teaching Reading Comprehension: Maximizing Your Impact* (ALA Editions, 2007). She serves as a literacies and libraries consultant, as an adjunct assistant professor, and as the Director of Business Development and Product Management for Star Bright Books in New York.

administrators to understand the impact of our instructional partnerships, then we must strive to practice various co-teaching roles rather than "do our part" separate from our colleagues in the classroom.

Using Collaborative Teaching to Lower Student-to-Teacher Ratios

Although there is no universal agreement on the precise ratio, a class size of fifteen or less has been described as optimal and the benefits of small class size are greatest for elementary-age students (Glass and Smith 1979). Recent research studies support the common-sense notion that reducing class size or lowering the student-to-teacher ratio has a significant impact on student achievement. The Student-Teacher Achievement Ratio (STAR) study conducted in Tennessee and Wisconsin's Student Achievement Guarantee in Education (SAGE) program both showed that student learning improved and that minority students made the greatest gains in small-sized class configurations (Reichardt 2001). Many school districts, however, have not made the commitment to provide more classrooms and more classroom teachers to implement this best practice.

Lowering the student-to-teacher ratio through co-teaching at the point of instruction, therefore, makes sense. Increasing opportunities for individual and small group support for learners may be particularly effective for children who are exploring divergent topics, or who are engaged in differentiated or inquiry learning, or who are learning a second language, or who enter formal schooling with fewer school-like literacy experiences. In *Interactions: Collaboration Skills*

for School Professionals, Friend and Cook describe various co-teaching approaches (1996, 47–50). Depending on the lesson, the students' prior knowledge and skill development, the expertise of the educators, and their level of trust, collaborators can assume one or more of the following roles during a lesson or unit of instruction.

One Teaching, One Supporting

In this approach, one educator is responsible for teaching the lesson while the other observes the lesson, monitors specific students, or provides assistance as needed. For example, a classroom teacher who has not previously taught note taking strategies may benefit from observing the lesson and learning these strategies with the students. Mainstreamed special education students or students learning a second language may benefit from the support of an educator who focuses attention on them. If the library media specialist/teacher-librarian does not speak the primary language of one or a number of students in the class, the English Language Learner (ELL) teacher's or bilingual classroom teacher's support may be necessary to help second language learners comprehend the lesson.

One teaching, one supporting scenarios provide job-embedded professional development. Rather than working with a coach or an administrator in a supervisory role or attending a workshop in after-school hours, educators can improve instructional practices by learning alongside a peer. With the addition of post-lesson reflection, educators practicing this approach can evaluate and refine their teaching to better meet students' needs

the next time they teach this or another lesson.

Center Teaching

Co-teaching makes center teaching more effective. During the planning process, educators can design small-group center rotations related to a specific instructional objective, topic, or theme. Each educator takes responsibility for facilitating one or more learning centers while students work independently of adult support in other centers. This approach offers students more individualized adult guidance and feedback.

The library media center in most schools is significantly larger than a classroom. Conducting center teaching in this environment, therefore, facilitates student movement and reduces distraction between centers. Educators can design lessons for students to explore information in a different media format in each center. Students may be independent at a listening or DVD viewing center while the educators provide guidance at the Internet and print resources centers. Library assistants, library student volunteers, and parents can facilitate centers to increase learner support. For example, young students who are learning about the five senses may benefit from rotating through centers, each one focused on a different sense and facilitated by an adult or older student.

Parallel Teaching

In parallel teaching, collaborators carefully plan lessons so each is teaching half the class the same or similar content. Educators may switch groups and teach the other half of the class as well. Parallel teaching can be especially effective if groups reconvene as a whole class to share, debrief, and reflect.

This approach is particularly useful if students are practicing identifying similarities and differences. Students can easily compare the experiences of characters in different books or they can look at a historical event from the perspective of two different groups. In working with half the class at a time, educators provide more opportunities for students to contribute their ideas, to pose questions, and to offer solutions.

Alternate Teaching

Alternate teaching is particularly valuable in classrooms where students have special needs or are learning a second language. In this model, one educator pre-teaches or re-teaches a concept to a small group while the other educator teaches a different lesson to the larger group. Pre-teaching vocabulary, background knowledge, or prerequisite skills may be essential to the success of individual or small groups of students in the class.

In the alternate teaching approach, educators can assume different teaching roles as needed to best support students. Educators may also create advance graphic organizers that support English language learners with foundational vocabulary or concepts. It can also be as simple as one of the educators working with students who were absent and need background information before they can tackle the lesson at hand.

Team Teaching

The team teaching approach requires more careful planning, understanding, and respect for each educator's style; the willingness to

experiment; and, above all, a shared belief in the benefits that this level of risk taking can offer both students and educators (Moreillon 2007). Team teaching at the point of instruction has many benefits for students. Educators can model using think-alouds and demonstrate to students that there are divergent responses to particular questions or problems. They can also show students how to perform cooperative tasks. They can assume different roles and demonstrate discussion or debate procedures.

Team teaching allows educators to be flexible during lesson implementation. With this approach, educators can provide effective support for inquiry learning and differentiated instruction. They can better monitor student and small group progress and offer individual and small group reading, writing, and researching conferences.

Making time to debrief and reflect on the lesson or unit after co-teaching is important for professional growth. Educators can share their assessments of the relative success of lesson components. They can strategize ways to improve their teaching. In addition, reflection helps educators articulate the relationship between learning objectives and student outcomes. Sharing the work of reflective practitioner helps educators improve both student learning and instructional practices.

Show Them!

Co-teaching is one approach to making WHAT library media specialists/teacher-librarians DO visible to students, classroom teachers, and administrators. When library media specialists/teacher-librarians co-teach and co-assess students' work, young people clearly SEE

the contribution we make to their learning. Classroom teacher colleagues see us as non-threatening instructional partners who are learners alongside them. Our colleagues will find that collaborative teaching makes their work easier and more fun. Our administrators can and should be invited to observe us while we are co-teaching. We can request that our annual evaluations be conducted during a collaboratively planned, taught, and assessed lesson. This approach gives administrators a tangible experience of the contributions of library media specialists/teacher-librarians to student learning, teaching practices, and the collaborative culture within the school.

We should approach all school library program stakeholders as though they are "from Missouri." Show them the value of our role as instructional partners. Then maybe we will no longer ask the question, "Why don't they understand what we DO?" Instead, these stakeholders can become our advocates and speak on behalf of integrated, effective school library programs because they will have SEEN it for themselves!

References

Friend, M., and L. Cook. *Interactions: Collaboration Skills for School Professionals.* 2d ed. Longman, 1996.

Glass, G. V., and M. L. Smith. "Meta-analysis of Research on Class Size and Achievement." *Educational Evaluation and Policy Analysis* 1, no. 1 (January-February 1979): 2–16.

Moreillon, J. *Collaborative Strategies for Teaching Reading Comprehension: Maximizing Your Impact.* ALA Editions, 2007.

Reichardt, R. *Reducing Class Size: Choices and Consequences* [policy brief]. Mid-continent Research for Education and Learning, 2001. ✋

Using Personality Traits and Effective Communication to Improve Collaboration

by Juanita Warren Buddy

A recurring topic at the end of school district meetings and state conference presentations is the proven success of collaboration. Yet, after more than twenty years as a library media specialist and a system-level library media coordinator, I recognize there are opportunities for greater collaboration between some library media specialists and teachers than has been accomplished thus far.

Components of successful collaborations between teachers and library media specialists have been identified through various research studies. Carol Kuhlthau (1993) concluded successful collaboration called for "a shared philosophy of learning... the development of an instructional team... a commitment to developing skills for living, working, and participating in changes in technology... and competent educators who creatively instruct, guide, coach, and assess students" (18). Aronson (1996) reported key factors influencing collaboration. The list included (1) educators' willingness to work together, (2) a joint sense of equality without hierarchical relationships, (3) mutual trust and open communication, (4) time for discussion and planning, (5) a school philosophy that encourages team work, and (6) role clarification.

As these studies indicate, collaboration is a process that involves working with others. Thus, it seems it would be beneficial to examine "soft skills," which are labeled in business literature as interpersonal skills or non-technical skills. It is wisely stated that, "Nearly every aspect of business, management in particular, requires an ability to interact effectively with others.... [Adopting] the approach of 'one size fits all' when it comes to people simply does not work in today's diverse workplace. Each individual must be treated as the unique individual they are. This requires investing time in getting to know each employee" (Buhler 2005).

It is advantageous for the library media specialist to view the library media program as a "micro-business" in the school community, where student achievement and lifelong learning are the primary products and sensitivity to the uniqueness of each teacher is paramount. Drawing on business as well as education research, this article addresses the importance of personality traits and effective communication in establishing, improving, and expanding collaboration with teachers as a means of designing and implementing enriched instructional activities and experiences.

Juanita Warren Buddy, Ph.D., is the coordinator for the Department of Educational Media, DeKalb County School System, Atlanta, GA. Email: juanita_buddy@fc.dekalb.k12.ga.us

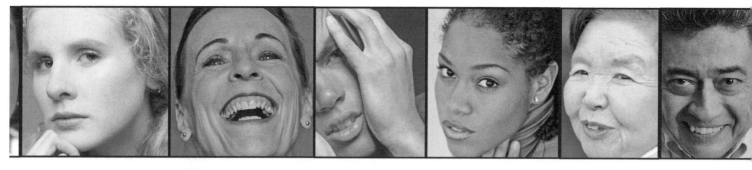

Common Beliefs about Collaboration

Most library media specialists understand and appreciate the integral role collaboration plays in the learning process. As outlined in *Information Power: Building Partnerships for Learning* (1998), collaboration is a central component in promoting partnerships with teachers to improve student achievement. Brodie (2006) reminds library media specialists that collaboration involves (1) familiarizing oneself with the curriculum, (2) attending grade level or departmental meetings, and (3) using various communication tools to inform teachers about resources and services available in the library media center that support the curriculum.

Dickinson (2006) encourages the library media professional to explore the potential of co-teaching. This delivery model allows the classroom teacher and the library media specialist to alternate the leadership role as an instructor for the entire class or to participate in a "station teaching" configuration where a portion of the class works in the classroom with the teacher and the other portion in the library media center with the library media specialist.

Hickel (2006) outlines the elements that lead to successful collaboration. These include (1) working cooperatively with teachers and administrators, (2)

realizing change does not happen overnight, (3) using an "ask" attitude, and (4) being attuned to the "next wave" of information technology. With the mechanics of collaborative planning in place, the library media specialist can strategize about how to incorporate the topic of personality traits and how to address diversity.

Personality Traits Impact Collaboration

President Theodore Roosevelt long ago observed, "The most important single ingredient in the formula of success is knowing how to get along with people" (*World of Quotes*). Establishing and maintaining close relationships with teachers and administrators remains critical to successful collaboration. In my conversations with library media specialists who consistently engage in collaboratively planned lessons with teachers, I've learned that there is a common strategy—the library media specialists know the teachers and have learned what they want. Educators must be cognizant of students' learning styles, must differentiate instruction to meet students' needs, and must learn about the personalities of students. Library media specialists must also take the opportunity to understand teachers' personality traits. These traits impact teachers' instructional styles and can reveal to the library media specialists vari-

ous approaches worthy of initiating to foster successful collaboration.

In answer to the question, "Who makes a good collaborator?" Brodie (2006) offers a variety of responses, but the following response underscores the importance of interpersonal skills in collaboration: "Certainly a mesh of personalities comes about as the collaboration grows, and it is almost essential to have a sense of humor" (28). Barron (1997) recommends that library media specialists complete self-diagnostic assessments to understand their individual temperaments and preferences and how their personality traits support or hinder the collaborative partnership. Having identified their personality preferences, the library media specialists are better prepared to understand teachers' preferred styles of interaction and organization.

Personality Diagnostic Tools

Educators across the nation have opportunities to discover their teaching styles, as well as identify their personality traits and/or temperament as strategies for improving their effectiveness in the classroom. Most educators are familiar with the *Myers-Briggs Type Indicators*, which provide information on sixteen personality types. The *Keirsey Temperament Sorter®* is used by many organizations to help individuals understand people in general and fundamental differences among individuals. The personality assessment for *Keirsey's Temperament Sorter®-II* is available online (http://www.advisorteam.com/temperament_sorter/register.asp).

In the DeKalb County (Georgia) School System, teachers, library media specialists, counselors, administrators, and students know their dominant color as determined by their responses to preference-type questions in the *TRUE COLORS®* inventory. This inventory helps determine behavioral and personality styles. Individuals are generally a blend of colors, with one color dominant but the dominant color changing over time with exposure to new experiences. Below are some characteristics attributed to each color.

- *Gold*—Likes structure, rules, and organization; Dislikes ambiguity and waste.
- *Orange*—Likes action, competition, sensational things; Dislikes inaction and rules.
- *Green*—Likes logic, structure, and the Big Picture; Dislikes routine and incompetence.
- *Blue*—Likes harmony between people and depth of feeling; Dislikes deception and competition.

Effective Communication Impacts Collaboration

Communication is a process that allows individuals to share ideas, information, and feelings. Through face-to-face conversations, email messages, cell phone text messages, and faxed messages, individuals share technology-rich communication networks. As a strategy for improving communication, Wheeler (2005) recommends examining personal communication styles to learn about individuals' "blind spots" in communicating with others. These "blind spots" can include interrupting the speaker before she or he completes a remark, forming a response before hearing the speaker's complete message, or not listening to others' viewpoints. Wheeler recommends communicating flexibly, which involves understanding the concept that in some situations, some listeners want "just the facts please," while in other situations their emotions should not be ignored. Being attuned to these differences can make the difference in launching a collaborative project.

Stephen Covey (1989) reminds us to "seek first to understand, then to be understood," habit number 5 in the book, *Seven Habits of Highly Effective People*. Adhering to this advice would position the library media specialist to be an active listener when communicating with teachers. Understanding the teacher's instructional needs permits the library media specialist to recommend creative instructional designs, appropriate resources, and effective evaluations for the instructional activity.

Numerous writers on the topic of effective communication recommend active listening as a practice to improve communication between the library media specialist and teachers. Harris (2005) offers the following tips:

- Begin by removing distractions and focusing your attention on the speaker.
- Restate what the speaker stated for clarification.
- Be aware of your body language and give eye contact to indicate that you are listening.
- Complete any tasks resulting from the conversation, which gives further affirmation of effective communication between the speaker and listener.

Garmston and Wellman (1998) broaden the discussion of effective communication by addressing the different ways of talking—dialogue and discussion. According to their model, "Dialogue leads to a collective meaning and shared understanding. It builds a sense of connection and belonging, and creates an emotional cognitive safety zone where ideas flow for examination without judgment. It connects individuals to their underlying motivations and mental models." On the other hand, discussion involves "rigorous critical thinking, mutual respect, weighing options and leads to confirmed decisions." Using both methods of conversing can lead to successes and pitfalls. Understanding when and how to use one or both methods will enhance collaboration.

Having a conversation "just for the sake of talking" can be ineffective communication and a misuse of time. Geller (2006) describes interpersonal conversations by using five labels, which can overlap based upon the needs and direction of the communication:

- A relationship conversation in one that focuses on the personal aspects of an individual's life, such as family and personal goals.
- A possibility conversation centers on shared visions among individuals who have a common goal, objective, or plan.

- An action conversation is behavior-driven and describes moving forward in the direction of achieving the goal.
- An opportunity conversation identifies the options and opportunities available to achieve the goal and the level of involvement of the team members in reaching it.
- Finally, a follow-up conversation represents the culmination of the goal or plan and sets the stage for evaluating it and discussing future possibilities or necessities for revamping it.

Collaboration between the library media specialist and teacher(s) involves combinations of these levels of conversation.

Buhler (2005) advises attending to the "small stuff" by taking a few moments to handwrite a note or send an email message to the teacher(s) about the success of the collaboratively planned lesson. It is appropriate and recommended that the library media specialist and teacher(s) share with the principal the instructional benefits of the collaboratively planned instructional activities. This communication provides the principal with an opportunity to observe the library media specialist in the teaching and information specialist roles. When a teacher makes a referral to a colleague about the success of the collaborative unit and recommends that the colleague visit with the library media specialist, the library media specialist should consider giving a "referral appreciation token" to the recommending teacher. Other golden opportunities to communicate about collaborative lesson plans and projects are the "Let Me Share..." column of the parent organization newsletter and the library media page of the school's website.

Summary

Collaboration is at the heart of the library media specialist's dual roles as instructional consultant and information specialist. Doll (2005) and Dickinson (2006) outline the levels of involvement the library media specialist experiences as moving from isolation through cooperation and coordination to true collaborative experiences with teachers. The brochure developed by the American Association of School Librarians entitled *Collaboration* also provides a comprehensive overview of collaboration that addresses the phases of cooperation, coordination, and collaboration. In addition, the brochure provides examples of lessons learned by library media specialists around the country (1996). Each of the publications supports the idea that the library media specialist is positioned to experiment with a variety of strategies to establish, improve, and expand collaboration with teachers.

Perhaps if the library media specialist were to combine information on collaboration with knowledge of personality traits and effective communication they might have greater success in collaborative endeavors with teachers. That information, combined with knowledge of the standards-based curriculum and available resources could result in powerful combined efforts that could impact student achievement in very positive ways.

References

American Association of School Librarians. *Collaboration.* Lessons Learned series. AASL, 1996.

American Association of School Librarians and Association for Educational Communications and Technology. *Information Power: Building Partnerships for Learning.* ALA, 1998.

Barron, D. D. "Doing It with Style or Different Stokes for Different Folks: Learning Styles for School Library Media Specialists." *School Library Media Activities Monthly* 14, no. 2 (October 1997): 48-50.

Brodie, C. S. "Collaboration Practices." *School Library Media Activities Monthly* 23, no. 2 (October 2006): 27-30.

Buhler, P. M. "Interpersonal Skills." *Super-Vision* 66, no. 7 (July 2005): 20-23.

Covey, S. *Seven Habits of Highly Effectively People.* Simon and Schuster, 1989.

Doll, C. A. *Collaboration and the School Library Media Specialist.* Scarecrow Press, 2005.

Dickinson, G. K. "When Does Collaboration Start?" *School Library Media Activities Monthly* 23, no. 2 (October 2006): 56-58.

Garmston, R., and B. Wellman. "Teacher Talk That Makes a Difference." *Educational Leadership* 55, no. 7 (April 1998): 30-35.

Geller, S. "The Power of Safety Communication." *ISHN* 40, no. 6 (June 2006): 16-17.

Harris, S. "Effective Communication Starts When You Don't Say a Word." *What Works in Teaching and Learning* 2, no 7 (February 2005): 10.

Hickel, D. "A Formula for Achieving Collaboration." *Library Media Connection* 25, no. 3 (November/December 2006): 30-31.

Keirsey's Temperament Sorter-II. http://www.advisorteam.com/temperament_sorter/register.asp (accessed January 11, 2007).

"Theodore Roosevelt Quotes." *World of Quotes.com.* http://www.worldofquotes.com/author/Theodore-Roosevelt/1/index.html (accessed January 11, 2007).

TRUE COLORS®. http://www.true-colors.com/ (accessed January 11, 2007).

Wheeler, P. A. "The Importance of Interpersonal Skills." *Healthcare Executive* 20, no. 1 (January/February 2005): 44-45. 🖐

Lesson Planning:
The Ticket to Successful Teaching

by Pat Franklin and Claire Gatrell Stephens

Collaboration

Library media specialists are first and foremost teachers. However, teaching in the library media center should not be done in isolation; it should be in collaboration with classroom teachers. An important component of collaboration is writing lesson plans for instruction. Unfortunately, because of so many other demands on the library media specialist, lesson planning often falls by the wayside. This is regrettable because good lesson planning or instructional design leads to stronger collaboration with partner teachers and, most importantly, improved student achievement. How can library media specialists, then, create good lesson plans?

Knowing the Standards

First, it is important to become familiar with the standards and benchmarks, including national, state, and local standards. Last October, the American Association of School Librarians (AASL) launched new *Standards for the 21st-Century Learner*. These standards can be used as a reference to design curriculum with state and district information literacy standards or used as a source if such standards are not available. It is also important for library media specialists in collaborating with teachers to know benchmarks for all subject areas.

The Big Picture

Classroom teachers need to use library media resources to make sure their students achieve success in their subject area. So, when developing collaborative lesson plans, library media specialists can help teachers look beyond the immediate subject and show ways to connect to nonfiction reading and learning outcomes for many subject areas. Integrating and combining these benchmarks with the specific subject area and information literacy standards can result in outstanding lesson plans. Library media specialists must also become familiar with the teaching style of the collaborating teacher, thus making it easier to identify how and where the library media resources and information literacy standards can be integrated within a proposed lesson. In discussing the options with the teacher, library media specialists should keep the focus on the curriculum standards and student learning while identifying the objectives of the lesson; they can also note the information literacy standards that can be met. They should define how assessment will be accomplished—how will it be known when students are successful? Possible activities should be identified to determine how data will be gathered to help refine the lesson for future use.

Endless Possibilities

The collaborative lesson might start in the classroom and then use library resources to find information to complete the instruction. Alternatively, the lesson might start in the library media center where students search for introductory information leading to an in-depth classroom discussion of the topic. The possibilities are endless. Will the teacher begin a unit on animals and a few days later have each student choose an animal for research in the library media center? Could the teacher launch the unit by bringing students to the library media center to research weapons, clothing, spies, food, transportation, and communication of the Civil War so that students have a background knowledge of this

▶The American Association of School Librarians (AASL) Web site provides access to its new *Standards for the 21st-Century Learner* (http://www.ala. org/ala/aasl/aaslproftools/learningstandards/standards.cfm).

▶Visit the *SLMAM* Web site for a comparison between the AASL information literacy standards of 1998/2007 (http://www. schoollibrarymedia.com/articles/correlations2008v24n6.html).

▶Join Kristin Fontichiaro at the *SLMAM* blog for ongoing discussion and information related to the AASL *Standards for the 21st-Century Learner* (http://blog.schoollibrarymedia.com/).

time period? Either way, the classroom teacher and library media specialist must decide the role each will play in the instruction and preparation.

Role Identification

The teacher's role can be defined through subject matter expertise. But, the role of the library media specialist, although linked to information literacy skill objectives, varies depending on the nature of the unit. It might involve gathering subject-related books to teach students how to use the table of contents and the index to find information. Or, it might involve teaching a lesson on how to find books on the shelves by using the library media management system.

Another option might be teaching students how to use a presentation program such as *PowerPoint*. It may involve teaching research skills with an emphasis on note taking and evaluation of resources or copyright issues. Whatever the identified roles, both the library media specialist and the classroom teacher must work together to ensure that all learning outcomes are met. A successful outcome assures the classroom teacher that collaborative instruction increases student achievement through and positively impacts future lessons.

Resources Needed

What resources are needed for the planned instruction? Will print and/or nonprint sources be used? Will specific software programs be needed? Will a print list of online databases or sample Web sites be necessary? Are craft materials required? Will displays need to be created in the library media center to support this lesson? Can clerks and student assistants help gather required materials? Answers to these questions are all part of effective lesson plans.

Meeting Learner Needs

As the library media specialist plans his/her part of the lesson, they must also consider adaptations needed for the students in the class. Are there exceptional education students in the group? This includes students who may be gifted, English language learners, hearing or vision impaired, or autistic. Each should be considered when designing and adapting the lesson. Flexibility is important as it may take more days than planned for a simple lesson. The goal is to help students succeed.

Assessment should be developed as part of the lesson plan and is as important for the library media specialist as it is for the students and the partner teacher. The library media specialist should be available to work with the classroom teacher to evaluate each student's work in acquiring information literacy skills. The assessment process can often lead to the last step in good lesson planning—extension activities for the original lesson. Future activities can be planned that allow students to review, apply, and expand on the knowledge gained in the instructional unit.

Making a Record

Lesson plans should be committed to paper and should be based on a lesson plan format of choice. Common templates include space for identification of standards and benchmarks, content goals, planned method of instruction, resources needed, assessment, etc. (See: "Use This Page." *SLMAM*, February 2008: 2). Writing the lesson plans increases communication with everyone involved in the instructional unit and helps ensure that the planning is complete. Written lesson plans also record a professional approach for instruction to be shared with not only the partner teacher but also administrators.

End Result

Through teaching partnerships and collaborative lesson planning, the library media specialist and the classroom teacher become a team and the students understand that the library media center is a place for enjoyable learning. As a result, other teachers see and hear about the fantastic results and become interested in collaborating, allowing even more students to be reached—a good outcome for any library media specialist!

Resources:

Logan, Debra Kay. *Information Skills Toolkit: Collaborative Integrated Instruction for the Middle Grades.* Professional Growth series. Linworth Publishing, 2000.

Rutherford, Paula. *Instruction for All Students.* Just ASK Publications, 2002.

Rutherford, Paula. *Why Didn't I Learn This in College?* Just ASK Publications, 2002.◄

Pat Franklin is a library media specialist at Timber Creek High School in East Orlando, FL, and is a National Board Certified Teacher in Library Media. Claire Stephens is also a National Board Certified Teacher in Library Media and has worked as a library media specialist first at the middle school level and most recently at Freedom High School in south Orlando, FL. Email: cgstephens@cfl.rr.com

Coteaching Published Lesson Plans: A Recipe for Success?

by Judi Moreillon

"Something magical happened among the villagers. As each person opened their heart to give, the next person gave even more. And as this happened, the soup grew richer and smelled more delicious."
—From *Stone Soup*, retold and illustrated by Jon J. Muth

Most cooks have tried and true recipes that are always successful. Some cooks experiment and invent their own recipes; others use recipes passed down from generation to generation. While some cooks like to substitute ingredients or leave out ones of which they are not fond, others follow the recipe verbatim. Ultimately, all cooks consider the diners who will savor and be nourished by their creations. Like cooking, teaching is a creative process that can be supported by "recipes" —published lesson plans. Teaching can also be more effective and even more exciting when educators team up with peers. Like the monks in Jon J. Muth's version of *Stone Soup*, library media specialists can cook up rich learning experiences for students when they coteach with colleagues (Scholastic 2003).

Coteaching

Coteaching with classroom teachers is one way for library media specialists to position the library program at the center of the school's academic program where it can contribute significantly to student achievement. Coteaching is ideal when educators co-plan, co-implement, and co-assess lessons and units of instruction. Library media specialists who coteach with colleagues develop both shared instructional practices and a common vocabulary for teaching. Classroom standards and information literacy skills are aligned and a common curriculum is taught, one of the cornerstones of effective schools. And most importantly of all, relationships with peers are developed that support the practice of job-embedded professional development.

Published Lesson Plans

Planning for coteaching, however, takes time, and many library media specialists and classroom teachers lament a shortage of joint planning time. Making time to co-plan lessons can be particularly problematic at the elementary level where teacher planning time is not often integrated into the daily schedule. To remedy this situation, educators can take advantage of published lesson plans.

By adapting these published plans, initial efforts can be focused on building rapport with colleagues. While coteaching involves taking a risk, educators can practice a shared responsibility for modeling the learning tasks, monitoring students' guided practice, and assessing students' processes and products. By building these collegial relationships, library media specialists can support future joint lesson planning, implementation, and assessment. Use of these published plans give educators time to work on developing skills to become effective educators in the company of their peers.

Benefits of Coteaching

Classroom-library collaboration has considerable benefits for students. There is a positive correlation between increased student achievement, particularly in reading, and fully-resourced, fully-staffed school library programs facilitated by professional library media specialists who collaborate with classroom teachers for instruction (Library Research Service 2008; Scholastic Research and Results 2008). When classroom teachers and library media specialists coteach, the student-to-teacher ratio is lowered. More students have opportunities for individualized attention, and groups of students can be better supported as they learn essential skills and content in different ways. Two or more educators can monitor, adjust, and assess the students' work as well as evaluate the lessons themselves.

If the best recipe for students' success involves classroom-library collaboration, what are the benefits to library media specialists and classroom teachers? Many library media specialists know from personal experience that coteaching with colleagues propels growth as effective educators. Learning is social for all human beings regardless of age; educators can grow and develop more fully and more quickly in the company of their peers. With rapidly growing information, changing technologies, and expanding curriculum standards, educators can provide appropriately challenging and engaging learning experiences for students while they maximize their own learning through joint teaching. Classroom-library collaboration is a natural, organic form of job-embedded professional development.

Achieving the Goal

There are many ways to benefit from having two educators in the room. For example, while one educator reads a text, the other can call on students and record their ideas. Flexible roles can be practiced. Classroom teachers can be the readers in the library media center, and library media specialists can be the readers in the classroom. When two or more educators provide think-aloud responses to questions and demonstrate other metacognitive processes, learners are shown the diversity of thinking. Coteaching also allows educators to jointly model the learning tasks. Cooperative learning can be effectively demonstrated, including partner sharing, discussion procedures, and debate techniques.

Benefits of Published Lesson Plans

The collaborative planning process is time-consuming. Although many educators find making time for collaborative planning a challenge, that should not be a reason to miss out on the benefits of coteaching. By using published standards-based lesson plans, attention can be focused on student learning and on building relationships with colleagues.

There are many print sources, including lessons available monthly in this magazine. There are also online resources for lesson plans that can streamline the planning process. Some school districts are also publishing downloadable exemplary lesson plans from their Web sites. Some published lesson plans require taking the initiative to integrate the *AASL Standards for the 21st-Century*

Learner. Even so, they provide a modifiable and adaptable framework to meet the needs of students. Using pre-existing lesson plans can streamline the planning process and give educators more opportunities and time for coteaching.

Conclusion

The organic nature of classroom-library collaboration offers on-site, just-in-time, job-embedded professional development integrated into the daily practice of educators (Moreillon 2007). When educators come together to teach and learn together, to share talents, and to share struggles and successes, the resulting sense of community and connectedness can support a collaborative culture. In this culture of collaboration, everyone is invested in the success of all learners.

For time-strapped educators, coteaching published lesson plans offers the opportunity to teach standards-based lessons and access essential materials such as graphic organizers and rubrics. Coteaching can be a great deal like the rich and delicious "stone soup" that the villagers collectively created after surviving hard times. Coteaching allows library media specialists and classroom teachers to cook up some tasty recipes for success for everyone.

References

American Association of School Librarians. *Standards for the 21st-Century Learner*. ALA, 2007. http://www2.scholastic.com/content/collateral_resources/pdf/s/slw3_2008.pdf (accessed October 16, 2008).

Library Research Service. *School Library Impact Studies*. 2008. http://www.lrs.org/impact.php (accessed October 16, 2008).

Moreillon, J. *Collaborative Strategies for Teaching Reading Comprehension: Maximizing your Impact*. ALA Editions, 2007.

Muth, J. J. *Stone Soup*. Scholastic, 2003.

Scholastic Research & Results. *School Libraries Work!* 3rd ed. Scholastic Library, 2008.◄

Judi Moreillon, Ph.D., is the teacher librarian in a combined junior high-high school library in Tucson, AZ. She is also a literacies and libraries consultant who teaches school library administration and children's and young adult literature at the School of Information Resources and Library Science at the University of Arizona. She is the author of *Collaborative Strategies for Teaching Reading Comprehension: Maximizing Your Impact* (ALA Editions, 2007) and two published children's books. Email: info@storytrail.com

Selected Free Online Lesson Plan Resources

Bertland, L. *Resources for School Librarians: Information Skills Instruction*. http://www.sldirectory.com/libsf/resf/libplans.html (accessed October 16, 2008).

Discovery Education. *Lesson Plan Library*. http://school.discoveryeducation.com/lessonplans/ (accessed October 16, 2008).

The Educators Network. *Lesson Plans 4 Teachers*. http://www.lessonplans4teachers.com/ (accessed October 16, 2008).

Information Institute of Syracuse. *The Educator's Reference Desk: Lesson Plans*. http://www.eduref.org/Virtual/Lessons/ (accessed October 16, 2008).

International Reading Association (IRA) & National Council of Teachers of English (NCTE). *Read, Write, Think: A Joint Project for the IRA and NCTE*. http://readwritethink.org/ (accessed October 16, 2008).

Library of Congress. *The Learning Page: Lesson Plans*. http://memory.loc.gov/learn/lessons/index.html (accessed October 16, 2008).

Moreillon, J. *Collaborative Strategies for Teaching Reading Comprehension: Maximizing your Impact*. ALA Editions, 2007. Downloadable Graphic Organizers: http://www.ala.org/ala/ourassociation/publishing/alaeditions/webextras/moreillon09294/moreillon09294.htm (accessed October 16, 2008).

Schrock, K. *Kathy Schrock's Guide for Educators*. http://school.discoveryeducation.com/schrockguide (accessed October 16, 2008).

Verizon Foundation. *Thinkfinity*. http://www.thinkfinity.org (accessed October 16, 2008).

Collaboration:

Classic Motown music is a universally recognized and iconic sound that represents a significant time in music history. The Motown sound is synonymous with the groundbreaking rock-n-roll, harmonic singing of such groups as The Four Tops, The Supremes, The Commodores, The Miracles, and The Temptations. Classic Motown crosses age groups, race, gender, culture, and socioeconomic barriers. How does Motown music connect to collaboration between the library media specialist and the classroom teacher? And, how can the library media specialist apply the basic fundamentals in Motown music to successful collaboration strategies?

Collaboration Can Intimidate

Collaboration between a library media specialist and a classroom teacher remains a relatively new concept to many classroom teachers. Components of co-planning, co-teaching, and co-evaluating leave many teachers nervous about the process and activities. Too often, they have not heard of collaboration or have not experienced working with a library media specialist during their professional training. No one wants to look silly or unskilled in front of students or fellow professionals.

The analogy of the Motown Method is an excellent way to explain collaboration to those classroom teachers who may be reluctant and fearful about the process. Basically with the Motown Method of collaboration, somebody always gets to be Diana Ross and others get to be the Supremes. While the Miracles harmonized, Smokey Robinson stepped up to take the lead vocals. Gladys Knight may be the lead vocalist, but she would be nothing without the harmony

The Motown Method

by Leslie Preddy

and teamwork of the Pips. All voices were needed to create the chemistry that made the songs so memorable to the listener. These examples help teachers easily see how important collaboration was to the success of the Motown sound. Smiles appear on nervous faces and heads begin to nod in understanding. The Motown Method is an entertaining vehicle for getting teachers to try something unfamiliar like collaboration with the library media specialist.

Taking Turns

With the Motown Method, Diana Ross (the library media specialist) may take the lead for the instructional segment with the other collaborating teacher or teachers in the role of the Supremes. Collaboration requires all educators just like Diana Ross and the Supremes to participate; otherwise it lacks the synergy necessary to make it effective, memorable, and entertaining for the students. Teamwork in the Motown Method also means taking turns. In collaboration, the lead changes whenever appropriate—whoever is better at a task or the expert for that

instructional strategy takes the lead. For example, the teacher who is great at organizing would take the lead when planning the unit's timeline. If another teacher has a talent for thinking outside the box, then that teacher would take the lead when teaching brainstorming or key words. In this approach, everyone gets a turn at being Diana Ross or Smokey Robinson.

Co-Plan

The Motown sounds were always harmonious and didn't just happen by chance. These sounds were the result of co-planning and recognizing individual strengths among the individuals in each group. This same fundamental applies to library media specialists and classroom teachers when they co-plan to develop curriculum based on collaboration. Co-planning harmonizes when the strengths of each member of the group are complemented.

Usually, the strength of the library media specialist is his or her knowledge and experience with print and nonprint resources—how to use them and how to provide the most effective instruction for students. The library

media specialist understands the information needs and abilities of the school population and keeps up to date on a range of educational best practices, education research, student interests, popular trends, and new and creative ways for students to share knowledge through final products.

The classroom teacher is more adept at understanding the individual student, classroom climate, state standards, and content area standards. The classroom teacher knows best practices for research goals in the content area and knows the students' attention span and whether something would intrigue them.

Communication is crucial during all phases of collaboration but especially during pre-planning. It is the responsibility of the library media specialist to keep the group organized and prepared—assuming the role of Diana or Smokey. This often involves initiating most of the email communications and responding quickly if emailed. The library media specialist, who is not responsible for doing all the work, may still be the one reminding others of what they need to have prepared for the next planning session, lesson, or week. The library media specialist is usually the one to plan meeting dates and can adapt to the classroom teacher's schedule.

Co-Teach

Using the Motown Method, co-teaching means that all educators participate in every instructional session. There is a lead teacher and a back-up teacher (it can switch, however, between the classroom teacher and the library media specialist). Somebody gets to be the lead singer (Diana Ross) and somebody gets to be the back-up singer (a Supreme). When the lead teacher is instructing, the back-up teacher is working the room, helping individuals and small groups stay focused. The back-up teacher is also watching the room for students who may not understand some part of the lesson. If the instruction used by the lead teacher does not seem to be working, the back-up teacher can speak up with a new perspective for going about the same thing a different way. The teachers play off each other and the students throughout instruction, thus facilitating learning and modeling teamwork. There may also be special times when the instructional team decides that both need to take the lead. In this scenario, one educator is working with one group of students while another educator is simultaneously working with another student group.

During co-planning, the location for instruction is specified (e.g., classroom or library media center) as well as who will take the lead instructional role for each lesson. The library media specialist and teacher should be thoughtful and consider teaching talents and skills.

Co-Evaluate

Just as the ground-breaking sounds of Motown music were constantly assessed and evaluated for new ideas,

so do collaborative projects in the media center need constant assessment and evaluation. The research unit and each lesson and mini-lesson call for assessment and evaluation of both the process and the final product. This involves another team effort from the library media specialist, classroom teachers, and students.

Assessment should be shared and communicated in an on-going manner. This can be done in a few moments of verbal communication with students at the end of the lesson during transition time. Other methods include reflection or exit slips written by students, quick emails as ideas arise, or jotting down ideas on sticky notes during the lesson. It is important to write these observations and assessments down as soon as possible so that there will be notes on what to change when planning future collaborative projects.

The library media specialist and teacher need to find out from students what they thought worked or didn't work both instructionally and collaboratively. This can be done through class discussion, written reflection, online survey, or small group or individual interviews. What do they think worked well? What was their favorite lesson? Which lesson helped the most? What lesson needs improvement, and what can be done to make it better? What skill did they learn and think they'll use the most? What sources were helpful/not helpful? What was most difficult about the project? What was the best thing that the classroom teacher did? What was the best thing the library media specialist did? What was a favorite experience? What did the educators do well? What can they do better?

Finally, educators must ponder the possibilities. There should be honest and open discussions with constructive criticism about what worked and what didn't work. The following questions should be answered: Will this unit

be taught again? What worked well? Which resources were most helpful when assisting students? What did students have difficulty doing properly, even after instruction? Did repeat instruction help? What was done very well this time, as a team and as an individual? Was there enough time to plan? Was there enough collaborative planning time? How well did the collaborative partners work together (e.g., classroom teacher, library media specialist)? What did educators learn about themselves when planning collaboratively? Will there be collaboration in the future?

Conclusion

Teaching today is a challenge. It is tough to design and build instruction every day. It is tough to find the balance between standardized tests, state standards, and best practices. It is tough to help students who think they are information literate understand that they are not. One of the best ways for educators to meet these tough challenges is to collaborate or work together as a team. The Motown Method can be used to quickly help fellow educators grasp the meaning of collaborative teaching. The library media specialist and classroom teacher can be one of the greatest teams by becoming the educational rock group equivalent of Diana Ross and The Supremes, Lionel Richie and The Commodores, Gladys Knight and The Pips, Smokey Robinson and The Miracles, or Martha Reeves and The Vandellas.◄

Leslie Preddy is the library media specialist at Perry Meridian Middle School in Indianapolis, IN. She is the author of *SSR with Intervention* (Libraries Unlimited, 2007) and co-author of *The Blue Book on Literacy and Instruction for the Information Age* (Libraries Unlimited, 2006). Website: http://www.lesliepreddy.com; Email: lpreddy@msdpt.k12.in.us

Collaboration: From Myth to Reality: Let's Get Down to Business. Just Do It!

by Ross Todd

Scenario: Miss Congeniality and Collaborations in Crisis

Miss Congeniality has been the library media specialist at ABC High School for twelve years. She manages a successful library media program. A core group of twenty teachers bring their classes to the library media center for at least one major project every year. There are almost 700 classes in the library media center for sustained work annually. It is difficult to find an empty seat, especially during the three lunch blocks when students drop in to socialize, read magazines and newspapers, and use the computers for recreation. She receives good support from her principal, who has been her colleague for several years. She is concerned, however, that her instructional program seems to have reached a plateau. There is little faculty turnover, so she does not have many new teachers to recruit. The resistors continue to

resist, but most are bringing their students for the Assured Experiences. The social studies department is the heaviest user; most 9th and 10th graders and about half of all 11th graders do at least one project every year. The social studies projects look like this: Project A—Choose a famous Renaissance person from the list. Research the life and work of this person. Create a "baseball card" that includes a picture of the person, biographical information, and his/her contributions. OR Project B—Choose a country from the list provided. Prepare a report on the natural resources, government, history, and geography, and include a picture of the flag. English teachers require students to research the historical periods relevant to the novels they read in class. Most science and math teachers do not use the library media center at all. The biggest concerns for this library media specialist are the

quality of student projects and the level of most of her collaborations.

Miss Congeniality's biggest worry is past individual collaborations that have ended in disaster. She worked with an English teacher to plan and teach a unit on contemporary New England authors. They met frequently for about two weeks. Miss C created a webpage for the project with a bibliography of multimedia resources and the packet students used to organize their work (visuals, graphic organizers, guides for their interviews, the schedule of library visits, formative assessments including a proposal form for focusing the thesis of the paper, a rubric for the students' rough drafts, a peer review form, and bibliography charts). She even invited one of the famous authors, who is related to one of the students, to speak to the class. After all the planning and designing of Web-based resources, the teacher did not take advantage of Miss C's knowledge of databases, but chose to do

Ross J. Todd, Ph. D., is Associate Professor in the School of Communication, Information and Library Studies at Rutgers, the State University of New Jersey. He is Director of Research of the Center for International Scholarship in School Libraries (CISSL) at Rutgers.

just an adequate job of instructing the students herself in the library media center. She did not acknowledge Miss Congeniality's work and avoided teaching with her.

Her collaboration with a social studies teacher was even worse. The teacher failed to show up for the scheduled library time after all the preliminary planning and collaboration with Miss C. Another social studies teacher, who is retiring next year, schedules her classes in the library media center but never collaborates with Miss C and does not even drop her lesson plan off in the library media center at least one day prior to the class visit. Sometimes this same teacher doesn't even notify Miss C that she is not bringing her class to the library media center at the scheduled time.

When Miss C did finally succeed in collaborating with a science teacher, who is head of the department, the class was a disaster. The low-level students in this homogenously grouped class had difficulty reading the most basic articles from a database and caused discipline problems. The teacher has not brought a class to the library media center since that disaster. What can Miss Congeniality do to improve her collaborations? She also fears that if she cannot show that she contributes to raising the quality of teaching in her school she will lose her comfortable budget.

(Thanks to Dr. Carol Gordon at Rutgers University for providing this scenario.)

Does this scenario sound familiar? I would make a calculated guess that most library media specialists can relate to it in some way. Collaboration is a pervasive force in school library literature and is on the minds of most library media specialists (at least the many thousands I meet and speak with each year). As illustrated in this scenario, however, collaboration emerges as a complex and polarizing notion. It is seen as a positive, enabling, and energizing approach to professional practice, and also as a negative, guilt-producing stumbling block to day-to-day practice. I will, in this article, provide some insights into library media specialist and classroom teacher instructional collaborations, with particular emphasis on strategies for building stronger partnerships resulting in realizing learning and achievement goals. These insights have emerged from a recent study undertaken to understand the dynamics of collaborative partnerships between library media specialists and classroom teachers through a systematic investigation of the partnerships established as part of the IMLS-Kent State University's Institute for Library and Information Literacy Education (ILILE) program over a three-year program from 2002-2005.

The ILILE program is based on the concept of collaboration between library media specialists and classroom teachers. Collaboration, a foundational principle, is the essential basis for the library media center's engagement in the learning goals of the school. While collaboration is certainly a complex and challenging concept, it has still been a pervasive concept in library media centers for at least two decades. The principle of collaboration is firmly embedded in school library literature and strongly endorsed and advocated by the American Association of School Librarians (AASL). A statement from AASL indicates that the library media specialist "provides leadership… in bringing an awareness of information issues into collaborative relationships with teachers, administrators, students, and others" (ALA 1998). Within a broader framework of educational leadership, the concept of collaboration is often articulated in terms such as "school library media specialist as teacher," "partnerships," "partner-leader," and "teams." Role statements of various school library associations often state, implicitly or explicitly, that the library media specialist is committed to the process of collaboration and works closely with individual teachers to integrate information and communication competencies in information and critical literacies into curriculum content. The benefits of collaboration typically center on instructional effectiveness and creativity, increased levels of communication and improved collegial relationships, increased job satisfaction, the development of information literate students, and improved profile of the library media center and role of library media specialist in the school. Since the importance of school library collaboration has been discussed for at least twenty years, it could be naturally assumed that examples of collaborations are frequent and ubiquitous in schools. Certainly, it has been identified as an important dynamic in student achievement (*School Libraries Work!* http://www.scholastic.com/librarians/printables/downloads/slw_2006.pdf).

However, there is also growing research evidence that suggests collaboration is more an elusive dream rather than an established and seamless practice. Lau's survey of principals' perceptions of library media specialists found that while 80% of principals believe that the library media center and library media specialist play a role in the school, only 37% of principals said that the library media specialist made them familiar with current research of library programs and student achievement, and 35% were made familiar with current research on library programs and reading development. In addition, only 50% of principals saw their library media specialist working in the classroom; indeed, 50% of principals saw the role of the library media specialist to be that of library "caretaker" (Lau 2002).

A study by Todd in 2005 of all 154 public school libraries in Delaware asked library media specialists to identify the nature and extent of their instructional involvement in relation to Delaware's core learning standards: English Language Arts, Social Studies, Science, and Mathematics. Given the blurry understanding of what collaboration actually is, the following categories were used in this study to identify the level of interaction: Cooperation—The teacher and the library media specialist may communicate informally about a short term project but work independently; Coordination—The teacher and library media specialist may meet together to discuss a lesson/unit of study, however, the individual goal setting, learning experience design, teaching, and evaluation are done independently; Collaboration—The teacher and library media specialist jointly set goals, design learning experiences, teach, and evaluate a comprehensive unit of study.

This study found that cooperations were the predominant mode of library media specialist's interaction with the school community. The data on the number of coordinations indi-cate that many library media specialists do not engage in any level of formal interaction with teaching faculty on curriculum activities that involve the library media center. Compared to the number of cooperations and coordinations, the number of collaborations is low. Callison's findings from surveys of library media specialists in Indiana show similar results (2005). His survey indicates that 48% of high schools, 44% of middle schools, and 25% of elementary schools reported that some teachers and the library media specialist collaboratively plan and teach curriculum units.

Meyers' recent study found that collaboration "as a proven practice remains elusive" (Meyers 2007, 94). This study examined the nature of collaboration in six high schools in Seattle and involved extensive site observations to capture the full range of activities in each library media center. This involved over 100 hours of directed observations and interviews with library media specialist and classroom teachers. According to Meyers, the research team did not see "deep collaborative activity." While 81% of the teachers involved in the study expected students to undertake research for their classes, only 37% of teachers involved the library media specialist in the creation of this task (Meyers 2007, 105). Meyers concludes that higher level collaborative effort may have greater impact on teaching and learning, but poses the challenge that library media specialists might better serve the information literacy agenda by managing instruction rather than directly delivering it.

Overall, available data show that the concept of collaboration is more espoused than practiced by library media specialists. Should we then, as library media specialists, even bother with collaboration? Should it be a key professional directive? After all, the whole practice of collaboration seems to be built on the assumption that teachers as a whole want to do this, and that they were actually consulted in the construction of this professional platform! I can find no evidence of such research however, though we acknowledge that the idea makes sound educational practice. Do instructional collaborations enable students to achieve better and/or more than traditional instructional methods such as isolated library lessons not linked to curriculum content? Should library media specialists be held accountable for not meeting professional expectations? Is an instructional intervention the most appropriate mode of collaboration? These are challenging questions that the profession as a whole needs to confront and address. The new AASL *Standards for 21st-Century Learners* reiterates the importance of collaboration, suggesting that collaboration continues to be a key modus operandi for the profession: "School librarians collaborate with others to provide instruction, learning strategies, and practice in using the essential learning skills needed in the 21st century" (p. 3, http://www.ala.org/aasl/standards). Even though there are questions concerning collaboration as a professional responsibility, statements such as those found in the new AASL *Standards* indicate it will be around for some time.

The highly successful ILILE program centers on classroom teachers and library media specialists developing instructional collaborations (http://www.ilile.org/). Over a three-year period, 170 library media specialist/classroom teacher collaborations (340 participants) have been mutually established. These teams from elementary, middle, and high schools in the content standards areas of social studies, science, language arts, and technology have engaged in integrating information literacy competencies into Ohio academic content standards, developing collaborative instructional units, and implementing planned instructional programs.

The ILILE program has provided a strong context for building a deeper understanding of collaborations: dynamics, processes, enablers, barriers; impact on perceptions of learning and instruction, effect on the nature of classroom practices; impact on learning outcomes, and the role in continuous improvement and school change. The research, undertaken by the Center for International Scholarship in School Libraries (CISSL) in 2006-2007 on behalf of ILLE (a research collaboration!) gathered data from 130 of the 340 participants who completed the extensive ILILE training program. It involved 85 library media specialists (65% of sample) and 45 teachers (35% of sample). The participants had an average of 12.5 years of professional experience in school librarianship or education.

An online survey instrument was used to collect qualitative data on the participants' first instructional collaboration as a result of the ILILE training program. The survey instrument was in six parts. Part 1: Background information; Part 2: The class details; Part 3: Planning your collaboration; Part 4: Implementing your collaboration; Part 5: The impact and outcomes of your collaboration; and Part 6: The future of your collaborations. The purpose here is not to present a detailed summary of the findings but to present seven key insights and lessons learned from the participants who had, from their perspective, undertaken successful collaborations in their schools. The following seven insights focus on strategies for building successful instructional collaborations:

1. Get over helplessness and grab the opportunities to develop and implement strategic collaborations. Helplessness is learned. Participants highly valued the professional training that ILILE provided. They recognized the sheer complexity of establishing instructional collaborations, the time involved, and the often sensitive and diverse negotiations that were needed to establish and set in motion a working collaboration. They came to understand that there are struggles involved—control, team work, self-interest, and self-doubt. Most importantly, they saw the opportunities to learn and to develop the shared experience of collaboration through engaging in extensive training. Professional opportunities helped build successful instructional collaborations.

2. Where there is a will there is a way. The participants in the collaborations encountered many school and situational issues typically presented as barriers to instructional collaboration or as factors that prevent even the initiation of collaborations. These barriers or factors included finding time and scheduling time; questioning the workability and viability of collaboration set against the daily competing pressures of schools; questioning whether they would be accepted by their partners as equals in the collaboration; questioning the level of commitment; and wondering how they could maintain the momentum of the partnership. Sometimes they felt uneasy because of the "unknowns" when two people rather than one lead the learning. However, the strong belief in the importance of the instructional collaboration provided the momentum to find solutions to the challenges, rather than to give up.

3. Giving up is not a solution. Participants were encouraged to see challenges and solutions, not problems. It was evident that the collaborating teams worked for solutions when they encountered barriers rather than wallowing in the setbacks or giving up. Solutions included being flexible, establishing priorities, valuing discussion, building a good working relationship, rearranging out-of-school schedules to accommodate the necessary planning, and closing knowledge gaps by making sure they understood the context and constraints of their collaborating partner. Participants saw that the pressures tested their belief in collaboration—at times it was much easier to simply give up, but there was recognition that the "I have no time" argument is a self-fulfilling prophecy. Essentially they saw that there are two choices—either they constructed solutions or they gave up. They realized that giving up was not in the best interest of library media centers.

4. The sum of the parts is greater than the whole. Participants saw that a successful strategy of collaboration was identifying complementary expertise, connecting them, and building on them. Often the coming together of expertise meant being open-minded and prepared to learn new skills as well as being responsive to the environmental pressures and stresses to provide mutual reassurance, support, and feedback. For example, library media specialists welcomed the opportunity to learn instructional strategies, observe a range of different teaching styles,

and learn classroom management techniques from teacher partners. Teachers saw information literacy in action and saw the opportunity for deep and wider learning for students by connecting the two areas of expertise. The experience of working together in the same learning space provided a supportive environment for taking risks, multitasking so that needs of students could be quickly met, and enabling deeper interaction with students. Participants thought that characteristics such as divergent and convergent thinking, creativity, flexibility, openness to experience, and organizational skills facilitated the working process by both partners.

5. Plan with mutuality of intent. One of the key dilemmas that surfaced in the study was at times an apparent disconnect in motivations. Some of the library media specialists expressed that the primary motivation for being involved in the collaboration centered on marketing library media services, increasing their status within the school, and spreading library-centered collaboration in the school. Some of the teachers expressed that collaboration with the library media specialist was a natural extension of social dynamic of teaching and their primary motive was one of socialization and developing networks. Is this collaboration? I would argue that the primary motivation and intention of collaboration must focus on student achievement and instructional collaboration as a key pedagogical mechanism for providing the best learning opportunities for students. It is certainly fine to hope that the library media center and the role of the library media specialist might

have a higher profile in the school as one outcome of the collaboration, but if that is what is driving the collaboration, then personal professional agendas, rather than learning agendas, take over and the real reason for collaboration becomes lost. There has to be a transcendent belief in collaboration as enabling quality learning outcomes. Instructional collaborations first and foremost are about learning and student achievement, not about boosting the role of the library media specialist. It is about the leading of learning and not authority-based leadership.

6. Plan with clarity of intent. The participants stressed the importance of careful and detailed planning before the instruction began: negotiating and formalizing the instructional goals, establishing the processes involved, and setting out the instructional sequence and structure. Such precision of planning, while time consuming, put focus on the team approach. It enabled refinement and reorientation, as needed, without stress and panic, and provided the necessary reassurance when spirits and energy lagged. Planning also involved anticipation of potential distractions and derailments, and having backup plans ready to go if needed.

7. Focus on collaboration as reflective learning. Acknowledge the complexity of collaboration and think through potential problems and potential solutions. Stay connected with the collaborating partner as the experience unfolds. Participants expressed the importance of taking the time to reflect, to hear their partner's expectations as the collaboration progressed, and to carefully con-

sider the evidence of student progress. Collaboration is not a linear process, but a recursive one, where roadblocks mean backtracking not stopping.

References:

American Association of School Librarians & Association for Educational Communications and Technology. *Information Power: Building Partnerships for Learning.* American Library Association, 1998.

American Association of School Librarians. *Standards for the 21st-Century Learner.* 2007. http://www.ala.org/aasl/standards.

Callison, Daniel. *Data from Indiana School Library Media Programs in 2004.* http://www.ilfonline.org/Units/Associations/aime/Data/navigate.htm

Lau, D. "What Does Your Boss Think about You?" *School Library Journal* 48, no. 9 (1998): 52-55.

Meyers, E. "The Complex Character of Collaboration: Current Practice and Future Challenge". In *Into the Center of the Curriculum. Papers of the Treasure Mountain Research Retreat,* edited by D. Loertscher and M. Mardis, 94-115a. Hi Willow Research & Publishing, 2007.

School Libraries Work! http://www.scholastic.com/librarians/printables/downloads/slw_2006.pdf

Todd, Ross. *Report of the Delaware School Library Survey 2004.* CISSL. http://www2.lib.udel.edu/taskforce/study.html🖐

Collaborative Planning

The process of collaborative planning involves creating partnerships so those involved can capitalize on each other's strengths and resources. The partners build the plan together. Here is an outline of the process:

Collaborate: Brainstorm and plan a curricular unit as a team:

- Identify goals and objectives (Curricular and information literacy)
- Identify learning goals, expectations, and guidelines for students
- Formulate the assessment: What are the learning targets? What standards are met (Harada, 27)?
- Identify resources
- Outline the lesson plan
- Outline the timeline
- Identify roles and responsibilities for:
    - Classroom Teacher, Library Media Specialist, Students, and Others
- Follow-Up: Reflection about student learning, collaborative efforts

Collaborative Planning Worksheet

Curricular Area: _____ **Grade Level:** _____ **Timeline:** _____

Curriculum Objectives:
Information Literacy Skills:
Learning Goal for the Lesson:
Assessment for Students' Learning: What must students do to demonstrate their learning goal (Harada, 27)?
Resources Needed:
Responsibilities: Classroom Teacher: Library Media Specialist: Students: Others:
Follow-Up: What evidence do you have that students achieved the learning targets (Harada, 25)? What went well? What needs work? How did the collaboration go?

This page was created in relationship to the articles "Building Evidence Folders for Learning through Library Media Centers" by Violet H. Harada (*SLMAM*, November 2006: 25-30) and "The Power and Spirit of Collaboration" by Susan Vanneman (*SLMAM*, November 2006: 31-32).

Assessment Tool: Levels of Communication, Cooperation, and Collaboration with Teachers

Use this chart to record the work you do with teachers over the course of the year. It will give you data to identify successes and gains as well as possible gaps. It will help you think about new approaches and set goals for the future. Compiled and summarized, it can provide important information to share with administrators about your work.

Identify the level of the working relationship with the teacher for:	Cooperation ◯ ◯	Coordination ◯◯	Collaboration ◯◯
Instructional Design			
Execution of Instruction			
Assessment of Student Work			
Reflection and Improvement			

Relationship
What do you want to remember?

Comments:

Teacher's Name:	Grade Level:	Date:	Curriculum Area:

Developed by Deborah Levitov in collaboration with Allison Zmuda (See Zmuda's article "Where Does Your Authority Come From?: Empowering the Library Media Specialist as a True Partner in Student Achievement," *SLMAM*, September 2006: 19-22). For more understanding of this page, see the articles: "When Does Collaboration Start?" by Gail Dickeson (*SLMAM*, October 2006: 56-57); and "Collaboration Practices" by Carolyn S. Brodie (*SLMAM*, October 2006: 27-30).

Chapter 9

Building a Toolkit of Instructional Strategies

Authentic learning involves exploring the world around us, asking questions, identifying information resources, discovering connections, examining multiple perspectives, discussing ideas, and making informed decisions that have a real impact."

—Daniel Callison and Annette Lamb, "Authentic Learning" (see page 247)

Library media specialists, by the nature of their collaborative work with teachers of varying styles and disciplines, need a robust toolkit of instructional strategies that complement those of their colleagues. Instructional approaches that promote meaningful learning can distinguish an outstanding school library media program from a mediocre one. Throughout this chapter, diverse instructional voices provide a variety of strategies that can provide more meaningful learning experiences for students. Specific lesson plans follow in chapters 10 and 11.

The Big Picture: The Value of Strong Lesson Design and Teaching/Learning Strategies

Unfortunately, many school library media specialists (SLMSs) have heard a comment similar to that which is echoed in the title of Clara Hoover's article, "We Don't Have to Learn Anything; We Just Have to Find the Answer" (beginning on page 244). The student who uttered that fateful statement was disengaged from the process of finding information because the task was superficial, disconnected, and without interest to the searcher. To counteract this learning-free anecdote, Hoover provides a rich overview of how deep instructional planning—inspired by the Backwards Design theories of Wiggins and McTighe (2005)—can reverse the sense of disconnect by asking meaningful questions that inspire engagement and learning that lasts.

Similarly, Daniel Callison and Annette Lamb promote "Authentic Learning" (beginning on page 247), with ideas that resonate throughout the AASL *Standards*. They build a definition of authentic learning as "real" learning. Authentic learning

- is student-centered, not merely the completion of tasks or worksheets designed by the teacher;

- uses resources that come from outside the school walls, with the school library media center as a clearinghouse;

- enables students to behave as information scientists who collect and verify information from a variety of sources;

- provides engagement as authentic researchers, not merely stringing together others' ideas but engaging in and analyzing primary sources and acquiring original data; and

- extends beyond the assignment into a lifetime of inquiry.

These articles set a foundation for meaningful instructional design. In "Differentiated Instruction," Gail Bush adds another layer (beginning on page 253). Differentiated Instruction (DI) is grounded in the idea that today's students cannot fully flourish in one-size-fits-all standardized instruction. With DI, educators can maximize student potential by customizing how students receive content, the process they use to make sense of that content, the types of products they use to demonstrate understanding, and the learning environment (Tomlinson 2003). Co-teaching to maximize the student–teacher ratio, acquiring collections for diverse interests and reading levels, and moving the learning environment from the classroom to a school library in which furniture can be flexibly arranged to meet many kinds of learning needs are ways in which school librarians are already supporting the needs of diverse learners. Bush's article extends that support by exploring how to further customize instructional design.

Strengthening the Students' Research Process

There are many research processes available that can be used to scaffold student inquiry. Regardless of any specific process, each student's research journey is built on awakening prior knowledge, developing strong question, interacting with resources, note-making, and student reflection. For a list of well-known research process models, see chapter 6.

Prior Knowledge and Questioning

Educators often say that inquiry begins with questions. But, as the teaching team of Kym Kramer and Connie Largent discovered, young students often struggle to create questions for topics about which they have little prior knowledge. In "Sift and Sort: The Answers Are in the Questions!" (beginning on page 256), they share their experiences in building background knowledge first, then facilitating student-generated questions. By doing so, the students' questions are built upon a stronger knowledge base and lead to more meaningful research investigations.

Once prior knowledge has been awakened, students have a foundation upon which to build new learning. But what will that learning be? Good questions are the key to strong inquiry. Ideally, the questions arise from the students' own curiosity. However, given the curriculum constraints of many classroom teachers, it is pragmatic to recognize that some questioning is led by the teacher in order to lead students to the conceptual understanding mandated by the curriculum. In "*Questioning* Revisited" (beginning on page 261), Daniel Callison gives many examples of types of questions that can be directed by teachers or asked by students.

Designing strong research questions and recognizing those questions in one's own work takes practice. Deborah Levitov shares an effective strategy for helping students in "Red Light, Green Light: Guiding Questions" (beginning on page 265). Using the metaphor of a traffic light, where green means "go" and red means "stop," students learn how to evaluate their own questions. "Red light" questions can be answered by discovering a simplistic factoid or with a "yes or no" answer, whereas "green light" questions propel the researcher forward.

Interacting with Resources

Questions lead the researcher to resources. Most school library media specialists are familiar with print material, reference books, and online databases and Web sites. Two areas that can be added to the toolkit to heighten the students' visceral connection with the topic are primary and graphical resources.

The proliferation of digital resources gives students unprecedented access to primary sources. From the Library of Congress's American Memory portal to countless engravings, documents, photographs, and multimedia resources (memory.loc.gov), to the blogs and photo streams of current American troops in Iraq, the eyewitness perspective, Marjorie L. Pappas shows how primary sources can make history vibrant and alive for students in "Primary Sources and Inquiry Learning" (beginning on page 267).

As chapter 1 points out, the 21st-century learner lives in a world rich with visual stimulus. Today's students love learning with visual resources. In their two-part series on graphic inquiry (beginning on page 271), Daniel Callison and Annette Lamb explore the power of images, charts, and graphs to stimulate student thinking and open new doors to understanding. Emerging readers, students with learning disabilities, and English language learners can particularly benefit from visual resources.

Organizing New Information: Taking Notes and Mapping Ideas

As practicing school library media specialists know, the vast quantities of information available are both a blessing and a curse. The curse can come when students struggle to make sense of the ever-flowing information stream.

Digital resources make it easier than ever for students to intentionally or unintentionally use another author's words or content as their own. Leslie Preddy, in "Cavemen Took Notes?" (beginning on page 280), shares a note-making strategy that condenses an author's ideas into a few simple words. When students create their project and use their notes, they then expand the idea using their own words. As Moreillon (2007) points out, "note-making" helps students understand content in a way that is more effective than highlighting or transcribing word for word.

Visualizing information is another strategy for helping students literally "see" the big picture of their gathered information. As Cristine Goldberg points out in "Brain Friendly Techniques: Mind Mapping ®" (beginning on page 282), using visualization techniques such as graphic organizers can help students make sense of and better retain information. Whether handwritten; created with software such as Inspiration, Kidspiration, or Microsoft PowerPoint; or created online with tools like Gliffy (www.gliffy.com), Webspiration (www.mywebspiration.com), or Lovely Charts (www.lovelycharts.com), visual note-taking can help students summarize, sort, and make sense of information.

Student Self-Reflection

Each of the four AASL *Standards* includes student self-assessment. Being able to accurately reflect on the process and outcome of one's learning is a lifelong skill. Whether a student enters college first or goes straight into the workforce, the ability to independently assess the quality of one's work is essential for success. Such metacognitive reflection should be embedded in library learning in order to scaffold the acquisition of that skill over time.

In "The Power of Reflection in the Research Process" (beginning on page 285), Peggy Milam builds the case for reflection in the research process; demonstrates how it is embedded in several popular research models; and presents several oral, digital, and print reflection strategies. Leslie Preddy's "Research Reflections, Journaling, and Exit Slips" and Deborah Levitov's "Sample Exit Slips for Elementary, Middle, and High School" (see chapter 8) demonstrate how a few simple exit questions can help students reflect on the dispositions, responsibilities, and self-assessments of the AASL *Standards*.

Minimizing Plagiarism

Truth be told, many school library media specialists hear regularly from classroom teachers about plagiarism. Indeed, with such easy access to information via the Internet, and with the ease of cutting and pasting, it is simple even for scholarly adults to plagiarize, either by accident or from lack of understanding about citation. In "Plagiarism" (beginning on page 289), Daniel Callison—with the cited help of others in the field—explores the important ideas behind plagiarism and the urgent need for instructional design that makes plagiarism impossible.

Technology Strategies

Never has the push to integrate technology into learning been stronger in American schools, and never has there been such a plethora of free or inexpensive tools that can be adopted. The school library media specialist is a technology leader in the school. Staying abreast of new tools and how they might be used to foster genuine student learning adds value to the role of the school library media specialist. The technology leadership role is complex, and the SLMS should take care when recommending tools to be certain that they will enhance—rather than detract from—student learning in the limited instructional hours available. It is somewhat paradoxical—yet true—that library media specialists both promote and carefully vet innovative technologies. The library media specialist also cannot afford to sit in judgment of the technology integration of his or her classroom colleagues. Just as the library media specialist wishes to be honored for a professional role as a teacher, respect must be shown for those who are slow to adopt technology or who have limited technology tools. As Deborah Levitov wrote in the *School Library Media Activities Monthly* editor's column "Cutting Edge?" in January 2009:

Pushing the edge, being innovative, thinking beyond what is known is important and necessary for all educators. Embracing new technology and Web 2.0 tools and putting them to the best use for students and staff is essential. It is also paramount that library media specialists put these new tools and modes of thinking into practice in ways that are instructionally sound. This can be encouraged in one of two ways.

One approach is to respect where people are, accept that there are real day-to-day limitations facing them, and acknowledge that good, solid, productive instruction and learning can still be accomplished with students and staff in these settings. This involves recognizing that what is being done has merit even though it may not be equal to the definition of cutting edge in terms of a Library 2.0 repertoire. It leaves room for thinking about possibilities.

The other approach is to dismiss and belittle people for where they are by undermining or ignoring existing successes that fit their settings. This approach involves lording over others the accomplishments of a few due to privileged settings without acknowledging the real restrictions and limitations that exist in individual schools or districts. This tends to shut down thinking rather than open minds to the possibilities.

Which approach would most people respond to? . . .

Library media specialists live in stressful times. Successful solutions that will make library media centers and schools more open and conducive to new 2.0 tools are needed. Ways to use the latest tools, incorporated within the library/educational settings must be implemented. Also, library media specialists must recognize when it is their own personal resistance that is preventing change and not their setting. But, above all, they need to be sure that what is done is instructionally sound. For those wanting to facilitate the shift to 2.0 environments, a positive, supportive approach seems more effective than lofty and extreme examples that make the possibilities seem impossible and the instructional approach seem less sound.

Library media specialists may also recognize that some tools are better suited to supporting the teacher (such as RSS feeds for a kindergarten teacher wanting to keep up on emerging literacy trends), some are better suited for student use (such as the learning games at PBSKids.org), some may benefit advocacy or public relations (such as using Issuu.com to create a virtual magazine about the school), and some may be used for multiple purposes (such as Voicethread.com or podcasting).

In "Podcasting 101" (beginning on page 294), Kristin Fontichiaro gives an overview of podcasting, an essentially free way for teachers to create content for oral learners and for students to demonstrate understanding that can be quickly shared with others both inside and outside the school community. Podcasting can be particularly powerful for libraries' youngest learners or those with learning disabilities, for whom written communication is time consuming and/or difficult.

To build collective knowledge, Annette Lamb and Larry Johnson recommend wikis, simple Web pages that allow many authors to contribute to the same document. In "Wikis and Collaborative Inquiry" (beginning on page 296), they provide several examples of how wikis, many types of which are available at no cost, can empower students to share knowledge and showcase their learning.

In "An Open Book: Life Online," Kathy Fredrick (beginning on page 300), a regular technology contributor to *School Library Media Activities Monthly*, identifies online tools that support students in their project management and creation. She identifies tools for individualized home pages; online word processing, presentation, and spreadsheet tools; collaborative planning and Web-conferencing sites; and calendaring tools. The AASL *Standards* promote learning activities that are collaborative, and these tools facilitate strong collective learning experiences. Even better, they can be accessed from anywhere, extending collaboration beyond the school day and the school walls.

Specific examples of technology integration in lessons are provided in the final two chapters of this book.

Beyond Academics: Developing Flexible Mindsets

On the road to developing healthy lifelong learners, it is easy to assume that the best way to build strong, emotionally healthy students is with high praise. "Great job!" and "You're brilliant!" are well-intentioned statements, but they have a surprisingly negative impact on students' self-perceptions. As renowned Stanford psychology professor Carol S. Dweck has learned, such statements can actually lead to students developing a fixed mindset, in which students believe that their intelligence has been "fixed" and is unchangeable. For some students, this means that they go through life assuming that they are not intelligent enough to tackle undiscovered territory. For others, too much early praise can lead to the alternative: a fixed mindset that one must always look successful, which can also lead to avoidance of challenge. Students with growth mindsets, on the other hand, see each new trial as an opportunity to learn. In "Mindsets: How Praise Is Harming Youth and What Can Be Done About It" (beginning on page 302), Dweck offers suggestions for how educators can reward process and effort and build growth mindsets that last a lifetime.

GETTING TO ADVOCACY

How can you use others' voices to tell the story of how students learn in your school library? Here are a few suggestions:

1. Keep a camcorder or portable podcasting recorder readily available and record students talking about their learning, for playback at a staff meeting or to share with parents and community members.

2. Invite students to promote their library "aha" moments on the school broadcast.

3. Collect student reflections and send them to administrators or the board of education, or share them with teachers to remind them of a successful unit. See Deb Logan's 2006 article, "Being Heard . . . Advocacy + Evidence + Students = Impact!" in the "References" section at the end of this book.

4. Ask a collaborating teacher to share the outcome of a successful collaboration with other teachers, administrators, or the board of education. If he or she shares via e-mail or in writing, request that a copy be placed in your personnel file.

5. Do visiting parents or volunteers rave about the learning they see happening in your library? Ask them to record their observations in a library guest book or open up comments on your blog so that they can share their feedback. Periodically ask them to share their perspective with administrators or the board of education.

THOUGHTS FOR THE JOURNEY

1. When debriefing with a teacher, save time to consider which instructional strategies are worth repeating and which might need to be changed or updated. Videotaping a class can be an illuminating way to reflect on the effectiveness of instructional design.

2. What is the best way to keep in touch with the latest and best instructional strategies? What blogs, listservs, or professional journals do you subscribe to?

3. How do you make time for continuous professional growth amid all of the other responsibilities of your job?

4. What are the major district, state, or regional educational buzzwords and trends? Check in with your district or intermediate school district's professional development office. They offer inexpensive professional development. If you are a student or work in a private school, ask if you may attend public school professional development.

"We Don't Have to Learn Anything; We Just Have to Find the Answer."

by Clara Hoover

A few years ago, prior to having Internet access in our library media center, a student needed to find the name of the current U. S. Supreme Court Chief Justice. I suggested the girl look in an almanac and showed her where the almanacs were located. She brought one to me but had no clue about how to use it. I told her to start with the index. She was flustered. I said, "I could tell you who the person is or I could find the answer for you, but then you wouldn't learn anything." She responded, "We don't have to learn anything; we just have to find the answer."

Later I relayed this conversation to her teacher, a colleague with whom I had collaborated on a variety of learning experiences. To say the teacher was disappointed would be an understatement. In this instance, the student's search was sparked by class discussion. Rather than telling the student the answer, the teacher asked the student to find the answer herself. The primary objective of the experiences we had planned was for students to be effective users of ideas and information. We wanted students to become resourceful. Although students were to find answers, the process of doing so was to be far more important than the answers themselves.

In today's society, how many people just want to know the answer? How many students are satisfied with accepting their first Internet hit without comparing information and validating sources? How many adults do the same? With today's technology, instant gratification and completing a task as quickly as possible seem to be the norm.

Two components of the learning process that help students focus on the process and not just the answer are asking essential questions and having students self-reflect on their learning. Often, in their haste to find answers, students miss these components that are so critical in an era in which information seems to explode every day.

Learning experiences should be designed with essential questions as their focus. Experiences that ask students to find disconnected facts or minute details might be fun for future detectives and Jeopardy contestants, but, for the most part, these experiences do not hold students' attention, contribute to their understanding of important concepts, nor prepare students to deal with tough questions in the future. Essential questions require deep thinking and ask students to "spend time pondering the meaning and importance of information" (McKenzie 1996). They are "provocative and multilayered questions that reveal the richness and complexities of a subject" (Wiggins and McTighe 1998, 28). They:

- Go to the heart of the discipline,
- Recur naturally throughout one's learning and in the history of a field, and
- Raise other questions (Wiggins and McTighe 1998, 29-30).

Essential questions help students understand what they learn in the context of their own lives and cause them to explore more broadly than they otherwise would. Additionally, these questions:

Formerly a library media specialist in Ames, IA, and Omaha, NE, Clara G. Hoover, Ed.D., is a curriculum facilitator for Millard Public Schools in Omaha and also an adjunct instructor in the Educational Administration Department at the University of Nebraska at Omaha. Email: choover@mpsomaha.org

- Reside at the top of Bloom's Taxonomy,
- Spark our curiosity and sense of wonder,
- Engage students in... real-life, applied problem solving, and
- Lend themselves well to multidisciplinary investigations (McKenzie 1996).

More importantly, answering essential questions takes a long time. Students don't just find answers;

they have to "construct their own answers and make meaning from the information they have gathered" (McKenzie 1996).

Let's examine two experiences. In the first, each student researches a different animal. Students are asked to identify its characteristics, where it lives, what it eats, and how it cares for its young. The activity culminates with students creating posters about their animals. In the second experience, students might find some of the same information, but their purpose for

doing so is to answer essential questions:

- What is an animal?
- How does an animal's characteristics help it adapt to its environment?
- How is this animal part of a system?
- Why are certain animals becoming extinct and what might be done to prevent this from happening?
- Why do people have animals as pets?
- Should something be done to prevent the overpopulation of some animals? Why?

When students read novels, they may be asked to write book reports and find information about authors. Students often simply summarize the story and provide a chronology of the author's life. They should focus on essential questions:

- Why did the author write this book?
- What in the author's life in-

fluenced the writing of the book?

- How was this book similar to or different from other books the author has written?
- How was this book similar to or different from other books you have read?
- Why did a certain character do what he or she did?
- What would you do if you were _____?
- Why is it important to read this book?

These essential questions will lead students to consider the book's themes and characters' thoughts and actions within the context of the students' own lives.

Asking students to answer essential questions requires substantial planning by the teacher/library media specialist partnership. This type of research may seem to have no end, will lead to a huge amount of information (often conflicting), and may be a challenge to manage, but it will be more fun and more rewarding for both students and the teaching team. It will provide students with a deeper understanding of the topic and a sense of how it applies to their own lives.

The second ingredient needed to ensure students learn, rather just find the answer, is for them to demonstrate their understanding through reflection and metacognition (Milam 2005; Wiggins and McTighe 1998; Wolf, Brush, and Saye 2003). Reflection is important if students are to understand what they have learned and retain that knowledge. Through reflection, students go beyond recalling, explaining, and applying information. They stretch to analyze, synthesize, and evaluate the information. In addition, they analyze and evaluate the research process and their role in it. They explain how they developed their sense of understanding, how their work has improved, and what they have yet to learn about the essential question (Wiggins and McTighe 1998).

Metacognition (thinking about thinking) is challenging. Adults seldom think about how they learn. Metacognition may be even more difficult for students. The teacher/library media specialist team can help develop these skills by providing a scaffolding structure, such as the Big6™, that takes students from where they are to the next level in thinking about their learning (Wolf, Brush, and Saye 2003). The final stage of the Big6™ includes two substages: judging the product and judging the process (Eisenberg and Berkowitz 1990). In the latter substage, students reflect on their role in the process, how they arrived at their understanding, and what they might do differently in the future. They explain their successes and challenges, as well as contemplate what they have yet to learn.

For teachers and library media specialists who suspect their activities focus on the answer rather than on learning and who are reluctant to give up their favorite units, how might they begin to change? Start with where you are—your current research projects. Perhaps your students research the thirteen original colonies or events such as the Louisiana Purchase, Lewis and Clark Expedition, and the Civil War. Some essential questions might be:

- How did historic and geographic factors contribute to the development of the United States?
- What is a country?

- How did events leading to the Civil War change history?
- How did various groups of people contribute to our country?

Instead of having students report on the U. S. Constitution or Bill of Rights, students could answer the following questions:

- Who is a citizen?
- What rights should a citizen have?
- What happens when people don't have these rights?
- What responsibilities do citizens have?
- What does equality mean?
- What makes our country unique?

Plan the research process by using the Big6™ model. Encourage students to select from all possible sources and then compare information by looking for recurring themes and supporting details. Challenge students to explore paths provided by unanticipated information. Once students have organized and presented their information and answered the essential questions, make sure they evaluate the product and reflect on the research process. Throughout their research, students can journal about their progress. They could blog with other students about the process. Along the way, ask students questions:

- Why did you do _____?
- What information do you still need or what do you still not know?
- What perspective did that source provide?
- What do you think would happen if _____?

At the end of the process (is there ever an end?), interview each student or hold small group discussions in which students ex-

plain what they've learned about the process, what questions they still have, how they would go about finding the answers, how their work has improved, and what they found challenging about the process—and why. A culminating activity would be for students to write an essay, journal/blog entry, or email describing themselves as learners.

If library media specialists and teachers collaborate on learning experiences that focus on essential questions and are conducted in an environment that fosters reflection throughout the process and requires students to self-assess at the end, then students should no longer be saying, "We don't have to learn anything; we just have to find the answer."

References

Eisenberg, M., and R. E. Berkowitz. *Information Problem Solving: The Big Six Skills Approach to Library and Information Skills*. Norwood, NJ: Ablex, 1990.

McKenzie, J. "Framing Essential Questions." *From Now On* 6, no. 1 (1996). http://fno.org/sept96/questions.html (Retrieved 23 June 2005).

Milam, P. "The Power of Reflection in the Research Process." *School Library Media Activities Monthly* 12, no. 6 (February 2005): 26-29.

Wiggins, G., and J. McTighe. *Understanding by Design*. Alexandria, VA: Association for Supervision and Curriculum Development, 1998.

Wolf, S., T. Brush, and J. Saye. "The Big Six Information Skills as a Metacognitive Scaffold: A Case Study." *School Library Media Research*. Vol. 6. AASL, 2003. http://www.ala.org/ala/aasl/aaslpubsandjournals/slmrb/slmrcontents/volume62003/bigsixinformation.htm (Retrieved 23 June 2005). ✋

Authentic Learning

by Daniel Callison and Annette Lamb

The term "authentic" refers to the genuine, real, and true. Authentic learning involves exploring the world around us, asking questions, identifying information resources, discovering connections, examining multiple perspectives, discussing ideas, and making informed decisions that have a real impact. An authentic learning environment is engaging for students because the content and context of learning are accepted by the student as relevant to his or her needs and deemed by the teacher as simulating life beyond the classroom.

Callison has suggested that information inquiry comes near authentic learning at the intersection of workplace information problems, personal information needs, and academic information problems or tasks.

```
Workplace or          Personal
Professional          Information
Info Problems         Needs

X ←——————————————— authentic learning

Academic Information
Problems, and Tasks
Assigned by Teachers

The Relationship among Workplace, Personal, and Academic
Information Problem Sets. 2001. Daniel Callison.
```

State and national learning standards found today across disciplines often attempt to stress real-world applications. Students are asked to make academic connections to ordinary life experiences. Rather than surface-level, fact-based tasks, learners are asked to question, interpret, and apply information and ideas that have value in a larger social context. Many students aren't aware of how reading, writing, and mathematics are part of their daily life, and one of the challenges for educators is to help students make such real-world associations.

A specific challenge of the library media specialist is to partner with other teachers to design learning activities and develop assessments that resemble constructive experiences beyond the school. Partnering and simulating real-world situations are not easy tasks and usually fall short of any ideal implied in definitions of authentic learning. Examples and situations given here may help teams of educators to consider how to move closer to developing authentic learning environments. Moving away from heavy use of common worksheets and skill drills, multiple-choice exams, and a standard formula applied to all student research projects is an evolution toward authentic learning.

Teaching teams who engage in information inquiry are most likely to create authentic learning environments when they act as mentors or master-level teachers who model for their learning apprentices. They engage in inquiry with their students, not simply assign tasks. They raise questions, seek information, interpret findings and draw conclusions, and illustrate their inquiry practices as they work with students. They discuss openly for students to hear and see the inquiry process and results, and share both personal inquiry successes and failures. As Carol Tilley has written, cognitive apprenticeship becomes the center of the learning tasks when students grow intellectually and eventually move to a near independent learning level.

Signs of Authentic Learning

Although this list probably is not exhaustive, the following are signs that teachers of information inquiry are reaching levels of learning that can be identified as authentic.

Learning Is Student-Centered. Not all of the questions for exploration are generated by the teacher, but most are raised, clarified, and become "owned" by the students working collaboratively to act more as problem-identifiers and not just problem-solvers.

Multiple Resources Accessed beyond the School. Questions are not answered to full satisfaction of the student, library media specialist, or other teachers by information provided in the school library media center alone. While some basic background information is accessible, the library media center is a clearinghouse for contacts to more in-depth resources and expertise in the community and beyond. Electronic documents and human experts are valued, monitored through master teacher guidance, and used extensively.

Student Acts as a Scientific Apprentice. As an "information scientist," the student is encouraged to be skeptical of the information located

Daniel Callison and Annette Lamb are Professors in library and information science at the Indiana University School of Library and Information Science in Indianapolis (http://www. slis.iupui.edu). Dr. Lamb teaches a graduate course in information inquiry over the Internet (http:// eduscapes.com).

and seeks to corroborate facts and gain a variety of perspectives on issues and to determine credibility and authority of sources. The student learns from several systematic information exploration approaches that can be applied to meet a variety of current and future information problems. With the guidance of the master teacher, the student evaluates approaches to match to information needs and documents the results for future uses. Mapping the results of information gained from different sources becomes as important as gaining information content itself because this will help in becoming more efficient in future information seeking practices.

Student Moves toward Real Research. The opportunity for the student to gather original data through surveys, interviews, or experiments helps to enhance the project and places the student in the role of not just "library researcher," but closer to that of authentic researcher. The student moves beyond just location of documents and organized data to one who deals with analysis of findings and identification of additional information needs. The student learns how primary sources, artifacts, and observations of human behavior can all contribute to useful data. The student learns the value of documenting through a research journal their feelings and findings and to do so in a constructive manner that can be shared with others. The student learns how to analyze his or her audience in order to best communicate findings in order to inform, persuade, or engage others in their information problem-solving pursuits.

Lifelong Learning beyond the Assignment. The student finds information problems and questions to be interesting, exciting, challenging, and personally meaningful. They move toward the intersection of personal, academic, and potentially future workplace information needs. The agenda of questions continues to evolve beyond the school assignment and becomes an inquiry set that they follow outside of school as well as in future academic experiences. The agenda impacts the student's selection of reading, viewing, and discussion both for pleasure and for intellectual growth.

Process, Product, and Performance Assessment. Attempts are made by the guiding educators as well as the reflective student researcher to evaluate all aspects of inquiry. The process and product are both valued as artifacts of learning. Actions taken or performance of application of the inquiry become evidence of learning success. Has the student's thinking changed? Has the student changed the thinking of others? Has the student mastered inquiry to make a difference in some constructive manner?

Instructional Collaboration and Interchangeable Roles. Students are more likely to learn the value of inquiry and collaboration with others when they see it modeled by master teachers. Library media specialists and other teachers of inquiry demonstrate collaboration as a team to select and implement a suitable approach to information problem identification and solving. They perform as information literate educators and share with their students how they have determined quality information sources or conducted original information gathering. As a team, they freely share responsibilities for lesson planning, instructional presentation, and performance evaluation. Each member of the team is information resourceful and fluent in matching search strategies to meet information needs. Master teachers display their ideas and inquiry work along with their apprentice students. They may present findings in visuals, speeches, papers, or other media displayed for audience examination and critical discourse.

Authentic Achievement

Fred Newmann and Gary Wehlage from the University of Wisconsin-Madison stress that meaningful learning is critical to engage students and transfer learning to new situations. Their research focuses on the direct connection between authentic instruction and student achievement. In a recent study, they concluded that students in classrooms with high quality, authentic assignments scored higher on standardized achievement tests. Three criteria were used to define authentic achievement:

- Students construct meaning and produce knowledge;
- Students use disciplined inquiry to construct meaning; and
- Students aim their work toward production of discourse, products, and performances that have value or meaning beyond success in school.

Newmann and Wehlage stress two problems that often result in conventional schooling not reaching authentic levels:

- Often school work does not allow them to use their minds well.
- The work has no intrinsic meaning or value to students beyond achieving success in school.

In their article "Five Standards of Authentic Instruction," Newmann and Whelage identified five continuous dimensional constructs that can be used to determine the authenticity of instruction. These are:

- Higher-order thinking,
- Depth of knowledge,
- Connectiveness to the world beyond the classroom,
- Substantive conversation, and
- Social support for student achievement.

There are many ways that students can demonstrate their understanding of academic content through authentic problems and projects. To demonstrate their skills in mathematics and social studies, students could develop a proposal regarding the use of a particular building or parcel of land in their city, create charts and graphs to speculate on whether racism or other factors impacted local home sales, or demonstrate the distribution of wealth and population on different continents by using ratio and proportion.

Authentic Assignments

Authentic assignments are grounded in reality and require students to create meaning from their experiences. Students are involved with communicating through e-mail, writing letters, and keeping journals. They may collect oral histories, write about current events, or conduct and report on experiments.

Molly Nicaise, a faculty member in the School of Information Science and Learning Technologies at the University of Missouri, stresses that authentic learning is anchored in real-world activities. Students access the information and resources needed to address essential questions. Assessments of these activities are directly related to the task.

Authentic Context. Assignments should be rooted in a meaningful situation. Educators use simulations, scenarios, and problems to provide this context. The closer the context can be to a real-world situation, the more likely it is that students will see the connection between academic context and practical applications. Leo Vygotsky used the phrase "zone of proximal development" to describe how learners use context to understand and create knowledge. He found that cultural and historical factors impact how we learn and that learners are not always able to transfer learning to new situations.

An effective strategy is to ask students to connect local with national or international information. Students might conduct a poll in their building to collect information about whether people recycle paper, glass, or aluminum. They then could compare this to the national average. Comparisons also could be made by using local versus national population statistics or immigrant data. The same could be done by comparing the stories of local veterans with those from other countries.

Authentic Questions. Assignments begin with authentic questions generated from personally relevant concerns, issues, and topics. Questions are framed in a real context that build on personal experience and extend to the larger world.

Authentic Tasks. Learning tasks often are not explicit, requiring students to identify problems, develop strategies, make decisions, and be in charge of their own learning. Students often feel uncomfortable with these types of assignments because they require independent thinking and metacognitive skills. These types of assignments require careful guidance to help learning through the processes of problem identification.

Scaffolding is a critical element of authentic learning environments. Students must connect new information to existing knowledge and experiences. Students need guidance in making these connections in inquiry-based projects. Authentic learning activities are not easy to manage.

Elliott Soloway, a professor at the University of Michigan, develops tools to provide the scaffolding needed for students to engage in authentic situations that require complicated subject matter. He stresses that teacher librarians must help learners evaluate digital content and use technology to access and use information. From handheld devices and science probes to software tools that help students with complex mathematics, he has worked with teachers to use technology to facilitate authentic learning. For example, middle school students have explored their own community environment through measuring the health of local rivers.

Tiffany Marra, the Program Manager for SmartGirl.org, asks the question, "Why should students learn how to solve problems about things that will never happen, when there is so much in their lives that already involves math, reading, writing, or any other subject matter?" Each year, SmartGirl.org along with the American Library Association conducts a reading survey to identify the interests of young women as part of Teen Read Week. Marra stresses that tasks can fall on a continuum of authenticity from reading books about art and going on virtual art museum visits to actually visiting an art gallery.

Authentic tasks often involve collaboration or competition with others. Many national writing contests, local media fairs, and science fairs provide opportunities to participate in a project that is shared beyond the school. Cyberfair (http://www.globalschoolhouse.com) is a well-known Web-based authentic learning programs that focuses on youth research connecting knowledge to real-world applications in categories including local leaders, businesses, community organizations, historical landmarks, environment, music, art, and local specialties.

Authentic Activities. These activities are natural, not contrived. Rather than reading about city government in a textbook, students write questions and interview local government officials. By providing meaningful contexts for learning, authentic learning closely resembles actual situations where knowledge and skills will be used.

Students read primary documents and original prose, create communications on meaningful topics for real audiences, and share work with real audiences. Students are asked to:

- Recall their prior knowledge and how it relates to a real situation;
- Articulate questions, problems, or a focus that are meaningful, relevant, and interesting; and
- Construct knowledge and discover connections in real-world contexts.

Authentic activities include working with the local chamber of commerce on promoting an annual event, natural resource, or historical building; providing nutrition and fitness information to seniors; or creating websites for local nonprofit agencies. Sometimes it is possible to become involved with large-scale projects such as identifying monarch butterflies, hummingbirds, or whooping cranes. In other cases, students might volunteer to participate in research being conducted by professionals at the United States Geological Survey or the National Park Service. For example, a middle school class in Idaho worked on a land survey at a local cemetery and a high school class in Washington assisted in identifying wildlife habitats.

Authentic Resources

A wide variety of information resources, materials, tools, and technologies are used in authentic learning. Students increase their understanding of the world by examining primary resources, interacting with members of the community, and connecting with real-world issues. Authentic materials can be traced back to the original author or idea. Students can be involved with generating this information through e-mail interviews or original reporting of events and experiments.

The library media specialist is essential in authentic learning environments. Students are expected to go beyond teacher-directed activities and textbooks. The library media specialist can collaborate with the teacher to locate and organize authentic materials and resources from community or online experts to primary source documents or photographs. Partnerships also may be formed with the public library, community organizations, museums, natural areas, aquarium, botanical garden, zoo, or planetarium.

Rather than simply reading the work of others, learners develop meaningful questions and gather information from many sources. They often generate new data and ideas by:

- Conducting oral histories with local senior citizens,
- Developing a plan to renovate a museum exhibit,
- Comparing local and national data on air and water pollution, or
- Interviewing a NOAA oceanographer through e-mail or video conferencing.

Technology can provide a bridge to authentic environments.

- Use webcams to video conference with experts at remote locations.
- Go on virtual field trips to historical locations, museums, and natural places.
- Interact with experts on group discussion forums.
- Access primary sources and real-world data sources.
- Communicate with students from other cultures through e-mail.
- Watch news broadcasts from other countries over the Web.
- Use a video camera to record oral histories.

Authentic Communications and Audiences

Students need a real-world audience for their work. Authentic audiences might include the student government, local agencies, civic groups, and government offices. The oral history projects could be shared with local and national historical societies and organizations. Teachers should help students seek out stakeholders who have the authority to take action based on student recommendations. Students also should be prepared to witness the frustrations of democratic government in action, or nonaction, and be prepared to understand that not all recommendations succeed. Many voices may influence decisions in some situations while other decisions may be made unilaterally. The authentic experience, however, is one in which students are encouraged to find a voice and to participate as constructively as possible.

When examining the work of professionals across disciplines, Fred Newmann found that adults rely upon complex forms of communication to conduct their work and present their results. These tools involve verbal, symbolic, and visual communication to provide "qualifications, nuances, elaborations, details, and analogies woven into extended narratives, explanations, justifications, and dialogue."

Newmann states that "when adults write letters, news articles, organizational memos, or technical reports; when they speak a foreign language; when they design a house, negotiate an agreement, or devise a budget; when they create a painting or a piece of music—they try to communicate ideas that have an impact on others. In contrast, most school assignments, such as spelling quizzes, laboratory exercises, or typical final exams, have little value beyond school, because they are designed only to document the competence of the learner."

Authentic Assessment

Assessment is a critical component of authentic learning. Students learn by applying knowledge to solve problems that mirror the challenges of tasks found beyond the classroom. Authentic assessment asks students to determine whether they've met their goal.

Authentic assessment values both the processes and products involved in learning. For example, journals, logs, and concept maps may be developed as the project progresses. Final products might include a letter to the editor, online book review, or presentation to a local nonprofit group. Students are asked to demonstrate their knowledge and skills in meaningful ways. Rather than testing isolated skills, authentic assessments effectively measure student capabilities through accurately evaluating learning by examining a student's performance in a natural situation. A variety of tools can be used in authentic assessment including checklists, portfolios, and rubrics.

Authentic assessment is used to evaluate student work as well as provide feedback for improvement. Rather than comparing students with each other, authentic assessment focuses on individual strengths and weaknesses. In other words, authentic assessment is criterion-referenced rather than norm-referenced. This aspect may prove to have limits however, compared to many real-world situations that are driven by human competition.

Grant Wiggins, well-known for his work with authentic education, places emphasis on selecting engaging problems that require students to develop effective, creative performances and products. By having a real-life context for product development, assessment has more relevance. Students are aware of the criteria used for evaluation and have opportunities for self-checking. They also have a chance to see and judge the impact of their product in the real world.

Authentic Learning and Information Inquiry

Information inquiry is at the core of authentic learning. The ultimate value of an inquiry project lies in its authenticity. Rather than exploring superficial questions and problems, students are asked to explore essential questions that require deep thinking.

Carol Gordon from the Educational Resources Library at Boston University conducted an action research study with high school English teachers and the library media specialist focusing on authentic research assignments. According to Gordon, most assignments ask students to report on the findings of others and draw conclusions based on readings. She stresses the importance of placing students in an active role as researcher by conducting interviews, administering questionnaires, and journaling observations. This data then is used to construct meaning. In other words, rather than asking students to simply be reporters, Gordon suggests that students become real researchers.

This idea has tremendous implications for teacher librarians. Rather than focusing on traditional information gathering approaches such as reading, taking notes, and summarizing, students become immersed in their research by using a variety of techniques to collect data, explore perspectives, and generate new ideas. Gordon notes that the ownership students feel for original work facilitates the construction process. Authentic inquiry may be an unreachable ideal, but the goal remains to raise the level educators should expect for student engagement and performance in meeting the information demands of their world both in and out of school.

Jinx Stapleton Watson from the University of Tennessee has written about higher expectations relevant to student inquiry in science fair projects:

Most "research" projects assigned at the senior high school level do not provide an authentic application of scientific methods. Students who are limited to simple models that outline a linear research process will not experience the more meaningful aspects of research: personal selection of problems and research questions, application of proper methods, collection of original data, and reaching relevant conclusions. ...[C]lean-cut exercises do not pretend to be about idea making or wondering, the essence of inquiry. Thus, teachers and school library media specialists who want students to pursue ideas that intrigue them enough to investigate must communicate different expectations from the step-by-step procedures. They must communicate that wrong turns and mistakes in thinking may offer as much information as successful efforts. They must support the approach that such inquiry might not be pursued with a single course or class schedule, but rather, across disciplines, across the day, in flexible schedules of classroom and library [access] with significant adults ready to assist at wrong turns, mistakes, and plateau periods in the investigation.

For Further Reading

Brandt, Ron. "On Teaching for Understanding: A Conversation with Howard Gardner." *Educational Leadership* 50, no. 7 (April 1993): 4-7.

Brown, John Seely, A. Collins, and Paul Duguid. "Situated Cognition and the Culture of Learning." *Educational Researcher* 18, no. 1 (1989): 32-42.

Brown, John Seely, and Paul Duguid. "Organizational Learning and Communities of Practice: Towards a Unified View of Working, Learning, and Innovation." *Or-*

ganization Science 2, no. 1 (1991): 40-57.

Bruner, Jerome. *Actual Minds, Possible Worlds.* Cambridge, MA: Harvard University Press, 1986.

Callison, Daniel. "Authentic Assessment." *School Library Media Activities Monthly* 14, no. 5 (January 1998): 42-43, 50.

Collins, A., J. S. Brown, and S. E. Newman. "Cognitive Apprenticeship: Teaching the Craft of Reading, Writing, and Mathematics." In *Knowing, Learning and Instruction: Essays in Honor of Robert Glaser,* edited by L. B. Resnick. Hillsdale, NJ: Lawrence Erlbaum, 1988.

Duffy, Tom M., and David H. Jonassen. *Constructivism and the Technology of Instruction.* Hillsdale, NJ: Lawrence Erlbaum, 1992.

Gardner, Howard. *The Unschooled Mind: How Children Think and How Schools Should Teach.* New York: Basic Books, 1991.

Gordon, Carol. "Students as Authentic Researchers: A New Prescription for the High School Research Assignment." *School Library Media Research* 2, 1999. Available from the American Library Association website (http://www.ala.org/aasl/SLMR).

Kuhlthau, Carol C. "Learning in Digital Libraries: An Information Search Process Approach." *Library Trends* 45, no. 4 (1997): 575–806.

Lafer, Stephen. "Audience, Elegance, and Learning via the Internet." *Computers in the School* 13, nos. 1-2 (1997): 89-97.

Lebow, David G., and Walter Wager. "Authentic Activity as a Model for Appropriate Learning Activity: Implications for Emerging Instructional Technologies." *Canadian Journal of Educational Communication* 23 (Winter 1994): 231-244.

Marra, Tiffany. *Authentic Learning Environments.* 2004. Available from the University of Michigan website (http://www-personal.umich.edu/%7Etmarra/authenticity/authen.html).

Mims, Clif. "Authentic Learning: A Practical Introduction and Guide for Implementation." *Meridian: A Middle School Computer Technologies Journal* 6, no. 1 (Winter 2003). Available from the Meridian website (http://www.ncsu.edu/meridian/win2003/authentic_learning/).

Newman, Delia. "Alternative Assessment: Promises and Pitfalls." In *School Library Media Annual,* Vol. 11, edited by Carol Collier Kuhlthau, 13-20. Englewood, CO: Libraries Unlimited, 1993.

Newmann, Fred M., and Gary G. Wehlage. "Five Standards of Authentic Instruction." *Educational Leadership* 50, no. 7 (1993): 8-12.

Newmann, F. M., A. S. Bryk, and J. K. Nagaoka. *Authentic Intellectual Work and Standardized Tests: Conflict or Coexistence?* Consortium on Chicago School Research, 2001.

Nicaise, M. "Student Astronauts Blast Off in the Midwest: An Example of an Authentic Learning Environment." *Space Times: Magazine of the American Astronautical Society* 34, no. 5 (1995): 18-20.

Stripling, Barbara K. "Practicing Authentic Assessment in the School Library." In *School Library Media Annual,* Vol. 11, edited by Carol Collier Kuhlthau, 40-56. Englewood, CO: Libraries Unlimited, 1993.

Tilley, Carol. "Cognitive Apprenticeship." In *Key Words, Concepts and Methods for Information Age Instruction.* LMS Associates, 2003.

Vygotsky, L. S. *Mind in Society.* Cambridge, MA: Harvard University Press, 1930.

Watson, Jinx Stapleton. "Examining Perceptions of the Science Fair Project: Content or Process?" *School Library Media Research* 6 (2003). Available from the American Library Association website (http://www.ala.org/aasl/SLMR).

Wiggins, Grant. "The Case for Authentic Assessment." *Practical Assessment, Research & Evaluation* 2, no. 2 (1990).

Wiggins, Grant. "Assessment: Authencity, Context, and Validity." *Phi Delta Kappan* 75, no. 3 (1993): 200-214.

Differentiated Instruction

by Gail Bush

Differentiated instruction (DI) is one particular approach to instructional strategies, the delivery of the curriculum, covered within the study of curriculum. It is not a form of curriculum design although it has recently been blended with the backward design model, the basis of *Understanding by Design* (Wiggins & McTighe 2005). Differentiated instruction requires that educators know their students in such a way that they can effectively plan for students' learning experiences prior to instruction. This is the major distinction from the Skillful Teacher Model where the teacher quickly reacts to the struggling student. In the DI model, the differentiation is planned within the lesson. Basically it is the difference between proaction and reaction. There is more flexibility built into the overall lesson plan and, therefore, more effective teaching delivery to more students.

Differentiated instruction is a learner-centered instructional design model that acknowledges that students have individual learning styles, motivation, abilities, and, therefore, readiness to learn. Within the learning environment, educators balance the three essential elements of content, process,

and outcome. In DI, whereas all these elements are differentiated, all students are held to standards that measure substantial growth and achievement. Pre-assessment as well as ongoing assessment become essential measures to determine where a student is in relation to the learning activity. The goal becomes

not only what content needs to be taught, but how to teach in a way that most effectively results in each student's ability to demonstrate understanding of the content.

There is a rhythm to differentiated instruction because this strategy allows for various groupings that are most effective within the learning process. For example, the teacher who starts with whole class discussion might move to individualized assigned tasks, back to whole class, then to small group, back to whole class, and so on. Students tend to have varying skills in readiness to learn based on the content, so a skilled math student might be in a particular small group in math but might be in a very different group for language arts. The fear of

Gail Bush is a faculty member and director of the Center for Teaching through Children's Books at National-Louis University in Chicago, IL. Email: Gail.Bush@nl.edu

stigma attached to ability grouping subsides as students feel fulfilled in reaching their potential in goals that match their abilities.

Differentiated instruction includes three essential elements of curriculum: what is worthwhile learning—content; how is the instruction best delivered—process; and what is evidence that demonstrates learning—product. The differentiation is planned according to the student's readiness, interests, and learning profile.

DIFFERENTIATING CONTENT

What knowledge, skills, attitudes, and values are most worthwhile to students? These basic questions of curriculum are answered by learning standards and standardized testing. However, there are a few ways to differentiate what is deemed desirable content: level of difficulty within the same unit of study; access to different sources that deliver the content; and different requirements of what is gleaned from the content, such as reading for factual information versus patterns or themes.

The School Library Media Connection: The mission of the library media center is to support the curriculum for every student which mandates that there will be resources available at the appropriate reading levels. There may be reference sources at different reading levels, nonfiction books, and access to online resources to serve all students, including English language learners and special education students. The library media center serves students of all abilities in accessing the general curriculum. The library media specialist is prepared to consult with teachers to match students with the appropriate resources.

DIFFERENTIATING PROCESS

Curriculum scholars ask what activities and strategies are most effective in enabling learners to acquire the knowledge, skills, attitudes, and values deemed worthy. In other words, if content is "what to teach," process then is "how to teach." "What to teach," or content, is when educators set goals and student behavioral objectives for learning. When this selection of content process works, students can make sense of what they are learning, apply it to prior knowledge, and seek categorization, thereby making it a part of their knowledge base. The most effective method for sense-making is to challenge students to reach to the next level by using what they know as a springboard for understanding. This process may be differentiated by a multitude of strategies including learning logs, graphic organizers, journals, literature circles, jigsaw, mind-mapping, and so many others to be explored.

The School Library Media Connection: Along with the library media center resource collection which is essential for differentiating content, the library media center has a physical space that can be used for learning centers or stations. As instructional partners, library media specialists guide and facilitate an understanding of instructional strategies and how they can be best utilized. Library media specialists continue to learn about strategies, education databases, and websites so that they may serve as resources for teachers.

DIFFERENTIATING PRODUCT

How do we know if the learners have acquired the knowledge, skills, attitudes, and values that are most worthy to learn? What provides evidence of students' understanding of the content? How do we know that they have made meaningful and substantive growth? In the DI model, assessment is ongoing to accommodate flexibility in guiding instruction. However, a product or outcome is necessary as evidence of understanding, and it also serves the student as a tangible representation of his or her learning achievement.

The School Library Media Connection: The library media center program provides resources not only for learning but also for development of learning products. The library media center is an appropriate learning environment for students to design webpages or quests, create public service announcements, prepare for a debate or town meeting, write a play, develop an advertising campaign, design and conduct experiments and research, tutor younger students, make video documentaries, hold press conferences, and so on. The library media specialist provides the instructional consulting, resources, and space to make differentiated products a reality in the school. Additionally, the library media center provides space that is inviting to other members of the school learning community, where they can join together in viewing or participating in these deeply textured demonstrations of understanding.

STUDENT READINESS

Matching the student's skills and understanding to the topic at hand is considered "readiness to learn."

Readiness differentiation focuses on the dynamics of moving a student beyond current knowledge to outside his or her comfort zone. Tomlinson identifies "The Equalizer," a tool listing eight variables, as a way to differentiate based on readiness:

Foundational ←→ Transformational
Concrete ←→ Abstract
Simple ←→ Complex
Single Facet ←→ Multiple Facets
Small Leap ←→ Great Leap
More Structured ←→ More Open
Less Independence ←→ Greater Independence
Slow ←→ Quick

(2001, 47).

These variables are adjusted to match students' readiness to be equally and appropriately challenged by the general curriculum. The more the teacher knows about his or her students, the more fluid these adjustments become throughout the course of the year.

The School Library Media Connection: As a learning environment that provides for independent learning and small group work, the physical setting of the library media center lends itself to the range of equalizing variables for student readiness to learn. Authentic and meaningful lessons, challenging comfort zones, and high expectations are important for all students and are also accommodated by the library media program.

STUDENT INTERESTS

We must be engaged to truly learn and be transformed. Student choice is, therefore, a good measure that satisfies many interests. As students enter the learning environment, differentiating by interest does not make the teacher captive to the interests of students, although learning about those interests can be a key method of engagement. Savvy teachers may, instead, create additional interest by sparking imagination through the artistry of inspirational teaching.

The School Library Media Connection: The library media center serves all students in support of the curriculum, but it also serves students' various interests. Facets of these varying interests may include real-life, authentic, local, global, pop culture, and hobbies that all stimulate student engagement and, therefore, have a place in the library media program. Displays, exhibits, programs, collaboration with the public library and local museums, and online communities all generate interest. By extending the meaning of "access to resources," the library media specialist can provide for this wide variety of students' interests.

STUDENT LEARNING PROFILE

How do we learn best? There are many measures, models, and studies to choose from including learning styles, multiple intelligences, brain-based learning, and domains (cognitive, affective/emotional, and psychomotor). The four categories identified in the DI model used to plan instruction include group orientation, cognitive style, learning environment, and intelligence preference. Other factors include culture-influenced preferences, gender-based preferences, and combinations of both culture and gender. Although it is tricky to accommodate all learning profiles at all times, it does behoove us to recognize that all students do not share our particular profiles. The challenge to many educators is to acknowledge those preferences different from one's own.

The School Library Media Connection: As teachers struggle to keep up with daily tasks both in the classroom and administratively, we in the library media center have the opportunity to assist them as instructional consultants. Identifying trends in learning profiles, providing ready access to professional education resources, and providing professional development in both the relevant features of the new research in classroom and school library applications all facilitate student learning.

Differentiated Instruction is simply an honest and mindful approach to teaching our diverse student populations. It acknowledges individual differences and seeks to make learning meaningful for all students. Our mission in the library media center mirrors these goals and matches this learner-centered instructional design model. Our role in the school strengthens our learning community's capacity for improving student learning.

Bibliography

Tomlinson, C. A. *How to Differentiate Instruction in Mixed-Ability Classrooms.* 2nd ed. Association for Supervision and Curriculum Development, 2001.

Tomlinson, C. A. *The Differentiated Classroom: Responding to the Needs of All Learners.* Association for Supervision and Curriculum Development, 1999.

Tomlinson, C. A., and J. McTighe. *Integrating Differentiated Instruction and Understanding by Design: Connecting Content and Kids.* Association for Supervision and Curriculum Development, 2006.

Wiggins, G., and J. McTighe. *Understanding by Design.* 2nd ed. Association for Supervision and Curriculum Development, 2005. ✋

Sift and Sort:

The Answers Are in the Questions!

by Kym Kramer and Connie Largent

Providing time and guidance to students as they "sift and sort" background information on a potential inquiry topic is important at any level of investigation, from grade school to graduate school. As the inquiring student moves through new information, discusses ideas with teachers and peers and, most of all, has time to reflect on the initial set of inquiry questions, the original questions begin to turn and new questions appear.

Guidance from the library media specialist and the classroom teacher should concentrate on assisting inquiry by providing tools, examples, and encouragement to the student to sift and sort new thoughts and insights—to manage reflection. This process often will include a recurring cycle of Question—Organize—Categorize (QOC).

A library media specialist/classroom teacher collaborative team have struggled with these ideas over recent years. Their experience has resulted in identification of elements of reflection necessary for effective pre-search activities for the elementary school student. In tandem, just as they conduct their inquiry classes, these two educators have written the following reflection on their QOC method.

The Answers Are in the Questions!

Due to their age and experiences, students in grades kindergarten through grade three have a limited amount of prior knowledge of any given topic. Therefore, teachers at one elementary school have begun experimenting with the placement of the questioning phase of the research process. They have found that it may need to be shifted in order to maximize children's learning and overall understanding of a topic. While questioning is still a vital part of the inquiry process, young children often need to build background about their topic before they engage in extensive question writing.

Teachers provide the impetus for inquiry by introducing broad topics, building conceptual understanding, and encouraging individual exploration of personal topics of inquiry. Once the students actively engage in inquiry, they need time

to gather and read resources on their topics to build their personal foundations.

Helping children identify what is critical information about the topic becomes the most important aspect of a successful inquiry for young children. Because everything is new and exciting, direct instruction on how to sift through all their factoids ensures that students will begin to understand what information is relevant versus what information is trivial. It is easy to think that learning to find facts is the most important stage in development, but the teachers in this article are discovering it is the least important part of all!

The following entries form a travelogue of sorts from an elementary teacher and a library media specialist who have been journeying on what they call "The Road To Research (RTR)." The entries are meant to shed light on the middle portion of the inquiry process which is particularly treacherous in the lower elementary level, but well worth the effort!

Kym—Get Your Motor Runnin'

Ten years ago when I started my first job as a media specialist, I embarked on a journey of helping children learn how to find answers to their information questions. During the course of the journey, we made many discoveries together, and the path we have been forging has taken many jogs and twists. However, one thing has remained constant: Children love to research. Truly, I have not run across a child in elementary school who was turned off by inquiry. It speaks to their natural curiosities, and teachers only need to exploit these tendencies to evoke learning rich in problem solving and higher-level thinking. The research model we currently use most closely resembles Virginia Rankin's inquiry process as described in *The Thoughtful Researcher*, but it is an eclectic collection of several inquiry models. I titled our variation "The Road To Research," which has enabled the development of a child-friendly analogy of the inquiry cycle. One of the most positive things to come out of this long journey is the realization that there is no one correct research model, and encouraging teachers to tweak any

Kym Kramer is school library media specialist and Connie Largent is a third grade teacher at Fishback Creek Public Academy in Pike Township Schools of Indianapolis. This article is based on a presentation by this collaborative teaching team at the American Library Association national conference in Orlando in 2004. E-mail: kkramer@ pike.k12.in.us or clargent@ pike.k12.in.us

model to fit their students' and their style has had a tremendous effect on the students' success. That success also correlates directly to how often teachers plan to incorporate inquiry projects during the school year, which we have found is critical to the internalization process for inquiry.

For the past seven years I have been lucky enough to be at a school with teachers who embrace activities requiring children to do more than fill in a blank or bubble on a test. These teachers are interested in engaging their students in multiple inquiry projects each year and have been willing to collaborate with me. This has translated into the use of a single research model, as well as the creation of a continuum of information literacy skills that begin developing in kindergarten and first grade. During our time at this school, we have been using The Road To Research and, by the end of the fifth grade, the majority of the students have completed the inquiry cycle four to six times.

Connie—Head Out on the Highway

For four years now, I have been engaged in different student inquiry projects in collaboration with my school's library media specialist, Kym Kramer. In one of our frequent planning sessions, she brought to my attention a student inquiry process she calls "The Road to Research." It fit nicely with the curriculum we planned to teach. In the world of education, standards have always driven curriculum. But now, in the world of No Child Left Behind, standards are attached with high stakes and punitive repercussions. Unfortunately, it is our children's ability to think for themselves and the questioning of our personal educational philosophies that are at stake. Using inquiry with our students would allow us to meet the outside demands without compromising what we know is good educational practice.

I first started implementing The Road To Research in a multi-age classroom with second and third grade students. In the state of Indiana, more and more standards were being added to our social studies, science, and health content areas. When they were taught through the traditional means of isolation and merely experienced through textbooks, students were not engaged, which also meant they were not truly learning.

However, with the introduction of the inquiry project to our curriculum of human body systems, our students were able to grasp some difficult concepts. I was immediately intrigued, excited, and engaged—better yet, so were my students, which translated to an increase in understanding. As an educator, this model is a perfect answer to "emotionally hooking" students with a broad knowledge platform and then allowing them to make a personal investment and take ownership of their work by allowing them to choose a topic related to the broader concept in which they are particularly interested in learning more. Inquiry also lends itself to being able to integrate content subjects such as science, social studies, and health with core skills in language arts and math. Research supports this as a highly effective way of teaching curriculum. Our first foray into inquiry as a team was a hit.

Kym—Lookin' for Adventure

For the better part of two years, Connie and I comfortably sailed along creating inquiry project after inquiry project. We basked in the children's successes and in their parents' adoration. We really felt we were on to something, and other teachers joined in and did collaborative inquiry projects, too. As everyone has heard: "Inquiring minds want to know!" I continued to think that this step needed tweaking or that stage needed changing to make inquiry more accessible to children. These questions led me on a quest for answers for myself. I read about many different inquiry models, attended workshops, poked and prodded, and "guinea pigged" my latest notions. But mostly, I simply thought a lot. Just like my students, I was discovering that the thinking part of the inquiry process is often the stage we cut. It simply doesn't seem to fit with a school timeline (i. e., it's time consuming and hard to quantify). Unfortunately, these types of activities are what are being taken out of classrooms in order to leave time for more "advanced skills" like how to correctly bubble the right answer for the test so the school can make acceptable yearly progress!

Connie—We're Going To Make It Happen

Helping children build a background for the topic being studied has become fairly easy. Educators at the lower elementary level understand that in order to engage their students they must help them experience broad curricular topics such as animals or communities in numerous ways. These often include introducing and reading print resources, viewing videos, going on field trips, doing experiments, or working with models, as well as discussing and helping children refine their core knowledge of the subject.

Setting the foundation soundly pays dividends when establishing individual inquiries on the broader topic later. It is important to help children move past this level, though, to do something with their learning. Unfortunately many teachers stop at this low level. They've covered the material, but as brain researcher Pat Wolfe said in a workshop, "If you are just going to cover the material, you might as well just dig a hole and throw the kid in it!" In other words, covering topics isn't enough. Children must be given the time and support to muddle through topics, and teachers must encourage and value this step—a message that must be conveyed to parents as well!

These early experiences help children build connections with existing learning. When children put the new learning into context with their existing knowledge base, gaps often surface if adequate time is given to this foundation building. For early elementary, this translates into an extended "pre-search" step that usually takes two to three weeks prior to individual inquiry projects.

Kym—Forging a New Trail

Ultimately what we discovered is that many of the inquiry models have a questioning stage at the beginning to jump-start the children's thinking. Theoretically this is correct; teachers must engage students at the beginning of the study. However, what we found was that at the elementary level, particularly in grades K-3, this initial foundation building is not always the perfect time to have students develop their questions for their personal inquiries. They often do not have a clear understanding of the depth and breadth of the broader topic. Quite simply, children often don't know what they don't know! They don't know what to ask, and they definitely don't know what is important to know when they get done with their study. Thus, came the development of QOC—a new take on an old step.

Once the topical foundation is sufficiently strong, children are able to move forward in the inquiry process. Our redesigned step teaches children how to sift through the information they are learning and extract the information that forms the core of a topic—the "critical" information. We've begun calling this stage "QOC", which stands for Question, Organize, and Categorize. This acronym also makes it very easy for children to remember as it's fun to mimic a duck and say, "QOC, QOC, QOC"! Children are encouraged to write any questions they have about their topic. At this point, some children have already discovered answers to some questions, but we encourage them to focus just on the questions—writing all that come to mind. Following are two models of ways to help children learn to sift through these questions and get themselves organized to find their answers. Also included are sample question evolutions that illustrate the students' growth and understanding of their topics.

Connie—Recording the Mileage

Once the phase of QOC evolved last year and became a permanent step in The Road To Research, I started tweaking this part so that this new addition would make an easy and natural transition for my classroom of diverse learners. After students chose their topics, gathered their resources, and started reading, Kym and I wanted a way for all students to begin recording any and all of the questions they had. Something as simple as Post-It Notes became my answer as well as a very useful tool in many ways.

By having students write out their questions onto Post-It Notes®, I could grasp how much or how little my students really knew and understood about their topic. It was a great way to pinpoint specific gaps or note solid foundations in their knowledge base. It enabled me to begin to know where they may need additional support. Often, the need was in the comprehension of the reading materials. An example of this would be second graders, Andrew and Nick. As a whole class, I was teaching the state standards relating to different cultures. During their self-chosen study of the Japanese culture, they were interested in the category of holidays. As adults, we recognized that often holidays are tied closely to religion, which is a much more complex category. We saw the boys answering their basic questions such as "What holidays are celebrated in Japan?" with short answers that led to additional, more complex questions. It required much adult intervention to help the boys "fill in the gaps" and build a basic understanding of the category. Luckily, the RTR allows for many "check points" that enable the teacher to catch comprehension holes before students proceed.

The students' Post-It® Notes served as a tangible organizational tool as well. Once they had all of their questions written out, students would sort their questions based upon similar categories. This is a great step for students to physically manipulate and organize the Post-It® Notes to see the category formation. For some, higher-level thinking was forced because they realized some of their questions could fit into more than one category. A conscious and purposeful decision had to be made regarding in which category they would place their question(s). They also discovered that some questions didn't fit at all and were therefore removed from the pool. This physical movement of sticky notes helped further cement their understanding of their topic, as well as create the beginning stages of what information is "critical."

Finally, the Post-It® Notes helped my students seek some balance in their project, if needed. Some students clearly saw they had numerous questions about one category in their topic versus having few questions for another category. Depending on the subject of focus, they would be able to stretch their curiosity to greater lengths than they had imagined by "digging deeper" into these other categories and provoking themselves with other questions, once again elevating critical thinking. Conversely, they sometimes discovered if they had only one or two questions, perhaps they didn't really have a "category" by our definition of the word. Our guidelines were that there must be several facts that go together to answer all the questions for a category. Therefore, if there were just one or two questions, it was likely the category was either too narrow or their questions fit under an umbrella of another category. For example, let's go back to second graders, Andrew and Nick. It was clear that several of their questions, such as What do their homes look like?, What do they use to build their houses?, How big are their houses?, and Do they live in neighborhoods?, naturally created the category of "Shelter." However, they had two more questions, and in their minds these two questions made a new category of "Furniture:" What do they sleep on? What do they have inside their homes? Clearly, these two questions formed too narrow a category and instead could be linked easily back to the category of shelter. The deliberate teaching of how to broaden and narrow categories of information seems to produce students who can later focus their research more easily.

Kym—The Scenic Route

Recently a second grade teacher took this questioning, sorting, and sifting step in another direction. She found that early in the school year her second grade students were having difficulty just identifying the critical questions let alone the critical categories for the topic of biography. As topics go, people's biographies are fairly concrete and can be linked directly to children's own experiences by first having them think about the stages of their own history. However, making the leap to another person proved difficult. Instead of having children work in partners or small groups as is the case in Connie's projects, Mrs. Bacon decided to do a whole group language experience lesson. As a whole class, the students brainstormed the questions they would need to answer about any famous person. They based the questions on the foundations they built by writing their own autobiographies, as well as on a biography project earlier in the trimester. These questions included things such as When was my person born?, What was my person's childhood like?, Were there events during childhood that caused my person to become the person s/he turned into?, and Why is my person famous? This foundation allowed them to come up with approximately twenty "critical" questions. With the questions in hand, they were able to cut apart and sort the questions into three categories: Childhood, Adult Life, and Famous. They understood that they should group questions, and together

the group equaled a category. It also helped to tie this type of thinking back to math activities that require sorting. By this point in their school career, most students have developmentally mastered sorting: sort by shape, color, size, etc. We transferred the thinking to sorting questions that would add up to a "chunk" of knowledge in a particular area of the subject. Mrs. Bacon's ultimate objective was to help her students discover that inquiry questions fit together to form distinct categories of information about the topic being studied.

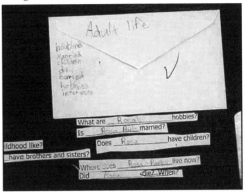

Connie—Caution: Dead End Ahead!

Additionally, at the QOC stage of The Road To Research, students are getting inundated with a large amount of information about their topic. Before my students really get into this stage, together we discuss in great detail that "cool" information does not deem it critical information, or what I like to quote to my students, "Cool does not mean critical!" Some information they can comprehend and some they simply cannot. This is where gaps begin to form when they are trying to bridge together all of their information.

Second and third grade students often come across information they simply find fascinating whether they understand it or not. This fascination feeds into their emotions and therefore they feel it necessary and, at times, become adamant that this piece of information must be a part of their research. Because they have been emotionally hooked by this fact, it is often difficult for students to let it go. For example, in a recent inquiry project on our local community, a group of four third graders were studying several war memorials. While searching on the Internet, they found and printed several pages listing all the Indiana soldiers who gave their lives in the Korean War. The students were thrilled with what they considered to be a "goldmine" of information. Rather than dismiss their find as irrelevant, I allowed them to continue working until they decided late in the project that the names were not critical.

Often, as students' research projects come to

fruition, they are able to step back and determine that their "cool fact" is a much better fit in a Jeopardy tournament than in their final project.

Kym—Mile Marker 1029

Our own inquiry has led us to believe that students who experience inquiry on a regular basis gradually begin to see that just because information is written down or documented in some way doesn't necessarily mean it is critical to their inquiry project. For most of our students, this skill continues to be fine-tuned throughout elementary school, and therefore we make it our mission to help children hone this portion of the process before they go on to middle school.

The unfortunate fact is that many teachers mistakenly assume that children know how to research, so rather than setting up projects collaboratively with their media specialists, they simply descend on the library media center and expect the children to be sufficiently capable of narrowing their topic, identifying their questions, and researching the answers. Little thought (and often no direct instruction) is given to whether the questions are even the correct ones to ask!

Kym—The Road Less Traveled

In addition to helping students sift and sort their questions, we also attempt to help them begin to synthesize their inquiry with facts of which they are already aware. We discuss things that our new learning might be related to in our brains. We encourage all of our students to try to synthesize after introducing this skill in second grade, but we go so far as to push our more ad-vanced students to reach this level sometime during third grade. We've found it is a very effective way to help children learn how to put information into their own words and steer farther away from plagiarizing material. By attaching their own knowledge, they are in effect creating original thought, which is what we are ultimately striving to reach! An example of this would be the third grade student who was studying an animal. Once she discovered the speed the animal could run, which was 25 mph, she proceeded to compare that to the speed a car can travel in a school zone. Obviously, we were very pleased with this synthesis, and after sharing with the class, many other students were able to begin synthesizing for themselves.

Kym and Connie—The Road Is Long

Inquiry with students takes tenacity, patience, and most importantly, curious minds on the parts of all involved. While there are plateaus and comfortable resting points along the journey, it's best embarked upon with the knowledge that it is a never-ending quest. The knowledge that teaching children to delve for answers to their questions, and helping them feel the sense of accomplishment when the thirst for knowledge is quenched is well worth any bumps along the way. Ultimately, inquiry allows children the freedom to become thinkers and doers rather than drones. It fits our school motto perfectly: Explorers of Today, Leaders of Tomorrow!

Bibliography
Rankin, Virgina. *The Thoughtful Researcher: Teaching the Research Process to Middle School Students*. Englewood, CO: Libraries Unlimited, 1999. ✋

Questioning Revisited

by Daniel Callison

The first key word defined for this regular column in *School Library Media Activities Monthly* was "Questioning." That was nine years ago in February 1997. Since then, additional ideas and concepts concerning the importance of guided, modeled, and free student questioning that drive the inquiry process have been raised. Some of these ideas are explored in this revisit of the very important element that triggers inquiry in each of us as teachers or students—asking meaningful questions.

Probably the most frequently stated reason for using a school library media center, besides finding a good book, is to "find an answer." Both of these reasons are important, but I want you to think about the idea that the library media center is the best place for students to raise ques-tions. Questioning is the first element of information inquiry. Questioning seeds all other pro-cesses. Without questions, the inquiry cycle stops, and learn-ing regresses to read and recite without any importance given to relevance and meaning.

The Art of Questioning

Dennis Palmer Wolf offered insights on how teachers in-fluence inquiry through their questioning behavior (1987). His comments were delivered to the College Board in Santa Cruz, Cal-ifornia, and drawn from Devel-opmental Theorist Erik Erikson (1975). Wolf said,

> "The very way in which teachers ask questions can determine, rather than build, a shared spirit of investiga-tion. First, teachers tend to monopolize the right to ques-tion—rarely do more than procedural questions come from students. Second, the question-driven exchanges that occur in classrooms almost uniformly take place between teachers and students. More-over, classroom questioning can be exclusive. It can easily become the private preserve of the few—the bright, the male, the English-speaking" (Wolf 1987, 2).

Wolf paraphrases a common Chinese proverb: "Ask a man a question and he may inquire for a moment or perhaps a day; teach a man to question [en-courage him, guide him, reward him, allow him ownership of more questions, give him the intellectual freedom to continue questioning] and he will prac-tice inquiry for life." Question-ing through inquiry becomes the very foundation of "lifelong learning" (Wolf 1987).

Types of Questions

Questions can be limited to recall of factual responses. Ques-tions also may involve processes or critical thinking such as:

- How are these alike or dif-ferent?
- Which is best and why?
- Which path do we take? Why?
- What are the advantages and disadvantages?

Questions may stimulate imagination and creative think-ing shown by the following ex-amples:

- What if you could change things?
- What will things be like in the future?
- What is your plan for action?

Daniel Callison, Ed.D., is a Professor at Indiana University School of Library and Information Science and Executive Associate Dean at Indianapolis; 755 W. Michigan Street; Indianapolis, IN 46212. Email: callison@iupui.edu; http://www.slis.iupui.edu

The Foundation for Critical Thinking describes various questions in the following manner:

- *Questions of Relevance* discriminate what does and what does not bear on an original question.
- *Questions of Accuracy* force evaluation and testing for truth and correctness.
- *Questions of Precision* lead to details and the specifics.
- *Questions of Consistency* examine for contradictions.
- *Questions of Logic* consider the synthesis of the whole and ask if conclusions make sense.
- *Questions of Interpretation* examine the organization and meaning derived from information.
- *Questions of Assumption* examine from several different perspectives what may be taken for granted.
- *Questions of Implication* test possible interpretations and challenge where evidence and arguments may be taking the investigation and may raise the value of the impact of the work. Are these questions worthwhile? Do these answers cause more harm than good?
- *Questions of Point of View* force consideration of other relevant perceptions, opinions, and evidence.
- *Questions of Depth* take the investigation under the surface level evidence and deal with hidden complexities.
- *Questions of Purpose* define the task and keep the investigation on target.
- *Questions of Information* force examination of the sources of information and the quality of the information

selected or rejected (http://www.criticalthinking.org).

To Wonder, To Learn

Jamie McKenzie, former school administrator and current international lecturer on educational technology innovations and other actions to improve student learning, draws his reader's attention to the questioning process by comparing it to yeast (2005). Questioning is to thinking as yeast is to bread-making. Unleavened bread is flat, hard, and unyielding. Unleavened thinking is uninspired. Questioning is what converts the stuff of thinking into something of value, acting as leaven to transform matter into meaning.

McKenzie often models the questioning process to allow the student's path for exploring information to become more challenging. Questions that will make the typical biographical assignment more personal and will lead to more insights about both the personality and the student writer push the extreme. Examples of some of these types of questions are as follows:

- In what ways was this person's life remarkable, despicable, admirable?
- What are several important lessons you or any other young person might learn from the way this person lived?

- An older person or mentor is often very important in shaping the lives of other people by providing guidance and encouragement. To what extent was this true of the personality you are exploring?
- Did this person make any major mistakes or bad decisions? If so, what were they and how would you have chosen and acted differently (McKenzie 2005)?

McKenzie also has rounded up one of the most diverse collections of different kinds of questions. A sample from his examples, some modified for sake of space, helps us see how much McKenzie's questioning process can enrich any standard school curriculum:

- *Clarification Questions:* How did they gather their data? Was it a reliable and valid process?
- *Sorting and Sifting Questions:* Which parts of the information gathered through the survey are worth keeping?
- *Elaborating Questions:* How could I take this further? What is the logical next step?
- *Planning Questions:* What have other groups before us done to address these issues?
- *Strategic Questions:* How can I best approach this next step? What resources do I have at hand and what others do I need to acquire?
- *Unanswerable Questions:* How can I maintain my

ideal when there is so much wrong with the world and so many greedy, evil people? What is the perfect solution that will bring world peace?

- *Irreverent Questions:* What can we do to change things? What social action can we take? Can we really trust the government?
- *Divergent Questions:* Beyond the information gathered so far, what else do we need in order to make our argument convincing (McKenzie 2005)?

McKenzie encourages educators to move from trivial questions to essential questions in order to engage students in learning that can be more authentic and meaningful. Traits of these recommended essential questions include the following:

- Probes a matter of considerable importance (relative to the learner's ability, environment, and needs);
- Moves the learner beyond mere understanding and toward action to solve a problem;
- The question cannot be addressed with a simple yes or no;
- The question endures and shifts or even turns and leads to larger questions as the inquiry progresses;
- The question is very likely one that cannot be answered completely; and
- The question creates frustration and mystery, but maintains the interest of the inquirer (McKenzie 2005).

Testing Your Research Questions

The Canadian instructional team of Koechlin and Zwann have developed a rubric to test the value of typical research questions raised by students. Components of this rubric are as follows:

- *Focus:* Does your question help to focus your research? At the highest level, focus targets a defined investigation and serves to examine all relevant perspectives.
- *Interest:* Are you excited about your question? Interest can inspire further investigation and more questions, and keep the student on task in difficult and confusing events in the inquiry process.
- *Knowledge:* Will your question help you learn? This can be a strong motivator as well as meet academic standards.
- *Processing:* Will your question help you understand your topic better? At the highest level, the question should be challenging and require analysis and synthesis to apply the information gained (Koechlin and Zwann 2001).

Questioning as Scientist and Information Scientist

Students who are guided by the scientific method will be problem-identifiers as well as problem-solvers (Harada 2003). Both the student scientist and the student information scientist will apply the systematic steps of the scientific method to their project. The student scientist will test his research question or hypothesis, and ask questions such as:

- What are the key research questions?
- What is the best method to test my hypothesis?
- What are the conclusions that I can infer?
- What audience needs do I address with my conclusions?

The student information scientist can experiment with information to see if it is convincing, entertaining, and/or understandable for the intended audience. The student information scientist needs space to draft, edit, and rehearse, as well as receive criticism on information selected.

The student information scientist can test the information and address questions such as:

- Is this project meaningful and does it meet a need or interest? Have I identified an important question or information need that merits my time and the time of others for me to explore possible answers?
- Are there likely to be useful sources that can be accessed and understood by me?
- Have I read widely and in the most relevant literature to inform myself for this project? Has this experience generated additional relevant questions, names, events, and other terms that will help in my information search?
- Have I found the most credible and authoritative information possible? If necessary, is this the most recent information available?
- Is my use of information to support my ideas convincing, understandable, and meaningful for the audience I am to address or for my own personal satisfaction?
- What information search paths and sources were most useful and perhaps likely for me to use again in similar

information-need situations?

- What information (book, website, magazine, person) was so important that it inspired me or convinced me I was learning and gaining excitement about what I would be able to report to others?
- What information have I found in this process that I enjoyed enough to return to for reading pleasure in the future?
- What information sources did I discover that were least useful and not authoritative enough for me to return to in the future for any reason?
- In what effective manner might I present or display the message I want to convey from my inquiry experience?

Brainstorm Questions

Students often need help and validation in development of questions. Exploring possible questions related to several typical student research topics can help students understand that it is possible to "test" questions with these criteria in mind:

- *High interest to themselves and their peers:* Is this something with which I really want to spend time and is relevant to what others are exploring as well?
- *Potential for resource support:* Are resources available within the time and location allotted for the project? Will others help me acquire special resources if necessary?
- *Age and ability level:* Does this topic and related questions meet my own level of understanding? Does it challenge me to move to the next level of exploration so that I

will really learn not only new facts, but also new investigative techniques as well?

Further, students may work in groups as well as with the guidance of the instructional media specialist and other teachers to raise issues to explore from the following question stems:

- *Which one (or more)?* Questions that force an informed choice. Which is the best or most recommended cure? What event influenced the final outcome the most? What five inventions during the past 100 years have changed the most how you live today?
- *Who?* Questions that ask who was "most or least" in given situations. Who was the President that promoted civil rights most effectively? (Hint: It was probably not Mr. Lincoln.) What three people in American history have most influenced the sort of job you now hold or may hold in the future?
- *How?* Questions are raised to address action. How might we address the problem of wasting water in our community? What are the best or most specific steps, and how should we take them?
- *What if?* Questions that pose a possible different path and raise different consequences. What if the authors of the United States Constitution had decided to abolish slavery?
- *When?* What are the milestone events leading to a cure for polio? Which of these events were by accident, and which were according to scientific methods? When did the Civil War

actually start? Was it started because of policy or because of armed conflict; when did one lead to the other?

- *Should?* Questions that often pose moral debate. Should we allow humans to be cloned? When should we go to war, and when should we not?
- *Why?* Perhaps the first and last stem for all inquiry questions and often the most difficult to answer. Asking why, however, often leads to questions of real value.

References

Erickson, E. "Gatekeeping and the Melting Pot." *Harvard Educational Review* 45, no.1 (1975): 40-77.

Foundation for Critical Thinking. *The Role of Questions – The Critical Thinking Community.* http://www.criticalthinking.org (accessed August 15, 2005).

Harada, V. "Empowered Learning." In *Curriculum Connections through the Library,* edited by Barbara Stripling and Sandra Hughes-Hassell, 41-64. Libraries Unlimited, 2003.

Koechlin, C., and S. Zwaan. *Info Tasks for Successful Learning.* Pembroke, 2001.

McKenzie, J. *Learning to Question, to Wonder, to Learn.* FNO Press, 2005.

Wolf, D. P. "The Art of Questioning." *Academic Connections* (Winter 1987): 1-7.

For Further Reading and Viewing

Barell, J. *Developing More Curious Minds.* Association for Curriculum Supervision and Development, 2003.

Dontonio, M., and P. C. Beisenherz. *Learning to Question, Questioning to Learn.* Allyn & Bacon, 2000.

Freedman, R. L. H. *Open-ended Questioning.* Addison Wesley, 1993.

How to Improve Your Questioning Techniques. Video. Association for Supervision and Curriculum Development, 1998. ✋

Red Light, Green Light:
GUIDING QUESTIONS

Formulating good questions for research is an essential step in the research process. Students need modeling and practice to become good at asking questions that will help them pursue new information, ideas, and directions. One way to begin this process is to think of questions as Red Light and Green Light Questions, a concept that can be introduced and modeled in primary grades and used throughout middle school.

To evaluate a question and to identify if it is a Red Light or a Green Light Question, ask the following:

- Does your question lead you to more information?
- Are you asking "why" or "what if"?
- Does your question make you investigate further?
- Does your question make you think of more ideas?

If the answer is "yes," then it is a Green Light Question!

- Does your question lead to a dead end?
- Does your question lead to only one answer?
- Does your question lead to only a "yes" or "no" answer?
- Does your question keep you from thinking about more ideas?

If the answer is "yes," then it is a Red Light Question!

Try these as examples:

How have Siberian tigers become endangered?
(Green Light Question)
Are Siberian tigers endangered?
(Red Light Question)

How are tarantulas different than other creatures?
(Green Light Question)
Is a tarantula an insect?
(Red Light Question)

What events could have influenced Lincoln's words for the Gettysburg Address?
(Green Light Question)
When did Lincoln write the Gettysburg Address?
(Red Light Question)

For Younger Students:

Create a graphic on tongue depressors with a red light on one side and a green light on the other. Have students display the appropriate side to identify examples of Red Light and Green Light Questions and discuss why. Do this exercise regularly to help students understand the difference.

For Older Students:

Display examples of questions on posters with a graphic of a Green Light or a Red Light with examples of questions listed under each. Revisit it whenever students are identifying or revising their guiding questions.

Print Resources:

Lincoln Public Schools Library Media Services. *Guide to Integrated Information Literacy Skills.* Lincoln: LPS, 2003.
McKenzie, J. "Framing Essential Questions." *From Now On* 6, no. 1 (1996). http://fno.org/sept96/questions.html
Milam, P. "The Power of Reflection in the Research Process." *School Library Media Activities Monthly* 21, no. 6 (February 2005): 26-29.
Wiggins, Grant. *Understanding by Design.* ASCD, 1998.

Websites:

Connecting Youth to a Brighter Future: The Art of Asking Good Questions. http://www.youthlearn.org/learning/teaching/questions.asp
Filling the Toolbox: Classroom Strategies to Engender Student Questioning (From Now On, The Educational Technology Journal). http://www.fno.org/toolbox.html
Jamie McKenzie: The Question Mark. http://questioning.org/
Kentucky Prism Partnership for Reform Initiative in Science and Mathematics. http://www.murraystate.edu/prism/kyprism/openrp1.htm
University of Delaware Center for Teaching Effectiveness. http://cte.udel.edu/TAbook/question.html

Assessing Questions

Formulating good questions for research is an essential step in the research process. Students need modeling and practice to become good at asking questions that will help them pursue new information, ideas and directions. One way to begin this process is to help them think of questions as Red Light and Green Light questions, a concept that can be introduced and modeled in primary grades and used throughout middle school.

Below is a simple guide that students, library media specialists, and classroom teachers can use to assess questions. (See the lesson plan "You Say It's Your Birthday" in this issue, pages17-19, and "Red Light Green Light Guiding Questions," *SLMAM*, October 2005: 25). For younger students create a graphic on tongue depressors with a red light on one side and a green light on the other. Have students display the appropriate side to identify examples provided of Red Light and Green Light questions and later for their own.

Do you have Red Light Questions?

Does your question lead to only one answer?	Yes	No
Does your question lead to only "yes" and "no" answers?	Yes	No
Does your question keep you from thinking about more ideas?	Yes	No

If the answers are "yes," it is a Red Light Question!

Which questions do you have?

Green Light Questions are questions that lead to more information and more investigation.

Red Light Questions are questions that lead to one answer and do not require further investigation.

Do you have Green Light Questions?

Does your question lead you to more information?	Yes	No
Are you asking "why" or "what if"?	Yes	No
Does your question make you investigate further?	Yes	No
Does your question make you think of more ideas?	Yes	No

If the answers are "yes," it is a Green Light Question!

Primary Sources and Inquiry Learning

by Marjorie L. Pappas

Scenario

Middle school students are studying Western Expansion beyond the existing United States in the mid-19th century with a focus on the Oregon Trail. They started their studies with a brainstorming session about the travelers using the Oregon Trail. Some of their questions included the following:

- How did they travel? What types of transportation did they use?
- Where were they going?
- What did they pack to take with them?

Their teacher suggested they needed more information before they could decide on a focus for their research. Using the background information section of the Western Expansion pathfinder developed by the library media specialist, they spent a day in the library media center reading from various general sources.

When they came back together to continue their brainstorming session, they discovered they had more questions:

- What routes did they travel? What maps did they use as a guide?
- How long did this journey take?
- How did they get food during the trip?
- What dangers did they encounter in their travels?

Eventually, they focused on three essential questions:

- How did these travelers plan for the journey?
- How did the travelers on the Oregon Trail survive the journey?
- How did the journey change their lives?

Their teacher divided them into several small groups based on the specific questions that interested them. The library media specialist suggested they use primary sources, e.g., maps used by the travelers, diaries or journals written by the travelers, newspapers from that time period, and pictures (photographs, drawings, etc.). She directed them to the section on their pathfinder that included primary source resources.

One group began to explore

Marjorie L. Pappas, Ph.D., is a writer, consultant, and virtual professor from Danville, KY. Email: mlpappas@adelphia.net

The Oregon Trail website which included a Trail Archive with entries from diaries and memoirs written by people who actually traveled the trail. One such diary was written by Amelia Stewart Knight who departed from Iowa in early April 1853, and reached the Oregon territory in September. The follow entries were part of her diary:

Saturday, April 9th, 1853—STARTED FROM HOME about 11 o'clock and traveled 8 miles and camped in an old house; night cold and frosty.

Wednesday, May 4th—Weather fair; travel 3 miles today, passed Kanesville and camp in a lane, not far from the Missouri River, and wait our turn to cross. No feed for the stock, have to buy flour at 3 per hundred to feed them.

Thursday, June 2nd—It has cleared off pleasant after the rain and all hands seem bright and cheerful again. We are going along the same old gait. Evening—traveled 27 miles today. Passed Court House Rock and Chimney Rock, both situated on the lower side of the river, and have been in sight for several days. We have camped opposite Chimney Rock.

Wednesday, June 29th—Cold and cloudy. The wagons are all crowded up to the ferry waiting with impatience to cross. There are 30 or more to

cross before us. Have to cross one at a time. Have to pay 8 dollars for a wagon; 1 dollar for a horse or cow. We swim all our stock. Evening—We crossed the river about three o'clock then traveled 10 miles and camp close to Slate Creek. It is cold enough to sit by the fire.

Thursday, August 25th—We will remain in camp today to wash, and rest the cattle. It is 18 miles to the next water. Cotton wood and willows to burn. We will start this evening and travel a few miles after dark. It is too hot and dusty to travel in the heat of the day. Camped about nine o'clock in the dry prairie (http://www.isu.edu/%7Etrinmich/00.n.trailarchive.html).

After reading parts of Knight's diary, students discussed and reflected using the following prompts:

- What can you infer from these diary entries that relates to your essential question?
- What predictions can you make about the dangers they will encounter along the trail?
- What "I wonder…" questions do these entries suggest to you?

Students continued to gather and evaluate information to answer their essential questions using note-taking organizers that encourage reflection. They used timelines to organize their information. Their next step was to decide on a format to communicate this new knowledge. Their teacher gave them a variety of formats from which to choose, and both the library media specialist and teacher worked with students to develop criteria to assess these final products. Students also engaged in both peer and self-assessment of their products.

What Is Inquiry Learning?

Inquiry learning puts students in the active role of investigators. If the content area is science, they become scientists; if the area is social science, they become historians. Questioning, authentic and active learning, and interactivity are a few of the characteristics of inquiry learning that put the teacher and library media specialist in the role of coaches while students are engaged in collaborative research. Teachers may establish the thematic parameters and broad essential questions to reflect standards and the curriculum, but students can question, brainstorm, and develop ownership in the investigation. "Inquiry learning is a dynamic process that uses questioning to actively involve students in their own learning" (Harada and Yoshina 2004, 11). Essential questions, an important element of inquiry learning, fuel curiosity, wondering, and critical thinking.

In the opening scenario, students are engaged in an inquiry learning experience. They develop the questions that will frame their research. They work in small groups and interact with peers and teachers (coaches) as they gather information and construct new understandings from that information. This learning experience is authentic because students are engaged in research in a manner similar to that of a historian. Students gather information that becomes evidence to enable a response to their essential question(s). Students engage in critical thinking as they wonder, investigate, construct new knowledge, express that knowledge, and reflect (Harada 2003, 10-17).

The disciplines of science and mathematics focus on the natural world and the focus of these researchers is to establish truths. Social scientists and historians, on the other hand, examine "human interaction with the world and other humans" (Stripling 2003, 24-25). When students assume the roles of social scientist and historian, their focus is on questions like "why do events occur?" or "what are the consequences of…?" Social scientists and historians often use primary sources as evidence in their research.

Context is, therefore, an important consideration when students gather information from primary sources. It can help students develop an understanding that various perspectives typically frame events. Context and resulting perspectives are not always easy to discern as events are actually occurring because personal biases get in the way, but looking backwards into history tends to neutralize those biases and enables a more neutral investigation. For example, the news media can put a slant on the reporting of an event today from either the conservative or liberal perspective. As consumers of the news, we read those accounts through the lens of our political perspectives because we are involved in these events. However, looking back into the events of history, we typically do not have the political biases of people in that time period, so we view the news accounts from a more objective perspective.

Context, or the "big picture," is important in our understanding of historical times. Teachers and the library media specialist can help students develop that context by suggesting resources to provide opportunities for discussion and reflection. For example, today we understand the perspective of Na-tive Americans who regarded the settlers as invaders of their land while the settlers living in that time period tended to regard the Native Americans as less civilized people who were impeding their ability to use the land for farming and raising cattle. Students need an understanding of these differing points of view through the use of context.

What Are Primary Sources?

Primary sources take different forms and formats, but were all created when the historical events actually occurred or shortly thereafter through the memories of people who lived during the events. Primary sources include newspapers, maps, diaries, journals, photographs, birth certificates, ship manifests, letters, speeches, memoirs, government documents, moving pictures, audio recordings, interviews, artifacts, etc. These documents and media depict historical events as the events actually occurred and, thus, are evidence for those historians who seek to tell the story of historical events. Typically, students are exposed to secondary sources such as textbooks which are written by authors who have interpreted information from primary sources. The value of using primary sources as part of the learning, therefore, is to provide opportunities for students to reach their own conclusions about historical events rather than view events through the writings of secondary source authors.

Consequently, it is important for students to learn to evaluate primary sources for accuracy, bias, authority, purpose, and origin of the document. The Web provides exciting opportunities today that did not exist even a few years ago for students to access primary sources because these documents were frequently buried in libraries (public and private), depositories, museums, and government agencies, or were the private property of people who stored the documents in their homes. Many of these documents are now being digitized and can be found within collections on the Web. However, students need to learn that not all documents described as primary sources are authentic so they should always apply evaluation criteria before accepting the information.

One of the most extensive collections of primary sources is the Library of Congress through the American Memory Project. States, too, are now developing their own memory projects and offering the digitized versions of documents on state virtual libraries. Public and specialized libraries are also developing digital collection of the works of various historical figures. The letters, speeches, and other documents of our presidents are rapidly becoming available on presidential websites as part of the collections within presidential libraries.

Finding Primary Source Documents

Primary source documents are now available on an expanding number of state digital libraries. For example, Kentucky, Indiana, Ohio, and Georgia all have digital collections that are freely available to users without the limitation of password access. Teachers and library media specialists can examine these websites for documents to support their curriculum. Many of these sites include content that is not state specific, and, thus, useful within regions and sometimes throughout the U. S. For example, *Kentucky Virtual Library* includes primary sources about Abraham Lincoln. *INFOhio*, Ohio's virtual library for K-12 schools, includes a digital collection of documents from the Underground Railroad and abolition. *INSPIRE*, Indiana's virtual library, includes cemetery records, obituary lists, and naturalization records. Historical societies have also begun to digitize some of their genealogical records. One of the largest of these collections has been digitized by historical societies in Utah, but those records are private and require a fee to access.

One of the most efficient strategies to use when searching primary source documents is to search under the name of the specific document. For example, when searching for the Emancipation Proclamation or Lincoln's Gettysburg Address, enter the title. Some library websites, both public and academic, include lists of historical resources (*RUSA History Section*: http://www.lib.washington.edu/subject/History/RUSA/).

Newspapers are now available on the Web, and some of the more prominent newspapers have begun to digitize their back issues. A fee may be involved, but it would still be worth checking on newspapers in larger cities to see if past issues are available.

Conclusion

Primary sources can be a fascinating medium for studying history. Often these documents give us a personalized view of historical events that is much more interesting and realistic than any textbook account. These resources also enable students to engage in inquiry

learning through the guise of an historian. This authentic learning experience fuels their natural sense of curiosity and gives them the motivation to engage in wondering and critical thinking, significant elements of standards today. Moreover, the use of primary sources as part of inquiry learning fosters collaboration between the classroom teacher and the library media specialist, putting both educators into the role of learning coach. This becomes a win/win scenario for everyone in the learning community.

For other ideas related to using primary resources, see "Inquiry and Living History, Part I" (*SLMAM*, December 2005); "Inquiry and Living History, Part II" (*SLMAM*, January 2006); and "Inquiry and Living History, Part III" (*SLMAM*, May 2006).

References

American Memory. The Library of Congress. http://memory.loc.gov/ammem/index.html (accessed May 23, 2006). Collections include Africa, Advertising, Architecture and Landscape, Cities and Towns, Culture and Folklife, Environmental Conservation, Government, Law, Immigration, American Expansion, Literature, Maps, Native American History, Performing Arts and Music, Presidents, Religion, Sports and Recreation, Technology, Industry, War, Military, and Women's History. These collections include photographs, artifacts, diaries, letters, government documents, films, scrapbooks, maps, etc.

GALILEO: Digital Library of Georgia. Digital Library of Georgia. http://dlg.galileo.usg.edu/ (accessed May 23, 2006). This site (part of GALILEO project) is a gateway to Georgia's history and culture found in digitized books, manuscripts, photographs, government documents, newspapers, maps, audio, video, and other resources. (Website description)

Harada, Violet H. "Empowered Learning: Fostering Thinking across the Curriculum." In *Curriculum Connections through the Library*, edited by Barbara K. Stripling and Sandra Huges-Hassell,

41-65. Libraries Unlimited, 2003.

Harada, Violet H., and Joan M.Yoshina. *Inquiry Learning through Librarian-Teacher Partnerships.* Linworth, 2004.

INFOhio: Ohio memory project. http://www.ohiomemory.org/ (accessed May 23, 2006). This website has Ohio historical treasures in an online scrapbook of primary sources. (Source: Website). *INFOhio* also includes OhioLINK's Digital Media Center.

INSPIRE: Hoosier Heritage Digital Library. INCOLSA. http://www.hoosierheritage.net/ (accessed May 23, 2006). The site includes many historical photographs; obituaries; cemetery records; naturalization records; maps; land records; genealogy collections from Brown County; historical newspaper articles from the *Zionsville Times Sentinel*; Native American portraits; Index of Indiana Marriages through 1850; Indiana University Sheet Music; postcard collection from Jackson County; a virtual tour of Muncie, Indiana; records of birth, marriage, and death announcements from Elkhart County; and Vevay newspapers from 1840-1901 (Switzerland County).

The Oregon Trail: Trail Archive. Mike Trinklein and Steve Boettcher. http://www.isu.edu/%7Etrinmich/00.n.trailarchive.html (accessed May 23, 2006). Designed by Mike Trinklein and Steve Boettcher to provide the historical information used for *The Oregon Trail* documentary aired on PBS, the site includes a free online teacher's guide.

Presidential Libraries. The U. S. National Archives and Records Administration. http://www.archives.gov/presidential-libraries/ (accessed May 23, 2006). This site includes presidential papers, records, historical materials, and artifacts from the Presidencies of Herbert Hoover through William J. Clinton.

RUSA. The Instruction & Research Services Committee of the Reference and User Service Association History Section in the American Library Association. http://www.lib.washington.edu/subject/History/RUSA/ (accessed May 23, 2006).

Stripling, Barbara K. "Building Independent Learners." In *Curriculum Connections through the Library*, edited by Barbara K. Stripling and Sandra Huges-Hassell, 3-39. Libraries Unlimited, 2003. ✋

Graphic Inquiry:
Standards and Resources, Part I

by Daniel Callison and Annette Lamb

Graphic inquiry involves extracting information from and presenting information in visual formats such as political cartoons, diagrams, maps, photos, charts, tables, and multimedia. Through a recursive process of questioning, exploration, assimilation, inference, and reflection, student information scientists and their instructional specialists use graphic inquiry as a means to answer questions, draw conclusions, solve problems, and make decisions.

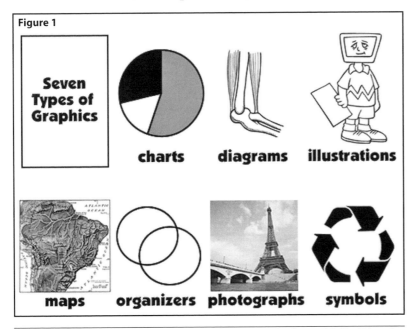

Figure 1

Seven Types of Graphics

charts   diagrams   illustrations

maps   organizers   photographs   symbols

Daniel Callison, Ed.D., is Professor and Dean of Continuing Studies and Online Education at Indiana University. Visit http://eduscapes.com/blueribbon for information leading to online school media certification. Email: callison@indiana.edu

Annette Lamb teaches in the School of Library and Information Science at Indiana University at Indianapolis. Email: alamb@eduscapes.com Website: http://eduscapes.com

Types of Graphics

Graphics are visual representations created on paper, the computer screen, or other surfaces to communicate information. Although graphics may simply provide a visual illustration of a concept, they often include numbers, words, and other symbols. Graphics may also represent fiction or nonfiction content. For example, an artist may create a 3-D picture of a fantasy world using imaging software, while a geologist may draw and label a cross section of a mountain.

Since graphics are used in many different contexts and involve overlaying techniques, it is, therefore, difficult to create a definitive list with distinct divisions. General categories are listed as follows (see Figure 1):

Charts. Numeric data are often represented using charts and graphs. Charts allow large quantities of data to be presented in a single visual. Bar charts, histograms, line charts, pie charts, and scatter plots are a few examples.

Diagrams. A simplified visual representation of an object, concept, or idea is often called a diagram. It is usually a line drawing and provides a quick reference to information that would otherwise be complex and difficult to understand. Diagrams often show the relationships among parts and wholes such as the anatomy of the human body or how something works such as the operation of a machine.

Illustrations. Drawings, paintings, sketches, and etchings are examples of illustrations. These visual representations are intended to communicate an informational or artistic message. In the case of an editorial cartoon, the message is often social or political. In graphic novels and picture books, illustrations are used to tell the story. Technical drawings provide accurate representations of objects used by architects, engineers, and machinists.

Maps. A map is a simplified, visual representation of the relationships among objects within a space and depicts a geographic location. Maps have traditionally represented three-dimensional space in two dimensions on paper. However, today's 3-D software and satellite imaging tools allow developers to visualize three dimensions.

Organizers. Mind maps, chains, webs, spider maps, decision trees, flowcharts, matrix, timelines, story maps, Venn diagrams, and KWL charts are a few examples of graphic organizers. These tools help students identify and classify information, so they can visualize the relationships and connections among these ideas, concepts, or issues.

Photographs. A photograph is simply a visual record of a moment in time and place. A photographer composes this visual record through techniques such as angle, field of view, and depth of field. Scanned images and photocopied visuals are also in this category.

Symbols. Symbols provide a simple visual representation and are used to represent abstract ideas or concepts. Pictograms, picture language, logos, icons, and traffic signs are a few examples.

Graphic Inquiry Found in Content Knowledge Standards

In addition to an obvious relationship with the information literacy standards for student learning promoted by the American Association of School Librarians, graphic inquiry can be found across all grade levels and subject disciplines. Examples drawn from *Content Knowledge: A Compendium of Standards and Benchmarks for K-12 Education* endorsed by the Association for Supervision and Curriculum Development are as follows (Kendall and Marzano 2000):

These standards support the following uses of graphics:

Document, argue, and persuade in order to make information more convincing.

Language Arts, grades 3–5. The student understands basic elements of advertising in visual media (e.g., sales approaches and techniques aimed at children, appealing elements used in memorable commercials, possible reasons for choice of specific language and visuals).

Language Arts, grades 6–8. The student uses a variety of criteria to evaluate and form viewpoints of visual media (e.g., evaluates the effectiveness of informational media such as websites, documentaries, news programs; recognizes a range of viewpoints and arguments; establishes criteria for selecting or avoiding specific programs).

Explain, define, instruct, report, and communicate information more clearly.

Language Arts, grades K–2. The student understands the main idea or message in visual media (e.g., pictures, cartoons, weather reports, newspaper photographs, visual narratives).

Language Arts, grades 3–8. The student uses strategies in editing and publishing of written works and multimedia. He/she considers format and layout for illustrations, charts, and graphs, and can edit for clarity to address an audience.

Represent, model, depict, and illustrate information.

Mathematics, grades K–2. The student uses a variety of strategies in the problem-solving processes such as draws pictures to represent problems; understands symbolic, concrete, and pictorial representations of numbers; understands that geometric shapes are useful for representing and describing real world situations.

Mathematics, grades 10–12. The student selects and uses the best method of representing and describing a set of data (e.g., scatter plot, line graph, two-way table).

History, grades K–4. The student knows how to develop picture lines of his own life and of his family's history. The student knows the origins and changes in methods of writing over time and how the changes made communications between people more effective (e.g., pictographs, cuneiform, hieroglyphics, alphabets).

Imagine, invent, tell story, entertain, or display information.

History, grades 3–4. The student knows the ways that families long ago expressed and transmitted their beliefs and values through oral tradition, literature, songs, art, religion, community celebrations, mementos, and visual crafts.

Language Arts, grades K–2. The student creates mental images from pictures and print. The student understands the similarities and differences between real life and life depicted in visual media.

Language Arts, grades 6–8. The student understands the use of stereotypes and biases in visual media (e.g., distorted representations of society, imagery, and stereotyping in advertising).

Illustrate navigate, map, chart, diagram, measure, organize, categorize, and classify information.

Mathematics, grades 6–8. The student understands procedures for basic indirect measures (e.g., using grids to estimate area of irregular figures); understands the defining properties of three-dimensional figures (e.g., a cube has edges with equal lengths).

Science, grades 9–12. The student understands how elements are arranged in the periodic table, and how this arrangement shows repeating patterns among elements with similar properties (e.g., numbers of protons, neutrons, and electrons; relation between atomic number and atomic mass).

History, grades 5–6. The student knows the migration and settlement patterns of peoples in the Americas and other regions of the world.

Language Arts, grades 6–8. The student knows how to organize information and ideas from multiple sources in systematic ways (e.g., timelines, outlines, notes, graphic sorting, and relationships).

Plan, predict, forecast, influence, and infer information.

Mathematics, grades K–5. The student understands that one can find out about a group of things by studying just a few of them. He/she understands that spreading data out on a number line helps to see what the extremes are, where the data points pile up, and where the gaps are.

Language Arts, grades K–5. The student uses a variety of strategies to predict content and meaning in visual media (e.g., uses knowledge of the structure of television programs such as cartoons, makes predictions based on program length, knows that a resolution will be reached and that the main character will overcome difficulties to return for the next episode; uses knowledge of cause and effect relationship to predict plot development).

Language Arts, grades 9–12. The student uses a range of strategies to interpret visual media (e.g., draws conclusions, makes generalizations, synthesizes materials viewed, refers to images for information to support point of view, deconstructs media to determine main idea).

Interdisciplinary Approaches, Individual Differences, and Graphic Inquiry

Individual differences among students can be addressed when matching information and content-area standards to the types of graphics used in activities as part of graphic inquiry. For example, a learner who has difficulty with a traditional written science log assignment may be more successful photographing the procedure (see Figure 2, below) or using a chart to trace his progress.

Use picture books to encourage young children to think visually. The book *The Great Graph Contest* by Loreen Leedy introduces students to bar graphs, pie charts, Venn diagrams, and other visual representations through a contest between two amphibian friends who both try to make the best graph. Use online tools such as *Create a Graph* (http://nces.ed.gov/nceskids/createagraph/) and *Grapher* (http://www.ambleside primary.com/ambleweb/mental maths/grapher.html) to help students build their own graphs for a class contest (see Figure 3, page 42).

Look for ways to combine standards from different subject areas

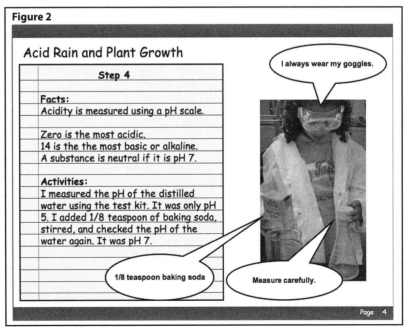

Figure 2

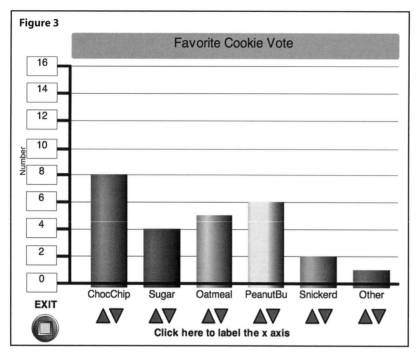

Figure 3

Favorite Cookie Vote

Number

16
14
12
10
8
6
4
2
0

ChocChip Sugar Oatmeal PeanutBu Snickerd Other

EXIT

Click here to label the x axis

such as language arts, science, and math. For instance, the book *Uno's Garden* by Graeme Base combines the science themes of balance in nature and biodiversity with math topics such as subtraction, multiplication, and prime numbers. Icons are used to represent animals, plants, and buildings in Uno's world. Students can explore their

Figure 4

Biodiversity in Indiana

270 birds species

99 butterfly species

51 mammal species

87 reptile & amphibian species

265 tree species

730 wildflower species

1 picture = 100 species

local natural world and represent their findings visually. The website *Enature's ZipGuides* (http://enature.com/zipguides/) can be used to help learners identify the birds, butterflies, mammals, reptiles and amphibians, trees, and wildflowers found in their region. Students can then create their own biodiversity visuals (see Figure 4).

Whether unlocking clues found in a historical photograph or creating a chart comparing reptiles and amphibians, graphics are powerful information resources for students. Below is a list of selected resources to help students think graphically:

Cooke, Donald. *Fun with GPS.* ESRI Press, 2005.

Each year our earth and universe is mapped in more detail and is readily available through the personal computer. This book shows how to keep up with kids who are already mapping their interests in sports, hiking, family history, conservation, animal life, and much more, not only internationally but soon universally.

Hanks, Kurt. *The Rapid Vis Toolkit: An Intriguing Collection of*

Powerful Drawing Tools for the Rapid Visualization of Ideas. Crisp Productions, 2003.

This is a highly inviting and contemporary guide to content framing, thumbnail sketches, storyboarding, schematic imaging, future visioning, graphic ideation, and other means to graphically tell stories and get the viewer to really see, imagine, and think.

Moline, Steve. *I See What You Mean.* Stenhouse, 1995.

This book has basic ideas to help the creative elementary school teacher and media specialist create graphic literacy activities that respect the ideas children bring to visually representing their world.

Lohr, Linda L. *Creating Graphics for Learning and Performance.* Merrill Prentice Hall, 2003.

This book is designed for teachers, computer programmers, and those who want to make presentations with sharp, focused illustrations that help the audience retain the main message.

Stein, Harry. *How to Interpret Visual Resources.* Franklin Watts, 1983.

Unfortunately, this book is seen as outdate and, therefore, weeded from many library media centers; this resource is, however, still relevant for thinking through activities that guide kids to extract information from photos, maps, and charts.

Zelazny, Gene. *Say It with Charts.* 4th ed. McGraw-Hill, 2001.

This is a standard guide for executives to convey data visually. It is presented clearly so that secondary school students can easily adapt the design principles given for charts, tables, and other data displays.

References

Kendall, John S., and Robert J. Marzano. *Content Knowledge: A Compendium of Standards and Benchmarks for K-12 Education.* 3rd ed. Mid-continent Research for Education and Learning, 2000. 🖖

Graphic Inquiry:
Skills and Strategies, Part II

by Daniel Callison and Annette Lamb

"Graphic Inquiry: Standards & Resources, Part I" by Daniel Callison and Annette Lamb was published in the September 2007 issue of *SLMAM*, pp. 39-42.

Children learn to read pictures before they read words. Unfortunately, we often stop teaching visually once children can read. In the Information Age, it's important to continue to help them interpret the visual world. From books and television to billboards and animation, children are bombarded with graphic images.

Just as children need to learn how to read text, young people also need to learn how to understand visual images. They need skills and strategies for not only reading and comprehending, analyzing and interpreting, using and applying, but also for designing and creating graphics that can be applied to inquiry experiences.

According to Donis A. Dondis in *A Primer of Visual Literacy*, "seeing is a direct experience and the use of visual data to report information is the closest we can get to the true nature of reality" (1973, 2).

Reading and Comprehending Graphics

Like reading a book, students should be able to translate the visual symbols and images in a graphic. They can look for clues to the main idea and support-

Daniel Callison, Ed.D., is Professor and Dean of Continuing Studies and Online Education at Indiana University. Visit http://eduscapes.com/blueribbon for information leading to online school media certification. Email: callison@indiana.edu

Annette Lamb teaches in the School of Library and Information Science at Indiana University at Indianapolis. Email: alamb@eduscapes.com Website: http://eduscapes.com

ing information in both the parts and whole of the picture. When reading a photograph, they can ask questions such as:

- What is the main subject?
- If there are people, can they be identified? What is their appearance (i.e., age, gender, race)? What are they wearing? What are they doing? What does their expression tell you? What do you think their lives are like? How are the people in the visual image connected?
- What is the setting? Is it inside or outside? What is the climate, weather, or season? How did the subject get into this situation?
- If there are objects, can they be identified? What is the purpose of these artifacts?
- What is in the background? Is it real or artificial? How do the background objects contribute to the overall setting?
- If the image is divided into nine visual sections, are there additional, close-up details?
- What is the age of the photograph? If not stated, what visual elements provide clues about the age?
- What might be happening beyond the scope of the camera?
- Why did the photographer choose this pose or action to photograph? What is the purpose of this visual?

Thousands of photographs at the Library of Congress can be used to bring history alive. Examine the photo of three women in Figure 1. When could the photo have been taken? What clues in the photo help identify the time period?

Full comprehension of graphics involves not only description, but also explanation and understanding. Picture books can be used to practice comprehension. Wordless books such as *Sector 7* by David Wiesner can be used as a basis to ask students to write the story (Clarion, 1997). The book *Right Here on This Spot*, by Sharon Hart Addy, is told visually and examines the changes that take place in a single location over thousands of years (Houghton Mifflin, 1999). Picture books with elaborate borders that tell stories or pro-

Figure 1

Library of Congress, Prints and Photographs Division

Figure 2

"We Can Do It." Color poster by J. Howard Miller. 179-WP- 1563.

vide information can also be used. For example, many of the books by Jan Brett, such as *The Mitten*, provide visual clues that anticipate later events in the book (Putnam, 1989).

Increasingly, text resources are being presented by using graphics. For instance, the *Visual Thesaurus* is an interactive dictionary and thesaurus displayed in a visual way to promote exploration (http://www.visualthesaurus.com/). By illustrating the meaning and relationship between words in a graphic format, students can easily identify words to meet their needs. A young inquirer, for example, might start with a question about the difference between responsibility and obligation. A series of clicks on the visual map may help refine his question and lead him to the words, "duty" and "liability." Similar visual tools are being introduced for Internet search engines and other search tools. For example, Grokker can be used to search Yahoo, *Wikipedia*, and Amazon and can be viewed in an outline or map form (http://www.grokker.com). Quintura for Kids is designed specifically for young searchers (http://kids. quintura.com/).

Marcy Driscoll in her book *Psychology of Learning for Instruction* states that "graphic representations have been particularly effective in facilitating encoding and memory storage of information" (2004, 105).

The master student information scientist should be able to effectively read and comprehend a wide range of graphic materials.

Analyzing and Interpreting Graphics

As students gain experience reading graphics, they become increasingly confident in retelling, describing, explaining, and critiquing visuals. For instance, an elementary student might describe the relationships she sees in a diagram showing life on a coral reef. Or, a teenager might identify the persuasive techniques used in a World War II propaganda poster (see Figure 2).

Graphics provide a great starting point for inquiry-based projects. Students can brainstorm questions based on a photograph found at the Library of Congress website or a chart in a *USA Today* article.

An effective analysis of graphics includes determining the meaning and quality of the visual presentation or argument. In addition, this analysis helps students seek out hidden assumptions, unstated facts, and misleading information leading them to the motives of a creator.

For example, if the topic of respiratory health is being explored, the following questions, criteria, and activities related to analyzing graphic materials can be examined:

Authority. What expertise does the author have in the subject represented by the graphic? Or, what resources did the author use to drawn the conclusions reflected in the graphic? When examining a map showing recent influenza outbreak in North America, it becomes apparent that it was produced by the United States Center for Disease Control (CDC) using data collected from state agencies during the past year. It is concluded that the CDC is an authoritative agency.

Sources. How was this graphic distributed? What individuals or groups support the communication of this information? The chart shows rates of lung cancer, asthma, tuberculosis, and sleep apnea. It is noticed that the chart is posted at an anti-smoking website and comes from the Canadian Lung Association. It is concluded that although the website may contain biased information in support of anti-smoking legislation, the content of the chart comes from a respected authority.

Context. In what setting is this graphic presented? Is it shown with other data representing a particular viewpoint or context? Are particular social, economic, or political agendas associated with the information? Information on rates of tuberculosis is discussed in the article "Health Issues in Africa," and it is determined that the chart is connected with research conducted in Africa by the World Health Organization.

Currency. Is the information in the graphic timely? When was the data collected? While examining a graphic on rates of tuberculosis, it is noticed that no date is provided. Is this historical or current information? Other information is sought to see how it compares to this chart.

Methodology. How was the data for the graphic collected? Was a systematic approach taken to experimentation? Were observations or eye witness reports used? Is the information valid and reliable? While examining the graph, an accompanying note is found indicating that the study tracked 1,000 teenagers during a six-month period to determine their smoking habits.

Assumptions. What are the hidden assumptions and unstated facts about the content of this graphic? Is misleading information conveyed in the graph? After viewing a photograph of a group of people smiling and smoking at a restaurant with the caption "Enjoy Fine Dining," further investigation reveals the group sponsoring the poster is opposed to legislation banning smoking in restaurants.

The mature student information scientist should carefully examine the evidence presented in a graphic, and then determine fact, value, and intent.

Using and Applying Graphics

Whether citing a chart as evidence in a debate on stem cell research or incorporating a historical photograph into a presentation on the Great Depression of the 1930s, students should carefully select, use, and apply graphics that best reflect their information needs. To do this, students need to be aware not only of the bias found in graphics, but the importance of considering alternative approaches to the same information. While students may use graphics found in print and electronic sources, they may also create original works and designs to meet a particular need.

Examine the following questions, criteria, and activities related to integrating graphic materials into communications.

Emphasis. What is the central idea represented? Is this a good choice for emphasis? What are the extraneous elements? What are the dominant and subordinate ideas? Highlighting essential features is an effective way to focus on the key ideas, but important elements may be left out. When presenting information about the functions of a human cell, what are the most important parts to illustrate? What differentiates a plant cell from an animal cell? Are the key components of the cell visible and clearly identified in the visual?

Selection. Does the data chosen for a graphic represent the entire population? Or, is it clear that only a particular group is represented? Is criteria provided for the selection of a subset of data? When selecting data for comparison, important examples may be omitted. When creating a graph to show the fat content found in meals at various restaurants, how are the restaurants chosen? Which menu items are represented? When showing population growth worldwide, which countries will be chosen and why?

Figure 3

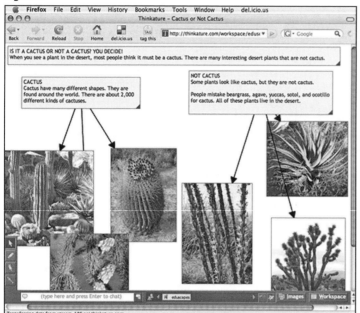

Proportion. Is all information equally represented? Do visuals accurately reflect the data? For example, images in the foreground of a photograph may look larger than those images in the background. Furthermore, a simple mountain icon may not adequately represent the difference between a mountain range at 5,000 feet and 10,000 feet.

Perspective. What facts and opinions are represented in this visual? Is a particular point of view most often represented? An illustration of a globe generally shows North America although there are many other views that could be presented. A visual representing Arizona often includes a Saguaro cactus even though this plant doesn't grow in all parts of the state.

Comparison. How does this graphic compare to other information that's been examined? Was the same or different data used? How do similarities and differences impact overall understanding? How does the method of presentation impact understanding? Which method best reflects the student's intent? For example, there's maybe space for only one diagram comparing the alligator and the crocodile. Would a Venn Diagram or labeled photo comparison be more effective? Each provides similar information, but each is presented in a different way.

Connections. How do the ideas in the graphic relate to each other? How do they relate to other ideas being presented? How do they address original questions posed by the inquiry? How do they support the con-

clusions being drawn in the communication? After examining many options, the concept map seems to do the best job showing the relationships among the characters in the novel *Of Mice and Men*.

The mature inquirer looks beyond the easy solution, common examples, and stereotypes to locate, integrate, or create unique ways for using graphics to represent ideas.

Designing and Creating Graphics

A high school student creates a list of pros and cons related to a summer internship, a second grader builds a Venn Diagram comparing birds and bats, and a team of middle school students take digital photos of the steps for a science experiment. They're all participating in graphic inquiry.

Starters. It is useful in some cases to provide students with prompts, templates, and resources to help them create graphics. Students could be provided with a *PowerPoint* or *Inspiration* template that has directions and a collection of photographs or clipart to stimulate thinking.

Tools. From markers and sticky notes to computer software and digital camera, a wide range of tools are available to student information scientists. Students should be helped to make good decisions about the best tool for a particular project. A piece of flip-chart paper and colored markers would work fine for creating a concept map as part of an idea generation session. If a group of students, however, from different class sections are working together, it might be more convenient to use the online tool *Thinkature* (http://thinkature.com) or *Gliffy* (http://gliffy.com). This website allows users in remote locations to collaborate on building a concept map (see Figure 3).

Composition. Like writing a poem, students need skills in composing visual communications. When using a digital camera, a student needs to consider the lighting, camera angle, depth of field, context, and other elements of composition. As the student edits the photographs, he or she may be cropping, extracting, or modifying the visual to best represent the idea for a particular audience.

In some cases, a graphic is created as part of the inquiry process, e.g., brainstorming or organization of evidence. At other times, a graphic is used as the final product or as part of a culminating communication, e.g., a report or wiki page. In both cases, basic skills in graphic design and development are essential. Regardless of whether the student is creating a timeline of events as he reads a novel or building a pictorial chronology for a report on the history of satellite communication, the student inquirer needs to understand the function and creation of effective graphics.

The mature student information scientist creates effective, efficient, and appealing graphics during both the process of inquiry and as a product to communicate results.

Graphics, Learning, and the School Library Media Program

Because graphics can incorporate multiple formats of information, they appeal to many learning styles and intelligences. For example, young people with strengths in verbal-linguistic intelligence are drawn to charts and graphs emphasizing key words and lists of text, while those with logical-mathematical intelligence choose bar graphs, timelines, logic maps, and other numeric visuals. Maps, sketches, and photographs suit those with visual-spatial intelligence. The classification aspects of diagrams and comparison charts appeal to those with naturalistic intelligence. The use of graphics for goal setting and meta-cognitive activities is associated with intrapersonal intelligence, while the social aspects of collaborative planning for graphics is associated with interpersonal intelligence.

Graphic novels and comics have become particularly popular with visual learners. According to Will Eisner, "the reading process in comics is an extension of text. In text alone the process of reading involves word-to-image conversion. Comics accelerate that by providing the image" (1996, 5). Using software such as *Comic Life* helps young people create their own visually-rich stories. Scott McCloud, author of *Understanding Comics*, notes that digital comics can take virtually any size and shape (2000).

The Pride of Baghdad is a high school level graphic novel by Brian K. Vaughan focusing on the impact of the War in Iraq on zoo animals (DC Comics, 2006). This graphic novel may inspire teens to create their own visual stories focusing on the consequences of war (see Figure 4).

Figure 4

Because of their many versatile uses, graphics are helpful in differentiating instruction. Visuals can provide concrete examples for students who have difficulty with abstract concepts. In addition, these visuals can present information in a variety of ways to meet individual needs. A learner, for example, who has difficulty communicating ideas through writing may excel at the development of graphic communications. The role of the library media specialist, then, is to connect the wealth of visual resources and tools with meaningful, inquiry-based experiences.

References

Dondis, Donis A. *A Primer of Visual Literacy*. The MIT Press, 1973.

Driscoll, Marcy. *Psychology of Learning for Instruction*. 3rd ed. Allyn & Bacon, 2004.

Eisner, Will. *Graphic Storytelling and Visual Narrative*. Poorhouse Press, 1996.

McCloud, Scott. *Reinventing Comics: How Imagination and Technology Are Revolutionizing an Art Form*. HarperCollins, 2000.

Cavemen Took Notes?

by Leslie Preddy

I'm feeling pretty good. The two classroom teachers and I have previously worked together and the power of our collaboration creates positive energy. Yesterday's lesson went well, so I assume that today's will go just as well. But, today's lesson seems to be all wrong, and I can see it in our students' faces. As my collaborators and I look at each other and try to figure out what has gone wrong, a student suddenly barks out, "I get it Mrs. P! You mean caveman talk!" I laugh, nodding encouragement for him to continue his explanation for the rest of the class as I acknowledge his analogy and watch the light of understanding sweep across the students' faces.

Caveman Talk

This student's simple, "caveman" explanation works to describe the essence of basic research notes. Taking notes for research is different from taking notes for any other purpose. Research notes are very simple with the researcher writing only the key facts in simple, informal, personal shorthand. Research notes should take the least amount of space and time necessary. The student writes only enough details to jog understanding and memory for later retrieval. For research, students take the information read from the source and break it down to its core meaning. A note is just a few words, including only the important facts, dates, and keywords.

Converting to Caveman Talk

Taking notes for research is an experience that is different from taking notes for other purposes. The popular characterization of a caveman in cartoons, movies, commercials, and comedy skits is a person that grunts and speaks simply. It is a good comparison for students to use as they gain a better understanding for how to abbreviate information from a source into a form appropriate for research notes. As we expanded to clarify understanding on our student's analogy, I said, "If I say, 'Mrs. Gunkel began her professional life as a teacher,' how would we convert that to caveman talk?" The shout-out from the students is the same, "Gunkel = teacher." They quickly understand how to take research notes as the image of a caveman runs through their minds.

Caveman talk is encouraged through a lesson that includes modeling extracting relevant information for students using a variety of resource types: online database article, book, Web page, magazine article, encyclopedia, or newspaper article. In a research project about the ancient culture and traditions of Native Americans, I might use a few paragraphs from page 28 of Raymond Bial's *Lifeways: The Apache* (Benchmark Books, 2008), while the class helps me as I work through how to extract only the relevant information and convert it into caveman talk (see Caveman Talk Example, below).

What we quickly realize while working together to analyze our two paragraphs is that each paragraph was about the training or education children received while growing up. After we figured that out, we go back through and break it down by re-reading the first sentence, asking ourselves if anything in that paragraph would be important to answering our research question and if there are any keywords about culture and traditions. Carefully and together we go through the paragraph one sentence at a time. We write down, caveman style, only as much as we need to, grouping like information together in order to remember what the information means days later when we review it and design the final product.

Simple and Plagiarism Proof

It is especially important that students take notes from text resources caveman style. This ensures a student can safely put things into his own words without too many of the author's sentences, paragraphs, and phrases. Through caveman talk, it becomes easy and uncomplicated to put research together into a final product using the student's own phrasing, sentence structure, and writing style.

References:
Callison, Daniel, and Leslie Preddy. *The Blue Book on Literacy and Instruction for the Information Age*. Libraries Unlimited, 2006.
Ranken, Virginia. *The Thoughtful Researcher*. Libraries Unlimited, 1999.◄

Leslie Preddy is the library media specialist at Perry Meridian Middle School in Indianapolis, IN. She is the author of *SSR with Intervention* (Libraries Unlimited, 2007) and co-author of *The Blue Book on Literacy and Instruction for the Information Age* (Libraries Unlimited, 2006). Website: http://www.lesliepreddy.com; Email: lpreddy@msdpt.k12.in.us

Caveman Talk Example

The book:	Caveman Talk:
"The Apache loved raiding and warfare, and from an early age boys were taught to be warriors. They learned to remain absolutely silent as they made their way across the land, raiding villages or avenging a death. Then they would go without sleep and they stood guard all night. They learned to send and read smoke signals. When the boys were about fifteen years old, they were ready for raids and warfare. From their mothers, girls learned to do the household chores—cooking and caring for the children. When they came of age, they underwent a puberty rite known as the Sunrise Ceremony. In this joyous event, girls danced for four days to the beat of water drums and songs. They were blessed in sacred rituals and honored for the strength they would need as wives and mothers." Bial, Raymond. *Lifeways: The Apache*. Benchmark Books, 2001.	Boys = warriors Training ►silent ►stand guard ►read & send smoke signals ►raid ►avenge deaths ►fight Age 15 = do raids & warfare Girls = wives & mothers Training ►cook ►childcare ►housekeeping Rite of Passage = Sunrise Ceremony ►4 days ►danced ▷water drums ▷songs ►sacred ritual blessing

Caveman Talk

►Read a line, sentence, or paragraph related to a research question or keyword.

►Write or draw on your source note only important:
▷Facts
▷Dates
▷Keywords
▷Your own thoughts, ideas, opinions about what you read
►Do not write sentences.

►If you need to quote or copy something exactly:
▷Put it inside quotation marks.
▷Write the page number next to the quote if it is from a book.

Brain Friendly Techniques:
Mind Mapping®

by Cristine Goldberg

Mind Mapping can be called the Swiss Army Knife for the brain, a total visual thinking tool or a multi-handed thought catcher. Invented by Tony Buzan in the early 1970s and used by millions around the world, it is a method that can be a part of your techniques repertoire when teaching information literacy, planning, presenting, thinking, and so forth. Building upon brain research from the early days of Dr. Sperry and others, Buzan has updated the technique constantly as more brain research has been completed. Mind maps all begin with a central image; branch out organically; and utilize color, images, codes, symbols, and key words in a hierarchical manner.

Some of the ways that Mind Mapping relates to what we know about the brain and how it works are:

- In its total form, a map is a visual image. Visuals are processed and remembered more (60,000 times faster) than text (Burmark).
- Other images within the total map increase the chances for memory.
- A map uses many colors because color is known to stimulate the brain. Black-and-white text turns the brain off rapidly.
- With all relevant points put together on one page, it is easy for students to see relationships as well as the big picture.
- The physical process of making a map produces better memory because of the kinesthetic involvement.

As always, what is difficult for many is to take research or verified facts and convert the ideas to everyday life in the library media center. Stated simply, from the drawing board to action often requires small steps or actions until a bigger picture emerges. Mind Maps are a great way to introduce an overall topic, increase student involvement, and get thoughts down quickly. I have used Mind Mapping with students in many settings. A few examples are discussed within this article: how to help high school students set up research papers or a paper in general, a discussion of Jacqueline Briggs Martin's *Snowflake Bentley* (Scholastic, 1999) with elementary students, and an overview of the Big6 process for middle and high school students.

In the case of *Snowflake Bentley*, I used a whiteboard map that I had prepared with pre-determined areas of discussion and main branches drawn before students arrived. Notice that main branches were established for illustrating Bentley, snow, storyline, and interesting (Figure 1).

Figure 1

An upper elementary class was able to add two more branches—history and family (Figure 2). After reading the book to the students, I began by asking specific questions about some of the branches. With younger students I filled in the words; upper elementary students were encouraged to come up with key words and write their own answers. Even young students readily adapt to the pattern as you move along.

Figure 2

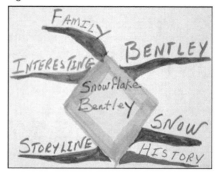

Figure 3 is a completed map by a first grade class. A week later we had a snowstorm (rare for these parts) and I was able to do a simple check with the same class. The Mind Map had not been erased, as they were the last class to discuss the book. I brought it out with paper covering all of the branches. I was amazed that the children could recreate it for me. All I said was, "Close your eyes and concentrate. Then think about the main branches and what words were on the main branches, and what was coming out from them." After about thirty-five seconds, I had the students open their eyes and we drew a new map. I asked them what was on a branch, then what came off the branch. Sometimes they would remember something else and I would go back and add it. When we were finished, I pulled back the cover and displayed the original map beside the new one. The retention displayed through this review activity was truly exciting and, to me, a testament to the use of this strategy.

Cristine Goldberg is a library media specialist with Whitfield County Schools in Dalton, GA and an adjunct faculty member of the Educational Media and Instructional Technology Department at the State University of West Georgia. Through the years she has taught all levels from pre-K to post graduate. E-mail: cgoldberg@whitfield.k12.ga.us

Any group reading or listening to the story activity can be more meaningful if students are allowed to Mind Map the experience. For example, M. C. Helldorfer's *Hog Music* (Viking, 2000) comes to mind as one where each of the stops on the journey could be a branch of a map. The students could fill in all the details from the illustrations and story onto a Mind Map. The library media specialist would have the first branch in place with a big B (for Baltimore, ultimately realized through context and clues) and the last one around the other side of the map would have the branch entitled Vandalia (Illinois). The students could complete the rest as the story progressed or after the story was finished on individual papers as a memory building exercise, sequence practicing, attention to detail of illustrations, and so forth.

The physical activity of drawing the story produces a strong kinesthetic experience and helps to engage more of the senses in the learning process. Note how *F.I.D.O.* was Mind Mapped with great detail by a reluctant learner from Seabrook Primary (Figure 4) and how the handwriting deteriorated when the student was asked to put the material into linear mode (Figure 5). L. Jobson of Seabrook (2003) states, "Normally when we go to the written form, we go straight into a very linear model. We don't allow students to do the processing in the written form using all of the senses that they can. If you allow them to go to a Mind Map format, you are allowing them to use as many senses as they possibly can to process their learning."

When I introduce or review the Big6, I hand the students a colored printout of a Mind Map created with a software program (Figure 6, page 24). As the process is discussed and we move from branch to branch, I encourage the students to add their own key words so they will be able to keep the map and make it work for them. The process of having something in hand, color and image utilization, an overview of the topic all on one page, and then adding more to it, generally helps to cement the process in a student's mind. From there I encourage students to Mind Map their research project.

A third situation that happens often in a high school setting is what I call the "confused student syndrome." Students arrive in the library media center and understand that they must produce a paper for a class. They know the number of words required and the subject of the paper, but for some reason they just cannot get a handle on the task at hand. Even if they have made a chart or used some type of different graphic organizer, there appears to be an element missing. I pull out a few samples of computer-generated and student-drawn Mind Maps on different subjects. I give a minimal explanation about the process and provide fine-line colored pens for them to produce a beginning map (approximately the same as a brainstorm but in a radiant pattern). What is happening is that the whole brain is engaged with the logical/analytical skills while incorporating visual/artistic skills. From there I have the student explore several resources and this encourages "the reflex brain" to kick into gear and get the oxygen pumping. When they incorporate the resources into the maps with key words, the limbic system becomes involved through the stimulation of memory channels. Some assignments lend themselves to the who, what, where, why and when map. As students realize how quickly they can work, the benefits of Mind Mapping are clearly realized. The

Figure 3

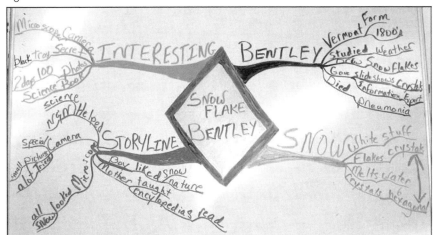

Figure 4

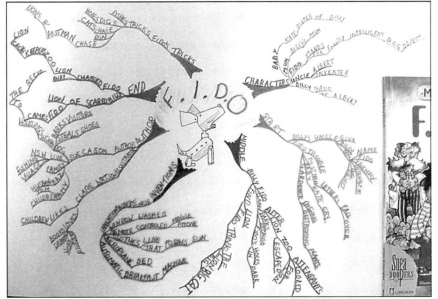

Figure 5

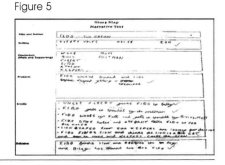

Figure 6 (Note: Contact the author for a color version.)

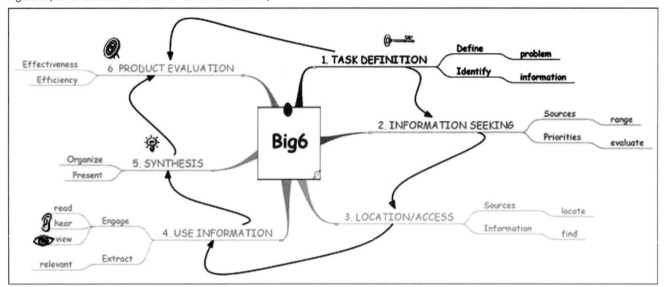

five Ws are appropriate for any age. Almost every student is able to produce a higher quality of work and get into the project more rapidly when exposed to this method.

An example in action is Suzanne Brion of Saline, Michigan, who trains her students each year in the process. This year her students completed an extensive family history/generations project. This project involved research of famous people who changed the course of history and time periods of fifteen-year segments from 1865 to the present. The purpose of the project was to understand the "big picture" of public history and interface this with their individual family histories. In addition to an individual project, the students produced a very large, group Mind Map of the people who changed history in four different areas—politics/government, sports/entertainment, literature/arts, and science/technology. The process of producing and seeing all of the famous people and their contributions on one huge map helped her students to comprehend the desired "big picture." During the entire process, her students used Mind Maps for note taking as well as being the prime graphic organizer of their units.

Another thing a library media specialist can do is to keep an inexpensive plastic container in the library media center with fine-line markers from discount stores and four-color pens (my favorite tool) stored inside. Ordinary unlined paper is almost always around in library media centers and I also keep one pack of large paper (11 X 17) for projects that are in-depth and therefore require more levels of detail. Have a color variety of dry-erase markers for whiteboards. Take the time to develop the skill yourself. Once you realize how powerful yet easily developed this skill is, you will understand the benefits for students. As you model for students, they will become increasingly involved.

In summary, Mind Mapping is a skill that cuts across ability levels and encompasses all subject matters. It can accommodate creative thinking while still adapting to linear tasks such as note taking, planning, and organizing. It will help your students make better use of information while providing a better platform for synthesis. The ability to grow and change is inherent in Mind Mapping, and definitely absent from linear note taking, while capitalizing on the common sense of using more of the senses.

References and Sources for Further Information:

Books

Burmark, L. *Visual Literacy; Learn to See, See to Learn.* Alexandria, VA: Association for Supervision and Curriculum Development, 2002.

Buzan, T. *Mind Maps for Kids.* London, UK: Thorson's, 2003.

Buzan, T. *The Mind Map Book.* London, UK: BBC Worldwide, 2003.

Buzan, T. *The Mind Map Book.* London, UK: Plume, 1993.

Mind Mapping®, the Learning Platform at Seabrook Primary School. Melbourne, AU: Seabrook Primary School report, 2003, revised 2004.

Mukerjea, D. *Brain Symphony; Brain-blazing Practical Techniques.* Singapore: Horizon Books Pte. Ltd., 2003.

Mukerjea, D. *Building Brainpower; Turning Grey Matter into Gold.* Singapore: Horizon Books Pte. Ltd., 2003.

Mukerjea, D. *Surfing the Intellect; Building Intellectual Capital for a Knowledge Economy.* Singapore: The Brainware Press, 2001.

Software with trial versions available

Mindjet: Visual Thinking. http://www.mindjet.com
  Distributes *Mind Manager*, a very flexible program with lots of bells and whistles; very professional; used around the world.

MindMapper. http://www.mindmapper.com
  Not as complicated to learn but without as many bells and whistles. There is also a *Mindmapper Jr.* version for younger children

Map it! Mind Mapping Software. http://www.mapitsoftware.com
  Fairly easy to use version for students; not a lot of bells and whistles but enough for most purposes.

HeadCase Mind Mapper® for Windows. http://www.bignell.de
  This is a beta version but the real version should be available by the time this article is published.

Websites

Big6: An Information Problem-Solving Process. http://www.big6.com

Buzan Centres - Mind Mapping. http://www.buzancentres.com

BrainDance.com. http://www.braindancing.com

For questions or a pdf copy of the Seabrook report, contact the author at: cgoldberg@whitfield.k12.ga.us ✋

THE POWER OF REFLECTION
IN THE RESEARCH PROCESS

by Peggy Milam

Recent research on the brain has identified a number of cognitive strategies for constructing knowledge and improving retention of new information. Classroom teachers have begun implementing many of these strategies in their teaching, but what about library media specialists? As leaders and learners in the Information Age, library media specialists must be change agents for introducing new research into practice and modeling best strategies defined by research. Noted cognitive researchers Robert Sylwester, Geoffrey and Renate Caine, and others have identified specific new instructional strategies that have a direct application to information literacy activities in school library media centers. One powerful strategy for constructing knowledge and improving retention of information is reflection.

What Is Reflection?

Webster's New International Concise Dictionary of the English Language (1997) defines reflection as "careful, serious thought or consideration." When students reflect on their learning, they carefully and seriously consider what they have gained from an activity. Reflection uses the higher order of thinking skills defined in *Bloom's Taxonomy* (1956): analysis, synthesis, and evaluation. As students reflect on their research, they analyze their

search results for the most accurate and relevant information, synthesize the information they have gathered from multiple sources into one organized product, and evaluate their products to determine if they have met their goals and produced the results they were seeking. Table 1 summarizes the higher order of thinking skills and the results of reflection during the research process.

Why Is Reflection Important?

Although several information problem-solving models incorporate reflection as a part of the process, reflection is not always regarded as an integral part of research—one that is crucial to the construction of new learning and the end product of research efforts. Recent brain research, however, indicates that not only is reflection vital to construction of knowledge, but it is also vital in retention of that knowledge. Noted brain researcher Robert Sylwester (2002) observes that reflection is a conscious and deliberate process. Reflective problem-solving, Sylwester says, can be used to solve challenging problems that don't require an immediate solution. One such application of reflective, conscious problem-solving might be a research question that requires continued searching and construction of new knowledge in order to reach a conclu-

sion. Geoffrey and Renate Caine (1997) elaborate on this conscious problem solving by noting that reflection makes the invisible visible. Much of our learning is unconscious, or processed below one level of awareness, note the Caines. In metacognitive reflection, students can bring to light their unconscious construction of learning so that they can recall it later. Reflection can promote connection building and ground learning, making it "stick."

What Information Problem-Solving Models Incorporate Reflection?

Recognizing the value of reflection, a number of information problem solving models have incorporated reflection as an integral part of the process.

In her book *Seeking Meaning*, Carol Kuhlthau (1993) explains her constructivist Information Seeking Process (ISP) model as one based on common feelings students experience as they research. Initially, students experience confusion, frustration, and uncertainty in their search results, but as they begin to construct knowledge with their results, students experience confidence. Kulthau asserts that an important step in the construction of knowledge is student reflection on their learning. Steps in this model include:

- Initiate a topic,
- Select sources,
- Explore information,
- Focus,
- Collect information,
- Prepare product, and

Peggy Milam, Ed.S., is a National Board Certified Media Specialist at Compton Elementary School in Powder Springs, GA, and author of *InfoQuest: A New Twist on Information Literacy* (Linworth Publishing, 2002).

• Assess results.

Striping and Pitts (1988) take a similar approach in their ten-step process, the Thoughtful Learning Cycle (TLC), detailed in *Brainstorms and Blueprints*. In this model, the authors include reflection points after nearly every stage. Reflection points guide students in analyzing completed research and determining if a step is completed satisfactorily before moving ahead to the next step. Steps in this model include:

• Choose a broad topic,
• Overview the topic,
• Narrow the topic,
• Develop a thesis,
• Formulate questions,
• Plan,
• Find/analyze/evaluate sources,
• Evaluate evidence/take notes/ compile bibliography,
• Establish conclusions, and
• Create final product.

Originally developed by Ken Macrorie (1988) and promoted by Joyce and Tallman (1997), the I-Search model incorporates student feelings and reflection throughout the research process and particularly at the end by having students write their reports in first person. Steps in this model include:

• Letting the topic choose you,
• Searching for information,
• Using information, and
• Presenting the final product.

Incorporating their thoughts and feelings about a topic encourages students to think deeply, analyze, and reflect on what they have learned.

Alice Yucht's (1997) FLIP IT! model was developed as a mnemonic device to assist students in remembering the steps. The acronym stands for:

• Focus,
• Link,
• Input,
• Payoff,
• Inform, and
• Tactical maneuvers and Thinking strategies (Reflection).

While the main steps are the first four, the last two, Inform and Tactical maneuvers and Thinking strategies, are where students assess their work metacognitively and reflect on its success.

Table 2 displays several problem solving models and the stages in which reflection occurs in each.

Implications for Practicing Library Media Specialists

How can library media specialists encourage reflection in library media center processes? A number of activities can be incorporated into student research activities that promote reflection before, during, and after the process.

• *Large group discussions.* Before students begin their research, a large group discussion may help define the process for students. Articulating goals before a group helps students reflect on and clarify their purpose, as well as become task-oriented. At this stage, some lesser-organized students also may benefit from other brain-based strategies such as developing graphic organizers or flow charts for the research project.

• *Small group discussions.* As students research, library media specialists can break up the process with occasional small group discussions. Small groups or panels allow students to connect to each other and their purpose, release their feelings, and refocus their efforts. Suggestions may come from a forum such as this to guide off-task students in a new direction. The small group can provide an emotional outlet for confusion and frustration and can provide support for those who are flailing.

• *Journaling.* Libary media specialists can collaborate with the classroom teacher to build journaling into an assignment. At strategic points throughout a research assignment, students write reflections into a journal on the stage they have completed. Journaling at regular points during the research process helps students to become more self-regulated in evaluating the progress they have made toward their goals.

• *Pair-sharing.* As students near completion of their research, they can pair up for some "pair-sharing," where each one reflects with their partner on thoughts, feelings, and what they have accomplished in the research process. Peers can objectively evaluate each other and determine if the end result satisfactorily meets the goals of the assignment. If

Table 1: Higher Order Thinking Skills and Reflection

Higher Order Thinking Skill	Results of Reflection
Analysis	Students reflect on goal for end product and sort and sift through information collected to retain only relevant data
Synthesis	Students carefully utilize relevant data gathered to create a new product
Evaluation	Students consider original goal and compare to end product

Table 2: Information Problem-Solving Models Incorporating Reflection

Author	Model	Reflection stages
Kuhlthau	ISP: Information Seeking Process	Reflection occurs throughout and at end as students assess work
Stripling and Pitts	TLC: Thoughtful Learning Cycle	Reflection occurs after most steps, beginning with step 3
Joyce & Tallman/ Macrorie	I-Search Model	Final product is written in third person, incorporating thoughts and feelings of researcher
Yucht	FLIP IT!	Last two steps involve metacognition and reflection on process

not, students can go back to make final changes before submitting their finished product. It may be helpful to pair older students with younger ones or more accomplished students with less accomplished ones.

• *Essays.* Reflection at the end of the research process leads to metacognition—thinking about learning. Reflections can be written in a brief essay on the process where students answer specific questions that lead to reflective thought. See Table 3.

• *Websites.* Students uncomfortable with writing or speaking may prefer to create a reflective webpage summary of their project, using the same specific questions as for the essay. See Table 3.

• *Chat room discussions.* Some students may prefer to reflect in an online chat room where they can respond to leading questions or comments of others that are metacognitive and encourage reflection on goals, the process, problem-solving techniques, the final product, successes/failures, etc.

• *E-mail or list-serv entries.* Alternatives to a chat room reflection are e-mail or list-serv entries, where students write a summary of their reflections on their research and final results.

• *Blogs.* Blogs are an appropriate as well as popular venue for student reflection, with over three million now in existence and more appearing daily. "Blog" is a nickname for weblog, an interactive website where viewers can post their thoughts and read the thoughts of others. Group blogs would be motivating, particularly for reluctant learners, and would allow for personal as well as group reflection.

• *Multimedia presentations.* For teachers who may want to place a grade on the student reflections and find grading a chat room or e-mail discussion difficult, a multimedia presentation may afford a more tangible format to assess. Student presentations might cover the stages of the project with each slide reflecting on one stage in the process.

• *Speeches.* A more traditional form of reflection could be requiring students to give a brief speech before a panel or a small or large group, or in front of a team of assessors such as the classroom teacher, the library media specialist, the instructional lead teacher, and/or an administrator.

• *Posters.* Another more traditional format for reflection is a display board or poster where students create three panels: Goals of the project, Strategies Used, and Results, with reflections on each.

In their reflections, students may consider what worked well, what did not work as well, what they gained from the experience, what they would do differently next time, and how they could avoid any problems they encountered. Table 3 lists sample questions that may lead students to reflect on their work.

Before beginning reflective activities with the students, library media specialists should consider all the options available and determine which styles fit best with students in their situation. Some library media centers may simply be too large or architecturally unsuited to facilitating small or large group meetings. For these media specialists, individual reflections in forms such as journaling, multimedia presentations, or even an annotated portfolio might work best. Schools with smaller student populations or smaller classes might be more suited to group activities such as peer sharing, small or large group discussions, or forums. Where adequate technology is available, library media specialists might simply facilitate chat room discussions, postings to a list-serv, or webpage development for student reflection. Whatever style of reflection is used, students still benefit from clarifying the purpose of the research, releasing their feelings during the process, determining if goals have been met, and evaluating the results. Table 4 provides a checklist for library media specialists who want to establish an environment conducive to reflection.

Purpose of reflection

Clarify the purpose of research

Determine if goals have been met

Release feelings

Judge quality of product

Metacognition

Conclusion

Reflection is a metacognitive skill that helps students analyze their research steps, synthesize their results into a final product, and evaluate their results in terms of meeting the project's criteria and their own goals. Numerous information problem-solving models incorporate reflection as an integral part of the process, including the ISP (Information Seeking Process) model, TLC (Thoughtful Learning Cycle) model, I-Search, FLIP-IT!, and others. Library media specialists can encourage students to reflect on their research by establishing suitable areas for pair-sharing, journal writing, small and/or large group discussions, or even setting up chat room discussion, facilitating e-mail or list-serv discussions, or posting student reflections to a website or blog. Library media specialists also can collaborate with classroom teachers to model effective strategies for reflection; assist with multimedia presentations, panels, or forums; and so on. When used properly, reflection is a powerful critical thinking skill that connects new knowledge to prior learning and helps ground the research process in students' minds.

References

Bloom, B. *Taxonomy of Educational Objectives: Handbook I. Cognitive and Affective Domain.* New York: David McKay, 1956.

Caine, G., and R. Caine. *Mind/Brain Learning Principles.* New Horizons for Learning, 1997. (Retrieved 12 April 2004: http://www.newhorizons.org/neuro/caine.htm).

Joyce, M., and J. Tallman, J. *Making the Writing and Research Connection with the I-Search Process: A How-to-Do-It Manual.* New York: Neal-Schuman, 1997.

Kuhlthau, C. *Seeking Meaning: A Process Approach to Library and Information Services.* Norwood, NJ: Ablex, 1993.

Macrorie, K. *The I-Search Paper.* Portsmouth, NJ: Heineman, 1988.

Stripling, B., and J. Pitts. *Brainstorms and Blueprints: Teaching Library Research as a Thinking Process.* Littleton, CO: Libraries Unlimited, 1988.

Sylwester, R. *The Downshifting Dilemma: A Commentary and Proposal.* New Horizons for Learning, 2002. (Retrieved 9 August 2004: http://www.newhorizons.org/neuro/sylwester2.htm).

Webster's New International Concise Dictionary of the English Language. New York: Doubleday, 1997.

Yucht, A. *FLIP-IT! An Information Skills Strategy for Student Researchers.* Worthington, OH: Linworth, 1997. ✋

Table 3: Reflective Questions

Identify your goals and objectives in this research. What strategies did you use to locate your supporting facts? How did you determine what research to keep and what to toss out?
What criteria were used to evaluate your work? Were your original goals/objectives in line with the evaluation? Explain the assessment and your answer.
What types of feedback did you receive as you progressed with your project? Did you meet in large or small groups, share with peers, reflect individually, or use some other method of evaluation? What changes did you make as a result of this feedback?
Were the final results of your project aligned with the goals you set at the beginning? If so, what process did you use to meet these goals? If not, what would you do differently next time?
What problems did you encounter? How did you solve them? What parts of this project made you feel most successful and why?

Table 4: Reflection Checklist for Library Media Specialists

Provide furniture arrangement in the school library media center that encourages students to pair up and reflect on their learning.
Have scrap paper and pencils on hand for students to jot down reflective journal entries.
Provide stimulating and organized work areas to encourage students to focus on the task at hand.
Display a variety of student research projects in different formats: posters, videos, webpages, demonstrations, poetry, multimedia presentations, etc. so that students can reflect on others' accomplishments.
Encourage use of mind-mapping techniques such as graphic organizers, webs, charts, and tables so that students can reflect on their own project goals.
Demonstrate research that crosses curricular boundaries to so that students can reflect on effective strategies.
Allow for effective use of time blocks to encourage productivity.
Empower students to research through technology.
Permit students to talk, share, discuss, and reflect on their work with each other.

Styles of Reflection

Individual Activities
Journal writing, oral presentation, report, e-mail, webpage, multimedia presentation, annotated portfolio of all work
Group Activities
Peer sharing, small group discussion, large group discussion, posting to chat room or list-serv, forum

Plagiarism

by Daniel Callison

I want to give Doug Johnson credit. Johnson, Director of Media and Technology for the Mankato Public Schools and international speaker on a wide spectrum of school library media management issues, has a very similar approach to mine on the subject of prevention and management of plagiarism. For the past thirty years and, probably even before Johnson became a library media specialist, I have believed that we should encourage what can be done rather than concentrate on what should not be done. By engaging students in projects that reward original ideas, the need to copy or cheat is discouraged. Student research should be presented as an opportunity to explore and share, not just learn how to follow another set of rules.

Even though I have paraphrased Johnson's comments and writings on plagiarism, he still receives credit. Even though his presentations and articles have come along several decades after my own similar ideas, he still receives credit. Why? He deserves credit because he has published these ideas in his books and other respected and widely read sources. In addition, he has achieved a respected status as a director of library media and as a national speaker. He has synthesized ideas and concepts that remain insightful and we both continue to wish they were common knowledge and hope they become common practice.

In addition to the standard citations, I give him credit within the text of my writing, speech, video, or website. Thus, I practice the opportunity to share with others my findings, my resources, and my links to what I have read and what I think others should read. Within the text, I give some measure of the value of expert opinions and evidence that I have worked hard to locate and organize. I give credit to those with whom I shared ideas, gleaned ideas, and combined ideas for new insights of my own.

I give credit both within my text and my references to help the reader identify my own knowledge trail so that they may learn more beyond what I write. By identifying experts, I can give the reader a key link to other resources of value that I may not even know about or that have not yet been written. For example, I would cite Carol Simpson, Associate Professor at North Texas University, and Kenny Crews, Law Professor at Indiana University-Indianapolis, in nearly any paper or presentation on copyright issues because their names trace to an established literature and can be counted on to lead the reader to future discussions. I would take the time to find relevant evidence from them to deliver to my audience, with much more in mind than a simple quotation. Links to experts help us keep on learning beyond the issues at hand.

Documentation of work, regardless of format, not only verifies that many sources have been examined, analyzed, and synthesized, but also expresses a judgment on these sources. The writer or speaker passes along to the audience his or her evaluation by stating relevance of the evidence and authority of the expert.

Daniel Callison, Ed.D., is a Professor at Indiana University School of Library and Information Science and Executive Associate Dean at Indianapolis; 755 W. Michigan Street; Indianapolis, IN 46212. Email: callison@iupui.edu; http://www.slis.iupui.edu

The information-literate student should know that giving credit to sources is not only the right thing to do, but also strengthens his or her final product. It serves to validate arguments and ideas. Plagiarism weakens the product and keeps it from addressing the following three-dimensional questions:

- What do I bring to the question?
- What can I assimilate from other sources?
- What do I now know and raise as a new question?
- Who helped me get there and how can I give them credit?

Peer Pressure, Procrastination, and Publish or Perish Often Equal Plagiarism

Plagiarism in the higher education circles has been widespread even before the temptations of electronic "cut and paste" (Hansen 2003). Macabe relates much of the plagiarism by college students to peer pressure and procrastination (1996). Surveys of college faculty indicate that nearly one third of college professors admit they have plagiarized at some time in their scholarly careers; another third indicate they have likely plagiarized but are not certain (Genereux 1995). Note that this information is cited, but the experts in each case are not of high relevance to my audience. They receive due credit, but not additional value through describing their authoritative standing within my text.

Recent charges of plagiarism against two prominent historians, Doris Kearns Goodwin and Stephen Ambrose, are common knowledge in popular reading circles. Their relatively minor transgressions are of much less importance than the extensive contributions both have made through primary interviews and tremendous firsthand research related to American presidential history. My opinion does not need documentation because similar opinions can be found easily in the popular news. However, if I were presenting detailed arguments to debate the Goodwin and Ambrose cases, I would cite resources extensively. These two examples serve to illustrate that even the best historians may not be the best role models, but the value of their contributions to history outweigh their minor transgressions of plagiarism.

Of course, this is not to say that plagiarism is not a serious ethical offense. *Plagiarius,* the Latin word for plagiarism, means kidnapper. Anyone who copies or even closely imitates another composer, artist, writer, or speaker without permission "kidnaps" or steals from the originator unless the original creator cannot be identified. Moreover, paraphrasing does not make an idea one that can be claimed by a new owner. Intellectual property in our society can be held by the creator for many years and for a profit.

The computerized cut-and-paste information world we live in today makes it easy to lift chunks of information from others and call them our own. This same computerized world, however, makes it easy to identify authoritative documentation and

to include it in our communications from the most basic of school reports to the most complex scholarly works.

So, with the following examples, let's see if I can apply some of these thoughts by reviewing issues as they pertain to plagiarism in the public schools.

Assign Inquiry, Not the Encyclopedia

David V. Loetscher aptly comments on traditional research projects by stating the need to "Ban the Bird Projects," because he believes critical thinking is called for in the design of student projects. His concept has become commonly understood due to the thousands of participants in his workshops, so it is not necessary to cite him formally in this article. His ideas may be accessed online by using the key term "Ban the Bird Projects" and his name. Because his statements have become classic within the context of the field, little more needs to be said.

Doug Johnson, proposed the following in *Phi Delta Kappan* (2004, 549):

Much effort is expended in education trying to "catch" plagiarism in student work. Teachers and library media specialists are using various web services and techniques using search engines to determine if or how much of student writing is lifted from online sources. Such tools are necessary and can be effective.

But our time as educators is better spent creating assignments, especially those that involve research, that minimize the likelihood of plagiarism in the first place. Rather than making assignments that can be easily plagiarized and then contriving methods for detecting or reducing copying, why not do a little work upfront to design projects that require original, thoughtful research?

Johnson has quoted Carol Tilley, formerly a school library media specialist in Danville, Indiana, who states that a good approach to discouraging electronic plagiarism is to "change the nature of the research assignment to utilize a higher level of thinking skills" (Johnson 1996). Johnson has built on Tilley's summary with examples that "lower [the] probability of plagiarism" or LPP projects. Some of Johnson's ideas related to inquiry-based approaches (also described in previous "Key Words in Instruction" columns, e.g., Callison, 2000; Callison and Lamb, September 2004; and Callison and Lamb, December 2004) are paraphrased as follows:

- Projects are based on student-raised questions associated with real-world questions concerning local issues. With guidance, topics that have relevance, meaning, and purpose effectively engage students.
- Projects should be based on such elements of research as data analysis, synthesis, and application of evidence. Evidence needs to include interviews, personal observations, experiments, or other primary source data. Answers can not be found based only on simple reference source searching.
- Projects should be partly written in narrative style to

include a description of how students formulated questions, gathered information, and determined the value of the information. The I-Search process originated by Macrorie (1988) and refined by Joyce and Tallman (1997) is useful.

- Projects should provide students with authentic assessment outlets involving a variety of presentation methods including multimedia. There should be a variety of audiences, not just the teacher, so students can adjust for differing ages and abilities.
- Another way to make projects relevant is for students to gather evidence and opinions to rank people, events, and opinions as they relate to them personally. Questions could be included as follows: What are the ten inventions that most influence your life and why? Who are the ten people who have influenced how you live and why? What are the ten events in history that have most affected how you live today and why? Assignments where the student must make judgments, evaluations, and choices and give justification are the goal.

Teaching More than Location and Citation

Joy McGregor, then Assistant Professor at Texas Woman's University, and Denise Streitenberger, then a doctoral student at TWU, observed high school juniors and found that they reduced their amount of copying

when taught how to paraphrase and correctly cite resources, but not by a great deal (1998). In a few cases, they suspected that students who copied, but provided a more clear and organized paper were graded higher than students who had messy, yet original papers. McGregor and Streitenberger concluded that teacher interventions regarding format and rules of correct citations seemed to limit the amount of blatant copying, but did not help students learn from the sources or construct their own understanding of their research topics (1998).

Their recommendations were that more time should be invested by the teacher collaborating with the library media specialist to work with students to understand the research process and to explore topics in more depth. Unfortunately, the most common instructional role of school library media specialist remains how to look up information and how to cite it.

Instructional library media specialists who approach projects based on inquiry principles know that their role with the teacher is to help stimulate many student-generated questions. These questions are intended to encourage students to read and explore background resources widely, and to demonstrate how such exploration leads to meaningful research project ideas from which students can make a choice. Proper citation style is taught at the point of need, when evidence is being gathered and documented.

In order to reduce the amount of cheating, teachers at the Lake Placid Central School of New York have adopted ideas originally developed in the Battle Creek Michigan School District and used with permission. Sara Kelly Johns, Director of School Library Media Services at Lake Placid Central, presented to ALA in 2005 a summary of the guidelines other teachers and she give to students:

- The best way to avoid cheating and plagiarism is to find ways to personalize your assignments. React in your writing about how your topic might personally affect you, your family, your school, or your community. An original conclusion supported by facts from other works that are properly cited is never cheating. Write in your own voice [style], not just in your own words.
- Organize your work so that you don't run into a last-minute time crunch that keeps you from studying, writing, creating, revising, reflecting, and making your work your own.
- Keep good records as you do research of where you found your supporting ideas. It's easier than doing research twice—once for finding the information and again for doing the bibliography.
- Always include a bibliography, list of resources, or acknowledgements whenever you use the work or ideas of others. If you can't provide a citation, don't use the source. If giving a presentation, credit your source verbally.
- Understand that using the work of others IS permissible and usually necessary to create a well-supported set of arguments, conclusions, or specific answers to questions. Give credit to the source of this work to avoid plagiarism.
- Make a large percentage of your work as original as possible. Use direct quotes or paraphrasing only when what you find is written in such a way that it clarifies or makes the idea expressed more understood.

Share Credit in the Media

Kym Kramer, library media specialist at Fishback Academy in Indianapolis, has engaged her elementary students over the years in many multimedia productions. During her annual celebration of the student products, she explains to an audience of parents all of the work that goes into planning and producing each individual student video. Above all, her students and she make sure parents and others know who was involved in each production as well as the resources that were used for scripts—especially student documentaries of local events and institutions.

Credit is given to the source of information, both within the narration of the student video and in print as credits roll at the end. Students who carried out technical duties also are credited. Kramer's students learn at an elementary school level the value and courtesy of giving credit to others who influence the product in any manner.

One of Kramer's graduate interns, Michelle Ward, recently assisted a group of students in writing a script to help them identify those who should be cited in a "video bibliography" (2005). The script was for two students who had completed, as a team, a report on the zoo. It is as follows:

My name is _____ and my name is _____.
We have been studying _____.
We got our live footage from the Indianapolis Zoo.
We got our information from _____,
We got our still shots from _____.
We got additional information from *Indyzoo.com*, *SIRS Discover*, and *EBSCO Animal Encyclopedia*.

I would add the following suggestions to Ward's script:

Zoo keepers interviewed were _____.
Video Director _____.
Script by _____.
Final Editing by _____ and _____.
Special "thanks" to _____ and _____ for their assistance, encouragement, and support.

As these elementary school students mature and do additional projects for science fairs, debates, and formal speeches, and to solve local community problems, they can build from these early experiences to give credit where credit is due both within the text of the presentation and at the end.

There is lots of credit to go around—just take the time to stay and view the credits as they roll after any major motion picture. Going that far may be too far, but encouraging students to practice the courtesy of acknowledging the work of others can certainly extend to all student products, not just the senior term paper.

References and Further Reading

Callison, Daniel. "Assignment." *School Library Media Activities Monthly* 17, no. 1 (September 2000): 39-43.

Callison, Daniel, and Annette Lamb. "Audience Analysis." *School Library Media Activities Monthly* 21, no. 1 (September 2004): 34-39.

Callison Daniel, and Annette Lamb. "Authentic Learning." *School Library Media Activities Monthly* 21, no. 4 (December 2004): 34-39.

Cheating: An Insider's Guide to Cheating at Lakeview High School. http://www.infotoday.com/MMSchools/jan02/Cheating.pdf (accessed August 18, 2005).

Genereux, R. L. "Circumstances Surrounding Cheating." *Research in Higher Education* 36 (1995): 687-704.

Hansen, Brian. "Combating Plagiarism: Is the Internet Causing More Students to Copy?" *CQ Researcher* 13, no. 32 (2003): 773-795.

Johns, Sara Kelly. "Information Ethics for the Net Generation." Presented at the American Library Association National Conference, Chicago, June 2005.

Johnson, Doug. *Head for the Edge.* http://www.doug-johnson.com/hfe.html (accessed August 16, 2005).

Johnson, Doug. *Learning Right from Wrong in the Digital Age.* Linworth, 2003.

Johnson, Doug. "Plagiarism-Proofing Assignments." *Phi Delta Kappan* 85, no. 7 (March 2004): 549-552.

Joyce, M. Z., and J. I. Tallman. *Making the Writing and Research Connection with the I-Search Process.* Neal-Schumann, 1997.

Macabe, D. "The Relationship between Student Cheating and Fraternity Membership." *NASPA Journal* 33 (1996): 280-291.

Macrorie, K. *The I-Search Paper.* Heinemann, 1988.

McGregor, Joy H., and Denise C. Streitenberger. "Do Scribes Learn? Copying and Information Use." *School Library Media Research* [online] 1 (1998). http://www.ala.org/aasl/SLMR (accessed August 16, 2005).

Ward, Michelle. *Journal of Internship with Kym Kramer for Certification as a School Library Media Specialist.* Indiana University School of Library and Information Science at Indianapolis, 2005.

Three useful websites to help you determine when and how to cite sources, avoid plagiarism, and present authoritative information as credible evidence are as follows:

Indiana University Writing Tutorial Services. http://www.indiana.edu/~wts/pamphlets.shtml

NoodleTools. http://www.noodletools.com/

Purdue University Online Writing Lab. http://owl.english.purdue.edu/handouts/research/r_plagiar.html ✋

Podcasting 101

by Kristin Fontichiaro

When I was in first grade, I could go to the recording corner of my classroom and dictate stories or other information into a cassette recorder. Sitting in the quiet corner, confidently speaking what was on my mind, I felt empowered, grown up, and expert, and I signed off each of my recording sessions with "This is Kristin Fontichiaro in Room 102" just as a real reporter might do on TV. These past feelings rushed back to me when I first heard about podcasting in the classroom.

What Is a Podcast?

A podcast is an audio file recorded on a computer and later shared with others. (The term "podcast" comes from combining the words "iPod" with "broadcast.") A microphone can be plugged into a computer microphone or USB jack and by using free or inexpensive software, multiple tracks can be recorded, making it easy to layer background music or sound effects over spoken text or narration. The digital format of podcasts makes editing errors or adding sound effects fast and easy. The real power, however, lies in sharing the final product. Podcasts aren't restricted to iPods since they can be uploaded to a web space, linked on a blog, burned to a CD, shared with parents and staff via email, downloaded to an mp3 player, or fed automatically into podcast-retrieving software like iTunes.

Well-designed podcasting projects help students develop oral fluency, write with an audience in mind, develop a "writer's voice," and increase confidence. Podcasting projects such as radio plays and mock news broadcasts invite high-level thinking and ask students to synthesize and showcase learning. Students are excited by this accessible technology and motivated to do great work for a real-world audience.

Equipment Needed

Podcasting equipment is very inexpensive. PC users with operating systems of Windows 98 or later can buy a combination microphone/headphone set for less than $10 and download the *Audacity* recording software for free (see Useful Websites). Mac users will need a more expensive USB microphone with the price starting at around $40. The *Audacity* software is available for Mac users with OS 9 or later. They can also use the fun and full-featured Garage Band that ships with new Mac computers. Lectures can be recorded with a wireless lapel microphone that costs around $150 and allows lecturers to move about the classroom while their presentations are recorded by the computer. Audio recording accessories such as these can turn newer-model iPods into portable recording studios.

If finances, however, prevent an equipment purchase, set up a free account with gabcast.com. Call Gabcast's toll-free number and leave a voice mail. After you review what has been recorded, Gabcast turns your message into an audio file online—an instant podcast! It will even post it to your blog.

Instructions for installing and using these options are available on each program's respective website (see Useful Websites).

Podcasting Projects for Beginners

When you begin podcasting, start simply by recording one child's voice at a time. As your confidence increases, add multiple voices, sound effects, or theme mu-

Kristin Fontichiaro is a library media specialist at Beverly Elementary in the Birmingham (Michigan) Public Schools and a free-lance arts education consultant. She can be reached at font@umich.edu, and her students' podcasts are online at http://www.birmingham. k12.mi.us/Schools/Elementary/Beverly/Media+Center/Podcasts.htm.

sic. The following project designs for podcasting can be implemented quickly and easily.

Create a class CD. Invite elementary students to record their research projects or creative writing stories. Create a separate audio file for each student. Burn the class's work onto a CD. An added benefit for elementary students is that reading aloud often doubles as an editing tool. As they read, students can find typographical, spelling, or grammar errors that might otherwise have been overlooked. Throw a launch party for this project during parent-teacher conferences!

Audio Tour. Visitors to museums can often take an audio tour of special exhibits. This idea can be used to invite a student to walk through your new school, an art show, or a book fair and narrate the highlights for visitors. Transfer the script for this tour onto an iPod or mp3 player for visitors.

Interview. PC users can purchase a Y-adapter that will allow two sets of headphones and microphones to feed into a single jack. This allows two people's voices to be recorded onto a single track. Invite a student to interview a school visitor such as an author, parent, fire fighter, dentist, college representative, superintendent, or politician. As a variation, create literature-based interviews in which one student plays a reporter and the other is the author, illustrator, or character from a book. Post the project on the Web for the community to enjoy.

Newscast. Invite students to research and co-host a school radio broadcast. You can also ask students to research a moment in history and report "live from the scene."

Students with Special Needs. Students who struggle with writing can quickly dictate assignments. Other students who, according to their IEPs, need to have tests read aloud can have them prerecorded onto an iPod so they feel "cool" instead of "different."

Foreign Language Practice. Foreign language teachers can use the *Audacity* software to record a series of questions for students to answer and leave a pause for responses after each question. The student can then open the file and configure *Audacity* to play back the teacher's track while recording responses onto a second track (FILE > PREFERENCES > AUDIO I/O > Check "Play other tracks while recording").

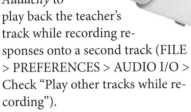

Radio Play. Ask students to recreate a moment from literature or to use research to create a radio play of historical fiction. Use student-created sound effects (or the sound effects built into Garage Band) to add dimensionality to the performance. The website *Creative Commons.org* can also be accessed to find music that does not require special permission to use in podcasts.

Podcasting and Personal Safety

Because digitally recorded audio projects can be transmitted so easily and cheaply, it is difficult to control exactly who will hear them. Consequently, for personal safety, students should use only first names or a pseudonym and should not include identifying details such as last names, addresses, student sports teams, or names of community or religious organizations. If a blanket media permission form is not already in place in your district, send a permission slip home to parents.

Conclusion

Podcasting is so simple to create, yet has so many potential uses. I think students and teachers in your school will be hooked! "This is Kristin Fontichiaro in Room 102."

References

Fontichiaro, Kristin. *Active Learning through Drama, Podcasting, and Puppetry.* Libraries Unlimited, 2007 (forthcoming).

Useful Websites
Software for creating or managing podcasts and audio files:
iTunes (Mac or PC). http://www.apple.com/iTunes
Garage Band (Mac only). http://www.apple.com/ilife/garageband
Audacity (Mac or PC). http://audacity.sourceforge.net
QuickTime Pro (one-button recording; Mac or PC). http://www.apple.com/quicktime
Websites that host podcasts for free:
Gabcast. http://www.gabcast.com
OurMedia. http://www.ourmedia.org
Source for royalty-free podcast music:
Creative Commons. http://www.creativecommons.org

Wikis and Collaborative Inquiry

by Annette Lamb and Larry Johnson

From exploring electronic databases to copying from *Wikipedia*, most students rely on the Internet for information. But, how many of these students really understand the origin of this information or the collaborative process used to create these pages?

Wikis Defined

Wikis are simply Web sites that provide easy-to-use tools for creating, editing, and sharing digital documents, images, and media files. Multiple participants can enter, submit, manage, and update a single Web workspace creating a community of authors and editors.

Wiki projects help young people shift from being *consumers* of the Internet to *creators* on the Web. Open-editing wiki tools engage students in exciting collaborative learning experiences that promote reading, writing, and high level thinking across content areas and grade levels. Wikis are a quick and easy way to energize reluctant learners, promote group synergy, and encourage authentic learning.

The Home of Sylvie wiki traces a Coho salmon, whose life story has been dramatized by the fourth and fifth graders of Harborview Elementary School (http://anadrama.wikispaces.com/). Students learned about the salmon and created a fact-based wiki in collaboration with community members.

While some projects are text-based, many incorporate a wide range of media including images, audio, video, and animation. *The Voices of the World* wiki involves participants in sharing ideas and information each month during the school year (http://votw.wikispaces.com/). Students exchange information about their countries, cultures, and varied languages through various media.

Wikis can be differentiated from other Web development software by their collaborative features including membership options, discussion tools, and history functions.

Membership options. Most wiki tools allow the Web site to be public, protected, or private. Public wikis can be viewed and edited by anyone. Protected wikis can be viewed by all users but only edited by members. Private wikis can only be viewed and edited with permission. Participants should select the best approach for their particular collaboration. For instance, an elementary class may become members of a protected wiki, while members of a community project might make their wiki public. Participants may choose to be notified of updates to monitor project progress.

Discussion tools. Many wiki spaces provide a discussion tab or comment option. In a collaborative environment, these tools can be used to provide feedback, note a connection, or explain changes that have been made to a page. These tools can be used to hold book discussions, to critique materials, or to vote for favorite content.

History functions. Additions and changes to wiki pages can be tracked using the history tools. This option is particularly useful in assessment. The contributions and comments made by each student can be viewed.

Successful Wiki Projects

Wikis provide new opportunities for students to share their findings. When studying Greek mythology, young people might read a classic such as *D'Aulaire's Book of Greek Myths* or the popular *Percy Jackson & the Olympians* series. Rather than simply writing a summary or taking a test, the content in social studies and language arts classes could be combined to address *AASL Standards for the 21st-Century Learner* and create a high impact learning experience.

Sixth grade students in southern Illinois collaborated on a project related to *Greek Mythology* wiki (http://mra-ancient-greece.wikispaces.com/). Their mission was to select a successor to Zeus's throne. After selecting a Greek god or goddess to nominate, students used Paint software to create a symbol representing their candidate. They also created informational wiki pages for their nominee and edited the pages of their peers (see Figure 1). Students were encouraged to read and link to peer postings. Pages were also created for fictional political parties where political posters and audio campaign ads were published. The six finalists took on the role of their god and participated in interviews using the "discussion" tab in the wiki. Finally, students voted on Zeus's successor. Using the "history" tab, the teacher was able to trace student writing and editing activities.

When working with wikis in teaching and learning, there are many options. Students can join an existing project, use another project as a model, or start one. Students can work independently, link to each other, peer edit, comment, and/or work collaboratively.

What Makes a Successful Wiki?

Unique Content. Why recreate the Web? The key to a successful wiki is identifying and filling a niche need. What can be created or organized that isn't available elsewhere? For example, a wiki can be based on one of the following topics:

- ►a small town or community without a Web site
- ►an interesting historical building, location, or event
- ►a lesser-known, regional, or note-worthy person
- ►oral histories or memories of a particular shared experience—an event that may have been overlooked by other Web sites
- ►an invented world or fictional work
- ►thematic resources for literature circles or book clubs with a unique focus

Structure. A project may quickly fizzle without good organization. An effective wiki makes good use of hyperlinks to connect information and ideas. Rather than one long page or a series of unrelated Web pages, a quality wiki provides an intuitive way to explore information. One idea is linked to another so that people can see the forest and the trees. Consider these factors for a wiki structure:

- ►How will people see the "big pic-

ture," but also understand all the elements?

- ►How can information be shared in an appealing, organized way?
- ►How can a consistent structure be developed through agreed upon guidelines?
- ►How can many people contribute while maintaining a sense of shared voice?

Flexibility. A well-designed wiki has both structure and flexibility. A wiki should not be started with all the information already in place. If it's complete, then why not just create Web pages? One of the best things about wikis is their versatility. Incomplete information or the beginning of an idea is viewed by the wiki community as an opportunity for another participant to contribute rather than seen as an omission. Although structure is important, it must be balanced with the opportunity to expand and dig deeper into the content. For instance, a wiki can be started about favorite illustrators. It can then be added to, developed, and refined over time. Or, a wiki abut a new park project might detail the plants found in the park, leaving year two for the animals, and year three for the geologic features.

Synergy. When people work together toward a joint goal, the result is often more comprehensive than when individuals work independently. Although

wikis work fine with small groups, larger projects require more commitment by individual group members or a larger writing pool. Contributors to wikis can be expanded to students or community members representing:

- ►Other class periods, schools, or countries
- ►Different age groups—young and old
- ►Varied perspectives, experiences, or points of view
- ►Different geographic areas
- ►Varied cultures
- ►Different academic fields

Enthusiasm. When engaging teen learners in a class project, it's important that the project provides a high level of interest. Participants need to be passionate about the content or the project activities will quickly become a chore rather than a quest for knowledge. One way to maintain enthusiasm is through questioning. Consider some of the following questions:

- ►What questions do we have about this topic?
- ►What do we still need to learn?
- ►Where can we go to collect more information?
- ►What can we create ourselves?
- ►What are different ways we can tell our story or share our information through varied media?
- ►How can we refine or expand what we have?

Figure 1. *Greek Mythology* wiki

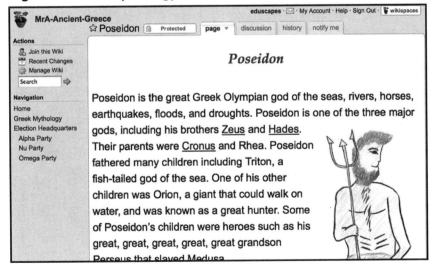

Wikis and Collaborative Learning

Wikis are effective in promoting collaborative learning within classes, between classes, among schools, with parents, and with communities.

Within Classes. Wikis work well as both whole class and small group activities. Since literature circles already contain collaborative elements, a wiki can be built for each group.

Nancy Bosch, a gifted facilitator in Kansas has used wikis for numerous classroom projects with her 4th through 6th graders. Her first wiki involved children sharing information about Frank Lloyd Wright and the book *The Wright 3* by Blue Balliett (http://thewright3.wiki-spaces.com/). In another project called *arrrpirates*, students learned about the Big6™ and explored pirates while reading *Peter and the Starcatchers* by Dave Berry and Ridley Pearson (http://arrrpirates. wikispaces.com/). Young learners not only worked on their own pages, but they also linked to the work of their classmates (see Figure 2).

Between Classes. Students always enjoy communicating with other classes. The library media specialist is in a great position to coordinate activities among classes. They can examine standards across content areas that might make interesting projects. For example, history students working on projects on Ancient Rome might work with a class learning to build model bridges.

Among Schools. Collaborative relationships can be developed among schools in different parts of the country or around the world. In *The Thousand and One Flat World Tales Project*, young people write stories and provide feedback for other student authors (http://burell9english.wikispaces.com).

With Parents. Parents can get involved with classroom activities through a library wiki project. For example, a project can be designed where people share ideas for places that families can visit within 100 miles of school. This type of experience allows parents to become involved with their children's computer activities.

With Community. Local community members or experts can also get involved with a wiki. A wiki can be used for a One Book, One Community Project. Local business representatives can also be asked to share experiences about starting a new enterprise or give their perspectives on local economic issues.

Wikis and Collaborative Information Inquiry

Wikis involve learners in asking increasingly sophisticated questions about a topic. After the initial excitement about the topic and exploration of essential questions, learners begin to assimilate new information and draw inferences. This leads to reflection and additional questions. This recursive process leads to increasingly complex questions, more in-depth analysis, and deeper understandings. These abstract connections can be made more concrete for learners through the creation of wikis. Features such as hyperlinks allow contributors to share their links to pieces of information.

The WebQuest approach to inquiry-based learning can be rediscovered through the use of wikis. In the *Goofy Global News* wiki, students are introduced to an inquiry task related to real and fictional news stories, then provided with online resources and activities (http://ggn.wikispaces.com/). Young people add their own pages to the wiki and use the discussion tab to review the pages of their peers (see Figure 3).

The Inquiry Process. Wikis encourage learners to think about how information

Figure 2. *arrrpirates* wiki

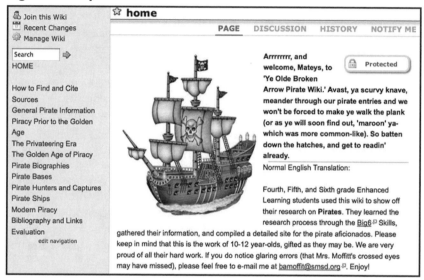

Figure 3. *Goofy Global News* wiki

can be organized to maximize understanding. For example, wikis can use alphabetical, chronological, hierarchical, geographical, or thematic approaches. Some people use outlines or visual maps (i.e., cluster map, flowchart, mindmap) for organization. Others design around regional locations, events, characters, key words, genres, categories, or other ways of thinking about a topic. Another approach is to focus organization around essential questions or problems.

The *CSI: Cemetery Scene Investigation*

wiki (http://csi.wikispaces.com/) and the *Weathering* wiki (http://weathering.wikispaces.com/) show how young people used wikis to organize and synthesize information during the inquiry process. Students recorded GPS coordinates, uploaded digital images, and wrote scientific and historical information about graves in their local cemetery. They also conducted research on burials. They finished by creating a Web site for the final project.

Collaborative Learning. Wikis allow learners to participate in a project larger

than their own. Participants can learn from each other and expand their thinking about a topic by working as a team. In addition, it's easy for them to go back and track who did what and when.

In the *Civil War Literature* wiki, participants begin by focusing on a historical fiction book set during the American Civil War (http://civilwarlit.wikispaces.com/). Once they have developed the informational wiki pages on their book, they started looking for connections with other Civil War themed books and found ways to connect their ideas and content to work created by others. For instance, if two books are about medicine of the Civil War, students collaborated on a single page rather than duplicating efforts. Participants were encouraged to connect with young people at other schools (see Figure 4).

Wikis in the Library Media Center

In addition to student-produced wikis, library media specialists are using wikis as part of library programs and professional development activities. For instance, Joyce Valenza's *Book Leads* (http://bookleads.wikispaces.com/) is a place where teacher librarians can share information about reading resources and ideas (see Figure 5).

Many free and low cost services are available for creating wikis. Web sites without advertising should be considered when choosing wikis for young people. Ads can be distracting and sometimes link to inappropriate sites for these young learners. *Wikispaces* is a site that currently provides ad-free wikis for educators (http://www.wikispaces.com/site/for/teachers).

Educators can learn more about wikis by exploring the online workshop, *Wiki World*, by the authors of this article (http://eduscapes.com/sessions/wiki/).◄

Annette Lamb, Ph.D., and Larry Johnson, Ph.D., are educational consultants and teach in the School of Library and Information Science at Indiana University at Indianapolis (IUPUI).

Figure 4. *Civil War Literature* wiki

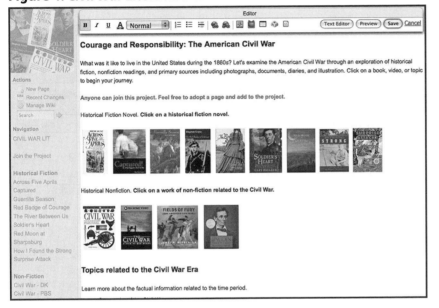

Figure 5. *Book Leads* wiki

An Open Book: Life Online

by Kathy Fredrick

A Wealth of Online Resources

Most people probably remember the slogan "everything is connected." People today have to look no further than the wealth of online tools available to create, store, and collaborate. Who would've guessed there would be an option to access personal medical records online? Who would have guessed that Web 2.0 would provide a host of resources to share information and ideas, as well as tools that allow people to access work wherever there is an Internet connection. The level of functionality is equal to suites like Microsoft Office with the cost minimal and sometimes even free.

What do these services and tools have to offer? They include software suites and document storage for minimal or no cost, the ability to share files with other users, the ability to conference with others using (high speed) Internet connection, and the opportunity to build a personal portal to the world.

It All Began…

How did all of this evolve? The granddaddy of all services, aimed to provide multiple tools in one place, emerged when AOL America Online provided an Internet connection, a web portal, email, and instant messaging services. It was the precursor to the more sophisticated tools now available. A host of other providers then followed suit. Google forged ahead, beginning with Gmail, then Google Docs, and now a seemingly endless list of must-have online utilities. With the advent of cell phones that allow Internet browsing and program applications, these Web 2.0 tools are a natural match.

The move to open source software shared worldwide has led some major software providers to join in this convergence of productivity tools. Adobe's Acrobat.com site has a free PDF creation tool, web conferencing software, and document sharing and storage. Microsoft has chimed in with Microsoft Live that extends Microsoft services for sharing documents, calendaring, and more. The educational version of their services can be found at live@edu. Most providers mentioned in this article also offer "enterprise" versions of their software for a fee based on number of users with a monthly or yearly charge. This fee-based level provides expanded capabilities for sharing of documents, including a way to track document changes. Some even use a check-in/check-out system—a familiar approach to library mavens. Educators are looking closely at these new options as a way to save money on software costs and still provide storage from any Internet connection.

A Look at Purpose

So what can be gained by looking at these new generation tools? And which ones could make life easier? There are three usage categories listed with some strong service providers for each function. The category "create and store documents online" can be provided by using such services as *Zoho*, Google-Docs, or *Glide*. The category "conference with others" can be provided through sites such as *Yugma*, *DimDim*, and *Vmukti*. The category "planner and calendaring tools for managing time" can be provided through such services as *Zoho* or iGoogle. The beauty of these providers is that information can be kept in a private workspace or shared with others—by invitation.

Document creation and storage online makes it possible to get documents from any Internet-connected computer. Sites like *Zoho* and Google require the user to set up a free account, and the user then has access to programs with features similar to any productivity software package. Word processing and spreadsheets will look familiar (Figure 1). Presentation software may not have all the bells and whistles of the software program installed on most computers (transitions and animations may be lacking), but, for the most part, are remarkably robust products ready for use.

Planner and calendar tools are great for those needing a way to keep track of time and stay organized. The calendar

Figure 1: *Zoho* Writer opening screen

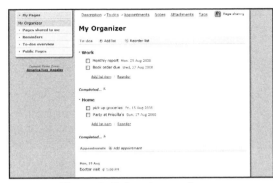

Figure 2: *Zoho* planner layout

tools in *Glide*, Google, and *Zoho* (Figure 2) are particularly useful. It is possible to track assignments and add specific notes for work. Calendars can be shared and updated by others on both Google Calendar and *Glide* Calendar. Library media specialists can use these tools to share the library calendar with teaching colleagues. It is also possible to create to-do lists with categories in *Zoho* planner, e.g., one list for home, one for work.

A Step Beyond Blogs and Wikis

Blogs and wikis both involve collaborating in a shared space. This can be taken a step further with sites like *Yugma*, *DimDim*, and *Vmukti*, where online space can be shared, work can be done simultaneously on shared documents, and conversations about work can be undertaken. These services allow communication with one person or whole groups. *Yugma* allows free connections for up to ten people at a time. A session can be started using their online tool (Figure 3), and others can be invited to

Figure 3: *Yugma* session controller

participate, granting them rights to both modify documents and act as moderator for the session. The whiteboard feature can be used to brainstorm, add information to documents for all participants to see, and record the session for posterity. Voice communication can be added through a partnership with Skype, a voice-over-IP (Internet protocol) telephone service.

Services can be brought together in one place using sites like iGoogle and *Glide*. The iGoogle portal lets users email and integrate all Google Docs services—word processing, spreadsheets, and presentation software—as well as integrate RSS feeds to favorite news and blogs. Tabs can be set up to reflect personal interests such as books, cooking, and skydiving on the user's personal iGoogle. Other options are also available. Many enterprising souls have created a widget and gadget world of add-ins. Users can also add a clock, set a birthday reminder list, and choose artwork of the day. These tools and hundreds more are available from Google. There is also a notebook tool for research process support. The online service *Glide* is described as a "complete mobile desktop solution" and, as such, provides software, email, calendaring, and conferencing —and lets the user move between desktop and portal to accommodate a wide range of tools.

Too Good to Be True?

Does this sound too good to be true? The answer is that these tools are available with few strings attached. Should users be hesitant to put their work out there? Despite promises of security and policies that state information will not be shared without express permission, it is advisable to investigate the sites to determine the level of security support. Is information truly private? Will others be able to see work posted? More providers are including encryption and

security measures. Can these tools be used at school? If such sites are blocked, it will require working with technical support staff to determine if access will be allowed since filters may block sites that allow collaboration. Despite these questions, there's no doubt that these online tools allow users to access information and share it from any Internet connection. Convenience and convergence mean great value for personal workspace—living online is the way to go.

Resources:

Van Horn, Roman. "Web Applications and Google." *Phi Delta Kappan* 88, no. 10 (June 2007): 727, 792.

VanderMolen, Julie. "Collaborative Writing." *Technology & Learning* (August 1, 2008). http://www.techlearning.com/story/show-Article.php?articleID=196605337 &page=1 (accessed September 14, 2008).◄

Kathy Fredrick is the Director of Libraries and Instructional Technology for the Shaker Heights City Schools in Ohio. She has worked in school libraries at all grade levels in Ohio, Wisconsin, Australia, and Germany. Email: fredrick_k@shaker.org

Web Sites

Acrobat.com. https://acrobat.com/

DimDim. http://www.dimdim.com/index#

Glide. http://www.glideos.com/

GoogleApps. http://www.google.com/intl/en/options/

Lifehacker. http://lifehacker.com/

Microsoft Live. http://www.microsoft.com/education/solutions/liveedu.aspx

Vmukti. http://www.vmukti.com/

Yugma. http://www.yugma.com/

Zoho. http://www.zoho.com/index.html

Mindsets:
How Praise Is Harming Youth and What Can Be Done about It

by Carol S. Dweck

Today's companies are reporting that their young employees need constant praise. Without it, they become morose and disgruntled. Coaches are complaining that their athletes can no longer tolerate corrective feedback. The athletes claim it undermines their confidence. Parents say that their children don't want to work hard in school. The children feel it should just come naturally.

What has happened in this country that used to be known for a solid work ethic and rugged individualism? Now, young people have a disastrous combination of entitlement and fragility. How did this happen and what can be done about it?

Research conducted at Columbia and Stanford Universities suggests that it could be well-meaning parent and teacher practices that have brought this on—practices that were meant to boost children's self-esteem. In the 1990s, parents and teachers, prompted by the self-esteem movement, decided that self-esteem was the most important thing in the world—that if a child had self-esteem everything else would follow.

The big problem came when they decided how to give children that self-esteem. In many cases, parents and teachers began telling children on a regular basis how smart and talented they were. In a survey done in the mid 1990s, over 80% of parents reported that they thought their children must be praised in order to give them confidence and motivation (Mueller and Dweck 1998). Most of them still seem to believe this. Recently, in an airport, the author observed a mother telling her 6-month-old son that he was brilliant.

Unfortunately, this commonly held belief of both teachers and parents isn't true. Research shows that children cannot be given self-esteem through this kind of praise (Mueller and Dweck 1998; Kamins and Dweck 1999). But, even worse, it also shows that this type of praise actually makes their self-esteem fragile—and undermines their motivation to learn. How can this be? How can the effect be just the opposite of what intuition or common sense seem to indicate?

Understanding Mindsets

The mindsets of students must first be understood to appreciate why praise for intelligence or talent might backfire. For over 20 years research has explored these mindsets and shown their impact on students' confidence and motivation (Dweck 2006).

Research indicates that some students have a fixed mindset because they believe that their intelligence

Carol S. Dweck is the Lewis and Virginia Eaton Professor of Psychology at Stanford University, Stanford, CA, and the author of *Mindset* (Random House, 2006).

is simply a fixed trait. They have a certain amount, and there's nothing they can do to change it. Not surprisingly, they worry about how much they have. Other students, however, have a growth mindset. They believe that their intelligence is a quality that can be developed. They don't believe everyone is the same, but they do believe that everyone can increase their intelligence through effort and education. Therefore, they don't spend their time worrying about how smart they are and instead spend it trying to get smarter.

Which view is correct? Although the answer to such questions is typically that both views have merit, more and more research indicates the following:

- Important aspects of intelligence can be developed (Sternberg 2005).
- The brain has enormous capacity to grow and change throughout life (Doidge 2007).
- Motivation and self-regulation often have more impact on achievement and the growth of ability than does a person's initial ability (Blackwell et al. 2007; Duckworth and Seligman 2005; Ericsson et al. 2006).

These differing mindsets affect students' achievement by creating different psychological worlds. Here is how these worlds work.

What do students care about?

In the fixed-mindset world, students care more about looking smart than about learning. In their world, every performance holds their intelligence up for judgment, so that learning takes a back seat to looking smart. In fact, research by Dweck and her colleagues has shown that students in a fixed mindset will even sacrifice learning that is crucial to their future success if they have to admit ignorance or risk showing de-

ficiencies (Hong et al. 1999).

On the other hand, in the growth-mindset world, students care first and foremost about learning. They don't have to worry about discrediting their permanent intelligence, so they can devote themselves to the task of getting smarter.

What do mistakes and effort mean?

In the fixed-mindset world, students worry about making mistakes. They see making mistakes as a sign of low ability. They also worry about effort and view it in the same way—as a sign of low ability. They believe that if they have high ability they shouldn't need any effort. These are both terrible beliefs because mistakes and effort are integral parts of learning. Because students with fixed mindsets make them into things to be avoided, they actually stand in the way of learning. In fact, research in psychology indicates that the main thing that distinguishes people who go to the top of their fields and make great creative contribution from their equally able peers is the effort they put in (Ericsson et al. 2006). The fixed mindset cannot take people to that level.

Students with a growth mindset understand that mistakes and effort are critical to learning. They, therefore, welcome challenges and seek critical feedback to help them learn.

When students are asked, "When do you feel smart?," students with a fixed mindset reply that they feel smart when something is easy for them, when they do a task quickly without mistakes, or when other people look dumb. But students with a growth mindset state that they feel smart when they are struggling with something hard and make progress or when they are helping someone else to learn (Dweck 2006).

Thus, it is the growth mindset that

helps students adopt the values that lead to intellectual growth.

How do students react to setbacks?

Students with a fixed mindset lose heart in the face of setbacks. If setbacks mean they lack ability and ability is fixed—and effort is distasteful—what can they do? Compared to students with a growth mindset, students with a fixed mindset indicate that after one failure in a class they would withdraw their effort, avoid similar courses in the future, and consider cheating. The fixed mindset provides no good recipe for recovering from a failure.

Students with a growth mindset say that after a failure they would simply study more in the future or study in a different way. Their failure is a spur to learning. As a result, these students end up earning higher grades—whether it's during their transition to junior high or the challenging organic chemistry course at the beginning of the pre-med college curriculum.

In short, students with a fixed mindset, no matter how bright, often develop values and habits that stand in the way of developing their abilities and doing well in school. In contrast, students with a growth mindset embrace learning, mistakes, and effort in a way that promotes their achievement.

Praise: How Do Students Learn the Mindsets?

What effects do praise and other well-meaning practices of parents have on their children? Modern parents want to give their children everything possible to build them up and ensure their happiness and success. The self-esteem movement told them that the secret lay in praise, especially in praise of the child's essential qualities. This has great intuitive appeal—

tell children they're smart and they'll have faith in their intelligence.

However, studies conducted over many years involving vulnerable students indicated that it was these very children who were overly concerned with how smart they were (Dweck 2006). It appeared that parents who place too much emphasis on intelligence or talent could send the wrong message. By praising a child's intelligence or talent, they could be conveying to their child that intelligence or talent is something deep and permanent that can be judged and quantified—a fixed mindset. They could also be conveying that brains and talent are what they value the child for, so that children become afraid that if they're not successful, they won't be considered smart anymore and they won't be valued anymore.

Research put this issue to the test (Mueller and Dweck 1998). Several hundred children—from different regions of the country and of different ethnicities—were given problems from an IQ test. After the first set of problems, some of them were given praise for their intelligence: "That's a really good score. You must be smart at this." Others were given praise for their efforts: "That's a really good score. You must have worked really hard." This one line or praise had a cascade of striking effects. First, the intelligence praise instilled more of a fixed mindset, making students believe that their intelligence was a fixed trait, whereas the effort praise instilled more of a growth mindset. Next, the praise changed students' desire for challenge and learning. Students praised for their intelligence now wanted easy tasks so they wouldn't jeopardize their label "smart." Students praised for effort wanted challenging tasks they could learn from, even if they would make mistakes.

When given more difficult problems, the intelligence-praised

students crumbled. They lost confidence, they lost their enjoyment of the task, and their performance—even on subsequent easier problems—fell significantly. In the public view, intelligence praise was supposed to hand them the gift of confidence, but instead it made them fragile. They were initially puffed up by the intelligence praise, displaying proud little smiles on their faces that weren't seen in the effort-praised group. But their pride evaporated quickly at the first sign of difficulty.

Effort-praised students, however, maintained their faith in their abilities, kept on enjoying the task, and showed markedly improved performance over time. The effort praise kept them focused on what mattered for their motivation and performance. Rather than worry about their intelligence, they focused on their efforts and kept on striving. This is reminiscent of the children who are puffed up by their parents' praise, but then are unable or unwilling to work hard in school. It is also seemingly reflective of the young workers who need constant praise and encouragement to keep up their confidence.

In the studies of praise, there was one more finding that was troubling. Students were asked to write anonymously to a child in another school, and a space was left on the sheet of paper for them to write in their score. Almost 40% of the intelligence-praised students lied about their score. (Only 13% of the students in the effort-praised group reported an incorrect score.) This means that praising children's intelligence makes them so invested in their intelligence that they cannot admit their mistakes. If they cannot admit their mistakes, they cannot correct their mistakes.

In several other studies, students in a fixed mindset did not confront

and remedy deficiencies—even when given the opportunity—whereas students in a growth mindset did (Hong et al. 1999; Mangels et al. 2006; Nussbaum and Dweck 2008). It is absolutely critical for people of all ages to honestly consider their mistakes and failings because there will always be mistakes and failings no matter how proficient people become. Without this capacity, intellectual growth is stunted.

This may well be why coaches are suddenly finding their young players to be uncoachable. Because these players are part of the overpraised generation, they may, like the intelligence-praised students in the research studies, have gotten the message that mistakes are unacceptable. They, therefore, may not be able to take even constructive criticism from their coaches—feedback that is essential for their continued growth and success.

How to Promote a Growth Mindset

What are the ways in which educators and parents can foster a growth mindset in children?

Feedback

Following up on the praise research, the first way is through process praise. That is, adults should praise the process the child engaged in—the effort, the strategies, the perseverance, the choices—rather than the intelligence or talent they think the child showed. Here are some examples:

"I really like the way you did those hard problems. You stuck to them until you figured out how to do them."

"Those are really interesting colors you chose for your painting. Tell me about them."

"You practiced a lot and you really improved. That's exciting!"

An important role for parents and

teachers is helping children to enjoy challenges and struggles:

"Wow, that was challenging. That was fun!"

"You chose a really hard one. You're going to learn a lot!"

"I like the way you struggled with that. I love a good struggle."

Parents and educators can also promote a growth mindset through process-focused criticism. Many adults are currently reluctant to criticize children, thinking that it will harm their self-esteem. But when this is taken too far, it deprives children of the helpful feedback that is essential to their learning and can make them unable to tolerate constructive feedback. Constructive, process-focused criticism is feedback that helps children understand how to do better the next time. Here are some examples:

"When you struck out your last time at bat I don't think you were keeping your eye on the ball. Let's try to make sure to do that next time."

"I really sympathize with you. I know you wanted to win a ribbon, but you're new at this and it looks like it will take a lot more hard work before it happens."

"Well, that didn't work—what are some strategies you could try now?"

Part of constructive feedback is helping children embrace and capitalize on mistakes. For example:

"That was a great mistake. It really helped us see what you don't understand yet."

"Class, who'd like to share an interesting mistake and tell us what they learned from it?"

"Let's go around the dinner table and each of us can tell about the best mistake we made today."

Brainology

As a part of the author's research,

workshops have been developed to teach students about the growth mindset. In one study, an eight-session program taught students many great study skills and also taught them the growth mindset. They read an article, "You Can Grow Your Intelligence," in which they learned that the brain is like a muscle that grows stronger with practice and that every time they apply themselves and learn something new their brain forms new connections. They also learned how to apply this lesson to their schoolwork. When compared to a control group that got eight sessions of only study skills, the students in the growth-mindset workshop showed an impressive increase in their engagement with school and in their math grades.

More recently, a computer-based workshop called "Brainology" is being developed. It teaches the growth mindset through six interactive computer modules and shows students how to engage with their schoolwork in ways that build new connections in their brains. When a pilot test of "Brainology" was conducted in twenty New York City schools, virtually every student reported noteworthy changes in motivation and behavior. The author and her colleagues are now working to make "Brainology" more widely available in the future.

Conclusion

Looking at mindsets has helped researchers understand how young people can become dependent on praise, fearful of challenges, allergic to effort, and demoralized by critical feedback. It has clarified why employers, coaches, and parents are having a hard time working effectively with these young people. Now that the power of mindsets can be understood, it is time to put this knowledge to work. It can help the next generation, not by trying to hand

them self-esteem, but by fostering in them a desire to stretch and, thereby, develop a capacity for resilience. This is the best gift anyone can give them.

References

Blackwell, L., K. Trzesniewski, , and C. S. Dweck. "Implicit Theories of Intelligence Predict Achievement across an Adolescent Transition: A Longitudinal Study and an Intervention." *Child Development* 78 (2007): 246-263.

Doidge, N. *The Brain that Changes Itself.* Viking, 2007.

Duckworth, A., and M. Seligman. "Self-discipline Outdoes IQ in Predicting Academic Performance of Adolescents." *Psychological Science* 16 (2005): 939–944.

Dweck, C. S. *Mindset.* Random House, 2006.

Ericsson, K.A., N. Charness, P. J. Feltovich, and R. R. Hoffman, eds. *The Cambridge Handbook of Expertise and Expert Performance.* Cambridge University Press, 2006.

Hong, Y. Y., C. Chiu, C. S. Dweck, D. Lin, and W. Wan. "Implicit Theories, Attributions, and Coping: A Meaning System Approach." *Journal of Personality and Social Psychology* 77 (1999): 588-599.

Kamins, M., and C. S. Dweck. "Person vs. Process Praise and Criticism: Implications for Contingent Self-worth and Coping." *Developmental Psychology* 35 (1999): 835-847.

Mangels, J. A., B. Butterfield, J. Lamb, C. D. Good, and C. S. Dweck. "Why Do Beliefs about Intelligence Influence Learning Success? A Social-Cognitive-Neuroscience Model." *Social, Cognitive, and Affective Neuroscience* 1 (2006): 75-86.

Mueller, C. M., and C. S. Dweck. "Intelligence Praise Can Undermine Motivation and Performance." *Journal of Personality and Social Psychology* 75 (1998): 33-52.

Nussbaum, A.D., and C. S. Dweck. "Defensiveness vs. Remediation: Self-Theories and Modes of Self-Esteem Maintenance." *Personality and Social Psychology Bulletin* (2007, in press).

Sternberg, R. "Intelligence, Competence, and Expertise. In *The Handbook of Competence and Motivation,* edited by A. Eliot and C. S. Dweck. Guilford Press, 2005.

Chapter 10

Elementary Lesson Plans

> *There is often a struggle in elementary schools between a desire for higher-order thinking and students' emerging reading skills. How do we simultaneously promote the new Standards for the 21st-Century Learner . . . and the call for independent, inquiry- oriented engagement when our students are just learning to read or write?*

> —Kristin Fontichiaro and Debbie West, "Promoting Inquiry with Emerging
> Readers Using Elephogs and Octobunnies" (page 313)

Chapter 9 outlines instructional strategies that could be employed in a variety of teaching and learning situations. In this chapter specific, field-tested lesson plans for the elementary learner are examined for each of the major academic areas: reading, writing, social studies, and science.

Reading

Judi Moreillon, whose articles about collaborative strategies are featured in chapter 8, models co-teaching of reading skills with two lessons. In *"Words Are Like Faces:* An Exploration into Language and Communication" (beginning on page 309), she demonstrates the power of co-teaching to help students in grades 2–5 connect emotions with poetic devices in Edith Baer and Kyra Teis's *Words Are Like Faces.* "Tricking the Trickster: Recording and Comparing Story Elements" (beginning on page 328) discusses several potential collaboration methods and includes guidance for how teachers and students can evaluate the students' collaboration, note-making, and compare-and-contrast skills. This multifaceted approach to assessment brings the *Standards for the 21st-Century Learner* to life by inviting students into the assessment process. Skills and dispositions are assessed.

Inquiry and Writing

"Promoting Inquiry with Emerging Readers Using Elephogs and Octobunnies" (beginning on page 313) demonstrates a collaboration between Reading Recovery™ teacher Debbie West and school library media specialist Kristin Fontichiaro. The goal was for students to think beyond the traditional "just the facts" animal report, and instead combine the features of two animals to create a new animal. The students then brainstormed reasons for including that animal in the local zoo and created a convincing letter to the zoo in the style of a formal paragraph. Team-teaching allows for frequent formative assessment and higher student writing mastery.

Social Studies

Remember the research of the past, which took place over an extended period and required a formal report? Twenty-first-century research can be more focused—and less time intensive. Consider the possibility of several shorter projects over a single long-term project. Maureen Tannetta's lesson plan (beginning on page 316) has a short research period followed by a short student response in the form of a historical letter. Long before e-mail, instant messaging, or push-to-talk cell phone technology, two revolutionary authors—the husband-and-wife team of Abigail and John Adams—were constant correspondents. In "Abigail and John Adams Online," Tannetta connects her Massachusetts students with their states' antecedents by introducing their letters as primary source material. Students move from merely reading letters to selecting one and crafting a historically accurate response. By doing so, students connect to the history of their state and practice writing in a different voice.

Science

The AASL *Standards* repeatedly refer to inquiry as a learning modality. This raises a question: Do school library media specialists support inquiry anywhere, or only when it is in the library, using library-procured materials? In chapter 6, Kristin Fontichiaro and Sandy Buczynski explore this question and suggest that school library media specialists supporting classroom-based, hands-on science inquiry, especially when using the science notebooking process for documentation and processing, could be a gateway to scientific inquiry with library resources. Buczynski and Fontichiaro's lesson plan, "Science Notebooking in Action: Where Does Condensation Come From?" (beginning on page 318), gives an example of classroom-based science inquiry, and "Science Notebooking in the Library Media Center: Alternative Energy," by Fontichiaro, Victoria A. Pascaretti, and Buczynski, demonstrates how the science notebooking approach can then transfer into scientific research by fifth-grade students in the library setting.

GETTING TO ADVOCACY

Maximize co-teaching opportunities when they arise!

1. Ask teachers to reflect on the co-teaching experience with you. If your co-teacher has had a positive experience, encourage him or her to share that perspective in a classroom newsletter or blog and to share that experience with the administration.

2. Maureen Tannetta's lesson focuses on famous citizens of her state. What famous state citizens are highlighted in your curriculum? Consider inviting a local politician or a representative from the historical society to participate in an inquiry unit focused on local history. That person's positive experiences will help him or her advocate for you and for your program in the future.

3. If teachers create a classroom display of final work, ask that your library or name be included on the display. If parents think that their child's work was done just with the classroom teacher, they will not know to advocate for your efforts!

4. When looking for collaborative partners, look to the classroom and beyond. Many schools have staff members who are not classroom teachers—such as Reading Recovery; special education; the school counselor or psychologist; or an arts, music, or physical education specialist—who are equally interested in a collaborative approach to teaching and learning. Advocacy extends beyond others speaking in support of you—these less-common collaborative partners give you a chance to advocate for others! As the saying goes, "What goes around, comes around": they may end up being advocates for the library media program.

THOUGHTS FOR THE JOURNEY

1. What are the most effective strategies for partnering with elementary teachers?

2. What strategies do you have for transforming outdated, copy-the-facts research projects into student-centered, inquiry-oriented lessons?

3. How do you differentiate at the elementary level to meet the needs of diverse learners?

Words Are Like Faces: An Exploration into Language and Communication

by Judi Moreillon

Information Literacy Skills Objectives:

AASL *Standards for the 21st-Century Learner:*

1.1.6: Read, view, and listen for information presented in any format (e.g., textual, visual, media, digital) in order to make inferences and gather meaning.

1.1.9: Collaborate with others to broaden and deepen understanding.

2.1.3: Use strategies to draw conclusions from information and apply knowledge to curricular areas, real-world situations, and further investigations.

Curriculum (subject area) Objectives:

Language Arts, Research, and Technology

The student will identify rhyme and sensory images in poetry.

The student will identify word choice for its impact on emotions and as a trait of effective writing.

The student will maintain a bibliographic record.

The student will use a keyboard effectively (to cut and paste).

At the end of this lesson, students will be able to:

- identify and categorize four poetic devices in a particular poetry book and infer the emotional impact of these word choices.
- apply this knowledge to a selection of poems and complete the poetic devices category matrix and bibliography.
- connect words with emotions and electronic communication symbols.

Grade Levels: 2-5

Resources:

Baer, Edith. *Words Are Like Faces*. Illus. by Kyra Teis. Star Bright Books, 2007.

A wide selection of children's poetry books

Poetry Websites:

Poetry: Resources for Studying and Writing Poetry. http://storytrail.com/Educator/poemresources.htm

Poetic Devices for Primary Students. http://storytrail.com/poetry/poetic devices_elementary.htm

Poetic Devices Category Matrix and Bibliography. http://storytrail.com/poetry/poetic_devices_category_matrix.doc

Emoticons Graphic Organizer. http://storytrail.com/poetry/emoticon_graphic_organizer.doc

Instructional Roles:

The classroom teacher and library media specialist team teach this lesson.

The classroom teacher copies the category matrix for student partners and loads the emoticon graphic organizer as a template on the classroom server.

The library media specialist bookmarks the poetic devices website and takes the primary responsibility for gathering a wide selection of poetry books and poetry websites (http://storytrail.com/Educator/poemresources.htm).

Activities and Procedures for Completion:

Brainstorm emotional states or feelings. The classroom teacher elicits students' responses. The library media specialist records them as a horizontal list (see Sample List, page 11), leaving room to add to the chart later in the activity.

Using the Poetic Devices for Elementary Students webpage, the educators teach or review these poetic devices: alliteration, metaphor, onomatopoeia, rhyme, and simile.

Judi Moreillon is a Literacies and Libraries Consultant in Tucson, AZ. She is also the author of *Collaborative Strategies for Teaching Reading Comprehension: Maximizing Your Impact* (ALA Editions, 2007). Email: info@storytrail.com

They can read the samples given on the website or offer additional examples from children's poetry.

The educators partner-read *Words Are Like Faces*. One educator re-reads the book while the other records an example of each poetic device on the category matrix (see Category Matrix below).

The educators lead a discussion about how words express emotions and affect communication.

Students work with partners or in small groups to read poems aloud and to complete a category matrix like the one below using other poetry books.

Return to the original brainstorm chart (see Sample List below) and add poetic devices from the students' graphic organizers and categorize them under the feelings they elicit in the listener. Example: "They glimmer and shimmer and shine from afar" from *Words Are Like Faces* would go under the feeling of "Joyful."

The educators share the emoticons graphic organizer (http://storytrail.com/poetry/emoticon_graphic_organizer.doc) and the example. They demonstrate electronically cutting and pasting the symbols. (See Emoticons Graphic Organizer below).

Students use the emoticons graphic organizer to create emotional equations in both symbolic and word formats. (Students can also draw faces to use in their emotional equations.)

Students share their equations with one another and check to see if their translations agree.

Assessment/Evaluation:

Students' completed graphic organizers will serve as assessments for their understanding of these poetic devices and their impact on emotions. Their ability to create symbolic and verbal sentences that signify emotions will further assess their understanding of the relationship between words and feelings.

Follow-Up:

Students will continue to identify poetic devices in the texts they read. They will add to the poetic devices found in literature to the class brainstorm.

The class can deepen their discussions by carefully selecting and responding to words in their communication with others.

Sample List

Emotion:	Happy	Sad	Angry	Joyful	Lonely	Cheerful
Poetic Device:						

Category Matrix

Poetic Device	Examples from *Words Are Like Faces*	Emotional Response
Metaphor	They *glimmer* and *shimmer* and shine from afar. (Metaphor: Words have the qualities of stars.)	Magical - Joyful
Onomatopoeia (and alliteration)	Some twirl on tiptoes, some *clatter* or *clink*, and some sound exactly the way you think!	Jarring - Annoyed
Rhyme	Passed as a secret from one to *another*— Words are what people say to each *other*.	Upbeat - Cheerful
Simile	Words can be plain *like a loaf of fresh bread*	Warm - Comforted

Emoticons Graphic Organizer

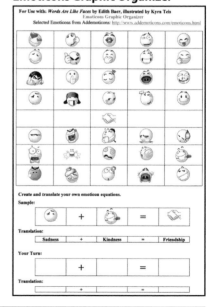

Tricking the Trickster: Recording and Comparing Story Elements

by Judy Moreillon

Library Media and Curriculum Objectives:

The student will identify story elements.

The student will use information accurately and creatively by recording notes in various formats.

The student will use a Venn diagram to compare story elements in two stories that have a similar theme.

The student will self-assess collaboration, notetaking, and comparison using a small group assessment rubric.

Grade Levels: 2-6

Resources:

"Tricking the Trickster" Text Set
Folktales

Aardema, Verna, retold by. *Borreguita and the Coyote: A Tale from Ayutla, Mexico.* Illus. by Petra Mathers. Knopf, 1991.

Confederated Salish and Kootenai Tribes. *Beaver Steals Fire: A Salish Coyote Story.* Illus. by Sam Sandoval. University of Nebraska Press, 2005. Note: This story should only be used in the winter months, November through February.

McDermott, Gerald. *Zomo the Rabbit: A Trickster Tale from West Africa.* Harcourt Brace Jovanovich, 1992.

Picture Books with Folktale Elements

Huggins, Peter. *Trosclair and the Alligator.* Illus. by Lindsey Gardiner. Star Bright Books, 2006.

Judi Moreillon, Ph.D., is the author of *Collaborative Strategies for Teaching Reading Comprehension: Maximizing Your Impact* (ALA Editions, 2007). She serves as a literacies and libraries consultant, as an adjunct assistant professor, and as the Director of Business Development and Product Management for Star Bright Books in New York.

Morales, Yuyi. *Just a Minute: A Trickster Tale and Counting Book*. Chronicle, 2003.

Wildsmith, Brian. *Jungle Party*. Star Bright Books, 2006.

Audiobook

Brer Rabbit and the Wonderful Tar Baby. Adapted by Eric Metaxas. Music by Taj Mahal. Rabbit Ears Productions, 1990.

Resources Created for this Lesson

Category Matrix: Comparing Story Elements - "Tricking the Trickster" Text Set (pdf). http://storytrail.com/Impact/Chapter_3/sample_category_matrix.pdf

Story Elements: Notemaking and Comparison Rubric (pdf). http://storytrail.com/Impact/Chapter_3/story_element_comparison_rubric.pdf

Story Elements: Venn Diagram (pdf). http://storytrail.com/Impact/Chapter_3/story_element_Venn.pdf

Types of Notes and Category Matrix Sample for Story Element Components. http://storytrail.com/Impact/Chapter_3/category_matrix_sample.htm

Educator Resource Online

Samuel, Stella. *Cultural Unity through Folktales*. Yale-New Haven Teachers Institute, 2007. http://www.yale.edu/ynhti/curriculum/units/1997/2/97.02.09.x.html#c

Background information for educators on trickster tales from several cultures.

Instructional Roles:

Depending on students' reading proficiency, the classroom teacher and the library media specialist can adopt various co-teaching strategies. Here are two options:

- With students who are not proficient independent readers, team teach one book to the entire class. Then divide the class in half. Each educator reads half of the book to half of the class and students work in small groups to complete the elements for the category matrix. Bring the students back together as a whole class to complete the lesson.
- If students are independent

readers, divide them into small groups or partners based on the resources. The educators first model the process using one of the books. Then both educators facilitate the small group or partner work. Work as a whole class to complete the lesson.

Preparation and Procedures:
Prior to the lesson:

Gather a text set of resources.

Create a large category matrix on butcher paper (see *Category Matrix* sample in Resources).

Cut pieces of paper for each book or audiobook title in six different colors (one for each story element) to fit the cells of the category matrix.

Photocopy one Venn diagram and one rubric for each group (see Resources).

During the lesson:

Teach or review these story elements: setting (where and when), characters (who), plot (what), cultural features (how), illustrations, and theme (message). Use a story with which all of the students are familiar as an example.

Teach or review types of notes. (Print out and show the online Cinderella sample if appropriate.)

Read aloud one of the books from the "Tricking the Trickster" text set to the whole class (Book A).

Reread and discuss the book's story elements with the class.

Educators record notes on six different colored papers for the category matrix. (Educators model taking turns, sharing ideas, and using different types of notes.)

Review the rubric and use it to assess the educators' sample.

Divide the students into small groups. In the groups, read aloud

another of the books, and then re-read and discuss the story elements. Record notes on the colored papers for the matrix (Book B).

Bring the whole class together to compile story elements on the category matrix.

Model using a Venn diagram to compare several story elements in Book A with Book B. (Use a different colored marker for each title. Use a third color for the similarities in the center of the Venn diagram.)

Reinforce that #1 for Book A should be the same story element as #1 for Book B.

Give a comparison example that does not work, such as comparing the setting from Book A with a detail from the illustrations in Book B.

Give the Venn diagram a title such as "Comparing the Story Elements in *Brer Rabbit and the Wonderful Tar Baby* and *Trosclair and the Alligator*."

Complete the assessment of the class sample using the rubric.

Students work in small groups to compare story elements from the whole class book with those in the title they read. The small groups then complete the rubric.

Evaluation/Assessment:

Model using the rubric for the whole class example.

Students and educators assess collaboration, notetaking, and comparison using the same rubric.

Follow-Up Extensions:

Rotate the books until students have read or listened to all of the titles. Students will select two titles to compare.

Gather inquiry questions about the cultures depicted in the stories. Conduct small group inquiry projects to answer students' questions. ✋

Promoting Inquiry with Emerging Readers Using Elephogs and Octobunnies

by Kristin Fontichiaro and Debbie West

There is often a struggle in elementary schools between a desire for higher-order thinking and students' emerging reading skills. How do we simultaneously promote the new *Standards for the 21st-Century Learner* by the American Association of School Librarians (AASL) and the call for independent, inquiry-oriented engagement when our students are just learning to read or write?

As the library media specialist and Reading Recovery teacher, we shared these concerns. Working together, we led our students on an engaging and deep-thinking exploration and writing project. Students explored animal books, then combined the characteristics of two existing animals to create and promote a new animal. A playful, imaginative atmosphere kicked off this four-day project that culminated in a letter to the local zoo. To best support the emerging skills of our students, each element of this story was team-taught, and we alternated roles as lead instructor and supporting instructor. Each of us conferenced with students and guided their thinking and writing. See "Meeting Standards with Elephog, Octobunny, and Other Animals," page 29.

Day 1

On the first day, Debbie, the Reading Recovery teacher, began with a story. Posting a hand-drawn sketch of an unusual animal with large flopping ears and an extended, fly-catching tongue, she told the students of a trip to central Africa, where she had befriended a most unusual animal. This animal, the elephog, was a most intriguing creature, and featured attributes of both the elephant and the frog (hence its name). Debbie was sad that she and the elephog were now separated by such a long distance. If only, she wished aloud, her friend could come to live at the Detroit Zoo, then, she could stop by and visit it regularly.

The students were enraptured by her tale. We then told them that they could create their own animal friend. We let them loose on dozens of animal books and encyclopedias that we had selected together. They pored over the images, seeking two "just right" animals. They would combine features from each into their new animal, so we encouraged them to select two very different animals.

They then sketched their new animal and named it, thus concluding the first day's work (one of the favorites was octobunny!). Each instructor circulated through the room, asking students to tell us about their new animal and its name.

Day 2

At the next session, Debbie led the class in revisiting their sketches, this time to begin to envision attributes based on what they had sketched. For example, long ears for the elephog might indicate good hearing, while the long frog-like tongue might give it incredible skill in fly-catching. Each student received a hamburger-shaped graphic organizer (which Debbie christened a "GO" Chart, because graphic organizers help you "go on" to the next step)—a bun at the top, then the lettuce, the tomatoes, the meat, and the bun at the bottom, enlarged to 11" x 17" to accommodate the students' beginning handwriting (see GO Chart, page 30). The items in the middle are what make the hamburger desirable to eat. Similarly, the students write an attribute on each layer that makes their animal interesting to explore.

We talked about how much we wanted to be able to visit our animals at the Detroit Zoo. The mother of one of our students is the zoo's veterinarian, and she agreed to let us write her with our requests. Kristin returned to the GO Chart, pointing out that just as the bun is important in holding a hamburger together, the opening and closing sentences will hold the paragraph (letter) together. As a class, we brainstormed intriguing opening and appropriate closing sentences. The opening sentence needed to let the audience (the Detroit

Zoo) know why we were writing and what we were asking for. The closing sentence would reiterate our hopes and thank the zoo for considering our offer.

Day 3

After Debbie's edits (checking for capital letters, periods, and complete sentences), the students used the GO Charts to create a letter to the Detroit Zoo. They followed the hamburger format, starting with the top bun, then the middle layers, then the bottom bun's closing sentence. Each instructor circulated the room to support students in this task. Since it was a letter, they included a signature line as well. Although the GO Chart may not have been filled out with complete sentences, teacher editing helped students change the information into complete sentences for the letter draft. Parent volunteers typed the letters.

Day 4

On the final day, the students illustrated the typed letter with their incredible animal creation. We encouraged the students to include the animal in its imagined habitat so the zoo could see the type of enclosure the animal would need if it were chosen to be displayed. One set of letters was displayed in the library media center, Debbie sent the other set to the zoo. We eagerly awaited a response, and the children were thrilled when a letter on formal letterhead was sent to the classes!

Conclusion

This project offered many benefits to our students. First, it was rooted in visual learning, which helps visual learners as well as emerging readers and writers who do not always think in terms of text. Images of real animals in research books provided a menu of potential animal features, and early sketches helped students "see" their animal before describing it in print. Secondly, by synthesizing the features of two existing animals, students practiced higher-order thinking that is frequently lacking in primary research projects. Next, by involving the Detroit Zoo, we involved the community in our students' learning. This gave students an authentic audience and made them highly motivated to do their best work. By working collaboratively, we were able to provide better writing support and guidance to each child, which resulted in greater levels of mastery and understanding. Working from students' areas of strength gave them more capacity for success. ◄

Meeting Standards with Elephog, Octobunny, and Other Animals

AASL Standards for the 21st-Century Learner:

1.4.2 Use interaction with and feedback from teachers and peers to guide own inquiry process.

1.4.4 Seek appropriate help when it is needed.

2.1.1 Continue an inquiry- based research process by applying critical- thinking skills (analysis, synthesis, evaluation, organization) to information and knowledge in order to construct new understandings, draw conclusions, and create new knowledge.

2.1.2 Organize knowledge so that it is useful.

2.1.6 Use the writing process, media and visual literacy, and technology skills to create products that express new understandings.

2.2.4 Demonstrate personal productivity by completing products to express learning.

Curriculum Objectives:

►Students will demonstrate an ability to synthesize information by taking attributes from two different animals and merging them into a new, fictional animal.

►Students will write in a persuasive voice.

►Students will structure their writing as a five-sentence paragraph (topic sentence, three supporting sentences, concluding sentence).

Grade Level: 1

Assessment:

Student work is formatively assessed throughout the process via instructor/student conferencing, students reading their work aloud to self-assess for errors, instructors' observations, and the instructor's written comments on draft writing. Because this lesson focuses on the writing process and was the students' first introduction to paragraph writing, there was no summative assessment. Instead, assessment efforts focused on achieving mastery via process-based feedback.

Kristin Fontichiaro is the library media specialist at Beverly School in the Birmingham (Michigan) Public Schools. She is co-author of the forthcoming book *Story Starters for Science Inquiry* (Teacher Ideas Press) and author of *Podcasting at School* and *Active Learning through Drama, Podcasting, and Puppetry* (Libraries Unlimited). She blogs for *SLMAM* at http://blog.schoollibrarymedia. com and can be reached at slmamblog@ gmail.com.

Debbie West is the Reading Recovery specialist for Beverly School. She has her Master's Degree in Reading and Language Arts and taught first and second grades for thirteen years.

GO Chart

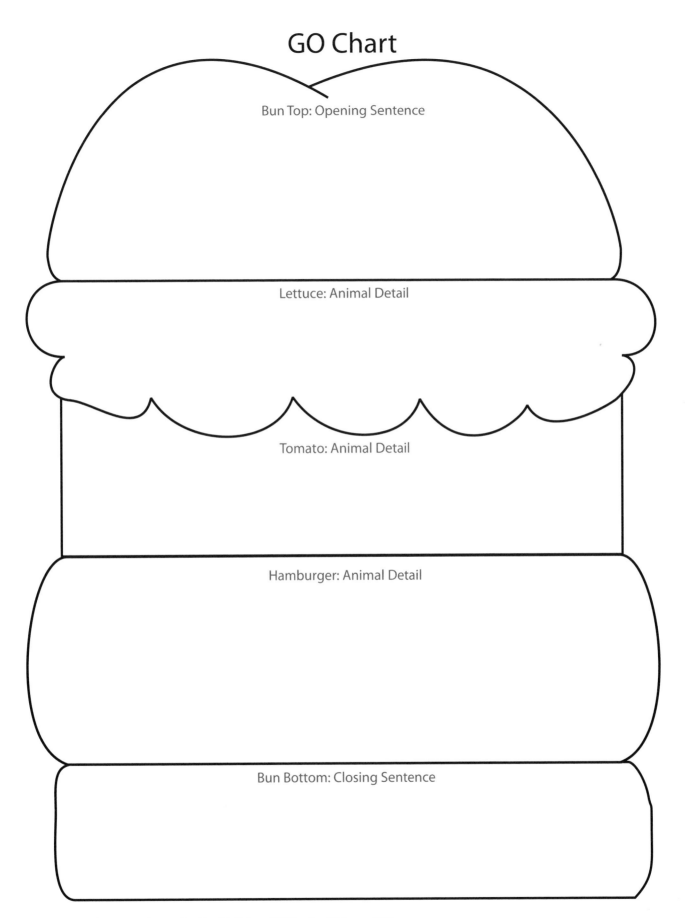

Bun Top: Opening Sentence

Lettuce: Animal Detail

Tomato: Animal Detail

Hamburger: Animal Detail

Bun Bottom: Closing Sentence

Abigail and John Adams Online

by Maureen Tannetta

Information Literacy Skills Objectives:

AASL Standards for the 21st-Century Learner:

Standard 1: Inquire, think critically, and gain knowledge. 1.1.6; 1.1.8.

Standard 2: Draw conclusions, create new knowledge: 2.1.1; 2.1.4; 2.1.6.

Standard 4: Pursue personal and aesthetic growth. 4.1.3; 4.1.8.

Curriculum (subject area) Objectives:

Students will perform a basic search on a historical database.

Students will locate, download, and print content from digital media collections for specific purposes.

Students will cite sources.

Students will identify and use terms related to the Internet.

Students will learn and practice letter writing format.

Students will study the biography and political leadership of John Adams and learn the important developments leading to and during the American Revolution.

Grade Levels: 3-5

Resources:

Web Sites

Massachusetts Historical Society. http://www.masshist.org

John and Abigail Adams' Timeline. http://www.masshist.org/adams/timeline.cfm

John and Abigail Adams' Letters. http://www.masshist.org/digitaladams/aea/letter/

Materials

Antiqued letter paper or materials for creating tea-stained parchment paper

Instructional Roles:

Despite the fact our famous presidential couple never experienced email, chat rooms, or blogging, their correspondence is now online thanks to the ongoing digitization of the Adams' papers by the Massachusetts Historical Society (MHS). In this collaborative language arts/social studies unit, the library media specialist teaches students how to access the MHS Web pages on John and Abigail Adams life and letters.

The teacher continues the lesson in the classroom during writing workshop time to help students develop a return letter to either John or Abigail Adams with proper format, grammatical structure, and penmanship.

Activity and Procedures for Completion:

Present a biographical talk on John and Abigail Adams while showing how

John and Abigail Adams Online Research and Writing Rubric

	Uninspired	Patriotic	Revolutionary
Database Research Skills	Printed letter only	Printed letter including 3 dates	Printed letter, dates, and cited the MHS website
Letter Writing	Responded to letter	Responded to letter using date, heading, salutation, and indents	Responded to letter using date, heading, salutation, and indents. No spelling errors.
Revolutionary Understandings	Wrote letter as either John or Abigail Adams	Wrote letter as John or Abigail and included convincing details of the times	Wrote letter as John or Abigail and included details of the times and an understanding of the Revolutionary Conflict

to access the timeline. (Note: The MHS online timeline will make just about anyone an Adams' expert in short time.)

Demonstrate how to use a date on the timeline to access an online letter to match the timeline date. Students will need to record a timeline event, use the back button, and click into the Adams' online letter database to choose a letter from the time of the event they choose. (Be sure to have a short form for students to record the research date, timeline event date, letter date, and the MHS Web address to underscore researching skills and citing sources.)

Show the MHS feature that allows visitors to see the actual Adams' script, actual size or enlarged, and view the transcribed version. Both are printable.

After students print the letter of their choice, they are ready to work with the classroom teacher to write own letter of response, posing as either John or Abigail Adams.

Evaluation/Assessment:

Teachers will provide a research and letter writing rubric for students to use for assessment. See: "John and Abigail Adams Online Research and Writing Rubric" page 17. (*AASL Standards for the 21st-Century Learner*: Self-assessment Strategies 1.4.2; 2.4.1; 2.4.2; 3.4.2; 4.4.5)

Follow-Up:

This lesson links students back to an earlier time through primary sources. In Massachusetts, we follow our Adams literature study with a visit to their homestead in Quincy. It's free! However, there are wonderful Adams' impersonators who make school visits. The Adams Homestead Web site also publishes a CD of information to study the Adams and the lifestyle of the time. Any of these follow-up options will allow teachers to extend this learning experience.

Maureen Tannetta is the library media specialist at Avery Elementary in Dedham, MA. Email: mtannetta2002@yahoo.com

Science Notebooking in Action: Where Does Condensation Come From?

by Sandy Buczynski and Kristin Fontichiaro

Information Literacy Skills Objectives:

AASL Standards for the 21st-Century Learner:

See "Connecting Science Notebooking to the Elementary School Library Media Center," Table 1, page 27.

Curriculum (subject area) Objectives:

Students will be able to explain that materials, such as water, can be changed from one state to another by heating or cooling.

Grade Levels: 3-5

Resources:

Containers made of glass, metal, Styrofoam, ceramic, and paper
Ice
Water
Soda
Food coloring
Thermometers
Weather forecast showing humidity level

Instructional Roles:

The library media specialist and classroom teacher co-teach this hands-on science inquiry unit. The science notebooking approach (see article, pages 24-27) helps students track their procedural and cognitive thinking. This hands-on inquiry develops the procedural and cognitive skills that can later be used in library research. Throughout, both instructors provide ongoing formative assessment via comments, conferencing, asking questions, and discussion with students.

Activities and Procedures for Completion:

Day 1: Introduction (45 minutes)

The classroom teacher leads a discussion with these questions:

► Does the cup holder in your car get wet when fast-food drinks are stored there?
► Have you ever exhaled on a mirror and seen your breath as water droplets?
► Do your glasses fog up when you go from a cool, dry room to the hot, humid outdoors?
► Does water form on the inside of your windows on a cold day?
► Why do you need a coaster underneath your cold drink?
► Is condensation formed on a water glass the same way that human sweat forms on skin?

The library media specialist records classroom contributions and makes notations on chart paper or a white board for future reference.

Connecting to Science:

Water vapor is water in a gaseous state (humidity). It only condenses (becomes liquid) onto another surface when that surface is cooler than surrounding air. Because warmer air holds more water vapor than cold air, condensation occurs when water vapor in air turns into liquid water droplets due to direct cooling of air. This process is also responsible for formation of clouds.

Inventory Walk:

Students view and discuss the materials available for use in the experiment to engage them in a common vocabulary (see Resources).

Vocabulary:

Some science terms are not represented by physical objects. These words and their definitions continue to develop students' science vocabulary: condensation, water vapor, and humidity.

Day Two: Experimental Design (60 minutes)

Questioning:

Student groups write a measurable question. It is not possible to pre-script this curiosity-driven process. Questions build on students' prior knowledge. Quantitative questions include, "How many/long/often/hot/much/strong?" Comparison questions focus on, "Which would be___?" "What would happen if ___?" Questions that deal with cause-and-effect and problem-solving questions begin with "Can you find a way to…?" or, "How can I…?" Save "why" questions for library research. It is important to note that groups of students will develop different questions to investigate. Some students may wonder, "Which would produce more condensation, a full glass of ice water or a glass half full?," while others may pose, "Which is a more likely surface for condensation: Paper or Styrofoam?" or "How can I stop condensation from forming?"

Formulating a Prediction:

The prediction takes a stand about an experiment's outcome. Students can use this template: "If I change ____, then I predict ____will happen because_____." What comes after "because" justifies or explains students' thinking. To serve as an example, we predict: "If blue food coloring is added to ice water in a glass, then the condensation will be blue because water is moving from inside the glass to the outside."

Identifying Variables:

The independent variable is the element that will be manipulated or altered. The dependent variable is what will be measured as a result of that manipulation. Constants are the elements that will remain stable and unchanged throughout the investigation. For our example, students might write:

Independent variable: Adding food coloring to a glass of ice water.
Dependent variable: Measuring the color of the condensation.
Control: Glass of ice water without food coloring.
Constants: Temperature and humidity of room, amount of ice and water in the glasses, measuring instrument.

Designing the Procedure:

Students write step-by-step instructions for conducting the experiment, using imperative sentences for clarity and economy of words. Each group's procedure will be different, depending on the condensation question being asked. For our example:

1. Set up two glasses (#1 and #2) with equal amounts of water and ice cubes.
2. Put two drops of food coloring in

	Glass #1	Glass #2
Initial Observations (baseline)	No condensation	No condensation
Color of condensation after 30 minutes	clear	clear

glass #2.
3. Record observations of the glasses (baseline data).
4. After 30 minutes, wipe condensation from each glass with a clean paper towel and record color.

Creating the Data Organizer:

Students need a place to record measurements and data during the experiment. Students design an organizer (T-chart, graph, table) that works for them and draw it in their notebook, such as the example shown above.

Day Three: Experiment and Reflection (60 minutes)
Conducting the Experiment and Recording Data and Observations:

Students follow the procedure, record data in the graphic organizer, and document the process with sketches and written observations.

Claims and Evidence:

Students study the data for patterns that lead to a claim, an assertion based on what they observed. They use evidence, concrete observations, and/or data to support their claim, using the template, "I claim _____ because _____." For example, "I claim condensation does not come from inside the glass because the wetness outside the glass was clear."

Conclusion:

Students look at their claims and evidence and their original prediction to decide if the claims and evidence support or do not support the original prediction. A sentence frame like "I learned that _____ because _____. My prediction was/was not supported." guides student thinking. Possible experimental error is also discussed in the notebook.

Days Three and Four (60 minutes each)
Project:

Students apply what they have learned to an authentic task: a lab report, or formal paper to the scientific community summarizing their findings. Lab reports have specific formats and use scientific vocabulary. Lab reports are written in third person and succinct (see http://www.geocities.com/chris_castellana/labreport.htm).

Assessment/Evaluation:

Use the Condensation Assessment Rubric to evaluate the lab report (see page 14).

Follow-Up:

Invite students to consider and write down additional hands-on or library inquiry they may wish to pursue about condensation. The library media specialist can suggest expert resources and meet with small groups to facilitate this ongoing learning.

Kristin Fontichiaro is an elementary library media specialist for the Birmingham (Michigan) Public Schools and author of *Podcasting at School* and *Active Learning through Drama, Podcasting, and Puppetry* (Libraries Unlimited) . She blogs about 21st-century learning in library media centers for *School Library Media Activities Monthly* (http://blog.schoollibrarymedia.com). Email: font@umich.edu

Sandy Buczynski is an associate professor of science education at the University of San Diego in San Diego, CA. She coordinates the Math, Science and Technology Education graduate program and teaches courses in science pedagogy and curriculum design. Email: sandyb@sandiego.edu

Note: This lesson plan evolved from a conversation on students' misconceptions with Lisa Baily of Scripts Elementary.

Condensation Assessment Rubric			
	Emerging Scientist (2 points)	**Practiced Scientist** (3 points)	**Accomplished Scientist** (4 points)
Introduction	What did you hope to discover from investigating condensation?	Be sure to indicate your purpose for conducting the investigation.	You clearly state what the investigation is about and give your predicted outcome.
Materials & Method	What did you do? Write a "how to" list of directions including all supplies that will be used.	Remember to give both step-by-step instructions and list materials needed.	Terrific! Another scientist could follow your procedure and repeat this experiment with similar results.
Results & Discussion	What happened? Make sure data gathered is related to prediction so that you draw a valid conclusion.	Think about how you could use charts, tables, or graphs to show data's patterns or trends.	Your data was very organized and easy to read. By making evidence-based claims, your conclusion was valid.
Word Choice	Consider where scientific words could replace common language to indicate the same action/event.	Try defining your scientific vocabulary first and then use it in your lab report.	Great use of science vocabulary in context!
Conventions	Can a friend help you proofread this for next time?	Make sure you spell check your paper!	It's a pleasure to see such great spelling, grammar, and punctuation.

Science:

Science Notebooking in the Library Media Center: Alternative Energy

by Kristin Fontichiaro, Victoria A. Pascaretti, and Sandy Buczynski

Information Literacy Skills Objectives:

AASL Standards for the 21st-Century Learner:

See "Connecting Science Notebooking to the Elementary School Library Media Center," Table 1, page 27.

Curriculum (subject area) Objectives:

Students will identify traditional and alternative energies used in the United States.

Students will discuss advantages and disadvantages of various types of alternative energies.

Students will develop decision-making criteria and use it to determine whether a particular alternative energy is beneficial for local use.

Grade Levels: 5-8

Resources:

Internet resources
Science notebooks

Instructional Roles:

The library media specialist and classroom teacher co-teach this research unit using science notebooking to track students' process and thinking. Throughout, both instructors provide ongoing formative assessment via comments (feedback), conferencing, asking questions, and discussion with students. This lesson is adapted from the work of Swartz (2008) and the science notebooking strategies outlined by Klentschy (2008).

Activities and Procedures for Completion:

Day 1: Awakening Prior Knowledge

In their notebooks, students brainstorm various energies they have observed, energy conservation efforts experienced, and reasons why people might be interested in reducing energy or saving natural resources. Students share their ideas, with the teacher facilitating and the library media specialist recording contributions on chart paper.

These views set context for a scenario: Imagine that the Board of Education must make budget cuts. They will have to dismiss teachers if spending cannot be reduced elsewhere. What kinds of alternative energy could realistically be implemented to save money for the school district?

Connecting to Science

One way to save money in the long term is to decrease our dependence on fossil fuels and other nonrenewable resources, and consider alternative energies. The Natural Resources Defense Council (n.d.) defines "alternative energy" as energy that is typically environmentally sound but has not gained popularity. Alternative energies include wind and water turbines, solar energy, hydroelectric energy, geothermal energy, nuclear energy, hydrogen, ethanol, and biodiesel fuels. Lack of mainstream adoption may be due to start-up costs, initial cost to the consumer for conversion from traditional energy, practicality of use, and aesthetic concerns (e.g., appearance or odor).

Ask students how they can learn about all of these kinds of energy. While a hands-on inquiry could be developed for solar energy, it certainly is not feasible for the study of nuclear energy. This would require library research.

Vocabulary

Students define new words in their notebook glossary as they discover them during research. Their vocabulary may include energy types (e.g., fossil fuel), units of measurement (e.g., barrel or miles per gallon), factors to consider (e.g., renewability or abundance), or specialty vocabulary (e.g., carbon credits or crude oil).

Developing Prior Knowledge

Ask students to search Google News using "alternative energy" as a search term (http://news.google.com) and print a resulting news article that piques their interest. They make notes as they read to summarize information, identify key ideas, develop questions, and make connections.

Working in the Science Notebook
Day 2: Pooling Knowledge

Students tape their article printouts into their notebooks. The teacher leads a discussion with question prompts such as: "Does your article discuss an energy that is already being used or just being developed?" "Are incentives offered for using that alternative energy?" The library media specialist records the discussion on the white board. If students express misconceptions, the teacher can quickly skim the article to identify the source and redirect thinking. By pooling their individual reports, students deepen their initial awareness of the extent of alternative energies and discover connections between their news research and that of their peers.

Now students work collectively to make meaning of the data and questions on the board. The teacher uses provoking questions such as: "What were the common hurdles or roadblocks to implementing alternative energies?" "What general applications of alternative energy uses have emerged from the collective articles?" Main ideas will emerge from this consensus building.

Schwarz (2008) identified four major areas for alternative energy research: abundance/renewability, accessibility, production and consumer costs, and safety. Additional considerations may include aesthetic impact, barriers, definition of the energy, or staffing issues.

Finally, students select a specific alternative energy to explore in more detail.

Day 3: Preparing for Research Question

Students begin by writing a measurable research question in their notebooks. For example, "How might _____ energy impact our district?" or "Where has this alternative energy implementation been most effective (success stories from other schools)? Least effective?"

Prediction

A prediction is a student's presumption, recorded in the notebook, about what might be found, supported by prior knowledge. For example, "I think that (alternative energy) will be effective/ineffective because _____."

Data Organizer

In their notebooks, students draw a series of columns across the spread. At the top of each column, students list areas to research (e.g., cost to consumer, cost to produce, barriers, aesthetics). A sample graphic organizer is available online (http://www.ascd.org/ASCD/pdf/el/Swartz%20Matrix.pdf).

Day 4: Procedure

In library research, the library media specialist models these procedural skills:
- Selecting appropriate sources.
- Organizing digital resources (such as a social bookmarking site; for example, http://del.icio.us/beverlyenergy).
- "Reading for research" using types of print, skimming, and scanning.
- Verifying information with additional sources.
- Documenting references.

Days 5 and 6:
Data and Information Collection

Students gather information, recording it in their data chart. Remind students of the objective: to convince the Board of Education that their alternative energy is—or is not—a viable means for long-term money savings for the school district.

Day 7: Making Meaning
Claim and Evidence

After students complete individual research, they share their information on a class wiki, building collective knowledge. (For an example, see http://beverlyenergy2008.pbwiki.com.)

To develop skills in evaluating the relevance or usefulness of a particular piece of information, Schwarz (2008) asks students to code each fact:

　　* important information
　　+ advantage
　　- disadvantage

We add a fourth code:

　　/ unimportant

Coding helps students identify and evaluate patterns. Overall, is the energy a good match with school district to save money? Or not? This leads to creating a claim along with its justification (evidence). A useful template is: "I claim that [type of energy] is / is not effective for our school district because _____."

Conclusion

The conclusion is a summary statement written in the notebook that answers two questions: Did the evidence-based claim support the prediction? What scientific knowledge has been learned?

Days 8–11: *PowerPoint* Project

Finally, the student's inquiry converges with the scenario. Working in groups, students carefully consider the audience (Board of Education) and craft a persuasive presentation encouraging the Board to take a particular action. To be persuasive, students must develop a clear position, using specific examples to explain key points.

Assessment/Evaluation:

Assess student work using the "Alternative Energy" Rubric (see below).

Follow-Up:

Invite students to consider and write down additional hands-on or library inquiry they may wish to pursue about alternative energy. The library media specialist can suggest expert resources and meet with small groups to facilitate this ongoing learning.

References:

Buczynski, S., Fontichiaro, K., and Pascaretti, V. "Alternative Energy: The Budget Crisis." In *Story Starters and Science Notebooking: Developing Student Thinking Through Literacy and Inquiry.* Teacher Ideas Press, in press.

Klentschy, M. *Using Science Notebooks in Elementary Classrooms.* National Science Teachers Association, 2008.

Natural Resources Defense Council. *Glossary of Environmental Terms.* http://www.nrdc.org/reference/glossary/a.asp (accessed December 13, 2008).

Swartz, R. J. "Teaching Students to Think." *Educational Leadership* 65, no. 5 (2008): 26-31. http://www.ascd.org/publications/educational_leadership/feb08/vol65/num05/Energizing_Learning.aspx (accessed December 15, 2008).

Kristin Fontichiaro is an elementary library media specialist for the Birmingham (Michigan) Public Schools and author of *Podcasting at School* and *Active Learning through Drama, Podcasting, and Puppetry* (Libraries Unimited) . She blogs about 21st-century learning in library media centers for *School Library Media Activities Monthly* (http://blog.schoollibrarymedia.com).

Vicki Pascaretti is a teacher at Beverly School in Beverly Hills, MI. Email: vp01bps@birmingham.k12.mi.us

Sandy Buczynski is an associate professor of science education at the University of San Diego in San Diego, CA. She coordinates the Math, Science and Technology Education graduate program and teaches courses in science pedagogy and curriculum design. Email: sandyb@sandiego.edu. Email: font@umich.edu

Alternative Energy Rubric			
Criteria	Points	Student's Self-Score	Teacher's Score
Student completed and coded the data organizer	10		
Student contributed to the wiki	10		
Student worked effectively in a group	5		
The title slide lists names and takes a stand on whether the energy is a good match for the district	5		
Presentation includes each category from data organizer	15		
Presentation is persuasive and takes a stand	10		
Students define and list advantages/disadvantages of alternative energy	25		
Presentation uses bullet points, not full sentences, to support the oral presentation	10		
Each teammate presents a portion of the slideshow with energy and poise	10		
TOTAL SCORE:	100		

Chapter 11

Secondary Lesson Plans

Questioning is at the heart of the learning experience. The nature and quality of the question is equally as important as the answer.

—Audrey Okemura, "Designing Inquiry-Based Science
Units as Collaborative Partners" (page 341)

Chapter 10 explores learning lessons for elementary students. This chapter presents seven lessons for secondary (intermediate and high school) students in the areas of language arts, social studies, and science.

It is at the high school level that school library media specialists (SLMSs) can see the fruits of their students' many years of labor, and the AASL *Standards for the 21st-Century Learner* can be seen as a kind of exit checklist for their work.

Language Arts

Secondary students are often more eager to leap into digital environments than bury their heads in a three-ringed binder. Roberta Sibley bridged this technology gap when she worked with a literature teacher to transform pen-and-paper reading journals into an online community using the social site LibraryThing (www.librarything.com). In "The Librarian Who Loves *LibraryThing*" (beginning on page 325), she explores her own journey to LibraryThing and how it was used effectively with a class of reading students. Her implementation supports Standard 4 of the AASL *Standards*, as it gives students a way to track their personal reading and see growth over time.

Government or Language Arts

Many secondary school librarians use a variety of book clubs, both within the classroom structure and as lunchtime or extracurricular activities. In "Yo Socrates! Amend This!" (beginning on page 327), Paula S. Eisen introduces the idea of Socratic Seminar, in which the adult poses a series of thought-provoking questions (and only questions!) for students to reflect upon and respond to. Because teachers refrain from giving feedback during the seminar, students practice self-assessment, a cornerstone of the AASL *Standards,* as they construct responses to the questions. In addition, the probing questions help students move beyond superficial understanding and into conceptual-level understanding. Her lesson plan includes application for both language arts environments and government class. Included are guidelines for participation as well as additional arenas in which to employ the Socratic Seminar format.

Social Studies

The social studies curriculum can come alive for students when two instructors guide the experience. In Ronda Hassig's "A Small World—Technology Connecting Kids to Kids," and the accompanying lesson plan, "A Small World" (beginning on page 331), she explores how the sixth-grade research project was transformed. Building on United Nations materials showing the lifestyles of children around the world, her students created their own public service announcements, which were broadcast and shared. By connecting her students with an authentic audience, and by building on their natural empathy for their global peers, she and her teaching team created a dynamic learning opportunity consistent with the technology and social collaboration goals found in the AASL *Standards*. Her lesson plans, which can be used with upper elementary students as well as middle schoolers, include a rubric.

Video is also at the heart of Alan McCarthy and Sandra Sterne's project. "Fighting the Civil War with Primary Sources" (beginning on page 355) describes how their students used research to create original Civil War films. Using technology to express learning is a theme found throughout the AASL *Standards,* as is collaboration.

The final social studies project used the local community as an expert resource. In a lesson plan originally published in 1989 and updated to incorporate podcasting in 2008, Sandra L. Ricker discusses how to conduct oral interviews. "Interviewing Older Americans" (page 340) can connect to units on civics, primary sources, or 20th-century history. It demonstrates how primary sources beyond text can be used effectively as learning tools for students.

Science

Science research can be particularly powerful because the inquiry methods espoused by scientists are so compatible with the inquiry values of school library media centers and with the AASL *Standards*. Hawaiian school library media specialist Audrey Okemura, in "Designing Inquiry-Based Science Units as Collaborative Partners" (beginning on page 341), discusses a collaborative unit in which students explored the chemistry of everyday objects—from Windex to Lactaid—and then discussed how those inventions had contributed to their own quality of life.

Finally, Catherine Trinkle uses Patricia Polacco's picture book *The Lemonade Club* as the springboard for a research project on health and diseases. "Text-to-Self Connection: *The Lemonade Club* and Research into Diseases" (beginning on page 346) demonstrates the power of a graphic organizer to lead students to new understanding. By asking students to provide a list of where people could find more information, she gives them an authentic reason for citation, and by asking them to describe the daily life of a patient with that disease, she asks them to synthesize the information they have learned in a meaningful way. Trinkle's lesson shows how scaffolding remains essential in planning 21st-century learning as SLMSs support students in pursuing new understandings.

GETTING TO ADVOCACY

Please see chapter 10.

THOUGHTS FOR THE JOURNEY

1. As a current or incoming secondary media specialist, you will work with far more teachers and students than will your elementary library counterparts. What strategies might you use to reach out to these larger numbers?

2. How do the rigors of the secondary curriculum affect the time available for meaningful research?

3. Some teachers have a predilection for "title and three bullet points" PowerPoint presentations, in which students can easily cut and paste content without inquiring, processing content, or synthesizing. What strategies might you recommend to these teachers to improve the instructional experience for students?

The Librarian Who Loves *LibraryThing*

by Roberta Sibley

A year ago, I attended a conference session on *LibraryThing*. In that session, this online tool was touted as a way to catalog a personal library collection. It looked like a great resource, but why, oh why, would I want to catalog on weekends? Wasn't cataloging during the week enough?

At the same time, however, I was having difficulty keeping track of all of the books I read. I used to have an index card file, but that's so 1980s! I got rid of the card catalog twenty years ago, so what in the world was I doing with a card file? Moreover, I would often forget to write up the cards after I read a book, so the system became outdated quickly. Then it hit me like a bolt of lightning: *LIBRARYTHING*! I remembered that conference session and realized that using *LibraryThing* would be a great way to keep track of my reading. Ditch the card file; welcome to Web 2.0.

Professional Use

LibraryThing is, indeed, a great way for library media specialists to keep track of the books we personally read. The account is free for the first 200 books or twenty-five dollars for a life-

time subscription. *LibraryThing* allows me to create a personal library, give my books tags, choose book covers, give star ratings, generate citations (MLA, APA, Chicago), and review books. I can also connect to other readers and see their reviews. Entries can be seen by anyone or made private if I don't want to share. The tags, which can be sorted alphabetically, are useful for remembering book topics and themes. When a tag is clicked, all of the books in the library tagged with that subject are displayed. When a student asks for a book about "love," for example, I can sort through my tags to find titles, cover art, and reviews to trigger my memory of which books to recommend.

LibraryThing with Students

I started experimenting with *LibraryThing* in our high school last spring. (One word of caution: according to the site's Terms of Use, children under the age of thirteen are prohibited from using *LibraryThing*. This limits its use to high school students.)

We have a senior elective in our school entitled "Reading in Literature." Students develop a personal reading plan, do booktalks, participate in literature circles, keep a log of responses to teacher-prompted questions, and review the books they read. It was the perfect place to try out *LibraryThing* with students. Teachers can go paperless and keep track of student reading logs, journals, and reviews online. They can also respond to students individually, and those responses can be private

communications between teacher and student.

I showed the students my personal bookshelf and taught them how to create an account. They immediately started adding books. By the end of the class, all students had an account, the teacher created a group, and every student joined the group.

Getting Started with Students

Go to the *LibraryThing* page (http://www.LibraryThing.com). On the right pane, click the Join Now button, and have students create a username and password. Email is optional, but if students don't put in an email address, they cannot retrieve lost passwords. I suggest that students enter their personal, rather than school email addresses, so that when they graduate and lose their school email, they will still have access to their *LibraryThing* account.

Groups

Over the summer I experimented with the Groups feature with several of my Birmingham media colleagues. We created a group and read a common book. We tried to post in real time, as well as asynchronously, to see how the discussion thread worked. This professional practice is also a great way for library media specialists to gain the experience needed to get classes started with groups.

Teachers can post a topic and have students respond to the journal prompts online. Students can sign their names at the end of the entry (John S.) so that the teacher does not have to look up each student's username to see who is responding. The other option is for the teacher to keep a spreadsheet with the real names and usernames for reference. Each entry is date and time stamped, so the teacher knows if the assignment is in on time.

It works well for the teacher to create a group while I get students started with their *LibraryThing* accounts. Students give the teacher their real names and usernames on a sign-up sheet or index cards. The teacher invites students to a group by username, and the students must accept the invitation.

If the screen is projected in the lab, we can watch the students join and double check that all of the students have accepted the invitation. I walk around the lab to provide support. The first time that I worked with a teacher to create groups, all of the students had created accounts, joined a group, and responded to a topic by the end of the period (see Figure 1).

Responding to Journals

Once the teacher posts a topic, they can see all student responses. When the student username is clicked, it leads to

a dialog box where a comment can be posted. This allows the teacher to give the students private feedback about their work (see Figure 2).

Assessment

LibraryThing allows for several assessment tools. Students can write book reviews, tag books, respond to journal topics, and participate in virtual book groups. The teacher can see each student's library as well as all of the journal entries.

With *LibraryThing*, my collaborating teacher could do all of his assessments online, "going paperless" for the class. The students can see one another's libraries just as they can see all of the group members' names.

Student Responses to *LibraryThing*

At first, students were varied in their responses. Some found it confusing the first day, but by the end of the semester, they all had positive comments. Many of the students like the book recommendations, and the ability to connect with others. The majority of the students enjoyed the online aspect of the class and wanted to enter all of the books they read into their library. Ah, to be a teenager and be able to recall of the books read!

What's Next?

I have worked with four English classes on *LibraryThing*, and I plan to work with several more next trimester. There is another English teacher who is interested in setting up a book group. It's definitely worth a try, and I think it's an exciting tool for teachers, students, and library media specialists. And, it's not really cataloging—or at least that's what I tell myself.◄

Roberta Sibley is a library media specialist at Birmingham Groves High School Media Center, Beverly Hills, MI. Email: rs02bps@birmingham.k12.mi.us

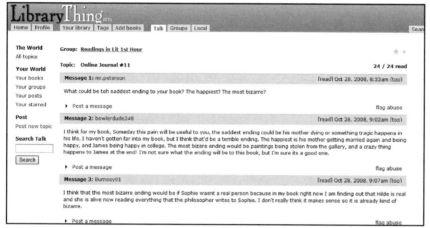

Figure 1. Group journal responses to teacher prompt.

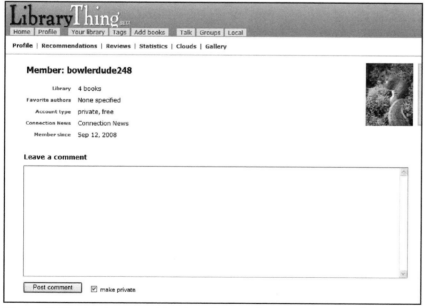

Figure 2. Student page with place for teacher comment and privacy check.

Yo Socrates! Amend This!

by Paula S. Eisen
This collaborative lesson was planned and taught with Helen Martin.

Library Media Skill Objectives:
Information Literacy Skills for Student Learning (AASL/AECT):

The student who is information literate:

- accesses information efficiently and effectively.

- evaluates information critically and competently.
- uses information accurately and creatively.

The student who is an independent learner is information literate and:

- strives for excellence in information seeking and knowledge generation.

The student who contributes positively to the learning community and to society is information literate and:

- recognizes the importance of information to a democratic society.

Paula S. Eisen is an English teacher at Granby High School, Norfolk Public Schools, Norfolk, VA. She is a graduate student in library science at Old Dominion University in Norfolk, VA. Email: peisen@nps.k12.va.us.

- practices ethical behavior in regard to information and information technology.
- participates effectively in groups to pursue and generate information.

Correlation with Virginia Standards of Learning:

GOVT.1. The student will demonstrate mastery of the social studies skills citizenship requirements, including the ability to:
- analyze primary and secondary source documents;
- analyze political cartoons, political advertisements, pictures, and other graphic media;
- distinguish between relevant and irrelevant information;
- evaluate information for accuracy, separating fact from opinion; and
- select and defend positions in writing, discussion, and debate.

GOVT.11. The student will demonstrate knowledge of civil liberties and civil rights by:
- examining the Bill of Rights, with emphasis on First Amendment freedoms; and
- exploring the balance between individual liberties and the public interest.

Curriculum (subject area) Objectives:

The student will identify issues inherent in selected amendments of the Bill of Rights.

The student will employ a variety of databases in order to examine and explore prominent points of view on the issues.

The student will interpret and analyze the implications of the various positions taken on the issues.

The student will select elements

of research to incorporate into a Socratic seminar.

The student will will lead and participate in a Socratic seminar.

Grade Level: 12

Resources:

Computer lab

Handouts
> Guidelines for Socratic Seminar Participants
> Seminar Question Writing Rubric

Databases to Use
> *Gale Gold Opposing Viewpoints*
> *SIRS Government Reporter*
> *Electric Library*
> *Facts on File News Services*

Instructional Roles:

The teacher and the library media specialist develop and deliver the unit collaboratively. The teacher provides information about Socratic seminars and what is expected of the students. The teacher has students break into collaborative groups of no more than four and helps students complete a list delineating research options. The library media specialist introduces students to databases to be used in conducting research for the assigned Socratic seminars.

Activities and Procedures for Completion:

On the board, the teacher writes FIRST, SECOND, FOURTH, FIFTH. The teacher guides the students so they ascertain that these numbers represent the amendments that will be studied. Students then list issues pertinent to each of the amendments.

The following essential question is posed: In what ways can Socratic seminars enhance understanding

> **Socratic Seminar**
> A Socratic Seminar fosters active learning as participants explore and evaluate their ideas, issues and values in a particular text. A good seminar consists of four interdependent elements: (1) the text being considered, (2) the questions raised, (3) the seminar leaders, and (4) the participants.
> —Excerpt from material developed by Cindy Adams, Vestavia Hills City Schools.

of the Bill of Rights? How can effective use of databases and the use of pre-screened databases improve the quality of research? What is the connection between effective research and a successful Socratic seminar?

Activity 1:

The teacher explains to students the nature of the Socratic seminar, the project they are about to undertake, expectations, responsibilities, and the handouts:
- Socratic Seminars (a handout needs to be prepared that helps students understand Socratic Seminars).
- Guidelines for Socratic Seminar Participants (see Handout #1, page 20).
- Seminar Question Writing (see Handout #2 page 20).

Activity 2:

The teacher guides students in completing the list from the anticipatory set delineating research options.

Activity 3:

Students break into collaborative groups of no more than four to work on the Socratic seminar assignment. Groups will be formed on the basis of interest in topics. Each group will address a different topic.

Activity 4:

The library media specialist introduces students to four distinct databases that will be particularly

helpful while conducting research for the assigned Socratic seminars:

• Socratic Seminar Research: Databases to Use (a list of databases, a summary of each

and access instructions should be provided).

Homework:

Students will read the newspaper,

Handout #1

GUIDELINES FOR SOCRATIC SEMINAR PARTICIPANTS

1. Refer to the text when needed during discussion. A seminar is not a test of memory; your goal is to understand the ideas, issues, and values reflected in the source.

2. It's okay to "pass" when asked to contribute.

3. Do not participate if you are not prepared. A seminar should not be a bull session.

4. Do not stay confused. Ask for clarification.

5. Stick to the point currently under discussion. Make notes about ideas that you want to revisit.

6. Do not raise hands. Take turns speaking.

7. Listen carefully.

8. Speak loudly so all can hear you.

9. Talk to each other, not to just the leader or teacher.

10. Discuss ideas rather than one another's opinions.

11. You are responsible for the seminar, even if you don't know it or admit it.

Handout published with permission of Cindy Adams, Vestavia Hills City Schools.

Handout #2

SEMINAR QUESTION-WRITING

When writing questions for your Socratic Seminar, include the following types of questions. You should encourage students to refer to the text in answering questions. The idea is not that students agree with the premises of the text, but that they refer to specific passages in agreement with them or in refuting them.

WORLD CONNECTION QUESTION:
Write a question connecting the text to the real world.
Example: If you were given only 24 hours to pack your most precious belongings in a backpack and to get ready to leave your home town, what might you pack? (After reading the first 30 pages of *Night* by Elie Wiesel [Holt, 1999].)

CLOSE-ENDED QUESTION:
Write a question about the text that will help everyone in the class come to an agreement about events or characters in the text. This question usually has a "correct" answer.
Example: What happened to Hester Prynne's husband that she was left alone in Boston without family? (After reading the first four chapters of *The Scarlet Letter* by Nathaniel Hawthorne [Macmillan, 1961].)

OPEN-ENDED QUESTION:
Write an insightful question about the text that will require proof and group discussion and "construction of logic" to discover or explore the answer to the question.
Example: Why did Gene hesitate to reveal the truth about the accident to Finny the first day in the infirmary? (After mid-point of *A Separate Peace* by John Knowles [Macmillan, 1960].)

UNIVERSAL THEME/CORE QUESTION:
Write a question dealing with a theme(s) of the text that will encourage group discussion about the universality of the text.
Example: After reading John Gardner's *Grendel* (Vintage, 1989), can you pick out its existential elements?

LITERARY ANALYSIS QUESTION:
Write a question dealing with how an author chose to compose a literary piece. How did the author manipulate point of view, characterization, poetic form, archetypal hero patterns, for example?
Example: In *Mama Flora's Family* by Alex Haley (Scribner, 1998), why is it important that the story is told through flashback?

Handout published with permission of Cindy Adams, Vestavia Hills City Schools.

---

check out recent or current news magazines, and listen to the national news to find anything pertinent to their topic. Each student should bring in at least one news report of some kind. The library media specialist should remind students of the resources that are available in the library media center to help them with the homework assignment.

Closure:

Students will respond on an exit card to the following question: How do you think the Socratic seminars will help you learn about the depth of the issues that fall under these various amendments we're addressing? (When the seminars have all been presented, students will review these answers and compare them with what they actually learned to distinguish expectations from actual accomplishment.)

Assessment or Evaluation:

Students will be evaluated on their use of the databases by the classroom teacher by presenting at least one valid source obtained from each database. They will ultimately be evaluated by the classroom teacher on the successful presentation of their Socratic seminars and on their participation in each of the individual seminars using the Socratic Seminar Rubric (at right). A participation log is helpful to keep track of student contributions. Teachers may also want to create a Socratic Seminar Evaluation Checklist that students could use to self-evaluate.

Follow-Up:

Possible extensions of this activity include exploring other amendments or narrowing research to a specific state. 🖐

Student _____

Seminar group _____

SOCRATIC SEMINAR RUBRIC

5=Excellent   4=Very Good   3=Good   2=Fair   1=Poor   0=No Evidence

PARTICIPATION IN GROUP PREPARATION _____

An active and equal participant in the preparation of the group's presentation
• Did the student contribute equally to the work necessary to put together the seminar?
• Did the student assist in brainstorming and strategizing?

PRESENTATION OF RESEARCH _____

Individual research materials include at least one valid resource from each of the following databases:
Opposing Viewpoints, SIRS Government Reporter, Electric Library, Facts on File

PARTICIPATION IN SEMINAR _____

Assessment of the role of the student during the presentation of his or her groups' seminar
• Did the student actively participate?
• Did the student assume a leadership role? If not, was there a reason?
• Did the student demonstrate knowledge of the issue being presented?
• When the group presented, was it evident that the student was a contributing member of the group?

PREPARATION OF GROUP _____

The preparation of the group as a whole
• Was an appropriate article, cartoon, or work of some kind given to the class in advance of the seminar?
• Was it apparent that the group had planned and prepared for the seminar?
• If necessary, was each member of the group assigned a designated role?
• Did the group function coherently, in a unified manner?

PARTICIPATION IN OTHER SEMINARS _____

Student's participation in all other seminars
• Total marks of participation: _____

TOTAL: _____/25 x 4 = _____/100 (This will be multiplied by 3)

A Small World—Technology Connecting Kids to Kids

by Ronda Hassig

An Accidental Discovery Have you ever been to a conference and not been able to get into the session you wanted? That happened to me at the very first session of the the National Social Studies Conference (NSSC) in 2005. I quickly learned that if the guest speaker is Jim Lehrer, you can plan on an overflow crowd. As part of my district's Social Studies Curriculum Revision team, I attended the conference with two other teachers, and the fact that we could not get into Mr. Lehrer's session is how we ended up in the United Nations (UN) session, "What's Going On?" This presentation is responsible for changing the way we teach our sixth grade research project.

Getting Started

The research project that evolved has come to be called the Public

Service Announcement Project by students. When we first introduce it as their sixth grade research project, they just roll their eyes and sigh real loud. However, once they see the ten UN clips or trailers for "What's Going On?" topics they're captivated!

Each trailer gives just enough information on the issue and its problems that students are eager to do the research and find out more. The clips can be found at *UN Works—For People and the Planet* (http://www.un.org/works). The ten 30-minute DVDs are the longer versions of the clips and can be found and purchased through Social Studies School Service. Each DVD costs $29.95 and includes a famous actor/actress and a young person living somewhere in the world and dealing with obstacles most of our students could never imagine.

Topics Covered

As teachers, the DVDs are pre-

ferred because several include Michael Douglas, Laurence Fishburne, and Richard Gere! The students like the DVDs because they can relate to the young people who look just like them. Topics include "Street Children in Mongolia,"

"Child Soldiers in Sierra Leone," "Child Refugees in Tanzania," "Indigenous Children in Australia," "Child Labor in Brazil," "Poverty in America," "Landmines in Cambodia," "AIDS in the Caribbean," and "Girls' Education in India." An added plus is that these topics are broad enough that students can take them in a variety of directions, e.g., poverty in America could lead to homelessness; street children in Mongolia could lead to runaways in America. Each of the ten topics has the possibility of subject flexibility.

Ronda Hassig, NBCT, is the library media specialist at Harmony Middle School in Overland Park, KS. In January, 2008 Ronda was chosen as a Kansas Master Teacher of the Year. Email: rhassig@bluevalleyk12.org

Research Process

Once students have chosen their topics, we begin the research process. I start with a lesson on the Big 6™ research model. The communication arts teachers work with the students on essential questions for their topics. The intent is to avoid questions like "how many," and work on "why" questions and how we can help make a difference in these children's lives. This is a suburban school district, very homogenous, and mostly high socio-economic. It is somewhat a life in a bubble. If students have time between soccer games and gymnastics practice they probably aren't watching the evening news. Consequently, the PSA project opens up the world to them. It not only gives students a chance to learn about the larger world, but to act on their new found knowledge.

The required resources for this research include periodical databases and Internet sites. The UN has multiple links connected with every DVD topic, as well as primary source reading materials that help to facilitate Internet use. The links include websites like UNICEF and Save the Child. Last year we collaborated with the social studies teachers for an almanac lesson on the topic country. The almanac work gave students the chance to make inferences about governments, war, and poverty, and their effects on the young people's lives as represented in the DVD. Many students used this information in their culminating piece, the PSA.

Skill Application

All lessons in the library media center and classroom are taught in context. Experience has shown that once a skill is taught, students need to use it—and use it immediately. Students are assessed on citing and completing a bibliography and encouraged to keep up with both as they proceed through their research. All of the research is done individually. However, once students finish their research, they meet with like-topic researchers in their class and begin to create their PSAs. We teach them to use *Movie Maker* or *iMovie*, if needed. Most have never used *Movie Maker* before so they learn a new technology skill that can be used again and again.

Topic groups then divide up the responsibilities of the PSA (e.g., photos, music, special effects, and transitions). Most importantly, they triangulate their research and decide as a team what information is worthy of placement in the PSA. They also decide if the information will convince their peers of the importance of their selected problem. Once they've made those decisions and prepared a storyboard they are ready to put their PSA together. We show examples of PSAs to give them ideas, including a PSA dedicated to Senator John Heinz, called the "Power of One." This PSA can be found at the *Caring Strangers* website (http://www.caringstrangers.com). Once they see the sample PSAs they are itching to get started.

PSA Work

Students work from a single rubric that assesses the research as well as the PSA (see A Small World: Research and PSA Rubric). Teachers work collaboratively to teach and assist students. The communication arts teachers assess the research content, and the library media specialist assesses the PSA work and the bibliographies. When students finish their PSAs, there is a popcorn party in the library media center for each class, and they watch their PSAs.

At least sixty or more PSAs are assessed every year, and the best PSA for each topic is chosen. The selections are based on the criteria and the rubric. The top ten are sent to the UN and are posted on their website (http://www.un.org/works/goingon/goinghome.html). The district superintendent and a school board member have attended an assembly the past two years to present certificates from the UN to those students that created the winning PSAs. It creates excitement for the project, and the results get better every year!

The Power of PSAs

There are also additional uses for the PSAs. For example, every year our building participates in the food drive for the metro food pantry. Throughout the designated collection time, the student-made Poverty in America PSAs are played at lunch to remind students of the national statistics on poverty. It is very effective.

In a Web 2.0 world, teaching our students new technology skills is imperative. This 2.0 world is their future and familiarity breeds comfort for most of our students. These new skills are also transferable from their school lives to their personal lives. Once they know these new technologies and how to access reliable information, they have the ability to truly change their world in an informed way. This is, after all, the goal of the PSA project. ✋

A Small World

by Ronda Hassig

Information Literacy Skills Objectives:
AASL Standards for the 21st-Century Learner:
Standards 1-4

Curriculum (Reading) Objectives:
Kansas State Standards:
Standard 1: The student reads and comprehends text across the curriculum.

Curriculum (Writing) Objectives:
Kansas State Standards:
Standard 1: The student writes

Ronda Hassig, NBCT, is the library media specialist at Harmony Middle School, Blue Valley School District, Overland Park, KS. In January 2008, Ronda was chosen as Kansas Master Teacher of the Year. The PSA project was featured in *The Librarian Won't Tell Us Anything!* by Toni Buzzeo (Upstart, 2006). Email: rhassig@bluevalleyk12.org

effectively for a variety of audiences, purposes, and contexts.

Benchmark 2: The student writes expository text using the writing process.

Benchmark 4: The student writes persuasive text using the writing process.

Grade Levels: 6-12

Resources:

Books:

Buzzeo, Toni. *Our Librarian Won't Tell Us Anything!* UpstartBooks, 2006.

Williams, Jessica. *50 Facts that Should Change the World.* Consortium Book Sales, 2004.

Videos/DVDs:

United Nations. *What's Going On?* RCN Entertainment, 2003. Titles include "AIDS in the Caribbean," "Child Labor in Brazil," "Child Soldiers in Sierra Leone," "Conflict in Northern Ireland," "Girls' Education in India," "Indigenous Children in Australia," "Landmines in Cambodia," "Poverty in America," "Refugees in Tanzania," and "Street Children in Mongolia."

Websites:

The Big 6™. http://www.big6.com/kids/3-6.htm

Caring Strangers. "The Power of One." http://www.caringstrangers.com/powerofone.htm

The Miniature Earth. "If the World Were 100 People." http://www.miniature-earth.com

Son of Citation Machine. http://citation-machine.net/

United Nations. What's Going On? (UN movie clips). http://www.un.org/works/goingon/goinghome.html

United Nations. "Declaration of the Rights of the Child." http://www.un.org/cyberschoolbus/humanrights/resources/child.asp

Databases:

EBSCO and *SIRS Discoverer*

Instructional Roles:

The communication arts teachers and the library media specialist

created, planned, and collaborated on the PSA project "Small World." The communication arts teachers taught the note-taking and graphic organizer piece, online quotation resources, and lessons on creating essential questions. The library media specialist taught lessons on the Big 6™, using the Internet wisely, library periodical databases, *Movie Maker/i-Movie*, and almanac, and reviewed citing and bibliography. The project isn't meant to bring them into the library media center to use books off a cart and write a report. Rather, this project is going to teach them how to come into the library media center, access information, and present the information in a way that can help them change the world!

Activities and Procedures for Completion:

This project takes at least five weeks. The library lessons and all of the research were completed in the library media center. When we taught students periodical databases or the library catalog we made sure they used those resources immediately.

Day 1: Prior to visitng the library media center, students have watched at least one of the United Nation's (UN) clips "What's Going On?" The library media specialist discusses *The Miniature Earth* webpage called "If the World Were 100 People." Under each student's chair is a piece of the "Declaration of the Rights of the Child." The document is cut into parts so that each student reads their piece out loud from beginning to end. The best current resources for this research are discussed. Required and extra credit resource lists are provided. Students will use at least three of

the required sources for their research. The library media specialist finishes with a review of the Big 6™.

Day 2: The communication arts teachers instruct students on the use of a graphic organizer using the "Cornell note-taking" method. The teachers and library media specialist then help students create essential questions on their topic. With three to five essential questions in place, students are ready to search for information. Through the research, they will need to identify a viable solution to their issue for the PSA.

Days 3–6: Lessons are provided by the library media specialist on library/district periodical databases and the Internet links at the UN website. Lessons are given one day and the next day students use newfound skills.

Days 7–8: Use of the almanac is taught by the library media specialist during social studies classes. Almanac information helps students understand issues related to the country (e.g., government, economy, and history).

Days 9–11: The library media specialist gives a lesson on intellectual property and the importance of crediting sources. Students review the website *Son of Citation Machine.* Students spend two days finishing research and completing the graphic organizer and bibliography.

Day 12: Students meet in like-issue groups. Research is individual, but PSA creation is in groups. The library media specialist shows the PSA "The Power of One" and discusses the purpose of a PSA and tips for what makes one truly meaningful. A successful PSA educates, offers a viable solution, and shows proof of knowledge in two minutes. Use of *Movie Maker* software is reviewed. If students know *Movie*

Maker, they can learn *iMovie*.

Days 13–15: Students meet in like groups and triangulate their research. Once done, they choose the information to share and the most viable solution. Students complete a storyboard and allocate jobs for creating the PSA. Video clips can be used within the PSAs. Transitions in *Movie Maker* and *iMovie* make the PSAs look professional. Students are reminded to cite all sources and each PSA must contain the Educational Fair Use statement. If PSAs are sent to the UN for possible posting, only first names should be on the PSA.

Assessment/Evaluation:

The students have a rubric that includes both the research and the PSA technology. The library media specialist will assess the bibliographies and the PSA piece of the project. The communication arts and/or social studies teachers will assess the research.

Follow-Up:

Every year we have a showing in the library media center for all of the PSAs. We do this by class and with popcorn! Every class then gets to sees the PSAs created by their classmates. Finally, based on the criteria and rubric, the top PSA for each issue is chosen and sent electronically to the UN. Award certificates are given at an assembly involving food donations for the local food pantry. "Poverty in America" PSAs are shown every day at lunch on a big screen, and statistics found by students are use as table tents in the cafeteria during the food drive. ✍

\multicolumn{4}{l}{**A Small World: Research and PSA Rubric**}			
CATEGORY	**5 - Highly Satisfactory**	**3 - Satisfactory**	**1 - Unsatisfactory**
Research Organization	Content is well organized using essential questions for your topic. KWL is complete with facts that thoroughly answer your essential questions.	Content is logically organized using at least 1 essential question. KWL is complete with facts that attempt to answer your essential question.	Content is not logically organized. KWL is incomplete and there is no attempt to answer an essential question.
Research Sources *	5 or more required sources were used to collect information on your topic.	3 required sources were used to collect information on your topic.	Less than 3 required sources were used to collect information on topic.
Research Bibliography *	All sources documented and cited in proper MLA format and typed in a bibliography.	All sources are documented and properly cited in MLA format but not in a bibliography.	Sources are documented but not cited or in a bibliography.
Research Content	Information collected in notes is essential (understands and identifies problem, explores viable solutions, and includes own solution) and is properly paraphrased.	Information collected in notes is essential, and attempts were made to paraphrase the information found.	Content in notes is not essential nor is it paraphrased properly.
Pre-PSA Organization	Storyboard for the PSA includes all 4 critical parts: an introduction, solutions, viable solutions, and a conclusion.	Storyboard for the PSA includes 3 of the critical parts.	Storyboard for the PSA includes only 1 of the critical parts.
PSA Movie	PSA shows an in-depth knowledge of your topic.	PSA shows information on your topic but at a surface level.	PSA is general and not on topic.
PSA Criteria	PSA lasts adequate time and uses pictures with music, transitions and visual effects to enhance the presentation.	PSA lasts adequate time and uses pictures with music, transitions, and even effects, but they often detract from the presentation.	PSA is too long or too short and does not include adequate pictures, transitions, music, or effects.
PSA Content	PSA content identifies and understands the problem and explores viable solutions for students.	PSA content attempts to identify and understand the problem as well as give viable solutions for students.	PSA content makes an attempt to identify and understand the problem, but no viable solutions are given to students.
PSA Creativity	PSA shows a large amount of original thought. Ideas are creative and inventive and hold audience's attention.	PSA shows some original thought. Work shows new ideas and insights.	PSA uses other people's ideas (giving them credit), but there is little evidence of original thinking.
PSA Bibliography	PSA bibliography includes required photo and music credits at the end for all sources used in making the PSA.	PSA bibliography includes some of the required credits at the end of the PSA for sources used.	No credits are listed at the end of the PSA.
\multicolumn{4}{l}{* Required sources include UN DVD, periodical using *EBSCO/SIRS*, almanac, quote book, and the Internet.}			

Fighting the Civil War with Primary Resources

by Alan McCarthy and Sandra Sterne

The calendar was creeping into June. It was late spring, a time when many students' thoughts were sliding toward summer vacation. But it wasn't a problem in Lori Lowe's classroom. Her students had bigger things on their minds—like whether or not the Civil War would turn out the way they hoped.

For many weeks, these fourth graders had been producing a sixteen-minute film documentary about America's bloodiest conflict. They had researched, written a script, recorded a soundtrack, and labored to fit together images gathered from the Library of Congress. The images were the key because they would tell the tale as much as the words.

These images—photos, drawings, maps, and posters—have a lot to say. They are all primary resources, artifacts derived directly from the time they describe and straight from the war itself. Their detail is revealing, their authenticity empowering.

With resources like these, students know they have done something more than play at filmmaking. They feel they are on par with Ken Burns, a man whose name they have all come to recognize. They feel a connection with his vision. They can appreciate the struggles of other artists and scholars, and they feel the happy anticipation of premiering their work.

The audience includes Dr. Mark Johnston, Arlington, Virginia's Assistant Superintendent of Instruction, and Dr. Rhonda Clevenson, Program Director for Adventure of the American Mind Northern Virginia Partnership. They and others have come to share in the excitement and to celebrate this achievement. The screen and projector are in place. The DVD is set to go. All that is left now is to press play…

Seeing the finished work of these students is impressive. Titles drift. Photographs bleed, float, and slide one into the next. Captions describe important places and events. The sound of an antique fiddle sings a sober melody. But to watch the film is to observe only half the story.

Like many large projects, this one began with collaboration. It started with workshops arranged by Liz Hannegan, our district's Supervisor of Library and Information Services, and conducted by personnel from An Adventure of the American Mind, a grant funded program promoting the use of the Library of Congress' digital primary resources within educational curricula. The workshops highlighted the materials available on the Library of Congress website

Alan McCarthy is the instructional technology coordinator (Email: alan_mccarthy@apsva.us) and Sandra Sterne is the library media specialist (Email: sandra_sterne@apsva.us) at Long Branch Elementary School in Arlington, VA.

School Library Media Activities Monthly/Volume XXIII, Number 4/December 2006

and how to locate them. The collections are enormous, covering a vast range of topics but specifically those connected with the American legacy. Anyone can access them, but training is a big help. We quickly found a theme for introducing the resources to our staff. The Civil War is a cornerstone of Virginia's fourth grade curriculum and the Library of Congress offerings on the subject are extensive.

Back at school, we plotted our next move. We needed a project that would dramatically package the materials we'd found and emphasize their efficacy. As our school's instructional technology coordinator and library media specialist, we wanted to introduce these digital resources to our colleagues. We agreed that a documentary film would be the best vehicle to meet our needs for three reasons. First, video is an excellent hook for our media-conscious students. It excites their creativity in ways that paper and pencil generally do not. Secondly, the documentary would be made with still images allowing students to control and edit their films. Finally, a Civil War documentary would result in a product that could be readily duplicated and shared with others, thereby lending a greater degree of authenticity to the students' work.

As we began assembling our team, we needed a class to pilot our project. Fourth grade teacher Lori Lowe was willing to let us test our idea with her students. We recognized a number of strong, independent learners in her group and knew they would be an asset in our experimentation. One of our goals was authentic learning, and we wanted the students to script their own film.

To help with the scripting process we recruited our school's writing specialist, Erin Watson. Her role would be to guide students through the writing process and to assist them in transforming their carefully researched, but disjointed facts into a polished script.

Dr. Rhonda Clevenson, Program Director for Adventure of the American Mind Northern Virginia Partnership, rescued us more than once as we groped our way through the Library of Congress' apparently limitless online resources chasing after just the right map or photograph or bit of music. With the support of these talented colleagues, we were ready to proceed.

Our first decision as executive producers was to download appropriate material beforehand. Recognizing the enormous scope of the available materials, we concluded that it would be impractical to expect students to sift through so much. It would prove too easy to get sidetracked and, in the interest of time, we wanted students to focus on understanding content rather than seeking it out.

We examined our district's curriculum guide and noted the relevant objectives. These considerations address causes and effects as well as key figures and events of the Civil War.

We searched the Library of Congress website for photos, maps, and other digitized artifacts relevant to the objectives and downloaded anything that seemed pertinent. We didn't want just enough material; we wanted more than enough. It would be up to the students to decide which images belonged in their film and which did not. To facilitate student decision making, we labeled all images and organized them into folders on our network's shared directory. Confident that we had ample material, it was time to introduce the project to the students.

We knew we would be asking a lot and wanted to get the students as excited as possible. Their excitement would need to sustain them through the challenging weeks ahead. As a hook, we showed them a Civil War video as an introduction to the subject and format. We also showed them an interactive documentary tool on the PBS website based on the Ken Burn's Civil War documentary which lets users select narrative, images, and a musical score to construct a mini-documentary. The model was very similar to what we hoped to achieve albeit on a smaller and more restricted scale, and it also gave the children an insight into what they would be doing. Their response was overwhelmingly favorable. They could not wait to begin.

Research was handled in the library media center where content was determined by the district's learning objectives. These were separated into four categories: people,  places, events, and issues. We elicited prior knowledge from the students concerning the listed topics. Concepts, personalities, and events were then each assigned to an interested student. The student's job was to gather as much information as possible on the topic using books, encyclopedias, and prescreened Web sources. The wording of the objectives served as the focus for research. Beyond that, the film would be a creative undertaking and the students would determine what aspects of the topic most appealed to them.

We took scripting seriously. The script would be the measure of student understanding and of the film's value to other classes. Mrs. Watson utilized a projector and laptop with *Kidspiration* software to collect the facts from the young researchers. Through an ongoing dialogue, the facts were sorted into a rough chronological order and built into complete sentences. Students asked tough questions. Having bought into the project, they now took interest in acquiring a full understanding of the subject. Throughout the process, new thoughts were interjected wherever students rec-

ognized a connection. In this way, each student became familiar with the full picture.

Students made a special effort to include poignant quotations from historical personages because they had seen for themselves the power of direct quotations when they viewed other documentaries. Students took home printouts of the rough script to review and edit. They gathered one last time to put the finishing touches to their script being careful to include only the information they could be sure of. A familiar mantra was "Do you think, or do you know?".

We wanted each student to own the film; therefore, it was essential that each child had a speaking role. We divided the script into topical sections. The classroom teacher identified our more confident speakers, those who might prove shy, and those who were working on their English. Roles were then assigned accordingly to ensure that each student would be challenged but not daunted. Some became narrators while others assumed the roles of significant personalities. Our Abraham Lincoln proved to be a born thespian. We provided the children with tips on projecting their voices and enunciating. Time was taken in class for practice and an assignment was given to continue practicing at home in front of parents, friends, or a mirror. They were well prepared for their big recording session.

The film's narration would drive the film. We recorded it on school computers. Many software applications exist for recording sound; we opted for Felt Tip Software's *Sound Studio* which was already loaded on our computers. In no particular order, we recorded each student reading his or her part. If they stumbled, they tried again. Individual recordings were then compiled into a single file using the same software.

To further engage their imaginations, we took the students into the gym to record some sound effects. They stomped in place while their young commander shouted marching orders. A few digital cannon blasts were added later. The narration and marching sound files were then placed along with the organized images on our network's shared directory. Everything was now in place for production.

Our ultimate goal was a single film, but we had twenty junior producers with whom to work. This was a challenge. We decided to match students up in pairs. Each pair would produce their own version of the film to take home. They would use the same narrative and choose from among the many images obtained from the Library of Congress. In this way, each film would tell the same story but would uniquely express it through different choices of photos, maps, and artifacts. In the end, we would be able to take the best bits of each film and blend them into one exemplary work to be shared with other classes.

Students began production by exploring the images housed on our shared directory. Following a printout of their script, they clicked through folders while discussing images and making note of items they wanted to use in their films. Once they felt comfortable with the file organization, they opened their movie editing software. At Long Branch that means working with Apple's free *iMovie* software. For those working with a PC, Microsoft's *Movie Maker* would serve the same purpose.

We instructed each pair of producers to select from between five to seven images for each section of the script. They were able to click and drag their selections directly into the movie software. At this point, sequence was not especially relevant. Having acquired the desired images, they next created titles and section headings for their movies. They had free choice of fonts and title effects with the caveat that they needed to consider their audience. Overly decorative fonts might be difficult to read. Elaborate title effects might convey the wrong message. Given the serious nature of the subject, the emphasis was on appropriate choices.

Narration came next. Again, the narration had already been recorded, compiled, and placed in the shared directory. Every student had contributed to the script. Every student's voice could be heard in the recording. All that was necessary was for each pair to click and drag the sound file from the shared directory into the film. The entire process required only a few minutes.

The most demanding portion of the project came next. Titles, pictures, and narration were all loaded into the movie, but they were not in synch. Images and titles did not yet correspond to the narration. Synchronizing audio and video required that the students work sequentially from beginning to end, adjusting the timing and

order of each image so that it corresponded with the film's narration. Fortunately, we were working with still images so adjusting timing was as easy as double-clicking a photo and changing its duration. Even so, it took a lot of trial and error to get the timing exact, and we had to be careful not to wear down student enthusiasm.

Finally, we were at the polishing stage. Effects, transitions, and music were all added. Students animated still shots using the "Ken Burns Effect," an option built into their software that allows for dramatic panning and zooming. They also added transitions between images and titles being careful to choose effects that would underscore the serious nature of their work rather than trivialize it. A credit sequence was built for them. We saw no reason to make each team keyboard in the lengthy and identical bibliographic information. This movie file was placed in the shared directory for them to drag into their film. Finally, students selected appropriate Civil War era music downloaded from the Library of Congress website. They dragged this into their film for the credit se- quence and moved the sound file con- taining their own marching into the open- ing title sequence. The films were then published as digital video and burned onto DVDs for the students to take home. A class version was distilled from the best of each production and shared with our special guests.

The premiere showing the final results of all this hard work has ended. For a moment, there is si-

lence then applause. The students exalt. Adults congratulate them on the excellence of their work. Dr. Johnston suggests that Ken Burns may be in trouble and offers the possibility of airing the film on the county's cable access channel. The mood is jubilant.

Following a celebratory snack of donuts and juice, we take time to debrief. Using the primary resources has been a tremendous success. The authenticity of the materials has conveyed a rich context of detail inspiring student imaginations and engaging their talents for reason. The students appreciate the professional caliber of the materials. They have been working with resources worthy of a professional and consequently feel professional themselves. Judging from the conversations, the children express a firm grasp of the people, places, and events they have studied. More importantly they demonstrate a mature understanding of the larger and subtler issues involved. Even without this discussion, their mastery of the content is evident from test scores. Having lived and breathed the Civil War, the content belongs to them. As one student puts it, "When we got ready to take the test on the Civil War I was a bit worried. But then when I saw the questions I said, 'This is easy. I learned all this making the movie.'"

The completed documentary is viewable online (http://www. arlington.k12.va.us/ schools/longbranch/ book_shelf/book_ media/Lowe_Civil_ War_05.mov). ✋

Interviewing Older Americans

by Sandra L. Ricker (*SLMAM*, May 1989)

UPDATED from 1989

Links to Key Words in Instruction:

Authentic Learning and Assessment, Collaboration, Inquiry-Based Teaching and Learning, Interview, Oral History, Primary Sources, Project-Based Learning, Questioning, Taking Notes, Technology. See *The Blue Book* by Daniel Callison and Leslie Preddy (Libraries Unlimited, 2006).

Information Literacy Skills Objectives:

AASL Standards for the 21st-Century Learner:

Inquire, think critically, gain knowledge: 1.1.1, 1.1.2, 1.1.3, 1.1.6, 1.1.9

Draw conclusions, make informed decisions, apply knowledge: 2.1.1, 2.1.2, 2.1.3, 2.1.5, Disposition: 2.2.4. Responsibility: 2.3.1. Self-Assessment: 2.4.1, 2.4.2.

Share knowledge participate ethically and productively: 3.1.1, 3.1.2, 3.1.3, 3.1.5. Dispositions: 3.2.2, 3.2.3. Responsibilities: 3.3.2, 3.3.4, 3.3.5. Self-Assessment: 3.4.2, 3.4.3.

Pursue person and aesthetic growth: 4.1.7, 4.1,8. Disposition: 4.2.3. Self-Assessment: 4.4.4.

Curriculum (subject area) Objectives:

English/Language Arts

Students will use a variety of forms to write for different purposes.

Social Studies

Students will demonstrate proficiency in information gathering skills, locating information from a variety of primary and secondary sources.

Students will demonstrate knowledge of technologies that support collaboration.

Students will collaborate with peers to contribute to an electronic community of learning.

Students will improve skills in historical research by using primary sources.

Grade Levels: 9-12

Resources:

Print:

Fontichiaro, Kristin. *Podcasting at School.* Libraries Unlimited, 2008.

Ratcliffe, Mitch, and Steve Mack. *Podcasting Bible*. Wiley, 2007.

Wigginton, Elliot. *Foxfire 2*. Anchor, 1973.

Web Sites:

How Podcasting Works. http://computer. howstuff works. com/podcasting

Interviewing Senior Citizens and Grandparents. http://www.emints.org/ethemes/ resources/S00000392.shtml

Instructional Roles:

The teacher and library media specialist work together to set the timeline, designate roles, create sample questions, and go over the steps to interviewing and creating a podcast.

Activities and Procedures for Completion:

Students will interview an older relative or friend, school employee, or other senior citizen. They will develop interview questions and create a podcast of the interview.

To create interest in the project, the teacher or library media specialist will show objects that belong to older family members (dishes, pictures, articles of clothing, etc.). They will generate questions about the objects and tell what they know about them. The library media specialist will tell about the Foxfire project started by Eliot Wigginton in the Appalachian mountains of Georgia where 9th and 10th grade English classes interviewed older people in the community in 1966. There are books, magazines, and recordings of the interviews. Read some selections from the Foxfire books. Collaborate on developing interview questions and teaching the podcasting process.

Evaluation/Assessment:

Students will be given materials to help them conduct the interviews and com-

plete the podcast (e.g., rubrics, guidelines, expectations).

Follow-Up:

Host an evening open house and invite the community to listen to the interviews in a lab (computer to computer) setting. Have students vote on the podcasts that should be posted on the school or library media Web site.

Do's and Don'ts of Interviewing

► Avoid "yes/no" questions. Pursue an issue.
► Come back to a question not fully answered.
► Engage in conversation. Be patient and listen carefully.
► Keep notes about things you forgot to ask.
► Act interested!
► Develop a plan, but remain flexible.
► Do not interject your own prejudices.
► Try to get complete, accurate, and candid information.

Interview/Podcast Assignment

Assignment: Interview an older person. It could be a parent, grandparent, neighbor or other community member.

Sample Questions:

► What is your name, where are you from, where did you grow up?
► What was it like when you were young? What games did you play? What jokes did you tell? What did you do in your leisure time?
► What did your parents do and how were they different from parents today?
► What do you remember about your grandparents?
► Did you travel or go on any trips?
► What is the oldest thing you own and does it have a story?
► What are some historical events that have happened and how have they affected you?
► What are the biggest changes you see from then to now? What was good and not-so-good?
► What do you miss about your early years?
► Who are your heroes?

The Podcasting Process from *Podcasting at School* **(Libraries Unlimited, 2008):**

Step One: Picture It—Who is the audience
Step Two: Plan It—Research, Prepare written notes, Rehearse
Step Three: Record It—Warm up your voice, get equipment ready
Step Four: Edit it
Step Five: Review It
Step Six: Distribute It

Designing Inquiry-Based Science Units as Collaborative Partners

by Audrey Okemura

Inquiry as a teaching and learning strategy is fundamental and deeply embedded within the content and teaching standards of science education (National Research Council 2000). Inquiry-based teaching and learning strategies guide students to explore and actively learn about the world around them. Now that No Child Left Behind is focusing on science education, it is crucial for science teachers to not only motivate this intellectual curiosity in their students through inquiry but for their students to demonstrate higher levels of understanding.

How can library media specialists play an active role in promoting and improving science learning? There has been little written about collaboration between teacher-librarians and science educators, and Mardis and Abilock each discovered that fewer than five percent of articles published between 1998 and 2003 were devoted to any aspect of working with science teachers or students (Mardis 2007; Abilock 2003; Mardis 2006).

Collaboration in science education has, therefore, become my challenge as a library media specialist in a suburban high school in Hawaii. This article is about how Judi Morton, a chemistry teacher, and I collaborated on science projects using an inquiry approach with approximately a hundred students in four general chemistry classes.

Inquiry and Science

Research shows that strong parallels exist between how students learn important science concepts and the processes of scientific inquiry that are used in inquiry-based classrooms (NRC 2000). Inquiry moves away from activities and tasks at the recall and simple comprehension levels to projects requiring the application of concepts and the synthesis, interpretation, and evaluation of information and ideas (Harada and Yoshina 2004). The following elements of inquiry emphasize what Wagner refers to as the 3 Rs that are essential for effective learning, i.e., rigor, relevance, and relationships (1997). They also reflect the major tenets of the *Standards for the 21st-Century Learner* (AASL 2007).

- Questioning is at the heart of the learning experience. The nature and quality of the question is equally as important as the answer. While fact-inducing questions are essential for eliciting basic information, questions that ask "what if," "why," "what else," and "who says this" provoke critical thought.
- Learning is social and interactive. Students work in peer groups; instructors team with colleagues. Both students and teachers frequently have mentors or seek information from community resources.
- Choice is crucial for students to feel ownership of the learning experience. Within the parameters of the assignment, students should be able to negotiate what is being learned and how learning will be demonstrated.
- Solving problems is an integral part of the process. Critical questions that might be confronted are: Why is this important? Why is this happening? What can I do?
- Students learn by doing. This is not referring to mindless physical tasks but "doing" that also requires rigorous intellectual engagement. The learning is both hands on and minds on (Costa and Kallick 1999).
- Learning is authentic and relates to students' personal lives. Quite often, the themes or issues are connected to larger social issues.
- Assessment is continuous and focuses on students participating in self-assessment that leads to empowering decisions about how to improve performance.

Designing for Inquiry-Based Learning

The catalyst for this collaborative initiative was a summer institute on inquiry-based learning. The benefits of an inquiry approach to learning were probed with the institute leaders and other participants. Instructional partners also planned an inquiry-based unit.

Making the learning relevant. Judi wanted her students to connect what they were learning in the classroom to their personal lives. She also wanted them to work in teams and exchange peer feedback. To accomplish these goals, we decided to have students (1) explore the chemistry behind everyday objects, and (2) connect these concepts to an explication of how these objects have improved their quality of life. We agreed that allowing choice was critical.

Linking to standards. One of our first tasks was to identify the content standards that would serve as the overarching concepts for the study. We identified two standards: the nature of matter and the relationship between science, technology, and society.

Starting with the end in mind. We had learned about the importance of using an outcome-based model of instructional design at the summer institute on inquiry-based learning (Wiggins and McTighe 1998). What did we hope students would be able to demonstrate by the end of the project? Starting with the end in mind was a new way of designing instruction for us. We devised a checklist (Figure 1) that described the goals as "I can" statements for the students and also served as a pre-assessment tool.

Key Activities Implemented

Our collaborative planning efforts continued after we returned from the institute. We refined our unit's essential question and designed lessons and activities to stimulate curiosity and invite differentiated paths of investigation. Once we thought that the attributes of inquiry-focused teaching and learning were incorporated, we were ready for implementation.

Hooking interest. We launched the unit as a team-taught lesson. Judi showed a film clip from *The Wizard of Oz* as an introduction to our foundational question, "What are things made of?" I then led a class discussion focused on the Tin Man's composition and used a K-W-L chart to visually connect our prior knowledge. Students then part-

nered with colleagues and brainstormed everyday objects and/or products they might research. To help them get started, Judi and I shared tangible examples, e.g., Lactaid, Windex, and Benefiber. Once students selected their objects, they started work on their K-W-L charts.

Clarifying goals and outcomes. Following the introduction, we explained the details of the project (e.g., plained the details of the project (e.g.,

expectations and timeline) and provided students with a copy of the project's poster rubric (Figure 2, page 49). Judi also shared clips from another video containing more examples of connections between chemistry and daily life.

Brainstorming questions. In the next lesson Judi explained a question web she had created using *Inspiration* to visually represent our essential and focus

FIGURE 1: Checklist of Goals			
I CAN...	Meets	Not Yet	Comments
Connect			
Identify the chemical composition of substances.			
List the characteristics and/or properties that make everyday objects useful.			
Distinguish the physical from the chemical properties of substances.			
Wonder			
Construct a question web that visually connects and organizes my thoughts and questions and possibly leads me to think of new questions.			
Investigate			
Use advanced online search strategies to locate and download information (e.g., key phrases, URL search).			
Apply strategies in online databases to make my searches more efficient and productive.			
Justify my selection of a Web site by citing at least three reasons for its use.			
Find scientific literature that is useful and relevant to my research.			
Create properly formatted citations documenting the variety of sources used.			
Construct/Express			
Produce an effective presentation suitable for the assignment.			
Present an object's usefulness based on the physical properties of its molecules.			
Relate an object's useful characteristics and properties to the chemical properties of its molecules.			
Invent new ideas of how technology can benefit society.			
Reflect			
Reflect on the research process (e.g., successes, areas to improve, what worked, what should be changed) and create a personal plan for future successes.			

questions. Judi also encouraged students to revisit their K-W-L chart and add their own questions to the web.

Conducting the investigation. I taught lessons to help students find and use appropriate resources (e.g., online search strategies, Web evaluation, and documentation). I also created a note-taking sheet (Figure 3, page 50) and a Web site evaluation checklist (Figure 4, page 51) that were influenced by similar forms created by Harada and Yoshina (2005).

Critiquing and reflecting. It was critical for students to provide constructive feedback to other teams prior to the gallery walk. To do this, they used the poster rubric. We were pleased with the exchanges. Many groups used the suggestions and comments from the peer assessment to improve their work. At various points in the unit, students also kept logs that helped them think about what they were learning and how they were learning which provided us with important feedback.

Midpoint Adjustments

Midway through the project our plans changed when we realized that students did not have the background knowledge

FIGURE 2: Poster Rubric

Category	4	3	2	1
Required elements ►Answers to 6 Focus Qs ►Two visuals ►Bibliography	Poster includes all required elements as well as additional information to enhance the research project.	All required elements are included in the poster.	One of the required elements is missing or incomplete in the poster.	Two of the required elements are missing or incomplete in the poster.
Content relevance, accuracy and suitability	All content is relevant, accurate, and appropriate to the object, and provides a thorough explanation in each section.	All content is relevant and appropriate to the object, and provides a general explanation in each section.	All content is relevant and provides a cursory explanation in each section.	Some content is relevant and provides a cursory explanation in each section.
Bibliography (Excludes citations for visuals)	Has more than three citations from a variety of sources, all correctly formatted.	Has three citations in the correct format from a variety of sources.	Has three citations from a variety of sources, but they are incorrectly formatted.	Has two citations from different sources.
Labels of each section	All items of importance are clearly labeled and can be read from 3 feet away.	All but one important item on the poster is clearly labeled and can be read from 3 feet away.	All but two important items on the poster are clearly labeled and can be read from 3 feet away.	Labels are too small to view from 3 feet away.
Graphics (Two visuals required: one of the object, one of the chosen compound's molecular formula or structure)	Has at least two graphics related to the object with relevant captions that describe each one. All borrowed graphics have a source citation.	Has two graphics related to the object with relevant captions that describe each one. One borrowed graphic has a source citation.	Has one graphic related to the object with a relevant caption that describes it. The graphic has a source citation.	Graphics are included, but no source citations are included.
Presentation	The poster is exceptionally attractive (grabs attention) in terms of design (theme and color use), layout, and neatness. It is very informative.	The poster is attractive in terms of design, layout, and neatness. It is informative.	The poster is acceptably attractive though it may be a bit messy. It is marginally informative.	The poster is distractingly messy or poorly designed, and/or not informative.
Grammar	There are no grammatical/ mechanical mistakes on the poster.	There are 1-2 grammatical/ mechanical mistakes on the poster.	There are 3-4 grammatical/ mechanical mistakes on the poster.	There are more than 4 grammatical/ mechanical mistakes on the poster.

to address our project's second standard regarding the relationship between science, technology, and society. We decided to address this standard in another inquiry project later in the year. Doing so gave us the opportunity to build on our first inquiry experience and try other ideas and strategies we had previously learned at the summer institute. Being able to reflect together as partners was essential to our understanding of the limitations of the first unit and the readiness levels of the students.

Scaffolding the learning experience. Our second inquiry project still focused on the relevancy of chemistry in people's lives, but this time the human body was selected as the focus. Students researched a chemical that was produced and used in the human body (e.g., insulin, adrenalin) and shared their findings in a *PowerPoint* presentation.

Students once again chose their topics, but this time, they created their own research questions, designed their own question webs, and used these webs as working documents to track new questions and thoughts. My lessons targeted choosing and narrowing a topic and asking critical questions.

Using assessment to adjust teaching. The limitations of self-perception data became apparent when data from the checklist (Figure 1) were reviewed. For example, while students indicated they already knew how to use advanced search strategies, my observations contradicted their perceptions. As a result, I devised a K-W-L chart to find out what they actually knew.

Student feedback also helped guide our instruction in our second project. In their journals, students admitted that they tended to copy when they were unsure about a subject. Therefore, a lesson on plagiarism was included and students were encouraged to include more personal connections and experiences in their presentations.

Insights Gained

Inquiry-based approaches led to learning that was more fluent, meaningful, and relevant. As instructors, we made the following critical discoveries.

Importance of background knowledge. Inquiry is based on constructivist principles. By paying thoughtful attention to students' prior understandings and gaps in content knowledge, we recognized that it was unrealistic to address both science standards in the first project and extended the work across two projects.

Impact of questions asked. Essential questions that frame the learning and capture the essence of a unit of study help students stay on track. We realized our need to conscientiously facilitate the questioning process rather than direct and tell.

Sharing control with students. We also realized that relinquishing control of the learning process was easier said than done. Students developed ownership for their projects when they selected their topic. At the same time, they were not ready to take full charge, e.g., determining goals, identifying critical tasks and appropriate resources, and devising feasible timelines for accomplishing the work. The sensible approach

---

FIGURE 3: Note-Taking Organizer for Web Sites

1. Name of object _____ *(fill in)*

Questions	Brief notes	Supporting details
Useful characteristics?		
Chemical composition of the object?		
Properties of these compounds: • Physical? • Chemical?		

2. Choose one of the major compounds or elements in your object and identify it here _____ *(fill in)*

Questions	Brief notes	Supporting details
Molecular formula?		
Other scientific and/or common names?		
Other uses for the compound?		
Relation of molecular or structural formula to its functions/properties?		

Citation Information for Web Site
Author's last, first name (if given): _____
"Title of Web page": _____
Title of Website: _____
Date (Day Month Year) posted/revised: _____
Name of institution or organization: _____
Date (Day Month Year) found: _____
Web address: http://_____

was to allow for greater student choice and voice in progressive steps.

Conclusion

Barbara Stripling states that "inquiry-based instruction that leads to student understanding is designed most powerfully when content and process specialists work together—a collaborative team of library media specialist and classroom teacher" (2007, 44). Mardis states that rather than working in "parallel universes," science classrooms and libraries must be "mutually reinforcing" as schools move in the direction of data-driven decision-making and practice (http://www.ala.org/ala/aasl/aaslpubsandjournals/slmrb/slmrcontents/volume10/mardis_schoollibrariesandscience.cfm). Our experiences confirm that by teaching and learning as curriculum partners, the teacher and library media specialist can integrate learning and motivational strategies to help students become more self-directed. We can assess and reflect together to co-create instruction that connects learning to personal levels of meaning.

Acknowledgments:
Thanks to Judi Morton, my teaching partner, and to Joan Yoshina and Violet Harada, who were the principal trainers for the summer institute on inquiry learning. I am also indebted to Violet Harada, who encouraged me to write this article and served as a valuable mentor and editor in the process.

References:
Abilock, Debbie. "Collaborating with Science Teachers." *Knowledge Quest* 31, no. 3 (January/February 2003): 8-9.
American Association of School Librarians. *Standards for the 21st-Century Learner.* ALA, 2007. http://www.ala.org/ala/aasl/aaslprof-tools/learningstandards/standards.cfm (accessed November 22, 2007).
Costa, Arthur L., and Bena Kallick, eds. *Discovering and Exploring Habits of Mind.* Association for Supervision and Curriculum Development, 1999.
Harada, Violet H., and Joan M. Yoshina. *Assessing Learning: Librarians and Teachers as Partners.* Libraries Unlimited, 2005.
Harada, Violet H., and Joan M. Yoshina. *Inquiry Learning through Librarian-Teacher Partnerships.* Linworth, 2004.
Mardis, Marcia. "Science Teacher and School Library Media Specialist Roles: Mutually Reinforcing Perspectives as Defined by National Guidelines." In *Educational and Media Technology Yearbook*, edited by M. Orey, V.J. McClendon, and R.M. Branch, 169-178. Libraries Unlimited, 2006.
Mardis, Marcia. "School Libraries and Science Achievement: A View from Michigan's Middle Schools." *School Library Media Research* 10 (2007). http://www.ala.org/ala/aasl/aaslpubsandjournals/slmrb/slmrcontents/volume10/mardis_schoollibrariesandscience.cfm (accessed December 27, 2007).
National Research Council (NRC). *Inquiry and the National Science Education Standards.* National Academy Press, 2000.
Stripling, Barbara K. "Teaching for Understanding." In *School Reform and the School Library Media Specialist*, edited by S. Hughes-Hassell and V. H. Harada, 37-55. Libraries Unlimited, 2007.
Wagner, Tony. *Making the Grade: Reinventing America's Schools.* RoutledgeFalmer, 1997.
Wiggins, Grant, and Jay McTighe. *Understanding by Design.* Association for Supervision and Curriculum Development, 1998.◄

Audrey Okemura is a library media specialist at Pearl City High School in Hawaii. Email: audrey_okemura@notes.k12.hi.us

---

FIGURE 4: Web Site Evaluation Checklist

Instructions:
▶Use two copies of the following checklist for two different Web sites on the same issue or topic.
▶Compare the two Web sites once you have completed the checklists. Which is more relevant and useful for your project? Why?

1. What is the name of the Web site? _____
2. What is the Web address or URL of the Web site being evaluated?

_____

Place a check in the appropriate column.

Criteria	Yes	No
Authority		
Is the name of the author and contact information stated?		
Do other experts in the field think this is a reputable page? (Conduct a link: command in Google to see who is linking to this page)		
Does the domain of the page (org, com, net, edu, gov) influence your evaluation?		
Currency		
Is the information current? (latest update is usually found at the bottom of the page)		
Content		
Do you understand what you are reading?		
Does the information relate to the topic?		
Is the information consistent with what you already know?		
Objectivity		
Are different points of view represented?		
Is the site free of advertisements?		
Overall		
Would you use this Web site in your research?		

3. Which Web site is more relevant and useful for your project? Why?

Text-to-Self Connection: *The Lemonade Club* and Research into Diseases

by Catherine Trinkle

Library Media Skills Objectives:

AASL Standards for the 21st-Century Learner:

1.1.1 Follow an inquiry-based process in seeking knowledge in curricular subjects, and make the real-world connection for using this process in own life.

1.1.8 Demonstrate mastery of technology tools for accessing information and pursuing inquiry.

2.3.1 Connect understanding to the real world.

4.1.1 Read, view, and listen for pleasure and personal growth.

4.1.5 Connect ideas to own interests and previous knowledge and experience.

Curriculum (subject area) Objectives:

Students will be able to:

▶ Explain the difference between communicable and noncommunicable diseases.

▶ Define hereditary diseases.

▶ Discuss ways in which technology can be used to help students find information about personal health.

▶ Analyze the ways in which peers influence healthy and unhealthy choices.

Grade Levels: 3-8

(This is an excellent lesson to introduce vocabulary to ELL students.)

Resources:

Print

Kehret, Peg. *The Year I Got Polio*. Albert Whitman, 1996.

Krull, Kathleen. *Wilma Unlimited: How Wilma Rudolph Became the World's Fastest Woman*. Voyager Books, 1996.

Polacco, Patricia. *The Lemonade Club*. Philomel, 2007.

Wolff, Virginia Euwer. *Make Lemonade*. Henry Holt, 1993.

Web Sites

KidsHealth. http://www.kidshealth.org

New York State Department of Health. *Communicable Disease Fact Sheets*. http://www.health.state.ny.us/diseases/communicable

New York State Department of Health. *Diseases and Conditions: Information about Diseases, Viruses, Conditions, and Prevention*. http://www.health.state.ny.us/diseases/

Instructional Roles:

The library media specialist reads aloud Patricia Polacco's *The Lemonade Club* to students at the beginning of the unit, and leads students in discussion. The classroom teacher and library media specialist introduce *KidsHealth* Web site and circulate while students are working, stopping to discuss findings with students; monitor comprehension; and are available to answer student questions.

Activity and Procedures for Completion:

Before Reading

To help students make text-to-self connections, ask them to think about health problems they have experienced or that a family member or friend has experienced. Ask them to write about these experiences, but tell them that what they write will be personal, unless they choose to share with the class. While students are writing, walk around the room, checking only to make sure that students are writing. Be available to answer any questions students might have.

During Reading

While reading aloud *The Lemonade Club*, stop to compare Miss Wichelman's classroom with this classroom.

Ask students what they dream about when they grow up. Have them think first, then turn and talk to another student about their future dreams, which may include career aspirations, where they might live, college choices, etc.

Stop to discuss the phrase, "when life hands you lemons, make lemonade." Ask volunteers to explain what this phrase means and seek volunteers to share a time they made something good out of a difficult situation. For older students, make a connection to Virginia Euwer

Sample Graphic Organizer and Rubric

Define Communicable and Noncommunicable Diseases

(Note: Points and comments for rubric assessment are shown in color).

Name of Disease		Symptoms of disease
_____ No credit given but be sure name of disease is spelled correctly.	_____ Communicable _____ Noncommunicable Three points.	1. Three points. Look for complete sentences. 2. Three points. Look for complete sentences. 3. Three points. Look for complete sentences.
If the disease is noncommunicable, how is it treated? Five points. Look for complete sentences and specifics provided to explain exactly how this disease is treated.	**If the disease is communicable, how can is it spread?** **How can it be prevented?** Five points. Look for complete sentences and specifics provided to explain exactly how this disease is spread and how it can be prevented.	**Profile of a patient: Describe how this disease affects the daily life of someone who has it:** Ten points. Look for a minimum of 5 complete sentences that explain in narrative form what it is like to be a carrier of this disease and how it affects daily life.
Statistics: How many people have this disease? Three points. Make sure the student writes in a complete sentence.	**Where does someone go for more information about this disease?** Ten points. Look for an annotated list of resources, which might be online, in print, or human resources. Encourage students to use the phone book and contact agencies to locate specific departments and phone numbers. This section should reveal the resources the student used to find information to answer these questions.	

Student Name: _____ Date: _____

Teacher comments:

Score: _____ /45

References

American Association of School Librarians (AASL) (2007). *Standards for the 21st-Century Learner.* www.ala.org/ala/mgrps/divs/aasl/aaslproftools/learningstandards/standards.cfm (accessed June 6, 2009).

Armano, David. Micro-Interactions (n.d.). www.slideshare.net/darmano/micro-interactions (accessed June 6, 2009).

Association for Supervision and Curriculum Development. (2009). Whole Child Web site. www.wholechildeducation.org (accessed June 6, 2009).

Costa, Arthur, and Bena Kallick (2009). Habits of Mind Web site. www.habitsofmind.net (accessed June 6, 2009).

Donne, John (n.d.). *A Valediction: Forbidding Mourning.* www.poets.org/viewmedia. php/prmMID/15468 (accessed June 6, 2009).

DuFour, Richard. (2004). "What Is a Professional Learning Community?" *Educational Leadership* 61, no. 8 (May): 6–11.

Eisenberg, Michael B., and Robert E. Berkowitz (1988). *Curriculum Initiative: An Agenda and Strategy for Library Media Programs.* Norwood, NJ: Ablex.

Fontichiaro, Kristin (2008a). "AASL Standards—Common Beliefs." *School Library Media Activities Monthly Blog.* blog.schoollibrarymedia.com/index.php/2008/07/16/aasl-standards-common-beliefs/ (accessed June 6, 2009).

Fontichiaro, Kristin (2008b). "Thinking More About the Standards' Common Beliefs." *School Library Media Blog.* blog.schoollibrarymedia.com/index.php/2008/07/17/thinking-more-about-common-beliefs/ (accessed June 6, 2009).

Gladwell, Malcolm (2000). *The Tipping Point: How Little Things Can Make a Big Difference.* New York: Little, Brown.

Gore, J. M., T. Griffifths, and J. G. Ladwig (2002): "Towards Better Teaching: Productive Pedagogy as a Framework for Teacher Education." *Teacher and Teaching Education* 20: 375–87.

International Society for Technology in Education (ISTE) (2007). *National Educational Technology Standards for Students.* www.iste.org/nets (accessed June 6, 2009).

Johnson, Doug (2007). "When Your Job Is on the Line." *Blue Skunk Blog* (July 10). www.doug-johnson.com/dougwri/when-your-job-is-on-the-line.html (accessed June 6, 2009).

Kuhlthau, Carol Collier (1994). *Teaching the Library Research Process.* 2nd ed. London: Scarecrow.

Levitov, Deborah (2009). "Cutting Edge?" *School Library Media Activities Monthly* 25 (5) (January): 2.

Lewis, Catherine, Rebecca Perry, and Jacqueline Hurd (2004). "A Deeper Look at Lesson Study." *Educational Leadership* 61 (5) (February): 18–22.

Logan, Debra Kay (2006). "Being Heard . . . Advocacy + Evidence + Students =IMPACT !" *School Library Media Activities Monthly* 23, no. 1 (September): 46–48.

McKenzie, Jamie (2000). *Beyond Technology: Questioning, Research and the Information Literate School.* Bellingham, WA: FNO Press.

Moreillon, Judi (2007). *Collaborative Strategies for Teaching Reading Comprehension.* Chicago: ALA Editions.

Pappas, Marjorie L., and Ann E. Tepe (2002). *Pathway to Knowledge and Inquiry Learning.* Greenwood Village, CO: Libraries Unlimited.

Partnership for 21st Century Skills (n.d.). *Framework for 21st Century Learning.* www.21stcenturyskills.org/index.php?option=com_content&task=view&id=254&Itemid=120 (accessed June 6, 2009).

Scholastic Library Publishing (2008). *School Libraries Work!* 3rd ed. www2.scholastic.com/content/collateral_resources/pdf/s/slw3_2008.pdf (accessed June 6, 2009).

Stripling, Barbara K., and Judy M. Pitts (1988). *Brainstorms and Blueprints: Teaching Library Research as a Thinking Process.* Englewood, CO: Libraries Unlimited.

Tomlinson, Carol Ann (2003). "Differentiated Instruction in the Elementary Classroom." *ERIC Digest.* www.ericdigests.org/2001-2/elementary.html (accessed June 6, 2009).

Wiggins, Grant, and Jay McTighe (2005). *Understanding by Design.* expanded 2nd ed. Alexandria, VA: Association for Supervision and Curriculum Development.

Yucht, Alice H. (1997). *Flip It! An Information Skills Strategy for Students Researchers.* Worthington, OH: Linworth.

Zmuda, Allison, and Violet H. Harada (2008). *Librarians as Learning Specialists: Meeting the 21st Century Learning Imperative.* Westport, CT: Libraries Unlimited.

Recommended Reading

Abilock, Debbie. "Applying Information Literacy Skills to Maps." *Knowledge Quest* 36, no. 4 (March–April 2008): 8–12.

    Maps often show up in students' textbooks, Web sites, and informational text. But how often do we stop and explore what those maps are showing us and what they mean? Several examples of how to bring inquiry to map reading are outlined.

Abilock, Debbie. " 'Portkeys' to Vocabulary." *Knowledge Quest* 35, no. 1 (September– October 2006): 8–11.

    Media specialists have always contributed to students' reading by distributing books. But how often do provide strategies for the acquisition of new vocabulary? Three strategies for vocabulary acquisition without drill are included.

Abilock, Debbie. "Visual Information Literacy: Reading a Documentary Photograph." *Knowledge Quest* 36, no. 3 (January–February 2008): 7–13.

    An excellent companion to the graphic inquiry articles included in chapter 9 of this book, this article includes examples for using photographs in the inquiry process and questioning the lens through which the image was taken.

Achterman, Doug. "Beyond Wikipedia." *Teacher Librarian* 19, no. 4 (December 2006): 19–22. Available at 0-find.galegroup.com.elibrary.mel.org/itx/start.do? prodId=AONE (accessed June 6, 2009).

    Discusses how to meaningfully implement wikis in student projects.

American Association of School Librarians. *Crisis Toolkit.* American Library Association. Available at www.ala.org/ala/mgrps/divs/aasl/aaslissues/toolkits/crisis.cfm (Accessed June 6, 2009).

    When your school library's budget or staffing is in jeopardy of being cut, consult this toolkit for advocacy strategies. For school libraries not yet in crisis, consider the preventative measures suggested in AASL's *School Library Program Health and Wellness Toolkit* (see below).

American Association of School Librarians. *Empowering Learners: Guidelines for School Library Media Programs.* Chicago: American Association of School Librarians, 2009.

    Provides an updated overview on the staffing, budgets, scheduling, and pedagogy necessary for a vibrant 21st-century library program.

American Association of School Librarians. *Reading4Life @your library®: Position Statement on the Library Media Specialist's Role in Reading.* American Library Association. Available at www.ala.org/ala/mgrps/divs/aasl/aaslissues/positionstatements/ roleinreading.cfm (accessed June 6, 2009).

    Adopted in February 2009, this document articulates the role of the 21st-century librarian in developing a vibrant, open collection for research and personal enjoyment; co-teaching reading comprehension strategies; leading literacy events that lead to lifelong reading habits; and continuing to engage in professional development to stay abreast of best practices.

American Association of School Librarians. *School Library Program Health and Wellness Toolkit.* **American Library Association. Available at www.ala.org/ala/mgrps/divs/aasl/aaslissues/toolkits/slmhealthandwellness.cfm (accessed June 6, 2009).**

To thrive, school libraries need ongoing support from stakeholders. This toolkit provides guidance on how to reach out and build that support before a crisis hits. For school libraries in jeopardy, consult AASL's *Crisis Toolkit* (see above).

American Association of School Librarians. *Standards for the 21st-Century Learner in Action.* **Chicago: American Association of School Librarians, 2009.**

Whereas the AASL *Standards* give a general overview of the types of activities in which learners engage, this document provides sample lessons designed to meet the standards at the elementary, middle school, and high school levels.

Barnett, Cassandra. "Creating Standards and Frameworks for Information Literacy." *School Library Media Activities Monthly* **24, no. 7 (March 2008): 21–23.**

After serving on the committee that authored the AASL *Standards,* Barnett worked at the state level to develop Arkansas's first State Framework for Information Literacy. She compares and contrasts the processes, contents, and committee compositions of the two projects. The article concludes with advice for others who are looking to generate state curriculum frameworks that incorporate the AASL or other standards documents.

Bower, Penny. "Battle of the Books!" *School Library Media Activities Monthly* **25, no. 3 (2008): 21–22.**

Battle of the Books programs aren't new, but putting students in the driver's seat is! This partnership between an all-girls' and an all-boys' school helped students read outside gender-preferred literature, and having students organize the event helped them practice the responsibilities outlined by the AASL *Standards.* Bower's students' sense of fun is infectious!

Brodie, Carolyn S. "Collaboration Practices." *School Library Media Activities Monthly* **23, no. 2 (October 2006): 25–30.**

Defines collaboration and identifies how summer workshops hosted by the Institute for Library and Information Literacy Education at Kent State University has worked to develop quality collaboration habits between teachers and school librarians.

Buczynski, Sandy, and Kristin Fontichiaro. *Story Starters and Science Notebooking: Developing Student Thinking Through Literacy and Inquiry.* **Westport, CT: Teacher Ideas Press, 2009.**

Libraries aren't a school's only home for inquiry. Hands-on science inquiry using the science notebooking process is a powerful way to develop deep thinking in elementary students. In this book, a short story sets up a problem for which students use inquiry to seek a solution.

Buddy, Juanita Warren. "Your Investments in Staff Development—An Open Letter." *School Library Media Activities Monthly* **25, no. 6 (February 2009): 21–23.**

Outlines a variety of strategies for school library media specialists to become more actively involved in staff development.

Bush, Gail. "Inquiry Groups for Professional Development and Information Literacy Instruction." *School Library Media Activities Monthly* **24, no. 10 (June 2008): 39–43.**

Inquiry groups are an approach to professional development in which a facilitator leads group members through an inquiry-oriented approach to problem solving. Bush models a sample protocol for convening an inquiry group for the purpose of discussing the AASL *Standards.*

Buzzeo, Toni. Collaborating to Meet Literacy Standards: Teacher/librarian Partnerships for K–2. Worthington, OH: Linworth, 2007.

Buzzeo, Toni. Collaborating to Meet Standards: Teacher/librarian Partnerships for K–6. Worthington, OH: Linworth, 2002.

Buzzeo, Toni. Collaborating to Meet Standards: Teacher/librarian Partnerships for 7–12. Worthington, OH: Linworth, 2002.

This trio of books pulls together successful collaborations for student learning in school libraries. Although published before the AASL *Standards* were released, many can be easily adapted to fit them.

Callison, Daniel. "Effective Instruction Based on Evidence-Based Strategies." *School Library Media Activities Monthly* 23, no. 8 (April 2007): 45–47.
>   Outlines past efforts to document evidence-based practice in school libraries over more than 20 years and outlines criteria for successful evidence.

Callison, Daniel, and Leslie Preddy. *The Blue Book on Information Age Inquiry, Instruction, and Literacy.* Westport, CT: Libraries Unlimited, 2007.
>   A thorough, comprehensive look at the many pedagogical elements of high-quality learning in school libraries.

Carmichael, Patricia. "The Pedagogy of the Heart and the Mind—Cultivating Curiosity and a Love of Learning, Part 1." *School Library Media Activities Monthly* (January 1, 2009): 55–58. Available at www.proquest. com.proxy.lib.umich.edu/ (accessed June 6, 2009).

Carmichael, Patricia. "The Pedagogy of the Heart and the Mind—Cultivating Curiosity and a Love of Learning, Part 2." *School Library Media Activities Monthly* (February1, 2009): 55–58. Available at www.proquest. com.proxy.lib.umich.edu/ (accessed June 6, 2009).
>   In this two-part series, an Australian school librarian describes her school's award-winning project, which develops research skills in students pursuing personal interests. The articles paint a progressive picture of implementing Standard 4 of the AASL *Standards.*

Coatney, Sharon, ed. *The Many Faces of School Library Leadership.* Westport, CT: Libraries Unlimited, forthcoming.
>   Examines the many types of leadership exhibited by SLMSs. Contributors include Ken Haycock, Violet H. Harada, Deborah Levitov, Doug Achterman, Jody Howard, Blanche Woolls, David Loertscher, and Helen Adams.

Coatney, Sharon. "What Is the International Flavor of Your library?" *Teacher Libarian* 36, no. 1 (October 2008): 59. Available at find.galegroup.com.proxy.lib.umich. edu/itx/start.do?prodId=ITOF (accessed June 6, 2009).
>   Reminds librarians of the need for collections that reflect the international languages and cultures of all their students.

Coatney, Sharon. "Why? (Primary Voices)." *Teacher Librarian* 35, no. 5 (June 2008): 66. Available at find.galegroup.com.proxy.lib.umich.edu/itx/start.do?prodId=ITOF (accessed June 6, 2009).
>   In response to high school librarians bemoaning their under-engaged students, Coatney reinforces the need for primary librarians to create an inquiry-rich world.

Costa, A. L., and Kallick, B. *Leading and Learning with Habits of Mind.* Alexandria, VA: ASCD, 2008.
>   The Habits of Mind are 16 characteristics correlated with successful adults. The Dispositions portion of the AASL *Standards* are compatible with the Habits of Mind. Naming and practicing dispositions or Habits of Mind in the school library can help students develop enduring life skills.

Darling-Hammond, Linda. *Powerful Learning: What We Know About Teaching for Understanding.* San Francisco, Jossey-Bass, 2008.
>   Summarizes many best practices that lead to deep conceptual understanding for students. Special emphasis is placed on awakening prior knowledge, organizing information so that it is useful, and metacognition, goals that are incorporated into the AASL *Standards* as well.

Dickinson, Gail K. "Yes, the *Standards* Are Different." Available at blogs.ala.org/ aasl.php?title=gail_dickinson_ yes_the_standards_are_dif&more=1&c=1&tb=1&pb=1 (accessed June 6, 2009).
>   Dickinson, a coauthor of the Standards, discusses strategies for implementation of the AASL *Standards* that include conversations about deeply held beliefs; a refreshed approach to curriculum (rather than "plop-and-go" or merely matching the new *Standards* to existing practice); reexamining instructional practices; and assessment of program, instruction, and student learning.

Diggs, Valerie, and David Loertscher. "From Library to Learning Commons: A Metamorphosis." *Teacher Librarian* 36, no. 4 (April 2009): 32–38. Educator's Reference Complete. Available at 0-find.galegroup. com.elibrary.mel.org/itx/ start.do?prodId=PROF (accessed June 6, 2009).
>   Discusses Diggs's library makeover to create a more welcoming and social learning commons for her students.

Donham, Jean. *Enhancing Teaching and Learning: A Leadership Guide for School Library Media Specialists.* rev., **2nd ed. New York: Neal-Schuman, 2008.**

Updated to reflect the new AASL *Standards,* this book focuses on aligning school libraries with instruction.

Fontichiaro, Kristin. *Active Learning Through Drama, Podcasting, and Puppetry.* **Westport, CT: Libraries Unlimited, 2007.**

Outlines a wide variety of dramatic strategies to enhance student learning and demonstrate understanding. Strategies include choral poetry readings, raps, radio play podcasts, improvisational drama, and shadow puppetry.

Fontichiaro, Kristin. "More Than Friendship: Social Scholarship, Young Learners, and the Standards for the 21st-century Learner (AASL Community)." *Knowledge Quest* **37, no. 4 (March–April 2009): 64–68.**

Discusses how elementary school librarians can develop social scholarship skills in their students to meet the AASL *Standards.*

Fontichiaro, Kristin. "Planning an Online Professional Development Module." *School Library Media Activities Monthly* **25, no. 2 (October 2008): 30–31. Available at www.proquest.com.proxy.lib.umich.edu/ (accessed June 6, 2009).**

Describes how the author adapted Helene Blowers's "23 Things" Web 2.0 online professional development module for use with elementary school staff.

Fontichiaro, Kristin. *Podcasting at School.* **Westport, CT: Libraries Unlimited, 2008.**

A comprehensive overview of podcasting projects for the K–12 environment. Includes instructions and sample instructional units.

Fontichiaro, Kristin. "The School Librarian as Instructional Partner for 21st-Century Learning." *The Connected Superintendent* **(March 2009). Available at www.remc. org/file.php?id=23 (accessed June 6, 2009).**

Unfortunately, many school administrators and superintendents are not aware that school librarians can contribute much more to student learning than the shushing librarians of their own childhood. This article works to bridge that misunderstanding.

Fontichiaro, Kristin, and Susan Ballard. "A Letter to Our Classroom Colleagues (AASL Community)." *Knowledge Quest* **37, no. 3 (January–Feburary 2009): 80–83.**

Discusses how a change to more open-ended instructional design could minimize student plagiarism.

Freeman, Judy. *Books Kids Will Sit Still For 3: A Read-Aloud Guide.* **Westport, CT: Libraries Unlimited, 2007.**

Make no mistake about it—reading and read-alouds are alive and well in 21st-century libraries. This encyclopedic collection of kid-tested read-alouds, plus strategies for bringing reading to life in the library, is a superb reference guide.

Friedman, Thomas J. *The World Is Flat: A Brief History of the Twenty-first Century.* **New York: Farrar, Straus & Giroux, 2005.**

Friedman's book on the rise and impact of a global economy became an international best seller. This book pushed many to reconsider whether American schools were up to the challenge of preparing students for this new world reality.

Gordon, C.A. "A Never-Ending Story: Action Research Meets Summer Reading." *Knowledge Quest* **37, no. 2 (November–December 2008): 34–41.**

Describes how Gordon and her successor created a summer reading program with a Web-based component based on a model of free and voluntary reading known as extensive reading. The extensive reading approach involves students reading voluntarily, with limited assessment or accountability.

Harada, Violet H. "Professional Development as Collaborative Inquiry." *Knowledge Quest* **25, no. 5 (May–June 2001): 13–19.**

When librarians speak about collaboration, they often frame it in terms of teacher–librarian partnerships. But powerful professional development can grow from librarian–librarian teams as well. In this article, a project to connect school librarians in Hawaii is discussed.

Harada, Violet H., and Joan M. Yoshina. *Assessing Learning: Librarians and Teachers as Partners*. Westport, CT: Libraries Unlimited, 2005.

Why do we assess, and what does assessment of learning look like in school libraries? This book provides practical guidelines for improving how assessment occurs in school libraries.

Hartzell, Gary. "Why Should Principals Support School Libraries?" *ERIC Digest* ED470034 (November 2005). Syracuse, NY: ERIC Clearinghouse on Information and Technology. Available at www.eric.ed.gov/ERICDocs/data/ericdocs2sql/ content_storage_01/0000019b/80/1a/84/84.pdf (accessed June 6, 2009).

Hartzell, a former school administrator, outlines why it is in principals' best interest to support school libraries.

Hartzell, Gary N. "The Invisible School Librarian, Part I." *School Library Journal.* Available at www.schoollibraryjournal.com/article/CA152978.html (accessed June 6, 2009).

Hartzell, Gary N. "The Invisible School Librarian, Part II." *School Library Journal.* Available at www.schoollibraryjournal.com/article/CA152979.html (accessed June 6, 2009).

These articles originally appeared in 1997, and alas, the "invisible" school librarian remains a concern today. School administrator Hartzell outlines how some of the deepest values of librarianship—such as empowering others above themselves— can lead to a perception that they are not seen as active teachers.

Harvey, Carl A., II. *No School Library Left Behind: Leadership, School Improvement, and the Media Specialist.* Worthington, OH: Linworth Publishing, 2008.

School librarians can be key to school improvement. Harvey suggests practical steps for deepening librarians' engagement with learning and the culture of the school.

Harvey, Carl A., II. *The 21st Century Elementary Library Program.* Worthington, OH: Linworth Publishing, in press.

Whether one is just starting out in the library media center or a seasoned veteran, the key is to look ahead so that the elementary library media program evolves as the needs of the students and staff evolve. This book provides strategies and ideas for creating the 21st-century elementary library media program those students and staff need.

Harvey, Stephanie, and Anne Goudvis. *Strategies That Work: Teaching Comprehension for Understanding and Engagement.* Portsmouth, ME: Stenhouse, 2007.

Though directed at classroom teachers, the reading strategies in this book focus on deepening meaning and comprehension for students, making it compatible with the AASL *Standards*. Harvey and Goudvis also portray the school librarian as a meaningful partner in developing reading comprehension.

Hughes-Hassell, Sandra, and Violet H. Harada. *School Reform and the School Library Media Specialist.* Westport, CT: Libraries Unlimited, 2008.

School librarians who envision themselves as "change agents" can have a profound impact on school reform. But how do we become agents of change? Hughes-Hassell and Harada provide practical suggestions for the journey.

Johns, Sara Kelly. "AASL Standards for the Twenty-First-Century Learner: A Map for Student Learning." *Knowledge Quest* 34, no. 1 (March–April 2008): 4–7.

Johns, who was president of the American Association of School Librarians at the time the *Standards* were released in 2007, gives an overview of the *Standards'* components and why they are so important to student learning.

Johns, Sara Kelly. "Sowing the Seeds of the New AASL Standards for the 21st Century Learner: AASL Standards and Guidelines Implementation Task Force." *Knowledge Quest* 37, no. 1 (September–October 2008): 72.

Johns and the AASL Learning Standards and Guidelines Implementation Task Force set forth a succinct list of suggestions for becoming acquainted with the *Standards*.

Johnson, Doug. "BLB or PLC?" *Library Media Connection 26,* no. 4 (January 2008): 98.

Explores strategies and technology tools that can help professional learning communities not become the blind leading the blind.

Jones, Jami L. "Promoting Resilience: Ways Library Media Specialists Strengthen Children." *School Library Media Activities Monthly* 22, no. 3 (November 2005): 25–27.

Jones, a leading thinker on the emotional health of children in school libraries, reflects on how school librarians can help children bounce back from challenges.

Knowledge Works Foundation. *2020 Forecast: Creating the Future of Learning.* **2009. Available at www.futureofed.org (accessed May 31, 2009).**

Examining current cutting-edge behaviors, businesses, and technology tools, the Knowledge Works Foundation predicts how these factors will impact learning in the coming years.

Koechlin, Carol, and Sandi Zwaan. *Q Tasks: How to Empower Students to Ask Questions and Care about Answers.* **Portsmouth, NH: Stenhouse, 2007.**

Part of creating a 21st-century school culture means creating a culture in which students—not just teachers—develop questions. Koechlin and Zwaan present a variety of strategies for developing questioning and curiosity in students.

Krashen, Stephen. *The Power of Reading, Second Edition: Insights from the Research.* **Portsmouth, NH: Heinemann, 2004.**

Those looking for an evangelist who supports free, voluntary reading in lieu of prescribed reading programs or software need look no further than Krashen, whose book synthesizes dozens of research studies on meaningful reading and reading comprehension.

Kuhlthau, Carol Collier, Ann K. Caspari, and Leslie Maniotes. *Guided Inquiry: Learning in the 21st Century.* **Westport, CT: Libraries Unlimited, 2007.**

Kuhlthau, a researcher on school libraries; and her daughters, a museum educator and a reading expert, move from the research on inquiry to practical implementation methods that will help you re-envision your library as an "inquiry laboratory."

Levitov, Deborah. "One Library Media Specialist's Journey to Understanding Advocacy: A Tale of Transformation." *Knowledge Quest* **36, no. 1 (September–October 2007): 28–31.**

Describes a personal career journey to advocacy and outlines five key roles for school library media specialists: professional learners, teachers, leaders, visionaries, and connectors.

Loertscher, David. "Flip This Library: School Libraries Need a Revolution, Not Evolution." *School Library Journal* **54, no. 11 (November 2008): 46–49.**

Loertscher challenges readers not to simply adjust current practices but to revolutionize them to reflect the very real digital world in which students live. Consider re-imagining your library as a "learning commons" rather than a repository of materials.

Loertscher, David, Carol Koechlin, and Sandi Zwaan. *Ban Those Bird Units! 15 Models for Teaching and Learning in Information-Rich and Technology-Rich Environments.* **Salt Lake City, UT: Hi Willow Research and Publishing, 2005.**

Have you ever been asked to collaborate in a project that simply required finding and copying information, such as the teacher assigning each child a bird to research and a graphic organizer asking them to find its habitat, number of eggs, migration pattern, and other facts? Then you've done a "bird unit." Loertscher and his coauthors look at several ways to up the instructional ante.

Mardis, Marcia A., and Anne M. Perrault. "A Whole New Library: Six 'Senses' You Can Use to Make Sense of New Standards and Guidelines." *Teacher Librarian* **35, no. 4 (April 2008): 34–39.**

Maps the AASL *Standards* to the six "senses" featured in Daniel M. Pink's *A Whole New Mind.* Pink gave the keynote address at the 2007 AASL National Conference.

McGhee, Marla W., and Barbara A. Jansen. *The Principal's Guide to a Powerful Library Media Program.* **Worthington, OH: Linworth Publishing, 2005.**

Research shows that many school administrators do not learn about the role of school librarians in their university coursework or other preparation programs. This guide outlines what principals should know to maximize the impact of their school library media centers.

Midland, Susan. "From Stereopticon to Google: Technology and School Library Standards." *Teacher Librarian* **35, no. 4 (April 2008): 30–33.**

An overview of school library standards over the past century.

Miller, Debbie. *Teaching with Intention: Defining Beliefs, Aligning Practice, Taking Action, K–5.* **Portland, ME: Stenhouse, 2008.**

Miller, author of the best seller *Reading with Meaning*, about developing reading comprehension in primary students using authentic texts, explores the importance of classroom environments and teacher beliefs in creating a powerful classroom learning community. Read this book for a chance to reflect on what your school library's furniture arrangement and collection say to your patrons about what your library is and what you value.

Mishra, Punya, and Matthew Koehler. (2006). "Technological Pedagogical Content Knowledge: A Framework for Teacher Knowledge." *Teachers College Record* **108, no. 6 (June 2006): 1017–54.**

In the past, teacher expertise was generally considered to be in the arenas of content knowledge (information that should be known) and pedagogical knowledge (teaching strategies). The authors argue that for technology to be effectively integrated into school curricula, a new type of knowledge, technological pedagogical content knowledge (TPCK or TPACK), is needed. TPACK represents the necessary understanding of how technology intertwines with instruction and content.

Moreillon, Judi, and Kristin Fontichiaro. "Teaching and Assessing the Dispositions: A Garden of Opportunity." *Knowledge Quest* **37, no. 2 (November–December 2008): 64–67.**

Provides several strategies for weaving the dispositions of the AASL *Standards* into the daily learning in a school library.

Morin, Melinda J. "Moving Towards Collaboration—One Step at a Time." *School Library Media Activities Monthly* **25, no. 8 (April 2008): 18–19.**

Discusses steps media specialists can take within a noncollaborative culture to promote partner teaching.

New Media Consortium. *Horizon Report 2009: K–12 Edition.* **2009. Available at www.nmc.org/pdf/ 2009-Horizon-Report-K12.pdf (accessed May 31, 2009).**

An annual report identifying new technologies and their potential use for teaching and learning in K–12 environments. This document can be useful to media specialists wanting to stay abreast of national trends and technology tools.

Palfrey, John, and Urs Gasser. *Born Digital: Understanding the First Generation of Digital Natives.* **New York: Basic Books, 2008.**

Observations and research about the generation born after 1980, from the perspective of law professors.

Pappas, Marjorie. "Standards for the 21st-century Learner: Comparisons with NETS and State Standards." *School Library Media Activities Monthly* **24, no. 10 (June 2008): 19–26.**

A comprehensive comparison of the *National Educational Technology Standards for Students* (NETS*S), produced by the International Society for Technology in Education, and the AASL *Standards for the 21st-century Learner.*

Partnership for 21st Century Skills. *Framework for 21st-Century Learning.* **2009. Available at 21stcenturyskills. org/documents/framework_flyer_updated_jan_09_final-1.pdf (accessed May 31, 2009).**

The Partnership, of which AASL is a member, worked with educators and business leaders to create this framework for the kind of educational experiences needed for success in the 21st-century workforce.

Partnership for 21st Century Skills. *Milestones for Improving Learning and Education (MILE) Guide.* **n.d. Available at www.21stcenturyskills.org/images/stories/otherdocs/ p21up_MILE_Guide_Chart.pdf (accessed June 5, 2009).**

Where is your school or district in meeting 21st-century learning goals? The *MILE Guide* can help schools chart a new vision for learning and assess where they are on the change continuum.

Pink, Daniel H. *A Whole New Mind: Why Right-brainers Will Rule the Future.* **Boston: Riverhead, 2006.**

As a result of the rise of Asia, a new sense of abundance, and increased automation, Pink postulates that America's future dominance is reliant on right-brained thinking. The AASL *Standards* are consistent with his vision of creative thinking and problem solving.

Prensky, M. "Digital Natives, Digital Immigrants." *On the Horizon* **(2001). Available at www.marcprensky.com/ writing/Prensky%20-%20Digital%20Natives,%20Digital%20Immigrants%20-%20Part1.pdf (accessed June 6, 2009).**

> An overview of millennials, referred to by Prensky as "digital natives," as compared to the adults in their lives, called "digital immigrants."

Prensky, M. "Digital Natives, Digital Immigrants, Part II: Do They Really Think Differently?" *On the Horizon* **(2001). Available at www.marcprensky.com/writing/Prensky%20-%20Digital%20Natives,%20Digital%20 Immigrants%20-%20Part2.pdf (accessed June 6, 2009).**

> Discusses differences in the brain function of digital natives.

Richardson, Ken. *Ken Robinson Says Schools Kill Creativity.* **Video from TED Talks, 2006. Available at www.ted.com/index.php/talks/ken_robinson_says_schools_kill_creativity.html (accessed June 6, 2009).**

> Both the AASL *Standards* and the refreshed NETS*S draw attention to the need for creative thinking, but as Sir Ken Robinson of the United Kingdom points out in this talk, schools currently do little to promote creativity in the classroom.

Richardson, Will. *Blogs, Wikis, Podcasts, and Other Powerful Tools for Classrooms.* **Thousand Oaks, CA: Corwin, 2008.**

> One of the first books for educators on the use of Web 2.0 tools to promote learning in classrooms. Richardson is a voracious reader and lecturer on educational trends; follow his Twitter feed at twitter.com/willrich45 .

Scholastic Library Publishing. *School Libraries Work.* **updated ed. New York: Scholastic, 2008. Available at www2.scholastic.com/content/collateral_resources/pdf/s/slw3_2008.pdf (accessed June 6, 2009).**

> Scholastic pulls together the research on the impact of school libraries in this one-stop shopping document. For the past several years, this document has been updated annually.

Shannon, Donna. "The School Library Media Specialist and Early Literacy Programs." *Knowledge Quest* **33, no. 2 (November–December 2004): 15–21.**

> Provides strategies for developing literacy among young library visitors, including learning centers, selection of "just right books" that appeal to children, and a variety of reading programs.

Taylor, Joie. "Transforming Literacy: The New Standards." *School Library Media Activities Monthly* **25, no. 4 (December 2008): 24–26.**

> Provides an overview and explanation of the *Standards'* structure and content and gives practical advice on how to integrate them into existing practice.

Todd, Ross J. "The Evidence-Based Manifesto for School Librarians: If School Librarians Can't Prove They Make a Difference, They May Cease to Exist." *School Library Journal* **54, no. 4 (April 2008): 38–43.**

> Drawing on the outcomes of the 2007 *School Library Journal* Leadership Summit, Todd reiterates the importance of having school librarians demonstrate how they positively impact student learning and achievement. He includes key questions that school librarians should ask.

Todd, Ross J. "A Question of Evidence." *Knowledge Quest* **37, no. 2 (November–December 2008): 17–21.**

> Ross defines evidence-based practice (EBP) in education and in school librarianship, breaking EBP into three arenas: evidence for practice, evidence in practice, and evidence of practice.

Truesdell, Ann. "Audiobooks on iPods: A Motivating Reading Strategy." *MACUL Journal* **(Fall 2007): 34–36. Available at www.macul.org/site/files/jfall2007.pdf (accessed June 6, 2009).**

> Discusses how the author used Audible.com and inexpensive iPod Shuffles to support the learning of students with special needs.

Valenza, Joyce, ed. *You Know You're a 21st-Century Librarian If . . . .* **Wikispaces. n.d. Available at informationfluency.wikispaces.com/You+know+you're+a+21+century+ librarian+if+.+.+. (accessed June 6, 2009).**

> Under the guidance of outstanding high school librarian and researcher Joyce Valenza, this collaborative wiki builds a definition of 21st-century school librarianship.

Valenza, Joyce, and Doug Johnson. "Reboot Camp: Get into Tech Shape." *School Library Journal* (2008). Available at www.schoollibraryjournal.com/article/CA6555547.html (accessed June 6, 2009).

Staying abreast of best practices and trends in school librarianship and educational technology requires the same kind of regular practice that gym exercise does. Valenza and Johnson discuss a variety of Web 2.0 tools that can connect you to others and keep you learning continually.

Vartabedian, M. L. "Social Studies: Maps, Finding our Way." *School Library Media Activities Monthly* 21, no. 5 (January 2005): 17–18.

Discusses how literature can help students understand maps and create their own.

Wiggins, Grant, and Jay McTighe. *Understanding by Design.* expanded 2nd ed. Alexandria, VA: ASCD, 2005.

A comprehensive view of backward design, which begins with student exit outcomes and then works backward to design the learning activities and assessments that will lead to those outcomes.

Williams, Robin, and David Loertscher. *In Command! Kids Build and Manage Their Own Information Spaces.* Salt Lake City, UH: Hi Willow Research and Publishing, 2007.

In the early years of the Internet in schools, school librarians created online structures such as pathfinders or WebQuests to organize possible resources for students. Williams and Loertscher argue that today's librarians, instead of organizing *for* students, teach students to organize for themselves, using free Web 2.0 tools such as customizable iGoogle pages.

Woolls, Blanche. *The School Library Media Manager.* 4th ed. Westport, CT: Libraries Unlimited, 2008.

A comprehensive overview of the many facets of administering a school library.

Zmuda, Allison, and Violet H. Harada. *Librarians as Learning Specialists: Meeting the 21st Century Learning Imperative.* Westport, CT: Libraries Unlimited, 2008.

Builds a powerful vision for how librarians can contribute more significantly to learning in schools. Highly influenced by Wiggins and McTighe's *Understanding by Design* (above), the book addresses both school administrators and school librarians. This slender volume is packed with ideas and questions that make it perfect for a librarian-administrator book club.

Recommended Blogs for School Library Media Specialists

American Association of School Librarians
AASL Blog
www.aasl.ala.org/aaslblog/

Posts on a variety of topics relating to school libraries and the initiatives of AASL.

Association for Supervision and Curriculum Development
ASCD Inservice
ascd.typepad.com/blog/

Media specialists need to be aware of the topics on their administrators' minds. ASCD's blog shares updates on educational research and writing. In addition, the blog announces calls for abstracts and links to articles from ASCD's flagship publication *Educational Leadership*, a journal read by many American administrators.

Diane Chen
Practically Paradise
www.slj.com

Perspective on middle school libraries and literature from a member of the American Library Association Council.

eSchool News
RSS feeds
www.eschoolnews.com/content-exchange-rss/

Though not technically a blog, *eSchool News* offers free RSS feeds that can be added into your blog reader so you can keep in touch with educational technology news.

Kristin Fontichiaro
School Library Monthly Blog
blog.schoollibrarymonthly.com
> Reflections on school libraries in the 21st century.

Buffy Hamilton, Ruth Fleet, and Tammy Beasley
The Unquiet Library
theunquietlibrary.wordpress.com/
> An outstanding high school library blog that pulls in several other Web 2.0 tools.

Christopher Harris
Infomancy
schoolof.info/infomancy
> A school library administrator, Harris's posts focus on systemic changes to school libraries and high-tech integration.

Doug Johnson
Blue Skunk Blog
doug-johnson.squarespace.com/
> A practical perspective, mellowed with humor, from one who thinks both deeply and practically about quality school libraries.

Joyce Valenza
The Never-Ending Search
www.slj.com
> Reflections on transforming high school libraries and on Web 2.0 tools to empower student learning.

Recommended Professional Journals

Educational Leadership
> **www.ascd.org**
>> To be a leader in a school means keeping up with what decision makers are reading. Each month, *Educational Leadership* brings together the voices of practitioners and academics on a chosen theme.

Knowledge Quest
> **www.ala.org/ala/mgrps/divs/aasl/aaslpubsandjournals/knowledgequest/knowledgequest.cfm**
>> This outstanding publication from the American Association of School Librarians takes a thematic approach to exploring issues that matter to school libraries. Authors may be practitioners or academics, school librarians or others. Of particular note are the November/December 2008 issue on evidence-based practice, the May/June 2009 focus on the Common Beliefs of the AASL *Standards,* and the November/December 2009 issue on the professional practice of the school librarian.

Learning & Leading with Technology
> **www.iste.org/Content/NavigationMenu/Publications/LL/L_L.htm**
>> The official publication of the International Society for Technology in Education (ISTE), author of the *National Educational Technology Standards.*

LMC Connection
> **www.linworth.com/lmc/**
>> A monthly journal focusing on school libraries, instruction, technology, and literature.

School Library Journal
> **www.slj.com**
>> Best known for its comprehensive reviews of books and media, *SLJ* also provides ongoing information about trends in school and public libraries.

School Library Monthly

schoollibrarymonthly.com

The articles in this book represent the scope of articles and lesson plans found in *SLMAM*'s pages.

Teacher Librarian

www.teacherlibrarian.com/

A journal reflecting on the many aspects of school librarianship for practitioners in both the United States and Canada.

Index

AASL. *See* American Association of School Librarians

AASL Affiliate Assembly, 218

AASL Fall Forum, 47

AASL Forum (listserv), 39

AASL Learning Standards and Guidelines Implementation Task Force, 4

AASL National Conference, 9, 47

AASL *Standards*, 3–4, 5, 6, 6-8, 9, 13–15, 16, 17, 20, 21, 22, 38–40, 41, 43, 62, 63–66, 67, 68, 72, 73, 86–88, 89, 102, 103, 105, 117, 118, 147–50, 159, 162, 163, 164, 203, 225, 234, 239, 241, 296, 307, 313–14, 316, 317, 323, 324, 327, 340, 341

AASL Standards Writing Committee, 11

"Abigail and John Adams Online," 308, 316–17

Abilock, Debbie, 79, 341

Abortion, 30

"About Mission," 41, 47–53

Abram, Stephen, 23, 25–30

Accelerated Reader, 90, 112

Access to information, 7, 40, 108–9

Accountability, 16, 45. *See also* Assessment; Standardized testing

Achievement gap, 82–83, 190

Achievement orientation, 30

ACT assessment, 93

Active learning, 127–28, 148

Adams, John, 307, 316–17

Adams, Abigail, 307, 316–17

Adaptability, 17, 18. *See also* Dispositions

Adaptation strategies, 18

Addy, Sharon Hart, 276

Adjusting instruction, 344. *See also* Formative Assessment

Administrators, 4, 42, 165, 205. *See also* Principals

Adobe Acrobat software, 300

"Adventure of the American Mind, An," 336

Advertising, 26. *See also* Promotion

Advocacy, 4, 24, 43, 68, 91, 118–19, 165, 205, 242, 243, 308, 324

AECT. *See* Association for Educational Communications and Technology

Aesthetic growth, 7, 10, 15, 17. *See also* AASL *Standards*

Affiliate Assembly, 218

After-school programs, 78

ALA. *See* American Library Association

"Alaska study," 200

Alice in Infoland blog, 78. *See also* Yucht, Alice

Alice in Wonderland, 86

Alignment of standards, 21

Alternate teaching, 220

Alternative energy, 320–22

Amazon.com, 32

America Online (AOL), 300

American Association of School Librarians (AASL), 1–2, 9, 10, 13, 15, 16, 20, 38, 42, 79, 147, 171, 180, 189, 203, 211, 218, 225, 233, 272, 296, 323. *See also* AASL *Standards*

American Library Association 1, 9, 10, 79, 233, 249

American Memory Project of the Library of Congress, 36, 269

Analysis, 106–7

Anderson, Chris, 33

Animal reports, 307, 313–15

Annotated bibliography, 143

AOL, 300

Application of knowledge, 14, 44

Are They Really Ready to Work?, 44

Arizona, 21

Art history, 203

Artifacts. *See* Primary sources

Artley, Sterl, 108

ASCD New Compact, 2,4

ASCD. *See* Association for Supervision and Curriculum Development

Asia Society, 44

"Assessing Information Fluency: Gathering Evidence of Student Learning," 163, 166–70

"Assessing Learning: The Missing Piece of Instruction," 164, 185–88

"Assessing Questions," 266

Assessment, 2, 6, 21, 83–85, 145–46, 156–57, 163–202, 231, 238, 248, 250, 310, 312, 314, 317, 319, 322, 325–27, 330, 340, 341,

"Assessment Tool: Levels of Communication, Cooperation, and Collaboration," 204–5, 238

Assignments, 249–51. *See also* Lesson plans

Assimilation, 121-22

Association for Educational Communications and Technology (AECT), 3, 9, 147, 171, 180, 211

Association for Supervision and Curriculum Development (ASCD), 2, 6, 13, 15, 86

Assumptions, 277

Audacity sofwtare, 294

Audio tours, 295

Audiobooks, 95

Ausubel, David, 182

Authentic Achievement, 248

Authentic learning, 37, 45, 171, 239, 244, 247–52

"Authentic Learning," 239, 247–52

Authenticity, 46, 54, 90, 247–52

Author visits, 91

Authority, 26, 54, 68, 82–85, 277
Autonomy, 23, 55
Avatars, 23

Background checklists, 168–69
Background knowledge, 54–56, 65, 88, 105, 109–10, 167, 256–60, 318, 321, 343–44, 346
Backward design, 164, 180, 195–96, 253, 342
Baer, Edith, 307, 309–10
Bandwidth, 35
Banned Books Week, 101
Bar graphs, 273
Barnes, 42, 57–59, 69–71
Barriers, 31, 109
Base, Graeme, 274
Battle Creek Michigan School District, 291–92
Bebo, 28, 29
"Being Heard . . . Advocacy +Evidence + Students = Impact!," 178, 243
Berkowitz, Bob, 20, 152, 246
Best practices, 130–31
Bibliographies, 143, 289–93
Big6, 20, 103, 246, 283
Bill & Melinda Gates Foundation, 38
Bill of Rights, 246
Biographies, 18
Bird units (Loertscher), 37, 290
Black Beat, 96
Blogs, 28, 29, 33, 78, 92, 97, 243, 287, 301
Bloom's Taxonomy, 17, 101, 104, 285
Book catalogs, 325–26
Book clubs and discussions, 36, 94, 118, 153, 327–30
Book Leads wiki, 299
Book lists, 112–16
Book logs, 325–26
Book reviews, 18, 94
Book trailers, 89, 115
Booktalks, 94, 99, 115
Boomers, 25, 26, 29, 30
Boston Globe, 63
"Brain Friendly Techniques: Mind Mapping," 241, 282–84
Brain function, 303
Brainology, 305
Brainstorming, 134, 156, 264, 310, 342–43
Brainstorms and Blueprints, 20, 286
Brett, Jan, 276
Brisco, Shonda, 78
Brodie, Carolyn S., 222, 238
Bruner, Jerome, 130
Buczynski, Sandy, 118, 159–62, 308, 318–22
Buddy, Juanita Warren, 204, 221–24
Budget cuts, 189
"Building Evidence Folders for Learning through Library Media Centers," 164, 189–93, 237
Bullying, 203
Bush, Gail, 24, 35–37, 42, 54–56, 240,253–55
Buzzeo, Toni, 79

Caine, Geoffrey, 285
Caine, Renate, 285
Calendaring tools, 300
Calendars, Web-based, 242
Callison, Daniel, 117, 121–29, 234, 239, 240, 241, 247–52, 261–64, 289–93
Cameras, 32, 278
Can You Find the Evidence-Based Practice in Your School Library?, 201
Candor, 46
Carbo, Marie, 99
Carey, James, 128–29
Carroll, Lewis, 86
Category matrix, 312
"Cavemen Took Notes?," 241, 280–81
CDs, 295
Cell phones, 23, 27, 35
Center for International Scholarship in School Libraries (CISSL), 232–36
Center of Education Policy Research, 44
Centers, 219
Centers-based instruction, 219
Chapman, Carolyn, 99
Charts, 174, 271
Chat room discussions, 287
Cheating. *See* Plagiarism
Checklists, 168–69, 172–73, 181, 182, 186, 251, 342, 344
Chelmsford High School Learning Commons, 63–66
Chen, Diane, 78
Children's welfare, 331–35
Choice, 27
Circulation policies, 119
Cisneros, Sandra, 97
Citation, 37, 241. *See also* Plagiarism
Citizenship, 14, 66
Civics, 324
Civil War literature wiki, 299
Civil War, 246, 299, 324, 336–39
Claims and evidence, 319, 322
Class size, 14
Classroom displays, 308
Classroom Instruction That Works, 102
Classroom–library collaboration, 227–28. *See also* Collaboration
Clevenson, Rhonda, 336, 337
Cloud computing, 300–301
Coatney, Sharon, 3, 10–11
Coding of information, 322
Cognitive apprenticeship, 247
Cognitive capital, 35
Cohen, Paul, 63
Collaboration, 14, 18, 28, 33, 44, 46, 54, 55, 61–62, 72, 83, 84–85, 105, 118, 150, 196–98, 203–38, 239, 248, 280–81, 296–99, 307. *See also* Teamwork
    Pyramid of, 204, 217
    ingredients of successful, 216
"Collaboration Connections," 203, 206–8
"Collaboration: From Myth to Reality: Let's Get Down to Business. Just Do It!," 204, 232–36

"Collaboration: The Motown Method," 204, 229–31
Collaborative inquiry, 242, 296–99
"Collaborative Planning for Information Literacy," 3, 12
"Collaborative Planning Worksheet," 204, 237
Collection development, 24, 96–97, 101, 108–9, 118, 119, 150, 241
Collective knowledge, 321. *See also* Wikis
College preparedness, 44, 45, 241
Collins, Jim, 45
Colorado Learner's Bill of Rights, 4, 24, 38–40
Colorado School Library Leaders Learner's Bill of Rights Committee, 38–40
Colorado School Library Leaders, 4, 24, 38–40
Colorado Study, 180, 200, 214
Comic Life software, 279
Comics, 279
Commodores, The, 229, 231
Common Beliefs, 3, 7, 11, 89, 117
Communicating evidence, 183
Communication, 14, 45, 71, 72, 87, 223–24, 230–31
Community resources, 140, 308
Community service, 23
Compare and contrast, 346
Comprehension. *See* Reading
Computer-based testing, 112–16
Concept maps, 251
Concerts in libraries, 28
Conclusions, 14, 319
Condensation, 308, 318–19
Conferencing, 62
Confidence, student, 123–24
Conley, David, 17, 44
Connecticut State Standards, 47, 51
"Connecting Science Notebooking to the Elementary Library Media Center," 118, 159–62
Connectivity, 23, 31, 46, 216, 248
Connectors, 68, 77, 78–79
Constructivism, 54–56, 127–29, 147, 216
Content knowledge, 55. *See also* Standards
Content Knowledge: A Compendium of Standards and Benchmarks for K-12 Education, 272
Content standards, 83
Context, 269, 277
Continuous learning, 88
Continuous partial attention, 35
Contract, research, 136–37
Convergent questions, 104
Conversations, informal, 208
Cooke, Lynne, 211, 213, 219
Cooperation, 212, 216, 234. *See also* Collaboration
Cooperative learning, 182
Coordination, 212, 216. *See also* Collaboration
Coordination, 234
"Core Curriculum Standards for New Jersey," 64
Correlation of the Information Literacy Standards, 171
Correlations, 8
Costa, Arthur, 17, 68, 68, 86–88, 341
Co-teaching, 227–28, 231, 308, 311–12. *See also* Collaboration

"Coteaching Published Lesson Plans: A Recipe for Success?," 204, 227–28
Covey, Stephen, 223
Cox, Ernie J., 89, 96–98
Create a Graph Web site, 273
Creative Class, The, 34
Creative Commons, 295
Creative thinking, 17, 45, 72, 261–62
Creativity, 2, 8, 22, 44, 46, 54–56, 63, 72, 86
Creativity literacy, 54–56
"Creativity Literacy: The Library Media Center as a Learning Laboratory," 42, 54–56
Creighton, Peggy Milam, 68
Crews, Kenny, 289
Critical inquiry, 151–54
"Critical Inquiry: Library Media Specialists as Change Agents," 118, 151–54
Critical thinking,4, 7, 10, 13, 17, 40, 44, 45, 46, 126–27
Critiquing, 343
CSI: Cemetery Scene Investigation wiki, 299
CSLA (California School Libraries Association), 34
Culture of reading, 108–11
Culture. *See* School culture
Curiosity, 17, 18, 40, 240, 268, 277
Curriculum, 2, 36, 150, 209, 324
Curriculum framework, 48
Curriculum mapping, 171, 207
Customization, 23
"Cutting Edge?," 241
Cyberfair Web site, 249

Dalbotten, Mary, 127
"Dancing Down the Rabbit Hole: Habits of Mind for Embracing Change," 68, 86–88
Daniels, Havey, 99
Data, 83–85, 87–88, 207, 319, 321. *See also* Graphic organizers
D'Aulaire's Book of Greek Myths, 296
Debate, 18
Decision-making, 3, 10, 14, 40
Declaration of the Rights of the Child, 334
DeKalb County School System (Georgia), 223
Delaware study,234
Delicious.com, 34, 79
Democracy, 7, 10, 11, 14, 21
Denver Public Schools, 39
"Designing Inquiry-Based Science Units as Collaborative Partners," 323, 341–45
"Designing Learning for Evidence-Based Practice," 164, 164, 180–84
Detroit Zoo, 313, 314
Dewey, John, 147
Diagnostic assessment, 163, 167
Diagrams, 271-72
Diaries as primary sources, 268
Dickinson, Gail, 78, 204, 211, 222, 224, 238
Differentiated Instruction, 89, 90, 91, 99–101, 253-55, 308
"Differentiated Instruction," 240, 253–55

"Differentiating Instruction in Reading: Easier Than It Looks!," 90, 99–101
Diggs, Valerie, 63–66
Digital citizenship, 2
Digital immigrants, 28, 32, 33
Digital learners, 24
Digital natives, 28, 31, 32, 34, 92–95
DimDim Web site, 300, 301
Dinosaurs, 11
Direct instruction, 182
Discovery, 63
Discussion, 28, 286, 294, 327–30
Diseases research, 324, 346–47
Disengagement, 60–62
Dispositions, 3, 7–8, 10–11, 16–19, 63, 90, 147, 148, 241, 307
"Dispositions: Getting Beyond 'Whatever'," 3, 16–19
Dissemination, 142–43
Divergent questions, 104
Diversity, 29, 44, 65, 66
DNA, 11
Document sharing, 300–301
Documentation of work, 226, 289–93
Dodge, Bernie, 126
"Doesn't Everyone Have Rights to a Learner's Permit?," 24, 38–40
Doll, Carol, 224
Donne, John, 3
Dresang, Eliza, 20
Driscoll, Marcy, 276
Drop Everything and Read (DEAR), 114–15
Dweck, Carol S., 243, 302–5

"Earning by Learning," 112
Eblen, Susan, 41, 47–53
E-books, 30, 32
Economics, 1
Educational Policy Improvement Center, 44
Eisen, Paula S., 323, 327–30
Eisenberg, Michael, 20, 119, 246
Elementary lesson plans, 307–12
Elmore, Richard, 44
E-mail, 2, 287
Emerging readers, 240, 307, 313–14
Emoticons, 310
Emotional resilience, 17
Emotions, 309–10
Enatrue's ZipGuides Web site, 274
Endangered animals and plants, 185–87
Engagement, 37, 63–66
"Engaging Students in Inquiry," 118, 155–58
England, 14
English Language Learners (ELL), 14, 160, 240
Enthusiasm for learning, 115, 297
Equitable access. See Access to information
Essays, 287
Essential questions, 244–45. See also Questioning; Questions
Ethical behavior, 7, 10, 14, 17, 20, 72

Evaluation of information, 7
Evaluation, 215, 231. See also Assessment
Evidence folders, 164, 183, 194
Evidence-based practice, 163, 164, 181–83, 200
Exit slips, 164, 176–79, 231
Exploration, 16, 136
Extrinsic motivation, 90, 112–16

Facebook, 28, 29, 78
Fargo, Susan, 63
Fast food, 27
Feedback, 302–5
Feedburner, 78
"Fighting the Civil War with Primary Sources," 324, 336–39
File sharing, 33
Film club, 36
Filtering of information, 28
Findlay, Christine, 164, 200–202
5E Model of science inquiry, 160
Fixed mindsets, 243, 302–5
Fixed schedule, 181, 203, 207, 205
Flexible mindsets, 242–43. See also Growth mindsets
Flickr.com, 43, 77, 79
Flip It!, 120, 286, 287
Florida, Richard, 34
Flow of information, 23
Fluency, 124–25
Flyy Girl, 97
Folktales, 311–12
Follett, 20
Fontichiaro, Kristin, 68, 86–88, 118, 159–62, 178, 225, 242, 294–95, 307–8, 313–14, 320–22, 340
Foreign language practice, 295
Formal paragraphs, 307, 313–14
Formanack, Gail, 3, 6–8
Format agnosticism, 26
Formative assessment, 163–64, 167–70, 232, 307, 313–14, 343–44
Four Tops, The, 229
Framework for 21st Century Learning, 13
Franklin, Pat, 204
Fredrick, Kathy, 242, 300–301
Friedman, Thomas, 38
Friend, Marilyn, 211, 213, 219
Friends, 28
"From Eyeballing to Evidence: Assessing for Learning in Hawaii Library Media Centers," 164, 194–98
Frustration, 23

Gabcast Web site, 294, 295
Gaming, 28, 29, 30, 32, 33, 89, 242
Gaps in understanding, 164
Garage Band software, 294
Garrison, Lois, 47
Gehrig, Jody, 39
Geitgey, Gayle, 201
Generation X (GenX), 25, 26, 30
George Mason University, 34

Gettysburg Address, 270
Ghost, 166
Gilmore-See, Janice, 23, 31–34
Gladwell, Malcolm, 68, 77–80
Glide Web site, 300, 301
Gliffy Web site, 241, 278
Global issues, 331–34
Global perspectives, 64, 66. *See also* Partnership for 21st Century Skills
Globalization, 2, 38, 46
Gmail, 23, 300
"GO Charts," 313–15
Goals and competencies chart, 52–53
Goals, 47–53, 131–32
Goldberg, Cristine, 241, 282–84
Good to Great, 37
Goofy Global News wiki, 298–99
Google calendar, 78
Google Docs, 300, 301
Google Earth, 77, 79
Google, 24, 26, 32, 300
Gordon, Carol, 63, 232, 251
Government, 323
GPS, 28
Graduation rates, 38
Grant, Jim, 99
Grant, Lillian, 99
Grapher Web site, 273
Graphic inquiry, 240, 271–79. *See also* Graphic organizers
"Graphic Inquiry: Skills and Strategies, Part II," 240, 275–79
"Graphic Inquiry: Standards and Resources, Part I," 240, 271–74
Graphic novels, 279
Graphic organizers, 102–3, 105, 172–73, 182, 192, 240, 282–84, 310, 315, 344, 347
Graphics, 271–79
    aesthetic qualities of, 277–79
    analyzing and interpreting, 276–77
    designing and creating, 278–79
    reading and comprehending, 275–76
    using and applying, 277–78
Great Graph Contest, The, 273
Greece, 15
Greek mythology, 296–97
Greene, Graham, 56, 57–59
Grimes, Nikki, 97
Grokker Web site, 276
Group discussions, 325–26
Group work, 207. *See also* Collaboration; Cooperation
Growth mindsets, 302–5
Guest book in library, 243
Guided practice, 182
Guiding questions, 265. *See also* Questions

Habits of Mind, 3, 10, 17, 63, 68, 86–88
Haley, Alex, 329
Hamburger chart, 313–15
Hands on learning, 341

Harada, Violet H., 7, 21, 62, 67, 68, 72–76, 118, 155–58, 164, 181, 185–99, 214, 237, 341
Harris, Christopher, 8
Harvey II, Carl A., 42, 57–59, 67, 69–71, 78, 203–9
Hassig, Ronda, 324, 331–34
Hawaii Association of School Librarians (HASL), 194
Hawaii Department of Education's School Library Services, 194
Hawaii experiment (assessment), 190
Hawthorne, Nathaniel, 329
Haycock, Ken, 79
Health research, 324, 346–47
Helicopter parents, 30
Helldorfer, M.C., 283
Higher order thinking, 65, 90, 248, 286, 313–14. *See also* inquiry, problem-solving, critical thinking
History, 307–8, 324, 336–39. *See also* Social Studies
"Hitch Your Wagon to a Mission Statement," 41, 44–46
Hitchhiker Web site, 78
Hog Music, 283
Home life, 97–98
Homework help hotlines, 78
Homework, 182
Hoover, Clara, 239, 244–46
Hughes-Hassell, Sandra, 89, 96–98
Humor, 55, 222. *See also* Wit
Hurricane Katrina, 118, 155–58
Hyperlinking, 23
Hypothesis, 318. *See also* Prediction

Idealism, 23
iGoogle Web pages, 300, 301
Illustrations, 272
Illustrator visits, 91
IMLS, 233
"Impact as a 21st-Century Library Media Specialist," 68, 77–80
"Importance of Language, The: The Partnership for 21st Century Skills and AASL Standards," 2, 6–8
Incentive programs, 89
Incentives, 95
Independent learning, 14, 36, 55
Independent thinking, 55
Indiana Department of Education, 69
Indiana's Academic Standards, 171
Indiana's Student Inquiry Model, 127
Indirect instruction, 182
Individualized instruction, 182
Inductive thinking, 160
Industriousness, 60
Inference, 122
INFOhio, 270
Infomancy blog, 8
Informal conversations, 208
Information fluency, 163, 166–70
"Information Inquiry," 117, 121–25
Information literacy, 2, 20, 21, 36, 83–85, 117, 118, 178, 225
Information literacy standards, 225

Information Literacy Standards, 180-81
Information Literacy Standards for Student Learning, 171
Information management skills, 14
Information Power: Building Partnerships for Learning, 2, 7–9, 171–72, 211, 222
Information problems, 123–24
Information Seeking Process, 285, 287
Information skills, 6
Information technology, 44
Information tools, 137
Information, Communications and Technology (ICT), 6
Information-centric learning paradigm, 63
Initiative, 17
Innovation, 2, 6, 44, 72
Inquiry, 3, 7, 10, 37, 45, 54–56, 63, 87, 115–62, 166–70, 182, 240, 251, 256–60, 267–70, 290–91, 296, 299, 307, 307, 313–15, 341–45
    vs. information literacy, 147
    educator's role in, 131
    evaluation of, 132
    planning for, 130
"Inquiry: Inquiring Minds Want to Know," 117, 147–49
"Inquiry-based Teaching and Learning—The Role of the School Library Media Specialist," 118, 150
Inquisitiveness, 45
Inspiration software, 241
INSPIRE (Indiana's virtual library), 171, 270
Instant messaging (IM), 23, 24, 27, 28, 33, 78, 79
Institute for Library and Information Literacy Education (ILILE), 77, 204, 232–36
Instructional design, 238, 241, 290–93, 341–45. *See also* Lesson planning.
Instructional methods, 182
Instructional objectives. *See* Curriculum
Instructional planning, 213
Instructional strategies, 239–306, 307
Intelligence, 64, 302–5
Intentional learning, 127–28
Interactions: Collaborative Skills for School Professionals, 219
Interdisciplinary connections, 64
Interdisciplinary learning, 6
International Society for Technology in Education (ISTE), 2, 13, 15, 22, 39, 86
Internet dangers, 32
Internet immigrants, 28
Internet natives, 28
Internet, 31, 97. *See also* Web sites
Interviews, 140, 295, 324, 340
"Interviewing Older Americans," 324, 340
Intrinsic motivation, 113–16
Inventory walk, 318
Investigating, 16, 17
Investigating, 343. *See also* Scientific method
Investigation, 139
iPod, 32, 294
IQ, 25, 304
Iran, 23
Iraq, 240, 279

I-Search, 286, 287
Issuu.com, 242
ISTE. *See* International Society for Technology in Education
iTunes, 294

Jackdaws, 36
Johns, Sara Kelly, 78, 292
Johnson, Doug, 78, 242, 289, 290–91
Johnson, Larry, 78, 296–99
Johnston, Mark, 336
Jonassen, David, 127
Journaling, 176–77, 251, 286, 325–26. *See also* Research journals
Just right books, 109

Kallick, Bena, 17, 68, 86–88, 341
Keene, Ellin (Oliver), 102
Keirsey Temperament Sorter, 222–23
Ken Burns, 336, 337
Kent State University, 204, 246
Kentucky Virtual Library, 270
"Kids 2.0," 23, 31–34
Kids in the Hall, 13
Kidspiration software, 241, 338
Kindergarten, 242
Klentschy, Michael, 318–22
Knight, Gladys, 229, 231
Knowledge attainment, 16
Knowledge construction, 60, 61–62
Knowledge creation, 14, 54–56
Knowledge, 7, 45, 105
Knowledge-building, 63–66
Knowledge-centric learning paradigm, 63
Knowles, Liz, 90, 99–101
Kramer, Kym, 240, 256–60, 292
Kuhlthau, Carol, 20, 119, 164, 200–202, 221, 285
Kumasi-Johnson, Kafi, 118, 151–54
Kuntz, Kelly, 80
KWL chart, 174, 182, 272

Lake Placid Central School, 291–92
Lamb, Annette, 78, 239, 242, 247–52, 296–99
Lance, Keith (Curry), 79, 214
Language arts, 323
Largent, Connie, 240, 256–60
Latina, 96
Leadership, 18, 23, 46, 67, 71, 72, 118, 150, 197–98
Learner's Bill of Rights, 24, 38–40
"Learner's Bill of Rights," 24, 40
Learning, quality of, 60–62
Learning centers, 204
Learning Commons concept, 63–66
Learning disabilities, students with, 14, 240, 242
Learning environments, 7, 15, 60–62, 66, 82–85, 118, 123, 247–52
Learning fairs, 185–87
Learning goals, 12
Learning laboratory, library as, 54–56

Learning networks, 40
Learning objectives, 12
Learning preferences, 255
Learning specialists, 67, 68
Learning standards. *See* Standards
Learning styles, 30, 222. *See also* Multiple intelligences
Leedy, Loreen, 273
Left brain, 86
Legislation, 22
Leisure reading, 89–90, 96–98
Lemonade Club, The, 324, 346–47
Lesson plan template design, 11–12
Lesson planning, 11–12, 18, 204. *See also* Planning.
"Lesson Planning: The Ticket to Successful Teaching," 204, 225-26
Lesson plans, 207, 227–28, 307–40
Lesson studies, 203
Letter writing, 313–15
Letters, 307, 316–17
Leveled readers, 100
"Levels of Collaboration: Where Does Your Work Fit In?," 204, 214–17
Levine, Mel, 61
Levitov, Deborah, 3, 164, 183, 205, 237–38, 240, 241, 265
Lewis and Clark Expedition, 246
"Librarian Who Loves Library Thing, The," 323, 325–26
Librarians as Learning Specialists, 62
Libraries as space. *See* Learning environents
Library 2.0, 29, 242
Library as laboratory, 36
Library as playground, 36
Library collections, 18
Library environment, 18, 26–28, 41, 54–56
Library of Congress, 36, 77, 79, 240, 275, 276, 336–37
Library Power, 211
Library space. *See* Library environment
LibraryThing.com, 77, 79, 323, 325–26
Life and career skills, 6
Lifehacker Web site, 301
Lifelong learning, 72
Lincoln, Abraham, 270
Linear learners, 55
Listservs, 243, 287. *See also* LM_NET listserv
Literacy trends, 242
Literature appreciation, 18. *See also* Reading
Little, Judith Warren, 214
LM_NET listserv, 79, 218
Local history, 308
Loertscher, David V., 37, 47, 63, 79, 178, 290
Logan, Deb, 178, 243
Logs, 182, 251. *See also* Journaling; Research logs
"Long tail," 31, 33–34
Longitudinal tracking, 183
Louisiana Purchase, 246
Lovely Charts, 241
Low Rider, 96

Macrorie, Ken, 286
Magazines, 96–97, 158

Mama Flora's Family, 329
Mankato Public Schools, 289
Maps, 272
Marcoux, Betty (Elizabeth L.), 4, 20, 204, 214
Mardis, Marcia A., 1, 4, 13–15, 341
Marketing, 79. *See also* Promotion
Marra, Tiffany, 249
Martin, Jacqueline Briggs, 282–84
Marzano, Robert [J.], 102, 106–7, 110, 126, 182, 272–73
Mashups, 33
Massachusetts Historical Society, 316–17
Massachusetts, 308, 316–17
Matrices, 182. *See also* Graphic organizers
Mavens, 68, 77–78
McCarthy, Alan, 324, 336–39
McCloud, Scott, 279
McGregory, Joy, 195
McKenzie, Jamie, 104, 120, 124–25, 129, 244–45, 262
McTighe, Jay, 21, 45, 47, 76, 164, 180, 190, 239, 244, 245, 253, 342
Measurement, 21
Media centers, student perception of, 200–202
Media literacy, 2, 72. *See also* Partnership for 21st Century Skills
Meetings, 207–8. *See also* Planning
Meier, Deborah, 17
Memorization, 24
Metacognition, 3, 8, 40, 88, 102, 172, 246. *See also* Reflection
Methodology, 277
Meyers, Eric, 234
Michigan, 14
Microphones, 294
Microsoft Live, 300
Microsoft Movie Maker software, 334–35
Microsoft PowerPoint software, 241
Milam, Peggy, 51, 285–87
Milbury, Peter, 78
"Millennial Learners Build Knowledge Communities," 24
Millennials, 23–40, 89, 92–95
"Millennials: Deal with Them, Part I," 23, 25–26
"Millennials: Deal with Them, Part II," 23, 27
Mind mapping, 174, 282–84. *See also* Graphic organizers
Minds on learning, 341
Mindsets, 302–5
"Mindsets: How Praise Is Harming Youth and What Can Be Done About It," 243, 302–5
Miniature Earth, The, 334
Mini-lessons, 231
Minnesota Department of Children, Families, and Learning, 127
Minnesota's Inquiry Process, 127
Miracles, The, 229
Mission, 43, 43, 47–53, 73–74, 76, 86
Mission statements, 41, 44–46
Mitten, The, 276
Mobile phones. *See* Cell phones
Modeling, 18, 89, 110, 115, 117, 182, 313
"Models, Part IV: Inquiry Models," 117

Moo Cards, 43
Moreillon, Judi, 90, 203, 204, 218–20, 227, 241, 307
Mosaic of Thought, 102
Motivation, 17, 18, 90, 108–9, 112–16, 303
Motown Method of collaboration, 229–31
Movie Maker software, 334–35
Mowry, Jess, 97
mp3 players, 23
MRI, 25
Multimedia presentations, 287, 292
Multiple intelligences, 279
Multiple literacies, 6
Multi-taskers, 28
Music, 336–37
Muth, Jon J., 227
MUVE, 78
Myers-Briggs Type Indicators, 222–23
MySpace, 28, 29, 32, 77, 79, 97

Narration, 339
Nation At Risk, A, 105
National Board certification, 78, 79
National Board of Professional Teaching Standards (NBPTS), 20
National Center for Education Statistics, 77–78
National Center for Educational Statistics (NCES), 77–78, 189
National Center on Education and the Economy, 8
National Conference on Differentiated Instruction, 99
National Council for Accreditation of Teacher Education (NCATE), 20
National Education Association (NEA), 6
National Educational Technology Standards for Students (NETS*S), 2, 4, 13, 22, 39, 86
National Educational Technology Standards for Teachers (NETS*T), 86, 87
National Geographic, 96
National Library Week, 101
National Park Service, 249
National Poetry Month, 207
National Research Council, 44
National Resources Defense Council, 321
National Social Studies Conference, 331
NATO, 35
NBPTS. *See* National Board of Professional Teaching Standards
NCATE. *See* National Council for Accreditation of Teacher Education
NCLB. *See* No Child Left Behind
NEA. *See* National Education Association
Nelson, Sandra, 21
NETS*S. *See* National Educational Technology Standards for Students
NETS*T. *See* National Educational Technology Standards for Teachers
Networking, 28, 29
New Jersey Department of Education, 64
New Learning Commons, The: Where Learners Win!, 63
"New Standards: Refreshing Our Work, *AGAIN!,*" 20

Newmann, Fred, 248, 250
News broadcast, 294, 295
News Web sites, 26
Newspapers, 158
Ning, 78
No Child Left Behind (NCLB), 2, 14, 20, 96, 105, 180, 190, 202, 214–15, 257, 341
Nomads, 28
Nonlinguistic representations, 182
North Elementary, 42, 57–59, 69–71
Note taking, 105–7, 182, 188, 241, 280–81, 344. *See also* Graphic organizers
Note-making, 241, 307. *See also* Note taking
"Nudging Toward Inquiry," 119

Objectives, 182
OCLC Perceptions report, 28
Office of Education Research and Improvement, 92–93, 108
Ohio Educational Library Media Association (OELMA), 164, 200–202
Ohio Study, 200–202
"Ohio's Foray into Evidence-Based Practice," 164, 200–202
Okemura, Audrey, 323, 324, 341–45
One Book—One School, 101
Online collaboration, 300–301
Online discussions, 325–26
Online Public Access Catalog (OPAC), 26, 29, 192, 193, 325–26
Online reading, 89
Online safety, 295
Open access, 218
"Open Book, A: A Life Online," 242, 300–301
Optimism, 30
Oral histories, 250, 340
Oregon Educational Media Association, 80
Oregon Trail. *See* Western Expansion
O'Reilly Media, 31
Organization, 142–43
Organizers, 172–73, 182, 272. *See also* Graphic organizers
Orientation, 133
OurMedia, 295
Outcome-based approach, 192, 193
Outreach, 209

Partnership for 21st Century Skills (P21), 2, 4, 6–8, 13, 15, 38, 39, 72
Paint software, 296
Pair-sharing, 286–87
Pappas, Marjorie L., 20, 120, 164, 171, 180–84, 240, 267–70
Parallel teaching, 204, 219–20
Parents, 243
"Parents as Reading Partners," 115
Partnership for 21st Century Skills (P21), 2
Pascaretti, Victoria A., 308, 320–22
Passive learning, 60–62
Pathfinders, 27, 36, 182, 267–70

Pathways to Knowledge, 20
Patrons, 119
Payne, Ruby, 94
PBSKids.org, 242
Peanut Butter Wiki, 77, 79
Pedagogical critique, 215
Pedagogy, 118
Peer coaching, 215
Peer conferencing, 141
Peer critique, 215
Peer evaluation, 143
Peer observation, 215
Percy Jackson & the Olympians book series, 296
Periodicals, 158
Perry Meridian Middle School, 92–95
Persistence, 17, 55. *See also* Dispositions
Personal growth, 10, 15, 17, 40. *See also* AASL *Standards*
Personal styles, 204
Personality diagnosis tools, 222
Personality, 204
Personalization, 31, 32
Pew Internet and American Life Project, 28, 29
Philosophy statements, 42, 47–53
Phonemic awareness, 100
Phonics, 100
Photographs, 18, 272
Picture books, 275–76
Pie charts, 273
Pink, Dan (Daniel M.), 22
Pitts, Judy M., 20, 119, 170, 286
"Plagiarism," 289–93
Plagiarism, 241, 281. *See also* Citation
Planning, 81, 140–41, 209, 213, 215, 218, 229, 237–38, 242, 300
Planning Guide for Information Power: Building Partnerships for Learning, A, 130
Plato, 35
Playfulness, 55
Playlists, 23
"Podcasting 101," 294–95
Podcasting at School, 178, 340
Podcasting, 2, 33, 79, 89, 242, 294–95, 324
Poetry, 207, 309–10
Polacco, Patricia, 324
Pooling knowledge, 321
Pop literature, 96–97
Portfolio, 164, 191, 251
Posters, 94, 287. *See also* Advocacy; Promotion
Post-It Notes, 258
Post-millennials, 25
"Power and Spirit of Collaboration, The," 203–4, 209–10, 237
"Power of One, The," 334
"Power of Reflection in the Research Process, The," 241, 285–87
Powering down, 36
PowerPoint software, 241, 322, 324
Praise, 302–5
    impact of, 242–43

Preddy, Leslie, 89, 91, 92–95, 117, 127, 130–46, 164, 176–77, 241, 280–81
Prediction, 318, 321
Prensky, Marc, 28, 32, 63
Pre-performance tasks. *See* Background knowledge
Pre-searching, 134
Presentation tools, 242, 300. *See also* Microsoft PowerPoint software
Preservice librarians, 5
Previous knowledge. *See* Background knowledge
Pride of Baghdad, 279
Primary sources, 139–40, 240, 267–70, 324, 336–38, 340
"Primary Sources and Inquiry Learning," 267–70
"Principal Perspective, Part 2: The Library Media Program," 42, 57–59
"Principal Perspective, Part I: The Role of the Library Media Specialist," 67, 69–71
Principals, 18, 19, 57–59, 67, 183, 234
Print reference, 31
Prior knowledge, 240. *See also* Background knowledge
Prison inmates, 93
Prizes, 112–16
Prizes, 90
Problem solving, 8, 26, 37, 40, 44, 72, 182, 285, 341
    models of, 285
Problem-based learning, 14, 37
Procedure, 319, 321
Productive Pedagogy, 43, 64–66
Productivity tools, 33
Productivity, 14
Professional development, 7, 19, 118, 150, 198, 214, 219, 243
Professional journals, 243
Professional learning communities (PLCs), 203
"Promoting Inquiry with Emerging Readers Using Elephogs and Octobunnies," 307, 313–15
Promotion, 90, 119, 165
Propaganda, 276
Prynne, Hester, 329
Psychology of Learning for Instruction, 276
P21. *See* Partnership for 21st Century Skills
Public libraries, 21, 97
Public relations, 242
Public service announcements, 331–32
Publicity, 39, 101. *See also* Promotion
Published lesson plans, 227–28
Pulitzer Prize, 30
Pyramid of Collaboration, 204, 217

Quality of learning, 60–62
Questioning, 13, 14, 17, 40, 88, 90, 102, 105, 117, 121, 134, 135, 147, 155–58, 182, 240, 244–45, 256–60, 261–64, 265–66, 318. *See also* Inquiry
"Questioning," 261
"Questioning Revisited," 240, 261–64
Questioning Toolkit (McKenzie), 104
Questioning Web, 186. *See also* Graphic organizers
Questioning worksheets, 135
Question-Organize-Categorize, 256–60

Questions, 106, 239, 249–51, 256–60, 261–64, 265–66, 321, 329, 344. *See also* Questioning
Questions to consider, 199
QuickTime Pro software, 295
Quintura for Kids Web site, 276

Radical Change, 20
Radio plays, 295
Rainie, Lee, 28
RAND Reading Study Group, 108
Rankin, Virginia, 256–60
Rating scales, 172
Ratios, student-to-teacher, 219
Read Across America, 101
Read for the Record, 101
Readers' advisory, 90, 109
Readers' cafe, 94
Reading, 7, 30, 89–116, 307
    research about, 108–11
Reading Across Continents, 101
"Reading at Risk," 93
Reading comprehension, 90, 91, 102–7, 108–11
Reading experts, 91
"Reading for Meaning: Questioning," 90, 102–4
"Reading for Meaning; Synthesizing," 90, 105–7
Reading for pleasure, 17, 101
Reading in school, 92–95, 97
Reading incentives, 90, 112–16
"Reading Incentives that Work: No-Cost Strategies to Motivate Studetns to Read and Love It!," 90, 112–16
Reading instruction, 90, 102–7
Reading lists, 112–16
Reading logs, 99, 325–26
Reading promotion, 90, 94
Reading Recovery, 307, 313
Reading skills, 105–7
Reading strategies, 102, 103
Reading teachers, 91. *See also* Reading Recovery
Realia, 36
Really Simple Syndication, 242. *See also* RSS feeds
Recording data, 319
"Red Light, Green Light: Guiding Questions," 240, 265
Reflection, 241. *See also* Self-reflection
"Reframing the Library Media Specialist as a Learning Specialist," 67, 72–76
"Refreshing our Standards—AGAIN!," 4, 20–22
"Research Reflections, Journaling, and Exit Slips," 164, 176–77, 241
"Research-Based Evidence: The Role of the Library Media Specialist in Reading Comprehension Instruction," 90, 108–11
"Road to Research," 256–60
Reeves, Martha, 231
Reflection checklist, 288
Reflection logs, 158, 172. *See also* Research journals
Reflection, 118, 122, 137, 139, 142, 147, 164, 167, 176–79, 182, 191, 192, 210, 231, 236, 238, 245–46, 285–87, 288, 308, 343. *See also* Metacognition
Reflective questions, examples of, 288

Refugee camps, 55
Relevance, 64–65
Reno, Nevada, 10, 38
Report of the National Reading Panel, 102
Research, rigorous, 60–62
Research Cycle (McKenzie), 120, 129
Research journals, 133–34, 158, 164
Research logs, 164
Research models, 286
Research process, 27, 106, 287, 320–22, 332–35. *See also* Information literacy; Inquiry
Research Process Model, 119
Research studies, 13–15
"Research-based Evidence: *The Role of the Library Media Specialist in Reading Comprehension Instruction,*" 108–11
Responsibilities, 3, 7, 10–11, 12, 147, 241
Rewards, 112–16
Richie, Lionel, 231
Ricker, Sandra L., 324, 340
Right brain, 22, 86
Right Here on This Spot, 276
Rigor, 194–95
Risk-taking, 87
Robb, Laura, 99
Robinson, Smokey, 229, 230
Role models, 68, 93–94. *See also* Modeling
Role of the school library media specialist. *See* School library media specialist, role of
Role-playing, 55
Roosevelt, Theodore, 222
Ross, Diana, 229, 230, 231
Rote learning, 24
Routman, Regie, 99
RSS feeds, 33, 242
Rubrics, 134, 144, 157, 251, 320, 322, 324, 330, 335, 343, 347
Rutgers University, 42, 200–202, 233

Salespeople, 68, 77, 79
"Sample Exit Slips," 241
Scaffolding, 154, 182, 240, 241, 249, 324, 344
Scarlet Letter, The, 329
Scenario-building, 55
Scheduling, 206. *See also* Fixed schedule
Scholastic, 205
School Advocacy, 205
School board, 5
School broadcast, 243
School culture, 19, 63, 92–95, 203,205
Curriculum meetings, 205
Collaboration, student benefits of, 205
School improvement, 58–59, 78, 205, 215
School leadership, 71
School librarian. *See* School library media specialist, role of
"School Librarians Help Students Achieve: Here's the Evidence!," 190
School Libraries Work!, 4, 204, 233
School Library 2.0, 31, 34

School Library Media Activities Monthly, 203, 241, 261
    blog, 79, 225
School Library Media Program of the Year, 42
School library media specialist, role of, 1, 8, 22, 25, 54, 56,
    67–88, 101, 109, 118, 149–54, 161–62, 203, 211–13,
    226, 241, 248, 310, 313–14, 328, 346
School Library Monthly, 119, 203
School library programs, 40
School reform, 5
School structures, 44
Schooling by Design, 45
Science, 307, 308, 318–22, 323, 324
Science inquiry, 162, 268–69, 308, 323, 341–45
Science notebooking, 118, 159–62, 308, 318–22
"Science Notebooking in Action: Where Does
    Condensation Come From?," 308, 318–20
"Science Notebooking in the Library Media Center:
    Alternative Energy," 308, 320–22
Scientific method, 118, 263, 308, 318–22, 341–45
Scottsdale School District, 21
Scripts, 338–39
Search Systems, 77
Second Life, 29
Second Life, 78
Secondary lesson plans, 323–48
Sector 7, 275–76
Seeking Meaning, 285
Self-assessment, 3, 7–8, 10, 11, 22, 86, 147, 196, 241
Self-direction, 72
Self-esteem, 302–5
Self-evaluation, 144–45
Self-reflection, 176–79, 241
Self-regulation, 303
Sensory input, 23
Seven Habits of Highly Effective People, 223
Sex, 30
Sharing of understandings, 40
"Show Them What We Do: Strategies for Collaborative
    Teaching," 203, 204, 218
Sibley, Roberta, 323, 325–26
"Sift and Sort: The Answers Are in the Questions!," 240,
    256–60
Sifting and sorting, 256–60, 262
"Silent Epidemic, The" 38
Simpson, Carol, 289
Simsbury Public Schools, 41, 47–53
Sister to Sister, 96
65% Solution, 189
Skillful Teacher Model, 253
SKILLS Act, 78, 79
Skills, 3, 7, 10–11, 47, 90, 307, 332
Skimming, 105, 134–35
Slam, 96
SLMAM blog, 225
"*SLMAM* Skills Correlations—New (2007) to Old (1998),"
    3, 21
Small, Ruth, 90, 91, 112–16
"Small World, A—Technology Connecting Kids to Kids,"
    324, 331–32

"Small World, A," 324, 333–35
SmartGirl.org, 249
Smartphones, 23 28. *See also* Cell phones
Snowflake Bentley, 282–84
Social bookmarking, 34
Social change, 118
Social engagement, 54
Social learning, 7, 54, 89
Social networking, 7, 28, 33, 92
"*Social Reading*: Promoting Reading in the Millennial
    Learner," 89, 92–95
Social reponsibility, 37, 72
Social studies, 307–8, 323, 324, 336–39
Socrates, 323, 327–30
Socratic Seminar, 323, 327–30
Son of Citation Machine Web site, 334
Soto, Gary, 97
Source notes, 139
Sources, 277
Special education, 219
Speeches, 287
Sports Illustrated, 96
Spreadsheets, 242
Stakeholders, 220
Standardized testing, 16, 35, 70, 89, 163, 247
Standards, 1–3, 47, 83, 130–31, 171, 180–81, 203, 218,
    225, 234, 247, 272–73. *See also* AASL *Standards*
Standards for the 21st-Century Learner. See AASL
    Standards
"*Standards for the 21st-Century Learner*" (article), 2,
    10–11
Stanford University, 242
State of Connecticut Information and Technology Literacy
    Standards, 47
Statistics, use of, 200–202. *See also* Data
Stephens, Claire Gatrell, 204
Stephens, Michael, 79
Sterne, Sandra, 324, 336–39
Stewart, Vivien, 44
Stone Soup, 227
Story elements, 307, 311–12
Story hours, 28
Storyboard, 140–41
Stover, Jill, 79
Strategies, 118
Strategy, 136–38
Street lit, 97
Streitenberger, Denise, 291
Stripling, Barbara, 3, 16, 20, 78, 117, 118, 119, 147–49,
    150, 163, 166–70, 286
Student achievement, 214, 218, 225
Student Achievement Guarantee in Education (SAGE), 219
Student engagement, 60–62, 97
"*Student Inquiry in the Research Process,* Part 1: Inquiry
    Research Basics," 117, 130–32
"*Student Inquiry in the Research Process,* Part 2: Inquiry
    Research Orientation," 117, 133–35
"*Student Inquiry in the Research Process,* Part 3: Inquiry
    Research and Strategy," 117, 136–38

"*Student Inquiry in the Research Process*, Part 4: Inquiry Research Investigation," 117, 139–41
"*Student Inquiry in the Research Process*, Part 5: Inquiry Research Conclusion & Reflection," 117, 142–46
Student learning, 60–62, 72–76. *See also* AASL *Standards*; Inquiry
Student learning profile, 255
Student perceptions of libraries, 164
Student readiness, 254–55
Student responsibilities. *See* Responsibilities
Student-centered learning, 5, 14, 239. *See also* Inquiry
Students as information scientists, 263–64
Students as scientific apprentices, 247–48
Students with special needs, 295
Student-Teacher Achievement Ratio (STAR), 219
Student-to-teacher ratios, 219
Summarizing, 103, 105–7, 182
Summative assessment, 163, 169
Summer reading, 97
Super Three, 20. *See also* Big6
Supremes, The, 229
Sustained silent reading, 89, 114–15
Swartz, 320–22
Swayze, Patrick, 166
Sylwester, Robert, 285
Symbols, 272
Synergy in learning, 297
Synthesis, 3, 105–7, 117, 172–73, 314
Systemic change, 44–46

Tannetta, Maureen, 307–8
T-charts, 175
Teacher evaluation, 70–71
Teacher Librarian wiki, 79
Teacher tasks, 14
TeacherTube, 79
Team teaching, 203, 204, 220. *See also* Collaboration
Teamwork, 44, 72, 84, 204. *See also* Collaboration
Technology, 2, 7, 14, 55, 58, 64, 72, 208, 241, 324
Teen Read Week, 101, 249
Teen Tech Week, 101
Teheran, 23
Teis, Kyra, 307, 309–10
Telecommunication, 33
Television commercials, 23
Temptations, The, 229
Tepe, Ann, 20, 120, 201
Testing, 111–16. *See also* Standardized testing
Text messaging, 28
"Text-to-Self connection: *The Lemonade Club* and Research into Diseases," 346–47
Texting, 23, 24, 92
"There Is Knowledge to Be Gained," 41, 42, 63–66
Thick and Thin Questions, 104
Thinkature Web site, 278
Thinking skills, 7, 17
"Thirty Helens Agree: 2007 Research Supports AASL's *Standards for the 21st-Century Learner*," 3, 13–15
Thoughtful Learning Cycle (TLC), 286, 287

Thoughtful Researcher, The, 256–60
Tilley, Carol, 247, 291
Tipping Point, The: How Little Things Can Make a Big Difference, 68, 77–80
Todd, Ross J., 41, 42, 63–66, 72, 79, 164, 181, 200–202, 204, 232–36
Tomlinson, Carol, 99, 240
"Tools for the Assessment of Learning," 164, 171–75
Transfer of knowledge, 86, 105
Transitions, 68
Treasure Mountain, 47
"Tricking the Trickster: Recording and Comparing Story Elements," 307, 311–12
Trinkle, Catherine, 90, 102–7, 324, 346–47
TRUE COLORS, 223
True to the Game, 97
Trust, 83
T-shirts, 47
Tsunamis, 118, 155–58
Television, 32
"Turning on the Lights" (Prensky), 63
21st-century learners, 1–22, 23–40, 50, 63–66, 82, 86, 240
Twitter, 23, 79, 92

Ubiquitous connectivity, 31, 32
Understanding, 65
Understanding by Design, 47, 253
Understanding Comics, 279
United Nations, 324, 331, 334–35
United States, 38
University of Hawaii
    Graduate School of Library and Information Studies, 21
    Library and Information Science Program, 194
University of Oregon, 44
Uno's Garden, 274
Urban Latino, 96
"Urban Teenagers, Leisure Reading, and the Library Media Program," 89, 96–98
Urban teens, 89, 96–98
U.S. Centers for Disease Control (CDC), 277
U.S. Constitution, 246
U.S. Department of Education, 108
U.S. Geological Survey, 249
USA Today, 277
Use of assessment results, 187
"Use This Page," 12
Using evidence, 183
"Using Personality Traits and Effective Communication to Improve Collaboration," 204, 221–24

"Valediction, A: Forbidding Mourning," 3
Valentine, Doug, 79
Valenza, Joyce, 78
Value of school library programs, 59
Vandellas, The, 231
Vanneman, Susan, 203–4, 209, 237
Variables, 319
Venn diagrams, 175, 272, 273, 312
Video booktalks, 89

Video games, 23
Video production, 243, 250, 331–39
Video resources, 336–37
Video streaming, 79
Video, 55, 79
Virginia Standards of Learning, 328
Virtual reference, 28
Vision, 42, 43, 83
Visioning, 41
VistaPrint, 43
Visual learning, 241, 313–14
Visual resources, 241
Visualization, 103, 241
Vmukti Web site, 300, 301
Vocabulary, 318, 321
Voice, 2, 294
VoiceThread.com, 242
Volunteers, 243

Warlick, David, 79
Warwick, Rhode Island, 47
Water cycle, 318–19
Watson, Jinx Stepleton, 251
"We Don't Have to Learn Anything; We Just Have to Find
    the Answer," 244–46
Web 1.0, 31–32
Web 2.0, 31–34, 242, 294–99, 300–301, 325–26
Web site evaluation checklist, 344
Web sites, 26, 28–31, 89, 287
Web-conferencing, 243
Webkins, 23
WebQuest, 126
Webspiration software, 241. *See also* Inspiration software
Wehlage, Gary, 248
Welch, Jack, 46
West, Debbie, 307, 313–14
Western (Westward) Expansion, 267–70
"What Does It Really Look Like When Students Are
    Learning in the Library Media Center?," 42, 60–62
"When Does Collaboration Start?" 204, 211–13, 238
"Where Does Your Authority Come From?," 68, 82–85, 238
Whole Child (ASCD), 86
Whole New Mind, A, 22
Wiesner, David, 275–76
WiFi, 35
Wiggins, Grant, 45, 47, 76, 164, 180, 190, 239, 244, 245,
    251, 253, 342

Wikipedia, 33, 77, 78, 79, 276
Wikis, 2, 33, 94, 242, 296–99, 301, 321
"Wikis and Collaborative Inquiry," 242, 296–99
Williams, Joan Frye, 79
Wired, 33
Wisconsin Educational Communications Board, 104
Wisdom of crowds, 31, 32
Wit, 55
Wizard of Oz, The, 342
Wondering, 268
Wonderment, 55
Woodson, Jacqueline, 97
Woolls, Blanche, 79
Word analysis, 100
Word processing, 242
    tools, 300
Word Up, 96
Wordless books, 275–76
"Words Are Like Faces: An Exploration into Language and
    Communication," 307, 309–10
Workforce preparation, 38, 45, 241
World Is Flat, The, 38
World War II, 276
World Wide Web. *See* Internet
Wright State University, 201
Writing, 14, 172, 307

XML, 28

Yahoo, 276
"Yo, Socrates! Amend This!" 323, 327–30
Yoeman, Donald, 68
Yoshina, Joan, 78, 118, 155–58, 164, 185–88, 341
Young adult literature, 55
YouTube, 28, 77
Yucht, Alice, 78, 120, 286
Yugma Web site, 300, 301

Zemelman, Steven, 99
Zeus, 296
Zimmerman, Nancy, 90, 108–11
Zmuda, Allison, 42, 44–46, 47, 49, 51, 60–62, 67, 68,
    72–76, 82–85, 180, 181, 183, 204, 238
Zoho Web site, 300–301
Zoo letters, 307, 313–14

About the Editor

Kristin Fontichiaro, MLIS, is an elementary media specialist and staff development facilitator with the Birmingham Public Schools in Birmingham, Michigan. She leads frequent workshops and professional development sessions for educators in the United States and abroad, focusing on creative teaching techniques to motivate learners into deeper explorations and more meaningful learning products.

She was a member of the inaugural (2007) class of the American Library Association's Emerging Leaders program and was named the 2008 Distinguished Alumna of the Wayne State University School of Information and Library Science. Along with Judi Moreillon, she was co-guest editor of the 2009 *Knowledge Quest* issue on the professional practice of school library media specialists.

She is the author of *Podcasting at School* (Libraries Unlimited, 2008) and *Active Learning Through Drama, Podcasting, and Puppetry* (Libraries Unlimited, 2007) and co-author, with Sandy Buczynski, of *Story Starters and Science Notebooking: Developing Student Thinking Through Literacy and Inquiry* (Teacher Ideas Press, 2009). Her picture book *The Mitten* (Mitten Press) and her informational text for children, *Go Straight to the Source!* (Cherry Lake Publishing), are both forthcoming.

She is a regular contributor to *School Library Monthly* (formerly *School Library Media Activities Monthly*), the source of the articles found in this book, and writes its blog on school library trends (blog.schoollibrarymonthly.com).